Instructor's Resource Manual

THE MAKING OF THE WEST

PEOPLES AND CULTURES

SECOND EDITION

DAKOTA HAMILTON
Humboldt State University

BEDFORD/ST. MARTIN'S   Boston ◆ New York

For information, write: Bedford/St. Martin's, 75 Arlington Street, Boston, MA 02116
(617-399-4000)

ISBN: 0–312–41774–8

Instructors who have adopted *The Making of the West, Peoples and Cultures,* Second Edition, as
a textbook for a course are authorized to duplicate portions of this manual for their students.

Preface

What first impressed me about *The Making of the West* when it was published in 2001 was its strong humanities-based approach to history and its vivid narrative, which I believed would capture the imagination as well as the attention of students. I was right on both counts. But I also quickly came to appreciate the ancillary materials as well because they addressed the needs of the Western Civilization instructor in direct and specific ways. Having used these ancillaries along with *The Making of the West* in all of my Western Civilizations' classes since their publication, I was asked (along with many other instructors) to respond to a survey questionnaire about the material. The editors wanted to know what worked, what did not work, and how the ancillaries could be improved generally. Many of those suggestions are now reflected in the new edition.

New to This Edition

In *The Making of the West*, some material has been condensed or deleted, and new material added. The accompanying *Instructor's Resource Manual* has been substantially edited, not only to reflect changes in *The Making of the West* but also to make the manual easier to use and more specific in its suggestions. The most significant change relates to the chapter summaries, which have been expanded in order to give instructors a more comprehensive review of chapters in the main text. Additional suggestions for lecture topics and student research and writing assignments have also been added, and references for these have been included to aid both instructors and students. Similarly, the *Building Historical Skills* activities have been expanded to accommodate new primary material in the textbook.

There are also some entirely new additions to the *Instructor's Resource Manual*. A comprehensive list of film and video material will be found for most chapters in the *Instructor's Resource Manual*. Brief summaries of these films and videos have been provided so that instructors can judge what will be most useful to them. The films fall into three main categories: dramatized biographies of prominent historical figures or events, fictional stories that are strong on historical detail, and adaptations of great works of literature. The video material is largely documentary in nature, although some videos also dramatize historical events. Another new feature is the *Making Connections* questions, based on questions posed at the end of each chapter in the textbook. These questions are aimed at getting students to think critically about primary material and sometimes link it to related issues in other periods of history. Model answers have been provided for these questions to aid instructors in evaluating responses. Lastly, the *Instructor's Resource Manual* features a new essay in its Appendix: *Active Learning Strategies for the Western Civilization Classroom*, by Dakota Hamilton. This essay discusses the ways in which instructors can depart from the traditional lecture format and liven up the classroom with direct student participation. It nicely complements the other essays that have been retained from the earlier edition.

We are grateful for the suggestions that we have received in revising *The Making of the West* and its ancillaries because the changes stemming from these will make these materials even more useful to the instructors.

Chapter Resources

Five to eight *Main Chapter Topics* open each chapter of the manual. These topics are broad enough for quick referencing and offer good starting points for lecture and discussion. Each chapter contains a *Summary* of the main themes presented in each chapter.

Suggestions for Lecture and Discussion Topics is composed of several paragraphs that flesh out chapter themes by suggesting ideas to get at the most significant topics in the chapter. Additionally, it provides bibliographic resources to consult for background information and interpretation for lectures and discussions.

Making Historical Connections provides answers to questions posed in the textbook at the end of each chapter, asking students to think more broadly about the West across different periods and to make connections between outcomes and themes.

Writing Assignments and Class Presentation Topics provides ideas that work well as paper assignments and ways to encourage student participation in in-class projects.

Research Assignments presents ideas that students can use to delve more deeply into topics mentioned in the text. Sources are supplied where necessary to give students a springboard when starting their projects.

Suggestions for *Literature* and *Films and Videos* provide lists of literature from the period covered in most chapters, available in translation and films or videos that can be used to give context or background on each period and its representation in the present.

Historical Skills targets selected maps, art, graphs, and primary documents from each chapter of *The Making of the West: Peoples and Cultures.* Students often merely glance at these visual, graphic, and topic-specific features of the text; yet these sources offer a unique way to get students thinking about the nature of history and how historians analyze evidence. This section discusses different ways you can help students develop their historical skills.

Essays: Enhancing the Western Civilization Classroom

Instructors may wish to try something new in the classroom, and these essays offer ways to change the dynamic of their courses. First-time instructors may find these short tutorials helpful to refer to as they employ different teaching techniques throughout the semester. The essays include:

"What Is 'The West'?," by Michael D. Richards (Sweet Briar College)
"Active Learning Strategies for the Western Civilization Classroom," by Dakota Hamilton (Humboldt State University)
"Working Primary Sources into the Western Civilization Syllabus," by Katharine J. Lualdi (University of Southern Maine)
"Visual Literacy: The Image in the Western Civilization Classroom," by Paul R. Deslandes (Texas Tech University)
"Literature and the Western Civilization Classroom," by Michael D. Richards (Sweet Briar College)

Also Available with *The Making of the West: Peoples and Cultures*

This *Instructor's Resource Manual* serves as the keystone to the comprehensive collection of ancillaries available for *The Making of the West: Peoples and Cultures*, Second Edition. Each chapter of this manual closes with a list of the specific components of the ancillary package relevant to that chapter.

Supplements

As with the first edition, a well-integrated ancillary program supports *The Making of the West: Peoples and Cultures.* Each print and electronic resource has been carefully revised to provide a host of practical teaching and learning aids.

For Instructors

Transparencies

A set of over 200 full-color acetate transparencies for *The Making of the West* includes all full-sized maps and many images from the text.

Using the Bedford Series in the Western Civilization Survey by Maura O'Connor, University of Cincinnati.
This short guide gives practical suggestions for using the volumes in the Bedford Series in History and Culture in conjunction with *The Making of the West*. Available online as well as in print, the guide supplies not only connections between the text and the supplements but also ideas for starting discussions focused on a single primary-source volume. **bedfordstmartins.com/oconnor**

Book Companion Site at bedfordstmartins.com/hunt

The companion Web site for *The Making of the West* gathers all the electronic resources for the text, including the Online Study Guide and related Quiz Gradebook, at a single Web address. It provides convenient links to such helpful lecture and research materials as *PowerPoint* chapter outlines from the textbook, *DocLinks, HistoryLinks,* and *Map Central.*

Computerized Test Bank, Joseph Coohill, Pennsylvania State University at New Kensington, and Frances Mitilineos, Loyola University Chicago, available on CD-ROM.

This fully updated test bank offers over 80 exercises per chapter, including multiple-choice, identification, timeline, map labeling and analysis, source analysis, and full-length essay questions. Instructors can customize quizzes, edit both questions and answers, as well as export them to a variety of formats, including WebCT and Blackboard. The disc includes answer keys and essay outlines.

Instructor's Resource CD-ROM

This disc provides instructors with ready-made and customizable *PowerPoint* multimedia presentations, built around chapter outlines, maps, figures, and selected images from the textbook. The disc also contains images in jpeg format, an electronic version of the *Instructor's Resource Manual,* outline maps in PDF format for quizzing or handouts, and quick start guides to the Online Study Guide.

Map Central at bedfordstmartins.com/mapcentral

Map Central is a searchable database of more than 750 maps from Bedford/St. Martin's history texts for classroom presentation and more than 50 basic political and physical outline maps for quizzing or handouts.

Blackboard and/or WebCT content is available for *The Making of the West.*

Videos and multimedia

A wide assortment of videos and multimedia CD-ROMs on various topics in European history is available to qualified adopters.

For Students

Sources of The Making of the West, Second Edition—Volumes I (to 1740) and II (since 1500)—by Katharine J. Lualdi, University of Southern Maine.
For each chapter in *The Making of the West,* this companion sourcebook features four or five important political, social, and cultural documents that reinforce or extend discussions in the textbook, encouraging students to make connections between narrative history and primary sources. Short chapter summaries and document headnotes contextualize the wide array of sources and perspectives represented, while discussion and comparative questions guide students' reading and promote historical

thinking skills. The second edition provides instructors with even more flexibility, as the nearly one-third new selections feature visual sources for the first time. This edition also features more attention to a geographic range beyond the core of Europe and includes an improved balance between traditional documents and selections that provide a fresh perspective.

Study Guide to Accompany **The Making of the West: Peoples and Cultures** — Volumes I (to 1740) and II (since 1500)—by Victoria Thompson, Arizona State University, and Eric Johnson, University of California, Los Angeles. The *Study Guide* offers for each chapter in the textbook: overview questions, a chapter summary, an expanded timeline with questions, a glossary of key terms with a related exercise, multiple-choice and short-answer questions, plus map, illustration, and source exercises that help students synthesize information and practice analytical skills. Answers for all exercises are provided.

Bedford Series in History and Culture—Advisory Editors Natalie Zemon Davis, Princeton University; Ernest R. May, Harvard University; David W. Blight, Yale University; and Lynn Hunt, University of California at Los Angeles.

European titles in this highly praised series combine first-rate scholarship, historical narrative, and important primary documents for undergraduate courses. Each book is brief, inexpensive, and focused on a specific topic or period. Packaged discounts are available. European titles include *Spartacus and the Slave Wars, Utopia, Candide, The French Revolution and Human Rights, The Enlightenment,* and *The Communist Manifesto.*

Online Study Guide at bedfordstmartins.com/hunt

The popular *Online Study Guide* for *The Making of the West* is a free and uniquely personalized learning tool to help students master themes and information in the textbook and improve their historical skills. Instructors can monitor student progress through the online *Quiz Gradebook* or receive e-mail updates.

DocLinks at bedfordstmartins.com/doclinks

This Web site provides over 400 annotated Web links with single-click access to primary documents online, including speeches, legislation, treaties, social commentary, essays, travelers' accounts, personal narratives and testimony, newspaper articles, visual artifacts, songs, and poems. Searchable by topic, date, or specific chapter of *The Making of the West.*

HistoryLinks at bedfordstmartins.com/historylinks

HistoryLinks directs instructors and students to over 500 carefully selected and annotated history-related Web sites, including topical sites, image galleries, maps, and audio and video clips for supplementing lectures or making assignments. Searchable by date, subject, medium, keyword, or specific chapter in *The Making of the West.*

A Student's Online Guide to History Reference Sources at bedfordstmartins.com/benjamin

This collection of links provides access to history-related electronic reference sources such as databases, indexes, and journals, plus contact information for state, provincial, local, and professional history organizations. Based on the appendix to Jules Benjamin's *A Student's Guide to History*, Ninth Edition.

We are grateful for the suggestions that we have received in revising *The Making of the West* and its ancillaries because the changes stemming from these will make these materials even more useful to instructors.

Dakota Hamilton

How To Use the *Online Study Guide* with Your Textbook

How the *Online Study Guide* Can Help You Learn Efficiently

Using the *Online Study Guide* (OSG), you can improve your comprehension of the course book and spend your time focusing on the areas you need the most help in. The best part is that you can evaluate your progress **as you learn interactively.**

1. Log on, click on "Recommended Study Plan" and take the first assessment quiz.
2. The plan tells you what you need to study and directs you to the right part of your book and shows you other interactive activities.
3. You take another quiz to double-check your mastery.
4. You do more practice on what you need to study.

How to get Started

Enter the URL for the *Online Study Guide* into your Web Browser http://bedfordstmartins.com/hunt.

Click on <u>Student</u> to set up an account.

First, we'll make an account for you so that you and your professor can see your progress on the assessment quizzes.

1. Click on "Student" in the left-hand frame to go to the next screen.
2. Provide your name and email address and create your own password.
3. Enter the password **twice** to verify it, and provide the email address of your instructor.*
4. Click **SUBMIT.**

Now you are ready to begin using the OSG.

---

*__Note:__ If your professor does not provide an email address or assign the quizzes, *you can still use the Online Study Guide.* Just enter a blank or nonsense address when prompted for "Instructor E-mail."

Using the Assessment Quizzes and Recommended Study Plan to Mark Your Progress...

A-1 Archaeology and History, pp. 4-6 Assessment score for this area: **100%** (4/4)	**Mastering the Building Blocks** * Defining Terms n/a * Chronology **Developing Historical Skills** * Map and Figure Activity 1 * Map and Figure Activity 2 * Reading Historical Documents * Visual Activity
A-2 The First Americans, pp. 6-8 Assessment score for this area: **75%** (3/4)	**Mastering the Building Blocks** * Defining Terms n/a * Chronology **Developing Historical Skills** * Map and Figure Activity 1 * Map and Figure Activity 2 * Reading Historical Documents * Visual Activity
A-3 Archaic Hunters and Gatherers, pp. 8-11 Assessment score for this area: **50%** (2/4)	**Comprehending the Narrative** * Chapter Summary Activity * True False * Fill-in-the-Blank * Reviewing the Text Activity **Mastering the Building Blocks** * Defining Terms n/a * Chronology **Developing Historical Skills** * Map and Figure Activity 1 * Map and Figure Activity 2

If you don't want to use the Recommended Study Plan, then just select the name of the activity or quiz you want to take from the main menu or the upper left-hand corner. Activities can be viewed by chapter or type.

(1) Click on "Recommended Study Plan" to go to the quizzes. You may be asked to confirm your instructor's email address. Take the first quiz.

(2) Click on **SUBMIT** when you are done to see the results. You will receive instant feedback on how well you did and what you did or didn't understand about each question. If you entered your instructor's email address, the quiz results will be sent to your instructor's online grade book.

(3) After viewing the results, you see how well you did and what activities you can do to improve. These are the "Recommended Study Plan Results." You can see them at any time by going to the "Recommended Study Plan" for chapters in which you've already taken the assessment quiz.

(4) You can take a second assessment quiz to check your mastery and see how much you have improved! Try our map quizzes to test your knowledge of maps or our defining terms quizzes to improve your understanding of key terms. Timeline activities help you to master the key events in each chapter. "Reviewing the Text" activities help you prepare for short-answer or essay questions on your exam.

Using the *Book Companion Site*:
Resources for Instructors

INTRODUCTION

The Book Companion Site *and* Online Study Guide

This guide is designed to help you get started using the *Book Companion Site* as an instructor. For students, we offer a similar guide, "How To Use the *Online Study Guide*" which helps students navigate the *Online Study Guide.*

The *Book Companion Site* consists of both an *Online Study Guide* for students and special resources for instructors. The *Online Study Guide* is a free web-based resource intended to provide customized feedback on students' comprehension of the textbook. Students take an assessment quiz that tells them which areas of the chapter they need to study most closely and offers them a variety of different interactive opportunities for more practice on what they need to study. These opportunities include quizzing in the form of multiple-choice, identification, and short-answer quizzes as well as interactive study activities based on key terms, maps, and timelines:

- *Recommended Study Plan.* A guided study system involving two sets of multiple-choice assessment quizzes that allow students to find out which specific parts of the text they need to review and then check their mastery.
- *Chapter Summaries.* Summaries of each chapter for students to read and review before and after taking online quizzes or to review textbook reading assignments.
- *Defining Terms.* A flashcard-style activity that helps students review key terms by viewing the content of each flashcard and then designing their own quiz to test their knowledge.
- *Multiple Choice.* Two multiple-choice exams per chapter. Detailed feedback helps the students understand the material.
- *Identification.* Up to four Identification quizzes (based on chapter sections) per chapter, containing seven or eight questions each, asking students to identify key terms and individuals.
- *Reviewing the Text.* A short-answer quiz that allows students to synthesize answers in response to essay questions guiding their textbook reading. Model answers to help them study for exams.
- *Timeline Activity.* Timelines that allow students to click on dates or events to view more detailed activity from a specific period, followed by a short quiz on the events shown on the timeline.
- *Map Activity.* Activities designed to improve students' geographic literacy, in which students answer various questions about a map or drag and drop place names onto the appropriate location.
- *Reading Historical Documents.* Questions pertaining to historical documents from the textbook, with model answers for comparison and exam preparation.

- *Visual Activity.* Short-answer questions pertaining to artifacts and images from the text-book with model for comparison and exam preparation.
- **Results of these quizzes and activities can be sent to the Quiz Gradebook for instructors to view.**

REGISTRATION

The *Book Companion Site* is **free** to adopters of our textbook. However, because the site contains sensitive information such as test banks, we require instructors to set up an account with their own login name and password. If you have already set up an account on any of our other sites, then you will not need to set up a new account for this book. Creating an account is easy and takes only a few moments:

Step 1: First, go to the website for your book: http://bedfordstmartins.com/hunt. Under "I am not registered. Sign me up," choose <u>Instructor</u>. You will then see a screen asking you to enter the instructor code or request an instructor code. Click on <u>Enter Instructor Code</u> and type in the instructor code provided to you by your sales representative, or by filling out a request form from the *Book Companion Site*.

Step 2: The form asks for your e-mail address and a password you create (entered twice for verification). **Be sure that the e-mail address you use to register is the same as the address you will give students to enter when they take the quizzes!** Note that your password is set by you and is not the same as the Instructor Code. Click <u>Submit</u> when you have completely filled out the form.

Step 3: You will be asked to confirm the data that you entered in Step 2 and to enter once more the Instructor Code provided by your Bedford, Freeman, and Worth Sales Representative. After entering the Instructor Code, click <u>Submit</u>.

Students can submit the results of their quizzes to a gradebook that you can view from the Instructor's Resources side of the Web site. To better protect their privacy and quiz security, students will have to set up an account in order to take quizzes. **They do not need an access code** in order to log on to the site. Furthermore, students can create an account **even if their instructors choose not to use the Web site**. Creating an account for students is described in our student guide to the site, "How To Use the *Online Study Guide*."

WHAT YOU WILL NEED

- An Internet Browser: Either *Internet Explorer* (version 5.5+ for Windows, 5.2 if you use a Macintosh) or *Netscape* (version 6.2+) is recommended. Note that most computers already come with one or both of these **already installed**. If your browsers are not current, you can download them from our Web site.

- Some Additional Internet Software: *Adobe Acrobat* (version 5.0 or higher) is required to read documents in PDF format (such as the online version of the *Instructor's Resource Manual*). *Shockwave* and *Flash Player* (version 4.0) is required to do the map and flash-card exercises. Many computers will already have these installed on them. You can also download them from our Web site.
- Microsoft PowerPoint is required for viewing PowerPoint outlines. We also provide these outlines in text format. You can download a free PowerPoint viewer for Macintosh or Windows from Microsoft's Web site at http://www.microsoft.com/downloads.
- Stuffit Expander (for Macintosh) or WinZIP (for Windows) is necessary to download some material from the site. If these are not already on your computer, you can install them from the link on our web site.

MONITORING STUDENT PROGRESS USING THE QUIZ GRADEBOOK

You can access the results of student's quiz-taking by selecting "Quiz Gradebook" from "Instructor Resources" in the main menu. You will then see the Quiz Gradebook menu. When students sign in, they are asked to supply their instructor's e-mail address. Only some types of student quizzes are reported to the instructor gradebook. To see which types of quizzes are reported, refer to the chart at the beginning of this handout.

Note: Although it is not necessary for them to provide your e-mail address in order to take the quiz, only students who supply your e-mail address will have their results posted in the quiz gradebook.

The **standard reporting option** allows you to view exercise results either one student at a time or for all your students at once. To track students in multiple courses or multiple sections, you can use the **custom reporting** feature.

Quiz Gradebook : Quiz Gradebook

View: **All Students, One Quiz** | One Student, All Quizzes | All Students, All Quizzes

	Delete Checked	Check All Clear All			Showing 1 to 3 of 3
	Detail Report	Quiz Name	Student	Score	When Started	When Finished
☐	🔍	Hunt Ch. 9 Assessment Quiz 1	Student, Good	19/20(95%)	5/10/2004 8:03:09 AM	5/10/2004 8:06:06 AM
☐	🔍	Hunt Ch. 10 Assessment Quiz 1	Student, Good	18/20(90%)	5/10/2004 7:57:52 AM	5/10/2004 7:59:13 AM
☐	🔍	Hunt Ch. 10 Assessment quiz 2	Student, Good	15/20(75%)	5/10/2004 7:43:19 AM	5/10/2004 7:44:18 AM
	Delete Checked	Check All	Clear All		Showing 1 to 3 of 3

When you look at a report, you can view **all the results from one particular exam** or **all the exams of one particular student**, or **exams by all students** by clicking on the links at the top of each column.

The report tells you the **Quiz Name**, the **Student Name**, their **Score**, when they **Started** and when they **Finished**. If you are viewing multiple students or quizzes, you can sort the quizzes by **Name**, **Student**, and **When Started**.

You can **delete** scores yourself, or wait until the system deletes the scores (usually once a year, around September). To delete all of the quizzes, select "Check All" and then click "Delete".

A **detailed report** will permit you to view student progress in a printer-friendly format for keeping paper records of student performance. It will also allow you to view students' free-response answers.

To **set up custom reporting**, select "Set up Custom Reporting" from the page immediately after you have selected "Quiz Gradebook" from the main menu. Enter the names of the courses or sections that you would like to have for custom reporting. When you have entered the names of the courses that you wish to create in custom reporting, click "Submit." You will be shown a page with a list of all students who have submitted your e-mail address as well as the names of your courses. To associate students with a specific course, first select the name of the course, then check the box next to the names of the students whose grades you want to be reported in that course. Then click "submit and refresh" to place those students in that course. Repeat this process for each course until you are finished. Then select "Return to the Instructor Main Menu" to return to the main menu.

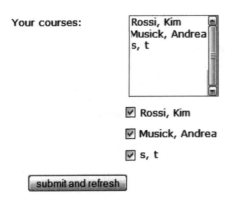

To **view your custom reports**, select "View a custom report of your students' practice activity" from the Quiz Gradebook menu. You will then be asked to choose which course's student activity you would like to view.

You can also sign up to be **e-mailed reports on Friday night** of students' activity. If you no longer want to receive these reports, then you can **unsubscribe from being e-mailed**. Both options are available from the Quiz Gradebook menu.

Contents

Prologue: Before Civilization
to 4000 B.C.E.

CHAPTER RESOURCES

Main Chapter Topics

1. Prehistoric human societies existed at the mercy of the environment and the constant search for food. By cooperating in hunting and gathering, members of Paleolithic societies ensured their survival.

2. With the discovery of agriculture and the domestication of animals, the Neolithic Revolution (c. 10,000–c. 4000 B.C.E.) marked the human transition from a nomadic existence as hunter-gatherers to a more settled lifestyle. It also led to an increasingly gender-based division of labor and the emergence of social hierarchy. By 6500 B.C.E., the invention of irrigation facilitated the establishment of settled agricultural communities in the Fertile Crescent.

Summary

New discoveries about our early development and reinterpretations of old discoveries are constantly being made. But one thing seems certain; people, physiologically identical to modern humans (*Homo sapiens sapiens*), emerged out of Africa more than fifty thousand years ago. During the later Paleolithic period (c. 50,000–c. 45,000 B.C.E.), *Homo sapiens sapiens* migrated from Africa via southwestern Asia to the European continent, displacing older hominids such as the Neanderthals. These new arrivals subsisted as nomadic hunter-gatherers, lived to be about twenty-five or thirty years of age on average, and congregated in groups probably numbering about twenty or thirty members. Although their small bands were most likely characterized by fairly egalitarian social arrangements, a mostly gender-based division of labor had emerged. Limited by childbearing, women usually engaged in gathering, leaving hunting to men. Each group probably kept to an area of no more than sixty miles across in any direction. Cooperative hunts were probably planned ahead of time. Frequently on the move, they lived in caves and temporary huts.

Control of fire making expanded the dietary base of Paleolithic people. They worked bone and stone into weapons, tools, and jewelry, and traded seashells—all items found in their graves and at sites far distant from their place of origin. They also had burial rituals that indicate some kind of religious belief. Their artistic skill is demonstrated by the famous cave paintings of France and Spain, which depict wild animals, and ubiquitous statuettes of female fertility figures, which again are suggestive of religion. Based on objects found in graves, Paleolithic societies may also have been hierarchical.

During the Neolithic Revolution (c. 10,000–c. 4000 B.C.E.), the development of agriculture in the ancient Near East (the Fertile Crescent area of modern Iraq in particular) provided the key step for the later development of large-scale civilizations because it relieved people from constantly searching for food and permitted them some leisure time. Women probably first deciphered the cycle of planting seeds that led to crop harvests. This was accompanied by the domestication of livestock. Sheep were the first animals to be domesticated for food, beginning about 8500 B.C.E. and, by about 7000 B.C.E., domesticated animals had become common throughout the Near East. People probably lived in permanent houses, which may have first been huts but later were built out of mud bricks. Initially, people lived in close quarters with their animals; this facilitated the spread of disease. Farmers moving outward looking for new lands helped to disseminate farming techniques.

More reliable and storable food supplies led to population growth and permanent settlements, such as those at Jericho and Çatalhöyük (by 6500 B.C.E.). The inhabitants of Çatalhöyük lived in closely packed brick houses that provided protection to the community. They diverted streams for irrigation to increase crop yields. Freed from agricultural work because of food surpluses, people diversified their occupations, such as metallurgy and textile work. The people of Çatalhöyük were also involved in trade, and it is likely that the community had a political and social hierarchy. A nearby volcano, regarded as being an angry god that had to be placated, destroyed Çatalhöyük about a thousand years after its foundation.

The Neolithic Revolution also witnessed a change in gender roles. The reason for this shift is not known for certain, but it is likely that men took over farming as inventions like the plow made farming more physically laborious. Sheep and cattle continually needed new grazing grounds, which meant the domesticated animals often had to be herded away from the home. Freed from having to nurse children, men took on this responsibility. Women, tied to the home to care for children, took on tasks related to processing the secondary products of agriculture and animal husbandry: spinning and weaving wool, and making yogurt and cheese.

Suggestions for Lecture and Discussion Topics

1. The need to rely on archaeological evidence when studying the pre-historical Paleolithic and Neolithic periods is obvious. Discuss the limitations and benefits of using archaeological evidence—tool types, materials, remnants of burial sites, artwork—to reconstruct early human societies. What do these reveal about the human relationship with the environment? Slides of the cave paintings of Lascaux, of the various Venus figurines, and of the early settlement at Çatalhöyük could facilitate discussion. Especially problematic is the frequent ascription of religious meaning or ritual use to representative artwork or to items for which no practical function is immediately apparent. Why do archaeologists and historians frequently resort to such identifications? For an introduction to archaeological methods aimed at the general reader, see Jane McIntosh, *The Practical Archaeologist: How We Know What We Know about the Past* (London: Paul Press, 1986).

2. Another common approach to deciphering prehistoric human societies is drawing conclusions based on parallels with anthropological studies of extant (though rapidly disappearing) Stone Age tribes, such as those of the Amazon basin or New Guinea. How valid are such comparisons? What biases might modern observers bring to their accounts of primitive peoples? Are some aspects of human organization less susceptible to the influence of modern civilization than others, and thus might they serve as better indicators of what early human societies might have been like?

Making Connections

1. Explain whether you think human life was more stressful in the Paleolithic or the Neolithic Age. It might be thought that life in the Paleolithic period was less

stressful because things were simple and basic, but the constant search for food would have made survival uncertain. Life was probably less stressful in the Neolithic Age because the introduction of animal husbandry and crop cultivation made the food supply more secure.

2. What do you believe were the most important differences and similarities between Stone Age and modern life? Why? The most striking difference is probably that Stone Age peoples lived in small groups numbering between twenty and thirty members, whereas people today tend to live on their own or within relatively small family groups. For Stone Age peoples, survival required that the entire community work together. To some extent, this is still the case today, as both members of any modern couple must work to maintain their households.

Historical Skills

Map 1, The Development of Agriculture, p. P-9

Have students scrutinize the location and spread of early agricultural sites. What geophysical features do most sites have in common? Are there differences between the locations of earlier sites and later ones? If so, why? What might account for the presence of later agricultural sites in what is now the middle of the Sahara desert?

Map 1.1, The Ancient Near East, p. 9

Have students identify and discuss the major geophysical features that characterize and surround ancient Mesopotamia and Egypt. How did these features both positively and negatively influence the development of settled, agriculture- and trade-based civilizations in these regions?

A Paleolithic Shelter, p. P-6

What do the building materials and construction methods used in this hut reveal about Paleolithic peoples' relation to resources and their environment? How were such structures adapted to their way of life? (Note the estimated date of the structure reproduced in the illustration.) Prehistoric "Venus" Figurine, p. P-7.

Female statuettes, such as this Venus, were produced throughout prehistoric Europe, whereas representations of males were relatively rare. What might account for this? Although the precise meaning of such figures is impossible to ascertain, ask students to explore what information such figures might suggest about gender roles and status during this period. A stimulating discussion on gender roles in the ancient world might be sparked by a comparison to the statue of Queen Hatshepsut (p. 25) after the class has covered the material on Egypt. Although Hatshepsut adopted the masculine role of pharaoh to rule Egypt and is depicted wearing the pharaoh's male dress, this likeness (intended for official public display) does not suppress her female physiology. What does this statue reveal about the complex, yet quite high position that women occupied in Egyptian society? What, if anything, does the statue have in common with the Venus figurine?

Prehistoric "Venus" Figurine, p. P-7

Although little is known about these kinds of figurines, they suggest a number of things about the cultures that created them. A discussion could focus on the fertility aspects of the statuette. The "Venus" may have symbolized human reproduction, or it might have signified fertility more generally—nature constantly renewing itself and producing the things that prehistoric people needed in order to survive.

OTHER BEDFORD/ST. MARTIN'S RESOURCES FOR THE PROLOGUE

The following resources are available to accompany the Prologue. Please refer to the Preface of this manual for detailed descriptions of all the ancillaries.

For Instructors

Transparencies

The following maps and images from the Prologue are available as full-color acetates:

- Map P.1: The Development of Agriculture
- *Lascaux Bison*
- *Venus of Willendorf*

Instructor's Resources CD-ROM

The following maps and image from the Prologue, as well as a chapter outline, are available on disc in both PowerPoint and jpeg formats:

- Map P.1: The Development of Agriculture
- *Lascaux Bison*

For Students

Study Guides

The print **Study Guide** and the **Online Study Guide** at bedfordstmartins.com/hunt (both by Victoria Thompson and Eric Johnson) help students synthesize the material they have learned as well as practice the skills historians use to make sense of the past. The following Map, Visual, and Document activities are available for the Prologue.

Map Activity

- Map P.1: The Development of Agriculture

Visual Activity

- *Lascaux Bison*

Reading Historical Documents

- New Sources, New Perspectives: Daily Bread, Damaged Bones, and Cracked Teeth

Foundations of Western Civilization

c. 4000–c. 1000 B.C.E.

CHAPTER RESOURCES

Main Chapter Topics

1. The term "western civilization" is not as simple as it may seem. The word *civilization* has lost its precision, and western civilization began not in Europe but in Africa and Asia. Moreover, these earliest civilizations borrowed from one another, and later societies borrowed from the earlier ones. Western civilization has never been isolated from other parts of the globe; rather, its pattern is to incorporate the ideas, arts, and technologies of other peoples and regions.

2. Mesopotamia contained the West's first large-scale civilization. Mesopotamians developed the wheel, the earliest writing system (cuneiform), complex mathematics, bronze, and the first empire (Akkad). Its numerous city-states, ruled by monarchs who claimed a divine connection, often warred with each other for control of territory and resources.

3. The west's second great civilization arose when Upper and Lower Egypt unified around 3000 B.C.E. Unlike Mesopotamia, Egypt enjoyed long periods of relatively isolated and peaceful development and was thus remarkably stable. Its society, which adhered to the principle of *maat* (the harmonious ordering of the world), was headed by a king (called pharaoh in the New Kingdom) who was considered to be the human incarnation of a god. The Egyptian belief in an afterlife is manifest in their magnificent tombs and pyramids, built to house their mummified dead. From 3000 to about 1100 B.C.E., Egyptian history was divided into three long periods of unification (Old, Middle, and New kingdoms), broken by two periods of internal revolts, foreign invasions, and the irregular flooding of the Nile.

4. Although they did not construct powerful, long-lived states, two groups from the Levant left lasting legacies for the west. The Canaanites, whose territory served as a major crossroads for long-distance trade, created the first true alphabet by about 1600 B.C.E. Early in the second millennium B.C.E., the semi-nomadic Hebrews laid the foundations of western monotheism. Their religious and moral teachings, contained in the Hebrew Bible, have similarities to and significant differences from Mesopotamian law codes like Hammurabi's. Their religion formed a basis for the younger monotheistic religions of Christianity and Islam.

5. The first Mediterranean civilizations emerged around 2000 B.C.E. Cretan (or Minoan) culture was prosperous, peaceful, and centered on palace complexes that controlled religious, economic, and political life. Minoan arts and writing influenced those of Mycenaean Greece, but the militaristic and independent Greek settlements had a distinct culture of their own. Mycenaean Greece was destroyed by civil war following an earthquake. During that same period, from 1200 to 1000 B.C.E., many Mediterranean and Near Eastern societies were stricken by a series of catastrophes, including invasions by the mysterious Sea Peoples, invasions by the Philistines, and internal turmoil. The cumulative effect of these events plunged the region into a widespread Dark Age.

Summary

Western civilization embraces complex ideas and circumstances. At the most basic level, *east* and *west* refer to where the sun rises and sets. The Latin words for rising and setting give us *orient* for the east and *occident* for the west. *Europe*, as a term for the western continent, comes from a Greek myth about the princess Europa who was carried off by the god Zeus from Asia to Crete. Over time, "the west" has come to imply a deep connection or relationship with the peoples and countries of Europe. "Civilization" has traditionally referred to cities or states with public buildings, diverse economies, a tradition of writing, and large populations with a collective identity. These criteria were, and continue to be, fluid depending on the period or area under discussion and the social, political, or economic perspective applied. The term "western civilization" puts into relief value judgments made about different cultures at various times in history. Cultural borrowing occurred at virtually all levels in western civilization from the very beginning.

The earliest foundations of western civilization were in Mesopotamia (c. 4000 B.C.E.) and Egypt (c. 2700 B.C.E.). Both societies were deeply religious and had clear—although different—concepts of justice rooted in their beliefs. By 2000 B.C.E., civilizations appeared in Anatolia, the Levant, the island of Crete, and Greece. (Although societies began emerging in India, China, and the Americas at differing times beginning about 2500 B.C.E., their development followed quite different patterns.) With the rise of metallurgy and the consequent improvement of tools and weapons, social divisions sharpened within these societies. Both trade and war increased contact among cultures, and this interaction led to a fruitful exchange of ideas and technologies. As a result, the history of western civilization begins in a mingling of diverse peoples and regions that were at times in conflict with each other.

After the Neolithic Revolution, agricultural surpluses freed many people to pursue work outside of farming. Metalworking, especially in bronze, not only was a vital craft that fed the wealth and power of society, it also led to political, economic, and social divisions between men and women and between rich and poor. Commerce grew to satisfy the increasing desire for goods and materials; meanwhile rulers drafted laws that justified the claim that their power was divinely ordained. Out of this framework came the first cities built by the people of Sumer in southern Mesopotamia.

The Sumerians settled first in the hills around the Tigris and Euphrates rivers in the Fertile Crescent, but the rivers were subject to floods that brought no water to the hot plains around them. Irrigation solved both problems. Canal systems limited flooding and turned the arid plains green, producing agricultural surpluses. These surpluses increased population and freed people from farming to specialize in crafts like weaving and metalworking. The Sumerians needed central authorities to organize maintenance of the canals, and this fostered the development of monarchy.

By about 3000 B.C.E., Sumer in Mesopotamia had twelve independent city-states (urban centers that dominated surrounding agricultural territories), ruled by kings who claimed divinely backed authority. Around 2500 B.C.E., Sumerian cities contained populations of twenty thousand or more. Within the city walls were large buildings, royal palaces, and ziggurats (temples to the Gods). City-dwellers lived in mud huts that varied in size depending on the wealth of their owners, and both rich and poor suffered the ill effects of overcrowding.

The Sumerians conducted long-distance trade as far away as India and constructed wheels strong enough for heavy transport. Goods were used to pay taxes and collected and redistributed according to the king's direction. To track the exchange of goods, the Sumerians created the west's first writing system (cuneiform). A mix of symbols and pictographs, cuneiform represented whole words or syllables. At first used only for accounting by professional scribes, cuneiform also preserved myths, epics, hymns, and king lists. In time, scribal schools further extended their curriculum to include mathematics and foreign languages. Later, Mesopotamians devised astronomy, used algebra and complex mathematics, and devised a system of reckoning time and the degrees of circles based on sixty still in use today.

Kings and their families topped Mesopotamian society, followed by their counselors and the priests and priestesses. Sumerians believed that the gods gave the king power so long as he ensured justice, established law, and defended his city-state from foreign attack. He and his family lived in luxury in a palace, which also served as the city-state's administrative center. At the bottom of society were slaves. Slaves were persons captured in war, born to slave parents, or sold into slavery to stave off starvation or to pay off a debt. They had no legal rights and were at the mercy of their owners. They worked at farming, domestic service, and craft production, and could be freed under certain conditions. It was once thought that slaves worked on state projects, but it is now believed that this work was performed by free persons who paid their taxes with labor.

The Mesopotamians worshiped anthropomorphic gods who possessed total control over human lives. Each god's and goddess's importance depended on the importance of his or her sphere of control, and each city-state had a patron god or goddess of its own. Soaring ziggurats were built to honor important gods and to bring their worshippers closer to them. The Sumerian *Epic of Gilgamesh* recounts how the semi-historical king Gilgamesh of Uruk searches for immortality after the death of his friend Enkidu. Ultimately, Gilgamesh realizes that only gods enjoy immortality; humans live forever only in the fame derived from performing mighty deeds. Still, priests were expected to discover the will of the gods by divination, by looking for astrological signs, interpreting dreams, and cutting open animals to examine their organs for deformities signaling trouble.

King Sargon established the first western empire from his home territory Akkadia (c. 2350–c. 2200 B.C.E.), which reached from the Persian Gulf to the Mediterranean. The fall of the Akkadian Empire has been ascribed to an invasion, but is now believed to have been the result of a civil war. Assyria advanced as the next dominant city-state because it controlled trade between Anatolia and Mesopotamia. Assyria broke with the pattern of redistributive state monopolies that characterized Mesopotamian economic life. By 1900 B.C.E., Assyrian kings permitted private individuals to buy and sell goods and to invest in commercial enterprises for profit. Babylon followed Assyria and generated the earliest known written laws: the code of King Hammurabi (r. c. 1792–1750 B.C.E.). These laws reflect the king's divinely ordained responsibility to maintain order and justice and to protect the weak as well as the strong. Hammurabi's laws codify the hierarchical ordering of Babylonian society and assign punishments accordingly. The justice of "an eye for an eye" applied only between equals.

Egypt constituted the other cradle of western civilization. Protected by deserts on the east and west, and nourished by the predictable annual flooding of the Nile, Egypt developed in relative isolation into a tremendously prosperous and stable kingdom. King Menes first unified Upper and Lower Egypt sometime between 3100 and 3000 B.C.E.

During the Old Kingdom (c. 2686–c. 2181 B.C.E.), Egyptians adhered to the concept of the harmonious ordering of society, a quality evident in their highly stylized artwork and hieroglyphs. This principle was expressed as *maat* (justice, truth, and balance), which uniformly guided the conduct of all people. Egypt's powerful kings were regarded as gods incarnate, but even they were held accountable for maintaining *maat*. The king's central duty was to invoke the annual flooding of the Nile, upon which the prosperity of his entire kingdom depended.

The Egyptian religious outlook differed substantially from that of the Mesopotamians. Egyptians believed that the soul was immortal and that those who lived just lives could expect a reward in the afterlife. To prepare for the afterlife, they mummified their dead; those who could afford it included provisions for the afterlife in their burial chambers. The most spectacular were the royal tombs, particularly the pyramids. The first monumental tomb was King Djoser's Step Pyramid (c. 2650 B.C.E.) at Saqqara, and the largest was King Cheops's Great Pyramid at Giza (c. 2575 B.C.E.).

Diminished flooding of the Nile and famines (c. 2350 B.C.E.) led to civic disruption and the loss of royal authority. Regional governors withdrew their support from the king, central government broke down, and the First Intermediate Period (c. 2181–c. 2050 B.C.E.) began. Thirty years later, King Mentuhotep II reunified Egypt in the Middle Kingdom period (c. 2050–1786 B.C.E.), with territorial expansion and increased trade contacts with the Near East and Crete. Invasion by the foreign Hyksos, accompanied by more irregular Nile floods, brought on the Second Intermediate Period (c. 1786–c. 1567 B.C.E.). Despite the chaos, Egypt benefited from the introduction of bronze, horses and chariots, hump-backed cattle, and olive trees.

Thebans from Upper Egypt reunited Egypt during the New Kingdom period (c. 1567–1085 B.C.E.). Warrior pharaohs energetically extended Egypt's borders and trade contacts. The New Kingdom also witnessed some aberrations in political and religious life. Queen Hatshepsut ruled Egypt as pharaoh during the minority of her stepson Tuthmosis III. Amunhotep IV (or Akhenaten, r. 1379–1362 B.C.E.) broke with deeply ingrained religious traditions by introducing the cult of one central god, Aten, and moving the capital to Amarna. His failed attempts at diplomacy could not stop the rise of the Hittites that threatened Egypt, and his religious reforms died with him. His successor, Tutankhamun (r. 1361–1352 B.C.E.), restored worship of the traditional gods.

Despite their differences, Mesopotamia and Egypt shared some important similarities, such as the relatively free status of women and the existence of slavery. Besides being priestesses, some Mesopotamian women became professional scribes and poets. The first author whose name we know was Sargon's daughter, the princess-priestess Enheduanna (twenty-third century B.C.E.). In both cultures, women could own property, enter into contracts, initiate legal proceedings, and sue for divorce. Egyptian women's freedom was almost equal to men's, although they did not partake fully of political authority. Women of the ancient Near East possessed a greater degree of freedom and status than virtually any other western women until recent times. Class, rather than gender, primarily defined social status. Slavery existed in both cultures, but most hard labor was performed as tax payments by free workers because coins did not appear until about 700 B.C.E. in Anatolia.

A very different culture arose in the Levant. Although its peoples — the Canaanites and the Hebrews — did not establish powerful empires, they did leave durable legacies. Around 1600 B.C.E., the Canaanites—who dominated trade at this crossroads between the Mediterranean and Near East—developed the first alphabet in which each letter represented only one sound. The Canaanite alphabet's simplicity made it adaptable to multiple languages, and modern western alphabets are based on it. Over several centuries, the semi-nomadic Hebrews established the west's first enduring monotheistic religion. Their foundation story is contained in the first five books of the Hebrew Bible (the Pentateuch), but the lack of contemporary records makes it difficult to ascertain the details of their earliest history.

The Hebrew Bible relates that the patriarch Abraham migrated with his followers (c. 1900 B.C.E.) from Ur in Mesopotamia to Palestine. During this period, the Hebrews remained loosely organized and did not form a political state. Their religion was founded when Abraham made a covenant with the Hebrew god Yahweh. The Hebrews agreed to worship Yahweh as their preeminent deity and to obey his laws; in exchange, Yahweh made them his chosen people. Hebrews moved into Egypt under Abraham's descendant Joseph. By the thirteenth century B.C.E., they were enslaved to labor on the pharaoh's building projects. Around 1250 B.C.E., their charismatic leader Moses led the Hebrews out of Egyptian bondage and, on Mount Sinai, he reestablished their covenant with Yahweh. The resultant moral and legal codes are specified in the Ten Commandments and elucidated in detail in the last four books of the Pentateuch. These texts resemble Mesopotamian laws, but differ from them in their lack of class distinction, lighter punishments for crimes against property, and protections afforded to slaves.

Two civilizations derive from Anatolian peoples: the Hittites and the Minoans. The Hittites had established an empire by 1750 B.C.E. From their capital Hattusas, Hittites maintained preeminence in the region by controlling trade routes and raw materials, especially metals, and engaging successfully in diplomacy and war. In Hittite society, women sometimes assumed positions of leadership in both peace and war. Hittite religion sought to maintain the gods' goodwill; the king served as high priest of the storm god and conducted religious services. Excelling at chariot-based warfare, the Hittites prevented Egyptian domination of the region by stopping Ramesses II at the battle of Kadesh (c. 1274 B.C.E.). Typically, the Hittites followed up Kadesh by negotiating a treaty with Egypt and sealing the alliance with an interdynastic marriage.

As early as 6000 B.C.E., Anatolian peoples began migrating out to the islands of the Mediterranean. These people are known as Minoans, after the mythological King Minos of Crete, and may or may not have been ancestors of the Greeks. By around 2200 B.C.E., a thriving civilization had emerged on Crete, where the Minoans had established a palace society; the island's sprawling royal palaces also served as political, economic, and religious centers. Archaeology has revealed a culture featuring highly specialized crafts, a redistributive economy, and sophisticated artwork depicting scenes of leisure and sports. Although Minoan rulers dominated politics and religion, they did not possess the absolute powers of a king.

Minoans spoke a language distinct from Greek though possibly Indo-European—it is still not completely deciphered—and wrote in a script called Linear A. Minoan farmers adopted Mediterranean polyculture, in which different growing seasons produce olives, grapes, and grains. The resulting food surpluses could be stored in enormous vessels and freed people to specialize in crafts. Olive oil, wine, and crafts also stimulated trade, which furthered economic interdependence. Minoan civilization came to an abrupt halt around 1370 B.C.E., when the palaces were destroyed for reasons not fully understood. But, before its demise, Minoan civilization came to be dominated by the Mycenaeans.

Early Greeks (known as Mycenaeans, after Mycenae on Greece's mainland) moved into the region by 8000 B.C.E., and established independent hilltop fortifications that competed with each other for resources and territory. Closely tied to the sea because Greece's mountainous terrain prevented easy overland travel, these centers reached their peak from about 1800 to 1100 B.C.E. As on Crete, the redistributive economy was regulated from palace centers

that served as storage and distribution points. The movement of goods was recorded in Linear B—which the Myceneans derived from Linear A—to record an early form of Greek. Mycenaeans clearly had close connections with Minoan Crete, and based some of their motifs on Cretan designs. Despite this cultural borrowing, the Mycenaeans and Minoans were distinctly different peoples in language, religious beliefs, and architecture. The Mycenaean *tholos* tomb was distinctive, and their palaces centered on a hearth and throne room: the *megaron*. Warfare and its accoutrements preoccupied Mycenaean men, war gods stood at the center of their religion, and spending on warfare exceeded spending on religion.

The flourishing and diverse Bronze Age civilizations came crashing to an end around 1200 B.C.E., when the region's political equilibrium was upset and most centers were dramatically wiped out. The exact reasons remain unknown. Egyptian and Hittite inscriptions reveal that foreign invaders, the mysterious Sea Peoples, toppled the Hittite Empire, severed trade routes, and set survivors on the move. Philistines from the north attacked the Canaanites and Hebrews; Minoan civilization disappeared; and Mycenaean centers collapsed, probably from internal discord created by major earthquakes, or the general chaos engulfing the region, or both. Egypt remained intact, but its repulsion of invaders left it with only a remnant of its former power and wealth. In the resulting Dark Ages, most traces of civilization disappeared for several centuries.

Suggestions for Lecture and Discussion Topics

1. Egypt is referred to as an *empire* only with the emergence of the New Kingdom. Discuss what is meant by the term, and how it applies to the New Kingdom (as opposed to the Old and Middle kingdoms). What distinguishes an empire? What are some of the problems typical of an empire? How does Egypt's empire compare to that of the Hittite Empire? Discussion of empire can be a running theme throughout the course, it would therefore be appropriate to foreshadow successive empires such as Greece and Rome.

2. The way in which rulers and their achievements were depicted reveals much about the nature of power and authority throughout history. King Hammurabi is depicted in an ancient carving receiving the laws from the god Shamash (the artifact is now in the Louvre). Not only was Hatshepsut regularly depicted as male, she also had the glories of her reign carved on obelisks erected throughout Egypt. Ramesses II had the treaty he negotiated with the Hyksos chiseled onto a public wall. The unusual depiction of Amunhotep IV (Akenaten) probably signaled that he was breaking away from the past. A discussion of how these representations both reflect and feed into concepts of power and authority would prepare the way for further discussions on the subject in later chapters.

3. Investigate with students the ingredients commonly thought essential for the emergence of civilization (urban settlements, religious cults, writing, diversified agriculture, organized political structures, etc.). Generate a list of justifications for the inclusion of each item on the "civilization list." Are some items more crucial than others? Have students identify additional, and perhaps intangible, factors that they believe also qualify as building blocks for civilization. One could also review the items characteristic of earlier human groupings, such as cooperation in obtaining food, toolmaking, and the division of labor. Are these exclusively human traits? Do they define *society*, if not *civilization*? This question also makes a convenient jumping-off point for an analysis of the very concept of civilization. (See "Terms of History: Civilization," p. 6.)

4. Religion was central to nearly all pre-modern societies and often closely tied to politics. Myths and religious practices furnish an interesting way to gain a broader understanding of the values and norms that governed the lives of both elites and commoners. Some choices for exploration include creation myths such as the Mesopotamian *Enuma Elish*; the Hebrew creation stories of Genesis 1:1–3:24; the Egyptian regeneration myth of Osiris, Isis, and Horus; and the Greek Cosmogonic myths retold in Hesiod's *Thogony* (which is a nice companion to Homer's stories about the gods). Comparisons are also illuminating. The class could contrast the Assyro-Babylonian creation story in the *Enuma Elish* with the Greek account of the generation of the gods, which involves the mutilation and overthrow of Cronos, father of the gods, by his youngest son, Zeus. Other kinds of comparisons involving so-called wisdom literature might be made between the Egyptian Book of the Dead; the Code of Hammurabi; and the Book of Exodus 20–24. Another theme that could be examined concerns epic struggles between the righteous and the wicked, for example, between Gilgamesh and death, Moses and the pharaoh of Exodus, and Theseus and the Minotaur (indeed, many figures from Greek mythology would be suitable for discussion here). Such stories frequently expose important aspects of a culture's political and social organization, familial structures, moral codes, views on warfare, and historical interactions with neighboring peoples. An example might be the investigation of Egyptian gender roles as reflected in the story of Isis and Osiris, with the central role played by the wife/sister/mother Isis in restoring her husband/brother Osiris to life after his murder and dismemberment by their brother Set.

For an overview of Mesopotamian religion, see Jeremy Black and Anthony Green, *Gods, Demons, and Symbols in Ancient Mesopotamia* (Austin: University of Texas Press, 1992); and Thorkild Jacobsen, *Treasures of Darkness: A History of Mesopotamian Religion* (New Haven, CT: Yale University Press, 1986). For Egypt, see Brian Shafer, ed., *Religion in Ancient Egypt: Gods, Myths, and Personal Practice* (Ithaca: Cornell University Press, 1991); and Aylward Blackmun, *Gods, Priests, and Men: Studies in the Religion of Pharaonic Egypt* (London and New York: Kegan Paul, 1993). For Minoan and Mycenaean religion, see Walter Burkert, *Greek Religion* (Cambridge, MA: Harvard University Press, 1985).

5. Mesopotamian, Egyptian, Hittite, and (perhaps) Cretan women enjoyed a higher status and greater legal rights than many western women would in later periods. Even the fictional women of Bronze Age Greece — Helen, Penelope, Clytemnestra — were represented as possessing more freedom than women had in later Greece with the exception of Spartan women. Are there features of dynastic, centralized monarchies, and redistributive economies that might have benefited women's social and legal standing? Why were mythical women depicted as possessing more freedom and power than ordinary Greek women? What sort of lessons for Greek women were embedded within these stories? In addition to the ample sources listed in the chapter bibliography, see Robin Gay, *Women in Ancient Egypt* (Cambridge, MA: Harvard University Press, 1993); Barbara Lesko, "Women of Ancient Egypt and Western Asia," and Marion Katz, "Daughters of Demeter: Women in Ancient Greece," both in *Becoming Visible: Women in European History*, 3d ed., R. Bridenthal, S. Stuard, and M. Kooz, eds. (Boston: Houghton Mifflin, 1998). Both articles have current and very solid bibliographies.

6. The environment determined much of the development of western cultures. Compare the topography, climate, and available natural resources of Mesopotamia, Egypt, the Levant, Crete, and mainland Greece with their social, political, and economic development. How central a role do the students believe was played by the environment? How did it affect intercultural contacts, economic prosperity, political organization, or artistic production? Is the role of the environment overemphasized? Especially when they must introduce a large volume of material in a compressed fashion, instructors often use broad-brush presentations of societies and assign to them a national character. (An exaggerated example might be that the rocky and mountainous internal terrain of Greece led to the individualistic, freedom-loving character of the ancient Greeks.) To what extent are generalizing schemas necessary in historical surveys? Conversely, what are the pitfalls of such depictions? These questions can help sensitize students to both the utility and the inadequacies of boiling down societies to their essential historical features and contributions.

7. Discuss the probable historical constants in the lives and work of ordinary people during this period. How were the lives of peasants, urban laborers, and slaves in Mesopotamia, Egypt, and/or Bronze Age Greece alike or dissimilar? This approach can lead to the subject of history viewed from the bottom up, rather than from

the top down, as well as introducing the role of technology as an agent of historical change. Useful studies (among many) of daily life include: Rosalie David, *The Pyramid Builders of Ancient Egypt*, 2d ed. (New York and London: Routledge, 1996); C. Snell, *Life in the Ancient Near East, 3100–332 B.C.* (New Haven, CT: Yale University Press, 1997). For women's work, often considered even more timeless than men's, see Elizabeth Wayland Barbara, *Women's Work: The First 20,000 Years* (New York: W. W. Norton, 1994).

8. Mesopotamian empires marked the appearance of the form of political organization that would typify much of the premodern west. Discuss the factors that led to their emergence. How did such empires function? What were the political, economic, and social consequences of empire? How was imperial power maintained, and what led to its loss? G. Stein and M. S. Rothman, eds., *Chiefdoms and Early States in the Near East: The Organizational Dynamics of Complexity* (Madison: University of Wisconsin Press, 1994) investigates the growth of political centralization in the early Mesopotamian city-states. Guillermo Algaze, *The Uruk World System: The Dynamics of Expansion of Early Mesopotamian Civilization* (Chicago: University of Chicago Press, 1993) argues that economic exploitation of peripheral areas was a key component of Sumer's rise. For a general history of political and social organization in Mesopotamia, see Amelie Kurht, *The Ancient Near East* (New York and London: Routledge, 1997).

9. The Hebrew religion was unique in the ancient east. Discuss how the character of this monotheism differed from the polytheistic religions of the time. How does monotheism reflect Hebrew attitudes toward social life? the environment? moral obligations? their perception of their historical identity? their place in the universe? How did it compare to the monotheism of Akhenaten in Egypt? For guides to reading the Hebrew Bible as a historical text, see John Bartlett, *Archeology and Biblical Interpretation* (New York and London: Routledge, 1997); and Bernhard Anderson, *Understanding the Old Testament* (Paramus, NJ: Prentice-Hall, 1986). For interactions between the ancient Hebrews and Egyptians, see Jan Assmann, *Moses the Egyptian: The Memory of Egypt in Western Monotheism* (Cambridge, MA: Harvard University Press, 1997).

10. The widespread crisis of 1200 to 1000 B.C.E. remains among the most absorbing puzzles of ancient history. Discuss the varying theories for the collapse and weigh their merits with the class. Major positions on the debate include N. K. Sanders, *The Sea Peoples*, rev. ed. (London: Thames & Hudson, 1985); and Eliezer D. Oren, *The Sea Peoples and Their World: A Reassessment* (Philadelphia: University of Pennsylvania Museum, 2000). Central older theories are contained in Colin Renfrew, "Systems Collapse As Social Transformation," in *Transformations: Mathematical Approaches to Culture Change*, C. Renfrew and K. I. Cooke, eds. (San Diego: Academic Press, 1979), pp. 481–506; and in Emily Vermeule, "The Fall of the Mycenaean Empire," *Archaeology* (1960): 66–75. Chapter 4 of Nancy Demand, *A History of Ancient Greece* (New York: McGraw-Hill, 1996) gives a quick introduction to the competing theories. For a more detailed synthesis, see Robert Drews, *The End of the Bronze Age: Changes in Warfare and Catastrophe circa 1200 B.C.* (Princeton: Princeton University Press, 1993).

Making Connections

1. *Compare and contrast the environmental factors affecting the emergence of the world's first civilizations in Mesopotamia and Egypt.* Both Mesopotamia and Egypt had fairly reliable access to water. The Tigris and Euphrates rivers flooded irregularly, necessitating the development of irrigation techniques, which required a high population density and organizational and bureaucratic institutions, or cities. The Nile River, however, flooded regularly and did not require the development of irrigation techniques. As a consequence, cities in Egypt developed more slowly. Deserts bordered the fertile areas of both Mesopotamia and Egypt and provided some limited degree of defense.

2. *What were the similarities and the differences in the notion of justice in the earliest civilizations?* Justice in early civilizations was often very harsh and frequently demanded exacting punishment in kind for the offense committed. Hebraic law differed from Mesopotamian law in its lack of class distinctions, lighter punishments for crimes against property, and the protection afforded to slaves.

Writing Assignments and Class Presentation Topics

1. The widely used *Epic of Gilgamesh* provides a highly engaging and accessible entry to a time and place that seems highly remote to most students. Good papers or presentations can be elicited by asking students to read for a very specific end. For example, gender roles and relations, or attitudes toward sexuality can be explored by examining the characters of Ishtar, the harlot, and the tavern maid, and their interactions with male characters. Students could investigate the relationship of humans to the environment as embodied in the presentation of Enkidu as wild man or the episode of the flood. Parallels with stories in the Hebrew Bible may also interest students, most obviously of the flood (and of Utnapishtim with Noah). Serpents play decisive roles in each work as well, with regard to the Plant of Life for Gilgamesh and the Tree of Life for Adam and Eve.

2. Many facets of Mesopotamian or Egyptian daily life can be approached via a reading of translations of cuneiform tablets or the personal poetry of ancient Egypt, some of which is presented from a female viewpoint. Many collections of Egyptian poems are included in the anthologies of Egyptian poetry in the chapter bibliography. An interesting selection is the "Collection of Contracts from Mesopotamia, c. 2300–428 B.C.E." at the site. For a glimpse into personal lives, see the collection of translated business and personal cuneiform letters by Leo Oppenheim, *Letters from Mesopotamia* (Chicago: University of Chicago Press, 1987).

3. A short essay comparing the "Negative Confession" from the *Egyptian Book of the Dead* and the Ten Commandments (Exodus 20:1–21) can orient students to similarities and differences between ancient Egyptian and Hebrew ethical proscriptions. For more extended explorations based on legal sources, students can compare Hammurabi's code and the Hebrew laws of the Covenant in Exodus 20:22–23:33. These sources furnish evidence for discussions of family, political organization, economic transactions, ritual observances, work, and slavery. Several translations of the complete Hammurabic code are available in the *Ancient History Sourcebook: Near East* (see "Writing Assignments and Class Presentation Topics" number 2), and there is also an excerpt of it in this manual in the section on "Fundamental Western Civilization Documents." The "Negative Confession" in abbreviated form can be found in Nels Bailkey, *Readings in Ancient History: Thought and Experience from Gilgamesh to St. Augustine*, 5th ed. (Lexington, MA: D. C. Heath, 1992), pp. 56–58, which provides a good selection of longer passages from many ancient works.

4. Have students explore the nature of early Hebrew monotheism and the presentation of the relationship between Yahweh and the Hebrew people. What textual evidence supports the view that, at this stage, the Hebrew faith did not constitute fully formed monotheism? Compare the accounts of the establishment of the covenant to Abraham (Genesis 17:1–27) and its reestablishment under Moses (Exodus 24:1–18, plus the laws in Exodus 20:22–23:33). Students can also compare Hebrew monotheism to the religion of Akhenaton as expressed in his "Hymn to the Aten" in Ancient Near Eastern Texts Relating to the Old Testament, James Pritchard, ed., 3rd rev. ed. (Princeton: Princeton University Press, 1969), pp. 370–371; reprinted in Bailkey, pp. 59–62 (see "Writing Assignments and Class Presentation Topics," number 3).

5. Later Greeks looked back to the Mycenaean Age as a heroic era, especially as it was reflected in *The Iliad* by Homer, who wrote from the other side of the Dark Age. Ask students to re-create the Greek heroic ideal as embodied in the Greek leaders. They would not have to focus exclusively on Achilles, although he provides a good model. The battles become ever more brutal as *The Iliad*

progresses, climaxing when Achilles finally fights in a frenzy of god-like *aretê*. How does the elite warrior relate to his social superiors? equals? inferiors? family? polis? How does the figure of the non-Greek Hector complicate this ideal? How is the ideal further complicated by the appearance of Patroclus's ghost? Was Homer wholeheartedly endorsing aristocratic aretê as personified by the Greeks? The recent translations by Robert Fagels are by far the best in modern English, *The Iliad* (New York: Penguin, 1990) and *The Odyssey* (New York: Penguin, 1996), both with helpful introductions and notes by Bernard Knox.

6. The proliferation of high-quality, academically solid visual resources for this period on the Internet can be mined by students to re-create daily life, to create their own travel guides for ancient visitors to ancient sites, and to aid in further research. While many facets of the institute's Web site are geared toward advanced academic users, undergraduates can use the "Museum Index" to launch other, less intimidating links.

Research Assignments

1. Scholars disagree about the origins of patriarchal institutions in the west. The debate over the causes of women's (greater or lesser) exclusion from positions of political, legal, and economic authority in ancient societies has continued for many years. A central, if controversial, place to begin is Gerda Lerner, *Creation of Patriarchy* (Oxford: Oxford University Press, 1987). For an opposing opinion, see Cynthia Eller, *The Myth of Matriarchal Prehistory* (Boston: Beacon, 2000). Collections of articles that focus on deciphering gender roles and relationships based on prehistoric archaeology include *Engendering Archaeology*, Joan M. Gero and Margaret W. Conkey, eds. (Oxford: Blackwell, 1991); *Reader in Gender Archaeology*, Kelley Hays-Gilpin and David S. Whitley, eds. (New York and London: Routledge, 1998); and *Reading the Body: Representation and Remains in the Archaeological Record*, Alison E. Rautman, ed. (Philadelphia: University of Pennsylvania Press, 2000).

2. New Kingdom Egypt witnessed the reigns of several fascinating and famous pharaohs, any of whom could serve as the focus for a more general investigation of the period. Students could focus on Ramesses II ("the Great," r. 1304–1238 B.C.E.), among the most powerful of all pharaohs, who left an impressive military, architectural, and personal history. Many believe it was during his pharaonate that the Hebrews left Egypt under Moses. Or students could investigate the experimental reign of Amunhotep IV (Akhenaten, r. 1379–1362 B.C.E.) and his wife Queen Nefertiti, under whom not only religion, but also Egyptian art, changed profoundly. Students could also explore the controversy over whether or not

Nefertiti became co-ruler with her husband, Amunhotep IV (Akhenaten). Hatshepsut (r. 1498–1483 B.C.E.) does, of course, garner much attention as the only female pharaoh. An absorbing and well-illustrated popular introduction to all the pharaohs is Peter Clayton, *Chronicle of the Pharaohs* (London: Thames and Hudson, 1994). Studies of individual pharaohs include Joyce Tyldesley's biographies of Hatshepsut: *The Female Pharaoh* (New York: Viking Penguin, 1996) and *Ramesses: Egypt's Greatest Pharaoh* (London: Viking, 2000); Bernadette Menu, *Ramesses II: Greatest of the Pharaohs* (New York: Harry Abrams, 1999); Donald Redford, *Akhenaten: The Heretic King* (Princeton: Princeton University Press, 1987); Eric Hornung, *Akhenaten and the Religion of Light* (Ithaca: Cornell University, 1999). Primary sources include Sir Alan Gardiner, *The Kadesh Inscriptions of Ramesses II* (Oxford: Oxford University Press, 1960) and *The Amarna Letters*, William Moran, trans. (Baltimore: Johns Hopkins University Press, 1992), both good for investigating Egyptian interactions with foreign powers. For an analysis of Egyptian diplomacy from a modern, political perspective, see Raymond Cohen and Raymond Westbrook, eds., *Amarna Diplomacy: The Beginning of International Relations* (Baltimore: Johns Hopkins University Press, 1999).

3. The contributions of the lands south of Egypt to the growth of ancient cultures have only recently been incorporated into broader surveys of western and ancient history. Surveys include Stanley Burstein, ed., *Ancient African Civilizations: Kush and Axum* (Princeton: Markus Wiener, 1998) and D. O'Conner, *Ancient Nubia: Egypt's Rival in Africa* (Philadelphia: University of Pennsylvania Press, 1994). A shorter introduction, with very solid bibliography, can be found in the special issue, "Nubia: An Ancient African Civilization," of *Expedition: The University Museum Magazine of Archaeology and Anthropology,* University of Pennsylvania 35.2 (1993).

4. The Indiana Jones films and their many offspring capitalized on the perennial romance of the archaeologist's profession. Students may be interested in the real-life explorations of Knossos, Mycenae, and Troy. Investigations of the findings as these relate to the historical sources can lead students to consider the complementary roles of archaeological and textual analysis in the reconstruction of ancient history. Students can also evaluate how the preconceptions of archaeologists like Arthur Evans and Heinrich Schliemann may have distorted their interpretations of their findings. A good place to start is William Biers, *The Archaeology of Greece,* 2d ed. (Ithaca: Cornell University Press, 1996), with specialized bibliographies for individual periods and sites. Also see Arthur Evans, *The Palace of Minos,* 4 vols. (London: Macmillan, 1964 [originally published 1921–1935]); and William A. McDonald and Carol G. Thomas, *Progress Into the Past: The Rediscovery of Mycenaean Civilization,* 2d ed. (Bloomington: Indiana

University Press, 1990). A basic work on the general subject is Paul MacKendrick, *The Greek Stones Speak* (New York: W. W. Norton, 1962). For an ancient Greek's comments on the Greek "sights," consult J. G. Frazer, *Pausanias's Description of Greece,* 6 vols. (Macmillan, New York: 1965 [originally published 1898]).

Literature

Dalley, Stephanie, and C. J. Fordyce, trans. & eds. *Myths from Mesopotamia: Creation, The Flood, Gilgamesh, and Others.* 1998.

Foster, John L. *Hymns, Prayers, and Songs: An Anthology of Ancient Egyptian Lyric Poetry.* 1996.

Lichtheim, Miriam. *Ancient Egyptian Literature.* 3 vols., 1973–1980.

Richardson, M. E. J. *Hammurabi's Laws: Text, Translation and Glossary.* 2000.

Sandars, N. K., trans. *The Epic of Gligamesh.* 1960.

Simpson, William Kelly, ed. *The Literature of Ancient Egypt: An Anthology of Stories, Instructions, and Poetry,* 3d ed. 2003.

Singer, Itamar. *Writings from the Ancient World: Hittite Prayers.* 2002.

Films and Videos

Egypt's Golden Empire (2002) (PBS: VHS/DVD, 180 min.). This excellent three-part series focuses on the period between 1570 B.C.E. and 1070 B.C.E. and covers the reigns of Ahmose, Hatshepsut, Amunhotep III, Akenaton, Tutankhamon, and Ramesses the Great.

Historical Skills

Mapping the West: The Calamities of 1200–1000 B.C.E., p. 38

Trace the paths of the Sea Peoples' invasions. What was their presumed point of origin? Based on what you know about their destinations, what might have led them to target such locations? How would their movements have affected trade and commerce in the Mediterranean and Near East?

The Ziggurat of Ur in Sumer, p. 10

The presence of monumental architecture is one of the hallmarks of a civilization. What motives would generate the production of such a massive edifice? What effect would the creation of this temple have for the reputation of Ur and its ruler, both on the city's own populace and on those of other city-states? What can the dedication of such a quantity of material resources and human labor indicate about the values of the societies that generated such structures or about their standard of living?

The Lion Gate to the Citadel at Mycenae, p. 35

The famous Lion Gate, with its cyclopean walls, furnishes another example of Bronze Age monumental architecture. It also constitutes the earliest surviving monumental sculpture in all of Greece. What realities of everyday life in Mycenae do the iconography and construction techniques reveal? Despite its size, Mycenae only possessed two entrances: the main Lion Gate and a northern gate. What impression would the Lion Gate have made on visitors entering the citadel for the first time?

Declaring Innocence on Judgment Day in Ancient Egypt, p. 26

The Egyptian concept of a "negative confession," where the dead listed not their accomplishments but the evil acts that they had *not* committed over the course of their lives, would be appropriate for discussion. Good works are neither always altruistic, nor can wicked acts necessarily be offset by kindness or achievement. The idea of "negative confession" could also form the basis of a comparison with concepts of contrition and repentance in Judaism and Christianity.

Terms of History: Civilization, p. 6

Comparison of the definitions given, including the proposed neutral definition ("any type of culture, society, etc., of a specific place, time, or group"), could generate a lively debate about what students understand the essential components of civilization (or "Civilization" or "a civilization") to be or what they should be. But instructors might also encounter some resistance or confusion from students upon even raising the question, especially in a highly diversified classroom.

You might ask whether the group can agree on a level of technological or artisanal achievement that should form the entry point for civilization. Or is the term more appropriately used in connection with moral, religious, or ethical content? Does the absence of war qualify a society as civilized? Or is conflict an inevitable concomitant to a civilized state? At what point does a society achieve civilization: when its elites attain the hallmarks of civilization, or when those hallmarks are more uniformly available to the populace at large?

OTHER BEDFORD/ST. MARTIN'S RESOURCES FOR CHAPTER 1

The following resources are available to accompany Chapter 1. Please refer to the Preface of this manual for detailed descriptions of all the ancillaries.

For Instructors

Transparencies

The following maps and images from Chapter 1 are available as full-color acetates.

- Map 1.1: The Ancient Near East, c. 4000–3000 B.C.E.
- Map 1.2: Ancient Egypt
- Map 1.3: Greece and the Aegean Sea, c. 1500 B.C.E.
- Mapping the West: The Period of Calamities, c. 1200–1000 B.C.E.
- *Standard of Ur*
- *Egyptian Hieroglyphic Writing*

Instructor's Resources CD-ROM

The following maps and image from Chapter 1, as well as a chapter outline, are available on disc in both Power-Point and jpeg formats.

- Map 1.1: The Ancient Near East, c. 4000–3000 B.C.E.
- Map 1.2: Ancient Egypt
- Map 1.3: Greece and the Aegean Sea, c. 1500 B.C.E.
- Mapping the West: The Period of Calamities, c. 1200–1000 B.C.E.
- *Standard of Ur* (chapter image, page 8)

For Students

Sources of The Making of the West

The following documents are available in Chapter 1 of the companion sourcebook by Katharine J. Lualdi, University of Southern Maine.

1. *King Hammurabi*, The Code of Hammurabi (Early Eighteenth Century B.C.E.)
2. *The Book of Exodus*, Chapters 19–24 (c. Tenth–Sixth Centuries B.C.E.)
3. *Egyptian Scribal Exercise Book* (Twelfth Century B.C.E.)
4. *The Epic of Creation* (c. 1800 B.C.E.)
5. *The Story of Sinuhe* (Late Nineteenth Century B.C.E.)

Study Guides

The print **Study Guide** and the **Online Study Guide** at bedfordstmartins.com/hunt, both by Victoria Thompson (Arizona State University) and Eric Johnson (University of California, Los Angeles), help students synthesize the material they have learned as well as practice the skills historians use to make sense of the past. The following Map, Visual, and Document activities are available for Chapter 1.

Map Activity

• Map 1.1: The Ancient Near East

Visual Activity

• *Standard of Ur* (chapter image, page 8)

Reading Historical Documents

• *Hammurabi's Laws on Surgery*
• *Declaring Innocence on Judgment Day in Ancient Egypt*

New Paths for Western Civilization

c. 1000–c. 500 B.C.E.

CHAPTER RESOURCES

Main Chapter Topics

1. The invasions by the Sea Peoples and concurrent disasters (1200–1000 B.C.E.) completely destroyed many Bronze Age settlements and left Egypt permanently weakened. When civilizations reemerged by the first millennium B.C.E., the competitive and militaristic Mesopotamian city-states returned to their old patterns of empire building, while the first participatory governments emerged in archaic Greece.

2. The Neo-Assyrian, then Neo-Babylonian, and then Persian empires, dominated Near Eastern history of the period. The Persian Empire established by Cyrus the Great, was the largest the west had yet produced. (In the fifth century B.C.E., the Persians would threaten to absorb the independent Greek city-states, which confronted their opponent in the later Persian wars.)

3. Scarce natural resources led the Greeks to establish colonies and trade networks throughout the Mediterranean and Black Sea. Rivalries between Greek city-states were common. Nonetheless, a common language, religion, cult centers, artistic conventions, and the Olympic Games (begun in 776 B.C.E.) created a pan-Hellenic sense of "Greek" identity and solidarity.

4. In the Levant, the Hebrews briefly established an independent monarchy under Saul, David, and Solomon. Their monotheism developed fully, and their scriptural corpus of the Torah and the prophetic books were set down in writing. Their religion and law served to sustain Jewish identity throughout the frequent periods of diaspora that characterized their subsequent history.

5. The Greeks reacquired literacy when they adapted the Phoenician (Canaanite) alphabet. Among the literary masterpieces of the era were the lyric poems of Sappho and the epics of Homer. Homer's depiction of warriors in the Trojan War in *The Iliad* vividly explores the nature of aretê ("excellence") embodied in Achilles and his enemy Hector and captures the essence of ideal Greek manhood that inspired future leaders including Alexander the Great. Hesiod's *Theogony* recounts the genealogy of the gods, their suffering, and their concern for justice among humankind.

6. The political organization of the Greek city-states varied, ranging from tyranny in Corinth, to military oligarchy in Sparta, to nearly complete democracy of male citizens in Athens. But whatever their political structure, city-states shared a concept of citizenship in the polis. Citizen women enjoyed various protections but were barred from direct political participation. Even legal protections were denied to slaves, who were prevalent throughout the Greek world.

7. Sparta's nearly totalitarian regime, based on strict subordination of the individual to the state and the subjugation of Helots—slaves who performed all manual labor—earned the polis its reputation for repression and made it the premier military force of archaic Greece. In contrast, Athens worked out a functioning democratic government. Solon and Cleisthenes reformed economic, political, and judicial laws to bring Athens closest to extending equal legal and political rights to all male citizens, regardless of class.

8. The dualism of the Zoroastrians of Persia and the monotheism of the Hebrews changed the religious composition of the west, and the rationalism of the pre-Socratic Greek thinkers offered a logical, empirical view of nature and the cosmos.

Summary

The Dark Ages that resulted from the mysterious, widespread calamities of 1200 to 1000 B.C.E., were relatively short-lived in Mesopotamia. After about a century, the region resumed its old patterns. City-states strove to establish imperial control over the region, culminating in the Persian Empire. In the Levant, Hebrew monotheism crystallized and their Bible was set in writing; the

Canaanites (Phoenicians) had invented the first true alphabet, which was adopted by the Greeks. The emergence of participatory, citizen-based governments in archaic Greece, particularly Athenian democracy, profoundly altered western politics. Finally, Greek rationalism laid the foundations of western science.

After the Dark Ages, Neo-Assyria appeared as the dominant power in Mesopotamia from 900 to 612 B.C.E. Assyria gained hegemony through military conquest, achieved with infantry-based tactics that replaced chariot-based warfare. Its territory encompassed even Babylon and Egypt — signaling Egypt's permanent loss of independence. The Neo-Assyrians ensured control by routinely deporting conquered peoples and exacting tribute. So many Aramaeans were deported that, by the eighth century, Aramaic had replaced Assyrian as the land's everyday language. Although King Ashurbanipal (r. 680–626 B.C.E.) considered himself an intellectual, Neo-Assyrian culture valued war and warlike pursuits over scholarship. Neo-Assyrian rule was so harsh, even its own people were alienated, and rebellions were frequent.

The brief but brilliant civilization of the Neo-Babylonian Empire was created when the Medes and Chaldeans rebelled against Assyrian repression, destroying the capital of Nineveh in 612 B.C.E. Under Nebuchadnezzar II (r. 605–562 B.C.E.), the Neo-Babylonians consolidated their victory by ousting the Egyptians from Syria at the battle of Carchemish in 605 B.C.E. Nebuchadnezzar's beautification of Babylon included the Ishtar Gate and the Hanging Gardens. The Chaldeans preserved Mesopotamian literature, like the *Epic of Gilgamesh*, while making their own contributions, especially in the area of wisdom literature. Their advances in astronomy were also passed on to other cultures, especially that of Greece.

Mesopotamian empires reached their height with the immense Persian Empire established by Cyrus the Great (r. c. 557–530 B.C.E.). Known for military and diplomatic skill, Cyrus also displayed religious tolerance, even permitting deported Hebrews to return to Jerusalem and rebuild their temple. Even though Persian rulers cultivated an aura of magnificence, they nonetheless permitted compliant subject peoples a great deal of internal freedom and placed relatively autonomous governors (satraps) in charge of provinces. The Persian Empire attained its greatest growth under Darius I (r. 522–486 B.C.E.), who extended it from the Indus valley to Thrace, just north of Greece. Darius instituted a system of roads and couriers to speed communications and control within his far-flung empire.

The dualistic Persian religion of Zoroastrianism, derived from the teachings of the legendary prophet Zarathustra (who may have lived as long ago as 1200–1000 B.C.E.), taught that all creation was locked in a continuous struggle between good led by Ahura Mazda and evil led by Ahriman. Zoroastrianism was monotheis-

tic and asserted a moral dualism whereby the exercise of human free will to pursue the way of truth or the way of lies determined one's salvation or damnation after death.

In the Levant, the Hebrew tribes briefly created an independent state. The monarchy created under Saul flourished under David (r. 1010–970 B.C.E.) and Solomon (r. c. 961–922 B.C.E.), whose reign witnessed the kingdom's greatest prosperity and the construction of the temple at Jerusalem. After Solomon's death, the kingdom split into Israel in the north and Judah in the south. Israel fell to the Assyrians in 722 B.C.E.; Babylon's Nebuchadnezzar II subdued Judah and its capital Jerusalem in 597 B.C.E., leveling the temple and deporting the Hebrews (later called Jews, from the Hebrew name for Judah) to Mesopotamia.

Although the Persian king Cyrus I allowed them to leave Babylon in 539 B.C.E., and return to their homeland, the Hebrews were usually politically subject to other peoples. Their prophetic tradition taught that their enslavement and political defeats were divine retribution for their failure to observe the Sinai covenant. An apocalyptic tradition also emerged that preached the end of the world and a final judgment by God, which would precede the coming of a better age.

Jewish law developed to help people follow divine precepts. Strict ritual purity had to be observed in all facets of life. Marriage to non-Jews was forbidden, diet was regulated, and work was not allowed on the Sabbath. The laws, which affected rich and poor alike, reinforced Jewish identity throughout their history of Diaspora (dispersion). Monotheism was consolidated, and their sacred texts were compiled into the Hebrew Bible, which formed a foundation for the Scriptures of Christianity and Islam.

Greece endured a much longer Dark Age (c. 1000–750 B.C.E.) than the Near East. Virtually all facets of civilization disappeared, including writing, urban settlements, and effective government. Trade survived although artistic production declined in sophistication and agriculture no longer produced the abundance of Minoan and Mycenaean times. Famine and warfare had decimated the population, and the survivors shifted to herding and subsistence agriculture. Their culture was kept alive via oral transmission.

By 800 B.C.E., the Greeks reestablished contact with eastern Mediterraneans. They adapted the alphabet of the Phoenicians (Canaanites), adding letters for vowel sounds. Trade burgeoned, and the Greeks learned to smelt iron ore and used it in place of bronze. Iron produced cheaper, more durable tools and weapons than bronze, and iron farming tools helped to produce larger harvests to support a growing population.

The return of literacy recorded masterpieces of epic and lyric. The earliest surviving written works were Homer's *Iliad* and *Odyssey* (c. 750 B.C.E.), originally preserved via oral tradition. Their re-creation of the semi-historical Trojan War (c. 1200 B.C.E.) and its aftermath reveals the central values of archaic society, particularly aretê. Elite men manifested aretê through military exploits and noble public speeches and women through fidelity to and preservation of the home and family. Despite the independence of the city-states, their common language, gods, and artistic conventions created a sense of Greek identity among them. Zeus headed the twelve Olympian gods. Every four years, the best elite, male athletes throughout Greece competed at the Olympic Games (begun in 776 B.C.E.) to honor Zeus. Separate games were held for women in which unmarried women could compete, in honor of Zeus's wife Hera. Greek leaders did not base their political authority on religion, but there were civic rites supported by the state. Each city-state honored one particular god especially as its protector. Ironically, both Sparta and Athens chose Athena as their defender. The gods suffered pain and unhappiness, though only temporarily. Greeks were expected to honor the gods to thank them for blessings received and to invoke their aid. Further, they were to avoid offending them, for fear of provoking misfortune. According to Homer, there was a plan for human existence in the form of Fate, which even Zeus does not overrule, but stories like the one about Bellerophon suggest that fate was not based on justice. Hesiod's stories, however, asserted a divine order for the universe that included a concern for justice. Hesiod identified Zeus as the fountain of justice, and lamented that unjust leaders of his own day caused unnecessary tensions between peasants and the elites.

Greece's mountainous terrain led to numerous isolated and fiercely independent city-states ranging from several hundred to several thousand inhabitants. Greece possessed few natural resources, and only about 30 percent of its land was arable, so Greeks relied on maritime trade for raw materials. By 750 B.C.E., entrepreneurs from many city-states had established settlements in the western and northern Mediterranean. These "colonies" (not to be confused with the modern version) were independent and supplied farmland, new markets, and increased contacts with Egypt and the Near East, which influenced archaic Greek art and thought.

Reemergent Greek city-states were unique in the ancient world. Many extended citizenship to free inhabitants and participation in governance to free adult males. In theory, poor and rich citizens alike enjoyed the same legal rights, but some city-states came closer than others to this ideal, most notably Athens. Although protected by the laws, citizen women were barred from political participation.

Why this distinctive system developed is not fully understood. Historians long attributed it to the shift from chariot-based to hoplite warfare, in which a citizen infantry militia furnished its own armor, made affordable by the introduction of iron equipment. These hop-

lites felt their voluntary defense of the city-state should be rewarded with greater political rights. However, because the hoplites were not laboring poor, the theory fails to account for the spread of civic rights to even the lowest strata of free society. Tyrants may have granted citizenship and rights to the poor in exchange for their support against elite rivals and opponents. Possibly the polis recognized the nonmilitary but essential contribution of the poorer members of the city-state. A likely theory is that men too poor to equip themselves as hoplites nevertheless played a crucial role in battles, fighting as "light infantry" armed with stones and arrows. This contribution may have earned them their rights and citizenship. Greek citizen liberty coexisted with widespread slavery: by the fifth century B.C.E., perhaps as much as one-third of the population consisted of slaves. Their lot varied considerably, from relatively valued positions as public servants and household tutors to the intolerable conditions experienced by mine and galley slaves.

Greek women's lives were quite secluded and restricted, except in Sparta. Their only public role was at certain religious festivals. Perpetually under male guardianship, a woman's primary duty was to produce legitimate children and to manage the household. Only poor women worked outside the home. Marriages were arranged, and daughters furnished with dowries. The sexual restrictions placed on women, who were expected to observe complete chastity within marriage, did not apply to Greek men. The prevailing misogynistic attitude was that women were a necessary evil to be tolerated for the propagation of family and city-state.

Citizens participated in government in distinct ways. In oligarchies, political power was held by a small group of citizens. Sparta developed the most distinctive oligarchy. Headed by two kings, the government was controlled by the council of twenty-eight elders and five elected ephors. Most citizens (the Alike) merely rubber-stamped legislation introduced into the assembly by the oligarchs, but could exercise a kind of mass veto. Strict adherence to Spartan laws was demanded and devotion to the state defined Spartan aretê.

Military skill and courage defined existence. By 700 B.C.E., Sparta conquered neighboring Messenia and reduced its entire population to Helots, or state-owned slaves, who were very harshly treated. Each Spartan received an allotment of the Helots' confiscated land to support himself and his family. Helots performed all manual labor, freeing Spartan men for training, warfare, and running their city-state. Spartan virtues were inculcated through rigid laws and a socialization process that prepared men for warfare and vigilance against the threat of Helot uprisings. From the ages of seven to thirty, males lived, trained, and fought together. Youths entered into exclusive, and often sexual, relationships with older males to reinforce bonds between fighting men, strengthen devotion to the state, and weaken links to their families. Eventually, the younger partner would marry, found a family, and become senior mentor to an adolescent "beloved."

Spartan women, who enjoyed extensive public freedom, could own land and other property. They underwent physical training that aided in bearing healthy children. When men went to war, women exercised wide latitude in running their households. Should a husband fail to provide a Spartan woman with children, she could—with her husband's permission—take a lover who might succeed.

Tyranny occurred if one family or individual monopolized political authority. The word *tyrant* did not necessarily imply abuse of power. Many tyrants ruled according to the laws, upgraded public works, and extended benefits to the lower classes to win their support. Tyrannies were often short-lived because unpopular tyrants were often driven out. Cypselus (r. 657–625 B.C.E.) and his descendants established the most well-known tyranny in the wealthy trade-center of Corinth.

Democracy achieved its most complete expression in Athens, the city-state that most influenced western history. Athens possessed a middle class, an unusual occurrence in the ancient world. Its development of democratic government required several centuries, but was secure enough by 632 B.C.E. to spark mass citizen opposition to the attempted tyranny of Cylon. Although elite Athenians initially dominated politics, full political rights were gradually extended to the middle class and poor. After Cylon's expulsion the citizens selected Draco (the "Snake") to harmonize society by reforming the laws, but his policies proved too severe (or "draconian") to endure. By 600 B.C.E., many farmers had fallen into debt slavery, and the situation threatened to disintegrate into civil war. In 594 B.C.E., Athenians chose Solon to further revise the laws. Most notably, he announced the "shaking off of obligations," which outlawed debt slavery and freed debt slaves. Solon struck a balance: debt cancellation angered the rich, while his refusal to redistribute farmland disappointed the poor.

Solon furthered democracy by reforming the basis of political participation. He divided the population according to income and tied eligibility for office-holding to wealth. The assembly, however, was open to even the poorest male citizens. Social mobility was now possible because if a man's income rose, so did his political opportunities. For efficiency, Solon instituted the Council of Four Hundred, whose members were chosen annually by lot as gatekeepers for issues to be brought before the assembly. Solon permitted all citizens to lodge criminal accusations on behalf of victims and to appeal legal judgments to the assembly. Again balancing class interests, Solon also created the elite Areopagus Council with membership restricted to ex-archons. This council tried the most serious cases.

Tyranny returned to Athens under Peisistratus (546

B.C.E.), whose benevolent rule and public works won approval. But his son Hippias's harshness generated opposition from the Alcmaeonid family, who enlisted Spartan intervention to expel him in 510 B.C.E. The Athenians then elected Cleisthenes, an Alcmaeonid later considered the "father of democracy," to draft further political reforms. By 500 B.C.E., Cleisthenes outlined a complex system for broader sharing of political power based on the geographical distribution of the population into demes and an expanded Council of Five Hundred.

The individualism displayed in Greek politics was expressed in the arts as well. Stimulated by renewed contacts with Egypt and the Near East, sculptors and vase painters demonstrated increasing realism and refinement. The personal idiom of human emotion characterized the new lyric poetry, in contrast to the military and mythical epics of Homer and Hesiod. Early lyric poetry achieved its pinnacle in the work of the female poet Sappho (b. c. 630 B.C.E.).

Influenced by Near Eastern mathematics and astronomy, the Greek pre-Socratics of Ionia created the first systematic philosophy. The contributions of Thales (c. 625–545 B.C.E.), Anaximander (c. 610–540 B.C.E.), and Pythagoras (active c. 530 B.C.E.) in physics, mathematics, and geometry marked the emergence of Greek rationalism, which taught that human reason could decipher the fixed and universal laws governing the natural world. The insistence that logical explanations based on evidence, rather than the arbitrary actions of the gods, could account for natural phenomena formed the foundation for western science.

Suggestions for Lecture and Discussion Topics

1. The scriptural tradition and laws of the Hebrews served not only to articulate their religious teachings but also to cement their identity as a scattered people nearly always under the political domination of others. Discuss the ways in which the stories contained in the Hebrew Bible serve this function throughout their history of Diaspora.

2. The emergence of hoplite warfare marked a significant transformation in the history of military tactics. Discuss the personal stake Greeks had in military prowess, as it was revealed in the elite martial culture of Homer's *Iliad*. Contrast the individualistic exploits of the Homeric heroes with the coordinated group effort required of hoplites. This idea can be impressed on students by having them (if they're willing!) re-create a hoplite phalanx formation. Also, compare the expense involved in chariot-based warfare to the relatively minimal equipment of hoplite infantry. Then debate both the merits and inadequacies of the "hoplite theory" of the origins of democracy. The class could also explore the hoplite as the ideal Spartan citizen. Useful details on mil-

itary techniques can be found in Victor Hanson, ed., *Hoplites: The Classical Greek Battle Experience* (London and New York: Routledge, 1998); *The Western Way of War: Infantry Battle in Classical Greece*, 2d ed. (Berkeley and Los Angeles: University of California Press, 2000); and J. F. Lazenby, *The Spartan Army* (Chicago: University of Chicago Press, 1985). For a sociohistorical perspective on Greek warfare, see John Rich and Graham Shiply, eds., *War and Society in the Greek World* (London and New York: Routledge, 1995).

3. Persian Zoroastrianism centered on dualism and on the role of free will in human salvation, concepts that continue to dominate western religious thought. Discuss these concepts as they appear in Zoroastrianism and then ask the students to comment on how they might relate to: earlier religious traditions encompassed by the Egyptian Book of the Dead and the Ten Commandments in Exodus; to later religious developments; and on western intellectual traditions in general. Mary Boyce provides a general introduction in *A History of Zoroastrianism: The Early Period* (Leiden: Brill, 1996). Translated primary sources can be found in the section on Persian Religion in the Internet Ancient History Sourcebook: Ancient Near East.

4. Another central theme in Greek history is the participation of citizens in the political life of the polis under the rule of law. To what extent was equality achieved, and at what costs? These questions can be explored through a comparison of Sparta and Athens, the two city-states for which by far the most information has survived. Were the Spartans with their identical social standing as citizen-warriors more equal than the more obviously class-stratified society of Athens? Did the women of Sparta really enjoy a more equal status with men than the quite secluded middle- and upper-class Athenian women? Do the students agree with the sentiment that, in a democracy, the citizen is the slave of the polis? Discussions of Athenian developments are found in Nicholas Jones, *Ancient Greece: State and Society* (Saddle River, NJ: Prentice-Hall, 1997), which despite its title focuses primarily on Athens; the more detailed Charles Hignett, *A History of the Athenian Constitution to the End of the Fifth Century B.C.E.* (Oxford: Clarendon, 1952); and for citizen involvement in the functioning of democracy, R. Sinclair, *Democracy and Participation in Athens* (Cambridge: Cambridge University Press, 1988). For Sparta, consult P. Cartledge, *Sparta and Laconia: A Regional History, 1300–362 B.C.E.* (New York and London: Routledge, 1979); and A. Powell, *Classical Sparta: Techniques behind Her Success* (Norman, OK: University of Oklahoma Press, 1988).

5. The text suggests that the emergence of a middle class in Athens was an essential ingredient in the development of its democratic institutions. Similarly, economic crisis provided the impetus for the early democratic reforms of Draco and Solon. What is the role of economic prosperity in the formation of participatory government? Contrast Athenian democracy with the empires of the Near East or the pharaonic dynasties of Egypt, both vastly more prosperous and powerful than archaic Greece. Did the nondistributive nature of the Greek economies entail an individual initiative that the subject peoples of Egypt or the Near Eastern empires lacked? Was minimal social welfare more precarious to sustain in the Greek city-states than in a redistributive economy? For the development of Greek democracy, see Victor Hanson, *The Other Greeks: The Family Farm and the Agrarian Roots of Western Civilization* (New York: Free Press, 1995), which considers the role of the independent hoplite-farmer. Also see Chester Starr, *Economic and Social Growth of Early Greece, 800–500 B.C.E.* (Oxford: Oxford University Press, 1977).

6. By the time of the Persian Wars, the Persians represented the threatening "other" to the Greeks, who characterized them as "barbarians." However, the Persian Empire and its rulers were widely admired in the ancient world. For example, the Hebrew Bible describes Cyrus the Great as the "anointed" of God (Isaiah II, 45:1–3). Review the generally tolerant and sophisticated policies the Persian leaders exercised to maintain their vast empire (the Romans would later follow similar practices in the administration of their own subject territories). The discussion can introduce the topics of European/Near Eastern cultural and political rivalries and interpenetration that would be important in subsequent eras (during the Persian Wars, the Hellenistic and Roman eras, medieval Christianity and Islam, etc.). The class can also address the issue of cultural vilification that often accompanies war. For further information on Persia, see J. M. Cook, *The Persian Empire* (New York: Schocken, 1987).

7. Painted vases, a major Athenian product, often featured vivid scenes from daily life. A slide or PowerPoint presentation could launch a discussion about virtually any aspect of this broad topic, or furnish the basis for an in-class writing assignment. Excellent collections are reproduced in John Boardman's *Athenian Black Figure Vases* (Oxford: Oxford University Press, 1974) and *Athenian Red Figure Vases* (Oxford: Oxford University Press, 1975).

8. Athenians possessed a reputation for litigiousness as great as that of modern Americans. Outline the central role that juries played in the civic life of this polis. Remember, serving on juries was one of the main political duties (and privileges) of every male citizen, including those who were poor. Personal reputation and rhetorical skill often played crucial roles in determining the outcome of a trial. In which ways did trials operate in this city-state, where for men, at least, there was very little distinction to be made between the "public" and "private" realms? How did the emphasis on public speaking con-

tribute to one's public career? How did reputation affect daily life in this face-to-face community, especially regarding gender roles? Many illuminating studies, often influenced by anthropology, have recently appeared: David Cohen, *Law, Violence, and Community in Classical Athens* (Cambridge: Cambridge University Press, 1995); S. Todd, *The Shape of Athenian Law* (Oxford: Oxford University Press, 1993); also the collected articles in P. Cartledge, P. Miller, and S. Todd, eds., *Nomos: Essays in Athenian Law, Politics, and Society* (Cambridge: Cambridge University Press, 1990), especially R. Osborne, "Vexatious Litigation in Classical Athens."

9. Given the emphasis on personal liberty in Greek history and writings, the phenomenon of tyrannies may seem strange. However, the inefficiencies of democracy may at times have made tyranny seem attractive, especially in periods of crisis. Explore the episodes of tyrannical rule in the archaic city-states, considering why some (those of Cepsylus and Peisistratus, for example) succeeded, while others (Cylon, Hippias) failed. What were the broader political and social realities that surrounded each episode? A standard study of Greek tyranny remains A. Andrewes, *The Greek Tyrants* (New York: Harper & Row, 1956). See also James McGrew, *Tyranny and Political Culture in Ancient Greece* (Ithaca: Cornell University Press, 1993).

10. The Homeric epics provide an inexhaustible supply of information about many facets of archaic Greek culture and society, as well as a reflection of its semimythical Mycenaean past. Selected passages from *The Iliad* and *The Odyssey* can serve as a basis for lectures on notions of masculinity and military virtue, the lives of women (mortal and immortal) and the family, religious beliefs of the early Greeks, inter-Hellenic conflict and cooperation in the face of a common adversary, relations between social classes, and the complicated Greek attitude toward the non-Greek (the "other," in this case, the Trojans). More specifically, the figure of Hector serves as an example of the warrior tempered by civilization; Nestor as the perfect heroic figure; Penelope as the epitome of constancy and faithfulness, etc. See Robert Fagels translations: *The Iliad* (New York: Penguin, 1990) and *The Odyssey* (New York: Penguin, 1996).

Making Connections

1. *What made the Greek city-state a new form of political and social organization?* Most Greek city-states shared a concept of citizenship whereby free adult male citizens participated in government. In theory, rich and poor citizens alike enjoyed the same legal rights, but some city-states came closer to this ideal than others.

2. *What were the differences between the ideas of the Ionian philosophers and the traditions of myth?* Ionian philosophers believed that unchanging natural laws,

rather than the whims of the gods, governed the universe. They believed the universe was ordered and knowable and separated scientific thinking from myth and religion.

Writing Assignments and Class Presentation Topics

1. The contrast between Athens and Sparta often fascinates students, especially the lifestyle of Sparta. Have students explore through a class presentation the fundamental distinctions and similarities of these rivals through a comparison of the reforms attributed to Lycurgus and Solon. The content of their reforms can be found in their biographies in Plutarch's *Parallel Lives*. Solon provides additional information in some of his poems; translations are contained in David Mulroy, *Early Greek Lyric Poetry* (Ann Arbor: University of Michigan Press, 1992).

2. Athens and Sparta differed radically from each other both socially and politically. A comparison between the cultures from an Athenian or Spartan perspective would be revealing of both societies. Students can assume a variety of roles—warrior, aristocrat, peasant, woman, slave—and compare them to their respective counterparts.

3. Have students track down a Greek god or goddess they can personally identify with. Have them briefly describe their particular god and discuss what their choice says about themselves. To ensure that students read beyond the obvious twelve Olympic gods, it may be necessary to restrict their selections to lesser figures. See J. E. Zimmerman, *Dictionary of Classical Mythology* (New York: Bantam Books, 1964; rpt. 1983).

4. Have the students explore the emergence of Greek individualism as expressed in Archaic lyric poems. How do they represent the "public" topics of military valor, arranged marriages, religious rituals, or civic service in politics? Conversely, what is the range of emotions and personal topics they discuss? Popular choices include Archilocus of Paros, whose poems were banned as subversive in Sparta; and Sappho, for a woman's point of view. Theognis, Alcaeus, and Tyrtaeus say many interesting things as well. Students could also compare the Greek lyrics with the personal poetry from ancient Egypt. Good collections of translations from the Greek are Andrew Miller, *Greek Lyric* (Indianapolis: Hackett, 1996); and Barbara Fowler, *Archaic Greek Poetry* (Madison: University of Wisconsin Press, 1992).

5. Students can approach the life of an independent, middle-class farmer as embodied in *Hesiod's Works and Days: A Translation and Commentary for the Social Sciences*, D. W. Hardy and W. C. Neale, trans. and eds. (Berkeley and Los Angeles: University of California

Press, 1996). Further background can be obtained from Alison Burford, *Land and Labor in the Greek World* (Baltimore: Johns Hopkins University Press, 1993). This collection of aphorisms and "common-sense" reflections on women, hired hands, sibling rivalry, and the corruption of those in political authority reveals a society far from that embodied in the Homeric epics. What constitutes a successful life, according to the speaker?

Research Assignments

1. The question of the origins of Greek civilization has recently generated considerable and heated scholarly debate. The study that sparked the controversy was Martin Bernal's *Black Athena: The Afroasiatic Roots of Classical Civilization,* vols. 1 and 2 (New Brunswick, NJ: Rutgers University Press, 1987 and 1991). Among the numerous responses to it is Mary Lefkowicz's pointed *Not Out of Africa: How Afrocentrism Became an Excuse to Teach Myth as History* (New York: Basic Books, 1996). Have students explore the merits of the argument on both sides. This topic provides a good introduction to historiography and revisionism in history.

2. Greek sexuality is another controversial topic that has generated numerous analyses from a wide variety of methodological perspectives. In addition to the works listed in the chapter bibliography, see J. J. Winkler, *The Constraints of Desire: The Anthropology of Sex and Gender in Ancient Greece* (New York and London: Routledge, 1989); David Cohen, *Law, Sexuality, and Society: The Enforcement of Morals in Classical Athens* (Cambridge: Cambridge University Press, 1992); David Halperin and John Winkler, eds., *Before Sexuality: The Construction of Erotic Experience in the Ancient Greek World* (Princeton: Princeton University Press, 1990); and K. J. Dover, *Greek Homosexuality* (Cambridge: Harvard University Press 1978; rpt. 1989). A unique examination of the metaphors Greeks used for the female body is Paige DuBois, *Sowing the Body: Psychoanalysis and Ancient Representations of Women* (Chicago: University of Chicago Press, 1988).

3. The Greek mystery religions, such as the cult of Demeter at Eleusis and the cult of Orpheus, provide an interesting contrast to the more well-known, official state cults of deities like Athena and Zeus. They also shed light on the religious role of Greek women. See E. R. Dodds, *The Greeks and the Irrational* (Berkeley: University of California Press, 1951). Two examinations by leading authorities are W. K. C. Guthrie, *Orpheus and Greek Religion: A Study of the Orphic Movement* (Princeton: Princeton University Press, 1993); and Walter Burkert, *Ancient Mystery Cults* (Cambridge, MA: Harvard University Press, 1987). See also Marvin W. Meyer, *The Ancient Mysteries: A Sourcebook of Sacred Texts* (Philadel-phia: University of Pennsylvania Press, 1999); and Thomas Carpenter and Christopher Faraone, eds., *Masks of Dionysus* (Ithaca: Cornell University Press, 1993). For information on sanctuaries and oracles, see Matthew Dillon, *Pilgrims and Pilgrimage in Ancient Greece* (London and New York: Routledge, 1997).

Literature

Barnes, Jonathan, ed., trans., *Early Greek Philosophy.* 1987.

Campbell, David A., trans., *Greek Lyric,* 5 vols. 1982–1993.

Fagles, Robert, trans., *The Odyssey.* 1999.

Fitzgerald, Robert, trans., *The Iliad.* 1989.

Greene, David, trans., *The History: Herodotus.* 1988.

M. L. West, trans., Hesiod's *Theogony, Works and Days.* 1999.

Lieber, David L., ed. *Etz Hayim: Torah and Commentary* 2001.

Malandra, William W. *An Introduction to Ancient Iranian Religion: Readings from the Avesta and the Achaemenid Inscriptions.* 1983.

Historical Skills

Map 2.5, *Phoenician and Greek Expansion, c. 750–500 B.C.E.*

How did the sea facilitate expansion while simultaneously limiting the territory targeted for colonization? Why did expansion occur to the west and north, rather than south and east? What do the distances from their mother city-states at which these colonies were established say about the availability of free land and the maritime technology and skills of the Greeks?

Mapping the West: *Mediterranean Civilizations, c. 500 B.C.E., p. 78*

This map provides a striking visual contrast of the relative size of Greece and the Persian Empire. Have students note all the civilizations that the Persian Empire encompassed under one central authority, composed with the often-squabbling and tiny Greek city-states. What does this comparison tell them about the resources, wealth, and manpower at Persia's disposal in the upcoming Persian Wars between the empire and a pan-Hellenic force? What added information might it lend to their understanding of the power of the Greeks' belief that they constituted a bastion of liberty against the "tyranny of eastern despotism"?

Taking Measure: Greek Family Size and Agricultural Labor in the Archaic Age, p. 65

This graph helps illustrate the way that agricultural production and the need for a sustainable food supply still governed the cycle of daily life for most families in the ancient world. How is family size tied to resources? What does the graph reveal about women's roles, considering that having a large family increased food production? How might the scarcity of arable land have impacted family size? Or, with the population recovery after the Dark Ages, how might this scarcity have contributed to the establishment of colonies, especially in the fertile lands of Sicily and southern Italy?

Black-Figure Vase from Corinth, p. 42

Animals were a popular motif in early Greek art, but the lion held a place of pride going back to the Mycenaeans (it was also important in Mesopotamian art). Which qualities were associated with this animal? Ask the students to characterize and comment on the stylistic qualities of the vase (for example, is it representational or abstract?). Have them compare the vase to the model granary (p. 54), done in the earlier Geometric style of Dark Age Greece, and with examples of the later black-figure style (p. 55) that Athens developed to steal vase-market share from their commercial rival Corinth. Discuss what the evolution of vase-painting styles might indicate about the recovery of Greek culture after the Dark Ages. Does an evolving naturalism and realism reflect greater advancement or sophistication?

The Great King of Persia, p. 48

This relief reveals the conservatism of Near Eastern art; the motifs, hairstyles, and dress are quite consistent with those in earlier works. Have students comment on the presentation of the ruler and the ways in which his divinely endorsed authority and the hierarchical ordering of society are emphasized. What does this adherence to the stylistic conventions of a long-established artistic canon suggest? Do the students find any similarities with Greek art of the same date? In which ways might similarities or differences be significant?

Athletic Competition, p. 55

Students may find it helpful to compare this painting with "A Greek Woman at an Altar" (p. 63), "Vase Painting of a Bride's Preparation" (p. 69), "Hunt Painting in a Spartan Cup" (p. 71), and "Vase Painting of a Music Lesson" (p. 76).

How does the subject of this Greek vase painting reflect the details of everyday life and Greek values? What about the medium on which it is displayed? The "Athletic Competition" forms a good contrast to the Persian relief (p. 48) regarding notions of hierarchy because these citizens are devoid of all marks of status (clothing, weapons, or other instruments); their only claim to superiority is their physical condition. The other vase paintings reveal much about the domestic versus public lives of women — both are depicted here in ritualistic activities. Contrast the active pursuits of the men (a race and hunting party, both competitive endeavors) with those of the women (religious observance and the propagation of the family through marriage, both reinforcing the social welfare). Then contrast these with the "Music Lesson." What does this vase painting further reveal about education? gender? culture?

A Hoplite's Breastplate, p. 66

Along with a hoplon (round shield) and helmet, the breastplate represented nearly the only armored protection of the hoplite, although he might also wear arm and shin guards. A hoplite's complete panoply—including arms, shield, spear, and short sword—weighed between fifty and seventy pounds. Most of a hoplite's protection came from the shield of the soldier standing next to him. In which ways did such vulnerability enhance the cohesiveness of the phalanx? How did the weight of the panoply, combined with the relative vulnerability of the phalanx on its flanks and rear, circumscribe tactical maneuverability? Because the chief purpose of hoplite infantry was defense of the polis if attacked, was strategic flexibility more important than the ability to stand one's ground and face the enemy head on? What does the custom-fitting of the breastplate reveal about the cost of this equipment, even when produced from economical iron, rather than bronze?

Homer's Vision of Justice in the Polis, p. 57

Homer's *Iliad* taught citizens of the Greek city-states valuable lessons on how to behave in the polis. Discussion could center on the principal lesson of this passage: the adjudication of an offence by the learned elders of society. Students should be especially familiar with this lesson because issues of justice and fairness are even more important today as entire groups of persons (like former employees of corporations that have folded, wiping out jobs and pension funds in the process) feel the weight of gross injustice. Ensuring justice in society is critical to maintaining peace and stability.

OTHER BEDFORD/ST. MARTIN'S RESOURCES FOR CHAPTER 2

The following resources are available to accompany Chapter 2. Please refer to the Preface of this manual for detailed descriptions of all the ancillaries.

For Instructors

Transparencies

The following maps and images from Chapter 2 are available as full-color acetates.

- Map 2.1: Expansion of the Neo-Assyrian Empire, c. 900–650 B.C.E.
- Map 2.2: Expansion of the Persian Empire, c. 550–490 B.C.E.
- Map 2.3: Dark Age Greece
- Map 2.4: Archaic Greece, c. 750–500 B.C.E.
- Map 2.5: Phoenician and Greek Expansion, c. 750–500 B.C.E.
- Mapping the West: Mediterranean Civilizations, c. 500 B.C.E.
- *Great King of Persia*
- *Archaic Greek Freestanding Sculpture of Male*

Instructor's Resources CD-ROM

The following maps and image from Chapter 2, as well as a chapter outline, are available on disc in both Power-Point and jpeg formats.

- Map 2.1: Expansion of the Neo-Assyrian Empire, c. 900–650 B.C.E
- Map 2.2: Expansion of the Persian Empire, c. 550–490 B.C.E
- Map 2.3: Dark Age Greece
- Map 2.4: Archaic Greece, c. 750–500 B.C.E
- Map 2.5: Phoenician and Greek Expansion, c. 750–500 B.C.E.
- Mapping the West: Mediterranean Civilizations, c. 500 B.C.E
- *Great King of Persia*

For Students

Sources of The Making of the West

The following documents are available in Chapter 2 of the companion sourcebook by Katharine J. Lualdi, University of Southern Maine.

1. *Inscription Honoring Cyrus, King of Persia* (r. c. 557–530 B.C.E.)
2. Tyrtaeus of Sparta and Solon of Athens, *Poems* (Seventh–Sixth Centuries B.C.E.)
3. *The Foundation of Cyrene* (Late Seventh Century B.C.E.)
4. Sappho of Lesbos, *Poems* (Sixth Century B.C.E.)
5. Hesiod, *Works and Days* (c. Eighth Century B.C.E.)

Study Guides

The print **Study Guide** and the **Online Study Guide** at bedfordstmartins.com/hunt, both by Victoria Thompson (Arizona State University) and Eric Johnson (University of California, Los Angeles), help students synthesize the material they have learned as well as practice the skills historians use to make sense of the past. The following Map, Visual, and Document activities are available for Chapter 2.

Map Activity

- Map 2.4: Archaic Greece, c. 550–490 B.C.E.

Visual Activity

- *Great King of Persia*

Reading Historical Documents

- *Homer's Vision of Justice in the Polis*
- *Cyrene Records Its Foundations as a Greek Colony*

The Greek Golden Age
c. 500–400 B.C.E.

CHAPTER RESOURCES

Main Chapter Topics

1. Persian invasions of the Greek mainland galvanized the independent Greek city-states into resistance and moved them toward the Golden Age of Greece. Because more of the art, literature, architecture, and other surviving products of the Golden Age have come down to us from Athens, discussion of the Golden Age is virtually a discussion of Athens.

2. Athens took full advantage of her naval leadership in the Persian Wars by establishing an Aegean Empire and political primacy in mainland Greece. The political institutions of Athens, in particular its direct democracy, are the most important and enduring legacies of Greece's Golden Age.

3. Greek art was intimately connected to the rituals of civic and religious life, epitomized by the Parthenon and its frieze and sculpture. Art, architecture, and theater were public affairs paid for by the wealthy and with the dues of the Delian League.

4. Greek women did not participate in politics, yet they were active and essential members of the city-state's domestic and religious life.

5. Although generally respectful of religious traditions, Greek philosophers, scientists, historians, and playwrights pioneered intellectual options that did not depend on accepted ideas or the caprices of the gods but rather on investigation of ethics and assumptions, logic and observation, consideration of cultural differences, political analysis, and the exploration of moral dilemmas and responsibilities.

6. The Peloponnesian War (431–404 B.C.E.) between Athens and Sparta ended the Golden Age by depleting the military and economic strength of Athens.

Summary

The Classical Age of Greece transpired from about 500 B.C.E. to the death of Alexander the Great in 323 B.C.E. The first part of this period, the fifth century B.C.E., is known as the Golden Age of Greece and Athens was at its center. This period has long been a touchstone for our ideas about western civilization. It began with Greeks at war against the Persians and ended with a war among the Greek city-states—specifically, between Athens and Sparta. In the period between these two great wars, a prosperous and confident Athens oversaw innovations in art, architecture, theater, education and philosophy. In particular, Athens experimented with a radical form of direct democracy and enjoyed a vibrant public life. But all of this was nearly destroyed by the Spartans in the Peloponnesian War, which lasted twenty-seven years.

In 499 B.C.E., Athens provoked the enmity of the mighty Persian Empire when Athens supported the revolt of the Ionian Greek city-states against King Darius I. Darius sent a formidable Persian force against Athens in 490 B.C.E. The victory at Marathon, important symbolically rather than militarily, increased Athenian self-confidence, giving them the courage to resist the second Persian invasion in 480 B.C.E. Xerxes I, the son of Darius, led an immense army into Greece, expecting the Greek city-states to surrender immediately. Instead, a relatively small coalition consisting of only thirty-one city-states united in the Hellenic League and, led by Sparta, successfully defended themselves against the world's greatest power. In a stunning display of courage, three hundred Spartans held back Xerxes' army in the narrow pass at Thermopylae for several days. Led by Themistocles, the Persian navy was tricked into sailing up the straights of Salamis where Greek triremes lay waiting to ram and sink them. The Persians were completely routed and suffered additional defeats on land at Plataea and Mycale. The Greeks' superior weapons, tactics, leadership, and knowledge of topography offset the superior numbers of the Persians. But, above all else, victory was due to the coalition of city-states, which was unique in Greek history, and the willingness of rich and poor alike to fight side by side for political freedom.

In the aftermath of victory, the unity of the Greek city-states splintered from the harshness of Spartan leadership, and Sparta and Athens created rival alliances. Sparta formed the Peloponnesian League, which included city-states on the Peloponnese; while Athens formed the Delian League, which consisted of city-states located in northern Attica, on islands in the Aegean, and along the Ionian coast. Members of the Delian League were theoretically equal, although in practice Athens dominated the alliance through its superior navy. Soon, Athens was the supreme naval power in the eastern Mediterranean. So complete was their dominance over Delian League members that modern historians have labeled Athens an "empire."

Athenian prosperity and power led to unprecedented accomplishments. In the mid-fifth century B.C.E., Athenian democracy differed to such an extent from most other governments that today political scientists consider it radical. A number of measures ensured direct participation by as many of the male citizenry as possible: most public offices were filled by lottery, term limits were applied to positions, power was shared, most officials of the Council of Five Hundred were paid, corruption was rooted out and prosecuted, equal protection under the law was extended to all citizens regardless of wealth, and jurors were randomly selected and paid for their work. At the same time, however, only elites were eligible for election to the ten generalships that were the highest offices in the Athenian government. They could be reelected multiple times, although they received no pay to ensure that financial gain was not a motivation for election. Another ingredient in Athens's democracy was the practice of ostracism by majority vote, which was intended to curb overpowerful politicians. There were, however, critics of democracy who were most vocal at times of crisis. They objected mainly to the inclusion of the poor in the democratic process.

Pericles, a spellbinding orator, became the most influential Athenian general of the Golden Age. His most important innovation was a per-diem stipend to men holding official posts, which allowed poorer men to leave their regular work to serve the government. Pericles also introduced social, economic, and military policies designed to improve Athenian life. He narrowed the definition of citizenship to those whose parents were both Athenian citizens. This had the effect of improving the status of Athenian women, who were now seen as potential mothers of citizens. He employed the poor, who generally manned the triremes, by increasing naval campaigns against Sparta and Persia. In the winter of 446–445 B.C.E., however, he signed a truce with Sparta

designed to freeze the balance of power in Greece for thirty years.

Despite the influx of wealth, even rich people continued to live modestly and to spend their money on public works. The wealth of Athens—and funds belonging to the Delian League—went mainly into public building projects, art, and festivals. Pericles began a large building project on the acropolis, the rocky hill at the center of the city. Its centerpiece was a new temple for Athena constructed from twenty thousand tons of Attic marble. The Parthenon ("the house of the virgin goddess") reflected Athenian self-confidence in its innovative proportions, design, and optical illusion of perfect straightness. Its elaborately carved marble frieze conveyed the message that Athens's citizens enjoyed the special goodwill of the gods. It has been estimated that the Parthenon and the new gateway to the acropolis together cost more than a billion dollars in today's money.

The new Parthenon reflected a revitalized interest in sculpture. Archaic statues had been stiff, formal, and largely motionless. But Golden Age sculptures represented the idealized human form more realistically. Motion was reflected through pose, and figures wore self-confident expressions. Whether paid for through public funds or by wealthy patrons, most statues were intended to be seen by the wider public, although some were made for private temples to specific gods.

Religious tradition in Athens involved participation in the sacrifices and public festivals associated with the cults of the Olympian gods. It also meant marking significant family moments such as birth, marriage, and death with prayers, rituals, and sacrifices. Individuals (men and women, adults and children) could also enrich their spiritual lives by joining mystery cults that offered a better life on Earth and blessings in the afterlife. The most famous of these was the cult of Demeter and Persephone at Eleusis. Persons also sought aid for this life from oracles and hero cults like the cult of Heracles.

The experiences of Greek women were somewhat mixed. While they were barred from politics, made dependent upon their male relations, and (except in Sparta) denied direct control of their property, they nevertheless were often considered their husbands' partners. The dowry they received on marriage was intended to be used to support them and any children they had, and men were frequently required to pledge collateral to guarantee the safety of this endowment. Upper-class women were expected to avoid close contact with men outside the family, but they were free to roam about their homes as they pleased, engaging in a variety of activities with male and female members of their household. If women ventured out in public, they were usually accompanied by their husbands or slaves. Women managed households, performed religious duties and, if poor, worked outside the home in crafts, business, or agriculture. There was a group of women in Athens, however, who stood outside traditional restrictions. A small number of *hetairas* (companions) moved freely in male society, sometimes selling sexual favors at a high price. Hetairas had a marginal place in society, yet they demonstrated that women could be educated, witty, talented, and valued by men like Pericles and Socrates. Euripedes, moreover, wrote plays that acknowledged the injustice of women's position. Only slaves and *metics* (foreigners who could reside in the city) were less free than women. Slaves accounted for 100,000 of the 250,000 residents of Athens during the time of Pericles. By the start of the Peloponnesian War in 431 B.C.E., metics numbered between 50,000 and 75,000 of the 150,00 free men, women, and children in Athens. Intellectual innovations caused tensions in Athenian society. Because public schools did not exist in Athens, only the wealthy could afford to educate their children well. Boys learned to read and write and also trained for athletic competition and military service. Young men from wealthy families learned even more by observing their fathers and other older men participating in public life, sometimes becoming the protégés of older men. It was not unusual for these older mentor/younger favorite relationships to become sexual. Such behavior was generally accepted in Athenian society. Girls from wealthy families were usually tutored at home by educated slaves. They were only trained to the extent that would prepare them to run a household and help their future husbands manage an estate. Poorer children learned by helping their parents or as apprentices to craftsmen. Illiteracy was not, however, the handicap that it is today because oral communication was central to Greek life.

Athenian democracy made the ability to speak persuasively a valuable skill. The Sophists ("wise men") appeared in Athens to teach oratory and debate to Athens's affluent youth. Athenians worried that the skills of these Sophists might be used to promote individual rather than communal interests and were therefore a threat to democracy. Protagoras, an agnostic and leading Sophist, also taught subjectivism, denying the existence of absolute truth, which some feared would lead to moral relativism. Scientific philosophers also affronted traditionalists by explaining the universe as a physical phenomenon governed by natural laws, not the will of the gods. Socrates (469–399 B.C.E.) was not a Sophist. He was principally interested in how one led a just life. Although Socrates wrote down nothing himself, his student Plato wrote about Socrates' questioning authority, traditional assumptions, and materialist values. Socrates' probing of the connections between personal virtue and public morality bred misunderstanding of his goals and resentment of his influence. Socrates' conclusion that virtue, not wealth and public success, led to happiness ran counter to the prevailing opinion in Athens. After the Peloponnesian War and the brief civil war that followed

it, powerful enemies of Socrates put him on trial. Officially, he was charged with impiety, although many believed that he had contributed to Athens's defeat by demoralizing the citizenry. After his conviction, he was executed by being forced to drink poisonous hemlock.

Other Athenian intellectuals achieved new approaches to history and medical practice. Herodotus's *Histories* and Thucydides' *History of the Peloponnesian War* inaugurated western history writing based on thorough research, cultural investigation, and analysis of power. They both rejected that gods intervened in human affairs. Hippocrates revolutionized medicine by insisting that a physician base his diagnosis and treatment on careful observation of his patient rather than on magical divination and ritual.

Theater was especially important to the Greeks and was publicly funded. Tragedy focused fierce conflicts between humans and powerful forces. Tragic playwrights used stories from myth and history to explore topics ranging from individual freedom and responsibility in the community to the nature of good and evil. The heroine of Sophocles' *Antigone* (441 B.C.E.), for example, must choose between her moral obligation to bury her brother and obedience to the state that forbids a traitor to be buried. Tragedy compelled audiences to observe the consequences of error, ignorance, and hubris (reckless arrogance). Tragic plays were highly stylized by modern standards. They had eighteen male cast members, three of whom played the principal characters while the remaining fifteen formed a chorus. All wore elaborate masks. Comedy offered direct, frank, often ruthless comment on current issues and personalities. Aristophanes wrote comedies that ridiculed pretentious citizens, political leaders, and the assembly's decisions. Typically, women were objects of ridicule and fun, although Aristophanes's *Lysistrata* (411 B.C.E.) breaks that tradition. In *Lysistrata*, the women of Athens and Sparta unite in a sex strike against their husbands that forces the men to end the Peloponnesian War, which they feel has weakened the family to the detriment of their respective city-states.

The Peloponnesian War between Athens and Sparta lasted a generation and ended Athens's Golden Age. Pericles' policies of expansion, his manipulation of the Delian League, and his aggression against Sparta's allies convinced Sparta that Athens must be stopped. Militarily, the city-states were at opposite ends: Sparta's preferred tactic was to fight on land, but Athenian strategy was to rely solely on naval forces. While Sparta ravaged the countryside, Athens retreated behind their city walls, keeping supplies flowing along a protected corridor to the sea. But just as the war began, an epidemic killed thousands of Athenians, including Pericles. Without his prudent leadership, Athens's squabbling leaders followed increasingly risky plans, culminating in a naval expedition against Sparta's allies in Sicily that ended in disaster and destroyed the better part of their navy. With the loss of so many ships, overseas commerce declined sharply. Agricultural production had virtually ceased through constant raids by Sparta and, at the end of the war, the people of Athens were virtually starving within their city's walls.

Sparta compelled Athens to surrender (in 404 B.C.E.) and installed a government of antidemocratic Athenians, the Thirty Tyrants, who put Athens through an eight-month reign of brutal repression and horrors. Within a year, Athenians had overthrown the tyrants. Fortunately for Athens, Sparta was having an internal struggle of its own and could not support their puppet regime. To end civil strife, Athens declared the first amnesty in history. But though free and democratic again, Athens was nevertheless exhausted, its military and economic strength depleted.

Suggestions for Lecture and Discussion Topics

1. The concept of radical democracy best expressed the politics of fifth-century Athens. But this democracy was not without its flaws. One approach to introducing students to Athenian political life was to ask them to identify who was omitted from of the Athenian polity and to explore why. What were the rules of Athenian democracy? Who established these rules? Additional discussion may come from comparing the participatory style of Athenian democracy to the representative forms of government currently practiced. A good introduction to this topic is Thomas R. Martin, *Ancient Greece: From Prehistoric to Hellenistic Times* (Princeton: Princeton University Press, 1996).

2. Slides of the Parthenon, its frieze, and its statues are an engaging way to introduce students to fifth-century Athens's contributions to public architecture. Ask students to identify ways in which Athenian art and architecture were used to inspire civic loyalty and other, similarly uplifting emotions. What were the connections between Greek architecture and politics? What is the role and function of public architecture in a democracy? Ask students to compare their reactions to contemporary public buildings with their reaction to the Parthenon.

3. It is important to talk about political concepts and the outstanding contributions of Athenians to art, architecture, and drama in the Golden Age, but students will probably also wish to know more about how ordinary Athenians lived. A good overview for nonspecialists is Chapter 2, "The Fountainhead: Athens 500–400 B.C.E.," by Sir Peter Hall, *Cities in Civilization* (New York: Pantheon Books, 1998). A far more detailed and authoritative study can be found in James Davidson, *Courtesans and Fishcakes: The Consuming Passions of Classical Athens*

(New York: St. Martin's, 1998). Also very readable is Robert Flaceliere, *Daily Life in Greece at the Time of Pericles* (London: Weidenfeld and Nicolson, 1965).

4. What did women do on a day-to-day basis? Which ideas prevailed about marriage and child care? What role did women play in religion? Why were female characters so often used in Greek drama and comedy to discuss difficult issues? Useful sources include Mary R. Lefkowitz and Maureen B. Fant, eds., *Women in Greece and Rome*, 2d ed. (Baltimore: Johns Hopkins University Press, 1992), which has short selections from documents illustrating the place of women in everyday life; the first four chapters of Elaine Fantham, et al., *Women in the Classical World: Image and Text* (New York: Oxford University Press, 1994), which offer lively accounts and contemporary images of the roles of Greek women during this period; and essays by Sarah Pomeroy — "Women and the City of Athens," "Private Life in Classical Athens," and "Images of Women in the Literature of Classical Athens" —in her very accessible *Goddesses, Whores, Wives, and Slaves in Classical Antiquity* (New York: Schocken Books, 1975). See also the broader context provided by the discussion of family life in Sarah B. Pomeroy's *Families in Classical and Hellenistic Greece: Representation and Realities* (New York: Oxford University Press, 1997).

5. Two wars bracket Greece's Golden Age: the Persian Wars (499–479 B.C.E.) and the Peloponnesian War (431–404 B.C.E.). In his history of the Peloponnesian War, Thucydides attributed the war to the hubris of Athens and Sparta's fear of Athenian power. Although not all scholars would endorse Thucydides' interpretation, this explanation can still be useful in discussing the ending of the Golden Age and the rise of Sparta. Donald Kagan's essay "The Peloponnesian War, 431–404 B.C.E.," pp. 15–74, in his book *On the Origins of War and Preservation of Peace* (New York: Doubleday, 1995), provides a helpful reflection on how and why the war occurred and also how it changed Greece forever.

6. Pericles' *Funeral Oration*, as recorded by Thucydides in about 429 B.C.E., is remarkably revealing of not only Athens but also more modern democracies. Ostensibly praising those who have died in the early campaigns of the Peloponnesian War, Pericles uses the opportunity to justify the war and prepare the citizens for more casualties. While the document is rhetorically brilliant, it has a classic tragic feel to it. Pericles, and indeed all of Athens, suffers from that tragic flaw, hubris. It is particularly illuminating to trace, first, where in the text Pericles exaggerates Athenian virtues and ambitions. Is Athens really that noble, or is the situation more gray than sharply black or white? Is there a modern equivalent to Athens? Can a reflection of the United States be found in this document?

Making Connections

1. *What were the most significant differences between Greece in the Archaic Age and in the Golden Age?* The liberal arts and sciences flourished in Greece's Golden Age like never before. Greek achievement in art, literature, drama, architecture, philosophy, and science distinguished it from the archaic period. Further democratic innovations made Athens more representative than it had ever been before. This tremendous artistic and scientific legacy continues to influence the world today.

2. *What did Greeks of the Golden Age believe it was worth spending public funds to pay for? Why?* Spending public funds on such things as buildings and festivals reflected in a very direct way the self-confidence and values of the community. The Parthenon, for example, with its elaborately carved frieze showing Athenians parading before the gods, conveyed the message that Athens alone enjoyed the special goodwill of the gods. That message was further emphasized through publicly funded commissions for religious statuary and the building of new temples. The values of the polis were further explored through publicly funded drama that often examined the nature of public and private behavior in the state.

Writing Assignments and Class Presentation Topics

1. Greek plays can form the basis of multiple assignments. One such assignment might be to have students read one of Sophocles' Theban plays. *Sophocles: The Three Theban Plays*, Robert Fagles, trans. (New York: Penguin Books, 1984 and later printings) is readily available. Many students will already be familiar with King Oedipus or Antigone. Both tragedies explore the twin themes of aretê and hubris. The tension between aretê and hubris is one of the underlying motifs of Sophocles' plays: while Oedipus and Antigone strive for aretê, both unwittingly succumb to hubris. Students can write an essay on the tension between these themes in Athens's Golden Age, making reference where appropriate to material from the play assigned. Many of the surviving Greek plays are also available on video. Keeping with Sophocles, the director Don Taylor produced all three of the Theban plays in 1984, with Michael Pennington as Oedipus, John Shrapnel as Creon, and Juliet Stevenson as Antigone. These would be appropriate for student review assignments. Or Taylor's *Oedipus* could be contrasted to Tyrone Gutherie's 1957 production of the play in which he keeps to performance conventions of Greek tragedy. The director Peter Hall has also produced filmed stage productions of *The Oresteia* (1983) and these would also be suitable for developing student assignments.

2. Greece in the Golden Age was fascinated by the tension between aretê and hubris, not only in its theater but also in the political struggle between Athens and Sparta. Was Athens's commitment to aretê ultimately an example of hubris? Did Athens fall victim to pride? In exploring the Greek's fascination with aretê and hubris, students might be asked to analyze what these two words reveal about the ideals of Greece's Golden Age. Additionally, students might comment on analogous situations in the contemporary period.

3. Milan Kundera once observed that if "you scratch a European you will find a Greek." This is true, especially in the sense that western thought is indelibly marked by Greece's Golden Age. Discuss this notion in class, with special reference to Socrates, Thucydides, Hippocrates, and Sophocles. Ask students to write an essay using one of the four as a means of commenting on connections between the Golden Age of Greece and western civilization.

4. Have students explore and then debate the complexities involved in the trial of Socrates. A mock trial can be set up where students are divided between the defense and prosecution. Some students can even be assigned specific roles to play, such as that of Socrates and his three principal accusers: Meletus, Anytus, and Lycon. Was Socrates justly charged and sentenced to death or was it a gross miscarriage of justice? Students will have to wrestle with contemporary Greek standards, which often clash with more modern sensibilities. See I. F. Stone, *The Trial of Socrates* (New York: Anchor Books, 1989).

Research Assignments

1. Men, not women, tell us what we know of Greek women. But even though we do not know exactly what Greek women thought, we do know that such women as Clytemnestra, Medea, Melanippe, Helen, Penelope, and Antigone commanded the respect of all Greeks. Have students write an essay or do a report in class on celebrated women in Greek mythology and theater, analyzing their authority, persona, and special powers. A good resource would be Mary R. Lefkowitz, *Women in Greek Myth* (Baltimore: Johns Hopkins University Press, 1986). Another useful resource is an essay by Sarah Pomeroy, "Images of Women in the Literature of Classical Athens," in her book *Goddesses, Whores, Wives, and Slaves in Classical Antiquity* (New York: Schocken Books, 1975).

2. The city-state of Sparta is often contrasted with Athens. Ask students to do a research project on political arrangements, social life, and values in fifth-century B.C.E. Sparta. Another possibility would be for students to debate the merits of Spartan and Athenian approaches to life. In addition to the sources listed in the chapter

bibliography, Anton Powell, *Athens and Sparta: Constructing Greek Political and Social History, 478–371 B.C.E.* (Portland, OR: Areopagitica, 1988) is a good introduction. Paul Cartledge, *Sparta and Lakonia: A Regional History Thirteen Hundred to Three Sixty-Two B.C.E* (New York: Routledge, 1979) will be helpful for students comparing Sparta and Athens.

3. Classical Greece is particularly well known for its beautiful vases, and this despite the fact that such pottery was viewed as utilitarian rather than works of high art. Have students research red figure pottery, answering such questions as why stories about both ordinary life and the exploits of the gods were depicted on vases; what such stories tell us about everyday life in Greece; what the shapes of vessels tell us about their use; and why potters competed among themselves for workmanship.

Literature

Fagles, Robert, trans., *Sophocles: The Three Theban Plays.* 2000.

Henderson, Jeffrey, trans., *Aristophanes: Acharnians, Lysistrata, Clouds.* 1997.

Hughes, Ted, trans., *Aeschylus: The Oresteia.* 2000.

Strassler, Robert B., ed., *The Landmark Thucydides: A Comprehensive Guide to the Peloponnesian War.* 1996.

Vellacott, Philip, trans., *Euripides: Medea and Other Plays.* 1963.

Films and Videos

Mystery of the Parthenon (2001) (VHS, 52 min.) – This is an excellent documentary about the building of the Parthenon. The Athenians lacked sophisticated tools or machinery, and yet constructed one of the most magnificent temples of the ancient world.

Historical Skills

Map 3.1, The Persian Wars, 499–479 B.C.E., p. 86

Ask students to locate and identify the following: Athens, Sparta, Marathon (King Darius's invasion), Themopylae, Salamis, and Plataea (King Xerxes' invasion). After the various sites have been located and identified, ask students to use this information in comparing and contrasting the invasions of Darius and of Xerxes. What can we see from the map that we might not notice in a written account?

Map 3.2, Fifth-Century Athens, p. 94

Ask students to locate and identify the following: the agora, Painted Stoa, acropolis, Parthenon, and Theater of

Dionysus. In addition to referring to the relevant illustrations in the text ("The Acropolis of Athens" [p. 93]; "Scene from the Parthenon Frieze," [p. 95]; and "Theater of Dionysus at Athens," [p. 112], what do the various sites suggest about public life in Athens during this period?

Mapping the West: Greece, Europe, and the Mediterranean, c. 400 B.C.E., p. 118

Ask students to examine the map and to reflect on where Greece is in the Mediterranean and also on what lies to the north and west of Greece (ask them to examine the inset map carefully and note the location of Macedonia). Students should compare this map to Mapping the West: Mediterranean Civilizations, c. 500 B.C.E. (p. 78) and note changes, not only for the Greek city-states but for other major centers of civilization as well.

Taking Measure: Military Forces of Athens and Sparta at the Beginning of the Peloponnesian War (431 B.C.E.), p. 117

Students should use this figure to reflect on Pericles' strategy for the Peloponnesian War. In which ways do the resources available to Athens and to Sparta appear to validate this strategy?

The Sculptural Style of the Greek Golden Age, p. 104

Ask students to compare this sculpture of a male nude with representations of the human body from the archaic period. What major differences do they note? What connections can fairly be made between this statue and Athenians' ideas about themselves?

Scene from the Parthenon Frieze, p. 95

Ask students to discuss the consensus that the frieze is a statement in stone that Athenians enjoyed the goodwill of the gods. Is this perhaps an example of hubris, or is it simply justifiable pride and confidence? Students should be encouraged to comment on similar statements in other contemporaneous cultures as well as in cultures from other time periods.

Athenian Regulations for a Rebellious Ally, p. 105

In theory, the Delian League was an alliance of equals; but in practice, Athens was the dominant power. Students should be able to recognize this from the threat inherent in the set of oaths Athens imposed on the Chalcidians after a failed rebellion. Students can be asked to point to the specific actions that will be taken if the Chalcidians rebel again: Athens will raze the city, exile or imprison the citizenry, abolish civil liberties and property rights, and otherwise destroy Chalcis.

OTHER BEDFORD/ST. MARTIN'S RESOURCES FOR CHAPTER 3

The following resources are available to accompany Chapter 3. Please refer to the Preface of this manual for detailed descriptions of all the ancillaries.

For Instructors

Transparencies

The following maps and image from Chapter 3 are available as full-color acetates.

- Map 3.1: Persian Wars
- Map 3.2: Fifth Century Athens
- Map 3.3: Peloponnesian War
- Mapping the West: Greece, Europe, and the Mediterranean
- *Vase Painting of Women Buying Shoes* (chapter image, page 99)

Instructor's Resources CD-ROM

The following maps and image from Chapter 3, as well as a chapter outline, are available on disc in both Power-Point and jpeg formats.

- Map 3.1: Persian Wars
- Map 3.2: Fifth Century Athens
- Map 3.3: Peloponnesian War
- Mapping the West: Greece, Europe, and the Mediterranean
- *Vase Painting of Women Buying Shoes* (chapter image, page 99)

For Students

Sources of The Making of the West

The following documents are available in Chapter 3 of the companion sourcebook by Katharine J. Lualdi, University of Southern Maine.

1. Thucydides, *The Funeral Oration of Pericles* (429 B.C.E.)
2. Plato, *The Apology of Socrates* (399 B.C.E.)
3. Euphiletus, *A Husband Speaks in His Own Defense* (c. 400 B.C.E.)
4. Overhead Views of a House on the Slope of the Areopagus (Fifth Century B.C.E.)
5. Aristophanes, *Lysistrata* (411 B.C.E.)

Study Guides

The print **Study Guide** and the **Online Study Guide** at bedfordstmartins.com/hunt, both by Victoria Thompson (Arizona State University) and Eric Johnson (University of California, Los Angeles), help students synthesize the material they have learned as well as practice the skills historians use to make sense of the past. The following Map, Visual, and Document activities are available for Chapter 3.

Map Activity

- Map 3.3: The Peloponnesian War

Visual Activity

- *Vase Painting of Women Buying Shoes* (chapter image, page 99)

Reading Historical Documents

- Athenian Regulations for a Rebellious Ally (page 105)
- Sophists Argue Both Sides of a Case (page 107)

From the Classical to the Hellenistic World
c. 400–30 B.C.E.

CHAPTER RESOURCES

Main Chapter Topics

1. Rather than creating a lasting peace, the end of the Peloponnesian War (431–404 B.C.E.) led to the decline of the independent Greek polis. Military rivalries among Athens, Thebes, and Sparta for control of the mainland weakened Greece and doomed the independence of the city-states.

2. The execution of Socrates disenchanted Plato with Athenian democracy, leading him to philosophical contributions to ethics, government, and metaphysics. Aristotle's pragmatism showed in his systemization of logical arguments based on observable evidence and his wide-ranging investigations.

3. Debilitated Greece was vulnerable to its historically weaker northern neighbor, Macedonia. Although held in contempt by southern Greeks, King Philip II and his son Alexander the Great saw themselves as the saviors of Greek culture and guaranteed its dissemination and ascendancy throughout the Mediterranean world, especially after Alexander's conquest of the Persian Empire.

4. Alexander's empire did not outlast him. Upon his death, his generals split the territory into three Hellenistic kingdoms, ruled by the Antigonid, Seleucid, and Ptolemaic dynasties. The successor kings governed through personal rule and were assisted by an elite class of administrators composed of Greek and Macedonian immigrants and local nobles.

5. Elite language and culture were Greek, yet extensive fusions with indigenous culture produced a vigorous combination of eastern and Greek elements. Cultural contacts inspired a more personal and emotive artistic style, especially in sculpture, whereas intellectual exchanges stimulated advances in science, particularly in the areas of geometry and mathematics.

6. The new philosophical schools of the time reflected political and social disorder and the waning of democracy. Focus shifted away from the metaphysical inquiries of Plato and scientific analyses of Aristotle to the more introverted approaches of the Epicureans, Stoics, Cynics, and Skeptics, all of whom tried to outline a program for the best manner in which to live daily life and achieve inner peace in turbulent times.

7. The Hellenistic Greeks adopted mystery cults of foreign deities (such as Isis), healing cults (such as that of Asclepius), the cults of Hellenized foreign gods (such as Serapis), and ruler cults. At the same time, many Jews emigrated from their homeland and established themselves in Hellenized cities like Alexandria and in Greece itself.

Summary

After the Peloponnesian War, the Greeks did not cease their inter-city wars. Athens, Sparta, and Thebes pummeled each other with all their remaining strength, crippling their ability to resist Philip II and Alexander the Great. Alexander in particular was inspired by the history and culture of the southern Greeks and epitomized the Homeric warrior-hero ideal. Alexander's generals divided his immense empire, building Hellenistic kingdoms for themselves. The successor kings installed Greeks and Macedonians at the top of the administration and also relied on local elites to keep old systems running smoothly. Alexander's conquests had spread Greek language and culture as far as India. Simultaneously, Greek traditions were transformed by the cultural matrix of Alexander's former empire. A new emotion and intensity characterized artistic expression, and patronage for intellectual endeavors led to numerous scientific discoveries. Meanwhile, new philosophical schools and religious cults spoke to the inhabitants of an uncertain world.

The Peloponnesian War plunged Athens into economic decline, exacerbated by the influx of rural refugees and the near exhaustion of its silver mines. But this dislocation generated greater flexibility in gender roles, as war widows were obliged to seek paid work to support themselves and their children and many men had to establish themselves in new occupations, sometimes working alongside women. Small businesses and cottage industries helped revive the economy, as did the rebuilding of Athens's long, protective walls to the coast, which made sea trade safe from attack. Still, daily life was a struggle for most individuals who usually could only provide for their immediate family and household. Economic revival, though, did not relieve political tensions.

Popular resentment over the rule of the Thirty Tyrants manifested itself in the persecution of Socrates (d. 399 B.C.E.) whose student Critias had been one of the tyrants. Condemned for impiety and corrupting the city's youth, Socrates chose to comply with the sentence of death by drinking hemlock. His death left an indelible impression on his most famous disciple, Plato (c. 429–348 B.C.E.), who lost faith in democracy and took up metaphysics and theories about ethics and idealized politics. Plato's student, Aristotle (384–322 B.C.E.) took a strictly pragmatic approach, focusing on logical argumentation, observation, and science.

Plato and Aristotle largely defined the trajectory of the development of western philosophy (and western science, as well). Plato amplified Socrates' teachings in a series of dialogues that explored the nature of virtues, such as beauty and justice, which Plato assumed to be universal and absolute. Although he never constructed an entirely coherent philosophical doctrine, Plato's ideas formed the basis of western metaphysics. Plato believed that humans could not understand the essential nature of virtue by drawing on their own experiences because all human experiences were relative, whereas the virtues in their pure form (which Plato often called Forms) were transcendent and universal. The level of the Forms was the level of reality, while matter reduced human perceptions of them to pale reflections.

Plato taught that humans possessed immortal souls on which the supreme creator or Demiurge imprinted knowledge. Plato's dualistic doctrine of the purity of the spiritual realm and the inferiority of the material realm fixed in western intellectual heritage its characteristic conception of a radical mind-body split.

Plato articulated his rejection of democratic government in a work titled "System of Government," which is more popularly known as *The Republic*. The selfishness of most citizens made democracy unworkable, so humans needed to be governed by an enlightened oligarchy or philosopher-king. *The Republic* outlined a highly authoritarian three-tiered society marked by the absence of private property, nuclear families, and gender discrimination.

Aristotle, who attended Plato's Academy in Athens (founded 386 B.C.E.), followed a path almost opposite from that of his teacher. He rejected Plato's abstract metaphysics to concentrate on scientific investigation of the natural world and on logical argument supported with evidence. Although also critical of Athenian democracy, Aristotle founded his own school (the Lyceum [or Peripatetic school]) in Athens. He later became tutor to the young Alexander the Great. Aristotle's work touched nearly every branch of human knowledge and stressed basing conclusions about reality on observations, rather than on abstract theories like Plato's Forms. He urged people to pursue the "golden mean" in all things. He argued that slaves deserved their enslavement. He also trumpeted the "natural" inferiority of women based on a faulty understanding of animal biology.

In 390 B.C.E., Athens, Argos, Thebes, and Corinth allied to block Sparta's attempts to subdue other Greek city-states. In a startling retaliation, the Spartans endorsed Persia's right to control Greek city-states in Anatolia (the "King's Peace" of 386 B.C.E.) in exchange for nonintervention in Sparta's mainland campaigns, thus undoing the Greek gains of the Persian Wars.

The Thebans defeated Sparta at Leuctra (371 B.C.E.), invaded Lakademia, and liberated the Helots, crushing Sparta's power base and seemingly leaving Thebes the ascendant power in Greece. Athens, a nearer neighbor to Thebes than Sparta, allied with Sparta in response. Thebes triumphed over their combined forces at Mantinea in 362 B.C.E., but lost its effective leaders in the process. Stalemate ensued, with Greek city-states able to control only their own respective local territories. Greek independence hung by a thread.

Macedonia, Greece's small and relatively unsophisticated northern neighbor, capitalized on Greek weakness. Propelled by the talents of two remarkable leaders, King Philip II (r. 359–336 B.C.E.) and his son Alexander the Great (r. 336–323 B.C.E.), Macedonia conquered Greece. Alexander then created the west's largest empire to date and dedicated himself to the spread of Greek culture.

According to the Macedonian tradition of limited military kingship, kings maintained power only by earning the goodwill of their nobles and the loyalty of their soldiers. At this, both Philip and Alexander succeeded brilliantly. Philip deployed cutting-edge siege engines and armed his hoplite phalanxes with long, thrusting spears that enabled them to outreach opponents. He also taught his phalanxes to move and maneuver as one cohesive unit. These innovations transformed ancient warfare, improved the morale of his soldiers, and contributed substantially to his victories. Philip defeated Athens and Thebes at Chaeronea in 338 B.C.E. He then granted the Greeks nominal independence on condition that they aid him in his mission to "avenge" Greece by joining a combined Greek and Macedonian force against the Persian Empire.

After Philip's assassination in 336 B.C.E., Alexander took power at age twenty and immediately subdued enemy forces to the west and north. He then forced the southern Greeks back into the alliance they had abandoned at Philip II's death. To remind Greeks of what disloyalty would bring, Alexander razed Thebes. He then turned his attention to Asia. In little over a decade, he accomplished the most impressive series of military conquests in ancient history. Alexander's idolization of the Homeric heroic ideal, combined with his willingness to share his soldiers' hardships, his chivalrous charisma, and his use of technological innovations in warfare, inspired his forces to follow him all the way to India (although his worn-out troops forced him to return to Persia at that point). By 326 B.C.E., Alexander's empire encompassed Greece, Macedonia, the Persian Empire (including Egypt), and vast tracts of the Asian steppes.

Alexander promoted Greek culture as the elite ideal throughout his empire. He consolidated control by establishing colonies in which he settled his veterans, while also retaining the local administration. By the end of his life, Alexander had come to believe that he was a son of Zeus and expected to be—and was—venerated as a god. He died of fever while planning further campaigns into Arabia and northern Africa. Historians differ wildly about Alexander's character and motivations. Most agree, however, that his explorations benefited a variety of disciplines, from geography to botany, and opened up lucrative trade routes that led to cross-cultural exchanges.

Because Alexander left no clear instructions for a successor, his generals rapidly murdered his mother, wife, and infant son and divided the empire among themselves. The successor kings presided over a world of Hellenistic culture—a fusion of Greek and indigenous elements. The Antigonids (Anatolia, the Near East, Macedonia, and Greece), Seleucids (Babylon and the East), and Ptolemies (Egypt) ruled from Alexander's death, in 323 B.C.E., until the advent of Roman domination in the mid-second to mid-first centuries B.C.E.

The successor kings governed by personal rule and maintained the Near Eastern tradition of vast bureaucracies and expensive mercenary armies. Amid the ongoing competition for territories, some smaller independent kingdoms like Attalid Pergamene and Greek Bactria managed to emerge. To acquire legitimacy for political stability, rulers adopted local customs and cooperated with both the Greek and Macedonian immigrants and the local elites. In these new dynastic houses, queens often achieved positions of great influence. The Hellenistic kings retained local elites, who often learned Greek, as mid-level administrators. They were entrusted chiefly with the collection of taxes (which were needed to fund vast bureaucracies, artistic patronage, mercenary troops and costly military elephants and technologies), mediation of local disputes, and administering royal monopolies. Although crucial to maintaining a ruler's control,

these local elites were not considered the equals of the resident Greek and Macedonian officials.

Cities underpinned the Hellenistic kingdoms. Although built and organized along Greek lines, Hellenistic city-states lacked real independence and had to adhere to policies set by their respective monarchs. Because of their economic importance, though, kings treated cities and urban elites respectfully, and this was true even with older cities in Anatolia and the Near East and their indigenous local leaders. Hellenistic society was hierarchical, with the king and his family at the top, followed by Greek and Macedonian elites. Hellenistic society's elites privately funded many public works and social welfare projects because they viewed such investments as their civic duty to contribute to the common good. Under the Greek and Macedonians on the hierarchy came local indigenous urban and rural leaders. At the bottom of the social scale were slaves. Reliance on slave labor increased, and up to ten thousand slaves were sold at Delos at the height of the period. A new form of semiservile peasantry (the "peoples") also appeared. The "peoples" were technically free tenants on royal estates who owed a quota of their produce as rent, but who found themselves increasingly bound to the land. Indeed, as many as 80 percent of all adult men and women—slaves as well as free people—worked in agriculture. The poor found some relief through the philanthropy of wealthier elites who distributed grain in times of shortages, funded state-sponsored schools, and subsidized medical care.

Elite Hellenistic women possessed potentially more freedom than their Greek predecessors. Hellenistic queens could influence their husbands' decisions, and even rule in their own right when no male heir existed. This was especially true of Egyptian queens. Most women, however, continued to be under the control of their fathers, husbands, and male relations. Elite women continued to live isolated lives; poor women often worked outside the home to support their family. Boys were more valued than girls, and the infant daughters of some poor families (perhaps up to 10 percent) were subjected to the practice of exposure.

The Hellenistic kingdoms finally fell to the ever-expanding power of Rome. The defeat of the Carthaginian general Hannibal brought Roman vengeance down on his Antigonid ally King Philip V, and Rome acquired Macedonia and Greece by 150 B.C.E. The Seleucid kingdom fell in 64 B.C.E. The Ptolemies survived the longest, but Rome won Egypt after Octavian (Caesar Augustus) defeated the Ptolemaic queen Cleopatra VII and Mark Antony at the battle of Actium in 30 B.C.E.

The political and social upheavals of the period and the increasing personalization of rulership transformed the arts, scholarship, and religion. Royal patronage of the arts and scholarship resulted in the foundation of centers such as the famed Alexandrian library (the Museum) in Ptolemaic Egypt. The division between the intellectual elite and illiterate masses was reflected in poetry, where allusions were often incomprehensible to all but the well educated. Ironically, poetry of the period also idealized country living over city life. Women also wrote poetry and excelled especially at epigrams, which were short, emotionally charged poems. They often wrote about other women, and love was frequently their topic. With writers increasingly under royal patronage, literature generally turned away from the political commentary of Attic drama toward romantic dilemmas and personal emotions, best exemplified by the popular comedies of Menander (c. 342–289 B.C.E.).

The visual arts shifted from the heroic, idealized calm of classical sculpture to the depiction of dramatic emotions, contorted poses, and diverse subjects often taken from ordinary life. Artists portrayed subjects formerly deemed scandalous or too undignified like drunkenness, old age, or nude goddesses.

The broad metaphysics and scientific ponderings of Plato and Aristotle gave way to new schools of thought like philosophical materialism—the belief that only things in the material world mattered or even existed. New schools included Epicureanism, which advocated "pleasure" (defined as an "absence of disturbance") and the withdrawal from public life; Stoicism, which taught that human suffering should be endured calmly in the pursuit of virtue; Skepticism, which argued that one must suspend judgment because human perception was arbitrary and unreliable; and Cynicism, which flouted convention by advocating that persons should strive for utter independence and act on their natural impulses. Some of these schools welcomed women and members of the lower classes, including slaves.

Alexander the Great's conquests, Hellenistic royal patronage, and a concentration of scientists in Alexandria in Egypt all stimulated notable achievements in the sciences, especially in geometry and mathematics. Among the numerous breakthroughs were Euclid's geometry, Archimedes' calculation of pi and discoveries in hydrostatics, and Aristarchus's postulation of a heliocentric solar system. Even with the lack of adequate technology, pneumatic and steam-powered machines were invented (though they had no practical application at the time), and the central nervous system was discovered. Improved designs for catapults and siege towers were introduced, and a giant lighthouse was built at Alexandria. Advances in medicine were made, although physicians continued to be limited by what could be observed directly rather than accurately measured (and this was especially true when it came to female anatomy).

Religion also underwent profound transformations, and many people turned to new cults for a sense of security and meaning in life in the face of the seemingly arbitrary divinities of Luck and Chance. The mystery cults of eastern deities such as Isis became popular, as did the healing cult of the Greek god Asclepius. Still others wor-shiped deified rulers, whose power on Earth was beyond question.

During this period, the Jewish Bible was translated into Greek, the common language of the Hellenistic world. Reacting to Seleucid support for an extreme Hellenizing faction of Jerusalem Jews, and attempts to suppress Jewish religious observances, Judah the Maccabee led a revolt for Jewish autonomy and recaptured the Jerusalem temple in 167 B.C.E.

Suggestions for Lecture and Discussion Topics

1. The career of Philip II of Macedonia was nearly as surprising as that of his celebrated son yet receives far less attention. Review the diplomatic, personal, and military tactics that paved the way for, and must have created a lasting impression on, Alexander. Compare their tactics and achievements and ask the class to identify those features of Philip's program that have the clearest parallels in Alexander's career and campaigns. What could Alexander have learned from his father about military strategy; "public relations" with his troops, allies, and enemies; and building and maintaining a strong personal image? For the background on Philip's reign, see E. Borza, *In the Shadow of Olympus: The Emergence of Macedon* (Princeton: Princeton University Press, 1990); on the character of his rule, see J. R. Ellis, *Philip II and Macedonian Imperialism* (London: Thames and Hudson, 1986).

2. In the Hellenistic Age, many things that had formerly given individuals a sense of identity and purpose in life (such as citizenship in the polis or belief in traditional religion) were eroded by foreign domination, the aftermath of war, and the rise of philosophical rationalism. Might Alexander have seemed to many to be a divinely appointed savior sent to restore order? In which ways was his proclaimed mission to create a "brotherhood of all mankind" a message particularly well-suited for his age? Was his being Macedonian, rather than Greek, an advantage in achieving his goals? On the superhuman persona of Alexander, see A. F. Steward, *Faces of Power: Alexander's Image and Hellenistic Politics* (Berkeley: University of California Press, 1993).

3. The Hellenistic era has often been labeled as "decadent." Ask students what reasons they can provide for and/or against that label. Compare the culture and artistic production of the cosmopolitan, dynastic Hellenistic kingdoms with those of the small-scale, independent city-states of Classical Greece. Why were the latter frequently believed to embody the pinnacle of western civilization? One of the best ways to make this comparison is through a survey of Hellenistic art. Background and illustrations can be found in two excellent overviews: Christine Havelock, *Hellenistic Art* (New York: W. W. Norton, 1981); and J. J. Pollitt, *Art in the Hel-*

lenistic Age (Cambridge: Cambridge University Press, 1986). See also J. Onians, *Art and Thought in the Hellenistic Age: The Greek World View, 350–50 B.C.E.* (London, 1979); A. F. Stewart, *Art, Desire, and the Body in Ancient Greece* (Cambridge: Cambridge University Press, 1997); and B. Brown, *Anticlassicism in Greek Sculpture of the Fourth Century B.C.E.* (New York, 1973).

4. Of the post-Alexandrine dynasties, the Ptolemaic kingdom endured the longest. Explore the reasons for this longevity by discussing its location in Egypt and the Ptolemies' adoption of Egyptian practices. How did the latter contribute to the status of several of their queens, most famously Arsinoe II and Cleopatra? Discuss Ptolemaic patronage of culture, especially the building of the lighthouse of Pharos and the great library (the Museum) at Alexandria. Were they trying to transform Alexandria into a "new Athens"? For a recent general introduction, see Gunther Hoelbl, *A History of the Ptolemaic Empire* (New York and London: Routledge, 2000). Other good overviews are Naphtali Lewis, *Greeks in Ptolemaic Egypt* (Oxford: Clarendon, 1986); and Alan K. Bowman, *Egypt After the Pharaohs, 332 B.C.–A.D. 642*, 2d ed. (Berkeley: University of California Press, 1996). The culture of Alexandria is explored from a variety of perspectives and disciplines in the collected articles in *Alexandria and Alexandrianism* (papers delivered at a symposium organized by the J. Paul Getty Museum in 1993; Malibu, 1996).

5. Despite the shift in the visual arts to a more emotive, realistic style, a greater diversity of subjects, and increased private patronage, monumental public sculpture programs still appeared. An outstanding example is the Telephos frieze from the great altar of Zeus at Pergamum. This work was commissioned by Eumenes II, monarch of the small, autonomous kingdom that existed alongside its much larger Seleucid neighbor. Use slides to discuss the altar's iconographic program. What political messages did the king hope to convey? Compare it to the Parthenon frieze. What similarities in subject and treatment do the students perceive? How do their styles reflect the eras in which they were composed? Does the difference in the political regimes that commissioned them (one a democracy, the other a monarchy) seem evident? See Nancy De Grummond, ed., *From Pergamon to Sperlonga: Sculpture and Context* (Berkeley and Los Angeles: University of California Press, 2000); and Elisabeth Rohde, *The Altar of Pergamon* (Berlin, 1983).

6. Women in the Hellenistic Age played a more prominent political role than they had in earlier Greek history. This topic can be explored by examining women's roles in the royal household of Philip II (his wives Olympias and Cleopatra), in Alexander's political dealings with conquered peoples (his selection of Ada to be satrap of Caria), and in the Ptolemaic dynasty (Arsinoe II, Cleopatra VII). Which features of dynastic monarchy, as opposed to the Greek participatory governments dom-

inated by male citizens, might account for women's more prominent role? Also consider the political uses of marriage, such as Philip II's polygamy or Alexander's policies for his soldiers. Would the influence of Near Eastern cultures in the Hellenistic world in part account for these practices? On women in Macedonia, see Elizabeth Carney, "Women and Basileia: Legitimacy and Female Political Action in Macedonia," *Classical Journal* 90 (1995): 367–391; and "The Politics of Polygamy: Olympias, Alexander, and the Murder of Philip," *Historia* 41 (1992): 167–189. For the Ptolemies, see Sarah Pomeroy, *Women in Hellenistic Egypt: From Alexander to Cleopatra* (New York: Schocken Books, 1984).

7. Alexander had a penchant for founding cities; in fact, such foundations constituted a key means by which Greek culture was spread. Cities, with their large immigrant populations, also served as the setting of social, intellectual, and cultural cross-fertilization. Review the founding of some of Alexander's "Alexandrias," and discuss with the class the ways in which urban planning was central to Hellenistic culture. How did the Hellenistic city differ — politically, architecturally, socially, and economically — from the Greek polis? There is a large amount of literature on this topic; the standard work is J. B. Ward-Perkins, *Cities of Ancient Greece and Italy: Urban Planning in Classical Antiquity* (New York: George Braziller, 1974). More recent works include E. J. Owens, *The City in the Greek and Roman World* (New York and London: Routledge, 1990); and R. Tomlinson, *From Mycenae to Constantinople: The Evolution of the Ancient City* (New York and London: Routledge, 1992).

Making Connections

1. *How did life differ, or not, for persons of all social classes in the Hellenistic kingdoms compared to life in the Greek city-state of the classical era?* Hellenistic cities reflected Greek culture, but they were not democracies in the way Greek city-states had been. Although some institutions of the Greek polis were kept, in practice, the king made all the important decisions. Monarchy created new, mutually beneficial relationships between rulers and social elites. Rulers behaved like patrons to elites who fulfilled mainly administrative duties. The poor continued to work the land. Life became more free for some Hellenistic women, especially those who were wealthy or in positions of power. Indeed, the wealthy in Hellenistic society took a renewed interest in bettering the lives of the poor and sponsored schools and medical care for their benefit.

2. *What are the advantages and disadvantages of governmental support of the arts and science, as in the Hellenistic kingdoms and in the United States today through the National Endowment for the Humanities, National*

Endowment for the Arts, and the National Science Foundation? One advantage is that publicly funded art and science is more accessible to the people at large. These programs also provide funding to creative and imaginative individuals and groups, who might not otherwise be able to pursue their projects, and demonstrate that the United States, like ancient Greece, values art and scientific discovery and believes that all people have a right to enjoy and derive benefit from them. One of the disadvantages is that art and scientific discovery can be controversial. Some persons may appreciate the work of a particular artist (indeed, they may even be offended), or they may object to certain kinds of scientific research.

Writing Assignments and Class Presentation Topics

1. Ask students to investigate the responses of Plato and Aristotle to the failure of Athenian democracy by comparing selected passages from *The Republic* and *Politics*. Do they blame the structure of democratic government or on human nature? What alternatives do they offer to democracy? What do they feel are the government's responsibilities to the people? What obligations must the people in turn fulfill?

2. The identity of those responsible for Philip II's murder remains a mystery. Students may want to attempt to solve it by comparing different historical versions of the event and weighing the evidence. See Plutarch, "Life of Alexander," 9.3–12; Arrian, *Anabasis*; and Aristotle, *Politics*, 5.1311.a25–1311.b3. Ask students whether they believe Alexander was in any way implicated in the affair. How convincing is the argument that Alexander's mother Olympias was behind the deed? Was the assassination the result of a conspiracy or did Pausanias act alone?

3. Have students reconstruct the "myth" of Alexander that had begun to disseminate during his lifetime, based on a reading of Plutarch's "Life" or Arrian's *Anabasis*. Among the questions they could address are: How did Alexander self-consciously cultivate this image? Did his tactics change depending on whether he was interacting with allies, followers, or enemies? What was Alexander's ostensible ideal? How did he try to live up to it? How had he been prepared for his position? Do students believe his persona was all artifice or a projection of his true personality? How laudable was Alexander's "mission"? Did he achieve it and, if so, how and at what cost? If not, why not? Did the benefits to the subjects of his conquered territories outweigh their loss of autonomy? Ask students to identify and evaluate a few of the episodes that contributed to the legend of Alexander during his lifetime (nearly every recorded episode might qualify). A few choices are his destruction of Thebes, sparing only the city's temples and the descendants of

Pindar; the Gordian knot; the taming of his horse Bucephalus; his restoration of Cyrus's tomb at Pasargadae; and his return of Poros's kingdom after the latter surrendered to him. For sources, see *Alexander the Great: Translation of the Extant Historians*, C. A. Robinson, ed. (Golden, CO: Ares, 1998).

4. Students could also approach the previous topic from the viewpoint of modern scholarship. Ask students to read one of the myriad, recent biographies of Alexander and present a summary report of the book to the class. This could lead to a discussion about the reasons for Alexander's enduring popularity and about why such divergent portraits of him have emerged. The following are among the better studies of Alexander to appear recently and all arrive at notably different conclusions about the man. Michael Wood, *In the Footsteps of Alexander the Great* (Berkeley and Los Angeles: University of California Press, 1997) is a discussion of Alexander's life and achievements formulated in the context of the author's personal retracing of the 22,000-mile route of Alexander's conquests. N. G. L. G. Hammond, *The Genius of Alexander the Great* (Chapel Hill: University of North Carolina Press, 1998) is a decidedly laudatory portrayal. Peter Green, *Alexander of Macedon, 356–323 B.C.E.: A Historical Biography* (Berkeley and Los Angeles: University of California Press, 1992) is written by a professor of classics who is also a published novelist. For some notable fictional accounts of Alexander the Great and the successor kingdoms, see Mary Renault's trilogy *Fire from Heaven*, *The Persian Boy*, and *Funeral Games* (New York: Pantheon, respectively, 1969, 1972, 1981; all three are in Vintage reprints, 2002).

5. Have students read one of the plays of Menander and discuss the elements of the central plot and stock characters. How does the play compare with romantic comedies of today? What accounts for the shift away from the lofty meditations on human fate and the political critiques that formed the subject matter of earlier drama? What might this shift indicate about the audience? The complete plays have been translated by David Sclavitt in *Menander* (Philadelphia: University of Pennsylvania Press, 1998), and include *The Grouch (Dyskolos)*, *Desperately Seeking Justice*, and *The Girl from Samos*.

6. With their almost gleefully irreverent disregard for social conventions, the Cynics are easily the most entertaining of all the philosophical schools that sprang up in the Hellenistic world. Outline their principles. Is there a serious message behind their unorthodox behavior or were they only trying to shock people? Why were they able to thrive when Socrates' less extreme message resulted in his condemnation? What were they reacting against? Unlike the schools of Plato and Aristotle, some of these new schools admitted women and even slaves into their circles. What accounts for this? Have students read "The Cynic" in Lucan's *Dialogues*, vol. 8, M. D.

MacLeod, trans. Loeb Classical Library (Cambridge, MA: Harvard University Press, 1967). The brief biography of the female Cynic Hipparchia by Diogenes Laertes ("Life of Hipparchia," in *Lives and Ideas of Eminent Philosophers*, vol. 6, pp. 96–98, Celia Luschnig, trans.) is at the Diotima Web site. Diogenes Laertes also has information on the Cynic Antisthenes, a pupil of Socrates, and Diogenes of Sinope.

Research Assignments

1. Remarkable discoveries characterized Hellenistic science, especially among the scholars who gathered at Alexandria. Many of these breakthroughs would be lost to the west for centuries, only to be rediscovered during the Renaissance or later. Students can explore the world of Hellenistic science in George Sarton, *Hellenistic Science and Culture in the Last Three Centuries B.C.E.* (New York and London: Dover, 1993); see also the chapters on Hellenistic science in Peter Green, *Alexander to Actium: The Historical Evolution of the Hellenistic Age* (Berkeley and Los Angeles: University of California Press, 1993); and David Lindberg, *The Beginnings of Western Science* (Chicago: University of Chicago Press, 1992).

2. The innovations in military technology and strategy of Philip II and Alexander have generated a substantial amount of scholarship. Philip's substitution of the sarissa transformed hoplite warfare and helped bring about its demise by opening up the possibility of military service to more men. Philip also pioneered the use of siege engines which, for the first time, made heavily fortified cities vulnerable to foreign attack, as well as escalating the financial costs of war considerably. Standard works on the topic remain F. E. Adcock, *The Greek and Macedonian Art of War* (Berkeley: University of California Press, 1967); D. W. Engels, *Alexander the Great and the Logistics of the Macedonian Army* (Berkeley: University of California Press, 1978); and N. G. Hammond and G. T. Griffith, *A History of Macedonia*, vol. 2 (New York: Oxford University Press, 1979), pp. 405–449. Among more recent works, see the section on Macedonian expansion in Victor Hanson, *The Wars of the Ancient Greeks and Their Invention of Western Military Culture* (London: Cassell, 1999).

3. Students could assess the extent to which Hellenistic culture constituted a truly "international" culture by investigating its manifestation in divergent parts of Alexander's empire and in the successor kingdoms. This topic would also permit students to examine the extent to which indigenous cultures influenced the shape of the imported Greek culture. Starting points for research include P. Bernard, "An Ancient Greek City in Central Asia (Ai Khanoum)," *Scientific American* 246.1 (1982): pp. 148–159; P. Bilde, et al., *Aspects of Hellenism in Italy: To-wards a Cultural Unity?* (Copenhagen: Museum Tusculanus Press, 1993); F. L. Holt, *Alexander the Great and Bactria* (Leiden: Brill, 1988); and the older, but informative, G. N. Banerjee, *Hellenism in Ancient India* (Calcutta, 1920). For various aspects of Hellenistic culture, see the articles in Peter Green, ed., *Hellenistic History and Culture* (Berkeley and Los Angeles: University of California Press, 1993).

Literature

Allen, Reginald, trans., *Plato: Euthyphro, Apology, Crito, Meno, Gorgias, Menexenus*. 1989.

Connor, Robert, trans., *Greek Orations: 4th Century B.C.: Lysias, Isocrates, Demosthenes, Aeschines, Hyperides and Letter of Philip*. 1987.

Cornford, Francis, trans., *Plato: Republic*. 1988.

Inwood, Brad, and Gerson, L.P., eds., *Hellenistic Philosophy: Introductory Readings*. 1997.

McKeon, Richard, ed., *The Basic Works of Aristotle*. 2001.

Page, D. L., ed., *Corinna*. 1953.

Page, D. L., and Gow, A. S. F., eds., *The Greek Anthology. The Garland of Philip, and Some Contemporary Epigrams*. 1968.

Thomas, I., trans., *Greek Mathematical Works*. 2 vols. 1953.

Verity, Anthony, trans., *Theocritus: Idylls*. 2003.

Walten, Michael, trans., *Six Greek Comedies*. 2002.

Historical Skills

Map 4.2, Conquests of Alexander the Great, 336–323 B.C.E., p. 137

Using the scale, calculate the approximate distances that Alexander and his men covered between campaigns and compare these with the dates of their military engagements. What does this tell students about the pace of Alexander's progress? About his effectiveness in motivating his troops? Ask students to identify the locations of the various "Alexandrias" founded by Alexander and comment on their placement, in light of his relations with the indigenous populations and the rulers of various conquered provinces. What might account for the places he chose not to found cities?

Mapping the West: Dissolution of the Hellenistic World, to 30 B.C.E., p. 157

Note the strategic position of Rome in the Mediterranean region. Compare this map to Map 4.2. Where did Alexander's conquests end? How did his conquests facilitate Roman development and expansion? How might the concentration of much of the Hellenistic world into fairly expansive, but consolidated kingdoms have simplified Roman conquests to the east? Ask students to evaluate the extent to which a highly developed, international community that spoke the same language (Greek) may have contributed to the foundations of Roman administration of its eastern provinces. How would this situation have differed if Alexander's empire had remained intact?

Dancing Figures on Gilded Bowl, p. 133

How does this uninhibited celebration of wine reflect the values and new stylistic conventions of Hellenistic art? In which ways are the influences of eastern cultures evident? Have the students contrast this scene with the disciplined restraint of high classical sculpture. In which ways might scenes such as this have contributed to the former interpretation of the Hellenistic age as one of "decadence"?

Mosaic of Alexander the Great at the Battle at Issus, p. 135

This scene represents yet another variation on a standard theme in Greek public art, the struggle between the Greeks and barbarians (most famously explored in the Parthenon frieze, which is an indirect representation of the Persian Wars). Here is a re-creation of the historical battle between Alexander the Great and King Darius of Persia. Which stylistic innovations, characteristic of Hellenistic art, has the artist incorporated to heighten the drama of the scene? (Point out the energy of the threatening lances, the barren tree trunk, and the use of frontal perspective and foreshortening.) How have the dynamics of that theme changed since the Parthenon's depiction? (Does this image portray a battle of equal forces, rather than the triumph of Greek rationalism over barbarian bestiality?) How has the enemy been rendered? Why is he given pride of place as the focal point of the composition? The caption states that Darius is "reach[ing] out in compassion for his warriors who are selflessly throwing

themselves in the way to protect him." But his gesture has also been interpreted as signaling retreat to his men.

Egyptian Style Statue of Queen Arsinoe II, p. 145

What does this statue reveal about the Ptolemaic assimilation of Egyptian norms and culture? Why is Arsinoe portrayed with the stylistic conventions normally reserved for the ancient Egyptian pharaohs? Can students detect any traces of Greek artistic influence in the work?

Praxiteles' Statue of Aphrodite, p. 151

This first depiction of a nude goddess was celebrated throughout the ancient world. Previously, the only unclothed females routinely portrayed in Greek art were prostitutes, nymphs, and half-nude (and crazed) maenads. What remarks do students have about the transfer of dignified and naturalistic nudity, usually reserved for male athletes and warriors, to the figure of a goddess? Does her identity as the goddess of love have any bearing? Is there an erotic tone in the piece, despite her gesture of modesty? Ask students what this statue might suggest about Hellenistic gender roles and norms of morality.

Aristotle on the Nature of the Greek Polis

Some discussion about Aristotle's concept of "nature" and its relation to the Greek polis would be fruitful. Aristotle states that "necessity" pairs or brings together elements that will not survive without the other. These partnerships are based on the idea that some people are naturally subservient and others are naturally masters. His examples are illuminating: men dominate the partnerships with their households, villages the partnerships with households, and the city-state the partnerships with the villages. By stressing that these partnerships are rooted in nature, few can argue with Aristotle's powerful political model.

OTHER BEDFORD/ST. MARTIN'S RESOURCES FOR CHAPTER 4

The following resources are available to accompany Chapter 4. Please refer to the Preface of this manual for detailed descriptions of all the ancillaries.

For Instructors

Transparencies

The following maps and image from Chapter 4 are available as full-color acetates.

- Map 4.1: Expansion of Macedonia Under Philip II
- Map 4.2: Conquests of Alexander the Great
- Map 4.3: Hellenistic Kingdoms
- Mapping the West: Roman Takeover of the Hellenistic World
- *Dying Celts* (chapter image, page 150)

Instructor's Resources CD-ROM

The following maps and image from Chapter 4, as well as a chapter outline, are available on disc in both Power-Point and jpeg formats.

- Map 4.1: Expansion of Macedonia Under Philip II
- Map 4.2: Conquests of Alexander the Great
- Map 4.3: Hellenistic Kingdoms
- Mapping the West: Roman Takeover of the Hellenistic World
- *Dying Celts* (chapter image, page 150)

For Students

Sources of The Making of the West

The following documents are available in Chapter 4 of the companion sourcebook by Katharine J. Lualdi, University of Southern Maine.

1. Arrian, *The Campaigns of Alexander* (Second Century B.C.E.)
2. *Funerary Inscriptions and Epitaths* (Fifth to First Centuries B.C.E.)
3. Map of Ancient Alexandria (Second half of the First Century B.C.E.)
4. Epicurus, *Letter to a Friend* (Late Third Century B.C.E.)
5. *The Book of I Maccabees*, Chapter 8 (c. 175 B.C.E.)

Study Guides

The print **Study Guide** and the **Online Study Guide** at bedfordstmartins.com/hunt, both by Victoria Thompson (Arizona State University) and Eric Johnson (University of California, Los Angeles), help students synthesize the material they have learned as well as practice the skills historians use to make sense of the past. The following Map, Visual, and Document activities are available for Chapter 4.

Map Activity

- Map 5.3: Roman Expansion

Visual Activity

- *Dying Celts* (chapter image, page 150)

Reading Historical Documents

- Aristotle on the Nature of the Greek Polis (page 131)
- Ethnic Tension in Ptolemaic Egypt (page 141)

The Rise of Rome

c. 753–44 B.C.E.

CHAPTER RESOURCES

Main Chapter Topics

1. From about 753 to 44 B.C.E., Rome developed from humble beginnings into the dominant power of its day. It incorporated much of Europe, northern Africa, Egypt, and the eastern Mediterranean within a single state system that was sustained for centuries and that left its traces in the history of all modern western societies.

2. Rome's social structure included class divisions and a patron-client system of benefits and obligations, whereas traditional morality emphasized virtue, fidelity, and devotion to the common good above personal interest.

3. Rome expanded its territory through conquest and alliances, incorporating former enemies into the state and its army and sharing with them the rewards of further expansion; this trend toward inclusiveness extended even to slaves who, once freed, became citizens.

4. Cross-cultural influences came to Rome via its central and accessible location on the Italian peninsula and in the Mediterranean Sea, which introduced new arts, ideas, and traditions into a relatively open and tolerant Roman system. Conquest extended the basin reach of influences even farther.

5. Rome's republic was shaped by the struggle of the orders—social and political strife between the patricians and the plebeians. Over time, the plebeians gained political and legal ground largely through a series of strikes in which they withdrew from the army, while shrewd patricians made concessions to stave off more severe consequences for the community.

6. Rome's territorial conquests were beneficial to many, but also crippled the economy, bankrupting farmer-soldiers, straining food supplies, and increasing the numbers of urban poor, which resulted in new political tensions.

7. Over time, ambition for personal power and wealth overrode traditional values and reduced the republic to a factionalized, sometimes violent state vulnerable to civil war and political upheaval at the mercy of autocratic generals and their client armies.

Summary

The legend surrounding Romulus and the "Rape of the Sabine Women" emphasized the very nature of the Roman Empire: it expanded by absorbing outside peoples, sometimes peacefully, sometimes violently. Rome also assimilated cultural traditions—particularly those of the Greeks—but reshaped them into something uniquely Roman. Romans firmly believed they were destined to rule the world by military might and law, and improve it through social and moral values.

Roman social order was a web of moral and social duties and obligations that connected all Romans to their gods and fellow citizens, legally and morally ordering of all facets of life: familial, social, and business relationships, religious matters, and politics. Romans trusted the time-tested *mos maiorum* ("way of the elders") and distrusted new or competing mores.

One such value was virtue (*virtus*), or willfully acting in good faith in all social dealings. Another was faithfulness (*fides*), which required one to fulfill one's obligations no matter the cost or risk of upsetting the gods and community order. Faithfulness was particularly nuanced along gender lines. For women, chastity before marriage and monogamy after were paramount examples, whereas men were held to their word and their debts and expected to treat persons with justice, by which Romans meant treating everyone according to their social status. Religious devotion, worshiping the gods faithfully and respectfully, was also a crucial element of faithfulness. By adhering to these values and observing moderation, self-control, and proper reverence for authority, Romans earned respect.

The reward for morality was status. For women, the ideal was the matron who bore and properly educated legitimate children. For men, status led to public office or official recognition. Initially, birth determined status, which gave children of elites advantages and the responsibility to live up to the highest standards. In time, though, wealth became overwhelmingly important because money was needed to live well, entertain friends, and support public projects.

The patron-client system carried social and legal obligations. Patrons provided political and financial benefits to those of lower status (clients) in return for the loyal fulfilling of duties, which could also be political and financial in nature. Possessing clients was another mark of status, so patrons welcomed as many as they could afford to maintain. The mutual obligations between clients and patrons could last over generations.

The family was the foundation of Roman society, the bedrock of property and the moral system; it was under the absolute authority of the patriarch (*patria potestas*). This authority extended from the economic affairs of his dependents, his children and slaves in particular, to the power of life and death over the entire household. This power, though, was usually only exercised over infants. Exposure was an accepted practice and used to control family size or dispose of imperfect infants. Abandoned babies might die, be adopted, or be raised by others as slaves. Infant girls probably suffered this fate more than boys. Roman men had a circle of friends and relatives who formed a kind of council that could be consulted for advice on important subjects, like a sentence of death over a family member.

"Free" marriages, where the wife technically remained in the power of her father, were the norm. After their fathers died, married women became fairly independent. They led lives that were less socially restricted than Greek women, especially among the higher classes, where they were even able to influence Roman politics. Women generally managed the household finances and were responsible for instituting values and learning in children. Some women, like Cornelia, who refused marriage to the king of Egypt in order to raise her two sons, earned enormous respect for carrying out her duties. Her sons, Tiberius and Gaius Gracchus, became prominent in the later republic. Women like Cornelia could indirectly influence politics through their husbands, sons, and male relatives. Women also contributed to family wealth, either by inheritance or entrepreneurship in the higher classes or by laboring in the lower classes.

Children were educated at home. Tutors were often educated slaves, ideally Greek slaves so they could teach their native language to their pupils. Only very wealthy families could afford paid teachers. Both boys and girls in wealthy families were taught to read and write, although the primary purpose of educating girls was to prepare them to instill traditional social and moral values in their own children. Fathers gave their sons physical training, but most important was teaching them rhetoric: the skill of persuasive speaking. Boys accompanied their fathers to the forum to learn the art from public speakers and wealthy families often paid professional teachers to tutor their sons. Greek techniques were especially studied.

Roman civic religion centered on the worship of Jupiter, Minerva, and Juno (who corresponded to the Greek gods Zeus, Athena, and Hera) and on tending the eternal flame of Vestia (Hesta). Romans looked to these deities not for models of behavior (the gods were unconcerned with human morality) but for the city's safety and agricultural success. Other cults celebrated personifications of virtue, fidelity, and other morals. Religious tolerance was high, and Romans imported new gods and cults from subject peoples. In their homes, Romans worshiped the Lares and Penates, spirits of the household and their ancestors. Ritual was an important aspect of Roman religious practices. The February 15 Lupercalia festival included a fertility ritual where naked young men, armed with strips of goatskin, ran around the Palatine hill striking women who had not yet borne children. The December 17 Saturnalia festival temporarily inverted the social order to release tensions between masters and slaves. Central Roman values were considered divine forces. Piety (*pietas*), for example, represented devotion and duty, and was personified as a female deity in human form. The personification of such abstract moral qualities provided a focus for cult rituals. There was no priestly class, and Roman religious officials were citizens who conduced sacrifices, festivals, and other rituals, to ensure the goodwill of the gods toward the state (*pax deorum*). Prominent men vied for the office of high priest (Pontifex Maximus), who served as head of the state religion and was the ultimate authority on religious matters affecting government.

For its first 250 years, Rome was ruled by kings who developed the Senate as an advisory council. The city quickly expanded, absorbing conquered enemies into its domain, while exhibiting a more liberal citizenship policy — even extended to freed slaves — than the Greek city-states. It was also ideally situated. It had fertile farmland, control of a major river crossing, and a nearby harbor on the Mediterranean Sea. Rome was greatly influenced culturally by the Greeks in Campania to the south, although the influence of the Etruscans just to the north is more widely disputed. Rome adopted and adapted some Etruscan customs and traditions, but both societies shared similar outside contacts, so it is difficult to determine Etruscan cultural influences. The Roman elites' distrust of monarchy is central in the legend of the republic's founding. Lucretia, a chaste and loyal wife, was raped by the son of King Tarquin, after which she committed suicide despite the pleas of her husband and family. Following this tragedy, her kinsman Lucius Junius Brutus led the Romans in a revolt and drove Tarquin out in 509 B.C.E., eliminating the monarchy and establishing a republic to prevent the tyrannical abuse of power.

The republic suffered from its own political tensions. For over two hundred years, the patricians (social elites) struggled with the plebeians (the rest of the population) over Rome's political organization in the struggle of the orders. The plebeians' strength in numbers worked to their advantage. They won concessions by refusing to participate in economic and military life, thereby crippling the smooth functioning of society. The Twelve Tables, Rome's earliest law code (c. 450 B.C.E.), instituted a rule of law and was the first of a series of reforms that included the creation of tribunes to protect the plebeians and the institution of new assemblies that redistributed electoral and legislative power.

The government consisted of numerous elected officials serving short terms. Officials worked their way up a ladder of offices to the highest offices of the consuls. Ten years of military service was the first prerequisite for office. The lowest ranking elected office was that of financial officer (quaestor). Then came election as one of Rome's aediles, who supervised the city's streets, sewers, aqueducts, temples, and markets. Few men achieved the office of praetor, which involved judicial and military duties. Consuls topped the ladder, and ex-consuls competed to become censors, responsible for taking the census and selecting new senators from among those who had won election as quaestors. Chafing over the patrician stranglehold on these offices, the plebeians forced the creation of a special panel of ten annually elected tribunes who collectively held the power to block official actions, veto legislation, and suspend elections. By 367 B.C.E., the plebeians broke the patricians' hold on offices, and required that at least one consul each year be a plebeian. In practice, only men of wealth could run for office because they were expected to spend lavishly to win election. Once in office they had to pay for public projects out of their own pockets. Initially, officeholders sought only status from their official positions; later, they sought wealth as well. Although mainly an advisory body, the opinions of the Senate nevertheless had the moral force of law. Many public decisions were voted in assemblies of adult males, although the status and wealth of the different segments of the crowd influenced the voting weight. Patricians dominated the Centuriate Assembly, which elected consuls and praetors. A separate Plebeian Assembly, which elected tribunes, was thus created to check patrician power. The Plebeian Assembly gained power in the struggle of the orders and, in 287 B.C.E., its resolutions (called "plebiscites") became legally binding on all Romans. The Tribal Assembly was soon created to mix patricians and plebeians (the latter outnumbering the former) and, in time, it became responsible for making policy, passing laws, and—until separate courts were formed—conducting trials.

The development of the Roman judicial system was marked by struggles within leading groups. Initially, praetors decided cases, although important cases could be transferred to the assemblies. At first, individuals often represented themselves in trials. But, in the third century B.C.E., jurists (senators with legal expertise) assumed a central place in Rome's legal system, offering advice as private citizens. Criminal law was simple, though civil law, involving as it did disputes over property and private issues, was complex. Still, ultimate legal authority was grounded mainly in tradition.

From the fifth through second centuries B.C.E., Rome first conquered the entire Italian peninsula and then dominated the entire Mediterranean region. Attacks were always justified as preemptive defense, but the desire for imperial spoils was often the decisive factor. Rome's chief opponents in Italy were the Etruscans with whom they had warred for one hundred years before victory in 396 B.C.E., at which time they faced invading Gauls. Rome's defeated opponents were shrewdly integrated into Roman society via enslavement, partial and full citizenship, and with promises of the spoils of future wars in exchange for aid and loyalty. To move its armies and goods, Rome constructed a monumental infrastructure, including roads—which further stimulated cultural interactions—and aqueducts.

Rome's most formidable foe was Carthage in North Africa, which controlled much of the southwestern Mediterranean and parts of Spain. The cities inevitably clashed in the three Punic Wars (from the Roman term for Phoenicians, *Punici*). With its victory in the First Punic War (264–241 B.C.E.), Rome captured Sicily and established its first province, subject to direct Roman rule and taxation. The battles, though, had been costly, as Rome developed its navy and learned to fight at sea. Success with the provincial system soon prompted Rome to seize Sardinia and Corsica from Carthage as well.

The Second Punic War (218–201 B.C.E.) was also costly to Rome, due to the Carthaginian general Hannibal's successful campaigns into the heartland of Italy. Yet, Rome's allies remained loyal and turned the tide. Rome invaded Carthage's territory and claimed victory in 202 B.C.E., after which it dismantled Carthage's navy and demanded enormous war indemnities and Carthage's holdings in Spain.

Fifty years later, Carthage had recovered financially and attacked an aggressive neighbor — and Roman ally — the Numidian king Masinissa. Rome resolved to demolish Carthage in the Third Punic War (149–146 B.C.E.) and added Carthage and its empire to the Roman dominions. Under its dominion, North Africa flourished economically and culturally.

In revenge for supporting Carthage, Rome conquered Macedonia and Greece and cemented Greek influence on Rome. Initially, Macedonia and Greece misunderstood their client status. Rome was eventually forced to raze Corinth for their show of independence and turn Macedonia and Greece into a province. In 133 B.C.E., the Attalid king Attalus III of Pergamene bequeathed Asia

Minor to Rome. In 121 B.C.E., the lower part of Gaul (France) became a province.

Although Rome believed Greece to be militarily inferior, it greatly respected its cultural traditions, especially in art and literature. The greatest writers of the period looked to Greek models: the poets Naevius (d. 201 B.C.E.) and Ennius (d. 169 B.C.E.), and the playwrights Plautus (d. 184 B.C.E.) and Terence (c. 190–159 B.C.E.). Yet, some influential Romans like Cato, decried the effect of "effete" Greek culture on "sturdy" Romans. Nonetheless, the Greek influence grew in a thoroughly Romanized manner, reflecting Roman values and traditions. Lucretius (c. 94–55 B.C.E.) wrote on death, and Catullus (c. 84–54 B.C.E.) on sexual scandal and unrequited love. Roman philosophy, especially that of Cicero and his concept of *humanitas* ("humanness, the quality of humanity"), adapted Greek ideas to Roman ethics, politics, and theology. Greek art and architecture influenced Roman styles. Buildings were based on Greek models, while Roman portrait sculpture, expanding on Hellenistic traditions of representing stereotypes realistically, depicted the physical reality of their subjects—long noses, wrinkles, receding chins—which demonstrated how hard they worked for the people.

Military success in the late republic caused hardship at home. Farmers were particularly hard hit because long military campaigns exhausted their resources and kept them away from their land, forcing many to later relocate to the cities as dispossessed poor. As food production was strained, the poor were in a state of crisis, forced into menial labor or prostitution. The glut of indigent persons created a tense political climate and Rome was forced to subsidize imported grain to feed the poor, much to the chagrin of politicians hoping to devote more resources to war efforts.

Meanwhile, the wealthy enjoyed the spoils of conquest, which elevated their social status. Spending lavishly on public works projects also further enhanced their reputations. Wealthy landowners also benefited from the plight of farmers, buying up failing farms at low prices to build huge farms (*latifundia*) worked by slaves and laborers. The irony in this was that poor farmers fought in wars that resulted in the enslavement of conquered peoples, who then displaced the farmers as workforce. Then, the unsupervised, provincial governors unleashed waves of corruption. In these ways, wealth and conspicuous consumption began to take precedence over traditional Roman values.

The intensifying struggle for power raised the threat of civil war. Some politicians, such as Tiberius and Gaius Gracchus, advocated concessions for the poor, pitting themselves against many of their fellow elites. After his election as tribune, Tiberius used his office to distribute public lands to landless Romans and further angered the Senate by devoting the gift of Pergamene by King Attalus III to equip new farms on the redistributed land. After

announcing he would run for an unprecedented second term, Tiberius was murdered by a group of senators led by his cousin Scipio Nasica under a cry of "save the republic." Tiberius's brother Gaius was elected in his place. Gaius followed policies similar to his brother's and also sought and won a second term. Gaius championed the poor and proposed a judicial body, composed of wealthy businessmen known as equites ("equestrians" or "knights"), to try senators accused of corruption as provincial governors—a blow against the senatorial class. Blocked by the Senate, Gaius armed his followers, but the senators sent the consuls after him. Rather than be captured, Gaius had a servant cut his throat; his supporters were killed. Tiberius and Gaius Gracchus introduced faction into politics. Members of the elite identified themselves as supporters of the people (populares), or supporters of the best (optimates).

The demand for effective military commanders throughout this turmoil gave rise to "new men," upper-class leaders arising without consular ancestors, who fought their way to the top on ability alone and challenged the elite's dominance. The first new man was Gaius Marius (c. 155–86 B.C.E.), an equestrian who rose on the strength of his military prowess. Marius was elected consul (in 107 B.C.E.) and, on the back of his continuing military victories, served an unprecedented six terms. His success, however, brewed resentment and deepened the divisions in Roman politics. He spearheaded reforms that allowed common people, including proletarians, to join the military. Armies began supporting their military commanders in all their ambitions, as clients would their patrons, thereby fracturing the republic further. In the early first century B.C.E., the Social War erupted when aggrieved Italians, lacking Roman citizenship and therefore a voice in deciding the allocation of spoils of war and other issues affecting them, rose against Rome. Even though the Italians lost the battle to the unscrupulous and ambitious Roman general Lucius Cornelius Sulla (c. 138–78 B.C.E.), they gained citizenship rights.

When the king of Pontus, Mithridates VI (120–63 B.C.E.), revolted against Roman control in Asia Minor (in 88 B.C.E.), killing tens of thousands of Italian officials there in a single day, the Senate set out for revenge, granting command to Sulla. His rival Marius, though elderly, attempted to revoke Sulla's command and, in retaliation, Sulla marched his troops on the city of Rome itself. While Sulla's officers fled in horror at this sacrilege, his common soldiers remained faithful, capturing Rome and killing Sulla's rivals. Sulla proceeded to Asia Minor, sacking Athens on his way to victory.

While Sulla was in Asia Minor, which his troops stripped bare, in Rome Marius attempted to regain his power and influence. Civil war broke out between Sulla and his enemies, and waged for two years, with Sulla eventually crushing all who opposed him. He initiated a process called "proscription," whereby all suspected of treason were listed and hunted down for execution. Because the property of those listed would be confiscated, victors fraudulently listed the names of men whose wealth they coveted. As a measure to stop the violence, the Senate appointed Sulla dictator. Sulla refashioned the government to suit his purposes and those of his peers, the "best people," in the highest social class.

Sulla's career made strikingly visible the cracks in the republic's façade. It highlighted the dissolution of Roman military, political, and social values, which earlier in the republic had been subordinated to personal ambitions. Leading generals after Sulla's retirement (in 79 B.C.E.) followed his example in the tactics of power. Gnaeus Pompey (106–48 B.C.E.) had been one of Sulla's generals and supporters. In 71 B.C.E., he won the final victories over a massive slave revolt led by Spartacus. In 70 B.C.E., Pompey demanded and won election as consul, bypassing an age requirement and before he had successfully won or held any other office. He defeated pirates in the Mediterranean, which made him extremely popular with the urban poor for securing the imported grain supply, and wealthy commercial and shipping interests. Pompey's victories extended Roman territory to the eastern Mediterranean, incorporating Judea. Favorable comparisons to Alexander the Great were made and he was nicknamed Magnus (the Great).

When the Senate tried to check Pompey's power, he entered into an alliance with his two most powerful rivals. The three dominant political rivals — Pompey, Marcus Licinius Crassus, and Julius Caesar (100–44 B.C.E.) — arranged an alliance, known as the First Triumvirate, to rule Rome. Pompey's eastern conquests were incorporated into the republic, Crassus was given financial breaks for tax collectors in Asia Minor loyal to him, and Caesar gained the consulship (in 59 B.C.E.) and was given special command of an army in Gaul. The alliance between Pompey and Caesar was further sealed by a series of marriages. But relations were increasingly strained as each member's quest for power intensified. Violence within Rome between supporters of Pompey and Caesar became so severe that elections became impossible. After Crassus's death in battle, the triumvirate dissolved, leaving the republic divided. The Senate demanded his command and, in response, Caesar led his troops into Rome to the great enthusiasm of the people of Italy, causing his enemies to flee. He followed them to Greece and defeated the army of Pompey and the Senate in 48 B.C.E. Pompey escaped to Egypt, where he was murdered by Egyptian petty politicians who wanted to curry favor with him. Caesar thus effectively ruled Rome and went on to victories in Egypt, where he established Cleopatra VII (69–30 B.C.E.) as ruler in an alliance that outraged those who insisted that Rome should seize power rather than yield it.

Republican institutions were maintained, but Caesar—in all essentials—was king. He embarked on an extensive campaign to rebuild Rome's crumbling social, physical, and economic infrastructure. Some debts were cancelled, citizenship was extended to more non-Romans, and non-Italians were admitted to the Senate. Clemency was extended to his enemies, the month of July was named after him, and the calendar was reformed and based on 365 days. Despite these massive and popular improvements, his power angered the political elite, many of whom joined in his assassination (44 B.C.E.) led by Marcus Junius Brutus. After Caesar's death, the fractured republic tumbled into chaos, with mass riots and political rivals attempting to fill the power vacuum.

Suggestions for Lecture and Discussion Topics

1. Rome's relationship to Classical Greece was one of reverence but not slavish or uncritical imitation. A revealing approach to the Roman republic could examine the role of Classical Greek traditions in Roman social, cultural, religious, and political life. In which ways did Rome absorb these traditions into its own system? In which form did they survive? In which ways did these Greek traditions transform Roman society?

2. The central Roman value of virtue, which encompassed uprightness, faithfulness, respect, and an adherence to tradition were gradually subordinated to a lust for power and wealth among social elites. But the hierarchical organization of society and an emphasis on social status as the measure of personal worth underlay the system throughout this transformation. In which ways might one view the crumbling of the republic as less a negation of traditional values than as a playing out of inherent contradictions? See the sections on the republic in Paul Veyne, *Bread and Circuses*, Brian Pearce, trans. (New York: Penguin, 1990). This discussion can fuel an examination of the causes of Roman social unrest, as well as the methods used to combat it.

3. Rome's devotion to a stable, social hierarchy in which all citizens knew and respected their proper roles entailed vastly different prescriptions for men and women. An examination of the differences in male and female roles and virtues as embodied in education, politics, morality, and so on, can help highlight some of the assumptions on which Roman society was based. The legends of the early Roman city and of the formation of the Roman republic can provide illuminating starting points. This discussion can also include an examination of the role of women in Roman politics. See the story of Lucretia in Livy, *The Early History of Rome*, A. de Sélincourt, trans. (New York: Penguin, 1960). On women in politics, see Richard Bauman, *Women and Politics in Ancient Rome* (London and New York: Routledge, 1992).

4. The family was, of course, the institution to which most Romans were most immediately subordinated. An

examination of the familial structure and its workings can serve as a good introduction to the daily life of average Romans. In which ways did the Roman family reinforce the broader social order? Such a discussion could involve both the internal familial functions, such as instilling education and values in children, and societal functions, including property distribution and social status. Useful information can be found in Jane F. Gardner, *Women in Roman Law and Society* (Bloomington: Indiana University Press, 1986); and Richard P. Saller, *Patriarchy, Property, and Death in the Roman Family* (Cambridge: Cambridge University Press, 1994). An excellent and wide-ranging selection of excerpted primary sources for all aspects of Roman social history can be found in Jo-Ann Shelton, *As the Romans Did: A Sourcebook in Roman Social History* (Oxford: Oxford University Press, 1988).

5. Geographically, Rome was particularly well situated for prominence in the ancient world. While examining maps of Italy and the Mediterranean in conjunction with an identification of Rome's chief rivals, discuss the factors that may have motivated, assisted, or inhibited Roman expansion. Such a discussion can incorporate economic considerations, military strategy, and political maneuvering. For an overview, see Chapter 3 of Lesley Adkins and Roy A. Adkins, *Handbook to Life in Ancient Rome* (Oxford: Oxford University Press, 1994).

6. Rome's expansionist foreign policy carried dramatic consequences for the city, its population, and other territories already within its domain. Because war and conquest were so central to Roman politics, students may be interested to learn how Roman foreign policy was related to domestic policy. Which factors propelled Rome's expansion? What were the effects of that expansion on Roman life? Which political alternatives existed at various points in Roman republican history in regard to foreign policy and the cultivation and distribution of resources? Which factors influenced the decisions that were ultimately made? An introduction to the topic can be found in Elizabeth Rawson, "The Expansion of Rome," in *The Roman World,* John Boardman, et al., eds. (Oxford: Oxford University Press, 1986).

Making Connections

1. *How do the political and social values of the Roman republic compare to those of the classical Greek city-state?* Roman political and social divisions were institutionalized in a way that differed from Classical Greece. Patricians were at the top, equestrians in the middle, and plebeians at the bottom of society; a person's political and legal rights depended on his or her class. There was the shared value of putting the common good over personal interests, but virtue, acting in good faith, and fidelity, fulfilling one's obligations at all costs, were more Roman values than Greek ones.

2. *What were the positive and the negative consequences of war for the Roman republic?* Many people suffered hardship during the Punic Wars (264–146 B.C.E.) and the conquest of Macedonia and Greece. Farmers were kept away from home for long periods of time during their obligatory military service, and many lost their farms and became destitute because they were unable to cultivate their land. With less production, food prices soared, forcing the poor into low paying jobs and even prostitution. This caused economic and political tension, especially in urban areas. While the poor got poorer, the rich got richer, buying up farms and enjoying the spoils of military conquests.

Writing Assignments and Class Presentation Topics

1. Ask students to write an essay on the phenomenon of the Roman "new man." One of the major characteristics of this development was the open encouragement of popular armies loyal to their commanders rather than to the ideals of the republic. Which factors gave rise to this phenomenon? What were its effects on Roman political life? What were the defining characteristics of these new notable Romans, as opposed to the notable figures of the past? An exceptionally useful source is the Roman historian Appian's *The Civil Wars,* particularly the first book.

2. Have students read the biographies of Tiberius and Gaius Gracchus and compare their lives and politics with those of Julius Caesar. In which ways were they similar, especially in their policies affecting ordinary Romans? Also compare the reaction of their fellow elites to their policies. Which factors made the Senate, ostensibly a popular organization designed to protect against tyranny, less popular than these "populist tyrants"? The biographies are found in Plutarch, *Lives of the Noble Greeks and Romans*: "Gaius Gracchus," pp. iii–ix; "Tiberius Gracchus," pp. viii.7–ix.5, xiv.1–2; "Julius Caesar," pp. lvii, lxiii–lxvii.

3. The notion of absolute patriarchal authority was the central tenet of family life. Yet the Roman republic was distrustful of such centralized, tyrannical authority in politics. Ask students to report on the tension between basing a republic adverse to unchecked power on a familial structure that demanded such power. How might this system have fed into Rome's political system? Did it contribute to the fall of the republic? Why or why not?

4. The Punic Wars were among the most important and influential events in the history of the republic's foreign conquests. What were the motivating factors of these conflicts? In which ways did they shape or transform Rome militarily? What were some of the economic consequences? This topic can involve discussion of the taxation of Sicily, the command of trade routes, the

development of the navy, the strains the wars placed on the Roman economy, and the means employed by Roman leaders to finance their efforts. For a general history of the wars, see Polybius's *Histories*. For a more detailed look at the financing of the war and related issues, see Livy's *History*.

5. On a more lighthearted note, you might have students discuss the portrayal of the late republic in such major Hollywood epics as *Spartacus* (1960), which deals with notions of slavery, freedom, the erosion of republican Rome, the spread of senatorial corruption, and the power of the "new man." Examine how well students can separate the fictionalized elements from history and how movements of the late 1950s and early 1960s, like the civil rights movement, fed into the production. Brent Shaw wrote a wonderful introduction to Spartacus and the Roman slave wars in his Bedford History and Culture Series Book, *Spartacus and the Slave Wars* (Boston: Bedford/St. Martin's, 2000). For a historical discussion of the events portrayed in the film, see Keith Bradley, *Slavery and Rebellion in the Roman World, 140 B.C.E.–70 B.C.E.* (Bloomington: Indiana University Press, 1989). As for the fictionalized elements or the portrayal of overall themes, an interesting discussion could involve the implicit comparison of Rome to the United States in such Hollywood films, including the values and morals represented.

Research Assignments

1. Although slavery was a fact of life throughout the Roman republic, it was a far more fluid condition than its modern variations, such as that in the antebellum American south. Have students write or report on the nature of slavery in the republic. What did it mean to be a slave? They might consider how Roman expansionist policies contributed to the creation of a slave state, not only through the conquest of other peoples, but also through the transformation of small, failing farms into estates for wealthy elites. A good place to begin is Keith Bradley, *Slavery and Society at Rome* (Cambridge: Cambridge University Press, 1994).

2. Have students research and report on the struggle of the orders. Which interests were pursued by each side of the struggle? In which values were those competing interests rooted? What measures were taken in advance of each faction's interests? In which ways were the political maneuvering of this struggle related to the overtly violent struggle between a small number of individuals for political power in the late republic? For many excerpts from primary sources, see the numerous sections indexed under "plebeians" and "patricians" in Naphtali Lewis and Meyer Reinhold, eds., *Roman Civilization, Sourcebook 1: The Republic* (New York: Harper & Row,

1966). On the general class structure of the republic, see chapters 1 and 10 in Jo-Ann Shelton, *As the Romans Did: A Sourcebook in Roman Social History* (Oxford: Oxford University Press, 1988). On the later nature of this struggle under the Gracchi, see chapters 44 and 45 in Nels M. Bailkey, ed., *Readings in Ancient History: Thought and Experience from Gilgamesh to St. Augustine*, 5th ed. (Lexington, MA: D. C. Heath, 1996).

Literature

Grant, Michael, trans., *Selected Works by Marcus Tullius Cicero*. 1960.

de Selincourt, Aubrey, trans., *Livy: The Early History of Rome*. 2002.

———. *The War with Hannibal by Livy*. 1965.

Latham, R. E., trans., *Lucretius: On the Nature of the Universe*. 1994.

Walton, J. Michael, ed., *Four Roman Comedies by Plautus and Terence*. 2003.

Waterfield, Robin, trans., *Roman Lives: A Selection of Eight Roman Lives by Plutarch*. 2000.

Films and Videos

Spartacus (1960) (VHS/DVD, 3 hrs., 16 min.), This lavishly produced film tells the story of the slave rebellion led by Spartacus against the Romans in 71 B.C.E. It nicely captures the feel of the period and the kind of political intrigues that were so much a part of the late republic.

Historical Skills

Map 5.1, Ancient Italy, c. 500 B.C.E., p. 173

Ask students to consider the location of Rome in regard to the geographical and cultural layout of the Italian peninsula. Which natural and cultural resources surrounded Rome in all directions? How might these considerations have factored into Rome's course of early expansion?

Map 5.3, Roman Expansion, c. 500–44 B.C.E., p. 184

Consider Rome's position in relation to both the Mediterranean and Europe. Which strategic interests fueled the course of its expansion? What were Rome's vulnerabilities, and how did it account for them? Ask students to locate Rome's major rivals and discuss the geographical and strategical considerations each had to face.

Taking Measure: Census Records of Adult Male Roman Citizens During the First and Second Punic Wars, p. 183

Ask students to examine the population figures as they relate to the events occurring in and between the years cited. What effects did the sudden increases and decreases in the population of adult males have on Rome's domestic and foreign policies? Based on the reading and these population figures, which factors, in addition to the Punic Wars, do students believe influenced Rome's politics?

Sculpted Tomb of a Family of Ex-Slaves, p. 167

Ask students to discuss the aesthetic features of this sculpture. What does the figure tell us about slaves in Roman society? What social purposes might such a sculpture serve?

Household Shrine from Pompeii, p. 171

Along with appeals to the gods, what other purposes might these shrines serve? Keep in mind that they in part portrayed the centrality of patriarchal authority. In addition, it would be well worth remembering the emphasis on status as a measure of personal and social worth.

Bust of the General Lucius Cornelius Sulla, p. 191

This bust captures the virtues of leadership as commonly portrayed in republic-era sculpture. This conservative style emphasizes the stern expression, direct gaze, weathered brow, and maturity of the subject. What do such features tell us about republican-era values of civic duty and leadership? Contrast these depictions with that of Augustus in Chapter 6 (p. 215).

Coin Portrait of Julius Caesar, p. 197

Ask students to consider the inconsistency between Caesar's insistence that he was not a king with his decision to place his portrait on the Roman coin, which flouted two Roman traditions: that coin portraits were rotated annually and that they would feature only dead persons.

Ides of March Coin Celebrating Caesar's Murder, p. 198

Ask students to discuss the implications involved in using coin minting as a form of journalism, as it is in this figure. Which ideas and values are portrayed in this coin? What are the meanings behind the portrayal of the freed slave's helmet? Is this coin in part a propaganda tool?

Livy on Liberty in the Founding of the Roman Republic

Ask students to consider the context of Livy's massive multivolume history of Rome. Commissioned by Augustus, Livy placed the foundation of the republic after Rome's "good" kings, thus reminding readers that Augustus, too, established a "republic" after good but dictatorial leaders. Instituting term limits and oaths, and expanding the Senate implied greater participation by the people in the early republic. Augustus had enacted similar measures. What Livy's account cleverly masked, however, was the fact that Augustus had actually established a monarchy and cloaked it with *images* of traditional republican government.

OTHER BEDFORD/ST. MARTIN'S RESOURCES FOR CHAPTER 5

The following resources are available to accompany Chapter 5. Please refer to the Preface of this manual for detailed descriptions of all the ancillaries.

For Instructors

Transparencies

The following maps and images from Chapter 5 are available as full-color acetates.

- Map 5.1: Ancient Italy
- Map 5.2: The City of Rome during the Republic
- Map 5.3: Roman Expansion
- Mapping the West: The Roman World at the End of the Republic
- *Aqueduct at Nimes in France* (chapter image, page 181)
- *Wolf Suckling Romulus and Remus* (chapter image, page 162)

Instructor's Resources CD-ROM

The following maps and image from Chapter 5, as well as a chapter outline, are available on disc in both Power-Point and jpeg formats.

- Map 5.1: Ancient Italy
- Map 5.2: The City of Rome During the Republic
- Map 5.3: Roman Expansion
- Mapping the West: The Roman World at the End of the Republic
- *Aqueduct at Nimes in France* (chapter image, page 181)

Using the Bedford Series with The Making of the West

Available in print as well as online at bedfordstmartins .com/oconnor, this guide by Maura O'Connor, University of Cincinnati, offers practical suggestions for using *Spartacus and the Slave Wars* by Brent D. Shaw, in conjunction with chapters 5 and 6 of the textbook.

For Students

Sources of The Making of the West

The following documents are available in Chapter 5 of the companion sourcebook by Katharine J. Lualdi, University of Southern Maine.

1. The Twelve Tables (451–440 B.C.E.)
2. *Roman Women Demonstrate against the Oppian Law* (195 B.C.E.)
3. Cicero, *On the Commonwealth* (54 B.C.E.)
4. *The Gracchan Reforms* (133 B.C.E.)

Study Guides

The print **Study Guide** and the **Online Study Guide** at bedfordstmartins.com/hunt, both by Victoria Thompson (Arizona State University) and Eric Johnson (University of California, Los Angeles), help students synthesize the material they have learned as well as practice the skills historians use to make sense of the past. The following Map, Visual, and Document activities are available for Chapter 5.

Map Activity

- Map 5.3: Roman Expansion

Visual Activity

- *Aqueduct at Nimes in France* (chapter image, page 181)

Reading Historical Documents

- Livy on Liberty in the Founding of the Roman Republic (page 176)
- Polybius on Roman Military Discipline in the Republic (page 190)

The Roman Empire
c. 44 B.C.E.–284 C.E.

CHAPTER RESOURCES

Main Chapter Topics

1. In 27 B.C.E., Octavian announced the restoration of the republic, but, with the Senate's cooperation, established himself as sole ruler of the principate. Titled "Augustus" and "princeps," he retained the Senate, consuls, courts, and other republican trappings to make his monarchy palatable to the Roman people.

2. Rome grew into a the western world's most populous city filled with crowded and dirty dwellings; new official forces and policies were designed to maintain order; and emperors provided expansive public amenities.

3. Imperial power was tightly bound to the loyalty of the army. Further, military operations continued to drive the economy. For a time, foreign conquests provided new revenue and slaves, but also required heavy expenditures. As time went on, defensive requirements increasingly strained the Roman economy.

4. Roman culture altered under imperial rule, reaching its literary peak in the first two centuries C.E. Lavish and violent spectacles such as gladiatorial combats were the focus of popular culture.

5. The first two centuries of the empire were relatively stable, with few major military conflicts and a strong economy. Increasingly, however, enemies and subjects on the imperial periphery exploited Roman weaknesses.

6. In the easternmost portion of the Roman Empire, political pressures and cultural and religious disputes among Jews moved them toward rebellion at the same time that Jesus of Nazareth's teachings produced Christianity. The new religion spread westward and suffered persecution, yet was still able to build institutional structures that coped with questions of doctrine and conduct.

7. In the third century C.E., economic instability, attacks from abroad, and natural disasters brought the empire to a crisis that would only resolve itself with yet another profound political and religious transformation.

Summary

Individual, personal ambitions began to take precedence over the good of the community in the late republic. Augustus tried to redress the balance and restore traditional values. He created a disguised monarchy, calling himself not king but rather princep, or "first man," an honorary title designating the leading senator. This was the modern equivalent of emperor, from the Latin *imperator* ("commander"). Augustus retained the Senate, consuls, and courts, giving the illusion of a republic, but in practice he and his immediate successors ruled like monarchs. Augustus ushered in a period of peace, known as the *pax romana*, that lasted about two hundred years, at which time the Roman Empire had to reorder itself once again. During the political and social turmoil following Julius Caesar's assassination (44 B.C.E.), three major figures emerged to rule the shattered republic. They were the Second Triumvirate: Mark Antony and Lepidus (both major generals), and Octavian, Caesar's young grandnephew. Octavian (63 B.C.E.–14 C.E.) marched Caesar's soldiers into Rome in 43 B.C.E., and demanded the consulship. The Senate, fearful of his power, granted it.

The Second Triumvirate disposed of rivals and confiscated their property through proscription. But soon Antony and Octavian forced Lepidus into retirement and began a civil war for sole leadership. Octavian claimed that Antony would make Cleopatra VII (69–30 B.C.E.) his queen and, to counter their alliance, Octavian demanded a loyalty oath from all residents of Rome and the western provinces. In 31 B.C.E., Octavian defeated Antony and Cleopatra in the naval battle at Actium, after which the pair committed suicide (30 B.C.E.). Octavian was now Rome's unrivaled leader.

In 27 B.C.E., Octavian possessed overwhelming power, yet shrewdly announced the restoration of the republic and appealed to the people and the Senate to decide Rome's political organization. The Senate implored Octavian to safeguard the restored republic, awarded him special civil and military powers, and bestowed on him the honorary title "Augustus" ("divinely favored").

Appearances were key to Augustus's success. The appearance of a republic was maintained through the continued elections of consuls and meetings of the Senate and assemblies. But Augustus was granted a tribune's powers without holding the office and could now use the power of the veto under the guise of protecting the people. Too wise to rub Roman noses in the loss of the republic, Augustus used the title princeps, hallowed in republican tradition, and maintained the dress and manner of an ordinary citizen, garnering the respect of the people. His power was based on his control of the army and treasury. Augustus further transformed the army from a citizen militia into a full-time professional force that was loyal to him personally. To pay for its maintenance, Augustus imposed an inheritance tax, which infuriated the rich but earned him the army's loyalty and gratitude. Another innovation was to station troops permanently in Rome to prevent rebellion in the capital. These soldiers were the praetorian guard and later played a significant role in determining the imperial succession.

Augustus paired displays of force with displays of symbols. Coins carried his image along with reminders of his accomplishments. Dedicated in 2 B.C.E., Augustus built a huge forum (public gathering space) emphasizing themes that justified his rule: peace through victory, devotion to the gods who protected Rome, respect for tradition, and unselfishness in dedicating his own funds for public projects.

Motivations for establishing the Principate are vague, but Augustus shrewdly balanced the need for peace, a traditional commitment to citizens' freedom of action, and his ambitions. The concept of the "first man" was transformed into a kind of pater familias: a ruler who looked after his people like a devoted father who expected obedience and loyalty in return. By the time of Augustus's death in 14 B.C.E. at age seventy-five, the transition from republic to empire had been solidified through forty-one years of peaceful rule.

During Augustan times, Rome's population was close to one million and many had no job and too little to eat. Ordinary, urban Romans lived in small apartments in multistoried buildings called "insula," which outnumbered private homes more than twenty to one. Small businesses operated on the ground floors and the rents for the apartments above grew cheaper the higher the floor. This was the case because ground floors might have had piped water, but upper ones did not. The primitive state of sanitation left city streets and the Tiber filthy and gastrointestinal illness was rampant. Public

fountains were primary sources of water for most people. Public baths were inexpensive and widely available for women and men, but these also helped to spread disease. While rich as well as poor suffered the effects of overcrowding, the wealthy had the wherewithal to alleviate them to some extent. Insula were often in danger of collapse due to imperfect engineering techniques and dishonest builders as well as fire. Augustus introduced limitations on the height of buildings and created the first fire department. He also established the first police force to maintain order.

As supreme patron of Rome, Augustus paid for imported grain to ensure the population had an adequate food supply, initiating the largest dole system by far in Roman history, perhaps encompassing as many as 700,000 people. He also introduced legislation that rewarded the propagation of legitimate children and severely punished adultery. In the social hierarchy, equestrians and provincials were elevated to senatorial rank as the old senatorial families died out.

Slaves were the foundation of the Roman labor force and were encouraged in their work by the hope of eventually being freed and achieving upward mobility. Notwithstanding, most Roman slaves suffered a harsh existence, especially in agriculture and manufacturing. Domestic slaves, who were often women, fared better. Some slaves ran their masters' businesses and were held in high regard. With enough extra money, saved through tips from their masters, some slaves could purchase slaves of their own or buy their own freedom.

Public entertainment, often paid for by the emperors, was extremely violent, featuring various kinds of gladiatorial combat and animals mangling condemned criminals. Women occasionally fought in these games until Emperor Septimus Serverus (r. 193–211 C.E.) banned their appearance. Crowds were passionate about these shows, betting was frequent, and popular champions became celebrities—famous and wealthy, but not respectable. To ensure class distinctions, the Senate barred the elite and freeborn women under age twenty from becoming gladiators. These entertainments, races, and theater displayed the emperor's generosity, but they also provided a place where the public could express their mood and will to the emperor, who was bound by tradition to attend festivals.

Elite culture was transformed by Augustus's rule. Oratory, once the height of republican arts and letters, lost its political purpose because criticism of the emperor and his policies was then dangerous and therefore unthinkable. Rhetorical skills were to be used to praise the emperor and argue cases in courts of law. Education was still an exclusive privilege of elite children; those persons who were not elites were taught only practical skills. Boys and girls age seven to eleven from wealthy families attended private schools and learned basic reading, writing, and arithmetic skills. Some continued three years after that, studying literature, history, and grammar. Only exceptional boys went on to study literature, history, ethical philosophy, law, and rhetoric in depth. Rich men and women employed educated slaves to read aloud to them.

Augustus vigorously supported literature, and his reign—the Golden Age of Latin literature—produced Horace (65–8 B.C.E.), who composed short poems celebrating Roman public and private life; and Virgil (70–19 B.C.E.), who wrote *The Aeneid*, which both praised and subtly criticized the Roman state. Inspired by Homer, Virgil's subject was the Trojan Aeneas, legendary founder of Rome. Livy (54 B.C.E.–C.E.) produced an openly critical but balanced history of Rome through Augustus's reign, but his support of Augustan traditional values saved him from punishment. Ovid (43 B.C.E.–17 C.E.), who irreverently mocked Augustan moral legislation in *The Art of Love* and *Love Affairs*, was tolerated, but his talent could not save him from exile in 8 B.C.E. when he was caught up in a sex scandal over Augustus's daughter Julia, whom Augustus also exiled.

Portraiture moved away from the unflinching realism of republican sculpture to idealized depictions reminiscent of Classical Greek models. For example, statues of Augustus reflected serenity and dignity, rather than his typical ill health.

To maintain political stability, Augustus initiated a tradition of grooming an heir to succeed to power, with a special emphasis on maintaining the loyalty of the army, presenting the emperor as stern but benign, and balancing local autonomy with universal Roman standards of law and culture. After Augustus's initial choices for heirs died, he eventually chose his stepson, the accomplished general Tiberius (42 B.C.E.–37 C.E.), to succeed him, thereby initiating the Julio-Claudian dynasty, named for Augustus's family. It was tacitly understood that the Senate would confirm each successor, which it did.

Tiberius's power (r. 14–37 C.E.) rested on the support of the military, and he built a fortified camp in Rome for the praetorian guard, thus giving them a de facto role in all future imperial successions. He maintained the façade of republican formalities but, being deeply unhappy, having earlier been forced to divorce a woman he loved to marry Augustus's promiscuous daughter, Julia (who was later exiled by her father), Tiberius neglected his duties and lived in isolation, allowing corruption to grow among his officials. His vices and political paranoia exposed the potential precariousness of one-man rule. Tiberius chose as his successor Caligula (r. 37–41 C.E.), Augustus's great-grandson, who added to violence and cruelty a penchant for cross-dressing, appeared in public attired as a god, and spent vast sums on personal whims. Caligula was murdered by two praetorian commanders. Because no successor had been named, the Senate considered restoring the republic until Augustus's grandnephew Claudius (r. 41–54

C.E.) won military support, and the Senate declared him emperor. Claudius shrewdly built loyalty by opening high positions to non-Italians and freeing slaves.

Claudius's successor, sixteen-year-old Nero (r. 54–68 C.E.), won favor with the poor through his lavish public festivals. The elite classes disliked and feared Nero who, having wasted public funds, falsely accused senators and equestrians of treason in order to seize their property. Nero failed to win the respect of the army and, after he was deposed by rebellious commanders, killed himself.

A year of violent civil war, which saw four emperors followed Nero's death. Vespasian (r. 69–79 C.E.) became the first Flavian emperor and worked to reinforce imperial power by promoting the worship of the emperor as a living god throughout the provinces. His two sons—Titus (r. 79–81 C.E.) and Domitian (r. 81–96 C.E.)—succeeded Vespasian with strong leadership and sound administrations and fiscal policies. The Flavians launched successful military campaigns against the northern tribes and left behind great public works, including the Colosseum, completed during Titus's rule. Domitian's arrogance, however, alienated the Senate. When a general in Germany revolted, Domitian executed a number of upper-class citizens as conspirators. His wife and members of the court, fearing they would be the emperor's next victims, murdered Domitian in 96 C.E. The empire had not escaped the power struggles and violence that had destroyed the republic.

Domitian's death ushered in the "five good emperors" of the empire's Golden Age: Nerva (r. 96–98 C.E.), Trajan (r. 98–117 C.E.), Hadrian (r. 117–138 C.E.), Antonius Pius (r. 138–161 C.E.), and Marcus Aurelius (r. 161–180 C.E.) who transferred power peacefully among themselves. Trajan extended the empire into Dacca (modern Romania) and Mesopotamia; Hadrian executed conspiratorial senators, put down a Jewish revolt, and turned Jerusalem into a military colony; Aurelius protected the Danube region from outside attack. These five emperors presided over a political and economic Golden Age.

In the two centuries following Augustus's reign, most provinces accepted Roman rule and therefore required minimal military presence. The exceptions were the northern and eastern frontiers facing hostile neighbors. The relative calm and prosperity within Rome's domain, however, did encourage long-distance trading for luxury goods from as far away as India and China. But with fewer new conquests, the empire lost its longstanding revenue from foreign plunder and new slaves, so agricultural taxes largely financed government and defense in the provinces. Administrative costs were actually quite minimal, given the size of provincial territories. Several hundred top officials governed a population of about fifty million. Most local taxes remained in the provinces. Provincial elites, serving as *decurions* (municipal senate members, later called *curiales*), collected the taxes, and had to make up revenue shortfalls from their personal funds. Still, these positions carried prestige, and might generate further reward by way of appointment as priests in the imperial cult.

The spread of Roman rule and culture (Romanization), increased trade, prosperity, and cross-cultural influence, and improved the standard of living for many in the provinces. The eastern provinces were least affected by Romanization because they largely retained their Greek and Near East character. Literature, especially in the Greek language and style, flourished; for example, the adventure novels of Chariton and Achilles Tatius, the satirical dialogues of Lucian (c. 117–180 C.E.), and the biographies of Plutarch (c. 50–120 C.E.). The late first and early second centuries are considered a "Silver Age" for Latin literature, and the most famous works of the period featured the critical histories of Tacitus (c. 56–120 C.E.), the satirical poems of Juvenal (c. 65–130 C.E.), and *The Golden Ass* of Apuleius (c. 125–170 C.E.).

Roman law stressed equity above the letter of the law, recognized fairness based on the intentions rather than the wording of contracts, and placed the burden of proof on the accuser. At the same time, the law assigned penalties based on social class. The "better people" enjoyed lighter sentencing under the law than the "humbler people," who comprised the remainder of the population.

The empire's stability depended on steady population growth. With scant reproductive knowledge and antibiotics nonexistent, women suffered to produce enough children to sustain the family line. Arranged marriages for very young women were commonplace, and their lives were often devoted to the bearing and rearing of children. Remaining single or childless represented social failure to Romans. Infant girls were more likely to suffer the practice of exposure because boys were more highly valued than girls. The emperors, with an eye to increasing the population, extended aid to needy children, as did private individuals.

Christianity, though, proved to be the most significant development in Roman history. In Judea, harsh Roman rule nursed apocalypticism — the idea that the one true God would send an "anointed one" (Hebrew, *Mashia* [or *Messiah*]; Greek, *Christ*) to right the injustices on Earth — and set a course toward a rebellion that would leave Jerusalem in ruins and its people enslaved. Jesus (c. 4 B.C.E.–30 C.E.) did not record his teachings and, it is only through his disciples—writing between 70 and 90 C.E.—that his messages, often conveyed in stories and parables, were recorded. Many viewed Jesus as the Messiah, but he did not preach the literal revolt the Jews had been expecting. Rather, Jesus taught that God's true kingdom was to be sought in heaven not on Earth. Jesus taught the primacy of love, the forgiveness of sins, and the transcendence and immanence of God's kingdom. Jesus earned a large following with his charisma and healings. His popularity

worried both the Jewish religious leaders and the Roman governor, Pontius Pilate (r. 26–36 C.E.), who ordered his crucifixion in 30 C.E.

Although Jesus' closest followers spread his teachings while remaining observant Jews, Paul (Saul) of Tarsus (c. 10–65 C.E.) opened Christianity to wider conversion by denying that Christians were bound by certain Jewish laws regarding diet and initiation rituals. Paul taught that belief in Jesus as the world's divine savior, not righteousness according to Jewish law, was the only requirement for salvation. The Romans executed Paul in 65 C.E. as a troublemaker. After an unsuccessful Jewish rebellion in Judea, the Romans destroyed the Jewish temple in Jerusalem in 70 C.E. and sold most of the Jewish population into slavery, hastening the division between Judaism and Christianity. The New Testament was compiled around 200 C.E. Early Christian communities were sometimes led by women.

Roman authorities exhibited contempt toward the new religion because its central figure had been executed as a criminal. To outsiders, the new Christian religion seemed to advocate cannibalism and free love through communal dinners, called "love feasts," where the body and blood of Jesus were symbolically consumed. All of these factors worried Roman officials who feared their own gods would be offended. Christians were therefore the first to be blamed for any disaster. On the whole, however, persecution was intermittent and employed when politically handy, even though adherents pointed out that, far from spreading immorality, Christianity taught an elevated moral code and respect for authority. Christians considered martyrdom the supreme act of faith, and stories of martyrs' courage and steadfast faith molded the Christian identity.

To sustain the new religion over the long term, Christians began building hierarchical organizations to impose order on the sometimes widely divergent beliefs. Bishops, supposedly the successors of Jesus' apostles (later referred to as "apostolic succession"), defined Christian doctrine and appointed priests to administer rituals. The appearance of urban bishops, who defined orthodoxy and heresy, constituted the beginnings of the Catholic or "universal" church.

With the rise of bishops, women were generally stripped of power and leadership in Christian congregations; some, however, continued baptising and prophesying in the second and third centuries. Some Christian women also eschewed traditional notions of female virtue by abstaining from sex and marriage in favor of a spiritual commitment to God, earning a type of independence largely unavailable in the Roman world and the admiration of Christians.

For three or four centuries after Jesus' death, most people were polytheistic, believing in multiple deities. "Paganism," as it is called today, did not conflict with Rome's traditional cults. The cult of Isis, from Egypt, promised followers life after death. As with many cults, it also required followers to behave righteously. The cult of Mithras was also popular, although little is known about it. Others took a more philosophical approach to religion: Stoicism, derived from the Greek Zeno (335–263 B.C.E.), emphasized personal discipline as a means of sharing in the one divine creative force in the universe; Plotinus (c. 204–270 C.E.) developed Neoplatonism from Plato's teachings, a philosophy that urged people to abandon the world and the pleasures of the flesh in favor of contemplation, which could align them with the universal soul. Both Stoicism and Neoplatonism had a strong influence on Christian intellectuals.

Catastrophe came with the Severan emperors. During the third century, northern and eastern invasions required more defense spending. Imperial expansion had once funded the military, now there was negative expenditure. Septimius Severus (r. 193–211 C.E.) pursued successful campaigns beyond Mesopotamia and northern Britain, and raised military pay. After his death, his son Caracalla (r. 211–217 C.E.) murdered his brother and seized power. He increased military pay by another 40 to 50 percent and, with deficit spending, entered into large building projects. Because only citizens paid taxes, Caracalla granted citizenship almost universally to everyone in the empire as a means of raising revenue. Political instability followed. Macrinus, a member of the praetorian guard, assassinated Caracalla to become emperor and, in turn, was himself murdered. A young Severan took his place and was also assassinated (in 235 C.E.). Fifty years of civil war followed. Rampant hyperinflation and foraging armies only worsened the crisis, decimating farmers and communities while foreign enemies took advantage. Imperial territories were seized by Zenobia of Palmyra and the Sassanids of Persia. Natural disasters made the situation even worse. With the empire in decline, many, such as Emperor Decius (r. 249–251 C.E.), blamed and persecuted Christians whose presence they felt had angered the gods. As the empire continued its downward spiral, the way was paved for a political and religious makeover.

Suggestions for Lecture and Discussion Topics

1. The Augustan era, in which Rome's political sphere was transformed definitively from republic to empire, provides an interesting study in the methods used to placate a public and consolidate and win support for a new political order. For example, Augustus was a shrewd propagandist and solidified his power in many cases by referring to the restoration of the republic while in fact strengthening his own position as sole ruler. Ask students to identify the different forms this propaganda assumed in the Augustan era. Why was it so important that Augustus shape the transformation in this way?

After so many years of one-man or three-men's rule in the late republic, why was it still necessary for Augustus to advertise his power in terms of old republican values? How did this propaganda coincide with other major innovations of the period, such as the inheritance tax or the development of a police force? In which ways were social allegiances realigned throughout this process? See Paul Veyne, *Bread and Circuses: Historical Sociology and Political Pluralism*, Brian Pearce, trans. (New York: Penguin, 1990). For a broader look at imperial propaganda, see Chapter 30 of Sir Ronald Syme, *The Augustan Aristocracy* (Oxford: Clarendon, 1986).

2. An examination of urban life in the early empire, particularly in Rome, can introduce students to the everyday lives of ordinary Romans. A discussion of Roman urban life could include an examination of the layout and structure of apartment dwellings; the local economy, employment, and consumer markets; the cultural aspects of cosmopolitan living; the functions of the public baths and other public amenities; and the measures used to remedy the growing problems of the tightly concentrated population, such as subsidized food, the development of a police force, and building specifications. Which types of inequalities were present in urban living, and in what ways were the social welfare measures implemented to deal with them? In which ways was the city stratified? An excellent source is Dave Favro, *The Urban Image of Augustan Rome* (Cambridge: Cambridge University Press, 1996).

3. Discuss family life in the Roman Empire. In which ways did it represent a continuity with republican norms? In which ways did family life change under the empire? In particular, you could examine Augustus's legislation on marriage, adultery, and sexuality. Which social, political, and economic conditions necessitated these legal changes? For example, you could examine the structure of the economy and how it related to the demand for increased population; the perceived importance of extending the lineage, particularly of upper-class families; and how the transmission of familial property related to the laws against adultery. Which moral issues were involved in the decision to enact this legislation? What were its effects? How did these changes affect women? There are several good sources for these issues, including Jane F. Gardner, *Family and Familia in Roman Law and Life* (Oxford: Oxford University Press, 1998); Beryl Rawson, ed., *The Family in Ancient Rome: New Perspectives* (Ithaca: Cornell University Press, 1986); and Chapter 11 of Elaine Fantham, et al., *Women in the Classical World: Image and Text* (Oxford: Oxford University Press, 1994).

4. Roman culture during this period was marked by extreme violence, particularly in its popular entertainment, such as the gladiatorial contests. Discuss the social, political, and cultural functions of this sanctioned violence. What purposes did it serve? Why were the

emperors so supportive of it? Because Roman emperors could exhibit their greatness and generosity through these circuses, what can we determine about the culture of violence that surrounded imperial Rome? Also discuss the social interchange at these events, in which there was a degree of communication between the populace and their rulers. Could these events be viewed in part as an outlet for the pervasive violent currents that had wrought so much havoc in the late republic? What does this tell us about the cultural and political climate of the period? Two excellent books on gladiators and the games are Roland Auguet, *Cruelty and Civilization: The Roman Games* (New York and London: Routledge, 1994); and Carlin Barton, *The Sorrows of Ancient Romans* (Princeton: Princeton University Press, 1993). See also Chapter 4, section 9, of Paul Veyne, *Bread and Circuses*, cited in "Suggestions for Lecture and Discussion Topics" number 1. Clips from films such as *Ben Hur* (1959), *Spartacus* (1960), and *Gladiator* (2000) could be used to illustrate the gladiatorial games.

5. A prerequisite to power throughout the first few centuries of the Roman Empire was the emperor's tight relationship with the military. When the loyalty and confidence of the army waned, the emperor found himself in a weakened position and was frequently killed. With tight control of the military, however, the emperor's position was relatively secure. In which ways does this feature of Roman imperial politics denote a sort of continuity from the late republic? Which factors influenced the prominence of the army? What effect did its prominence have on Roman society? What does this tell us about the underlying nature of Roman politics? See J. B. Campbell, *The Emperor and the Roman Army: 31 B.C.E.– 235 C.E.* (Oxford: Clarendon, 1984); and Ramsay MacMullen, *Corruption and the Decline of Rome* (New Haven, CT: Yale University Press, 1998).

6. While Christianity's message resonated with a great number of people throughout this tumultuous period, first among Jews in the east and then gradually among Gentiles in the west, this dissemination was also greatly aided by its position within the Roman Empire. For instance, the communication and travel infrastructure of Rome greatly facilitated the new religion's spread. What effects did this feature have on the Christian message, as related by both the Gospels and the teachings of Paul of Tarsus? Which factors shaped the various audiences' receptivity? How did the new religion's coming of age within Rome affect its early development? For instance, the development of Christian institutions, such as the hierarchical organization of bishops to decide orthodoxy, could be seen as a reflection of the Roman political and social structure. You can also relate these developments to the overall climate of the period as it affected Christians, leading to their persecution. See Harry Y. Gamble, *Books and Readers in the Early Christian Church* (New Haven, CT: Yale University Press, 1995); and Ram-

say MacMullen, *Christianizing the Roman Empire, C.E. 100–400* (New Haven, CT: Yale University Press, 1994).

7. Roman art in the imperial period connotes an interesting shift in substance and form. With tighter control at the very top of the social hierarchy, reflecting imperial values through art became more necessary in order to project the proper image of imperial power. In sculpture, for example, rugged realism gave way to glorified idealism. Students may be interested in the ways that the demands of politics influenced artistic expression. This idea can be related to the vigorous promotion—both in Rome and in the provinces—of the worship of the emperor as a living deity. In which ways were imperial values brought to bear in art? See J. Lendon, *Empire of Honour* (Oxford: Clarendon, 1997). In addition, see the pictures online of Augustan-era art and architecture at Augustus: Images of Power, maintained by the Classics Department of the University of Virginia.

8. The development of Roman law is important not only for its central place in Roman social life, but also for its effect on subsequent western legal systems. In particular, the notion of intent as the decisive factor in settling disputes, rather than the "mere" facts, represents a profound alteration in legal concepts of guilt and justice. What effect did this new idea have on the development of the legal system? For example, how were the works of legal practitioners and their place in society changed? What advantages and disadvantages did this focus on intent have on ordinary citizens? For a brief overview of this period of Roman legal development, see Chapter 2 of Peter Stein, *Roman Law in European History* (Cambridge: Cambridge University Press, 1999); and Olga Tellegen-Couperus, *A Short History of Roman Law* (New York: Routledge, 1993).

9. The development of Christianity was one of the most influential landmarks of western history, a discussion of the conditions that gave rise to this new force can therefore provide valuable insights into the social, cultural, and political climate of the postclassical world. Which conditions helped spur the development of this new religion? How did Jesus' message fit into the context of the contemporary struggle between Jews and Romans? In which ways are the Jewish traditions from which Jesus' teaching sprang related to its subsequent development in Christianity? See Martin Goodman, ed., *Jews in a Graeco-Roman World* (Oxford: Clarendon, 1998); and Robert Louis Wilken, *The Christians as the Romans Saw Them* (New Haven, CT: Yale University Press, 1984).

Making Connections

1. *What were the similarities and differences between the crisis in the first century B.C.E. that undermined the republic and the crisis in the third century C.E. that undermined the Principate?* Although there were serious power

struggles among some of the military generals, the Roman republic in the first century B.C.E. was essentially prosperous and strong internally. By the third century C.E., however, Rome was suffering economic instability largely because of overexpenditure by the military, attacks from abroad, and natural disasters. There was also a crisis in leadership as several successive emperors were assassinated.

2. *If you had been a first-century Roman emperor under the Principate, what would you have done about the Christians and why? What if you had been a third-century emperor?* Most people today would probably have extended some degree of toleration to the Christians in the first century on the grounds that this might have warded off the religious conflicts that occurred later in the third century. For instance, Christians might have been allowed freedom of worship on the payment of a special tax. Some aspects of Christianity might have been incorporated into traditional Roman religious practices, given the similarities between them. This would have been in keeping with Roman policies in other parts of the empire.

Writing Assignments and Class Presentation Topics

1. Have students read Augustus's *Res Gestae* and write an essay comparing Augustus's reign as it is portrayed by Augustus himself with the assessment that students can surmise by a close reading of the text. The point of this exercise is to get students to develop skills to critically analyze primary sources and identify biases and euphemisms.

2. The legal institution of the orders is an important event in the development of the Roman legal system. Have students write briefly on the effects this policy had on the social hierarchy. Of particular interest are the clues it gives concerning Roman notions of justice. What does this development reveal about expectations of behavior and the value of individuals in Roman society?

3. Have students give a class presentation discussing the extent to which the Roman economy was based on the military. In particular, ask them to analyze the effects of relying on military conquest as a basis for revenue. How did this reliance place stress on public expenditures? What constraints did a heavily militarized system place on the society? More broadly, how might this economic foundation of conquest and slavery have affected the culture at large?

4. Ask students to compare and contrast the two major philosophical systems that emerged in this period: Stoicism and Neoplatonism. In which Roman and Greek traditions were these philosophies steeped? What were

their similarities and differences? In which ways did they influence Christian theology and philosophy? See Martin L. Clarke, *The Roman Mind: Studies in the History of Thought from Cicero to Marcus Aurelius* (New York: W. W. Norton, 1968).

5. Have students watch a film dealing with the Roman Empire, perhaps *Ben Hur* (1959), *Gladiator* (2000), or part or all of *I, Claudius* (1976). Students should consider issues of historical accuracy in their essay: Are the characters, both real and imaginary, appropriately drawn? Has the filmmaker gotten the plot, whether historically or fictionally based, correct? What about the setting? Students should also consider the larger question of whether such films *should* be historically accurate. This essay assignment could be the basis of an online and/or in-class discussion.

6. Compare and contrast the character studies made by Tacitus (c. 55-117 C.E.) in *The Annals*; and Suetonius (c. 69–140 C.E.) in *The Lives of the Caesars*, of Tiberius, Claudius, and Nero. How similar is their approach? Do they have any bias? What is Suetonius's approach to the other emperors?

Research Assignments

1. An examination of the changing face of Roman literature during the imperial period can provide a useful glimpse into the relationship between politics and culture. Have students research and write on the substantive and formal changes in literature in Roman imperial society. Students can also incorporate the effects of literacy patterns on literature. A useful source on imperial-era literature is John Wight Duff, *Literary History of Rome from the Origins to the Close of the Golden Age* (London: Ernest Benn, 1953). On the effects of literacy patterns, see Chapter 7 of William V. Harris, *Ancient Literacy* (Cambridge, MA: Harvard University Press, 1989).

2. Pagan Roman and Christian belief systems differed markedly in their conceptions of the status of women and of female virtue. Have students report on the contrasting views of women's autonomy and sexuality. Of particular interest is the relationship between sex and freedom for both systems. How did sex relate to the control of women and toward what specific ends in each system? Which assumptions about gender and sex were shared by both systems? What do these ideas tell us about the underlying social structures of the period? Two invaluable sources are Aline Rousselle, *Porneia: On Desire and the Body in Antiquity* (Cambridge, MA: Blackwell, 1983); and Peter Brown, *The Body and Society: Men, Women, and Sexual Renunciation in Early Christianity* (New York: Columbia University Press, 1988).

Literature

Arrowsmith, William, trans., *Petronius: The Satyricon.* 1990.

Graves, Robert, trans., *Suetonius: The Twelve Caesars.* 2003.

Green, Peter, trans., *The Erotic Poems: The Amores, the Art of Love, Cures for Love, on Facial Treatment for Ladies by Ovid.* 1983.

Hays, Gregory, trans., *Marcus Aurelius: Meditations.* 2003.

Mandelbaum, Allen, trans., *The Aeneid of Virgil.* 1981.

Martin, Charles, trans., *Ovid: Metamorphoses.* 2003.

Radice, Betty, trans., *The Letters of the Younger Pliny.* 1976.

Wellesley, Kenneth, trans., *Tacitus: The Histories.* 1972.

Films and Videos

Quo Vadis? (1951) (VHS, 171 min.). The conflicts between the Roman Empire and the new religion of Christianity are played out between a slave girl and a Roman officer during the reign of Nero.

Ben Hur (1959) (VHS/DVD, 3hrs., 32 min.). This dramatization of Civil War General Lew Wallace's 1880 novel about the struggles a Jewish aristocrat faces in the Roman Empire in the first century is the best of the three adaptations that were made. Although the plot is fictional, the period has been fairly accurately re-created. The film is most famous for the magnificent chariot race scene.

Fall of the Roman Empire (1964) (VHS/DVD, 153 min.). Although based on Edward Gibbon's monumental history of Rome, the film focuses mainly on the period surrounding the death of Emperor Marcus Aurelius and the succession of his unbalanced son, Marcus Aurelius Commodus Antoninus.

I, Claudius (1975) (VHS/DVD, 740 min.). Robert Graves's novel has been dramatized in thirteen episodes of about 55 minutes each. It is an excellent and lucid account of the Roman emperors of the first century, beginning with Augustus and ending with Claudius.

Jesus of Nazareth (1977) (VHS/DVD, 6 hrs., 22 min.). This is Franco Zeffirelli's lavish miniseries about the life and death of Jesus.

Gladiator (2000) (VHS/DVD, 2 hrs., 35 min.). Set in the second century, a Roman general is falsely accused of treason and made a slave. Trained to be a gladiator, he waits for an opportunity to avenge himself on the emperor. This film is good at re-creating life, especially the gladiatorial games, during the Roman Empire.

Empires: Peter and Paul (2003) (DVD, 3 hrs, 14 min.). This PBS documentary focuses on Peter and Paul and their influence on the early years of Christianity.

Historical Skills

Map 6.1, The Expansion of the Roman Empire, 30 B.C.E.–C.E. 117, p. 219

Augustus's conquest of Egypt and the subsequent conquest of Mesopotamia gave Rome ample breathing room around the entire Mediterranean Sea. This period represented the height of Rome's territorial dominion. What kept it from spreading beyond these regions?

Map 6.3, Christian Populations in the Late Third Century C.E., p. 229

Have students identify and consider the varying geographic proliferation of Christian peoples in the Roman Empire. Which factors may have contributed to these variations? Why might the new religion have become so popular in some areas and less so in others?

Taking Measure: The Value of Roman Imperial Coinage, 27 B.C.E.–C.E. 300, p. 235

This chart showing the devaluation of Roman coinage can provide students with a glimpse of the economic strains that influenced policy throughout the period, and particularly during the third century. Have students discuss the effects this devaluation and the economic policies associated with it had on the lives of ordinary Roman citizens, from elites and soldiers to farmers and the urban poor.

Portrait of a Married Couple from Pompeii, p. 214

This painting of the couple in their own home likely conveys how they ideally saw themselves. Stemming from what we know of the Roman class structure, what can we conclude about the position of this couple in Roman society? What were their aspirations? Which features of the painting signify these aspirations?

Priests on the Altar of Augustan Peace, p. 206

Have students identify the representations of this sculpture. What are the elements of propaganda? What is their significance, both in the representation itself and in the context of its setting in the Altar of Augustan Peace?

Violent Shows, p. 233

Have students discuss the representational elements in this mosaic. What do these themes, displayed in the home of well-to-do Roman citizens, tell us about Roman social values and virtues? Who are the human figures in the mosaic?

Marble Statue of Augustus from Prima Porta, p. 215

This famous sculpture of Augustus represents him as a dignified, bold, and youthful leader, in many ways reverting sculptural values back to the Classical Greek era. Why might the powerful and blatant symbolism in this sculpture have been so welcomed by Augustus? Why might it have resonated so loudly with Roman people during this period?

Catacomb Painting of Christ as the Good Shepherd, p. 226

Have students identify the major differences in this depiction of Christ from the later, standard western representations. What might account for the differing depiction in this early catacomb painting? What styles and features are evident?

War Scenes on Trajan's Column, p. 234

Ask students to locate the features of Roman military styles and equipment in this sculpture. What does this column tell us about Rome's military culture? Which values are evident? What effect would such columns, constructed as historical narratives, have on Roman culture? Remind students that most of the population was illiterate.

Augustus, Res Gestae (My Accomplishments), p. 208

Augustus composed the *Res Gestae* to describe the glories of his rule, and ordered it to be engraved and erected outside his mausoleum after his death. Ask students asked to consider the kinds of things valued by both Augustus and Roman citizens. Augustus expanded the empire, relieved the tax burdens of his people, staged public entertainments, donated land for public use, and built and repaired public structures. Every Roman could take pride in, and enjoy the fruits of, the growing empire. Augustus's failures, which he does not mention, can make an interesting comparison. The loss of three legions on the Germanic borders had been a serious blow to the Roman psyche. Finally, issues of immortality are wrapped up in the *Res Gestae*. Immortality was achieved by being remembered and, in effect, by writing his own obituary, Augustus ensured that he would be remembered very well indeed.

OTHER BEDFORD/ST. MARTIN'S RESOURCES FOR CHAPTER 6

The following resources are available to accompany Chapter 6. Please refer to the Preface of this manual for detailed descriptions of all the ancillaries.

For Instructors

Transparencies

The following maps and images from Chapter 6 are available as full-color acetates.

- Map 6.1: The Expansion of the Roman Empire
- Map 6.2: Natural Features and Languages of the Roman World
- Map 6.3: Christian Populations in the Late Third Century
- Mapping the West: The Roman Empire in Crisis
- *Marble Statue of Augustus from Prima Porta* (chapter image, page 215)
- *Portrait of a Married Couple from Pompeii* (chapter image, page 214)

Instructor's Resources CD-ROM

The following maps and image from Chapter 6, as well as a chapter outline, are available on disc in both Power-Point and jpeg formats.

- Map 6.1: The Expansion of the Roman Empire
- Map 6.2: Natural Features and Languages of the Roman World
- Map 6.3: Christian Populations in the Late Third Century
- Mapping the West: The Roman Empire in Crisis
- *Marble Statue of Augustus from Prima Porta* (chapter image, page 215)

Using the Bedford Series with The Making of the West

Available in print as well as online at bedfordstmartins .com/oconnor, this guide by Maura O'Connor, University of Cincinnati, offers practical suggestions for using **Spartacus and the Slave Wars** by **Brent D. Shaw**, in conjunction with chapters 5 and 6 of the textbook.

For Students

Sources of The Making of the West

The following documents are available in Chapter 6 of the companion sourcebook by Katharine J. Lualdi, University of Southern Maine.

1. Seutonius, *The Life of Augustus* (c. 69 c.e.–c. 122 c.e.)
2. *Notices and Graffiti Describe Life in Pompeii* (First Century c.e.)
3. Tacitus, *Agricola* (98 c.e.)
4. *Interrogation of Christians* (189 c.e.)
5. Flavius Josephus, *The Jewish War* (70 c.e.)

Study Guides

The print **Study Guide** and the **Online Study Guide** at bedfordstmartins.com/hunt, both by Victoria Thompson (Arizona State University) and Eric Johnson (University of California, Los Angeles), help students synthesize the material they have learned as well as practice the skills historians use to make sense of the past. The following Map, Visual, and Document activities are available for Chapter 6.

Map Activity

• Map 6.4: Mapping the West: The Roman Empire in Crisis, c. 284 c.e. (page 238)

Visual Activity

• *Marble Statue of Augustus from Prima Porta* (chapter image, page 215)

Reading Historical Documents

• Augustus, *Res Gestae* (page 208)
• *The Scene at a Roman Bath* (page 211)

The Transformation of the Roman Empire
284–600 C.E.

CHAPTER RESOURCES

Main Chapter Topics

1. In an attempt to halt the damage caused by the late imperial period civil wars, Diocletian (r. 284–305) created the authoritarian dominate. His creation of the tetrarchy divided the empire into two eastern and two western administrative sections. Although abandoned by his successors, the tetrarchy prefigured the final split between the Latin west and the Greek east.

2. Constantine (r. 306–337) converted to Christianity and passed the Edict of Milan, which granted religious freedom throughout the empire in 313. Augustine, bishop of Hippo (354–430), laid much of the doctrinal groundwork for the newly recognized faith in his influential writings. Still, Christians divided over Arianism, Monophysitism, Nestorianism, and Donatism. In response, the councils of Niceea (325) and Chalcedon (451), met to distinguish orthodoxy from heresy.

3. Christianity developed an administrative hierarchy modeled on the Roman imperial bureaucracy. The bishop of Rome claimed preeminence among bishops as the apostolic successor of Peter but was recognized as pope only in the west. Ascetic monasticism attracted Christians wishing to withdraw from the world to devote themselves to contemplation. Monasticism, at first eremetical, became conobitical under Pachomius in Upper Egypt. Basil the Great in the east and Benedict of Nursia (c. 480–553) in the west developed different regulations for monastic life—some service oriented and some contemplative.

4. The flight of multi-ethnic tribes was set in motion by the westward migrations of the Huns beginning in the 370s. Unable to accommodate the influx, the eastern empire drove those fleeing into the west. In 410, the Visigoths sacked the city of Rome. Afterward, they and the tribes that followed established their own kingdoms

within the old borders of the empire, gradually replacing imperial government while replicating many of its features—especially Roman law. By the time Theodoric (r. 493–526) established his Ostrogothic kingdom in Italy, there would never again be an officially recognized western Roman emperor.

5. The Germanic kingdom of the Franks (Francia) proved the most enduring. The Frankish king Clovis (r. 485–511) rejected Arianism in favor of Orthodox Christianity, strengthening his relations with the western church. Under his descendants, the Merovingians, the Frankish kingdom became the largest in western Europe, occupying an area that became most of modern France.

6. In the west, cities and the infrastructure decayed. Meanwhile, wealthy provincials withdrew to rural Roman villas, which were usually self-sufficient and fortified, and served as centers of civilization and learning, thus preserving the written legacy of classical antiquity. In the east, multilingual, multi-ethnic urban centers flourished.

7. The Byzantine Empire combined a Greek-speaking culture with a determination to be the preserver of Rome's imperial greatness, which it retained until its capture by the Ottoman Turks in 1453.

8. The Byzantine emperor Justinian (r. 527–565) briefly reclaimed western Roman territory, launched a monumental building program, and systematized Roman law. The enormous cost of the wars and the escalating taxes required to cover these conflicts drained the east of resources. In the west, the ravages of the Gothic wars destroyed much of the remnants of the ancient Roman infrastructure.

Summary

In the third century, the strain of fifty years of civil war over who should become emperor, and the conflict between Christianity and traditional Roman religion, left the Roman Empire drastically weakened, requiring strengthened defenses and new infusions of revenue. The damage was halted by Emperor Diocletian (r. 284–305), an uneducated soldier from Dalmatia who rose through the military and elevated by his soldiers to the imperial throne. Shunning the republican title Princeps, adopted by emperors since Augustus, Diocletian styled himself *dominus* ("master"). From Diocletian onward, Roman rule would be known as the "dominate." Diocletian insisted on autocracy, refusing to share power with the elite whose positions as senators and consuls became honorary, relying instead on able administrators from the lower classes loyal only to him. The imperial style became more majestic and immersed in ceremony. Subsequent emperors increased the brutality of legal punishments, especially for the lower classes, while simultaneously placing themselves above the law.

In 293, Diocletian enacted his most dramatic remedies for the failing empire by splitting it into two eastern and two western quarters and establishing the tetrarchy ("rule of four"). He chose three others to share in governing, with himself as supreme ruler. Power was further subdivided by separating military and civil authority and by sectioning the provinces into almost one hundred subdivisions. These subdivisions were grouped into twelve dioceses under regional governors who reported to praetorian prefects. The four prefects, in turn, reported directly to the tetrarchs.

After the death of Diocletian's successor Constantius I, his son Constantine I (r. 306–337) then claimed the throne. Constantine struggled to consolidate his position until 324, when he made Byzantium (renamed Constantinople) his imperial base. After Constantine's death, his three sons fought for power. Eventually, the empire split on a north-south geographical line along the Balkan peninsula. When Theodosius (r. 379–395) died, the division between east and west became permanent, with his son Arcadius ruling the eastern half, and his other son Honorius I ruling the western side. Constantinople was the capital in the east and, after 404, Ravenna was the capital in the west, chosen because it was more defensible than Rome and had its own seaport.

Third-century civil wars had created hyperinflation, and Diocletian's rescue of the empire was costly. Diocletian tried to cope by imposing price controls and a new tax system. The Edict on Maximum Prices (301), a response to rampant inflation, mandated price ceilings for numerous goods and services, but failed when merchants refused to cooperate. Diocletian also revised the tax system, ruling that some taxes were to be paid in goods rather than in coin, and adding a land and a head tax. This, too, proved ineffectual because the taxes were not uniformly imposed. To guarantee tax payments, Diocletian restricted the movements of the coloni ("tenant farmers") who formed the backbone of the empire's agricultural economy. This mandate transformed agriculture into a hereditary occupation because, henceforth, the coloni and their descendants were tied to a particular plot of land. Other essential professions, such as baking and soldiering, also became hereditary and compulsory.

The *curials* ("urban, propertied classes") served as unpaid city councilmen. Already expected to foot the bill to repair the infrastructure, feed troops, and—especially burdensome—make up shortfalls in taxes due from their communities, the curials were now crushed by soaring taxes. The curials' characteristic spirit of willing public service evaporated; they frantically evaded public office. Escalating taxes battered the rural poor as well. Widespread discontent and occasional rebellion ensued throughout the western empire.

Blaming the empire's troubles on Christianity, in 303, Diocletian set in motion a sweeping attack on Christians known as the Great Persecution. Although unevenly enforced, it removed Christians from office, destroyed churches, and martyred many, especially in the east. In the west, violence against Christians lasted about a year; in the east, it lasted a decade. Even so, the persecution failed: it further corroded public morale while failing to decrease the numbers or devotion of the Christians.

Constantine settled the status of Christianity in the empire after his victory over his imperial rival Maxentius at the battle of the Milvian Bridge (312), which won him the throne. On the eve of battle, Constantine had dreamed of a Christian cross surrounded by the words, "In this sign you shall conquer." He attributed his victory to the Christian God and converted. In 313, his Edict of Milan granted freedom of religion throughout the empire. Constantine blended Christian and Roman religious traditions in an effort to embrace as many people as possible.

Polytheism persisted long after Christianity's legalization. Julian the Apostate (r. 361–363) returned the empire to polytheism for a brief period. Succeeding emperors diminished polytheism's influence by gradually removing its official privileges. Emperor Theodosius (r. 379–395 [in the east]) made Christianity the official state religion (391) and banned all polytheist sacrifices. Some ancient shrines remained open for a time, but temples were slowly converted to churches during the fifth and six centuries. Non-Christian schools, like Plato's Academy, also survived for a time, but Christians received advantages in official careers.

The status of the Jews within the empire was precarious. A long-standing imperial privilege permitted Jews to practice their religion, and Christians were mindful that Jesus had been a Jew, yet Christian emperors burdened them with legal and financial obligations and thrust them out to the margins of society. Harassment notwithstanding, synagogues remained open, Jewish law was studied, and the monumental Palestinian and Babylonian Talmuds and the Midrash were produced.

Christianity spread rapidly between 300 and 600. Imperial conversion particularly relieved soldiers, who found reconciling their faith and military careers easier. The Christian emphasis on a universal community and on personal salvation attracted converts. Jesus' injunction to practice charity also enhanced the religion's appeal to those who lacked wealth.

As the church's hierarchy solidified, women were edged out of positions of authority within the Christian community. Some, however, donated their wealth to support the church and others found an alternative to established social expectations by living as consecrated virgins or widows who refused to remarry.

The hierarchy that replaced the informal organization of earlier centuries helped to spread the young religion. Bishops ordained priests, supervised the congregation's members and finances, and eventually supplanted the secular curials as local, imperial administrators. Bishops' councils determined orthodox doctrine. The bishop of Rome claimed primacy over other bishops by right of apostolic succession from Peter (Matt. 16:18–19), widely believed to have been Rome's first bishop, and took the title pope (Greek *pappas*, "father"). The pope's supremacy was not recognized in the eastern empire.

No longer subjected to persecution, the Christian community was rocked by disparate views among its members. For example, the Alexandrine priest Arius (c. 250–336) claimed that Jesus was neither coeternal nor consubstantial with God the Father, a proposal that threatened absolute monotheism. The Arian heresy prompted Constantine to call the Council of Nicea (325), which rejected Arius's teachings and insisted that Jesus was "of one substance with the Father." But even Constantine was unsure and changed his mind twice on the issue. His son Constantius II (r. 337–361) favored Arianism, which was embraced by many Germanic tribes who later entered the western empire in hordes.

Other heresies were popular in the east, such as Monophysitism, which argued that Jesus possessed a single, divine nature. Monophysites broke away from the orthodox hierarchy in the sixth century to found independent churches in Egypt, Ethiopia, Syria, and Armenia. Nestorius, consecrated bishop of Constantinople in 428, claimed that Jesus was born human and acquired his divine nature later, which offended those devoted to Mary as *theotokos* ("god bearer"). The bishop was deposed and his doctrines officially rejected at church councils in 430 and 431, but the Nestorians broke away and formed a separate church in the eastern empire. The most troublesome heresy was Donatism. Donatus (bishop of Casae Nigrae) and his followers wanted to bar the church from those Christians who had cooperated with imperial authorities during the Great Persecution. They also declared that sacraments administered by priests and bishops tainted in this way were invalid—a

recipe for chaos among the faithful. The Council of Chalcedon (451) again tried to define Christian orthodoxy; its tenets are still accepted by most western Christians today. But it failed to eradicate diverging views that continued to spread—particularly in the east.

The most influential thinker to shape Christianity was Augustine, bishop of Hippo (354–430). He converted to Christianity (386) after following several philosophical schools and heresies in his long search for meaning, which he chronicled in his autobiographical *Confessions* (c. 397). Augustine was one of the prominent early Christian writers known as the patristics ("church fathers"), a group that also included Jerome (c. 345–420) and Ambrose (c. 339–397), bishop of Milan. In *The City of God*, Augustine postulated the notions of free will and original sin and justified the establishment of earthly governments by citing inherent human sinfulness. Augustine greatly feared that social disorder would erupt without government authority. He also promoted asceticism (the practice of self-denial) and virginity as the highest states of human existence. Sexuality, he taught, had been irreparably damaged by the Fall: intercourse was justifiable only for procreation, not for pleasure.

Specialized forms of ascetic Christian life were practiced by eremetic monasts who passed solitary lives in self-denial and prayer. These ascetic monks (e.g., Symeon the Stylite [390–459], who lived thirty years on a tall pillar) became models of Christian heroism and suffering after the era of martyrs had ended. Their reputations for holiness led many to regard their relics as imbued with protective and healing powers.

In 323, the hermit Pachomius brought together Egyptian ascetics into communal life to encourage their devotion and self-discipline, thus forming the basis for cenobitic ("communal") monasticism. Whereas severe austerity characterized eastern monasticism, and some western counterparts followed suit—especially the followers of Martin of Tours (c. 316–397)—the west generally developed a more moderate tradition based on the rule of Benedict of Nursia (c. 480–553). This monastic code, developed c. 540, stressed a regulated day balanced between prayer, study, and work, but avoided extreme self-denial and forbade corporal punishment. The Benedictine order attracted thousands of men and women . Parents sometimes dedicated their babies to the monastery, a practice known as oblation. Bishops, however, often disapproved of monasteries, because their independence challenged the bishops' authority.

Political and cultural development in the western and eastern empires also diverged. Around 370, the Huns —raiders renowned for their exceptional skills on horseback — were displaced from the Asian steppes into the eastern regions of the empire and in turn spurred the first widespread migrations of non-Roman peoples into eastern Europe. The Huns attained their greatest power under Attila (r. c. 440–453) who controlled territory from the Alps to the Caspian Sea. Attila even led his cavalry into northern Italy, but his warriors left Rome undisturbed. Despite their infamy, the Huns largely disappeared after Attila's death.

Economic hardship rooted in third-century crises made it difficult to control persons pushed into the empire by marauding Huns. Territory was ceded to the immigrants as a way of maintaining order. These new kingdoms were "ruled" by chiefs who led raids to capture cattle and slaves and distributed gifts to followers to reinforce bonds of fellowship. Both matrilineal and patrilineal kinship lines were important, and society was based on clans loosely arranged into tribes. Family life was patriarchal; men were occupied with warfare, iron-working and animal husbandry; women concentrated on agriculture, pottery, and textile production. A woman could inherit and control property, and was entitled to one-third of her husband's property.

The first major immigrant group that coalesced after entering into imperial territory came to be called the Visigoths. In 373, the eastern emperor Valens (r. 364–378) permitted the Visigoths to enter the Balkans if they joined him against the Huns. However, their maltreatment by Roman military officers generated a revolt in 378, in which Valens was killed. The Visigoth experience was typical of the disparate peoples fleeing the Hun advance, petitioning Roman government for asylum in exchange for military service, then rebelling against their Roman "protector" after being mistreated. Valen's successor, Theodosius I (r. 379–395), acceded to Visigoth demands for annual payments and permanent settlement within imperial borders in individual kingdoms under tribal laws. However, pressure from the eastern emperors who reneged on their annual payment and threatened full-scale war, continued to push non-Roman peoples west. In 410, the Visigoths under King Alaric I sacked Rome itself — the first time in eight centuries that had occurred. In 418, the western emperor Honorius reluctantly agreed to settle the Visigoths in southwestern Gaul, from where they later expanded into Spain.

Few other non-Roman tribes matched the Visigoths' organization. The Vandals, for example, who also fled the Hun advance into Europe, earned a reputation for lawlessness after their conquest of northern Africa (429) and a raid on Rome (455). The Danish Angles and Germanic Saxons invaded Britain (440s) after the Roman army's recall to defend Italy against the Visigoths. Their domination of the island subjugated the Celts and suppressed Celtic culture and Christianity except in Ireland and Wales.

The transformation of western Europe from empire to multiple kingdoms occurred under a succession of weakened emperors who hired mercenaries: Germanic officers and troops. Eventually, these men set up and deposed emperors as they chose. Romulus Augustulus was the last emperor to hold the western throne. Augustulus

was the son of a former aid to Attila the Hun (Orestes), who was deposed by the Germanic leader Odoacer in 476. Odoacer established himself as the western viceroy of the eastern emperor Zeno. Zeno later supported the competing general Theodoric, who killed Odoacer and created an Ostrogothic capital at Ravenna in 493. The Ostrogoths were converts to Arian, rather than orthodox, Christianity, although Theodoric exercised a policy of religious toleration. He retained the symbols of Roman rule—the Senate and consuls—and appropriated Roman traditions that supported his own power. Hence, scholars refer not to the "fall" of Rome but rather its transformation with the advent of the Ostrogoths.

In 507, King Clovis (r. 485–511) and his Franks overthrew the Visigoths in Gaul with the backing of the eastern emperor. Clovis established the largest Germanic kingdom in the west. Clovis also converted from Arianism to Orthodox Christianity, fostered good relations with his bishops, and founded the Merovingian dynasty, which ruled France for over two centuries.

An intermingling of Roman and Germanic elements characterized western society. Germanic kings issued written codes of their customary laws modeled on the Roman legal heritage, and imposed fines such as the wergild to maintain order while discouraging the blood feud. But several centuries of migration, invasion, and warfare had significantly altered western Europe. Urban life declined, and independent, fortified Roman villas increasingly served as centers of community, agricultural production, and defense. Tax collection and officeholding disappeared and, with them, communication and trade. Education was also largely lost, except for a few monastic centers, such as the monastery founded by former statesman Cassiodorus (c. 490–585) whose library preserved many ancient texts from destruction.

A combination of force, bribes, and diplomacy spared the eastern portion of the empire from the direct impact of the Germanic tribes and the Sassanid military. Rulers of Constantinople considered themselves the heirs of Roman imperialism. Urban life flourished, and the Byzantine Empire enjoyed great wealth, based largely on its prosperous trade with places as far away as China and India. But, while "Romanness" was emphasized, the multi-ethnic Byzantines spoke Greek rather than Latin, and many embraced Monophysite heresy.

Under the control of their fathers and husbands, Byzantine women were severely limited. They rarely ventured beyond their homes or socialized with men outside their family circle. They could not witness wills, divorce was virtually impossible, and remarriages were discouraged. Women in the imperial family, though, like Theodora (c. 500–548), did possess influence at the highest levels. Social divisions were aggravated by the government's providing services according to people's wealth. Only the wealthy could afford fees and bribes, which in turn supplemented the salaries of underpaid officials.

Emperor Justinian I (r. 527–565), with his ambitious and talented wife Theodora, wanted to reunite the Roman Empire, but the populace balked at the escalating taxes required to finance the project. Their discontent erupted in the Nika riot of 532, which had to be quelled forcefully, leaving Constantinople in ruins and thirty thousand rioters dead. Justinian wanted to flee in the face of these riots, but Theodora made him stand firm. Later, an onslaught of plague further reduced the population by a third in the 540s.

Justinian did briefly reconstitute the territory of the ancient Roman Empire. His generals—first, Belisarius, then Narses who replaced him—defeated the Vandals in North Africa, then subdued the Ostrogoths in the Gothic wars, regaining Italy and the west in 562. But Justinian's plans were too ambitious, and the wars demolished what remained of the west's infrastructure and financial stability.

Justinian sought further stability through the strengthening of imperial authority, which he did by emphasizing his closeness to God and increasing the autocratic power of his rule. In a mosaic at San Vitale, Ravenna, Justinian was depicted shoulder to shoulder with figures of Christ and Abraham. He also intended to restore the imperial grandeur of earlier times. The ancient dedication to monumental public building programs found expression in his commission for the Hagia Sophia ("Holy Wisdom"). A huge dome, reminiscent of the Roman Pantheon, adorned the structure, which was covered inside by four acres of gold mosaics. This, too, proclaimed Justinian's overpowering supremacy as well as his religiosity. He reduced the autonomy of the provinces, dispatching imperial officials to replace local leaders. Justinian's most durable achievement, however, was the systematization of centuries' worth of Roman law. The Codex (534) attempted to unify decisions earlier emperors had made. Justinian's legal scholars also produced a handbook for expediting court proceedings, the *Digest*; and the *Institutes*, a textbook for students of law.

Justinian acted to enforce religious purity, which included enforcing laws against polytheists and male homosexuals. Religious leaders under Justinian tried to stem the growing tension between Orthodox Christians and Monophysites, whose disagreements reflected the increasing disunity between the Byzantine and Roman church leaders. Their efforts, however, only drove the parties further apart.

Because service in the vast Byzantine governmental bureaucracies required a liberal education, traditional Roman schooling in Greek and Latin continued to flourish in Byzantine east. Its schools, which provided a home for Latin scholars who fled the chaos in the west, preserved much of the learning and literature of western antiquity. Christian thinkers produced their own literature, however, which overshadowed the pagan classics as popular reading even though it was based on classical models. Polytheistic, artistic traditions were also incorporated into Christian art. In place of papyrus scrolls, which were difficult to use and damaged texts, Byzantine scholars invented the Codex, the precursor to the modern book. This new form reduced the wear and tear of using old texts, thus preserving them. Although knowledge of Latin survived, knowledge of Greek died out in the west, and education in general suffered a dramatic decline. Plato's Academy finally closed in 530, and the classics were suppressed in favor of Christian-based curricula. The Neoplatonist school in Alexandria, however, survived, because its leader—John Philoponus (c. 490–570)—was a Christian.

Suggestions for Lecture and Discussion Topics

1. A perennially fascinating topic for students is: What really caused the decline and fall of the Roman Empire? Outlining the numerous scholarly (and less scholarly) theories that have been advanced frequently leads to lively discussions about their relative merits and the dangers of oversimplification when debating historical causality. If you lack the time to read all of Gibbon's classic, you can start with Donald Kagan, ed., *The End of the Roman Empire: Decline or Transformation?*, 3d ed. (Lexington, MA: D. C. Heath, 1992), which offers a first-rate selection of competing viewpoints taken from the works of leading scholars, including Gibbon. For passages from relevant primary sources, refer to the *Internet Ancient History Sourcebook*. Other excellent studies, among the myriad that discuss this topic, are Peter Brown, *The World of Late Antiquity* (London: Thames & Hudson, 1971), which views the era as one characterized by Christianity's rise rather than Rome's fall. Arther Ferrill, *The Fall of the Roman Empire* (London: Thames & Hudson, 1988), treats the fall largely as a result of military factors. There is also a highly informative set of essays in Part 1 of *Debating the Middle Ages: Issues and Readings*, Lester Little and Barbara Rosenwein, eds. (Malden, MA: Blackwell, 1998), including Chris Wickham's "The Fall of Rome Will Not Take Place."

2. Students often hold the misconception that most early Christians faced persecution and eventual death in the arena at the hands of Romans. You can illuminate the complexity of the development of Christianity during these centuries by stressing the range of Roman responses—both official and unofficial—to Christianity and the ways in which Christianity coexisted with the polytheistic religions of the late Roman Empire. Ramsey Macmullen, *Christianity and Paganism in the Fourth to Eighth Centuries* (New Haven, CT: Yale University Press, 1999), is a good place to begin. For a detailed presentation of the beliefs of ordinary pagans and Christians, see Robin Lane Fox's massive *Pagans and Christians* (New York: Alfred A. Knopf, 1989), which forms an interesting

contrast to E. R. Dodds, *Pagan and Christian in an Age of Anxiety: Some Aspects of Religious Experience from Marcus Aurelius to Constantine,* rpt. (Cambridge: Cambridge University Press, 1990). A short treatment that argues for the distinctly Christian character of martyrdom is G. W. Bosersock, *Martyrdom and Rome* (Cambridge: Cambridge University Press, 1995).

3. The legalization of Christianity generated the problem of defining exactly what constituted its religious orthodoxy. In the process, many conflicting opinions on fundamental questions of faith were declared heresy. Students may be interested to learn more about the wide diversity of beliefs that fell within the purview of Christianity and about the attempts to establish orthodox doctrine in the early church councils. Discussion should also include *why* such doctrines were perceived as being destructive. Very useful introductions to the intricacies of the early doctrinal dispute include Stuart G. Hall, *Doctrine and Practice in the Early Church* (Grand Rapids, MI: William Eerdmans, 1992); the *Encyclopedia of Early Christianity*, E. Ferguson, M. P. McHugh, and F. W. Norris, eds., 2d ed. (New York: Garland, 1998); and *Encyclopedia of the Early Church*, A. Di Berardino, ed. (Oxford: Oxford University Press, 1992). Two general surveys of early church history that contain helpful sections on the role of the councils and the content of various early heresies are Henry Chadwick, *The Early Church* (New York: Viking Penguin, 1993); and W. H. C. Frend, *The Rise of Christianity* (Minneapolis: Augsburg Fortress Publications, 1984). Primary-source selections online can be found at the *Internet Medieval Sourcebook.*

4. Monasticism, while not invented in the west, became the preeminent expression of ideal Christianity in western Europe during the early Middle Ages. Explore the development of monasticism in general in the fundamental work by David Knowles, *Christian Monasticism* (New York: McGraw-Hill, 1969). For a recent study focused on the early medieval period, see Marilyn Dunn, *The Emergence of Monasticism: From the Desert Fathers to the Early Middle Ages* (Malden, MA: Blackwell, 2001). See also the materials available on the *Internet Medieval Sourcebook* on the Benedictine movement, including the complete text of Benedict's rule and Gregory the Great's biography of Benedict. For the participation of women in early western monasticism, see Susanna Elm, *Virgins of God: The Making of Asceticism* (Oxford: Oxford University Press, 1994).

5. Theodoric was perhaps the most accomplished of the early Germanic leaders ruling in western Europe. A discussion of his reign can illuminate the difficulties connected with the establishment of Germanic states in the postimperial west and the ways in which some Germanic rulers set out to assimilate and utilize the accomplishments of their Roman heritage. A very solid treatment, with excellent discussion of diplomatic policy, is John

Moorhead, *Theodoric in Italy* (Oxford: Oxford University Press, 1993). Primary sources containing remarks on Theodoric are Jordanes's *History of the Goths* and Sidonius Apollinaris's letters. A standard history of the Goths is Herwig Wolfram, *The History of the Goths* (Berkeley: University of California Press, 1990). Theodoric patronized some of the leading intellectuals of his time, including Boethius and Cassiodorus.

6. Augustine's impact on the development not only of Christianity but also on western thought in general is profound. Discussion of his life can serve to introduce many central themes in the history of late antiquity. The classic biography of Augustine is Peter Brown, *Augustine of Hippo,* rpt. (Berkeley: University of California Press, 2000), which can be read in conjunction with Gary Wills's very well-received study, *Saint Augustine* (New York: Penguin, 1999). For an introduction to Augustine's ideas, see Eugene Portalie, *A Guide to the Thought of Saint Augustine* (Washington, DC: Regnery, 1960); and Robert Markus, *Saeculum: History and Society in the Theology of Saint Augustine* (Cambridge: Cambridge University Press, 1970). Finally, consult the very helpful resources available at James O'Donnell's Late Antiquity site at <http://ccat.sas.upenn.edu/jod/augustine.html>.

7. The transformations that occurred during the late empire occasioned drastic measures in the realms of administration, law, finances, and the military. Ask students to assess the effectiveness of Diocletian's reforms and their impact on the empire. See G. H. Stevenson, *Roman Provincial Administration* (Oxford: Oxford University Press, 1975 [originally published, 1939]). Stephen Williams's biography *Diocletian and the Roman Recovery* (New York and London: Routledge, 1996) argues for the overall success of Diocletian's policies. For the establishment and political history of the tetrarchy, see Simon Corcoran, *The Empire of the Tetrarchs: Imperial Pronouncements and Government, A.D. 284–324* (Oxford: Oxford University Press, 1996). The overviews provided by A. H. M. Jones, *The Later Roman Empire 284–602: A Social, Economic, and Administrative Survey* (Norman: University of Oklahoma Press, 1964); and Averil Cameron, *The Later Roman Empire, A.D. 284–430* (Cambridge, MA: Harvard University Press, 1993) place Diocletian's policies in their broader historical context.

Making Connections

1. *What were the main similarities and differences between the political reality and the political appearance of the Principate and the dominate?* Augustus called himself princeps, which harkened back to the days of the republic. He held no more formal authority than any other leader and guided Rome solely by virtue of the respect and moral authority he merited. In practice, however,

Augustus created a hereditary monarchy masked by republican traditions and emblems. Diocletian, however, did not attempt to cloak his authority in republican trappings; rather, he called himself *dominus* ("master"), making clear his imperial authority.

2. *What were the main similarities and differences between traditional Roman religion and Christianity as official state religion?* Both Roman religion and Christianity tried to impose their beliefs on others and often harshly repressed dissenting views. Both believed in the concepts of sacrifice and eternal life. Religious figures in both traditions often played prominent secular roles in society and government. Although the local traditions of conquered peoples were often assimilated into Roman practices, aiding in the acceptance of Roman religion, local customs were not incorporated into Christianity as frequently. Sacrifices were often literal in traditional Roman religion, whereas the sacrifice central to Christian service was metaphorical. Women sometimes had official, leading roles in Roman religion, but were abrogated from similar positions in Christianity.

Writing Assignments and Class Presentation Topics

1. Students can explore the impact of developing Christianity on the roles and lives of women in late antiquity. Pertinent primary-source selections from the Bible and early church fathers on the "nature" of women are gathered in Alcuin Blamires, ed., *Women Defamed and Women Defended: An Anthology of Medieval Texts* (Oxford: Oxford University Press, 1992). The diversity of female responses to Christianity is evident from an analysis of the texts that concentrate on individual women's lives; among the most moving is the "Passion of St. Perpetua," notable also for containing a first-person account of her imprisonment leading up to her martyrdom. Other excellent texts are the travelogue to the Holy Land of the pilgrim Egeria and the life of the St. Macrina. Background information can be found in Gillian Clark, *Women in Late Antiquity: Pagan and Christian Lifestyles* (New York: Oxford University Press, 1993).

2. Have students form groups and assign each group a Germanic tribe to research. Then each group should present its findings to the class on its tribe's history and what can be discerned from archaeological remains. Good choices include the Vandals, Goths, Saxons, Lombards, and early Franks. The sometimes legendary histories of many of these tribes were chronicled by contemporary Christian writers. See, for example, Paul the Deacon (*History of the Lombards*), Jordanes (*History of the Goths*), Gregory of Tours (*History of the Franks*), and Isidore of Seville (on the Visigoths). In addition to the works cited in the chapter bibliography, students can

consult the following studies for additional information: E. A. Thompson, *Romans and Barbarians* (Madison: University of Wisconsin Press, 1982); M. Todd, et al., *The Early Germans* (Malden, MA: Blackwell, 1992); N. Christie, *The Lombards* (Malden, MA: Blackwell, 1995); and Alberto Ferreiro, ed., *The Visigoths: Studies in Culture and Society* (Leiden: Brill, 1999).

3. Have the class debate the nature of Constantine's conversion to Christianity: Was it prompted by true religious devotion or political expediency? Samuel Lieu and Dominic Montserrat, eds., *From Constantine to Julian: Pagan and Byzantine Views, A Source History* (New York and London: Routledge, 1996), considers Constantine's reign from the perspective of non-Christian sources. H. A. Drake, *Constantine and the Bishops: The Politics of Intolerance* (Baltimore: Johns Hopkins University Press, 2000), discusses the political motives behind Constantine's religious policies. Constantine's conversion could also be compared to the conversion of the Frankish leader Clovis, two accounts of which are located in the *Internet Medieval Sourcebook.*

4. It is difficult to resist the attraction of the history of Theodora and Justinian. Have the class compare Procopius's characterizations of them in the *Buildings and the Wars* to the lurid version he presents in the *Secret History.* For more in-depth information, students may want to investigate the standard study by Robert Browning, *Justinian and Theodora* (London: Thames & Hudson, 1987). For an analysis of Procopius's works, see Averil Cameron, *Procopius and the Sixth Century* (New York and London: Routledge, 1996).

5. Representing a far-flung portion of the empire that was never fully Romanized, the British Isles are of interest to students for more reasons than merely the Arthur legend. Which special problems did the British Isles present to the Romans? This subject is well-documented on the Internet, and many primary sources are available there. Standard studies for Roman Britain include Peter Salway, *Roman Britain* (Oxford: Oxford University Press, 1993); and P. H. Blair, *Roman Britain and Early England, 55 B.C. to A.D. 871* (New York: W. W. Norton, 1978).

6. Students can increase their knowledge about Roman attitudes toward Germanic and other barbarians, and about the Romans' views of themselves, by analyzing Roman commentaries on the peoples who lived on the edges or beyond their empire. Tacitus's *Germania*, which can be found in Patrick Geary, *Readings in Medieval History*, 2d ed. (Peterborough, Ont.: Broadview, 1998), gives students a glimpse of a Roman's assessment of the Germanic peoples as a whole, even though Tacitus describes individual tribal groups. Attila and the Huns also form an excellent subject for this kind of assignment.

7. Have students research the Roman military in late antiquity, its major battles, and the conditions on the

frontiers. A broad survey of tactics is contained in Edward Luttwak, *Grand Strategy of the Roman Empire* (Baltimore: Johns Hopkins University Press, 1990). Michael Dodgeon and Samuel Lieu, eds., *Roman Eastern Frontier and the Persian Wars, 226–323* (New York and London: Routledge, 1994), provides a documentary history of battles on the eastern border of the empire. Thomas Burns, *Barbarians within the Gates of Rome: A Study of the Roman Military Policy and the Barbarians, ca. 375–425* (Bloomington: Indiana University Press, 1994), discusses the use of Germanic troops within the Roman army.

Research Assignments

1. Students may want to consider the slow decline of urbanism in the western empire and the shift of the imperial capital to Constantinople in the east. John R. Curran, *Pagan City and Christian Capital: Rome in the Fourth Century* (Oxford: Oxford University Press, 2000), explores the emergence of Rome's rise as the center of western Christendom even as it lost its status as center of the Roman Empire. J. Rich, *The City in Late Antiquity* (London and New York: Routledge, 1996), combines historical and archaeological perspectives to examine the decline of urbanism in some parts of the empire after the third century and its survival in other regions. N. Christie and S. Losebly, eds., *Towns in Transition: Urban Evolution in Late Antiquity and the Early Middle Ages* (Burlington, VT: Ashgate, 1996), examines the ongoing vigor of some urban centers but argues they ultimately lost their Roman character.

2. Late-antiquity Jews occupied a problematic position within the Roman Empire because they were accorded a status that differed from other non-Roman religions. Students can investigate primary-source documents in Margaret H. Williams, *The Jews among the Greeks and the Romans: A Diasporan Sourcebook* (Baltimore: Johns Hopkins University Press, 1998). The legal status of Jews in the empire is considered in Alfredo Mordechai Rabello, *The Jews in the Roman Empire: Legal Problems, from Herod to Justinian* (Burlington, VT: Ashgate, 2000). See also Louis H. Feldman, *Jew and Gentile in the Ancient World: Attitudes and Interactions from Alexander to Justinian* (Princeton: Princeton University Press, 1993). An online collection of primary sources and links can be found at the *Internet Jewish History Sourcebook.*

3. The history of magic long predates the witch crazes of the early modern era. An influential survey of the subject can be found in Valerie Flint, *The Rise of Magic in Early Medieval Europe* (Princeton: Princeton University Press, 1994), which argues that the necromantic traditions of late antiquity became assimilated into the beliefs of early medieval Christianity. J. Gager, *Curse*

Tablets and Binding Spells from the Ancient World (Oxford: Oxford University Press, 1999), examines the history of magical incantations in antiquity. For an overview of magical beliefs and practices in the Byzantine Empire from the fourth century until the Ottoman conquest, see Henry P. Maguire, ed., *Byzantine Magic* (Washington, DC: Dumbarton Oaks, 1995).

Literature

Chadwick, Henry, trans., *Augustine: Confessions.* 1991.
Cruse, C.F., trans., *Eusebius' Ecclesiastical History.* 1998.
Dods, Marcus, trans., *Augustine: City of God.* 1994.
Whiston, William, trans., *The Works of Josephus.* 1980.
Williamson, G.A., trans., *Procopius: The Secret History.* 1982.

Historical Skills

Map 7.2, The Spread of Christianity, 300–600, p. 256

Ask students which factors helped to account for the spread of Christianity to the farthest reaches of the Roman Empire. Have students locate the geographical distribution of monasteries. What conclusions can they draw from the concentrations of monastic centers in the British Isles? Gaul? portions of North Africa? the Near East? Asia Minor?

Map 7.3, Germanic Migrations and Invasions of the Fourth and Fifth Centuries, p. 266

Discuss the general direction of the movements of the groups represented on this map. Why did these peoples focus on the western, rather than the eastern, portion of the empire? Which kinds of information are obscured by the presentation of large waves of migration and invasion that occurred over two centuries in a static format, such as a map? Why are virtually no battles represented? Which groups covered the most ground? What do students know about the lifestyles of these groups?

Mapping the West: The Byzantine Empire and Western Europe, c. 600, p. 278

Have students identify the key cities and their locations that Justinian controlled after his reunification of the empire. Which areas remained independent of imperial control? Did these areas pose a threat? Which historical factors were present in 600 that prevented the continued existence of the reunited empire after Justinian's death? Given the conditions in Rome and western Europe in 600, what, if anything, did Justinian's military conquests achieve?

Taking Measure: Peasants' Use of Farm Produce in the Roman Empire, p. 249

What can students deduce about an average peasant family's daily life based on the information presented in this graph? With about 60 percent of produce required merely to feed the family, and another 20 percent set aside to guarantee the next year's yield, what margin — if any — would be available if the family's tax burden was increased? Which strategies might have been employed to enable a family to meet rising fiscal obligations and to continue to feed its members?

Upper-Class Country Life, p. 270

This mosaic depicts the leisure activities of a wealthy couple in the Roman provinces. Beyond the obvious material prosperity pictured here, what other lures might such villas have offered to Germanic invaders? What does the existence of this Roman villa in North Africa reveal about the international spread of imperial culture? In which ways did the exportation of Roman affluence to all of the empire reinforce the legendary status of Rome as the center of the "civilized" world? What impressions might Roman villas, churches, and urban centers — which were located throughout imperial territory — have made on Germanic and other tribal peoples who were entering the empire's borders in increasing numbers?

Christ as Sun God, p. 255

Discuss the mingling of polytheist and Christian motifs in this mosaic. What might account for the adoption of pagan iconography in a portrayal of Christ? This phenomenon can be placed in the broader context of Christianity's borrowings from Roman political, cultural, and polytheistic traditions (such as the hierarchical organization of the church) that imitated Roman bureaucracy, or the date of Christmas. Could the use of polytheistic imagery, such as the vine leaves that often appear in depictions of Bacchus, have been intended to make Christianity more familiar to recent polytheistic converts? Or, was such a portrayal of Jesus less the result of a conscious adaptation of polytheistic motifs than the simple generation of Christian art according to then-current stylistic conventions?

Adam and Eve on the Sarcophagus of Junius Bassius, p. 260

The choice of theme (Adam and Eve after the Fall) is unusual for a sarcophagus. What message might this picture be intended to convey? Ask students to consider the approximate date of the sarcophagus, and discuss the recent historical events that might be connected to this very open rendering of Christian themes on a high-ranking

Roman's sarcophagus. Even though overt polytheistic elements are absent, which influences of classical art are evident in this work? This piece forms an interesting contrast to the mosaic of Jesus as sun god (p. 255).

Monastery of St. Catherine at Mount Sinai, p. 263

The features of the architectural design and setting of this monastery reinforce which ideals that underlay monasticism (such as self-sufficiency, withdrawal from the world, proximity to a sacred site)? Which practical and spiritual functions did the prominent walls serve? How would outsiders regard this community?

New Sources, New Perspectives: Looking for the Decline and Fall of the Roman Empire, pp. 268–269

Ask students whether or not they agree with the text's statement that Gibbon "lived to regret his choice of a title because his work continued telling the empire's story far beyond A.D. 476" (and, in fact, he ended with the conquest of Constantinople in 1453). In which ways might Gibbon's title be considered apt? Can the students suggest other phrases to encapsulate the changes that the Roman Empire experienced during the time period covered in this chapter? To what extent did the Germanic migration to and domination of the former imperial territory in the west signal a "transformation" as opposed to the creation of something entirely new?

Justinian and His Court in Ravenna, p. 275, and Theodora and Her Court in Ravenna, p. 274

These mosaics rank among the most famous artworks of late antiquity. Ask students to identify elements in the iconographic scheme that reinforce a message of divinely sanctioned imperialism backed by military force. In which ways is the cult of the deified emperor, begun by Diocletian, continued in these works? Was this theme compatible with the Christianization of the empire? In which ways are the close cooperation of church and state (and, indeed, the church's dependence upon the Byzantine state) stressed? Which stylistic elements harken to the artistic traditions of classical Rome? Which reflect Byzantine influences? Ask students to comment on the representation of Theodora and her status compared to those of Justinian.

The Edict of Milan on Religious Liberty, p. 252

Ask students to consider what Constantine and Licinius might have gained by granting religious toleration. Internal security would have been a priority. Officially favoring of one religion over another divided society in ways that could result in civil uprisings, or so it was feared.

OTHER BEDFORD/ST. MARTIN'S RESOURCES FOR CHAPTER 7

The following resources are available to accompany Chapter 7. Please refer to the Preface of this manual for detailed descriptions of all the ancillaries.

For Instructors

Transparencies

The following maps and images from Chapter 7 are available as full-color acetates.

- Map 7.1: Diocletian's Reorganization of 293
- Map 7.2: The Spread of Christianity
- Map 7.3: Visigothic Migrations and Invasions
- Map 7.4: Peoples and Kingdoms of the Roman World
- Mapping the West: The Byzantine Empire and Western Europe
- *Christ as Sun God* (chapter image, page 255)
- *Hagia Sophia* (chapter image, page 277)

Instructor's Resources CD-ROM

The following maps and image from Chapter 7, as well as a chapter outline, are available on disc in both Power-Point and jpeg formats.

- Map 7.1: Diocletian's Reorganization of 293
- Map 7.2: The Spread of Christianity
- Map 7.3: Visigothic Migrations and Invasions
- Map 7.4: Peoples and Kingdoms of the Roman World
- Mapping the West: The Byzantine Empire and Western Europe
- *Christ as Sun God* (chapter image, page 255)

For Students

Sources of The Making of the West

The following documents are available in Chapter 7 of the companion sourcebook by Katharine J. Lualdi, University of Southern Maine.

1. *The Nicene Creed* (325 C.E.)
2. Quintas Aurelius Symmachus and St. Ambrose, *The Altar of Victory Sparks a Religious Debate* (384 C.E.)
3. St. Jerome, *Letter 107* (403 C.E.)
4. *The Burgundian Code* (c. 475–525 C.E.)
5. Procopius, *Buildings* (c. 553–554 C.E.)

Study Guides

The print **Study Guide** and the **Online Study Guide** at bedfordstmartins.com/hunt, both by Victoria Thompson (Arizona State University) and Eric Johnson (University of California, Los Angeles), help students synthesize the material they have learned as well as practice the skills historians use to make sense of the past. The following Map, Visual, and Document activities are available for Chapter 7.

Map Activity

- Map 7.4: Peoples and Kingdoms of the Roman World, c. 526 (page 271)

Visual Activity

- *Christ as Sun God* (chapter image, page 255)

Reading Historical Documents

- Diocletian's Edict Controlling Prices and Wages (page 250)
- The Edict of Milan on Religious Liberty (page 252)

The Heirs of the Roman Empire
600–750

CHAPTER RESOURCES

Main Chapter Topics

1. Adaptation and transformation characterized the western world during the seventh and eighth centuries, a period that marked the end of antiquity and the beginning of the Middle Ages.

2. Despite the short-lived gains of Justinian, the Byzantine Empire was soon losing territory. By 750, new invasions by Lombards, Slavs, Avars, and Bulgars had diminished its power and robbed it of the Balkans; it then entered a period in which life centered on rural estates instead of urban centers. New opposition to the veneration of icons led to an imperial policy of iconoclasm (prohibition of icons) imposed on the Byzantine Empire from 726 to 843. Wars with the Sassanids regained previously lost territory in the Near East and Egypt, but left both sides exhausted.

3. Islam, a new monotheistic faith founded by the Meccan prophet Muhammad (c. 570–632), arose in the Arabian desert and unified the Bedouin tribes of the region. Its clear teachings (set down in the Qur'an) and emphasis on individual devotion won converts and displaced polytheism.

4. In the century after Muhammad's death, Muslim armies under the Umayyad caliphs took the Near East and northern Africa from the Byzantine Empire. The ummah was triumphant, but, in 656, the caliph Uthman was murdered by soldiers hoping to replace him with Ali, a son-in-law of Muhammad. Civil war followed until Ali's death in 661. Those loyal to the Umayyads were called Sunni; followers of Ali were called Shi'ite.

5. In western Europe, many Germanic tribes moved from Arian to Orthodox Christianity. Roman and non-Roman traditions mingled in Visigothic Spain and Lombard Italy, where the ancient institutions remained especially vigorous. The most powerful of the Christian-ized Germanic peoples were the Merovingian Franks who would dominate western Europe for several centuries.

6. Irish monks and Roman missionaries reintroduced Christianity to Anglo-Saxon England. England effectively elected the Roman over the Irish church when it accepted the Roman date of Easter at the Synod of Whitby (664). Roman customs and learning were reintroduced at Christian schools, but the English, unique among European kingdoms of that time, also developed a flourishing vernacular language used in literature, preaching, and law.

7. Under Pope Gregory the Great (r. 590–604), the Roman papacy laid the foundations of its future political power in Europe. Moreover, the Roman church broke with the Byzantine church over clerical celibacy and Lenten fasting. Iconoclasm in the eastern church further exacerbated the rift. Gradually, the popes came to represent the only political power in Italy other than the Lombards.

8. In Byzantium, Islam, and western Europe, warfare led to the flattening of social hierarchies and the replacement of secular political authority and classical learning with religiously allied leadership and education.

Summary

Justinian's reunified Roman Empire proved short-lived and superficial. From 600 to 750, the Byzantine Empire endured attacks from Persian Sassanids and new groups, such as the Muslims, Slavs, Lombards, Avars, and Bulgars.

Since the third century, the Sassanid Empire in Persia had been the rival of imperial Rome. When the Sassanids shifted their economic and military capital westward to Ctesiphon in Mesopotamia, they also began to pay and arm new warriors. The imperial bureaucracy introduced Persian intellectuals to Byzantine and western writers. Nestorian Christians were numerous in the area and tolerated by the Zoroastrian kings.

The Sassanid king Chosroes II (r. 591–628) tried to restore the Persian Empire to the glory it had experienced under Xerxes and Darius. He captured Damascus, Jerusalem, and Egypt, but the Byzantine ruler Heraclius successfully reclaimed this lost territory by 627. Both sides were exhausted by the wars, which left them more vulnerable to Arab attacks from 630 to 730. Both Syria and Egypt fell under Islamic control.

Byzantium was not even able to secure its own borders. The Germanic Lombards quickly seized much of the Italian peninsula after Justinian's death; Slavs and Avars overran the Balkans; and the Bulgars created the independent kingdom of Bulgaria, which Byzantium ceded to them in 681. The loss of the Balkans severed most political, cultural, and economic ties between east and west, and Latin gradually disappeared as a living language in the east.

The diminished Byzantine Empire suffered a near total shutdown of urban life. Fortifications arose, and public baths and other social centers closed. Constantinople remained the exception to urban stagnation, and its silk manufacturing industry continued. Elsewhere, rural life was the rule and, unlike in the European countryside where the elite remained in control, it was controlled by a free peasantry. The nuclear family grew in importance as grounds for divorce became more limited, sexual indiscretions for both men and women were more severely punished, and mothers acquired equal power to fathers over the management of their families. The Byzantine military—especially the navy—made its reputation with the introduction of Greek fire, a flammable liquid dispensed through an early version of a flamethrower. In the seventh century, the emperor divided the empire into military districts ("themes"), and placed all civil matters for each theme under the direct control of a *strategos* ("general") whose primary function was to halt frontier attacks. *Strategoi*, who also collected imperial taxes, represented the new Byzantine rural elite.

The focus of education shifted from classical to religious texts, especially the Book of Psalms (the Psalter), and both girls and boys were educated. This shift mirrored political realities: bishops had replaced the curiales as administrative officials. Bishops were appointed by metropolitans who oversaw provinces; and metropolitans were appointed by patriarchs who oversaw entire regions. Still, the emperor exercised considerable religious control through his right to appoint the patriarch of Constantinople, convene church councils to set doctrine, and employ bishops as local governors. Religious policies became stricter when Emperor Heraclius (r. 610–641) began the forced baptism of Jews. Only the monasteries functioned outside the control of the emperor and the episcopal hierarchy.

The status of icons split Byzantine Christians into two factions. Popular religious devotion centered on veneration of depictions of holy beings and saints (icons) that were believed to be holy and possess power. Muslim victories over Byzantine forces led many soldiers to view the veneration of icons as idolatry, and they promoted the destruction of the images (iconoclasm). The emperors, needing the army's support, agreed. But independent monasteries, which often possessed icons that drew pilgrims, became seats of power to rival imperial centers. Matters came to a head in 726, when Emperor Leo III the Isaurian (r. 717–741) defeated the Muslim forces. He besieged Constantinople and ordered all icons destroyed. From 718 to 787, icons were banned throughout the empire, despite much popular opposition. A modified ban was revived from 815 to 843. Iconoclasm led to attacks on the monasteries that were seen as potential threats to imperial power and authority. Some monasteries were closed.

In the seventh century, the Arabian peninsula was inhabited by Bedouins—loosely confederated nomadic tribes who survived by herding and trading and who preserved their history orally. Clans, the central organizational units, were grouped into larger tribes that often warred against each other. Men valued manliness (defined as courage in battle), avoidance of shame, and generosity in sharing the booty taken in intertribal warfare. The religious heart of the Bedouin was Mecca, the site of the ancient Ka'ba shrine of 360 idols. Because Mecca was under a kind of permanent religious truce, commerce flourished there along with religion.

Muhammad (c. 570–632) was born at Mecca into the Quraysh tribe, which controlled the Ka'ba. Orphaned while young, Muhammad became a caravan trader and married his former employer, the widow Khadija. Beginning in 610, Muhammad listened to the voice of the angel Gabriel, who commanded him to recite the will of God (Allah), whom Muhammad identified as the God of the Jews and the Christians. After his death, these messages were written down, forming the Qur'an, the central religious text of Islam. The Qur'an also encompasses Islam's history, law, and ethics. Islam elevated familial over tribal loyalties and stressed the community of true believers ("ummah"). Islam lacked clergy and emphasized instead the individual's belief and direct access to God. Those who worshiped Allah and lived according to the precepts of the Qur'an could anticipate eternal reward in paradise.

Muhammad gained few early converts in Mecca, and his teachings were rejected by the Quraysh, whose control over the polytheistic Ka'ba had made them wealthy. In 622, Medina invited him to become its political leader. Muhammad's journey to Medina, the Hijra, marks the year one in Muslim reckoning. Muhammad established his military authority at the battle of Badr in 624, when he and his followers ambushed a Meccan caravan, thus grafting Bedouin raiding onto the Muslim duty of jihad ("striving"). In 630, Muhammad led thousands of troops into Mecca. By his death in 632, many Arabic-speaking tribes were united by Islam.

As Islam grew, Muhammad distanced it from Judaism because, contrary to his expectation, the Jews of Arabia refused to convert to Islam. Muhammad instituted the five pillars of Islam: the Fatihah, the first or opening sura of the Qur'an; the *zakat*, a tax used for alms; fasting from sunrise to sunset during the month of Ramadan; the hajj, a devotional pilgrimage to Mecca; and *salat*, formal prayer at least three times daily (later five). Initially, women's status was enhanced and they prayed alongside men but, beginning in the eighth century, women's participation in community life was circumscribed.

Operating as a kind of "supertribe," with energies focused away from intertribal warfare, Islam spread rapidly, advanced by battle and by trade. The caliphs, successors to Muhammad, subdued Egypt by the 640s; and the Sassanids, weakened by their skirmishes against the Byzantines, by 651. Many in those areas whose beliefs differed from Orthodox Christianity welcomed the change in leaders. Conquests were made permanent through garrisons and the settlement of Muslims in vanquished territories.

The first two caliphs reigned securely, but the third, Uthman (r. 644–656), who was one of Muhammad's sons-in-law, was murdered by dissatisfied soldiers who joined with another son-in-law, Ali, husband of Fatimah. The Ummayads and Ali's forces warred until Ali was killed (661). The Umayyads retained control of the caliphate until 750, while Ali's supporters (the *Shi'at Ali*, now "Shi'ite") broke away, claiming that he had been the true successor to the prophet. They awaited the true leader—the *imam*—who had to be descended from Ali.

From their capital in Damascus, the Umayyads transformed the Islamic world into a cohesive state unified by religion and the Arabic language. They established financial and bureaucratic institutions based on Byzantine and Persian models. The caliphs extended religious toleration to Jews and Christians who paid a special tax for the right to freedom of worship. An Arabic literary canon developed, including the definitive version of the Qur'an and literature about Muhammad's life (*hadith*). Conquest brought wealth and artistic traditions flourished, especially calligraphy and poetry.

In western Europe, kinship, ecclesiastical patronage, royal courts, and land-based wealth replaced Roman imperial institutions. The most notable royal dynasty was the Frankish Merovingian dynasty. Although vestiges of the Roman past remained, like amphitheatres and villas, cities virtually vanished from the region, and the majority of the semifree peasantry lived on small holdings (manses), often clustered around villages near wealthy and powerful men (religious as well as secular) who could offer some semblance of protection. The few remaining vital cities were focused on church society. Usually the seats of bishops, cities like Tours treasured the relics of Christian saints (in their case, those of St. Martin), thought to protect the community and sometimes work miracles, especially healing the sick.

From the fifth to the mid-eighth centuries, glaciers advanced, causing a drop in the mean temperature and subsequent crop shortages, famine, and plague. Many existed on the edge of starvation, because the agricultural tools manufactured at that time were inadequate to produce enough to feed even the relatively reduced population regularly. By the seventh century, a gift economy system had replaced commerce: booty, tribute, and gift exchanges accounted for most of the circulations of goods.

Some economic activity, though, was strictly commercial and impersonal, like long-distance trade, which helped maintain contact with faraway lands. Because Jews were involved in trade, they were usually more fully integrated into Christian societies, and most lived in urban centers. Hebrew was used in religious ceremonies but, in everyday life, Jews spoke the same languages as Christians, gave their children Christian names, dressed like everyone else, and engaged in similar trades. Only later, during the eleventh century, did their status change. Women also experienced more social integration than they had in Roman times, some possessing considerable wealth and influence. The aristocrats included ecclesiastical officials and warlords who held power through inherited wealth, status, and political influence. They conducted hunts, raids, and banquets at which they redistributed their valuables among their followers to enhance their status.

In Merovingian society, the most formal type of marriage was costly. Husbands gave dowries of lands, livestock, and clothing to their brides, as well as a formal morning gift of furniture. In informal marriages, no dowry was paid. The church did not play a significant role in making marriages, which were considered to family matters. Because marriageable, aristocratic women were scarce, daughters enjoyed a high status and could dispose of their dowries as they wished if they were childless; they often inherited family property equally with their brothers. Women sometimes attained great wealth, and widows especially wielded great influence through property and by arranging careers and marriage alliances for their children. Some women became abbesses of important, wealthy monasteries.

By the eighth century, religious culture supplanted classical learning, and the vestiges of the classical past had largely been lost, except for the Latin language. About 591, St. Columbanus (d. 615) emigrated from Ireland to the continent, establishing monasteries in Gaul and Italy that stressed exile, devotion, and discipline. The deepened religious devotion appealed to aristocrats. Bishops, who were among the most powerful men in society, were the chief administrators of the few cities that remained.

Merovingian kings, who ruled the Frankish kingdom from 486 to 751, maintained close alliances with local aristocrats and the clergy. Stability was achieved with the formation of the Merovingian kingdoms of Austrasia, Neustria (centered in Paris), and Burgundy. The monarchs were assisted in ruling by the mayors of the palace who could, over time, become very powerful.

Learned monastic culture in the British isles merged Roman and non-Roman traditions. After being conquered by Anglo-Saxons (440–600), England consisted of twelve independent kingdoms, and British Christianity disappeared except in Ireland, Wales, and parts of Scotland. In the north, Christianity was reintroduced from Ireland, which had converted under St. Patrick in the fifth century. The organization of Irish Christianity copied the power structure of its rural clans, with abbots or abbesses heading monastic *familiae*. Control of specific monasteries was often hereditary. Monasteries, not cities, formed the centers of settlement, and bishops came under the authority of the abbots.

From Italy in 597, Pope Gregory the Great (r. 590–604) sent missionaries to southern England under Augustine of Canterbury. Their Roman practices stressed links with the papacy, a local organization headed by bishops rather than abbots, and division into dioceses rather than monasteries. The Irish and Roman churches recognized different dates for Easter, and this caused conflict. When King Oswy of Northumbria determined to follow the Roman date at the Synod of Whitby (664), he placed England in the orbit of Roman, rather than Irish, Christianity.

The intellectual traditions of the Roman church also appealed to English clergy who imported relics and books to enrich their monasteries and cathedrals. Benedict Biscop (c. 630–690) was especially dedicated to endowing his two monasteries in this way, and England became a leading center of Christian learning. Biscop's pupil, the monk Bede (673–735) is famous for his *Ecclesiastical History of England*. Although most religious texts were written in Latin, Bede and others also promoted Anglo-Saxon and helped transform it into an important written language. Unlike continental Europe, England developed a tradition of religious and secular texts written in the vernacular instead of in Latin.

On the continent, King Clovis defeated the Visigoths in 507, absorbing most of the Gallic portions of their kingdom. In Spain, the Visigothic king Reccared (r. 586–604) finally converted from Arianism to Catholic Christianity in 587, with Arian bishops following suit at the Third Council of Toledo, thus ensuring their ascendancy on the Iberian peninsula. The cooperation between the king and bishops was closer than elsewhere in Europe. The bishops even underscored the sacral status of the king by anointing him with holy oil at his coronation. Unfortunately for the Visigoths, this tightly unified kingdom facilitated the Muslim capture of Spain in 711, when they took the capital city of Toledo and killed the king.

In contrast, the Lombards in Italy, who converted from Arianism in piecemeal fashion, remained disunited and hostile to the pope. They remained strong in northern Italy, especially around their capital of Pavia, where a strong and wealthy kingship and the remnants of Roman urbanism and traditions provided the basis for royal authority. But, as the Lombard kings solidified their hold on the south of the peninsula and encroached on Rome, the papacy looked to outside assistance to protect and maintain its independence.

Around 600, the pope occupied an indeterminate status. The pontificate of Gregory the Great (r. 590–604) laid the groundwork for the office's future political power. Europe's greatest landowner, Gregory organized the military defense of Rome, conducted diplomatic relations with the secular European powers, and sent missionaries to convert the Germanic peoples. He popularized the teachings of the church fathers and developed a practical guidebook for clergy, the *Pastoral Rule*.

The pope, however, still remained under the authority of the Roman emperor who ruled from Constantinople. Byzantine hegemony, however, began to decline during the seventh century, when pope Sergius I (r. 687 or 689–701) endorsed most, but not all, 102 rules for the church devised by a council called by Emperor Justinian II. When the emperor tried to have the pope arrested, the populace resisted. Imperial authority declined further in the early eighth century when Pope Leo III protested imperial tax increases and Byzantine iconoclasm, which clashed with the Roman support for veneration of holy images.

Simultaneously, the pope experienced increased friction with the neighboring Lombards whose advances on southern Italy threatened the papal territories. In 753, Pope Stephen II (r. 752–757) asked the Frankish king, Pippin III the Short (r. 751–768), who had just deposed the last Merovingian, to invade Italy against the Lombards. This act strengthened papal ties with the Franks and signaled the end of close links with the emperor in the east.

Suggestions for Lecture and Discussion Topics

1. The Byzantine Empire's transformation and internal struggles demonstrate how precarious these centuries were even for a region usually thought to have escaped the "dark ages" of the west. In particular, the controversy over icons highlights the tenuous peace in the area. Good guides to this period of Byzantine history include Mark Whittow, *The Making of Byzantium, 600–1025* (Berkeley: University of California Press, 1996); and John Julius Norwich, *Byzantium: The Early Centuries* (New York: Knopf, 1989). For a focused study on the role of icons in Byzantine history, see Kenneth Parry,

Depicting the Word: Byzantine Iconophile Thought of the Eighth and Ninth Centuries (Boston: Brill, 1996).

2. The success of Islam depended in part on its simplicity of teachings, its appealing message, and its compatibility with Bedouin life. Explore the world into which Muhammad was born and the reasons for Islam's spectacular expansion in its first century. Hugh Kennedy provides a general introduction in *The Prophet and the Age of the Caliphates: The Islamic Near East from the Sixth to the Eleventh Century* (White Plains, NY: Longman, 1989). On the code of honor in Bedouin societies, see Frank Henderson Stewart, *Honor* (Chicago: University of Chicago Press, 1994). Patricia Crone, *Meccan Trade and the Rise of Islam* (Princeton: Princeton University Press, 1986) discusses the economic world of Mecca during Islam's early years.

3. The disputes over the Islamic succession were quite complex, especially those surrounding the formation of the Shi'ite sect. The establishment of the Umayyads and the fragmentation of Islam in its first century can be investigated in Bernard Lewis, ed., *Islam: From the Prophet Muhammad to the Capture of Constantinople*, vol. 1 (Oxford: Oxford University Press, 1987); and P. Holt and Bernard Lewis, eds., *Cambridge History of Islam*, vol. 1a (Cambridge: Cambridge University Press, 1978).

4. Outline the particular advantages that the Merovingians enjoyed during this period and the legacy they developed for subsequent Carolingian rulers. An excellent introduction is Patrick Geary, *Before France and Germany: The Creation and Transformation of the Merovingian World* (Oxford: Oxford University Press, 1990). For a treatment that combats the common assessment of the Merovingians as quintessential barbarians, see Ian Wood, *The Merovingian Kingdoms, 450–751* (White Plains, NY: Longman, 1994).

5. Gregory the Great's pontificate was one of the most influential in history and set the course for an independent western Christendom. Explore his policies on both secular and ecclesiastical matters and the historical circumstances that might have influenced the increasing politicization of the papacy. Would it have been possible for the pope to have remained an exclusively, or even predominantly, spiritual authority during the early Middle Ages? The best fundamental biography is J. Richards, *Consul of God: The Life and Times of Gregory the Great* (New York and London: Routledge, 1980). For an investigation of his religious thought, see Carole Straw, *Gregory the Great: Perfection in Imperfection*, rprt. (Berkeley: University of California Press, 1991).

Making Connections

1. *What were the similarities and differences between the three "heirs" of the Roman Empire?* Byzantium, west-
ern Europe, and the Islamic world were all marked by war. Each of these societies also professed monotheistic religions, emphasized the nuclear family and religion as the most important aspects of human life, and adopted or maintained Roman institutions such as a coinage. However, only Byzantium had an emperor, and only in the Islamic world did rulers (caliphs) serve as both political and religious leaders. The three societies were not equally centralized, and each treated religious minorities differently within their respective territories.

2. *Which of the heirs seemed most poised for success (economic, political, cultural) around the year 750? Why?* All three seemed poised for success. Islam controlled vast territories and enormous natural resources, was supported by some of the conquered population, and inspired by religious fervor. Byzantium relied on proven Roman institutions, had a reorganized army, and a strong infrastructure. Western Europe had plentiful natural resources, strong relations between church and state, and rich cultural diversity.

Writing Assignments and Class Presentations

1. Ask students to re-create the debate surrounding icons in the Byzantine Empire, using relevant primary sources to enumerate the arguments on both sides of the issue. John of Damascus's statements in defense of icons and the decrees of the Iconoclast Council of Constantinople (754) are available in the "Byzantium" section of the *Internet Medieval Sourcebook.*

2. In early medieval Islamic societies, both Jews and Christians enjoyed religious toleration as "peoples of the Book." Ask students to discuss the relationship of Islam to its sibling monotheistic religions, Judaism and Christianity, as presented in the Qu'ran. Several translations of the complete text are available in the *Internet Islamic History Sourcebook.*

3. The status of women and the role of the family in early Islam can be explored through numerous primary texts and Web sites. For a scholarly discussion, students can also consult Leila Ahmed, *Women and Gender in Islam: Historical Roots of a Modern Debate* (New Haven, CT: Yale University Press, 1992), which, among other topics, discusses the influence of Bedouin societal norms and practices on the dynamics of gender roles within Islam.

4. The Merovingians, with their long-haired kings, possessed an often brutal and highly colorful history that students may want to explore. Ask them to re-create that history by reading Gregory of Tours, *History of the Franks.*

5. One of the most influential legacies of ancient Rome for the Germanic societies that superseded it was

its law. Numerous Germanic kings issued their own codes in imitation of the ancient compilations. These laws, many of which survive, can help students reconstruct the norms and values of the early medieval Germanic kingdoms. The Lombard codifications are translated, with commentary, in Katherine Fischer Drew, *The Lombard Laws* (Philadelphia: University of Pennsylvania Press, 1973).

6. The Christianization of western Europe occurred over a long period of time and, in the process, its new converts transformed the religion. Ask students to discuss the impact that the norms of Germanic warrior culture had on the Christian faith (and vice versa) as Germanic peoples abandoned their traditional polytheism for the new religion. Excellent sources for this question are the histories of the various Germanic groups that were written by contemporary churchmen (but remind students of the point of view from which these works were produced). Relevant portions of Bede's *Ecclesiastical History*, Jordanes's *History of the Goths*, and Gregory of Tours's *History of the Franks* are contained in *Readings in Medieval History*, Patrick Geary, ed., 2d ed. (Peterborough, Ont.: Broadview Press, 1997).

Research Assignments

1. Students interested in military history might want to investigate the reorganization of the Byzantine military during this troubled period in its history. See the studies by J. F. Haldon, *Recruitment and Conscription in the Byzantine Army c. 550–950: A Study on the Origins of the Stratiotika Ktemata* (Vienna, 1979); and W. E. Kaegi, *Byzantine Military Unrest, 471–843: An Interpretation* (Amsterdam: A. M. Hakkert, 1981).

2. Abbesses and elite women frequently occupied influential positions in the Christianized Germanic kingdoms of western Europe. Among the numerous books on this subject are Suzanne Wemple, *Women in Frankish Society: Marriage and the Cloister, 500 to 900* (Philadelphia: University of Pennsylvania Press, 1981); Dick Harrison, *The Age of Abbesses and Queens: Gender and Political Culture in Early Medieval Europe* (Nordic Academic Press, 1998); and Jo Ann McNamara, John Halborg, and Gordon Whatley, eds., *Sainted Women of the Dark Ages* (Durham, NC: Duke University Press, 1992).

3. Religious practices, such as the veneration of relics, of early medieval Christianity often seem quite superstitious and alien to students. An excellent, short introduction to the role saints occupied in early Christendom is Peter Brown, *The Cult of the Saints: Its Rise and Function in Latin Christianity* (Chicago: University of Chicago Press, 1981). On relics, see Patrick Geary, *Living with the Dead in the Middle Ages* (Ithaca: Cornell University Press, 1995). For comparisons of similar practices in

a slightly later period, students can consult Lester Little, *Benedictine Maledictions: Liturgical Cursing in Romanesque France* (Ithaca: Cornell University Press, 1994); and Patrick Geary, *Sacra Furta: Thefts of Relics in the Central Middle Ages* (Princeton: Princeton University Press, 1990).

Literature

Dawood, N.J., trans., *The Koran*. 1990.
Guillaume, A., trans., *The Life of Muhammad*. 1955.
Sherley-Price, Leo, trans., *Bede: The Ecclesiastical History of the English Peoples*. 1991.
Thorpe, Lewis, trans., *Gregory of Tours: The History of the Franks*. 1983.

Historical Skills

Map 8.2, Diagram of the City of Ephesus, p. 289

Discuss the transformation of the city reflected in this map. Ask students to contrast the nature of the central sites of the ancient city (such as the agora and embolos) with those of the medieval city. What do they reveal about the quality of urban life in the earlier period? Its institutions?, Occupations? How cosmopolitan do the students judge ancient Ephesus to have been? What might account for the adaptation of older structures for new uses, such as transforming ancient baths into medieval residences? Compare this map to the map of Tours, c. 600 (p. 303).

Map 8.3, Expansion of Islam to 750, p. 296

Have students identify the regions that were acquired by the Muslims during the first great wave of Islamic expansion. How might control of these areas have aided in the further conquest of new territories? What can students surmise about the effectiveness of the Arabic language and Islam as unifying forces across such a great geographical expanse, much of it consisting of mountainous, desert terrain?

Mapping the West: Europe and the Mediterranean, c. 750, p. 314

Ask students how this map reflects the changed balance of power that characterized the west during this period. Which portions of the former Roman Empire were now under Byzantine control? Under Islamic control? How might Islamic hegemony over so extensive a portion of the formerly great ancient empires of Rome, Persia, and Alexander have affected the preservation of the learning and cultures of the past in these areas?

Taking Measure: Church Repair, 600–900, p. 288

Ask students to compare the fluctuations in church repair at Constantinople with those at Rome and to discuss them in light of historical circumstances at that time. For example, what was occurring in the Byzantine Empire around 500 that might be related to the high rate of repairs there? Conversely, what were the times like in the west? How useful do students believe the frequency of church repair might be as an indicator of overall social stability or economic prosperity?

Mosque at Damascus, p. 283

Ask students what the incorporation of Byzantine artistic production in this mosque, located in postconquest Syria, reveals about the interpenetration of cultural and commercial influences during the Umayyad caliphate. Could it indicate a willingness on the part of both conqueror and subject people to cooperate while respecting each other's religious differences?

Amphitheater at Arles, p. 301

What impression of the Roman past might this amphitheater, which dominates the urban landscape, have made on the early medieval city's residents or visitors? What can students say about the ambivalent attitude many early Christians might have had toward the pagan, but more materially and culturally sophisticated, past still extant in such remains?

York Helmet, p. 308

What does this object suggest about the penetration of Christian ideals in early Germanic medieval societies in the west? How might the helmet's owner, who very likely was illiterate, have expected the inscription — an invocation to the Trinity for protection in battle — to function? Ask students to compare this helmet with other items of Germanic production decorated with Christian motifs.

Lindisfarne Gospels, p. 310

The lettering of this text is so stylized that the script becomes a work of art in itself. How does this artistic quality underscore both the sacral nature of the text's content and the symbolic power of writing in a culture that was largely illiterate? Do students note any similarities between this Gospel and the elaborate calligraphic style used for copies of the Qur'an, such as that on page 294, which could not include depictions of the human form?

Santo Stefano Rotondo, p. 312

Discuss the intermixed influences of classical Rome (the architecture) and early medieval Byzantium (the artistic decoration) in this structure. Why do the saints occupy a more prominent visual position than Christ in this mosaic? How can students account for the elaborate inscription?

Terms of History: Medieval, p. 286

What does this discussion about terminology indicate about the relativism of historical periodization? What does it say about notions of "progress" in history? What might account for the frequent emphasis on those aspects and events of the past that seem to be forerunners of modern institutions and values, whereas those that seem unrelated to our modern society are ignored or denigrated?

The Fatihah of the Qur'an, p. 295

The Qur'an is a compilation of the messages Muhammad received during his life from the archangel Gabriel. Ask students to consider how god is described in the text and how it relates to the way God is portrayed in the Old Testament and the New Testament. The relatively short phrases emphasize the poetic nature of the Qur'an, but there were other reasons for brevity. Muslims were expected to memorize as much of the Qur'an as possible, and keeping passages brief aided that task. Simplistic verses were also appropriate for uncomplicated messages about God's love.

OTHER BEDFORD/ST. MARTIN'S RESOURCES FOR CHAPTER 8

The following resources are available to accompany Chapter 8. Please refer to the Preface of this manual for detailed descriptions of all the ancillaries.

For Instructors

Transparencies

The following maps and images from Chapter 8 are available as full-color acetates.

- Map 8.1: Byzantine and Sassanid Empires, c. 600
- Map 8.2: Diagram of the City of Ephesus
- Map 8.3: Expansion of Islam to 750
- Map 8.4: The Merovingian Kingdoms in the Seventh Century
- Mapping the West: Europe and the Mediterranean, c. 750
- *Christ as Sun God* (chapter image, page 255)
- *Hagia Sophia* (chapter image, page 277)

Instructor's Resources CD-ROM

The following maps and image from Chapter 8, as well as a chapter outline, are available on disc in both Power-Point and jpeg formats.

- Map 8.1: Byzantine and Sassanid Empires, c. 600
- Map 8.2: Diagram of the City of Ephesus
- Map 8.3: Expansion of Islam to 750
- Map 8.4: The Merovingian Kingdoms in the Seventh Century
- Mapping the West: Europe and the Mediterranean, c. 750
- *Christ as Sun God* (chapter image, page 255)

For Students

Sources of The Making of the West

The following documents are available in Chapter 8 of the companion sourcebook by Katharine J. Lualdi, University of Southern Maine.

1. Theophanes Confessor, *Chronicle* (Ninth Century)
2. *Islamic Terms of Peace* (633–643)
3. Muhammad ibn al-Harith al-Khushani, *The Qadi' Abd al-Rahman ibn Tarif al-Yahsubi* (Tenth Century)
4. Pope Gregory the Great, *Letters* (598–601)
5. *The Life of Lady Balthild, Queen of the Franks* (Late Seventh Century)

Study Guides

The print **Study Guide** and the **Online Study Guide** at bedfordstmartins.com/hunt, both by Victoria Thompson (Arizona State University) and Eric Johnson (University of California, Los Angeles), help students synthesize the material they have learned as well as practice the skills historians use to make sense of the past. The following Map, Visual, and Document activities are available for Chapter 8.

Map Activity

- Map 8.5: Mapping the West: Europe and the Mediterranean, c. 750 (page 314)

Visual Activity

- *Christ as Sun God* (chapter image, page 255)

Reading Historical Documents

- The Fatihah of the Qur'an (page 295)
- A Portrait of Pope Gregory the Great by Bishop Gregory of Tours (page 313)

Unity and Diversity in Three Societies
750–1050

CHAPTER RESOURCES

Main Chapter Topics

1. From 850 to 1050, the Byzantine, Islamic, and western Christian worlds experienced the rise of powerful, but short-lived empires that were quickly supplanted by the dispersal of power under the control of numerous local rulers. In all three regions, new military elites also arose. Despite these stressful times, each realm witnessed a corresponding period of artistic and intellectual renaissance.

2. After a century of defensive warfare against the Muslims, the Byzantine Empire went on the offensive (c. 850) and recovered some of the territory it had lost. These victories led to a revival of court life during the Macedonian renaissance (c. 870–c. 1025).

3. The new states of Bulgaria, Serbia, and Kievan Russia emerged from the Slavic polities established from 850 to 950. These were heavily influenced by Byzantine religion and culture.

4. Civil war in the Islamic world ended the Umayyad caliphate in 750, which was succeeded by the Abbasid caliphate based in Baghdad. Islamic political and religious unity splintered into regional Islamic states during the ninth century. These states remained united by commerce and the Arabic language. The entire Islamic world experienced an artistic and scientific renaissance from about 790 to 1050.

5. In France, the Carolingian mayors of the palace deposed the Merovingian kings (c. 750). The military conquests of Charlemagne (r. 768–814) created the largest empire since the fragmentation of the western Roman Empire in the fifth century.

6. Hoping to combine Germanic and Roman strengths in a new Christian empire, Charlemagne imitated ancient imperial practices by conducting a building campaign at his capital of Aachen, standardizing weights and measures, promoting education, and improving communication and law enforcement throughout his realm. Pope Leo III endorsed his efforts on Christmas day, 800, crowning him "Emperor and Augustus" in Rome. This action marked a definitive papal swing away from the Byzantine emperor and toward the west.

7. The gains of the Carolingians were largely lost in the chaos of intrafamilial struggles that followed under Charlemagne's successors (814–911). This conflict resulted in the three-part division of the empire with the Treaty of Verdun (843), which roughly defined the divisions of modern Europe.

8. As the Carolingian Empire disintegrated, foreigners invaded: Vikings from the north, Muslims from the south, and Magyars from the east. Vikings eventually settled in the Danelaw in England, halted by King Alfred the Great (r. 871–899). In France, they settled in Normandy after the conversion of their leader, Rollo, to Christianity in 911. During that same period, Muslims began to conquer Sicily. The Magyars were defeated in 955 at Lechfeld by the German king Otto I (r. 936–973).

Summary

By 800, Byzantium, the Islamic world, and the Christian west were relatively centralized empires. All three experienced renaissances, in which literacy and ancient learning were revived and scientific advances made, particularly by Islamic scholars. All three also contained forces of internal division that led to the reorganization of social, familial, and economic structures, and to the rise of new military elites. The Byzantine emperor lost sway over the countryside, the Islamic caliphate fragmented into regional centers under local powers, and the west saw feudalism and the partitioning of the Carolingian Empire into smaller kingdoms that helped set the political contours of modern Europe. A last wave of foreign invasions entered Europe but, by 1000, many of these groups had converted to Christianity and established settled kingdoms of their own.

From 850 to 1025, after a century on the defensive, the Byzantines returned to offensive warfare on all frontiers, recapturing Antioch, Crete, and Bulgaria. These victories brought wealth and prestige to the Byzantine emperors. To quell the threat of uprisings among his own forces, the emperor employed eunuchs in civil and military service. Eunuchs posed no personal or dynastic challenge because they lacked independent power bases.

Byzantine imperial wealth depended on imperially controlled guilds and entrepreneurially run trade fairs. Trading privileges were granted to key "nations" of foreign merchants resident temporarily in Byzantine territory in exchange for services rendered. The Venetians, for instance, promised to transport troops when necessary in exchange for a reduction in customs dues. Byzantine officials also negotiated favorable treatment for their own merchants in other countries.

This renewed prosperity financed the Macedonian renaissance (c. 870–c. 1025), which flourished during the dynasty established by Basil I of Macedonia (r. 867–886). The scholarly elite pursued and sponsored classical studies, and icons began to be restored in 843. The mingling of classical and Christian influences manifested itself particularly in manuscript illumination.

Outside the capital, but especially along the borders of Anatolia, a new elite consisting of dynatoi ("military families") emerged. The dynatoi acquired land and booty in the imperial wars, and became powerful enough not only to take over or buy up entire villages, but also even challenged the emperor. They constituted a hereditary landowning class closely resembling that of western Europe, where their lands were worked by a subject peasantry.

Emperor Nicephorus (r. 802–811) launched a Byzantine offensive against the Slavs. Although he recaptured Greece, Nicephorus was killed in the move against the Bulgarian ruler Krum (r. c. 803–814). The war endured until Basil II the "Bulgar-Slayer" (r. 976–1025) conquered the region and forced it to convert to Byzantine Christianity. The Byzantine religion often accompanied territorial conquest. The Serbs also converted and settled into the region that would become modern Serbia. In 863, the brothers Cyril and Methodius, sent as missionaries to the Slavs, created a Greek-based alphabet for the Slavic language. Their innovation would become the modern Cyrillic alphabet.

Although outside Byzantine political dominion, Russia fell within its religious and cultural orbit in the ninth and tenth centuries. A descendant of Vikings, the chieftain Oleg founded a tribal association that later became Kievan Russia. In 905, it forced Byzantium to welcome Russian traders or suffer attacks. Russia converted to Byzantine Christianity under Vladimir (r. c. 980–

1015), prince of Kiev. This move cemented Russian links with the Christian world and further alienated it from western Europe. Although Prince Iaroslav the Wise (r. 1019–1054) had forged some cultural contact with western Europe, disunity between his heirs erupted in Russia with his death.

In the Islamic world, civil war ended the Umayyad caliphate in 750, which was replaced by the Abbasids who were supported by Shi'ites and non-Arabs. They relocated their capital to Baghdad, near the former Sassanid capital; as a result, the Muslims adapted Persian bureaucratic administration and court culture. The Abbasid caliphate reached its apex under Harun al-Rashid (r. 786–809). Afterward, the dynasty declined, suffering from revenue shortages needed to fuel the burgeoning bureaucracy and army. Many former soldiers, disgruntled with their pay, backed rival caliphs. But the caliphs became mere figureheads after a series of civil wars; by the tenth century, new rulers emerged. They relied on the support of a new military elite, the Mamluks ("Turkish slaves or freedmen who served as highly trained, mounted troops"). Unlike their Byzantine and western European counterparts, they often changed allegiance because they were paid in cash rather than land.

The local Islamic states followed regional customs and were highly diverse, despite the western Christians' tendency to characterize all their inhabitants as "Saracens" (from the Latin for "Arabs"). The Fatimids, a Shi'ite group named for Ali's wife, rose to control Tunisia in 909 and, by 969, Egypt, which they held for two centuries.

Sunnis had ruled al-Andalus (central and southern Spain) since 756, when the Umayyad Abd al-Rahman fled the Abbasid revolution and his army subsequently conquered Spain. He founded the emirate of Córdoba, where Jews, Muslims, and Christians ("Mozarabs") resided together under a policy of religious toleration. Al-Andalus flourished under Abd al-Rahman III (r. 912–961) who guaranteed freedom of worship, opened civil service to all, and sent ambassadors to Byzantium and Europe. But, in 1031, this region also shattered into many independent regions (taifas).

Despite this fragmentation, commerce and the Arabic language still united the Islamic world. Goods were traded from the Atlantic to Persia over a vast international network. The Islamic world also experienced its own renaissance during the period from about 790 to 1050, when Arabic scholars wrote important commentaries on Greek, Persian, and Indian classics. Islamic mathematicians also made great strides, with al-Khwarizmi's development of equation theory (al-jabr, from which the word algebra is derived) around 825 and Al-Hasan's development (c. 1000) of quadratic cubic equations. Muhammad ben Musa (d. 850) introduced Hindu numbers, including zero, into the Islamic world; the west later adopted them to replace Roman numerals. Among the most versatile of Islamic scholars was Ibn

Sina (or Avicenna, 980–1037) who wrote on logic, natural science, physics, and medicine. Higher education also emerged much earlier than in the west. Schools for Qur'anic and related studies (madrasas) proliferated because literacy was necessitated by the Islamic injunction that all believers should read the Qur'an. While western Europe and the Byzantine Empire used parchment that restricted access to documents to the rich, Islamic scholars used paper, making their work widely available to all who could read.

In western Europe, the Carolingians rose to prominence as the mayors of the palace in Merovingian France. Charles Martel (mayor from 714–741), founder of the dynasty, earned his fame by defeating Muslim forces at the battle of Tours in 732. Charles and his family kept power by pitting aristocratic competitors against each other and supporting monasteries, which in turn supported them. His son Pippin III (d. 768), who deposed the Merovingian king in 751, won papal sanction by defending the pope against the Lombards. The formation of this Franco-papal alliance was sealed in 756 with the Donation of Pippin, which granted to the pope the Papal States, carved out of former Lombard territory.

The most famous Carolingian was Pippin's son Charlemagne (r. 768–814). A man of contradictory impulses, Charlemagne built on his father's legacy by forging through conquest the largest territorial base seen since the fall of the western Roman Empire. After defeating the Lombards, Charlemagne annexed northern Italy in 774, warred against the Saxons for more than thirty years and in victory forced them to be baptised, battled the Avars in the southeast, and established a buffer march between the Franks and al-Andalus. Inspired to create a Christianized fusion of the Roman and Germanic worlds, he emulated Roman imperial practices by inaugurating a building program at the capital Aachen, standardizing weights and measures, and creating the missi dominici. These messengers rode on circuit throughout his realm, delivering Charlemagne's directives and checking on his regional representatives (the counts) by inquiring about their performance among the local populace. Pope Leo III (r. 795–816) formalized Charlemagne's status in Rome on Christmas day, 800, crowning him "Augustus and Emperor." This act, which may have been intended to exalt papal power as much as elevate Charlemagne, signaled a decisive papal shift away from Byzantium and toward the west. Meanwhile, the papacy was laying the foundations for its own claims to imperial authority with the Donation of Constantine, a forged document that claimed the emperor had bequeathed to the pope the imperial crown and dominion over both Rome and the entire western empire.

Charlemagne's reign also marked the beginning of the Carolingian renaissance (c. 790–c. 900) noted for its revival of classical learning and its emphasis on overall education. Many of its achievements can be attributed to the Anglo-Saxon scholar Alcuin (c. 732–804), Charlemagne's tutor and adviser. Alcuin was brought from England to supervise Charlemagne's educational efforts that advocated universal literacy through monastic schools. The era was reflected in innovative development of Carolingian minuscule, the prototype of modern letter fonts.

Charlemagne's son Louis the Pious (r. 814–840) continued his father's administration and ordered that the rule of St. Benedict be imposed on all monasteries, making it the monastic standard in the west. Louis's sons quarreled over the succession, fomenting intrafamilial warfare. In 843, the three surviving brothers split the empire into eastern, middle, and western kingdoms; the Treaty of Verdun set the basic divisions of what would become modern western Europe. The western third, ruled by Charles the Bald (r. 843–877), would eventually become modern France; the eastern third, ruled by Louis the German (r. 843–876), would become Germany; and the middle kingdom, governed by Lothar (r. 840–855), would form parts of France and Germany, and the modern states of the Netherlands, Belgium, Luxemburg, Switzerland, and Italy.

The Carolingian economy, although based heavily on agriculture, still encompassed long-distance trade. Landholding was reorganized among western aristocrats into self-supporting manors worked by free peasants, who also tilled the manses on which they settled. All peasants owed obligations of produce or labor to their landlords, and worked the demesne (very large manse of the landlord). This arrangement represented an advance over ancient, slave-powered *latifundia*, where slave families could be separated. The origins of the modern, nuclear family may lie in this manor system because the peasant families resided together. A new form of farming also emerged: the three-field system, in which peasants sowed two-thirds of their fields with two different crops, while the third field remained fallow. This practice increased production yields and encouraged soil regeneration.

After Charlemagne's death, Europe experienced its last foreign incursions. From the north, the Vikings swept along the coast, raiding and pillaging for a century. Superb maritime navigators, they also moved into the open Atlantic, reaching Iceland, Greenland, and even North America by about 1000. The Vikings were subdued in England by King Alfred the Great of Wessex (r. 871–899) who had previously bought them off with dangeld ("tribute"). In 876, the Vikings settled in the northeast of England under their own laws in the Danelaw. The Vikings also settled in Normandy, which the Frankish king Charles the Simple granted to their leader, Rollo, when he converted to Christianity (911). The kingdom of Denmark was also established; it converted to Christianity by 950 and later gained control over Norway, Sweden, and England under King Cnut (r. 1017–1035).

From the south, mercenary armies of Muslims began to conquer Sicily, which took a century to subdue (827–927). Throughout the Mediterranean, Muslims established themselves as fearsome, cutthroat pirates.

From the east, the nomadic Magyars, a Slavic people, entered the Danube region (c. 899) and settled in modern Hungary. They launched aggressive raids westward until the German king Otto I (r. 936–973) stopped them at the battle of Lechfeld (955). This victory brought Otto fame and marked the last foreign invasion the west endured. There is debate, however, about whether Magyar containment had more to do with them settling down as farmers than with their military defeat.

The breakdown of centralized authority in the post-Carolingian world, the rise and usage of vernacular languages in place of Latin, and foreign invasions caused people to seek protection from the local counts. Counts slowly became powerful landlords, controlling local castles, maintaining law and order, and monitoring the local economy. As they evolved into regional rulers, they dominated the local peasantry and emerged as a new military elite in the west.

Social order was cemented by personal loyalty. Carolingian kings relied on their fideles ("faithful men") who were granted land (fiefs) in exchange for their service. These grants often became hereditary. The fideles frequently gained retainers of their own (vassals) who also received fiefs for service. The military, social, and economic order based on this system is called feudalism. Its hierarchy involved promises of mutual obligation and loyalty and evolved to substitute for the lack of public authority in post-Carolingian Europe.

Feudal society contained three broad groupings: those who fought, those who prayed, and those who labored. Knights and members of the church were free and often the vassals of other lords while having vassals of their own. Even some women and monasteries became high-ranking military vassals and granted fiefs to others to render their military service. Vassalage was marked by the rituals of homage, in which the vassal promised to be the lord's man, and fealty (a promise of service, fidelity, and trust) to the lord by swearing on relics or a Bible. This exchange worked as a public, oral contract between the two parties with reciprocal obligations.

Many farmers — the vast majority of the population — were gradually reduced from free peasantry status to involuntary servitude as serfs. They inherited this status and lost ownership of their manses to lords; they exchanged their manual labor for basic security. As landlords grew more powerful, they increased their control over not only services, but also access to mills, ovens, and breweries. Agricultural innovations, such as the three-field system, the substitution of horses for oxen as draft animals, and the introduction of heavy plows to work the claylike northern soil increased crop yields to feed a growing population. The peasants lived in villages, the social life of which centered on the local church and its religious feast days. Regular tithes, equal to one-tenth of their crops or income, supported the church. As the villages expanded, some even negotiated land-lease rights from the local lords. Village life, though, could complicate loyalties and obligations, especially when they were owed to persons outside the community.

Especially in France, local lords often consolidated their power in castles by 1000. These castellans extended their influence through the ban (the jurisdiction over taxation, legal matters, fines, and defense). Castellans enjoyed near-autonomy in their localities.

All those who fought (kings, counts, castellans, and knights) did so on horseback, wearing heavy chain-mail armor and equipped with stirrups, a lance, and shield. Lords and vassals often lived and feasted together. Many remained unmarried. This lifestyle provided an option for elite males who found it increasingly difficult to marry and to support families on estates of their own, due to changed inheritance patterns. With rising population and cessation of great conquests, the former system of partible inheritance (with family property divided among all children) became impractical because splintering an estate would impoverish elite families. Instead, the entire estate was bequeathed to one child, usually the eldest son, a system called "primogeniture." The heir claimed descent from the father, rather than from both parents. This practice denied younger sons an inheritance and thus the opportunity to found a family; instead, they became knights (called "youths" regardless of their age) or joined the church. This new system also disinherited most daughters who lost the power that came from inheriting land, and who became increasingly rare as feudal vassals. Women did continue to serve as links between powerful families through marriage and had to manage estates when their husbands went to war.

The peasants' and church's opposition to the spreading violence that accompanied the rise of an exclusively warrior class found expression in the Peace of God, a movement that began in southern France and spread widely by 1050. Regional councils issued decrees prohibiting violence against noncombatants and their property upon pain of excommunication. The Truce of God prohibited fighting between knights on Thursdays through Sundays. Mediation between placita ("parties") was also encouraged. These innovations also sanctioned the use of force to contain those who violated the peace, the truce, or mediated settlements.

Regional differences became more pronounced during this period. Italy, with its vestiges of Roman infrastructure, diverged from the rest of western Europe. Italian cities remained centers of influence, and powerful lords often based themselves within urban palaces from which they directed their rural affairs. Markets continued, and a cash economy was more vital here than elsewhere on the continent. Familial organization focused not on patrilineages but on consorteria. These formal contracts stipulated that all male family members shared equally in a family's profits and inheritance, from which women were excluded.

As the Carolingian kings in France lost prestige, kings in England and Germany gained it. In England, Alfred the Great (r. 871–899) did much to unify the island by building fortifications (*burhs*), a navy, and promoting the Anglo-Saxon language. He also produced the first English code of law since 695, in which he drew on laws from all preceding kingdoms and merged them into a code for all English people. Alfred and his successors pushed back Danish influence in England, although many Vikings settled there permanently and converted to Christianity. New administrative units of shires and hundreds were created. This centralization was fragile, and England was conquered by the Danish king Cnut (r. 1017–1035), who allowed many Anglo-Saxon institutions to continue.

In France, the Carolingians died out and were replaced by the Capetians when Hugh Capet was elected king (r. 987–996). His dynasty would control France until the fourteenth century.

In Germany, five duchies emerged. When the last Carolingian, Louis the Child, died in 911, the dukes elected Henry I of Saxony (r. 919–936) as the next monarch. His victories against the Magyars were continued by his son Otto I who also seized the Lombard crown in Italy. The pope crowned him emperor in 962, and Otto claimed the old Carolingian Middle Kingdom, announcing himself the restorer of the Roman Empire. He founded the Ottonian dynasty, which continued through the reign of Henry II (r. 1002–1024). The Ottonians adopted patrilineal inheritance and rewarded nobles in exchange for their military and political support. Revolts by minor royals and discontented nobles against Ottonian kings were common. The Ottonians enjoyed better relations with the church and often named bishops as royal officials. Increasingly, the Ottonian kings even claimed the right to invest bishops and the pope. Ottonian Germany enjoyed its own renaissance, especially under the royal tutor Gerbert (later Pope Sylvester II, r. 999–1003). Women participated to an extraordinary extent in this revival of classical learning.

Dissent among the German aristocracy plagued the Ottonians' successors: the Salians. In fact, the German monarch never succeeded in subduing factionalism as the French king did because Germans considered vassalage beneath the dignity of free men. To circumvent the nobles, the Salian kings relied on ministerials (serfs who often rose to high positions but retained their servile status) for administrative assistance.

The German kings expanded their borders into Russia, creating an "elastic bishopric" without an eastern boundary that could stretch to accommodate future conquests. German monarchs and the papacy supported newly converted Christian rulers in eastern Europe. These included the Czech Václav (r. 920–929) who became Duke of Bohemia (and that country's patron saint after being murdered by his brother), and Mieszko I of Poland (r. 963–992). He placed Poland directly under papal protection, and his son Boleslaw the Brave (r. 992–1025), who eventually controlled territory to Kiev, was proclaimed king. In Hungary, the Magyars also settled down, subjugating local Slavs. The Magyar ruler Stephen I (r. 997–1038) converted to Christianity, receiving a royal crown in return from the pope. The Christianization and settling of eastern Europe led to the spread of agriculture, and with it, the growth of internal division.

Suggestions for Lecture and Discussion Topics

1. The scholars of the Islamic renaissance produced an impressive legacy for the development of western science because they were responsible for transmitting much of the knowledge of classical antiquity and also for generating important scientific discoveries. A survey of this topic can be found in C. A. Qadir, *Philosophy and Science in the Islamic World: From Origins to the Present Day* (New York and London: Routledge, 1988). For more in-depth information, the essays in *Religion, Learning, and Science in the Abbasid Period*, R. B. Serjeant, J. D. Latham, and M. J. L. Young, eds. (Cambridge: Cambridge University Press, 1990) cover the gamut of Islamic philosophy and science during that period, and includes a survey of the classical Greek works that were translated into Arabic.

2. The Byzantine Empire faced attack throughout most of its history, yet managed to maintain its independence until the end of the Middle Ages. Discuss the details and successes of Byzantine military strategy and organization and the social or political consequences that features such as the dynatoi might have entailed. Warren Treadgold, *Byzantium and Its Army, 284–1081* (Stanford, CA: Stanford University, 1995) covers the organization and functioning of the themes; and John Haldon, *Warfare, State, and Society in the Byzantine World* (London: UCL Press, 1999) provides a general overview. Eric McGeer, *Sowing the Dragon's Teeth: Byzantine Warfare in the Tenth Century* (Washington, DC: Dumbarton Oaks, 1995) contains the texts of two Byzantine military treatises on tactics used against Muslim forces, the *Praecepta militaria* by Nikephoro Phokas, and the *Takitka* by Nikephoros Ouranos.

3. The achievements of Charlemagne's reign and the Carolingian renaissance are sometimes credited with bringing Europe out of the early Middle Ages. Discuss the innovations of the period and the extent to which they imitated Roman imperial precedents. A recent collection that evaluates the Carolingian renaissance in

political theory, education, art, and music, in addition to literary production, is Rosamond McKitterick, ed., *Carolingian Culture: Emulation and Innovation* (Cambridge: Cambridge University Press, 1994). On the Carolingian education initiative, see Bernhard Bischoff and Michael M. Gorman, *Manuscripts and Libraries in the Age of Charlemagne* (Cambridge: Cambridge University Press, 1994). On the spread of literacy in the Carolingian world beyond the clergy and monasteries, see Rosamond McKitterick, *The Carolingians and the Written Word* (Cambridge: Cambridge University Press, 1989). John Beckwith, *Early Medieval Art: Carolingian, Ottonian, Romanesque*, rpt. (London: Thames & Hudson, 1988) contains information and illustrations for artistic production. For primary sources, refer to Paul Edward Dutton, *Carolingian Civilization: A Reader* (Peterborough, Ont.: Broadview, 1993). For the broader political and historical context of Charlemagne's reign, see E. James, *The Origins of France: From Clovis to the Capetians, 500–1000* (New York: St. Martin's, 1982).

4. Scholars continue to question the very existence of feudalism. One of the most influential studies arguing against the existence of ninth- or tenth-century feudalism is Susan Reynolds, *Fiefs and Vassals: The Medieval Evidence Reinterpreted* (Oxford: Oxford University Press, 1996). Another overview of the scholarly debate is contained in Part 2 of *Debating the Middle Ages: Issues and Readings*, Lester Little and Barbara Rosenwein, eds. (Malden, MA: Blackwell, 1998), particularly the introduction and Elizabeth Brown's "Feudalism: The Tyranny of a Construct."

5. Medieval Spain under Muslim rule represented one of the most diverse and vibrant cultures in the west, described by the term *convivencia* — the coexistence of Jews, Christians, and Muslims under the Muslim caliphs of Córdoba. Recent studies of the intermingling of the three religions include Mark D. Meyerson and Edward D. English, eds., *Christians, Muslims, and Jews in Medieval and Early Modern Spain: Interaction and Cultural Change* (Notre Dame, IN: University of Notre Dame Press, 1999); and Roger Collins, *Early Medieval Spain: Unity in Diversity, 400–1000*, 2d ed. (New York: St. Martin's, 1995). David Wasserstein, *The Caliphate in the West: An Islamic Political Institution in the Iberian Peninsula* (Oxford: Clarendon, 1993) examines the establishment of Muslim authority in early medieval Spain. Vivian B. Mann and Thomas F. Glick, eds., *Convivencia: Jews, Muslims, and Christians in Medieval Spain* (New York: Braziller, 1992) is the catalog of an exhibition at the Jewish Museum in New York, featuring images of objects that reflect the cultural and intellectual flourishing of the age.

6. The apocalyptic predictions made during the first millennium were hardly less dire than those made for the second. See Richard Landes, "Lest the Millennium Be Fulfilled: Apocalyptic Expectations and the Pattern of Western Chronography, 100–800 C.E.," in Werner Verbeke, Daniel Verhulst, and Andries Welkenhysen, eds., *The Use and Abuse of Eschatology in the Middle Ages* (Leuven University Press, 1988), pp. 137–211. For the lack of impact the millennium made on the minds of Anglo-Saxon England, see Zacharias Thundy, *Millennium: Apocalypse, Antichrist, and Old English Monsters c.1000 A.D.* (Notre Dame, IN: Cross Cultural Publications, 1998). For a history of medieval millenarianism, which covers this period, see Bernard McGinn, *Visions of the End: Apocalyptic Traditions in the Middle Ages* (New York: Columbia University Press, 1998); and for millenarian traditions beginning in the new millennium, see Norman Cohn, *The Pursuit of the Millennium* (Oxford: Oxford University Press, 1990).

7. The Christianization and emergence of the eastern Slavic states is a topic of particular interest in light of recent historical events. A standard introduction to Kievan Russia is George Vernadsky, *Kievan Russia* (New Haven, CT: Yale University Press, 1973). For the process of Christianization of the Slavic peoples, see Boris Gasparov and Olga Raevsky-Hughes, eds., *Slavic Cultures in the Middle Ages*, vol. 1 of *Christianity and the Eastern Slavs* (Berkeley: University of California Press, 1993).

Making Connections

1. *How were the Byzantine, Islamic, and European economies similar? How did they differ? How did these economies interact?* Land was the main source of wealth for the Byzantine, Islamic, and European economies. All knew of and used money (coins) for local and long-distance trade, although long-distance commerce was far more important and widespread in the Islamic world than elsewhere. Byzantine control over commerce, centered at Constantinople, was unmatched. There were interactions between these economies. Scandinavia was the hinge between the silver of the Islamic world and western Europe, whereas Venice served as the intermediary between Byzantine products and those of Europe.

2. *How were the powers and ambitions of castellans similar to, and different from, those of the dynatoi of Byzantium and of Muslim provincial rulers?* The dynatoi and the castellans were generally military men. The castellans, like many of the Muslim provincial rulers, controlled land and men without concerning themselves much about a "central power." Muslim provincial rulers who took the title caliph were, like the Byzantine dyantoi, competing with the ruler at the top. In Byzantium, dynatoi competed with the emperor in a very direct way because they wanted to be emperor themselves, but the castellans had only local claims. Muslim provincial rulers depended on Mamluk warriors who worked under their own leaders and could move as a group from employer to employer. Castellans, however, depended on their

vassals, some of whom lived with them and were dependent upon them in every way.

3. *Compare the effects of the barbarian invasions into the Roman Empire with the effects of the Viking, Muslim, and Magyar invasions into Carolingian Europe.* The barbarian invasions into the Roman Empire ended with the creation of many new kingdoms. Magyar was the only kingdom created by invasions into Carolingian Europe by the ninth and tenth centuries, and most of these invaders were thieves who came not to settle, but to plunder. The invaders who stayed were absorbed into the Roman Catholic culture of western Europe. The Viking invasions led to settlements in Normandy and Danelaw (in England). Scandinavia itself was converted to Roman Catholicism (c. 1000), as was Magyar.

Writing Assignments and Class Presentation Topics

1. The Vikings rival the crusades and the Black Death in popularity as a topic. Have students explore Viking history and culture (and perhaps dispel a few myths about them). Although recorded at a later date, the sagas form a powerful literary tradition and serve as an entertaining introduction to many of the norms and practices of Nordic cultures. Students interested in Viking women can read Jenny Jochen, *Women in Old Norse Society* (Ithaca: Cornell University Press, 1995). An introduction to Viking interactions with Europe is P. H. Sawyer, *Kings and Vikings: Scandinavia and Europe, A.D. 700–1100* (New York: Barnes & Noble, 1994). The treasures found at the Sutton Hoo burial site in East Anglia, England, well illustrate the culture reflected in this literature.

2. Students can investigate the Islamic world of the Abbasid caliphate, which they probably know only from the fame of *The Thousand and One Nights*. See Guy LeStrange, *Baghdad During the Abbasid Caliphate: From Contemporary Arabic and Persian Sources* (Westport, CT: Greenwood, 1983).

3. Einhard's biography of Charlemagne makes entertaining reading for students, in large part because of the author's lively and opinionated remarks on his subject. If students read the biography in conjunction with Charlemagne's letters and capitularies, they can begin to piece together this renowned leader's achievements, motivations, and impact on western European history. Students can also compare the versions of Charlemagne that emerge from two different biographies (Einhard's and Notker the Stammerer's) in *Two Lives of Charlemagne* (New York: Viking Penguin, 1976). For a reassessment of Charlemagne's reign and the "Pirenne thesis," based on archaeological evidence, see Richard Hodges and David Whitehouse, *Mohammad, Charlemagne, and the Origins of Europe* (Ithaca: Cornell University Press, 1983).

4. Have students research the daily lives of "those who worked." Useful introductions to the topic of peasant life include: J. A. Raftis, ed., *Pathways to Medieval Peasants* (Toronto: University of Toronto Press, 1981); David Herlihy, *Medieval Households* (Cambridge, MA: Harvard University Press, 1990); Barbara Hanawalt, *The Ties that Bound: Peasant Families in Medieval England* (Oxford: Oxford University Press, 1988); and George Duby's important *Early Growth of the European Economy: Warriors and Peasants from the Seventh to the Twelfth Centuries* (Ithaca: Cornell University Press, 1990). For an interesting perspective on medieval childhood, see John Boswell, *The Kindness of Strangers: The Abandonment of Children in Western Europe from Late Antiquity to the Renaissance* (New York: Pantheon Books, 1989).

5. Even though they may strike students as rather "low-tech," the technological innovations of this period (such as the three-field system, the adoption of the horse as a draft and military animal, the heavy plow, and the stirrup) precipitated wide-ranging transformations in western European life. Have students research and report on the various facets of this technological revolution. The classic text is Lynn White, *Medieval Technology and Social Change* (Oxford: Oxford University Press, 1962). Other useful studies include R. H. C. Davis, *The Medieval Warhorse* (London: Thames & Hudson, 1989); and, on changes in construction, John Kenyon, *Medieval Fortifications* (New York: St. Martin's, 1990). For military innovations, see the video *NOVA: Secrets of Lost Empires II: Medieval Siege*, where modern scholars and craftsmen build a trebuchet using the same technology available two thousand years ago.

6. Ask students to explore the flowering of the Macedonian renaissance. The Suda, an encyclopedic compendium of knowledge dating from the late tenth century, provides a fascinating entry into the intellectual world of the Macedonian renaissance.

7. Many notable "national" epics were composed in these centuries. These texts can be mined for numerous topics, such as notions of warfare, masculinity, the "other," kingship. See Seamus Heaney, *Beowulf: A New Verse Translation* (New York: Farrar, Straus, & Giroux, 2000). Two scholarly studies that consider the history behind these epics are Peter Haidu, *The Subject of Violence: The Song of Roland and the Birth of the State* (Bloomington: Indiana University Press, 1993); and R. Fletcher, *The Quest for El Cid* (Oxford: Oxford University Press, 1991).

Research Assignments

1. Islamic law forms an excellent source for information about Muslim society. For an introduction, see Ann K. S. Lambton, *State and Government in Medieval Islam: An Introduction to the Study of Islamic Political Theory:*

The Jurists (Oxford: Oxford University Press, 1981); and the collected essays in Muhammad Khalid Masud and Brinkley Messick, eds., *Islamic Legal Interpretation: Muftis and Their Fatwas* (Cambridge: Harvard University Press, 1996). For the status of women under medieval Islamic law, see Nikki R. Keddie and Beth Baron, eds., *Women in Middle Eastern History: Shifting Boundaries in Sex and Gender* (New Haven, CT: Yale University Press, 1993).

2. Byzantine civilization during the flowering of the Macedonian renaissance has received a fair amount of scholarly attention in the past few years. Students might find it intriguing to compare the culture of the Greek east to that of the post-Carolingian west. A survey of social groups in Byzantine society is presented in the articles assembled in Guglielmo Cavallo, ed. *The Byzantines* (Chicago: University of Chicago Press, 1992), which discuss all social strata and many occupations. Each selection contains a useful bibliography for further research. A standard historical overview of the period is Mark Whittow, *The Making of Byzantium, 600–1025* (Berkeley: University of California Press, 1996). A stimulating group of essays that explores gender roles and identity in Byzantium is Liz James, ed., *Women, Men and Eunuchs: Gender in Byzantium* (New York and London: Routledge, 1997). Serious bibliographic researchers should access the online library catalog of Dumbarton Oaks, the foremost center for Byzantine studies in the United States.

3. The status and lives of women in the west changed with the emergence of regional centers of power, economic transformation, and the Carolingian renaissance. A very good overview can be found in the collected essays of David Herlihy in *Women, Family, and Society in Medieval Europe* (New York: Berghahn Books, 1995); and his short introduction to women's work, *Opera Muliebria* (Burr Ridge, IL: McGraw-Hill, 1991). For royal women, see P. Stafford, *Queens, Concubines, Dowagers: The King's Wife in the Early Middle Ages* (Athens: University of Georgia Press, 1983). Women in Carolingian France are discussed in Suzanne Wemple, *Women in Frankish Society: Marriage and Cloister, 500–900* (Philadelphia: University of Pennsylvania Press, 1981). For an intriguing series of essays on women and religious life in the period, see Jane Tebbits Schulenberg, *Forgetful of Their Sex: Female Sanctity and Society, ca. 500–1100* (Chicago: University of Chicago Press, 1997). The advice of Dhuoda to her son is translated in Carol Neel, trans., *Handbook for William: A Carolingian Woman's Counsel for Her Son* (Washington, DC: Catholic University of America Press, 1999).

4. The cultural differences between Islamic and western European countries during this period are striking. With Córdoba as a reference point, students should make comparisons between it and an English and Carolingian "city." Where would they have preferred to live?

Compare Islamic and western Europe medical theories and practices. Which are nearest to modern medicine?

Literature

Chickering, Howell D., *Beowulf: A Dual-Language Edition.* 1977.
Haddawy, Husain, trans., *The Arabian Nights.* 1990.
Harrison, Robert, trans., *The Song of Roland.* 2002.
Neel, Carol, trans., *Handbook for William: A Carolingian Woman's Counsel for Her Son by Dhuoda.* 1991.
Thorpe, Lewis, trans., *Two Lives of Charlemagne.* 1969.

Historical Skills

Map 9.2, Islamic States, c. 1000, p. 327

Ask students to identify the regions that border the edges of Muslim-controlled territories. What advantages in the region (such as control over much of the Mediterranean) did the various Islamic powers enjoy?

Map 9.3, Expansion of the Carolingian Empire under Charlemagne, p. 333

How far do Charlemagne's conquests replicate the constitution of the ancient Roman Empire in the west? Which forces might have prevented him from enlarging his subject territory even further? Which portions of western Europe lay outside his control? Which groups dominated those areas?

Map 9.4, Muslim, Viking, and Magyar Invasions of the Ninth and Tenth Centuries, p. 339

Discuss the range and impact of this series of invasions that struck western Europe from all sides at roughly the same time. What negative consequences might have resulted? How did these contribute to the rise of the new warrior class? The transformation of agricultural society? The fragmentation of political authority in the west? What possible positive effects might these invasions have occasioned, even if unintended?

Mapping the West: Europe and the Mediterranean, c. 1050, p. 354

What were the internal weaknesses of these apparently balanced geographic powers? How many smaller territories can students identify that would emerge as powers in their own right? Do students note the presence of numerous urban centers throughout the region, not merely along the Mediterranean? What might the increased number of cities indicate and imply for the future development of the region?

Taking Measure: Viking Coin Hoards, c. 865–895, p. 340

What do students conclude from the presence of coin hoards outside the Danelaw (the area settled by the Vikings)? Do these artifacts necessarily indicate that Vikings lived outside the Danelaw? Why might the hoards be concentrated at the area's perimeter? What does the use of coins indicate about changes in the Vikings' lifestyle once they became settled in England?

Andromeda C, p. 330

This manuscript reflects the flourishing of science that occurred during the Islamic renaissance. What clues does it give concerning the Muslim transmission and extension of the ancient Greek scientific heritage? What does the identity of the astronomer's "pupil" — the ruler of Iran — indicate about the prestige that scientific learning and patronage commanded in the Islamic world?

Charlemagne's Throne, p. 332

How does Charlemagne's establishment of a new capital city reflect the practices of western emperors who preceded him? Ask students to comment on what the placement of the throne might suggest about Charlemagne's relationship to ecclesiastical authority.

Two Cities Besieged, p. 344

Ask students to describe the military equipment employed in these illuminations. What kinds of tactics were employed when attempting to take a fortified city? How do the strategies and equipment used relate to the rise of a specialized warrior class — "those who fight" — in western Europe? What broader social ramifications did the emergence of that group involve?

St. Matthew, p. 335

Compare this illumination with any of the examples of classical, Byzantine, or Islamic art found in the textbook. What similarities do students find? What seems uniquely Carolingian in this work?

Hard Work in January, p. 346

Why would the depiction of peasant labor have been included on a liturgical calendar? What does this illustra-
tion reveal about the labors of the common peasant and the centrality of agriculture in medieval life? Ask students to comment on the workers' clothing, especially the lack of shoes on the young man leading the oxen. How much energy do students believe would have been expended in a day spent at work such as this? What does that tell them about the need for calories, the likelihood of long-term good health, and the outlook on life in general of the average peasant?

Otto III Receiving Gifts, p. 353

The iconography and stylistic conventions of these illustrations are highly suggestive. Have students remark on the identities of the four female figures presenting gifts to the emperor. Does their gesture suggest any parallels to those of the magi? Which similarities to Byzantine art can the students list? Who is seen accompanying Otto? What were the political circumstances of his relations with the Byzantine Empire and with the papacy in Rome?

Terms of History: Feudalism, p. 343

Discuss the differences intended in the two systems that are described by manorialism versus feudalism. Why did the different terms emerge? What are the current scholarly criticisms of feudalism? What does its adoption by earlier historians indicate about the historians' concerns? Which realities about the past did the term obscure? Do students believe that the recent abandonment of the term facilitates our understanding of the period? Why or why not?

Fulbert of Chartres, Letter to William of Aquitaine (1020)

Bishop Fulbert of Chartres Cathedral was a serious, well-respected classical scholar interested in education and church reform. Students might consider why Fulbert was in a position to give Duke William advice on vassalage. High-ranking churchmen like Fulbert often operated like secular lords in the administration of church land, and this included protecting their vassals while expecting the usual loyalty and faithfulness in return. Fulbert also understood the lord–vassal relationship in religious terms because everyone stood as vassals in relation to God. This connection is particularly clear in Fulbert's instructions, which have decidedly religious overtones.

OTHER BEDFORD/ST. MARTIN'S RESOURCES FOR CHAPTER 9

The following resources are available to accompany Chapter 9. Please refer to the Preface of this manual for detailed descriptions of all the ancillaries.

For Instructors

Transparencies

The following maps and images from Chapter 9 are available as full-color acetates.

- Map 9.1: The Expansion of Byzantium, 860–1025
- Map 9.2: Islamic States, c. 1000
- Map 9.3: Expansion of the Carolingian Empire under Charlemagne
- Map 9.4: Muslim, Viking, and Magyar Invasions of the Ninth and Tenth Centuries
- Mapping the West: Europe and the Mediterranean, c. 1050
- *Crowning of Constantine Porphyrogenitos* (chapter image, page 323)
- *Macedonian Renaissance* (chapter image, page 323)

Instructor's Resources CD-ROM

The following maps and image from Chapter 9, as well as a chapter outline, are available on disc in both Power-Point and jpeg formats.

- Map 9.1: The Expansion of Byzantium, 860–1025
- Map 9.2: Islamic States, c. 1000
- Map 9.3: Expansion of the Carolingian Empire under Charlemagne
- Map 9.4: Muslim, Viking, and Magyar Invasions of the Ninth and Tenth Centuries
- Mapping the West: Europe and the Mediterranean, c. 1050
- *Crowning of Constantine Porphyrogenitos* (chapter image, page 323)

For Students

Sources of The Making of the West

The following documents are available in Chapter 9 of the companion sourcebook by Katharine J. Lualdi, University of Southern Maine.

1. *General Capitulary for the Missi* (802)
2. Liutprand of Cremona, *Report to Otto I* (968)
3. *Digenis Akritas* (Tenth or Eleventh Century)
4. Ahmad al-Ya'qubi, *Kitab al-buldan* (Ninth Century)

Study Guides

The print **Study Guide** and the **Online Study Guide** at bedfordstmartins.com/hunt, both by Victoria Thompson (Arizona State University) and Eric Johnson (University of California, Los Angeles), help students synthesize the material they have learned as well as practice the skills historians use to make sense of the past. The following Map, Visual, and Document activities are available for Chapter 9.

Map Activity

- Map 9.5: Mapping the West: Europe and the Mediterranean, c. 1050 (page 354)

Visual Activity

- *Crowning of Constantine Porphyrogenitos* (chapter image, page 323)

Reading Historical Documents

- Dhuoda's Handbook for Her Son (page 337)
- Fulbert of Chartres, *Letter to William of Aquitaine* (page 345)

Renewal and Reform
c. 1050–1150

CHAPTER RESOURCES

Main Chapter Topics

1. The new profit-based economy in Europe gave rise to social, cultural, and political changes; created cities structured around and rebuilt for commerce, extensive international trade, money for trade and exchange; and advances in technology that increased production and further altered social relationships.

2. The wealth and power of the church prompted calls from within it for reform and inspired new monastic movements. Reformers altered the level and nature of church involvement in everyday life. Popes and others called for the abolition of simony (purchase of church offices) and nicolaitism (clerical marriage).

3. In the name of reform, the church—especially the papacy—extended and increased its power and took on the character of a political monarchy, raising armies and institutionalizing its authority as it vied with secular rulers for control of Europe.

4. This rivalry was epitomized by the Investiture Conflict, in which pope Gregory VII and emperor Henry IV contended for the right to appoint men to high church offices. In this intense political battle, the emperor outmaneuvered the pope temporarily, but the overall dynamics of the conflict consolidated church supremacy and shifted imperial power into the hands of German princes.

5. In 1095, Pope Urban II proclaimed the First Crusade, calling on Christians to expel the Muslims from the Holy Land. This call stirred both piety and bigotry, greed and self-sacrifice. Crusaders, following Peter the Hermit, slaughtered Jews who were living peacefully in Europe. In the Near East, the crusaders eventually defeated the Muslims at Jerusalem and established the states of Outremer.

6. Monarchs in western Europe set about consolidating their rule. The king of France advanced his standing. In England, the Norman conquest brought English society into the purview of continental politics and established a regime that combined Norman and Anglo-Saxon traditions of government and law. In the Byzantine Empire, the arrival of the Seljuk Turks brought a new dynasty and a call for military aid from the west but also a renaissance of the study of ancient Greek classics.

7. Education, art, and scholarship flourished in Europe after the First Crusade. The discipline of logic, the liberal arts, and the beginning of an infusion of classical learning transformed the way westerners realized their faith and conceived of themselves and God. Romanesque and Cistercian architecture, plainchant, and a system of musical notation similarly enriched cultural life but also made uneasy those committed to conservative or alternative visions of correct Christian life.

Summary

The century spanning 1050 to 1150 was marked by an explosion of commercial activity and new wealth; struggle between popes and secular kings; dramatic breakthroughs in the arts, letters, and learning; and the church's crusades to the east. All these factors profoundly changed medieval life and provoked a wide range of actions and reactions.

The growth of the profit-based economy coincided with population increase, agricultural improvements, and enhanced trade, and produced the prototypes of corporations, banks, and accounting systems. New cities, meanwhile, grew around these new commercial bases. Feudal lords shifted their activities to take advantage of this change, converting feudal services to cash for use in market-based exchange, converting agricultural surpluses into luxury goods, and levying taxes on local merchants.

Further, they encouraged traders and craftspersons to settle nearby. New commercial centers took root especially around castles, monasteries, churches, and ancient Roman towns.

Local merchants tended to sell staples, whereas long-distance traders specialized in the luxurious and exotic goods enjoyed by lords and vassals. Long-distance trade was the special domain of Jews, many of whom turned to commerce upon being barred from landownership; and Italians, who had remained relatively urbanized since Roman times, and whose contacts with the eastern world and maritime trade, prepared them for this endeavor.

The commercial explosion produced an urban construction boom to accommodate marketplaces, the attendant population, and their churches and other institutions. Typical cities were surrounded by walls and lined with narrow streets containing wattle and daub buildings that housed the family and its business. Specialized buildings for trade and government were erected, as were community houses, warehouses, and charitable houses for the sick and indigent. Although roads were somewhat improved, cities proliferated along key waterways and seacoasts, the main arteries of a busy international economy.

The displacement of the gift economy and its direct transfer of goods and property by a profit economy with currency as its medium of exchange comparatively depersonalized social relations. Contracts and partnerships formed the basis around which resources and labor were pooled for specified projects, and carried various methods for allocating risk and benefits. A compagnia, usually formed by extended families, shared profits but also assumed joint and unlimited liability for losses and debts. Meanwhile, the surge in new businesses created a market for credit and risk, requiring creative means of collecting interest to avoid the church ban on usury.

New technologies generated mass production and industries. Particularly affected were cloth-making, which benefited from water-driven machinery; and agriculture, which now had wide access to iron plows and other tools that made farming less labor-intensive and more productive.

The cramped living conditions and new social category of townspeople—distinct from workers, warriors, and clerics—brought a new desire for local self-government, and cities developed local legal and administrative systems. Some cities—particularly those in Italy, France, and Flanders—formed communes, in which a community aligned without social and economic distinctions among its inhabitants, and in which land and goods were held in common for the benefit of all. But interest in self-government was also fueled by religious as well as economic concerns. Some tradespersons worked to free their cities and towns from the control of powerful clerics, who often exercised some degree of secular authority over them.

The rise of commerce affected the church, which was tied to cities for political, religious, and economic purposes. But with every step toward commercial involvement came calls for church reform and even withdrawal from secular life. In the tenth century, Cluny's Benedictine monastery was a precursor of the reform movement; Cluny's monks eschewed possessions and lived off of the donations of land by the pious. The abbots of Cluny enforced clerical celibacy and eventually even papal reform, asking the pope to defend their lands from encroachment.

The major reform movement was built upon clerical and monastic criticism of two common practices: nicolaitism (clerical marriage) and simony (the buying of church offices). Emperor Henry III (r. 1039–1056) supported the reform and, at the Synod of Sutri (1046), backed like-minded Leo IX (r. 1049–1054) as pope, settling three conflicting claims to the papacy. Leo quickly mobilized the power of his office: he sponsored the creation of a cannon law textbook (*Collection in 74 Titles*), which emphasized papal powers; and recruited the most zealous reformers of the day. At the council of Reims, he set about rooting out bishops who had purchased their offices. Leo's sweeping claims and intractable spirit alienated the Byzantine church hierarchy. After a few rounds of mutual excommunication, the Great Schism of 1054 completed the split of Christianity into the Roman Catholic and the Greek Orthodox churches.

The popes still continued to assert their primacy, however, building their position politically and militarily. The papacy made its most dramatic move under Pope Gregory VII (r. 1073–1085) whose insistence on papal authority to appoint (invest) church officials set him at odds with Emperor Henry IV (r. 1056–1106). Gregory styled himself as the savior of the church, but Henry, convinced that he and his bishops were the rightful leaders of the church, denounced Gregory as an ambitious and evil man.

Pope and emperor collided over the investiture of the archbishop of Milan: Gregory denied the emperor's right to appoint him, but Henry appointed him anyway. After a series of mutual, bitter, public denunciations, Gregory revoked Henry's title and excommunicated him, authorizing rebellion in Germany. The sentences mobilized Henry's enemies, both within and without his empire. Finding himself cornered, Henry traveled to Gregory's fortress in northern Italy, where he stood in the snow and begged forgiveness as a penitent, which Gregory had no power to refuse. Henry had forced the pope's hand, but the church had won the symbolic battle by forcing the emperor to grovel before the pope.

The Investiture Conflict lingered on for years—rebellious German princes elected an antiking and Henry and his supporters elected an antipope—until the Concordat of Worms (1122), where a compromise was reached dividing the secular from the spiritual aspects of church appointments: the pope conferred spiritual appointments, the emperor its worldly property and place. Decisive electoral influence in Germany was conferred on the emperor and, in Italy, on the pope. But the overall effect was to solidify the papacy's supreme authority over the church. The German emperor lost out in other ways, too. German princes consolidated their lands and positions at the expense of royal power, and in Italy the emperor lost power to the cities.

Church reform institutionalized the sacraments and the role of priests in everyday life. Heretofore, the number, nature, and purposes of the sacraments had been unclear. Now the church clarified these matters, placing increased emphasis on the role of the priests by whom the sacraments were administered. The church—for the first time—assumed authority over marriages, performed weddings, and decided the legality and validity of marriages. The church also stressed the importance of the holy communion at mass. The elevation of priests coincided with increased demands—from reformers and congregations—for clerical celibacy, which many clerics in many places resisted strenuously. Notwithstanding, the church declared it law in 1123. Many of these reforms required study and standardization of canon law: the accumulated decisions and doctrines of councils, bishops, church fathers, and popes. Gratian, a monk trained in law, selectively systematized canon law according to the papacy's agenda, and it was published under the title of *Harmony of Discordant Cannons* but was more commonly known as the *Decretum*. The papal curia (government) centered in Rome, resembled a court of law with its own collection agency. Papal lands were insufficient to support this growing bureaucracy; churchmen newly appointed to office had to pay for their consecration, and litigants had to pay to have their petitions heard. All of this was widely resented. With his law courts, bureaucracy, and financial apparatus, the pope had, in effect, become a monarch.

In the late 1000s, the Byzantine Empire faced mounting invasions by Muslims. In 1071, Emperor Romanus IV and his mercenary army met the Seljuk Turks at the battle of Manzikert and were soundly defeated. Byzantine domination in Asia Minor came to an end. In 1095, as the Seljuk Turks encroached on Jerusalem, the emperor Alexius I asked Pope Urban II (r. 1088–1099) to send an army of mercenaries to repel the Muslims. Urban, however, used this opportunity to call on the Franks to conquer the Holy Land around Jerusalem, promising salvation to all who died in that effort. The First Crusade (1096–1099) seduced hordes of people from all walks of life with all sorts of motives, ranging from salvation to riches, land, and adventure to unfettered violence. The separate militias from disparate regions were loosely organized; one faction of peasants led by Peter the Hermit made a detour specifically to massacre European Jews before pressing on to fight Muslims in Asia Minor, where they were promptly annihilated.

An active part of many Christian communities, urban Jews were, however, largely segregated from Christians and thus were a relatively easy target. The pope's appeal to fight the "wicked race" unleashed horrifying atrocities against Jews by crusaders remaining in Europe, who killed and plundered Jews as persons no better than the Muslims and much closer to home. Jews had generally had a tenuous position in Christian Europe, but it was not until the crusades that systematic pogroms began.

Disunity left Muslims unusually weak and vulnerable. The crusaders captured the Holy Land in 1099 and held it, tenuously, until 1291. By 1109, the crusaders had established the four states of Outremer ("beyond the sea")—Edessa, Antioch, Jerusalem, and Tripoli—on the western Mediterranean coast of Muslim lands. Western Europeans ruled as feudal lords over populations of Muslims, Jews, and Greek Orthodox Christians. These western outposts encouraged trade, but their military preoccupations led to the creation of the Knights Templar: Christian monks pledged to warfare for protection of the crusader states. As the sole transporters of money from Europe to the Holy Land, the Templars, who opened what were in essence branch banks in major cities, became fabulously rich. Despite their initial success, the crusader states slowly crumbled, particularly following the ludicrous Second Crusade (1147–1149) in which quarreling crusaders abandoned the siege of Damascus after four days. Six more crusades followed until the end of the thirteenth century. But, by 1291, the crusader states were securely back in Muslim hands.

The growing power of the pope was matched by a similar reemergence of monarchical power elsewhere. Byzantine Emperor Alexius I (r. 1081–1118), first of the Comnenian dynasty (1081–1185) consolidated his power by amassing an army of soldiers whom he rewarded with large imperial estates, and by placating the elites with new offices. The Comnenian dynasty presided over a culturally and materially rich Byzantium, in which philosophers revived Plato and Aristotle and classical forms resurfaced in literature—trends that would have profound influences on Europe in the high Middle Ages.

By the twelfth century, England boasted western Europe's most powerful monarchs. In 1066, Edward the Confessor died childless, and William of Normandy (1027–1087) claimed that Edward had promised him his crown. When Harold, named successor by Edward on his deathbed, was crowned, William invaded England in the fall of 1066 with a papal endorsement and about eight thousand men. Harold and William clashed in the battle of Hastings, decisively won by William who supplanted the old Anglo-Saxon aristocracy with his own family and supporters arranged in a graded Norman hierarchy. William and his Norman successors nevertheless retained significant Anglo-Saxon legal and administrative institutions, such as the use of the writ (terse, written instructions) and shires (counties).

By right of conquest, all of England was technically William's property. In 1086, William ordered a survey and census of England, popularly called "Domesday" because, like the records of people judged at doomsday, it provided facts that could not be appealed. It was the most extensive inventory of land, livestock, taxes, and population that had ever been compiled in Europe. The Norman conquest also propelled cultural and economic ties between England and the continent. Indeed, the kings of England often spent more time on the continent than in England. For a time, England's archbishop of Canterbury was St. Anselm (1033–1109), an Italian by birth.

In France, meanwhile, the monarchy similarly consolidated power. Although maintaining that the pope was head of the church, royal supporters placed the king on equal footing by depicting the pope as consulting with the king for advice. Louis VI the Fat (r. 1108–1137), with the help of his biographer Suger (1081–1152), set the framework for the future role of the French king.

Education and innovative scholarship increased dramatically during the twelfth century. Students flocked to the schools that developed out of the monasteries, and the "wandering scholars" changed the face of university cities, which were obliged to add infrastructure to accommodate them. Latin was their common language. By the end of the eleventh century, the best schools were at Reims, Paris, Bologna, and Montpellier.

The seven liberal arts were divided into the trivium (grammar, rhetoric, and logic) and the quadrivium (arithmetic, geometry, music, and astronomy). The most popular of the liberal arts in the twelfth century was logic (or dialectic), which scholars looked to for a philosophical confirmation of beliefs, including those concerning the nature and existence of God. The use of logic was propelled by the translation of Aristotle into Latin, facilitated by contacts with Muslims, who had been studying Aristotle for centuries. Students could pursue further studies at specialized schools of medicine, theology, and law.

Peter Abelard (1079–1142) was destined for a career as a warrior and lord, but instead pursued the life of a scholar. He studied with William of Champeaux and challenged his tutor's position on "universals." Abelard introduced dialectic by juxtaposing contrasting positions and their respective supporting claims (including passages from the Bible) in order to reconcile them and find the truth. Abelard stressed that logic and knowledge were the true pathways to faith. Abelard's ideas, however, were too radical for his time; his logical treatise on the Holy Trinity was condemned by the church in 1121 and he was forced to burn it.

Abelard's student and lover, Heloise (c. 1100–c. 1163[1164]), was herself exceptionally learned, one of the few such women of the period known to historians. When Heloise's uncle suspected a romance between the young couple (they had married clandestinely), he had Ablelard castrated. The pair retired to separate monasteries. Although she eventually became abbess, Heloise never lost her regard for Abelard. Another leading female scholar was Hildegard of Bingen (1098–1179), perhaps the only authorized female preacher of her time. A scientist, composer, and playwright inspired by visions, Hildegard, like Abelard, viewed knowledge as a hallmark of faith. She describes and interprets some of her visions in *Scivias* (1151), which also includes illustrations, fourteen pieces of music, and a play.

Monastic tradition and monastic reform likewise gave rise to flourishing artistic expressions. Benedictine monks specialized in Gregorian plainchant that preserved, modified, and notated ancient melodies, which became the core music of the Catholic church. Architecture, at this time, embellished the Romanesque style of the monastery, featuring enormous structures, brightly colored paintings, and elaborate sculptures. Altars and reliquaries similarly showcased the aesthetic eloquence favored by the monastic tradition.

Some monks rebelled against this opulent artistic trend, unable to separate it from the world of commerce. They enacted a new devotion to poverty and seclusion. Monks of the Carthusian order, founded by Bruno of Cologne, lived out their lives in silence and seclusion. They were, however, devoted to education and renowned for copying manuscripts as part of their devotion to spreading God's word. Each Carthusian house was limited to no more than twelve members. One of the most successful of such monastic orders was the Cistercian order, particularly under the leadership of St. Bernard (c. 1090–1153). The Cistercians were devoted to simplicity, and their churches were therefore unornamented, their liturgies greatly simplified, and their habits remained undyed. They kept the natural color of wool and were known as white monks. Devoted to prayer and the management of their farms, the unworldly Cistercians ironically flourished. Besides emphasizing the humanity of both Jesus and his mother Mary, they elevated Mary's status in Christian expression.

Suggestions for Lecture and Discussion Topics

1. The commercial economy in western Europe was one of the most influential developments of medieval history, but is taken for granted today. Students might find it interesting to see how this system affected those who lived during its early stages. By which mechanisms did the commercial economy develop? Who were its primary champions and opponents? Why? How did it affect social relationships? Demographics? Urbanism? Daily life? How did it affect the political order? There are a

handful of classic studies on this topic, including Henri Pirenne, *Economic and Social History of Medieval Europe* (New York: Harcourt Brace Jovanovich, 1933). Chapter 1 details the revival of commerce, the growth of European cities, and the role of the crusades in economic growth; Chapter 4 outlines the emerging role of money. One of the best general overviews is Georges Duby, *The Early Growth of the European Economy: Warriors and Peasants from the Seventh to the Twelfth Century* (Ithaca: Cornell University Press, 1978), which includes a discussion of the general social context as the economy emerged from the feudal period.

2. Another development of eleventh- and twelfth-century western Europe that would have a crucial, lasting impact on Europe was the centralization of authority in the western kingdoms. An overview will provide a useful understanding of the basis of the modern state system. For a look at the general features of state building in the medieval west, see Joseph Reese Stayer, *On the Medieval Origins of the Modern State* (Princeton: Princeton University Press, 1970), an outstanding short overview of the development of national political institutions during this period. For more detailed studies of particular national systems and their development, see H. G. Richardson and G. O. Sayles, *The Governance of Medieval England from the Conquest to Magna Carta* (Edinburgh: Edinburgh University Press, 1963); and Alfred Haverkamp, *Medieval Germany, 1056–1276*, H. Braum and R. Mortimer, trans. (Oxford: Oxford University Press, 1992). Compare and contrast the development of centralized royal authority in these countries. What are the factors that influenced the pace and extent of consolidation? How did the rulers of these countries confront these considerations?

3. The crusades were among the most dramatic and harrowing events of the Middle Ages, characterized by brutal warfare, ugly racial and religious bigotry, and military expansionism. Examine the crusades from varying perspectives: religious, social, cultural, economic, and political. How did the crusading spirit fit contemporary Christian beliefs? What motives, emotions, and incentives did the pope offer the people to induce them to join the crusade? What might have been some of the pope's ulterior motives? How did the crusades fit into the political climate of western Europe at that time? How did the crusades affect relations between the west and Byzantium? Between the west and Muslims? What if anything can explain the behavior of the crusaders toward the Jews? What were some of the economic and cultural outcomes of the crusades? For a good overview, see Jonathan Riley Smith, *The First Crusade and the Idea of Crusading* (Philadelphia: University of Pennsylvania Press, 1986); and Thomas F. Madden, *A Concise History of the Crusades* (Lanham, MD: Rowman & Littlefield, 1999). For the contribution of the crusades to the cross-cultural contact and mutual enrichment of both Muslim and Christian societies, see Bernard Lewis, *The Muslim Discovery of Europe* (New York: W. W. Norton, 1982); and M. R. Menocal, *The Arabic Role in Medieval Literacy* (Philadelphia: University of Pennsylvania Press, 1990).

4. The increasing hostility in church-state relations during this period crystallized in the Investiture Conflict. The growing ambitions and territorial and jurisdictional claims of the emperor and the pope revealed the growing chasm in what was once a much more harmonious relationship. What might have given rise to this hostility? In analyzing the Investiture Conflict, compare the behaviors of Henry and Gregory. How did they each appeal to the people for recognition of their authority? What rhetorical and propagandistic devices did they use? Who actually "won" the Investiture Conflict? What does all this tell us about the underlying nature of people's notions of authority at the time? See Gerd Tellenbach, *Church, State, and Christian Society at the Time of the Investiture Conflict* (Oxford: Blackwell, 1940), an older but excellent overview that includes much useful discussion of religious worldviews, conceptions of freedom, and notions of hierarchy. Also see Brian Tierney, *The Crisis of Church and State, 1050–1300* (Englewood Cliffs, NJ: Prentice-Hall, 1964), a good introduction to vital documents.

5. The reform movement within the church reflects problems that some perceived in the church, aggravated by the church's interaction with a rapidly changing social reality. How did the church react to the reform movements? In which ways were the calls for reform accommodated? Modified? Ignored? What was the basis for the criticisms? How did this movement fit into the growing church-state conflict? An excellent source is I. S. Robinson, *The Papacy, 1073–1198: Continuity and Innovation* (Cambridge: Cambridge University Press, 1990). Also see Gerd Tellenbach, *The Church in Western Europe from the Tenth to the Twelfth Century* (Cambridge: Cambridge University Press, 1993), which details the Catholic church's religious, social, and political development through the reform movement and into the high Middle Ages.

6. The Norman conquest transformed the face of England and set the country on its course to rapid, royal consolidation. Normans shrewdly integrated their own practices and institutions with those already in place in Anglo-Saxon England. What paths did the Normans take in solidifying their conquest? How effective were they? What were the reactions of the various groups within England? See R. Allen Brown, *The Normans* (Rochester, NY: Boydell & Brewer, 1994).

7. Examine the intellectual development of western Europe as it entered the high Middle Ages. What contributed to the rapid emergence of scholasticism? Who were its proponents? enemies? Explain why. How was scholasticism received in the church and by the laity?

How exactly did it break with intellectual systems that preceded it in the west? More broadly, what accounts for the fantastic cultural enrichment that characterized the period? How was this cultural change related to the major events of the day, including the crusades, the Investiture Conflict, and the commercial economy? For many useful essays on the intellectual culture and its development, with special discussions on philosophy, science, law, history, literature, and the arts, see Robert L. Benson and Glies Constable, eds., *Renaissance and Renewal in the Twelfth Century* (Cambridge, MA: Harvard University Press, 1982). Also see John Baldwin, *The Scholastic Culture of the Middle Ages, 1000–1300* (Lexington, MA: D. C. Heath, 1971), a great introduction to the topic.

8. Students may better appreciate the profound alteration of culture in the high Middle Ages through direct examination of the products that emanated from it. Have students examine a range of such images and identify the emergent patterns of features and how they relate to the contemporary context, with its rapidly changing conceptions of humanity, God, appropriate behavior, and so on. How did the move toward elaborate aestheticism—especially in architecture—play against the simultaneous striving for religious modesty? A good introduction to the descriptive changes in architecture is Louis Grodecki, *Gothic Architecture* (New York: Harry N. Abrams, 1977).

Making Connections

1. *What were the similarities and differences between the Carolingian renaissance and twelfth-century schools?* The Carolingian renaissance was localized and short-lived in comparison with the impact of the twelfth-century schools, and there were more differences than similarities between the two periods. The Carolingian renaissance took place at the royal courts or was sponsored by royal patronage, whereas twelfth-century schools arose in cities. The Carolingian renaissance was not very interested in logic, but it was a key interest of the twelfth-century schools. The participants in the Carolingian renaissance were few by comparison with the number of masters and students involved in the twelfth-century schools.

2. *What were the similarities and differences between the powers wielded by the Carolingian kings and those wielded by twelfth-century rulers?* Both Carolingian kings and twelfth-century rulers relied on vassals to administer their territories while retaining highly developed personal powers, but they differed in that twelfth-century rulers controlled much smaller territories than Carolingian kings and had a more adversarial relationship with the papacy. And, while Carolingian kings largely depended on the wealth from their estates and warfare to support themselves, twelfth-century rulers collected taxes, received dues from their vassals, and benefited (through taxes on commerce) from the rise of cities and the expansion of trade.

Writing Assignments and Class Presentation Topics

1. Have students write a short essay on the causes and consequences of the movement to centralize church authority. Which conditions within the church and the broader society gave rise to this movement? What form did this development take? How was it related to the church's broader political, religious, and economic ambitions? This could include a discussion of the militarization of the church and what it meant for religious life and for western society. For an overview, see I. S. Robinson, *The Papacy, 1073–1198: Continuity and Innovation* (Cambridge: Cambridge University Press, 1990). See also Colin Morris, *The Papal Monarchy: The Western Church from 1050 to 1250* (Oxford: Clarendon, 1989), a sweeping study of the church's political development and centralization, its economic dealings, territorial expansion, and governmental structure.

2. Using "Four Accounts of the Crusades," in Patrick Geary, ed., *Readings in Medieval History*, 2d ed. (Peterborough, Ont.: Broadview Press, 1997), have students write a concise history of the crusades drawing on the western Christian, Byzantine, Jewish, and Muslim accounts. The purpose of this exercise is to teach students how to use primary sources; identify biases, inaccuracies, and differing perspectives; and construct a sensible history of their own using disparate available data. In addition, such an exercise will instruct students about the degree to which history is not simply one person's version of what occurred, but that a historian's or contemporary's own perspectives are embedded in his or her writing.

3. Ask students to deliver a presentation on the role of technological development in the eleventh and twelfth centuries. This presentation should include some of the major causes and consequences of technological innovation. What effects did technological change have on social relations, the economy, and so on? An excellent study of the role of technological development in economic growth and commercialization is Frances Gies and Joseph Gies, *Cathedral, Forge, and Waterwheel: Technology and Invention in the Middle Ages* (New York: HarperCollins, 1994), which includes a useful section on Asian contributions to western medieval technological development.

4. Students may be curious about what life was like for ordinary persons during this period of dramatic transformation. Assign a short writing assignment on the social history of the period. Students could approach

the topic from a variety of angles. There are several useful sources for such an assignment: Robert Fossier, *Peasant Life in the Medieval West* (Columbia: University of South Carolina Press, 1988); David Herlihy, *Medieval Households* (Cambridge, MA: Harvard University Press, 1985), which includes excellent discussions of marriage patterns, family size, sexual relations, and emotional life; and Georges Duby, ed., and Arthur Goldhammer, trans., *A History of Private Life,* vol. 2, *Revelations of the Medieval World* (Cambridge, MA: Harvard University Press, 1988), which features an interesting assessment of the concept and nature of private life.

Research Assignments

1. Ask students to research and report on the changing role and status of women in the medieval west. There are a variety of possibilities for such a paper, and a wealth of excellent sources from which to draw ideas and perspectives. Christiane Klapisch-Zuber, ed., *A History of Women,* vol. 2, *Silences of the Middle Ages* (Cambridge, MA: Harvard University Press, 1992) includes excellent essays on various topics related to women in the Middle Ages. Emilie Amt, ed., *Women's Lives in Medieval Europe: A Sourcebook* (New York: Routledge, 1993) is a collection of primary sources that is valuable for its particular focus on legal developments and legacies that shaped women's lives. Another good collection of essays appears in Patricia H. Labalme, ed., *Beyond Their Sex: Learned Women of the European Past* (New York: New York University Press, 1980). A related reading that may be of use to students is Caroline Bynum, *Jesus as Mother: Studies in the Spirituality of the High Middle Ages* (Berkeley: University of California Press, 1982). Bynum interestingly frames key social and religious institutions and practices that, she argues, manifest an increasing feminized character, and discusses the effects this had on social life.

2. Students today may not be aware of how profoundly revolutionary the introduction of logic as the central tenet of human beliefs was when it resurfaced in Europe in the twelfth century. Ask them to write a research paper on the topic discussing how logic emerged and how it transformed western philosophical systems. See Michael T. Clanchy, *Abelard: A Medieval Life* (Oxford: Blackwell, 1997), a very wide-ranging source that discusses Abelard's role as scholar, teacher, logician, theologian, and heretic, along with an extensive discussion of the social context. Also see Richard William Southern, *Scholastic Humanism and the Unification of Western Europe,* vol. 1, *Foundations* (Oxford: Blackwell, 1994), an essential text on the broader, revolutionary aspects of the scholastic movement.

Literature

Atherton, Mark, ed., *Selected Writings: Hildegard of Bingen.* 2001.

Cusimano, Richard C., trans., *Abbot Suger: The Deeds of Louis the Fat.* 1992.

Peter, Edward, ed., *The First Crusade: The Chronicle of Fulcher of Chartres and Other Source Materials.* 1998.

Radice, Betty, trans., *The Letters of Abelard and Heloise.* 1998.

Sewter, E. R., trans., *The Alexiad of Anna Comnena.* 1979.

Thompson. Augustine, trans., *Gratian: The Treatise on Laws.* 1993.

Historical Skills

Map 10.1, Medieval Trade Routes in the Eleventh and Twelfth Centuries, p. 362

This map gives students a glimpse of the "global economy" of the day and can thus be useful in discerning some general patterns that have survived or been abandoned in the years since in the development of the modern global economy. Have students identify major regional specialization and routes of trade. How might such production and trade patterns affect rulers and their policies, as well as the societies' social and economic development?

Map 10.2, The First Crusade, 1096–1098, p. 373

This map identifies the geographical disparities within Europe at the launching of the First Crusade. In light of the contemporary political situation, with the Investiture Controversy still fairly recent, what advantages might the pope have seen in launching a crusade against non-Christians outside of Europe and building sentiment against such "outsiders"? How might such activities have contributed to the slaughtering of the Jews inside Europe by the crusaders?

Taking Measure: Slaves in England, p. 383

Have students identify the geographical disparities in the English slave populations. Why were slaves less widely used in the east of lower England than in the west? This discussion could serve as an introduction to the differences between farm-based and industry-based labor.

Leo IX, p. 367

Have students consider the demeanors of the characters and discuss which messages are being conveyed. Why might such manuscript portraits have been produced at that time? What is the importance of the pope's granting of a church to the abbot in light of the contemporary context?

Bayeux Tapestry, p. 382

Have students identify the different factions of the battle scenes depicted here. What are their respective characterizations meant to convey? What is the significance of the figures along the top?

St.-Savin-sur-Gartempe and Eberbech, p. 393

Have students compare the two structures and their features. How do their characters differ? What is the significance of these differences? Which values does each building convey? Which values are common to both?

Did You Know?: Translations, p. 387

This example illustrates how cross-cultural contact allowed for the dramatic acceleration of cultural production in Europe during the twelfth century, including most of the revolutionary and influential developments in several disciplines. Why might such contact and cultural and linguistic diversity help spur innovation and lead to cultural development?

A Byzantine View of Papal Primacy, p. 370

The public debate between Anselm of Havelburg and Nicetas of Nicomedia was but the first of many through the centuries concerning the primacy and power of the bishop of Rome (otherwise known as the pope). A discussion can be based on the central issue of Nicetas's argument, that there is a difference between the office of bishop of Rome and the officeholder. Nicetas recognizes the primacy of the one but not the other. The bishop of Rome acts as though he is personally in authority over all other bishops, which is unacceptable to Nicetas because only God can occupy that position. But what also seems to be very much at issue is hurt pride: the eastern bishops resent that they are not consulted over decisions, which places them in an inferior position in relation to the western church.

OTHER BEDFORD/ST. MARTIN'S RESOURCES FOR CHAPTER 10

The following resources are available to accompany Chapter 10. Please refer to the Preface of this manual for detailed descriptions of all the ancillaries.

For Instructors

Transparencies

The following maps and images from Chapter 10 are available as full-color acetates.

- Map 10.1: Medieval Trade Routes in the Eleventh and Twelfth Centuries
- Map 10.2: The First Crusade, 1096–1098
- Mapping the West: Major Religions in the West, c. 1150
- *Bayeaux Tapestry* (chapter image, page 382)
- *Eve of Autun* (chapter image, page 391)

Instructor's Resources CD-ROM

The following maps and image from Chapter 10, as well as a chapter outline, are available on disc in both PowerPoint and jpeg formats.

- Map 10.1: Medieval Trade Routes in the Eleventh and Twelfth Centuries
- Map 10.2: The First Crusade, 1096–1098
- Mapping the West: Major Religions in the West, c. 1150
- *Bayeaux Tapestry* (chapter image, page 382)

Using the Bedford Series with The Making of the West

Available in print as well as online at bedfordstmartins.com/oconnor, this guide by Maura O'Connor, University of Cincinnati, offers practical suggestions for using *Power and the Holy in the Age of the Investiture Conflict: A Brief History with Documents* by Maureen C. Miller, in conjunction with Chapter 10 of the textbook.

For Students

Sources of The Making of the West

The following documents are available in Chapter 10 of the companion sourcebook by Katharine J. Lualdi, University of Southern Maine.

1. *Urban Charters of Jaca, Spain* (c. 1077) and *Loriss, France* (1155)
2. Emperor Henry IV and Pope Gregory VII, *Letters of the Investiture Conflict* (1076)
3. *The Anglo-Saxon Chronicle* (1085–1086)
4. Hildegard of Bingen, *Selected Writings* (Twelfth Century)

Study Guides

The print **Study Guide** and the **Online Study Guide** at bedfordstmartins.com/hunt, both by Victoria Thompson (Arizona State University) and Eric Johnson (University of California, Los Angeles), help students synthesize the material they have learned as well as practice the skills historians use to make sense of the past. The following Map, Visual, and Document activities are available for Chapter 10.

Map Activity

- Map 10.3: Mapping the West: Major Religions in the West (page 394)

Visual Activity

- *Bayeaux Tapestry* (chapter image, page 382)

Reading Historical Documents

- *A Byzantine View of the Papacy* (page 370)
- *Genoese Traders in Palestine* (page 378)

An Age of Confidence
1150–1215

CHAPTER RESOURCES

Main Chapter Topics

1. The cultural, economic, technological, and intellectual developments of the twelfth century transformed human affairs in western Europe, affecting everything from the everyday patterns of life to the conception of humankind's position in the universe. These changes, in turn, altered the political divisions of Europe and initiated a movement toward a new social order characterized by nationalistic sentiment and pride.

2. The western European kingdoms underwent rapid and significant institutionalization and bureaucratization to solidify royal authority and stabilize their societies. The pace and extent of these transformations varied due to local political conditions; it was most pronounced in England, whereas the eastern European countries slowly fragmented and drifted into instability, further weakening their positions.

3. In some cases, this institutionalization and extension of royal authority met with considerable opposition. In England, leading barons rebelled against the irresponsible use of authority by King John (r. 1199–1216), forcing him to sign Magna Carta in 1215. This document for the first time placed formal restrictions on the extent of royal power and established legal guarantees of the rights of free men, setting a precedent for later democratic, constitutional governments.

4. Prosperous courts patronized troubadour poetry in vernacular language, rather than in clerical Latin. These poems transmitted values and ideals that emphasized the importance of women and men's proper conduct toward them. Chivalry instituted new codes of behavior for the upper classes that included the courtly behavior celebrated in troubadour poetry and added a code of conduct for the battlefield, a code that distinguished the knightly class from the mercenaries who were replacing them.

5. The accelerating commercial economy produced new patterns of daily life, as more persons from the countryside moved into the cities, furthering the division of labor between societal groups. New industry gave rise to hierarchical guilds in which children first served apprenticeships for their future occupations; then as journeymen who worked for wages, and finally earned the rank of master—all coordinated by guild officers.

6. Universities began as guilds of teaching masters but came to include students and schools as well. Universities in different cities excelled in particular branches of learning—law at Bologna, medicine at Montpellier, and so on.

7. The era witnessed the emergence of several new religious movements. Some of these, such as the Franciscans, were able to win recognition by the church as monastic orders, whereas others—Albigensians or Cathars and Waldensians—were charged with heresy by a church now organized enough to define and attack heretics.

8. The rise of nationalism and the increasingly strict nature of Christian identity generated bitterness against the "others" of western European societies. Jews were particularly singled out for both social and physical harsh persecution.

Summary

By the middle of the twelfth century, rulers and institutions had a new confidence and consciousness of their place in the world. As new sources of personal and collective identification arose, new cultural forms were found to express them. Royal authority shifted from personal rule over a populace to institutional rule over a territory, thus initiating the nation-state. This institutional structure, which grew bureaucratic in many countries, enabled kings both to extend their power among their subjects and to leave their subjects at times under a smoothly running government. The kings of England

and France were particularly proficient at centralizing and institutionalizing their power.

This centralization was less pronounced in Germany, however, where political fallout from the Investiture Conflict had weakened the king and opened opportunities for ambitious princes to secure a domain of autonomy. The leading political factions—Welf and Staufer (Hohenstaufen)—in the civil wars that ensued eventually ousted the current ruler and elected as king the son of a Welf mother and a Staufer father, Frederick I Barbarossa (r. 1152–1190). Frederick required the German princes to acknowledge that their territories and near royal privileges stemmed from him and, in so doing, strengthened the king's power in Germany while coordinating kingly and princely rule. Frederick also insisted that he held the title of emperor by conquest and emphasized the sacred connotations of that office. Frederick increased his territories by marrying Beatrice of Burgundy who brought estates in Burgundy and Provence to the marriage.

Frederick continued the emperor's tradition of wrangling with the pope over Italy, whereas northern Italian communes guarded their independence. The commercial centers in Italy made it a valuable territorial prize, and northern Italy also attracted Frederick for its strategic value. By 1158, the prize belonged to Frederick who appointed magistrates (*podesta*) to govern the communes and collect taxes. These rulers, Germans with no consideration of the communes' traditions, were heavyhanded and arrogant. In 1167, the cities allied with Pope Alexander III (r. 1159–1181) to form the Lombard League and defeated Frederick at the battle of Legnano (1176), after which the emperor withdrew from Italy.

Among the powerful German princes of the day was Henry the Lion (c. 1130–1195), noted for his wideranging power that he had secured in part by marrying the daughter of England's King Henry II and Eleanor of Aquitaine. Henry expanded his territory and felt secure enough to defy the Concordat of Worms and appoint bishops. Henry developed an institutional body under his rule that was largely staffed by ministerials. His ambition was his undoing, however; Frederick confiscated the powerful prince's holdings for failure in his duty as a vassal to appear before his overlord.

England's government, the most institutionalized during this period, was based on the exceptional wealth and mixture of Anglo-Saxon and Norman traditions in the ruling structure. As in Germany, royal feuding after the death of Henry I (r. 1100–1135) allowed strong barons and churchmen to erode the king's power. Henry had no male heir, and forced the barons to swear to recognize his daughter, Matilda, as queen after his death. When the king died, the barons, fearing Matilda's husband, Geoffrey of Anjou, transferred their allegiance to Stephen of Blois (r. 1135–1154), Henry I's nephew by his sister Adela. Civil war raged, and Stephen eventually

recognized Matilda's son, Henry of Anjou, as his heir. When Henry II (r. 1154–1189) inherited the throne, he set about to tirelessly consolidate and expand his power, particularly through his marriage in 1152 to Eleanor of Aquitaine.

Eleanor, the duchess of Aquitaine, was the most powerful woman of her day, first as the wife of King Louis VII of France, then as Henry II's wife. Having met her match in the irrepressible Henry, Eleanor plotted with their eldest son to overthrow him in 1173. For this failed attempt, Henry had Eleanor imprisoned until his death in 1189.

Henry dismantled the power of the barons and appointed sheriffs to police the shires, muster military levies, and bring criminals to justice. He further boosted royal legal authority under the eyres system, in which royal justices traveled throughout the county to handle legal violations of the "king's peace"—murder, rape, and arson—as well as civil cases involving disputes over such things as inheritances, dowries, and property. The expansion of common law was praised, even as it increased royal authority and the royal treasury.

Not everyone, though, was enthusiastic about the legal reforms. King Henry met perhaps his greatest opponent in his former friend, archbishop Thomas Becket (1118–1170). Henry claimed he had the right to try the clergy and others traditionally under church protection, who were then being tried in clerical, more lenient, courts. Becket refused to concede the church's legal jurisdiction, and their struggle culminated when Becket was murdered at the hands of Henry's men. Henry, his popularity severely damaged, was forced to perform public penance.

Henry's sons Richard (r. 1189–1199) and John (r. 1199–1216) presided over an opulent monarchy with a variety of revenue sources. But Richard, having been captured on his return home from the Third Crusade, depleted the treasury, leaving John to scrounge for the money he needed to protect his French possessions. Defeated by Philip II (r. 1180–1223) at the battle of Bouvines (1214), John returned to find his barons at home in rebellion. In 1215, the barons forced him to sign Magna Carta, which put into writing the "customary" constraints on the king's power and also established legal rights for all free men. The "free men" of the day were largely members of the elite but, in time, the term came to mean all the king's subjects.

In France, Philip II (r. 1180–1223) inherited, at age fourteen, a kingdom dominated by powerful counts and England's Henry II. But Philip strengthened his position and his territory by playing his rivals against each other. He wrested Vermandois and Artois from Flanders in the 1190s; and Normandy, Anjou, Maine, Touraine, and Poitou from King John of England in 1204. Philip soon became the most powerful French ruler, keeping a firm grip on all his territories and centralizing his authority.

A contemporary chronicler dubbed him Philip Augustus ("the augmenter"). Philip Augustus instituted a new kind of French administration, run by officials who maintained written records and accounts. Like the kings of England, he relied on lesser nobles—especially knights and clerics—to serve as officers of his court, tax collectors, and overseers of the royal estates. While central governments strengthened western countries, eastern European rulers, such as Bela III (r. 1172–1196) of Hungary and Grand Prince Vsevolod III (r. 1176–1212) of Russia, did not entrench the institutions that assured stability as power transferred from one ruler to another. Even the strongly bureaucratized Byzantine Empire began to erode; its economy fell to competition from western traders, and its authority became increasingly nepotistic until the final disgrace of its conquest by western Europeans on the Fourth Crusade in 1204.

In the west, national, social organization was paralleled by the birth of a new vernacular culture. Lyric love songs written in the vernacular flourished in southern France and spread to northern France, England, Germany, and beyond. Eleanor of Acquitaine's grandfather, Duke William IX (1071–1126), was a notable composer of poems in Occitan, the language of southern France. Troubadour poets wrote sophisticated lyrics featuring intricate meters and rhyming patterns. Love, both human and sacred, was often their subject but, more broadly, these courtly songs centered on the power of women, reflecting the growing influence of many women as lords political players, and patrons of the arts. Music was part of troubadour poetry, which was typically sung by a *jongleur* ("musician").

Another topic featured widely in twelfth- and thirteenth-century vernacular literature was warfare, prominent in the long, narrative poems called chansons *de geste* ("epics"). These epics, developed out of a long oral tradition, centered on heroic deeds and provided a code of conduct for nobles and knights who were actually beginning to lose their supremacy to mercenary infantry.

Romances, such as the Arthurian poems by Chrétien de Troyes (c. 1150–1190), explored relationships between men and women. These tales often played with the resonances between religious and romantic adoration. These stories spread the code of chivalry (from the French *cheval* ["horse"]) through elite medieval society, outlining the proper role of knights as strong and brave yet refined and courteous.

The commercial revolution continued to transform life for peasants and lords alike. As business became more complex, specialists created new professions for those who maintained the wealthy lords' finances. Farmers and peasants still performed the grueling labor needed to sustain growing populations and their commercial wants and desires. Peasants were offered incentives for clearing and farming marginal land. Major irrigation projects transformed the landscape and pro-

vided more space. The rural population was growing too large to be sustained on the Carolingian-era manse—twenty peasant families might crowd onto a manse intended to support only one family. Peasants and their lords renegotiated labor services and dues, converting them into annual payments of cash. This enabled peasants to assume control of their own plots of land, even through their taxes were increased to support the royal administrations.

Guilds mirrored the move toward administrative order, developing into corporations defined by statutes and rules and engaging in political negotiations. Guilds and town governments negotiated over wages, material and product standards, working hours, and so on. Because production often involved numerous guilds, negotiations also took place between guilds. Guilds (Latin *universitas*) were organized into a hierarchy with masters at the top who controlled hiring, policies, and education; apprentices at the bottom learning their trades; and journeymen who worked for wages in the middle. Journeymen were thus free to go wherever they wished, being the west's first free and independent wage earners, neither slaves nor dependents.

Women's position in the economy declined. When occupations traditionally filled by women were moved into the cities, men began to perform many of these jobs. Still, girls were sometimes apprentices, and women did belong to guilds, although female guild officers were unheard of, and women earned far less than men for performing identical tasks. Sometimes husbands and wives worked together in the same trade.

Universities developed in central locations, such as Paris, Bologna, and Oxford, out of guilds of masters and students. Universities regulated students' discipline, scholastic proficiency, housing, and even masters' behavior. Major universities tended to specialize and attract students accordingly: law at Bologna, medicine at Montpellier and Salerno, the liberal arts and theology at Paris. Oxford taught the liberal arts and theology and, unusual for the time, science. Each school developed its own curriculum, and learning centered on lectures, rather than on expensive and rare books. Some students formed themselves into groups called "nations," which were linked to their places of origin. Each nation served to protect members, enact statutes, and elect officers. Because masters and students were considered clerics, women were excluded from universities, and men were subject to church, rather than secular, courts. On occasion, there was friction between "town" and "gown," but because of the strong drawing power and influence of scholars, they were usually able to negotiate their differences.

New religious movements in the period formed new organizations. Some were reactions to dissatisfaction with the church; some were quests for greater personal piety, and some focused on points of theology. Women were especially attracted to these new movements. Some of these movements found their niches within the church, whereas others were condemned as heretical. The most famous religious movement was led by St. Francis of Assisi (c. 1182–1226). The son of a wealthy merchant, Francis experienced visions and illnesses that led him to renounce all possessions, valorize poverty, preach penance, and perform good works. A charismatic figure, Francis attracted many followers. Franciscans or friars ("brothers") broke with monastic tradition by remaining in, rather than fleeing from, cities and by refusing to be cloistered, and were instead mendicants. A companion of Francis, Clare, founded her own order for women: the Sisters of St. Francis. But because both St. Francis and the pope disapproved of them being "of the world," they were forced behind the walls of the convent, adhering to the order of St. Benedict. The Franciscans were recognized as a religious order by the pope who was aware of Francis's tremendous popularity. Franciscans traveled throughout Europe to preach, help the ill, and beg for food.

The Beguines were women who chose a life of chastity and earned their living by tending to the ill and weaving cloth. They did not, however, take vows as nuns did and were free to leave their communities and marry if they chose. Like other contemplatives, the Beguines' religious life was essentially mystical and imbued with emotion.

When a number of movements promoted ideas that ran directly counter to church doctrine and even Scripture, the church took action. The Cathars (also known as the Albigensians), for instance, believed that the world had been created not by God, but by the devil. As if dualism (a struggle between two great forces) were not enough, the Cathars flouted social norms—forswearing wealth, sex, and meat—and elevated women to leadership positions. Followers of Waldo of Lyon (Waldensians), who anticipated St. Francis's radical poverty and preaching, were denied papal authorization, denounced, and excommunicated.

Emergent national and other collective identities also led to demarcating more clearly "outsiders" who became scapegoats and targets of persecution. The denunciation of these groups by popes and kings provided a rallying point, while also inciting militant action against these "outsiders" across borders.

A long tradition of anti-Jewish laws and customs had nevertheless allowed the Jews to integrate into society for centuries. But, forced from their lands in the eleventh century, Jews ended up in cities either as laborers, merchants, or moneylenders. Moneylending was necessary to provide the capital for commercial development, but the church prohibited Christians from usury; that is, lending money at high interest. As a result, this essential service became one of the few occupations open to Jews. Jews were nonetheless stigmatized as sinners for performing it, and debt-ridden kings and lesser men did not shrink from persecuting or even murdering Jews to avoid repayment. Economic and physical persecution was commonplace, and rulers and nobles propelled and exploited anti-Jewish sentiment to their advantage. Depictions of Jews began to feature demeaning stereotypical features, while fabricated tales of ritual Christian-child murders by Jews (the "blood libel") led to massacres of Jews via pogroms conducted throughout Europe.

Similarly, attacks against heretics grew in frequency and severity. A peaceful counter to the Cathars was the Dominican order, founded by St. Dominic (1170–1221), which, in many ways, mirrored the Franciscans but was established specifically to stem the tide of heresy by preaching. Whenever and wherever these efforts failed, the church summoned armies to crush heretics by force. The Albigensian Crusade (1209–1229) was the first crusade waged in Christian Europe that gave crusaders the same economic and spiritual benefits as any crusade waged in the Holy Land. As with many of the previous crusades, there were political dimensions at play, and the southern French princes were pitted against northern leaders who wanted to demonstrate their piety while expanding their territories.

In the Holy Land, Saladin (1138–1193), the Muslim ruler of Syria, defeated the armies of the Christian king of Jerusalem, leading to the pope's call for the Third Crusade (1189–1192), in which all the major national rulers of the day played a leading role. Thus, European political tensions were injected into the crusade, which did little but exacerbate tensions with Byzantium.

The Fourth Crusade (1202–1204) brought the previous crusade's tensions to a boil. Engaged first by the Venetians to attack their Christian trade rival Zara, the crusaders continued the Venetian agenda by attacking Constantinople. In 1204, it fell to the crusaders, who plundered the city, brutalized its inhabitants and, on the pope's instructions, remained to solidify their control. Thus ended the major period of eastern crusades, leaving countless dead and little changed politically save for the dismantling of the Byzantine Empire. The Byzantines recovered their city in 1261.

Elsewhere in Europe, however, similar campaigns were waged. Most notable was the *reconquista* in Spain in which Spain's Christian rulers united to combat and expel the Muslims to the south. The rulers of what remained of al-Andalus also faced Muslim enemies: the Almohades from North Africa. Relentlessly, the kings of Portugal, Aragon, and Castile won victory after victory in Muslim Spain. Finally, Aragon and Castile decisively defeated the Almohades at the battle of Las Navas de Tolosa (1212). In northern Europe, Christians channeled the crusading spirit into fighting the fishing, trading, and raiding peoples of the Baltic coast, whom the pope added to his list of heathens to attack. In these cases, however, local populations became Christianized, local elites prospered, and German traders, craftsmen, and colonists poured into the area, integrating the Baltic region into the western model.

Suggestions for Lecture and Discussion Topics

1. Discuss the ways the church reacted to the changing face of western culture in the twelfth and early thirteenth centuries. Which policies did it implement? Why? How did the church's crusades—both inside and outside Europe—affect the church and European society? Why was the movement to weed out heresies so vociferous? Why were some dissident orders eventually integrated into the church? Some excellent introductory sources for this discussion are Colin Morris, *The Papal Monarchy: The Western Church from 1050 to 1250* (Oxford: Clarendon, 1989); and I. S. Robinson, *The Papacy, 1073–1198: Continuity and Innovation* (Cambridge: Cambridge University Press, 1990).

2. Students would benefit greatly from an in-depth discussion of Magna Carta, a central document in the history of constitutional government that has particular relevance to the United States. Which major factors led to the drafting and signing of Magna Carta? Which interests represented the groups involved? How are these interests reflected in the document? Was it a comprehensive assurance of civil liberties? Why or why not? What were its strengths and weaknesses? J. C. Holt, *Magna Carta*, 2d ed. (Cambridge: Cambridge University Press, 1982) is one of the best-known studies of the history, context, significance, and range of this document. (The text of Magna Carta is reprinted at the back of this manual, in Appendix 4.)

3. This period had a substantial impact on women, their work, their positions in society, and their relationships. Discuss how all these things changed during the twelfth and thirteenth centuries. Which factors contributed to these changes? How did the commercial development of the economy affect women? Did the trends toward nationalism, or concurrent campaigns against outsiders, have any implications for women's status in society? Numerous sources are available for detailed discussions of these topics. See Christiane Klapisch-Zuber, ed., *A History of Women*, vol. 2, *Silences of the Middle Ages* (Cambridge, MA: Harvard University Press, 1992); and Emilie Amt, ed., *Women's Lives in Medieval Europe: A Sourcebook* (New York: Routledge, 1993). These books contain revealing readings on the development of women's status, the former through contemporary essays and the latter through primary sources. For the changing economic roles of women, see Barbara Hanawalt, ed., *Women and Work in Pre-Industrial Europe* (Bloomington: Indiana University Press, 1986), which contains descriptions of and discusses on women in diverse occupations.

4. Universities as cohesive institutions grew to prominence during this period, giving a geographical center to the flourishing scholastic movement and the developing intellectual culture generally. What role did the universities play in shaping the development of knowledge and learning? Which residual functions did the universities serve? How did they interact within their communities and contribute to the economy? How might such interaction have affected the universities? See John Baldwin, *The Scholastic Culture of the Middle Ages, 1000–1300* (Lexington, MA: D. C. Heath, 1971), which analyzes the broader development of scholasticism; and Hilde de Ridder-Symoens, ed., *A History of the University in Europe*, vol. 1, *Universities in the Middle Ages* (Cambridge: Cambridge University Press, 1992), an outstanding and comprehensive study of the topic.

5. Students may be interested in the extent to which there existed a "global economy" of sorts as far back as the twelfth century. Discuss the role of international commerce and economic development on the political, cultural, and social development of Europe. How did this pattern emerge? By which mechanisms did it function? How did it affect the nature of work? Demographics? Social interaction? Class development? A classic study is Georges Duby, *The Early Growth of the European Economy: Warriors and Peasants from the Seventh to the Twelfth Century* (Ithaca: Cornell University Press, 1978), which includes a discussion of the development of bourgeois freedom, local legal systems, the effects of monetary circulation, and international trade. See also Robert S. Lopez and Irvin W. Raymond, *Medieval Trade in the Mediterranean World* (New York: Columbia University Press, 1990), a good outline of the medieval global economy, its trade practices and mechanisms, and the development of commercial contracts and international markets.

6. The high Middle Ages was a period of fantastic technological progress that contributed greatly to the flourishing of culture and economic production. Students' appreciation of the revolutionary character of the period can be greatly enhanced by a discussion of the manner in which technological change came about, as well as its affects on society. How did technology alter the nature of work? The relationship between human beings and their environment? See Frances and Joseph Gies, *Cathedral, Forge, and Waterwheel: Technology and Invention in the Middle Ages* (New York: HarperCollins, 1994). Another excellent study is Jean Gimpel, *The Medieval Machine: The Industrial Revolution in the Middle Ages* (New York: Holt, Rinehart & Winston, 1976). Gimpel's book centers on the role of technological development in the production of energy, agriculture, and the movement into industrial production, with some discussion of its affects on environmental and labor conditions.

7. The monastic movements of the high Middle Ages were an integral component of European spiritual

and cultural life, providing an alternative to the norms of everyday work and religion. What was the nature of these alternatives as embodied in the different recognized orders of the time? Why were these movements able to integrate themselves into the Catholic orthodoxy? What was their appeal? What were their economic contributions? How did they encourage and propel cultural enrichment? For a general overview, see C. H. Lawrence, *Medieval Monasticism: Forms of Religious Life in Western Europe in the Middle Ages* (New York: Longman, 1988). Chapters 1 and 2 of Lester K. Little, *Religious Poverty and the Profit Economy in Medieval Europe* (Ithaca: Cornell University Press, 1978) discuss the transformation from a gift economy to a profit economy and its affects on people's social relations and religious thought. The book also contains interesting discussions of reactions that the religious had to commercial urbanism; monks, hermits, major orders, and heretical sects; and monasteries and their economic contributions. Finally, Part 1 of John Moorman, *A History of the Franciscan Order from Its Origins to the Year 1517* (Oxford: Clarendon, 1968) considers Francis and the development of the Franciscan order during his lifetime.

8. The anti-heretical campaigns within the church were among the most startling events of this period. Why was the church so threatened by these movements? Which alternatives did the heretical movements propose? What impact did the social context of the individual movements have on the church's decision to uproot them? What differentiated these movements from other religious dissidents who were accepted by the church? See Edward Peters, ed., *Heresy and Authority in Medieval Europe* (Philadelphia: University of Pennsylvania Press, 1980).

Making Connections

1. *What were the chief differences that separated the ideals of the religious life in the period 1150–1215 from those of the period 1050–1150?* In the latter period, many more people pursued the religious life, even though the cloistered life was repudiated and life in the world embraced. Heresy was also a new concern in the later period, and new doctrines were condemned as heretical.

2. *How did commercial interests enter into the crusading movements of the thirteenth century?* Venetian trading interests determined the course of the Fourth Crusade. In the Northern Crusades, German merchants and craftspersons followed in the wake of the crusading armies, taking over and expanding Baltic trade.

Writing Assignments and Class Presentation Topics

1. The development of chivalry and courtly love is among the most celebrated features of medieval lore.

The precise nature of these trends and ideas embodies a very rich and complex mixture of romantic idealism, conceptions of nobility and proper behavior, ideals of love and honor, and an emerging consciousness of the roles of men and women. Have students write a short essay on courtly love and chivalry from any of these perspectives, illustrating the factors that helped bring these to life and make them so popular. Why were these ethical codes, transmitted through poetry, stories, and norms of behavior, so important at the time? A good starting place is Andreas Capellanus, *The Art of Courtly Love*, John Jay Parry, trans. (New York: Columbia University Press, 1960), a veritable handbook of love among the noble classes, with a vivid portrayal of life in a medieval French court. Georges Duby's *The Chivalrous Society* (C. Postan, trans.) (Berkeley: University of California Press, 1977) is an excellent overview of chivalric development in its social context. See also Roger Boase, *The Origin and Meaning of Courtly Love: A Critical Study of European Scholarship* (Manchester: Manchester University Press, 1977). A good collection of troubadour songs is James L. Wilhelm, ed., *Lyrics of the Middle Ages: An Anthology* (New York: Garland, 1990).

2. Have students deliver a presentation on the shifting work patterns in the twelfth and thirteenth centuries. Such a presentation could include a discussion of the influence of wage-based labor, shifting production patterns, the emergence of an urban industrial economy and its affects on city dwellers and country dwellers alike, the patterns of apprenticeship, workers' mobility, the importance and influence of the corporate guild structure, and so on. Sources to help students prepare include Georges Duby, *Rural Economy and Country Life in the Medieval West* (Columbia: University of South Carolina Press, 1968). One of the classics in the field, this is an intriguing study of the economic mechanisms of the period, the process of work and wealth creation, labor practices and social relations, trade patterns and effects, class differentiation, and the evolution of wages and prices. See also M. M. Postan, *The Medieval Economy and Society: An Economic History of Britain, 1100–1500* (Berkeley: University of California Press, 1975).

3. The medieval persecution of Jews throughout Europe may strike a chord with modern students, familiar as they are with the horrors of the Nazi Holocaust. They might benefit from an assignment that asks them to trace the conditions and policies that gave rise to such practices during the Middle Ages. What was the rationale for the anti-Semitic hysteria that grew increasingly common in Europe throughout this period? How was such sentiment transmitted, exacerbated, manipulated, and exploited by those in power? What might have been some contributing factors to these feelings among the Christian populations? R. I. Moore, *The Formation of a Persecuting Society: Power and Deviance in Western Europe, 950–1250* (Oxford: Blackwell, 1987) is an outstanding

work analyzing the social conditions of Europe, particularly its developing relationship of people to authority and how it contributed to the emergence of a persecuting society, the primary victims of which were heretics, Jews, and lepers. For a history of Jews in particular, James W. Parkes, *The Jew in the Medieval Community* (London: Sepher-Hermon, 1976) is one of the best general overviews on Jews in the Europe during the Middle Ages.

4. Have students write an essay on the Third or Fourth Crusades. What were the stated objectives of these crusades? To what extent were these objectives achieved? Why? How did the internal dynamics of the crusading armies affect not only the outcome of the crusades, but also the character of western Europe? How did the crusades change relations with Byzantium and the Islamic countries? What role did the crusader states play in the Third and Fourth Crusades? Good introductory materials include Malcolm Cameron Lyons, *Saladin: The Politics of the Holy War* (Cambridge: Cambridge University Press, 1997); and Donald E. Queller and Thomas F. Madden, *The Fourth Crusade: The Capture of Constantinople* (Philadelphia: University of Pennsylvania Press, 1999).

Research Assignments

1. Assign a research paper on the institutionalization of national governments in this period. What was the general affect of this trend across Europe? How precisely was this movement carried out in England? Germany? France? What accounted for the different levels and paces of bureaucratization? For the general trends and a precise overview across Europe, see Joseph Reese Stayer, *On the Medieval Origins of the Modern State* (Princeton: Princeton University Press, 1970), a concise overview. For more detailed studies of individual governments, see H. G Richardson and G. O. Sayles, *The Governance of Medieval England from the Conquest to Magna Carta* (Edinburgh: Edinburgh University Press, 1989); Benjamin Arnold, *Princes and Territories in Medieval Germany* (New York: Cambridge University Press, 1991); and John W. Baldwin, *The Government of Philip Augustus: Foundations of French Royal Power in the High Middle Ages* (Berkeley: University of California Press, 1986).

2. Have students give a detailed analysis of family and social life. How were social and familial relations configured? How did daily life differ among peasants? Laborers? Merchants? and royalty? See Georges Duby, ed., *A History of Private Life*, vol. 2, *Revelations of the Medieval World*, Arthur Goldhammer, trans. (Cambridge, MA: Harvard University Press, 1988); Robert Fossier, *Peasant Life in the Medieval West* (Columbia: University of South Carolina Press, 1988); Michel Mollat, *The Poor in the Middle Ages: An Essay in Social History*, Arthur

Goldhammer, trans. (New Haven, CT: Yale University Press, 1986); David Herlihy, *Medieval Households* (Cambridge, MA: Harvard University Press, 1985); and Frances Gies and Joseph Gies, *Marriage and Family in the Middle Ages* (New York: HarperCollins, 1989).

Literature

Goldin, Frederick, ed., *Lyrics of the Troubadours and Trouvères: Original Texts, with Translations*. 1973.

Meirow, C. C., trans., *Otto of Freising: The Dessds of Frederick Barbarossa*. 1990.

Parry, John Jay, trans., *Andreas Capellanus: The Art of Courtly Love*. 1960.

Raffel, Burton, trans., *Chrétien de Troyes, Yvain: The Knight of the Lion*. 1987.

Terry, Patricia, trans., *The Song of Roland*. 1992.

Wilhelm, James L., trans., *Lyrics of the Middle Ages: An Anthology*. 1990.

Videos and Films

Becket (1964; Peter Glenville, dir.; with Peter O'Toole and Richard Burton). This excellent film charts the stormy relationship between King Henry II and his archbishop of Canterbury, highlighting the growing tensions between church and state during the Middle Ages.

The Lion in Winter (1968; Anthony Harvey, dir.; with Peter O'Toole and Katherine Hepburn). This excellent film nicely captures the tumultuous relationship between Henry II and his wife, Eleanor of Aquitaine, as they and their surviving three sons fight over the succession.

Cadfael (1990s; VHS/DVD). Ellis Peters's mystery novels about brother Cadfael, a twelfth-century monk in Shrewsbury, England, are dramatized in thirteen, 50-min., self-contained episodes. The episodes, especially the later ones, are historically accurate in their settings, and details about everyday life in the Middle Ages have been interwoven seamlessly into the plots.

Historical Skills

Map 11.1, Europe in the Age of Frederick Barbarossa and Henry II, 1150–1190, p. 403

Have students identify the various domains and what their relationships were to the rulers of western Europe at the time. How did France fit into these relationships? How might a French ruler in this situation endeavor to secure his own autonomy?

Map 11.2, Crusades and Anti-Heretic Campaigns, 1150–1204, p. 426

This map details the emergence of a profoundly changed Europe and is based on cultural and political patterns that would have a tremendous influence on the development of modern Europe. How might the emerging social conditions within the western European nations have contributed to the zeal for aggressive expansion at this time?

Frederick Barbarossa, p. 401

This figure depicts Frederick in several roles: military, authoritative, and paternal. How does this image project changing attitudes toward kingly authority? Which kingly values are emphasized and championed?

Hanging Thieves, p. 407

This grisly picture depicts criminal punishment during the emergence of the "king's peace." Why were the crimes, such as breaking into a shrine, considered offenses against the king? How might such a conception of criminality affect social relationships among citizens and between a citizen and the king? Why would the king resort to capital punishment for such offenses?

A Weaving Workshop, p. 417

Have students discuss the representations of work in this picture. What view of monastic life does this drawing present? Which values are represented? How do the religious connotations interact with the subject of work?

The Jew as the Other, p. 424

Have students discuss the marked differences in the depictions of Jews and Christians, including faces, hair, and clothing. What role might such a portrayal of group differences have played in medieval society? What might have given rise to these depictions of "types"? How might this image be related to the anti-Jewish sentiment and persecution in the context of the period?

Hardships of the Poll-Tax

Poll taxes were often a special hardship because they taxed individuals, not what individuals earned. Many people, like Der'a, were unable to earn enough to pay the tax. Ask students to consider Maimonides's position in society and why the authorities might have granted his request to relive Der'a. Maimonides, a Jewish scholar, has compassion for co-religionists, and carries influence with town authorities, otherwise Der'a probably would not have approached him. Minyat Zift was a Muslim town with Jewish inhabitants. In this kind of situation, it was wise for the authorities to remain on good terms with the leaders of minority groups in order to ease community tensions and keep the peace.

OTHER BEDFORD/ST. MARTIN'S RESOURCES FOR CHAPTER 11

The following resources are available to accompany Chapter 11. Please refer to the Preface of this manual for detailed descriptions of all the ancillaries.

For Instructors

Transparencies

The following maps and images from Chapter 11 are available as full-color acetates.

- Map 11.1: Europe in the Age of Frederick Barbarossa and Henry II, 1150–1190
- Map 11.2: Crusades and Anti-Heretic Campaigns, 1150–1204
- Map 11.3: The Reconquista, 1150–1212
- Mapping the West: Europe and Byzantium, c. 1215
- *Murder of Thomas Becket*
- *Frederick Barbarossa*

Instructor's Resources CD-ROM

The following maps and image from Chapter 11 as well as a chapter outline, are available on disc in both Power-Point and jpeg formats.

- Map 11.1: Europe in the Age of Frederick Barbarossa and Henry II, 1150–1190
- Map 11.2: Crusades and Anti-Heretic Campaigns, 1150–1204
- Map 11.3: The Reconquista, 1150–1212
- Mapping the West: Europe and Byzantium, c. 1215
- *Murder of Thomas Becket*

For Students

Sources of The Making of the West

The following documents are available in Chapter 11 of the companion sourcebook by Katharine J. Lualdi, University of Southern Maine:

1. *Medieval University Life* (Twelfth and Early Thirteenth Centuries)
2. Chrétien de Troyes, *Erec and Enide* (c. 1170)
3. Saints Francis and Clare of Assisi, *Selected Writings* (Thirteenth Century)
4. Thomas of Monmouth, *The Life and Miracles of St. William of Norwich* (c. 1173)
5. Illustration of Christ Casting out Synagoga (c. 1100–1120)

Study Guides

The print **Study Guide** and the **Online Study Guide** at bedfordstmartins.com/hunt, both by Victoria Thompson (Arizona State University) and Eric Johnson (University of California, Los Angeles), help students synthesize the material they have learned as well as practice the skills historians use to make sense of the past. The following Map, Visual, and Document activities are available for Chapter 11:

Map Activity

- Map 11.1: Europe in the Age of Frederick Barbarossa and Henry II

Visual Activity

- *Murder of Thomas Becket*

Reading Historical Documents

- *Frederick's Reply to the Romans*
- The Children's Crusade (1212)

The Medieval Search for Order and Harmony
1215–1320

Chapter Resources

Main Chapter Topics

1. Under Pope Innocent III (r. 1198–1216), the Roman church continued its mission of reforming society with a refocusing on both clergy and laity. The Fourth Lateran Council (1215) undertook the harmonious unification of all Christendom through the systematization of Christian ritual, law, and practice. The council also called for the extirpation of heretics. They and other marginal groups endured systematic exclusion and persecution.

2. The church integrated scholasticism into the defense of doctrines and dogmas, particularly through the work of Thomas Aquinas (c. 1225–1274). In turn, scholasticism influenced, directly or indirectly, new vernacular expressions of faith and philosophy, manifest in such works as the *Divine Comedy* of Dante Alighieri (1265–1321).

3. The arts flourished. Literature was produced in vernacular languages, rather than just Latin, which was increasingly reserved for scholarship and the church. Gothic architecture was refined, reflecting the integration of reason and faith to which scholastic philosophy aspired, while musical notation was improved to record duration of notes and rhythm.

4. Despite the church's attempts to promote unity, Christendom continued to splinter into regional factions as secular polities developed into nation-states, such as those of England and France. The emergence of parliaments and the continued institutionalization of royal authority reorganized western Europe and renewed conflict between church and state.

5. The disempowerment of the church relative to the nation-state was highlighted by the conflict between France's king Philip IV the Fair (r. 1285–1314) and Pope Boniface VIII (r. 1294–1303). Boniface's concessions to Philip and Edward I of England and the following Babylonian Captivity of the papacy in France marked the end of papal dominance in the west.

6. While the centralized nation-states ascended, Italy and Germany failed to unify, remaining divided by internal factions and small but independent states. Spain, meanwhile, was divided along religious lines with Muslims and Christians vying for power. The fragmentation of eastern European countries left them vulnerable to attack by invading Mongols.

7. Invasions by the Mongols overran the eastern periphery of Christendom but also bridged the gap between the west and the east for the first time in history. This opened a new era of intercultural exchange, including vast new trade routes, to form an integrated, Eurasian economy.

Summary

Papal power attained its apogee during the pontificate of the university-educated Innocent III (r. 1198–1216) who promoted reforms, most notably at the Fourth Lateran Council (1215). Its legislation touched nearly all aspects of society. Major legislation ("canons") included regularizing the sacraments, mandating annual confession, and declaring doctrine of transubstantiation, which stated that the bread and wine used in the Eucharist became the actual flesh and blood of Christ. This doctrine enhanced the authority of the priest who alone could perform this transformation. The church further claimed greater control over marital matters, reserving to itself judgment over marital disputes and forbidding clandestine marriages. It also declared that any child born out of an illicit relationships could not inherit his or her father's property or become priests.

The Fourth Lateran Council also distinguished members of the Christian community from nonmembers by requiring Jews to wear a distinctive insignia on their clothing. Regulations against heresy increased in severity, and secular authorities were required to punish convicted heretics. Military force, in the form of the Albigensian Crusade (1209–1229), was also invoked to combat false beliefs. The Inquisition, a pattern of inquiry used in secular criminal investigations, was adopted by the church to root out heresy; entire communities fell under suspicion. Punishments ranged from penance to imprisonment to burning at the stake.

By about 1250, Franciscans and Dominicans lived in monasteries but ventured out during the day to preach; laypersons connected themselves to the friars by becoming tertiaries who adopted many of the practices of the friars (such as frequent prayer and acts of charity) but otherwise lived in the world, tending to their families and businesses. Preaching gained popularity as the friars applied the church's teachings to daily life. Female religious fervor found an outlet in the growth of nunneries. Others lived as Beguines in independent spiritual communities rather than under the rule of an established monastic order, or simply infused their daily life with devotional practices. The Fourth Lateran Council's stress on the Eucharist inspired a bizarre form of piety among women: some highly devout women ingested only the Eucharist for food. Control over their food gave some holy women a way to gain social and religious power outside the exclusively male church hierarchy.

Scholasticism flourished in the thirteenth century. It was used to investigate all fields of knowledge, gathered in systematic compendia called *summa*. Building upon the *sic et non* technique of Abelard, the scholastics parted company with Abelard by proposing answers for the questions they posed. Among those who used Aristotelian logic to reconcile faith and reason was Albertus Magnus (c. 1200–1280), who explored natural phenomena such as motion. His student Thomas Aquinas (c. 1225–1274), the greatest of the scholastics, was a Dominican friar and professor at the University of Paris. In his majestic *Summa Theologiae* (1273), Aquinas divided each topic into questions, citing apparent support for affirmative answers, followed by arguments for the opposite position. He then reconciled the two camps in his own synthetic answer and refuted counterarguments. Aquinas's approach did not go unchallenged, and thinkers like John Duns Scotus (c. 1266–1308) argued that only divine will, not human reason, could lead humans to comprehend God.

Secular writers also sought to intertwine reason and faith, heaven and earth, God, and man; among them was the Florentine poet Dante Alighieri (1265–1321). His *Divine Comedy* (1313–1321) incorporated scholasticism, faith, and courtly love into a tale of his imagined voyage through Hell, Purgatory, and Heaven—a journey that mirrored the soul's journey to God. Written in the dialect of Florence, the *Divine Comedy* helped turn Dante's Tuscan dialect into modern Italian. Another vernacular poem, *The Romance of the Rose*, explored human and divine love,

and *The Quest for the Holy Grail* (c. 1225) turned transubstantiation into the stuff of romantic quests.

In music, the new motet (from the French *mot*, meaning "word") blended the conventions of sacred and secular polyphony. Typically, the thirteenth-century motet had two or three melody lines; the lowest was usually derived from a liturgical chant and might have been sung or played on an instrument. The other two lines might have been in Latin, French, or even both at the same time with different texts. Vernacular music was thus combined with sacred music. Franco of Cologne (c. 1280) devised the precursor of the modern system of musical notation using different notes to designate the varying durations of musical beats. Written music could now express new and complicated rhythms. In architecture, Abbot Suger inaugurated the Gothic movement in art with his design for the remodeled choir of the church of St. Denis in Paris (c. 1140). This architectural style spread rapidly across Europe. Like scholastic philosophy, Gothic architecture was intended to unite the physical and spiritual worlds in an orderly and elaborate whole through its interconnected pointed arches, flying buttresses, ribbed vaults, and stained glass. Gothic three-dimensional sculpture followed suit, depicting biblical stories and human interactions. Large churches—especially cathedrals—were community projects; townspeople and clergy alike contributed financially to their construction while local craftspersons were employed to do the actual building. Especially grand cathedrals attracted pilgrims who boosted the economy. Sculptured figures in the round decorated Gothic cathedrals; they turned, moved, and interacted with each other and, taken altogether, were often meant to be read like a scholastic summa. In Italy, the Florentine artist Giotto (1266–1337) introduced the illusion of three-dimensional depth and the intense emotion of the Gothic style into painting, combining once more the natural and divine realms.

The attempt at harmonious social unity was lost in the world of politics, however, as popes and emperors butted heads over Italy. After Frederick Barbarossa's failure to control northern Italy, the unexpected death of his son Henry VI (r. 1190–1197) left three-year-old Frederick II on the throne. The child's uncle, Duke Philip of Swabia, tried to seize control but was blocked by the German nobles and Innocent III who backed Otto of Brunswick, an enemy of Frederick's Hohenstaufen family. Innocent crowned Otto as emperor, but Otto promptly reneged on his promise to the pope to leave Italy and invaded Sicily. Innocent excommunicated Otto in 1211. The following year, Innocent tried his luck with Frederick II as emperor (r. 1212–1250), but he relentlessly vied with Innocent for Italian hegemony. Both emperor and pope saw control of Italy as being key to their power and authority. To solidify his power base, Frederick granted concessions to the German princes in 1232, making their principalities into independent states. These concessions effectively delayed

German national unification until the nineteenth century. Frederick also reformed Sicilian government and administration, and followed tradition by trying to invade Italy through Lombardy. Although the four popes who followed Innocent III excommunicated Frederick several times, the most serious confrontation came in 1245, when the pope and other churchmen at the Council of Lyon excommunicated and deposed Frederick. The emperor's vassals and subjects were absolved of their fealty and forbidden to aid him. By 1248, churchmen were preaching a crusade against Frederick, who died two years later. The German princes splintered into factions, electing two foreigners who spent their time fighting each other.

In 1273, the princes finally united and elected Rudolph Habsburg to hold the newly created and strictly ceremonial title of Holy Roman Emperor (r. 1273–1291). Rudolph's focus on his home province of Swabia, rather than on expansion into Italy, freed the Italian states to develop autonomously. The papacy impeded German control in Sicily by inviting others to rule there. When Charles of Anjou took Sicily, the Staufer (Hohenstaufen) claimants sought aid from the king of Aragon, which led to a long war between Aragon and the Anjou for the kingdom. Although the papacy eventually triumphed in the struggle between church and emperor, this overt, political maneuvering damaged its religious credibility.

France attained prominence under King Louis IX (r. 1226–1270) and his mother, Blanche of Castile (d. 1252), who ruled as regent while the king fought in two crusades. Renowned as a lawgiver, Louis based the parlement permanently at Paris, regularized judicial administration, and pursued a policy of concession to protect domestic peace. He also insisted on separate spheres of authority for church and state. Canonized in 1279, Louis IX was revered as a model of Christian chivalry and pious devotion. He had, however, instituted repressive measures against the Jews, such as prohibiting their profession of moneylending. Although involved in two unsuccessful crusades, Louis greatly enhanced the prestige of the French monarchy.

Representative parliaments across Europe developed from ad hoc advisory bodies into formalized, administrative institutions. These contained members from broad-based social categories ("orders") consisting of the clergy, the nobles, and commoners. In Spain, the parliamentary *cortes* was the first to include townsmen, albeit only those wealthy enough to engage in mounted warfare (*caballeros villanos*). In England, where Magna Carta (1215) limited monarchical power, Henry III's reign (r. 1216–1272) provided representative experience for the barons during the king's sixteen-year minority and for commoners during the brief government of Simon de Montfort, leader of a successful civil war against Henry at the end of his life. The idea of representative government grew out of these uncertain times.

The French Estates General emerged during the church-state conflict between Pope Boniface VIII (r. 1294–1303) and King Philip IV the Fair (r. 1285–1314). Philip taxed the French clergy to support his war against England's King Edward I. But Boniface opposed taxation of the clergy without papal approval and threatened French clerics who complied. Further, Boniface threatened to excommunicate kings who taxed prelates without papal permission. In response, Edward declared that clerics who refused to pay taxes would be considered outlaws, while Philip effectively closed France's borders, cutting off revenue to the Vatican. Boniface backed down, allowing clerical taxation in emergencies. To test his powers further, Philip arrested Bernard Saisset, bishop of Pamiers, on a charge of treason (he had compared the king to an owl). In 1302, Philip called together the representatives of the French "estates" (nobles, clergy, and commoners) to build support for his position that clerics were subject to secular law. This assembly developed into the Estates General, which met sporadically until 1789. When Boniface claimed in the bull Unam Sanctam (1302) that he enjoyed plenitude of power as the spiritual and temporal overlord of kings, Philip responded with a list of trumped-up charges against Boniface. Philip circulated antipapal propaganda and ultimately sent his agents to arrest Pope Boniface and bring him to France for trial. Boniface was spared that indignity, but died soon afterward. The whole episode demonstrated the limits of papal power. When, shortly thereafter, civil strife in Rome forced the papacy to move to Avignon in southern France, this Babylonian Captivity (1309 to 1378) signaled the pope's loss of control over Christendom and the separation of church and state in western Europe.

Italy developed along a different course and did not unify until the nineteenth century. Local interests asserted themselves, resulting in small-scale communal governments dominated first by nobles and then by non-nobles (called *popolo*) incorporated into craft guilds and civic organizations. These popular associations claimed a share in urban government, especially concerning taxation. But the power struggle between the popolo and the nobles exacerbated the civic factionalism that haunted the Italian city-states. In many cases, regional nobles eventually asserted themselves as *signori*, overlords who maintained order by suppressing opposition.

In eastern Europe and Russia, internal fragmentation left the indigenous populations vulnerable to Mongol invasions. Around 1200, local tribes in Mongolia coalesced under Chingiz (Genghis) Khan (c. 1162–1227) into a powerful, highly mobile military force. Their aggression brought them control of Beijing and northern China by 1215. In the 1230s, they also attacked eastern Europe under one of Chingiz's sons, Ogodei (1186–1241); Germany was spared a concentrated attack only because Ogodei died. In the 1250s, the Mongols captured

Iran, Iraq, and Syria, then pushed all the way to Egypt where they were at last stopped. Mongol tactics, involving flanking maneuvers conducted by cavalry, permitted them to dominate Russia from Kiev (captured in 1240) for two centuries, an empire later called the Golden Horde. The Mongols adopted local administrative practices and left many of the old institutions in place. Russian princes were allowed to rule their territories if they paid tribute, and the Orthodox church was tolerated and exempted from taxation.

The Mongols opened China to westerners, who came to trade, spread Christianity, and forge alliances against the Muslims. The accounts of the Venetian trader Marco Polo (1254–1324) stimulated widespread interest in Asia. These contacts between east and west motivated further European explorations that would reach the Americas.

Suggestions for Lecture and Discussion Topics

1. Innocent III's pontificate represented the apex of papal authority in the medieval west. His ambitious program for the renewal of western Christendom, much of it included in the decrees of the Fourth Lateran Council, addressed all facets of society. Even though he was not the first pope to assert such power, in many ways he was the most effective in having his message heeded. Discuss the factors that may have enabled him to succeed where earlier and later popes failed. A very comprehensive collection of essays that examines many facets of Innocent's pontificate and its historical context is John C. Moore, et al., eds., *Pope Innocent III and His World* (Aldershot, Eng.: Ashgate, 1999). For a recent biography that stresses the political and legal dimensions of Innocent's career, see Jane Sayers, *Innocent III: Leader of Europe, 1198–1216* (Harlow, Eng.: Addison-Wesley Longman, 1993). An older collection of short essays that debate the merits of Innocent's papacy is James Powell, ed., *Innocent III: Vicar of Christ or Lord of the World?* 2d ed. (Washington, DC: Catholic University of America, 1994). Key primary sources can be found in Brian Tierney, ed., *The Crisis of Church and State: 1050–1300*, rpt. ed. (Toronto: University of Toronto Press, 1994).

2. France's early cohesion into a nation-state and Germany's failure to unify form an interesting contrast in the political fates of two important regions. What were the political and social conditions in each that contributed to their differing political outcomes? Besides the biographies of Louis IX and Frederick II listed in the chapter bibliography, the essays in William Tronzo, ed., *Intellectual Life at the Court of Frederick II Hohenstaufen* (New Haven, CT: Yale University Press, 1998) are useful for researching Germany. For an innovative analysis of how the symbolism of medieval French monarchy contributed to the growing sense of French nationalism, see

Colette Beaune, *The Birth of an Ideology: Myths and Symbols of Nation in Late-Medieval France* (Berkeley: University of California Press, 1991).

3. As European contact with the rest of the world increased and nation-states centralized, the social marginalization of certain groups within Europe was also on the rise. Heretics, Jews, and prostitutes all became the focus of exclusionary legislation, official prosecution, and even mob violence. Discuss with students how these phenomena might be related. Two highly influential studies on the topic are Norman Cohn, *Europe's Inner Demons: The Demonization of Christians in Medieval Christendom*, rev. ed. (Chicago: University of Chicago Press, and R. I. Moore, *The Formation of a Persecuting Society* (Oxford: Blackwell, 1990). Several excellent studies supplement them, particularly David Nirenberg, *Communities of Violence: Persecution of Minorities in the Middle Ages* (Princeton: Princeton University Press, 1996), which concentrates on France and Spain.

4. During this period, popular governments emerged in the west for the first time since the end of the Roman republic. Examine this trend and the reasons for the rise of the Italian communal city-states, including growing internationalism, commercialism, and the spread of secular education. Good introductions are provided by Daniel Waley, *The Italian City-Republics* (Harlow, Eng.: Addison-Wesley Longman, 1988); and Giovanni Tobacco, *The Struggle for Power in Medieval Italy* (New Haven, CT: Yale University Press, 1990). For a detailed account of culture, society, and economic life in late-medieval Italy, see John Larner, *Italy in the Age of Dante and Petrarch, 1216–1380* (White Plains, NY: Longman, 1980). A 1995 collection of essays highlighting the various dimensions of state-building in Italy, including legal and fiscal aspects, is Julius Kirshner, ed., *The Origins of the State in Italy, 1300–1600* (Chicago: University of Chicago Press, 1995).

5. Scholars have often viewed the tall Gothic cathedrals as architectural manifestations of the intellectual search for harmony that was expressed philosophically in scholasticism. Debate the merits of this interpretation. A beautifully written, highly personal version of this approach can be found in Henry Adams, *Mont Saint Michel and Chartres*, rpt ed. (Princeton: Princeton University Press, 1981). A modern assessment of how the innovations of Gothic art were perceived in the high Middle Ages is Michael Camille, *Gothic Art: Glorious Visions* (New York: Harry N. Abrams, 1996). For information on the construction techniques used in building the cathedrals, see John Fitchen, *The Construction of the Gothic Cathedrals* (Chicago: University of Chicago Press, 1981).

6. Magna Carta and the nascent national parliaments can be viewed as precursors of modern, western political ideals and institutions. Talk about the development of the division of power between king and parliament and its

contemporary analogues in the doctrines of the separation of powers and of individual rights. How did these institutions serve to balance the array of political interests present in western European societies? What were their shortcomings as "representative" institutions? The development of constitutional government in medieval England has received much attention. Two important works are H. G. Richardson and G. O. Sayles, *The English Parliament in the Middle Ages* (Rio Grande, OH: Hambledon Press, 1981); and J. R. Lander, *The Limitations of English Monarchy in the Later Middle Ages* (Toronto: University of Toronto Press, 1989). For France, see Joseph Strayer, *The Reign of Philip the Fair* (Princeton: Princeton University Press, 1980); and John Baldwin, *The Government of Philip Augustus: Foundations of French Royal Power in the Middle Ages* (Berkeley: University of California Press, 1991). For Spain, see Joseph O'Callaghan, *The Cortes of Castile-León, 1188–1350* (Philadelphia: University of Pennsylvania Press, 1989). For Germany, see Benjamin Arnold, *Princes and Territories in Medieval Germany* (Cambridge: Cambridge University Press, 1991). On developments in medieval political theory and their importance for succeeding centuries, see Brian Tierney, *Religion, Law, and the Growth of Constitutional Thought, 1150–1650* (Cambridge: Cambridge University Press, 1982); and James Blythe, *Ideal Government and the Mixed Constitution in the Middle Ages* (Princeton: Princeton University Press, 1992).

7. Another fundamental, scholarly interpretation of the period concerns the courtly love tradition as the source for modern notions about romantic love. A central investigation of the topic is Denis de Rougemont, *Love in the Western World* (Princeton: Princeton University Press, 1983). Students frequently view the troubadour's idealization of women as reflecting a gain in women's social status. And yet this idea might have been double-edged because placing a lady on a pedestal may have also substituted one set of restrictive, normative assumptions for another. On this theme, see R. Howard Bloch, *Medieval Misogyny and the Invention of Western Romantic Love* (Chicago: University of Chicago Press, 1991). On the social and political context for the courtly tradition, see Linda Paterson, *The World of the Troubadours: Medieval Occitan Society, c. 1100–c. 1300* (Cambridge: Cambridge University Press, 1995). The courtly love literature found an earthy analogue in the French fabliaux and numerous studies investigate their import for understanding gender roles in high medieval French society. Among the studies discussing this literature are Norris Lacy, *Reading Fabliaux* (New York: Garland, 1993); and E. Jane Burns's controversial *Bodytalk: When Women Speak in Old French Literature* (Philadelphia: University of Pennsylvania Press, 1993).

8. The rise of the Cathar heresy signaled spreading discontent with the Catholic church at the height of its greatest power under Innocent III. Discuss the content of this heresy, its similarity to earlier heretical movements such as Manichaeanism, and the church's often highly repressive moves to contain it, including crusade and inquisitorial prosecution. In addition to Ladurie's Montaillou, see Michael Costen, *The Cathars and the Albigensian Crusade* (Manchester: Manchester University Press, 1997). A standard overview of medieval heresy is Malcolm Lambert, *Medieval Heresy: Popular Movements from Bogomil to Hus* (New York: Holmes & Meier, 1977).

Making Historical Connections

1. *Why was Innocent III more successful than Boniface VIII in carrying out his objectives?* Innocent III was a proactive pope, whereas Boniface VIII was a reactive one. Aware of the need for consensus, Innocent used a council to promulgate his views. In addition, kings were not as powerful in Innocent's day as they were in Boniface's time.

2. *What impact did the Mongolian invasions have on the medieval economy?* Devastating to eastern Europe and Russia, the invasions ultimately brought about new prosperity as the Mongolians welcomed European traders. As a result, China became part of a wider economy that included Europe and the Muslim world.

Writing Assignments and Class Presentation Topics

1. The late-thirteenth to early-fourteenth centuries were a time of great international travelers, some of whose accounts still survive. An examination of the insights and prejudices these writers express can help students to appreciate just how international the world was and also to discern the dynamics of cultural confrontations that occurred, even when travelers explored regions dominated by their own religious and political traditions. Wonderful paper or presentation topics can be based on the observations of Ibn Battuta (a Muslim) concerning his travels in Africa, and on those of Marco Polo (an Italian) concerning China. Recent editions of their works are *Ibn Battuta in Black Africa* (Williston, VT: Markus Wiener, 1994) and *The Travels of Marco Polo* (London: Wordsworth, 1997). Students can also compare these two authors with the twelfth-century Jewish travel writer, Benjamin of Tudela, whose journeys are discussed in *The World of Benjamin of Tudela: A Medieval Mediterranean Travelogue* (Madison, NJ: Fairleigh Dickinson University Press, 1995).

2. The Inquisition usually generates great interest among students. Have them outline the inquisitorial procedures that they find in the *Inquisition Manual of Bernard Gui*, available with additional primary sources in the *Internet Medieval Sourcebook*. You can also ask

students to reconstruct the historical events that lay behind the records of an Inquisition trial, such as that of Beatrice de Planissoles. The transcripts of that investigation are reproduced in Patrick Geary, *Readings in Medieval History*, 2d ed. (Peterborough, Ont.: Broadview, 1997).

3. Despite its highly challenging content, the thoughts of Thomas Aquinas can lead students to confront the power and limits of applying logic to theological questions. What do the documents reveal about the state of empirical inquiry in the west? The parameters of the questions that scholastics asked? The ability of the church to adapt to new intellectual paradigms? The section on "Intellectual Life" of the *Internet Medieval Sourcebook* gives excerpts from Aquinas's works, as well as from those of earlier philosophers, which students can access and use for comparative essays.

4. Ask students to evaluate how "courtly" the courtly love tradition was. How much did it affect ordinary society? To what extent was it restricted to the amusements of the elites? Students can write brief analyses of troubadour poems, short romances, or treatises on courtly love. They can also compare selections, perhaps noting similarities and differences between troubadour poems penned by male and female authors. A recent, bilingual selection of poems by female troubadour poets is Sarah White and Laurie Shepard, *Songs of the Women Troubadours* (New York: Garland, 2000). For treatises on courtly love, see Andreas Cappellanus, *Art of Courtly Love*, John Jay Perry, trans. (New York: Columbia University Press, 1990); a late-twelfth-century work that can be compared to Juan Ruiz (archpriest of Hita), is Elizabeth Drayson McDonald, trans., *The Book of Good Love* (New York: Everyman, 1999) from the fourteenth century.

5. Have students investigate the development of the international Gothic style and its spread throughout medieval Europe. Few movements in history have so skillfully combined engineering prowess, artistic expression, and intellectual content. There are extensive visual and textual resources available on the Internet. Also of interest is David Macaulay's *Cathedral* (New York: Houghton Mifflin, 1985), available on video, which demonstrates the construction of the Gothic cathedral Notre Dame de Beaulieu.

6. The propaganda war between Philip the Fair and Boniface VIII dramatically illustrates how tensions between church and state came to a head at the turn of the fourteenth century. Students can trace the escalation of the conflict by investigating the alternating claims to universal authority and accusations launched by the two; students should also consider the role that public opinion played in the outcome of the conflict. Key primary sources and secondary commentaries are contained in Charles Wood, ed., *Philip the Fair and Boniface VIII: State vs. Papacy*, 2d ed. (Melbourne, FL: Krieger, 1976).

7. Despite its magnificent poetry and biting commentary on contemporary events, Dante's *Divine Comedy* is a difficult text for the uninitiated to comprehend. However, with a little guidance, students often find the landscape of the Inferno to be fascinating, especially because they can read the poem in two excellent translations: John D. Sinclair (Oxford: Oxford University Press, 1990); and Robert Pinsky (New York: Farrar, Straus & Giroux, 1994).

Research Assignments

1. Have students investigate the cultural history of the Mongols, the creation of the Yuan Mongol dynasty in China, or the rule of the Golden Horde. Were they in fact savage, nomadic horsemen, as they are often deemed in the popular imagination? In which ways did they adapt to the societies of their subject territories? What were their contacts like with the powers of the west? The earliest major Mongolian source is Paul Kahn's translation of the thirteenth century's *Secret History of the Mongols* (Boston: Cheng & Tsui, 1999). A good, general introduction is David Morgan, *The Mongols* (Oxford: Blackwell, 1986). Two scholarly biographies of the most famous of the Mongol rulers are: Morris Rossabi, *Khubilai Khan: His Life and Times* (Berkeley: University of California, 1988); and Paul Ratchnevsky, *Genghis Khan: His Life and Legacy* (Oxford: Blackwell, 1993). For Mongolian conquest and imperial rule, see John Joseph Saunders, *The History of the Mongol Conquests*, rpt. ed. (Philadelphia: University of Pennsylvania Press, 2001); and Charles J. Halperin, *Russia and the Golden Horde: The Mongol Impact on Medieval Russian History* (Bloomington: Indiana University Press, 1987).

2. The cult of the Virgin Mary and the celebration of the lady in the courtly love tradition signaled new ways of conceptualizing female nature and the status of women. Ask students to explore how such changes were manifested in the devotional practices of high medieval Christianity in the west. The works of Caroline Bynum are central to any exploration of this topic, especially *Holy Feast and Holy Fast: The Religious Significance of Food to Medieval Women* (Berkeley: University of California Press, 1987); and *Jesus as Mother: Studies in the Spirituality of the High Middle Ages* (Berkeley: University of California Press, 1982). A different perspective on female devotional practices and food is presented in Rudolph Bell, *Holy Anorexia* (Chicago: University of Chicago Press, 1985). On women and mysticism, see the essays in Ulrike Wiethaus, ed., *Maps of Flesh and Light: The Religious Experience of Medieval Women Mystics* (Syracuse: Syracuse University Press, 1993).

3. The study of medieval women has generated a corresponding and growing interest in changing definitions

of masculinity in the high Middle Ages, especially as it relates to the development of courtly romance and troubadour poetry. A fundamental source for a range of perspectives on the topic is Clare Lees, ed., *Medieval Masculinities: Regarding Men in the Middle Ages* (Minneapolis: University of Minnesota Press, 1994). See also Jeffrey Jerome Cohen and Bonnie Wheeler, eds., *Becoming Male in the Middle Ages* (New York: Garland Publishing, 1997).

4. The opening of trade routes and the push to missionize the east indicate that cross-cultural contacts were occurring at a rapid rate during this period. Students might want to investigate the international economy and this world of exploration that occurred before the more well-known "Age of Exploration." A substantial collection of primary documents is Robert Lopez and Irving Raymond, eds., *Medieval Trade in the Mediterranean World* (New York: Columbia University Press, 1990). A broad perspective of cross-cultural interactions prior to Columbus is Jerry Bentley, *Old World Encounters: Cross-Cultural Contacts and Exchanges in Pre-Modern Times* (Oxford: Oxford University Press, 1993).

5. There is a wealth of information on everyday life for the Medieval period, and students can be asked to research any number of subjects, including food, armory, clothing, medicine, children, music, and so on. Students can present their findings in class, thus collectively forming a picture of what life, in all of its varieties, was like in the thirteenth and early fourteenth centuries. Students can begin with the work of Joseph and Frances Gies, who have published widely on the Middle Ages.

Literature

Horgen, Frances, trans., *Guillaume De Lorris and Jean De Meun: The Romance of the Rose*. 1999.
Latham, Ronald, trans., *The Travels of Marco Polo*. 1958.
Matarasso, Pauline Maud, ed., *The Quest of the Holy Grail*. 1969.
Shaw, M. R. B., trans., *Jean de Joinville and Geoffroy de Villehardouin: Chronicles of the Crusade*. 1963.
Singleton, Charles S., trans., *The Divine Comedy*. 1970.

Films and Videos

Robin Hood (1991; John Irvin, dir.; with Patrick Bergen and Uma Thurman). This is a largely faithful retelling of the Robin Hood story in a fairly accurate setting.
Braveheart (1995; Mel Gibson, dir.; with Mel Gibson and Sophie Marceau). This film is a largely inaccurate depiction of the life of thirteenth-century Scotsman, William Wallace.

Historical Skills

Map 12.1, Europe in the Time of Frederick II, r. 1212–1250, p. 451

What made the Italian peninsula such a coveted area? Why would the papacy have felt consistently threatened by foreign powers? Ask students to identify the territorial anomalies on this map, given the general trend toward the consolidation of regions under the control of a handful of major political powers.

Map 12.3, The Mongol Invasions to 1259, p. 459

Have students identify the Mongols' routes of conquest in the order in which they occurred. What are the implications of the fact that this process, which integrated disparate cultures and tied economies together, was achieved by violent conquest? How might this conquest have influenced cultural exchange and notions of collective identities?

Mapping the West: Europe c. 1320, p. 460

Ask students to see how many individual nation-states and other political entities they can identify on this map. What was the likely impact of the increased number of relatively small, politically autonomous states for the economic reality of the medieval west? What was its likely effect on political ideologies and foreign political relations? What was the significance of western empires, such as the Holy Roman and Byzantine empires, when their actual geographical dimensions were relatively modest in comparison to the former Roman, Persian, or Carolingian empires?

Taking Measure: Sentences Imposed by an Inquisitor, 1308–1323, p. 439

Ask students to discuss their perceptions of the effectiveness of the various modes of punishment meted out by Gui's tribunal. What was the motive for imposing some penalties (prison, burning) posthumously? Do students agree with scholars who conclude that 50 pronouncements of burning at the stake, out of a total 633 punishments, means that the "Inquisition was not particularly harsh"? What might account for the large percentage of prison sentences, especially when imprisonment was not a routine method of punishment? What additional data might help with the interpretation of the statistics presented in this table?

Christianizing Aristotle, p. 435

This manuscript illumination reflects the Catholic church's attempt to adapt the newly introduced pagan learning—especially the works of Aristotle—that reinvigorated intellectual life during this period. What "Christianizing" effect, if any, did placing a depiction of a Christian religious ceremony have on the reader's perception of this classical text? (In other words, did the picture really Christianize the content of the text in the reader's mind?) What does the juxtaposition of pagan text and Christian illumination suggest about the necessity of the church's accommodating classical thought into its curriculum? Is there an irony associated with depicting the Christian requiem mass for the dead in a section of Aristotle's works contained under the heading *De Vita* ("On Life")?

Host Mold, p. 437

After the Fourth Lateran Council's declaration of the doctrine of the transsubstantiation of the Eucharist, the adoration of the host gained momentum. What function might the impression of religious scenes onto the surface of the host have served? Might the increased veneration of the host have fueled criticism of the church? In which ways did this doctrine elevate the role of the priest and perhaps alienate the ordinary believer? Alternatively, might the idea that the communicant actually received the physical presence of Christ during the taking of the host have strengthened the faith of the laity, especially women?

Boniface VIII, p. 457

As the caption suggests, this sculpture highlights one of the functions of art, especially political art: it stresses the difference between the mere representation of the actual subject depicted (in this case, Pope Boniface) and the expression of certain ideas. Why would fostering an image that masks the actual physical attributes of the subject be important to rulers? Might the similarity between this portrayal of Boniface and that of Innocent III (p. 436) be intentional, especially given Boniface's papal ambitions?

The Debate between Reason and the Lover

Jean de Meun's portion of the *Roman de la Rose* (*Romance of the Rose*) explores a philosophical consideration of love, as this passage demonstrates. Students can consider the writer's definition of *reason* and *love*, and how women fit into this picture. There is nothing dispassionate about Reason's response, and this keeps it from being "reasonable." Reason epitomizes "Eros" (physical love), which contrasts unfavorably with "agape" (divine love), the kind of love that transcends the physical and is therefore the highest kind of love. In Meun's view, the affection of women is fleeting and superficial, concerned only with the physical.

OTHER BEDFORD/ST. MARTIN'S RESOURCES FOR CHAPTER 12

The following resources are available to accompany Chapter 12. Please refer to the Preface of this manual for detailed descriptions of all the ancillaries.

For Instructors

Transparencies

The following maps and images from Chapter 12 are available as full-color acetates.

- Map 12.1: Europe in the Time of Frederick II, r. 1212–1250
- Map 12.2: France under Louis IX, r. 1226–1270
- Map 12.3: The Mongol Invasions, to 1259
- Mapping the West: Europe, c. 1320
- *Louis IX & Blanche of Castile*
- *The Last Judgment*

Instructor's Resources CD-ROM

The following maps and image from Chapter 12, as well as a chapter outline, are available on disc in both PowerPoint and jpeg formats.

- Map 12.1: Europe in the Time of Frederick II, r. 1212–1250
- Map 12.2: France under Louis IX, r. 1226–1270
- Map 12.3: The Mongol Invasions, to 1259
- Mapping the West: Europe, c. 1320
- *Louis IX & Blanche of Castile*

For Students

Sources of The Making of the West

The following documents are available in Chapter 12 of the companion sourcebook by Katharine J. Lualdi, University of Southern Maine.

1. Abbot Suger, *The Abbey Church of St.-Denis* (1144)
2. Hadewijch of Brabant, *Letters and Poems of a Female Mystic* (1220–1240)
3. Dante Alighieri, *Human and Divine Love* (Late Thirteenth–Early Fourteenth Centuries)
4. Nikonian Chronicle, Russia: The West and the Golden Horde *(1241–1381)*

Study Guides

The print **Study Guide** and the **Online Study Guide** at
bedfordstmartins.com/hunt, both by Victoria Thompson (Arizona State University) and Eric Johnson (University of California, Los Angeles), help students synthesize the material they have learned as well as practice the skills historians use to make sense of the past. The following Map, Visual, and Document activities are available for Chapter 12.

Map Activity

- Map 12.1: Europe in the Time of Frederick II, r. 1212–1250

Visual Activity

- *Louis IX & Blanche of Castile*

Reading Historical Documents

- The Debate between Reason and the Lover
- Municipal Legislation at Pisa (1286)

The Crisis of Late Medieval Society
1320–1430

CHAPTER RESOURCES

Main Chapter Topics

1. The population growth and economic expansion of Europe during the Middle Ages collapsed in the fourteenth century under a series of overlapping economic, demographic, political, and religious crises.

2. The Hundred Years' War caused widespread destruction in France and Burgundy, but it also created a new sense of nationalism and accelerated changes in the nature of warfare with the advent of cannons and the use of mercenaries. France and Burgundy emerged at the end of the war as powerful rivals, while England entered into civil war at home.

3. Social, economic, and political transformations—such as the decline of the wool industry—caused social upheaval, violent persecution of Jews, and peasant and worker revolts across Europe.

4. The Holy Roman Empire fragmented further as power shifted eastward and the communes of the Alps formed the independent Swiss Confederation. Lithuania and Poland united under one crown, Muslim influence in the Iberian peninsula declined, and the Ottoman Empire expanded westward into Europe.

5. The loss of up to one-half the population during the Black Death altered the dynamics of feudalism and decreased overall production, but increased individual wealth and the demand for luxury goods. As grain prices fell, farmers diversified their crops, which resulted in a better overall diet for Europeans. The Black Death also fueled further persecution of the Jews.

6. The Avignon papacy extended its powers and curia, but the Great Schism split the papacy between Avignon and Rome from 1378 to 1415. Popular religious groups, such as the Lollards and Hussites (or Taborites), questioned the conduct of the church hierarchy, the validity of church teachings, and the nature of the church itself.

7. The household and home were focal points in the lives of most medieval persons. As trade and commerce declined, merchants invested their resources into luxury goods. The middle class prospered, with women working side by side with their husbands, but there was also a large, prominent underclass where women especially were exploited. Vernacular literature, produced by middle-class writers for an educated laity, became popular. There was a parallel revival in classical literature.

Summary

Between 1320 and 1430, the tenuous medieval order that had developed throughout the twelfth and thirteenth centuries collapsed in the face of political, demographic, religious, social, and economic crises.

The agrarian crisis that followed in the wake of the plague helped to alter the mechanisms of warfare. As food prices declined, land ownership became less profitable and the nobility—knights especially—became mercenary soldiers fighting for profit. Knightly codes of conduct were increasingly emphasized, perhaps to disguise the cynical reality of warfare for personal gain. Arthurian romances became vogue and, in 1344, Edward III of England created the Order of the Garter to revive the idea of chivalry. By the end of the fourteenth century, in the wake of new military technologies, well-equipped forces counted more than valor on the battlefield, and commoners often joined the ranks. Chivalry and warfare remained intimately linked during and after the Hundred Years' War but, in practical terms, winning rather than acquiring honor became the ultimate goal.

Political crises took forms that differed from region to region. For England and France, the crisis was the Hundred Years' War. Started in 1337 as a dynastic conflict between Philip IV of France (who claimed the English fief of Aquitaine) and Edward III of England (who claimed the French crown in response), the Hundred Years' War spread havoc far beyond the contested duchy. Captured nobles and knights were well treated, following the conventions of chivalry, but commoners were brutally slaughtered. Although the English won important battles, Agincourt (1415) being among the most notable, they were greatly outnumbered by the French. As French and English fought, Burgundy altered its allegiance at critical moments during the conflict. The war witnessed innovations in tactics and weaponry, which further changed warfare. English yeomen used longbows that decimated infantry and cavalry. Cannons were also becoming common as siege weapons. Larger armies consisting of commoners who had to be paid, and cannons all increased the cost of the war, which increased taxes and stirred discontent. The efficacy of the aristocracy in actual combat decreased, yet the French were slower than the English to arm their peasantry.

In 1429, Joan of Arc ("The Maid"), a sixteen-year-old peasant girl, had a vision that she was destined to save France. Dressed in men's armor, Joan rode at the head of the French army to break the siege at Orléans. The Maid also persuaded the dauphin to venture into Burgundian territory to be anointed and crowned King Charles VII at Rheims. But her troops began to lose faith in her when Joan could not deliver on her promise to take Paris. When Joan was captured by the Burgundians (1430), Charles did little to save her, even though she may have helped to turn the tide of the war in his favor. Joan was tried and burned at the stake (1431) by Charles's enemies, the Burgundians and English, who declared her a heretic. Within two decades of her death, the English were driven from French soil. By 1453, nearly all the European territories that the English had claimed were lost to the French. Joan's sentence was rescinded by a second trial organized by the French, and she was canonized and declared the patron saint of France (1920).

The Hundred Years' War exacerbated the demographic and economic crises of the fourteenth century; the countryside was torn apart by pillage and warfare, and fields remained uncultivated. The war also resulted in a change in the political landscape; France and Burgundy emerged as strong rivals, while England grew weaker through civil war at home. Finally, the war prevented a quick resolution to the spiritual crises of this period.

Social unrest also followed in the wake of the Hundred Years' War. The Jacquerie rebellion of 1358 began in Paris as a movement for political empowerment. Merchant Étienne Marcel led the Parisians (who had lost patience with heavy taxes), the nobility, and vicious mercenaries. A political struggle between commoners and nobles surged into a massive uprising and savage class war. Commoners destroyed manor houses and castles near Paris, sometimes killing entire noble families. The nobility put down the uprising with equal savagery. In

England, rebellion (the Peasants' Revolt) broke out in 1381 over a poll tax imposed in 1377 to raise money for the war. This revolt quickly gathered steam among non-peasant members and soon extended to the urban workers of London. Richard II promised reforms, but rescinded these after the revolt had been brutally put down. Popular uprisings shook the Low Countries, especially Flanders, the most densely urbanized region of Europe. Flanders was a French fief, but workers, dependent upon English wool, opposed their count's pro-French policy. Beginning in 1338, Ghent was in rebellion and, in time, fielded an army. They suffered a disastrous defeat (1382), but were not completely subdued until the fifteenth century.

There were uprisings in Italian cities as well. In 1347, after a failed mission to Avignon to get the pope to return to St. Peter's, Rome's Cola di Rienzo was hailed by the citizens as "tribune of the people." In the ensuing uprising (1347–1354), the nobility fled the city, and Rienzo and his cohorts tried to remake the city into the image of classical Roman republicanism. The Roman nobility ultimately suppressed the uprising. In 1378, in Florence, as the wool industry declined and unemployment became prolific, the Ciompi (lower classes) revolted against the regime. Joined by artisans and merchants, they demanded a role in government and took to the streets, burning the homes of the wealthy, and insisting on the right to form a guild. Alarmed at this radical turn of events, the guild artisans turned against their fellow workers, defeated them, and restored the old regime. The Ciompi continued to plot worker revolts into the 1380s.

While England and France struggled, the Holy Roman Empire fragmented. With the succession of three emperors from the house of Luxembourg—Charles IV (r. 1347–1378), Wenceslas (r. 1378–1400), and Sigismund (r. 1410–1437)—power shifted from the Rhineland to the Luxembourg power base in east central Europe, and Prague became the imperial capital. German institutions became more closely allied with eastern rather than western Europe. The first universities in German territories were established in Prague (1348) and Vienna 1365. The Golden Bull (1356) required the German king to be chosen by seven electors: the archbishops of Mainz, Cologne, and Trier; and the king of Bohemia, the elector of Saxony; the count of the Palatine; and the Margrave of Brandenburg. Often, as was the case of Charles IV, regional nobility would not recognize the emperor's authority. Urban economic confederations, such as the Swabian League and Hanseatic League, were at the forefront of economic growth, but never formed independent communes. In the Alps, self-governing communes linked together under the Swiss Confederation, removed themselves from imperial authority, and defeated a Habsburg army in 1315. The Swiss continued to acquire new member communes and to defeat German armies sent against them. In contrast to Germany, Poland and Lithuania expanded, prospered, and wrested territories from Russia and the Holy Roman Empire. In 1386, the previously pagan Lithuanian prince Jogaila (also spelled Jagiello) accepted Roman Catholic baptism, married the young queen of Poland, and later assumed the Polish crown. Under the Jagiellonian dynasty, Catholicism and Polish culture marked the upper classes, whereas most Lithuanian villagers remained pagans for several centuries.

The Iberian peninsula encompassed five Christian kingdoms: Portugal, Castile, Navarre, Aragon, and Catalonia; and one Muslim state: Granada. All had religiously and ethnically diverse populations but, at the end of the fourteenth century, pogroms against Jews and Muslims became more common; Muslims were gradually driven out of urban areas and toward the south. Others were captured by Castilian armies and worked as slaves on large Christian estates (*latifundia*) that were given to the crusading orders, the church, or noble families. Jews congregated in urban centers, practicing trades and even serving in the Castilian administration but, in 1391, there was an extreme backlash against Jews. Of the 200,000 Jews who were rounded up, half converted to save themselves, while 25,000 either fled to Portugal and Grenada or were murdered.

Under Osman I (r. 1280–1324) and his son Orhan Gazi (r. 1324–1359), the Ottoman Empire expanded into the Balkans. Murat I (r. 1360–1389) solidified these gains by making Constantinople a vassal state and defeating the Hungarians and Serbs at Maritsa River in 1364. By the end of the fourteenth century, the Ottomans threatened Europe and the remnants of the Byzantine Empire, now reduced to the city of Constantinople. The Ottomans exploited Christian disunity and even incorporated Christians into its rule. Christian slave children (also known as "Janissaries") were raised by the sultan as Muslims, Christian women became part of the sultan's harem, and Christian princes who acknowledged the sultan as their overlord extended their services to him. Further, existing religious and social structures in conquered Christian areas were left intact as long as the population recognized Ottoman overlordship and paid taxes. Although there were calls for another crusade, with the Hundred Years' War in progress, Europe was in no condition to respond in a concerted effort to the Ottoman menace.

In 1300, the population of Europe had increased to a level that was barely sustainable. All arable land was already under cultivation. The ever-growing population crowded even marginal lands and subdivided plots into smaller parcels. Towns and urban centers also grew, and the surplus population from the countryside only added to urban crime, filth, disease, and unemployment. In the early fourteenth century, Earth's climate cooled and reduced agricultural output. The standard of living declined, famines became common, and food prices rose sharply. In 1348, just when many Europeans were malnourished and weak, the bubonic plague struck. The Black Death destroyed at least one-third of the popula-

tion within fifty years; in some areas, as many as 90 percent of the population died.

The plague arrived from central Asia and swept through all of Europe, affecting urban and rural, rich and poor. The plague was known as the Black Death because it turned victims' bodies black when the disease broke down their blood vessels. It came in three forms: bubonic, pneumonic, and septicemic. The bubonic form was most common and acquired its name from the large black swellings, known as buboes, which first appeared in the groin or armpits. The disease was contracted from the bite of a flea that was infected with the bacteria. The pneumonic form was transmitted via the air (pneumos) with coughing and sneezing; the septicemic form was most likely passed by the bite of a heavily infected flea directly into a human vein.

The plague outbreak caused widespread political, social, and economic chaos as massive numbers of persons died. Aristocrats and political leaders died at the same rate as everyone else, often creating a political vacuum. Social classes were upset and total economic production plummeted. Cities often lost 50 percent of their population. No one at that time could explain the cause of the plague, and physicians tried desperate but useless cures. Some attributed the disease to God's displeasure, and out of this mindset came an extreme group known as the flagellants, people who through extreme piety whipped themselves publicly to appease God's anger. Although soon condemned by the church, flagellants stirred up anti-Semitic sentiment and Jews across Europe were persecuted, sometimes savagely and often for mainly economic reasons. In some areas, anti-Semitic violence preceded the outbreak of plague. In many instances, local authorities colluded in the violence against Jews. The plague kept returning in new outbreaks throughout the fourteenth century and, with less frequency, even into the seventeenth and eighteenth centuries.

The plague also began the decline of serfdom, the rise of the middle class, and the erosion of aristocratic power because their source of wealth—land—was no longer in high demand. In the depopulated countryside, marginal areas were abandoned and the good lands consolidated. In the towns and cities, demand for skilled labor forced up wages. Because wealth was concentrated in fewer hands, those who survived the plague were economically better off. The total output from the land and manufacturing declined, but only because there were fewer people producing and fewer people buying the products. The material life of the middle class improved. More disposable income made luxury goods affordable to more than a tiny elite. Although the Bardi and Peruzzi banks of Florence were bankrupted by bad loans in the middle of the fourteenth century, more affluence generally meant more investments. Not everyone, though, was better off. The traditional woolen industry, which had produced for a mass market, collapsed; and Flanders, which relied heavily on the textile manufacturing, saw civil unrest into the fifteenth century. As economies shrank generally, more restrictions were placed on women's labor. The Black Death also changed the survivors' worldview. Some responded with increased religiosity and joined monasteries, the clergy, or new radical groups.

In 1309, the papal residence relocated to Avignon in southern France. Most members of the Sacred College of Cardinals were French, and much of the papacy's income came from France. The papacy had quietly gathered the appointment of benefices to itself, established an entrenched bureaucracy to collect religious taxes, and expanded its army as it sought to restore control over the Papal States in Italy. In many ways, the papacy's government and institutions were more sophisticated than their secular counterparts. Further, popes often gave preferential treatment to their extended families. Trenchant criticism of the papacy's wealth and worldly power came from William of Ockham (c. 1285–1349) and Marsilius of Padua. Ockham rejected Aristotelian principles and argued that universal concepts had no reality in nature but rather existed only as mere representations. This thinking became the basis of nominalism. Imprisoned for heresy (1328) by Pope John XXII, Ockham escaped to the court of the emperor Louis of Bavaria. Marsilius was already with the emperor, having been driven there in 1327 by the pope for questioning papal power in *The Defender of the Peace* (1324). Because both Ockham and Marsilius argued that the real church was constituted by the faithful, they became vulnerable to charges of heresy.

The determination of Pope Gregory XI, elected in 1371, to return the papacy to Rome was hastened when Florence declared war on the Papal States (1375). When Gregory died (1378), mobs clamored for an Italian; the bishop of Bari was elected and became Urban VI. When the new pope tried to curb the cardinals' power, thirteen cardinals elected a rival pope, Clement VII, and returned to Avignon. The Great Schism exacerbated secular, political rivalries as Charles V of France recognized his cousin Clement as pope, while Richard II of England acknowledged Urban VI. The rest of Christendom was equally divided: Catherine of Siena (1347–1380) sided with Urban; while Vincent Ferrer (1350–1419), a popular Dominican preacher, supported Clement. Each pope excommunicated the followers of the other. At the Council of Pisa, cardinals who had defected from both popes elected a third, Alexander V, who went unrecognized by both Urban and Clement. Alexander's successor, John XXIII, pressured by Emperor Sigismund, convened a church council at Constance (1414–1417). The council deposed John XXIII and Clement's successor, Benedict XIII; whereas Urban's successor, Gregory XII, resigned on his own. Although Benedict refused to acknowledge his removal, the rest of Christendom recognized the new pope, Martin V, and the Great Schism came to an end.

Laypersons began to seek spiritual fulfillment outside the church. The Free Spirits who believed that humans and God were of the same essence, began attracting converts among the Beguines who lived in community houses ("beguinages"), and Beghards, men who did not belong to a religious order but who lived pious lives and begged for their sustenance. Their beliefs, and their threat to ecclesiastical control, were deemed heretical and Pope Urban V exposed them to the Inquisition. They were brought under church control and, over time, their numbers declined.

Yet, dissidents grew in number and became more difficult to silence. John Wycliffe of Oxford (c. 1330–1384) gradually came to question the very foundations of the Roman church. His treatise, *On the Church* (1378), viewed the true church as a community of believers, not a clerical hierarchy. His anticlerical followers were the Lollards (after *lollar*, or "idler"). Wycliffe repudiated pillars of the Roman church including the Mass and the priesthood, believing instead in Bible reading and conscience as sufficient guides to salvation. At the time of his death, Wycliffe had been working on an English translation of the Bible. Further dissent at Oxford was suppressed, but Lollard ideas smoldered underground and resurfaced during the Reformation.

The Hussites in Bohemia challenged the church more directly. Economic downturns and socioethnic rivalries (between Czechs and a German minority) fed into religious dissent. In Prague, critics of the clergy, often clergymen themselves, decried the priests and prelates who held multiple benefices, led dissolute lives, and ignored their pastoral duties. Reformers particularly wanted the right to receive the wine as well as the bread at Mass to achieve a measure of equality between laity and clergy. A leading dissenter was Jan Hus, an ethnic Czech and Prague professor. Despite a guarantee of safety, Hus was burned at the stake in 1415 by the Council of Constance, which he had been attending. This tragedy caused a national uproar, and the religious movement exploded into a national revolution. Hussites (later called Taborites) seized territory in southern Bohemia, ministering to their community in the Czech language and exercising moral, judicial, and even military leadership (they defeated five attacks from Germany). Ultimately, the pope gave them special permission to receive the Eucharist as both bread and wine.

House and home were focal points for both urban and rural residents. Small, nuclear families were the norm. Shopkeepers and craftspersons often lived above their shops whereas in rural areas families might have shared quarters with their livestock. Life was generally crowded. Although excluded from guilds, women often worked side by side with their husbands in agriculture and commerce, and engaged in unorganized retail trade in such things as dairy products, textile production, and brewing. Women in Mediterranean Europe generally lived more circumscribed lives than women in northern

Europe. Quick remarriages were the norm, especially in rural areas. Italian and Flemish paintings reflected the improved material life that the middle classes now enjoyed. There was also a large and prominent underclass. Crime and violence were common, especially at the extreme bottom of the social strata. Women featured prominently in the underclass as slaves and prostitutes, reflecting the unequal distribution of power between the sexes. The crises of the period affected trade. Hardest hit were Italian bankers who financed the Hundred Years' War. When Edward III defaulted on his loans, the Bardi and Peruzzi banking houses fell. Trade decreased as merchants avoided the dangers of travel and stayed closed to home. Historians argue that merchants invested their capital instead in the arts and luxuries for immediate consumption.

Vernacular literature blossomed in the fourteenth century. Most late-medieval writers were of urban middle-class origins, and wrote for a literate laity. Francesco Petrarch (1304–1374) and Giovanni Boccaccio (1313–1375) were both from middle-class Florentine families. Boccaccio's *Decameron* popularized short stories and, in his novella, persons fleeing the plague tell stories to each other to pass the time. Geoffrey Chaucer (c. 1342–1400) came from a wealthy family of wine merchants and worked as a servant for the king and controller of customs in London. In his *Canterbury Tales*, individuals from all walks of life tell stories to each other as they travel as pilgrims to Canterbury. Even writers who celebrated the life of nobility were children of commoners, like Jean Froissart (c. 1333–c. 1405), who wrote of the Hundred Years' War; and Christine de Pisan (1364–c. 1430), the official biographer of the French king Charles V and author of *The Book of the City of Ladies* (1405). Royal or noble patronage was vital to the careers of all these writers. There was a revival in classical literature alongside the popularization of vernacular works. Latin remained a vital language in the academy as well as in the church, but it was overly formal. There was a move to recapture the essence of Latin as a vernacular language, to get back to its origins. This fascination with the classical past gave rise to the humanist movement. Roman rhetorical styles were studied and emulated, while the classical ideas from Roman literature resonated with contemporary events.

The period from 1320 to 1430 was one of crisis, but it was also a decisive turning point in history.

Suggestions for Lecture and Discussion Topics

1. To help students understand the impact and implications of the Black Death in the fourteenth century, discuss the changes that would be placed on contemporary society, especially their university town, if the population of the class rose constantly. Rents would increase, competition for housing would become fierce, employment would be difficult to find, and special payments or bribes might be required to obtain a job or apartment. Then ask students to work through the same scenario with the student population plummeting by 50 percent within a few years. Question how they might react to widespread death if they did not know its cause. Reactions might include a rise in spirituality or an urge to live for today. Next, apply all these scenarios to the fourteenth century. David Herlihy, *The Black Death and the Transformation of the West* (Cambridge, MA: Harvard University Press, 1997) is by far the best short and readable work for students on the subject.

A lecture on the disease itself is also effective. The plague came in three related strains: the bubonic, pneumonic, and septicemic. The bacteria reproduced in the digestive tract of fleas living on black rats. Fleas are animal-specific, but when the preferred host is unavailable, they will bite another host, such as humans. When they bite, they first regurgitate into the bloodstream, depositing the bacteria. The pneumonic plague was transmitted via air (pneumos) if one coughed or sneezed. Little is known about the septicemic (blood-transmitted) strain because victims died within a few hours of contraction. Read Robert S. Gottfried, *The Black Death: Natural and Human Disaster in Medieval Europe* (New York: Free Press, 1985). The results of recent DNA research should be included in any discussion of the plague. Geneticist Dr. Stephen O'Brien of the National Institutes of Health in Washington, DC, convincingly argues that a mutated gene, CCR5, known colloquially as Delta 32, determined whether or not someone became infected. Interestingly, Delta 32 seems to play a similar role with HIV. The results of his work are available on PBS video *Secrets of the Dead: Mystery of the Black Death.*

With the Hundred Years' War and the emergence of the plague, people of the fourteenth century were constantly surrounded by death. For a look at the various issues related to death in the Middle Ages, see Christopher Daniell, *Death and Burial in Medieval England* (London and New York: Rouledge, 1997); and Rosemary Horrox, "Purgatory, Prayer and Plague: 1150–1380" and Philip Morgan "Of Worms and War: 1380–1558" in Peter C. Jupp and Calre Gittings, eds., *Death in England: An Illustrated History* (Manchester: Manchester University Press, 1999; rpt. New Brunswick: Rutgers University Press, 2000).

2. Each social and political group of the fourteenth century attempted to defend and advance its position during a climate of change and realignment. Divide the class into groups representing peasants, urban workers, artisans, merchants, aristocracy, clergy, and monarchy. Ask each group to develop an argument for their group's defense and advancement. What do they want? Why should they get it? Who is disadvantaged by their

advancement? What leverage do they possess? What power should they have? Why? What power are they willing to concede? Why? Have them read George Huppert, *After the Black Death: A Social History of Early Modern Europe*, 2d ed. (Bloomington: Indiana University Press, 1998).

3. The larger towns and cities of Europe during the fourteenth and fifteenth centuries often purchased their independence from feudal aristocrats; yet, as soon as they did so, the wealthy merchants who had supplied the money began acting like aristocrats. Discuss what provided status in medieval society. The class might begin by discussing what provides status in contemporary American society. Read Sylvia Thrupp, *The Merchant Class of Medieval London, 1300–1500* (Ann Arbor, MI: University of Michigan Press, 1989); and Paul Fussell, *Class* (New York: Summit Books, 1983).

4. Geoffrey Chaucer's *Canterbury Tales* provides numerous examples of challenges to authority, from ridicule of aristocracy and clergy to the power of women and the humor derived from examining existing social structures. The best parts to illustrate these points might be the "Prologue," "The Miller's Tale," and "The Wife of Bath's Prologue."

5. In the cases of the Peasants' revolt of 1381 in England, and the Ciompi rebellion of 1378 in Florence, peasants and workers lived under difficult conditions and the Black Death surrounded them; but, in fact, economic conditions were on the rise and the standard of living was improving. Compare these two revolts to the civil rights "rebellion" of African Americans in the United States in the 1950s and 1960s. One can see that revolts often occur not when conditions are getting worse, but when they are not getting better as rapidly for one group as for another group of society. Read R. H. Hilton, *Class Conflict and the Crisis of Feudalism: Essays in Medieval Social History*, 2d ed. (London: Verso, 1990).

6. Thomas à Kempis's *The Imitation of Christ* illustrates the more personal Christianity of the fifteenth century. It calls on individuals to strive for goodness in daily life and to become intimate with God, conditions that are strikingly similar to those of the Reformation of the sixteenth century. This work, which can be read in short pieces or as a whole, can be compared to paintings by Pieter Brueghel the Elder, such as *Land of Cockaigne* or *Carnival and Lent*. Although Brueghel was painting in the middle of the sixteenth century, his works illustrate the religious view that living for today is sinful and corrupt. A book that presents a woman's view is Louise Collis, ed., *Memoirs of a Medieval Woman: The Life and Times of Margery Kempe* (New York: Harper, 1983).

7. Records concerning medieval women (albeit usually queens and women of the upper classes) survive in some quantity beginning in the Middle Ages. It might surprise students to discover that, despite a deeply patriarchal society, some women—even those from the middle and lower classes—could exercise considerable power and influence. Begin with a discussion of what medieval society believed women's roles to be and how women were supposed to behave. Counter these perceptions with Christine de Pisan's contemporary defense of women contained in *The Book of the City of Ladies* (1404). This can be followed by a discussion about how reality differed from or conformed to the ideal. For primary sources, see Emilie Amt, ed., *Women's Lives in Medieval Europe: A Sourcebook*. (New York: Routledge, 1993); and Carolyne Larrington, ed., *Women and Writing in Medieval Europe* (New York: Routledge, 1995). See also Eileen Power, *Medieval Women*, M. M. Postan, ed. (Cambridge: Cambridge University Press, 1975; rpt. 1989); John Carmi Parsons, ed., *Medieval Queenship* (New York: St. Martin's Press, 1998); David Herlihy, *Women, Family and Society in Medieval Europe* (New York: Berghahn Books, 1995); and Peter Coss, *The Lady in Medieval England 1000–1500* (Stroud: Sutton Publishing Ltd., 1998).

Making Connections

1. *Is it reasonable to state that the late Middle Ages experienced a general crisis in society? Why or why not?* After a century of population growth and economic expansion, significant elements of late-medieval Europe collapsed in the face of a series of overlapping crises that decimated the population, killing one-third of Europeans and one-half of urbanized persons. The previous century's spirit of confidence vanished with the loss of the people. The plague and economic decay set off violent persecution and murder of Jews, sometimes with governmental approval. The economic downturn prompted a series of worker revolts. The Hundred Years' War caused widespread destruction in France and destabilized taxes on both French and English citizens. The Holy Roman Empire fragmented, allowing communes in the Alps to form an independent confederation. The church itself was split between Avignon and Rome (the Great Schism), while heretical groups like the Lollards and Hussites challenged church teaching and practice. On the other hand, the decrease in population and demand for grain led to a much improved European diet; the sudden labor shortage meant increased wages for many workers; the deaths from the plague increased resources and property for the survivors; and a prosperous middle class who enjoyed, for the first time, luxuries and vernacular literature. France and Burgundy emerged from the Hundred Years' War immensely strengthened. And, from one point of view, heretics and schism weakened the church, but the church's crisis was the reformer's opportunity.

2. *To what extent was Christendom less tolerant and open in the fourteenth century than in the high Middle*

Ages? The thirteenth century had witnessed the Albigensian Crusade (1209–1229) launched in Southern France. The Fourth Lateran Council (1215) had systematized Christian ritual, law, and practice and established the Inquisition to root out heresy to such an extent that entire communities sometimes fell under suspicion. Complicating the fourteenth-century church's tolerance was the Great Schism between Avignon and Rome. The church was not more tolerant or open, but it also was not as successful at combating dissent. Lollards in England were not persecuted until after John Wycliffe's natural death and even then survived only by hiding. Jan Hus was treacherously arrested and burned at the stake, but the Hussites mounted a successful armed rebellion and won their central demand from the church. Free Spirit heretics and flagellants were successfully suppressed, but they had been extremist groups, relatively few in number. Beguines, who had the added disadvantage of being women, were forced into cloisters. Christendom, as distinct from the church establishment, was less tolerant and more successful in its attacks on non-Christians, especially on the Iberian peninsula. Jews by the tens of thousands were forced to convert to Christianity or flee; Muslims were captured and enslaved on latifundia.

Writing Assignments and Class Presentation Topics

1. Assign students any of Chaucer's *Canterbury Tales*, such as "The Knight's Tale," "The Wife of Bath's Tale," "The Nun's Priest's Tale," or "The Miller's Tale." Ask students to write a synopsis of the tale that includes what can be learned about medieval European society from literature that cannot be learned from other historical documentation. Then, do the same for one of the stories by Boccaccio in *The Decameron*. How are the stories similar? How do they differ? What differences can you discern between Florentine and English society?

2. Have students log on to one of the major medieval Web sites, such as the *Internet Medieval Sourcebook*, and evaluate the primary documents available for the period. Students should address the types of information that might gleaned from them.

3. Assign small groups of students to research different classes in medieval society, such as peasants, merchants, aristocracy, clergy, and even the monarchy. Then, have them devise a justification for their class's existence, the power they hold, and why they should be given greater rights or income within society.

4. Examine the illustrations "Siege Warfare" (p. 470) and "The Spoils of War" (p. 472). In which ways would warfare change with the advent of cannons? Consider the viewpoints of aristocrats, town dwellers, and commoners.

5. Refer to "The Burning of Jews" (p. 467) and "Burning of a Heretic" (p. 491). Although these two scenes depict similar occurrences, the way in which they are constructed gives us additional insight into each event. In "The Burning of Jews," who is most prominent: the victims? The onlookers? The executioner? Whose features and clothing contain the greatest detail? Can you distinguish the social rank or official position of any of the onlookers? Why has the emphasis been placed where it is? Then, contrast this with "Burning of a Heretic." Who is most prominently placed in this woodcut? Who has the artist depicted in the most detail? Can you distinguish the social rank or official position of any of the onlookers? After you have observed these differences, how would you analyze the messages to the audience incorporated in these illustrations? How do these messages differ from one another?

Research Assignments

1. Ask students to write an essay or present a report answering the following question: If you were a wealthy merchant from Baghdad visiting Europe in 1385, what would be most noticeable and distinctive? Then, turn the scenario around: What would be most noticeable and distinctive to a wealthy European merchant visiting Baghdad or Córdoba? Students should discuss the physical world as well as attitudes.

2. Ask students to write an essay or present a report on the following question: If this chapter is about the collapse of medieval order, what "order" collapsed?

3. Ask students to read Christine de Pisan's *The Book of the City of Ladies*. What is her "defense" of medieval women? Based on that defense, how are women perceived by medieval society? Describe Pisan's ideal woman. Is she very much like a modern woman of today? Would Pisan be satisfied with what women have achieved today?

Literature

Benson, Larry D., *The Riverside Chaucer*. 1987.

Brereton, Geoffrey, trans., *Jean Froissart: Chronicles*. 1979.

McWilliam, G. H., trans., *Giovanni Boccacio: The Decameron*. 2003.

Quillen, Carol, trans., *Petrarch's Secret*. 2003.

Videos and Films

The Return of Martin Guerre (1982; DVD, 2 hrs., 3 min.). Gerard Depardieu stars in this film about a soldier who returns from war and assumes the identity of a fellow fighter. Based on a true event, it nicely captures peasant life in sixteenth-century France. The film is in French with English subtitles.

The Name of the Rose (1986; Jean-Jacques Annaud, dir.; with Sean Connery and Christian Slater). A medieval monk applies deductive reasoning to solve a series of murders within a monastery. The film is remarkably accurate in its details both large and small, but especially in its depiction of medieval tensions between faith and reason.

The Anchoress (1993; VHS/DVD, 91 min.). A young woman who commits herself to the life of an anchoress must deal with the conflicting influences and ambitions of the local priest, a local administrative officer, and her mother. The story is based on the letters of a fourteenth-century anchoress and care has been taken to re-create life in the countryside in medieval England.

Messenger: The Story of Joan of Arc (1999; DVD, 2 hrs., 38 min.). A dark and somewhat speculative account of Joan of Arc, this film captures the dirt, grime, and extreme religiosity and intrigue of the period.

Joan of Arc (1999; DVD, 3 hrs.). This miniseries closely follows the traditional story of Joan of Arc. Careful attention has been paid to the minutia of medieval life.

Historical Skills

Map 13.1, The Hundred Years' War, 1337–1453, p. 471

Map 13.2, Central and Eastern Europe, c. 1400, p. 478

Map 13.3, Ottoman Expansion in the Fourteenth and Fifteenth Centuries, p. 481

Mapping the West: Europe, c. 1430, p. 501

Growth of the Swiss Confederation to 1353, p. 479

Christian Territory in Iberia, c. 1350, p. 480

These maps demonstrate much of the political development of the fourteenth and early fifteenth centuries. In northern Europe, France barely exists in the early fourteenth century but, by the end of the Hundred Years' War, France expands to become a huge and dominant player in European affairs. In central and eastern Europe, the Holy Roman Empire is a fragmented confederation of states and remains so beyond the fifteenth century. In the alpine region, small states begin to join together under the Swiss Confederation. In the Iberian peninsula, there is relative fragmentation that does not change until the end of the fifteenth century, but consolidation of Christianity is taking place. In the Balkans, the Ottoman Empire is expanding rapidly into Europe, surrounding

the remnants of the Byzantine Empire and threatening to overrun Christianity. These maps demonstrate that simple statements about political consolidation or fragmentation, or the expansion or fragmentation of Christianity, cannot be made. The history of Europe during the fourteenth and fifteenth centuries was highly complex and sometimes contradictory.

Map 13.4, Advance of the Plague, 1347–1350, p. 484

How can one explain the rapid transmission of the plague from the Black Sea in 1347, to all of Europe by 1350? What responses to the plague would have actually accelerated its spread?

Map 13.5, The Great Schism, 1378–1417, p. 490

The Great Schism may have weakened the west during a period of Islamic expansion. What does this say about the mentality of the church in the west during the fourteenth and fifteenth centuries? How does the Great Schism foreshadow the Reformation of the sixteenth century?

Siege Warfare, p. 470

With the introduction and use of cannons, many elements of warfare changed. Heavier fortifications were needed, as were engineers both for the cannons and the design of fortifications. The mentality of warfare also changed from defensive to offensive thinking and planning. All of these changes required huge financial commitments.

Joan the Warrior, p. 473

What is there about a simple maiden, portrayed both as defenseless and warlike, that caught the emotions of the French people?

June, p. 495 and February, p. 495

The farm was probably the arena of greatest equality between the sexes. However, some tasks required more physical strength than women could provide. What appears to be the division of labor in these two illustrations? What sort of agricultural enterprises are illustrated in these scenes? In the February illustration, who is the most important person in the picture? How can you tell?

William Langland, Piers the Ploughman

Langland's *Piers the Ploughman* is as much a critique of society as it is an extended religious allegory. A discussion can center on church corruption, as it was experienced firsthand by the common people. The clergy are more interested in worldly things than fulfilling their Christian vows. Some of the clergy actually go out of their way to cheat people in order to live worldly lives, thus depriving the genuinely needy in the community. More to the point, such clergy imperil the souls in their keeping by twisting and distorting Scripture, and promoting blasphemous practices.

OTHER BEDFORD/ST. MARTIN'S RESOURCES FOR CHAPTER 13

The following resources are available to accompany Chapter 13. Please refer to the Preface of this manual for detailed descriptions of all the ancillaries.

For Instructors

Transparencies

The following maps and images from Chapter 13 are available as full-color acetates.

- Map 13.1: The Hundred Years' War, 1337–1453
- Map 13.2: Central and Eastern Europe, c. 1400
- Map 13.3: Ottoman Expansion in the Fourteenth and Fifteenth Centuries
- Map 13.4: Advance of the Plague, 1347–1350
- Map 13.5: The Great Schism, 1378–1417
- Mapping the West: Europe, c. 1430
- *June*
- Joan the Warrior

Instructor's Resources CD-ROM

The following maps and image from Chapter 13, as well as a chapter outline, are available on disc in both Power-Point and jpeg formats.

- Map 13.1: The Hundred Years' War, 1337–1453
- Map 13.2: Central and Eastern Europe, c. 1400
- Map 13.3: Ottoman Expansion in the Fourteenth and Fifteenth Centuries
- Map 13.4: Advance of the Plague, 1347–1350
- Map 13.5: The Great Schism, 1378–1417
- Mapping the West: Europe, c. 1430
- *June*

Using the Bedford Series with The Making of the West

Available in print as well as online at bedfordstmartins.com/usingseries, this guide offers practical suggestions for using **John Aberth, *The Black Death: The Great Mortality of 1348–1350: A Brief History with Documents***; and **Carol Quillen, *Petrarch's Secret*** in conjunction with chapters 13 and 14 of the textbook.

For Students

Sources of The Making of the West

The following documents are available in Chapter 13 of the companion sourcebook by Katharine J. Lualdi, University of Southern Maine.

1. *The Black Death* (Fourteenth Century)
2. Thomas Walsingham, *Peasant Rebels in London* (1381)
3. Catherine of Siena, *Letters to the Papacy* (1376–1417)
4. Geoffrey Chaucer, "The Prologue of the Pardoner's Tale" from *The Canterbury Tales* (1387–1400)
5. Marsilius of Padua, *Defender of the Peace* (1324)

Study Guides

The print **Study Guide** and the **Online Study Guide** at bedfordstmartins.com/hunt, both by Victoria Thompson (Arizona State University) and Eric Johnson (University of California, Los Angeles), help students synthesize the material they have learned as well as practice the skills historians use to make sense of the past. The following Map, Visual, and Document activities are available for Chapter 13.

Map Activity

- Map 13.4: Advance of Plague, 1347–1350

Visual Activity

- *June*

Reading Historical Documents

- Piers the Ploughman
- *The Book of the City of Ladies*

Renaissance Europe
1400–1500

CHAPTER RESOURCES

Main Chapter Topics

1. The tragedies of the latter Middle Ages were shaken off as the Renaissance ("rebirth") of European civilization produced a revolution in art and learning in Italy that spread to other countries. The humanist movement embodied a renewed interest in classical antiquity and was central to the Renaissance. Man now became "the measure of all things." The invention of movable type helped disseminate the many ideas—political as well as artistic—that underpinned the Renaissance.

2. The status of artists changed; they were no longer viewed as mere artisans. Artists idealized the human form and introduced visual perspective into their work. Architects imposed order on space, and composers reached new heights through polyphonic music.

3. Renaissance society in Florence was stratified: the "little people," or small shopkeepers and artisans, made up 60 percent of the population; whereas "fat people," wealthier merchants and tradesmen, made up 30 percent. The elites of Florence—bankers and extremely wealthy merchants—controlled the government. Marriages were seen as political, social, and economic contracts; and women, who had little say in the matter, were often married at a young age to older men. Women in Northern Europe had more freedoms than their Mediterranean counterparts.

4. Under the Milanese example, diplomacy became a feature of fifteenth-century politics.

5. Burgundy consisted of French, German, and Dutch territories and was held together for much of the fifteenth century by two able dukes. It was a center of Renaissance culture, but it declined when Charles the Bold (1433–1477) was killed in battle. Louis XI seized Burgundian land and further expanded French territory when he inherited Anjou. England grew economically

strong in the fifteenth century despite a civil war known as the War of the Roses. Hungary-Bohemia and Poland remained weak through the dominance of the nobility. The Ottoman Empire continued to expand and captured Constantinople in 1453. Under Ivan III, Moscovy also expanded its territory and consolidated its control.

6. The Portuguese were the first to undertake long-distance voyages of exploration. They rounded the Cape of Good Hope and settled forts along the African, Sri Lankan, and Indian coasts. Columbus persuaded the Spanish that a new route to India lay across the Atlantic. He discovered the Bahamas instead, and Spain began a long exploitation of the native population and sugarcane industry. Spain soon conquered the Aztecs, Incans, and Mayans, and took advantage of the precious metals found in Mexico and Bolivia. Other countries explored North America, but did not establish permanent communities there until the seventeenth century. The slave trade began to be concentrated in West Africa.

Summary

The Renaissance, from 1400 to 1500, brought about rapid change as European civilization shook off the tragedies of the latter Middle Ages. After the fourteenth-century devastation by the Black Death, a new sense of growth, expansion, and intellectual renewal spread throughout Europe. The Renaissance ("rebirth") of civilization produced a revolution in art and learning in Italy that began expanding to other countries. At the same time, European power grew, and new influences developed from beyond Europe's former boundaries.

Continuing in the tradition of Petrarch, a reawakening to classical learning via the fashionable, late-medieval study of Latin and Greek revolutionized culture under the added influx of scholars and texts after the fall of Constantinople (1453). Classical Roman manuscripts were rediscovered; classical statues excavated. Classical ideals of the value of the individual and of the importance of civic life inspired Italian writers and artists in what became known as "humanism": the study of liberal arts—grammar, rhetoric, poetry, history, moral philosophy, and music. Humanism celebrated the glory of human achievements and most humanists saw no conflict between this idea and their Christian faith. Indeed, Cosimo de Medici (1388–1464) sponsored the Platonic Academy in Florence, which was headed by the priest Marsilio Ficino (1433–1499), the foremost Platonic scholar of the Renaissance. Ficino argued that the concept of an immortal soul was a Platonic idea, and that ancient wisdom prefigured Christian teaching. The primacy of original texts revitalized Latin, which had become stilted in the painstaking logic and abstract language of scholastic philosophy. Humanists advocated elegance and style in discourse in the fashion of Cicero. By the end of the fifteenth century, one had to know Latin and some Greek in order to be considered educated. Renaissance humanism influenced school curricula well into the nineteenth century.

The advent of printing with movable type, invented by Johannes Gutenberg (c. 1400–1468) in the 1440s, greatly aided both the dissemination of classical learning and the expansion of European power in a communications revolution. Two preconditions to printing — the industrial production of paper and commercial production of manuscripts — were available to printers by the middle of the fifteenth century. With these two innovations, a single printing press could produce volumes at a rate that had previously required the labor of one thousand scribes. Printing spread rapidly from Germany to other European countries and expanded to uses other than classical or religious texts. The dissemination of the wisdom of the times could be done rapidly and cheaply, but because printed material could also promote political ideas that challenged the status quo, censorship soon followed the invention of the printing press.

A revolution also occurred in the arts, both in the social standing of the artist and in technique. Because of the Renaissance emphasis on the arts and the accomplishments of the individual, the creator of art was transformed from artisan to artist. Many artists became famous and wealthy, acquiring a new status in European society. Yet, even the most successful of the artists required continued support by wealthy patrons, such as the Medici family of Florence or the Gonzaga family of Mantua, whose input on the rendering of a work of art could be considerable. The human form took on a new prominence in Renaissance art. The paintings of Masaccio (1401–1428) exemplified the new emphasis on expressive human emotions and movement. The ideal of feminine beauty was reflected in the classical pagan figures and allegories of Sandro Botticelli's (c. 1445–1510) *The Birth of Venus* and *Springtime* (*Primavera*) and in the many Madonnas by Raphael (1483–1520). Portraiture of individuals from all walks of life also reflected the new, ele-

vated view of human existence. Portraits by Jan van Eyck (1390?–1441) and other painters from the Low Countries achieved a sense of detail and reality unsurpassed until the advent of photography. Man's central place within the Renaissance worldview was articulated by Giovanni Pico della Mirandola (1463–1494) in *On the Dignity of Man*. Mankind was at the center of the universe and served as the measure of all things. Sculpture especially embodied this idea. Donatello (c. 1386–1466) used Roman emperors on horseback as the model for his sculpture of a mounted Venetian general The idealized human form was also represented in Michelangelo's (1475–1564) magnificent eighteen-foot sculpture, *David*.

Visual perspective further distinguished Renaissance paintings from art produced by earlier artists. Humans asserted themselves over nature in painting and design by visually controlling space. Lorenzo Ghiberti (c. 1378–1455) used linear perspective to create a sense of depth and space in the bronze panels for the doors of the San Giovanni baptistery in Florence; Michelangelo described these doors as "the Gates of Paradise." Andrea Mantegna's (1431–1506) frescos in the bridal chamber of the Gonzaga palace created the illusion of the room opening up to the landscape depicted on the walls. Piero della Francesca's (1420–1492) detached and expressionless figures sat amidst a geometrical world of columns and tiles. Renaissance architects like Filippo Brunelleschi (1377–1446), especially renowned for the dome of Florence's cathedral, united artistic creativity and scientific knowledge in their work. In *On Architecture* (1415), Leon Battista Alberti (1404–1472) argued for large-scale urban planning in which monumental buildings would be set in open squares. His theories helped transform medieval Rome into a great Renaissance city that reflected its classical roots.

Motets had long been a part of church music, but purely secular polyphonic music was not common until the fourteenth century, and did not reach its height until the fifteenth century. Guillaume Dufay (1400–1474) was among the most noted composers of the period and wrote music to celebrate the completion of Brunelleschi's dome on Florence's cathedral in 1438. Employed for a time by the papal court, Dufay also composed music for the French and Burgundian courts. Patronage of composers like Dufay and his younger rivals—Johannes Ockeghem (c. 1420-1497) and Josquin des Prez (1440-1521)—commonly were of noble birth. There were three main genres of music during this period: the cannon (or central texts) of the Catholic Mass, the motet, and the secular chanson ("song"). Folk melodies were often adapted for sacred music, and new keyboard instruments, like the harpsichord and clavichord, complemented tambourines and lutes.

Florence was one of the most urbanized regions in Europe, with a population of 260,000 in 1430. Florentines divided society into two classes: "little people" —

workers, artisans, and merchants with small shops — who composed roughly 60 percent of the population; and "fat people" — more successful merchants and professionals — who made up approximately 30 percent. The elite, at the apex of this hierarchy, were the wealthiest merchants and bankers who also controlled Florence's government. Wealthy families were often large and extended, whereas poor families were usually small and nuclear in form. Women, who outnumbered men in Florence, had little power politically or economically except as a marriageable commodity. Because Italian marriages were generally arranged for social and economic gain, women were married at a very young age, usually to much older men. Widows were often pressed by their families to remarry to form new alliances, but they lost control of any children from previous marriages if they did so. In Florence, the Dowry Fund was an investment account into which wealthy families could save money to use to marry off their daughters.

In northern Europe, women enjoyed a relatively more secure position because of their economic contributions to the family. There, women tended to share inheritances with their brothers, retain control over their dowries, and could represent themselves before the law. Issues of sexuality were closely regulated in Florence. Middle-class women could afford to have their children cared for by nurses; whereas the poor often abandoned children, especially girls, to strangers or to a public charity. Many abandoned children were illegitimate. Prostitution was tolerated but homosexuality was not. Violence against women was treated less seriously than illegal, male sexual behavior, and penalties were based on social class; noblemen often escaped without punishment, while poor men received harsher penalties. After years of observing Italian politics, Niccolò Machiavelli (1469–1527) produced *The Prince*, a treatise that addressed the acquisition and exercise of power without reference to an ultimate moral or ethical end. It scandalized Europe, in spite of (or perhaps because of) the fact that it was an accurate reflection of Renaissance power politics.

The states of Renaissance Italy were either republics or principalities. Venice, a republic, was a maritime, mercantile power with an extensive empire and a large merchant fleet. In the mid-fifteenth century, Venice faced threats from Milan and the Ottoman Turks but was able to ward off both with its navy. One of the city's great strengths was that it was internally stable. Florence, also a republic, was less stable than Venice even though it was a center for Renaissance artists and scholars. The Medici family, whose power rested in its banking empire, constantly vied with the rest of the merchant elite for control of Florence. Cosimo de Medici (1388–1464), the founder of the family, wielded tremendous power, and his grandson Lorenzo became especially known as a patron of the arts. After Lorenzo's death in 1494, the Medici were twice driven from Florence, and twice restored, the last time in

1530 when the Medici declared the city a duchy and became its dukes. Milan was a duchy ruled first by the Visconti and later, after a brief republican experiment, by the Sforza families. It had an enormous military and, under the Visconti, tried to gain dominance of northern Italy. The duchy reached its height under Ludovico Sforza (1451–1508), but eventually came under Spanish rule. The kingdom of Naples came under Aragonese rule between 1435 and 1494 but, in practice, it was dominated by feudal barons. Although invaded by France in 1494, it, too, eventually came under Spanish rule. In the Papal States, the pope endeavored to restore papal authority, which had earlier been undermined by the Great Schism and the conciliar movement.

Diplomacy became an integral part of fifteenth-century European politics. Foremost in the development of diplomacy was Milan, who sent representatives to Aragon, Burgundy, France, the Holy Roman Empire, and the Ottoman Empire. Ambassadors were expected to send home a steady stream of information, usually in cipher, not just serve on diplomatic missions.

Outside Italy, large territorial states—Burgundy, England, France, Spain, the Ottoman Empire, and Muscovy—would soon overshadow the Italian states because they had far greater economic and military resources. Situated between France and Germany, Burgundy was an artificial creation of astute use of diplomacy and military might by the Burgundian dukes. Its territory included the Netherlands, German lands from the Swiss border in the south to Friesland in the north, and the Burgundy region of France. It was ruled for much of the fifteenth century by two able dukes: Philip the Good (r. 1418–1467), and his son Charles the Bold (r. 1467–1477), both of whom used elaborate ceremonies to enhance their power. Burgundy began to decline in power after Charles was killed in battle; France seized much of Burgundy, while other Burgundian lands, including the Netherlands, were subsumed into the Holy Roman Empire. England, after its defeat in the Hundred Years' War and civil wars between the Lancastrians and Yorkists (known as the "War of the Roses") nonetheless suffered little damage and enjoyed a thriving economy despite the quarrels of its royalty. Along with the English economy, the middle class expanded and, at the same time, Parliament gained in importance and authority. This parallel development increased the tension between the two. Spain began its meteoric ascent with the marriage of Ferdinand of Aragon and Isabella of Castile in 1469. A united Castile and Aragon concluded the reconquista by 1492, but directed extreme intolerance toward the Jews and the *conversos* (Jewish converts to Christianity) who were subjected to the Spanish Inquisition and driven out in large numbers or forced to convert to Christianity. France slowly added the territories that had been removed from control of the king during the course of the latter Middle Ages. Louis XI (r. 1461–1483) seized

Burgundian territory when Duke Charles was killed in 1477, and later acquired the southern area of Anjou when the Angevin dynasty died out. Louis XI promoted commerce and industry, maintained the first standing army in Europe (which had been created by his father), dissolved the Estates General, and gained important papal concessions. The Sanction of Bourges (1438) established what would be known as "Gallicanism," whereby French kings had control over church revenue and ecclesiastical appointments in France. The rise of powerful monarchies in the west contrasted with the weakness of states in central and eastern Europe.

Under King Matthius Corvinus (r. 1458–1490, Hungary-Bohemia was strong and on the verge of becoming an empire. But after his death, everything crumbled when the nobles refused to recognize his son as king. Polish nobles, who deliberately elected weak kings, maintained their power and kept centralization at bay. The Ottoman Empire, however, continued to expand during the fifteenth century with the crossing of the Bosporus into Europe and the conquest of Constantinople in 1453. Muscovy emerged from Mongol control in the fifteenth century to become the largest state on Earth, adding Novgorod and its vast territories under Ivan III (r. 1462–1505), who was the first Muscovite prince to claim an imperial title, referring to himself as "tsar." Dynastic rule was autocratic in Muscovy, and its rulers held absolute rights over all lands and peoples.

The fifteenth century inaugurated the first period of world history. Although the Chinese and the Ottomans were in contact with large areas of the known world, Europe had been relatively isolated (and insignificant) until the fifteenth century. The area of the Mediterranean was multicultural and multiethnic; the resulting divisions, along with Ottoman incursions into areas of European trade (such as the Black Sea and the eastern Mediterranean) forced Europeans to seek new trade outlets. Exploration was led by Portugal and financed in large measure by the royal family. Prince Henry of Portugal, after seeing more of the world when his father attacked Ceuta in North Africa (1415), established a center for the study of navigation at Sagres on the southern tip of Portugal (1419). Missions left Portugal by sea in the 1430s and traveled down the west coast of Africa in the hope of finding a possible route to spices in South and Southeast Asia. Another hope was to find allies in the European struggle with the Muslim world. During 1497–1499, Vasco da Gama (1469–1524) rounded the Cape of Good Hope and made it to Calicut in India. In 1512, Ferdinand Magellan (a Portuguese sailor in the Spanish service), circumnavigated the globe. By 1517, the Portuguese had ports in Mozambique, Hormuz, Goa, Sri Lanka, and Malacca (modern Malaysia). Maritime competition between Portugal and Spain prompted the Treaty of Torsedillas in 1494. Mediated by Pope Alexander VI, the treaty divided the Atlantic world between the two countries.

Christopher Columbus (1451–1506), though born in Genoa, trained in the Portuguese navy. Columbus proposed, first to the Portuguese and then the French, to take a fleet across the Atlantic in search of an eastward route to reach the east. Only Ferdinand of Aragon and Isabella of Castile were willing to support the venture. Setting sail in August 1492, Columbus reached in October what he believed to be the East Indies near Japan but had actually come upon the Bahamas. Subsequent trips would prove to others, if not to Columbus, that he had in fact discovered a new continent. When the expected spices and gold mines were not found, the Spanish began enslaving many of the native inhabitants, shipping some to Europe and forcing others to work in the sugarcane fields. Slavery had existed in Europe since antiquity and, during the Renaissance, the slave population included Greeks, Slavs, Europeans, Africans, and Turks. Beginning in the fifteenth century, however, the slave trade began to center on West Africa. From the Caribbean, Hernan Cortez (1485–1547) and Francisco Pizarro (c. 1475–1541) subdued the Aztecs and Incans respectively in their search for gold. The Mayans were also conquered. Gold and silver were discovered in Mexico, and the area of modern Bolivia yielded vast silver deposits. The Dutch, English, and French followed in trips of exploration and established trading bases upon discovering the New World and routes to the Far East. With these discoveries came an extensive slave trade, transmission of disease, dissemination of plants and animals, and a new era of European domination.

Suggestions for Lecture and Discussion Topics

1. Slides of Gothic and Renaissance architecture, especially churches, are readily available. Comparing the architecture of a Gothic cathedral and a Renaissance church to classical Greek or Roman architecture dramatically illustrates the idea of a rebirth. To be fair, one should point out that the comparison should be between Italian Gothic and Italian Renaissance, not northern Italian Gothic and Italian Renaissance. This comparison can be made with slides of any of the late-medieval Italian palaces. The best way to have students analyze a Renaissance building is to have them study it level by level. The classical features will then be readily apparent.

2. A number of important English letter collections from the fifteenth century survive, and provide a fascinating array of information on a wide variety of subjects: the relationship between men and women, parents and children; women's roles; state and local politics; and everyday life in general. The best known of these collections is the Paston letters, the bulk of which cover the years 1440 to 1500. For examples of strong, industrious women, none better can be found than Agnes, Margaret, and Margery Paston. Norman Davis has produced the

most recent editions: *The Paston Letters and Papers of the Fifteenth Century*, 2 vols. (Oxford: The Clarendon Press, 1971); and *The Paston Letters: A Selection in Modern Spelling* (Oxford: Oxford University Press, 1999). James Gairdner's six-volume, 1904 edition, has also been reprinted in one volume: *The Paston Letters* (Gloucester: Alan Sutton, 1986). The wide range of subjects that can be illuminated by these letters is suggested by Roger Virgoe's *Illustrated Letters of the Paston Family: Private Life in the Fifteenth Century* (London: Macmillan, 1989). For a narrative account of the Pastons, see Frances Gies and Joseph Gies, *A Medieval Family: The Pastons of Fifteenth-Century England* (New York: HarperCollins, 1998). The Stoner collection, which concentrates on the fifteenth century, also provides rare insights into the period. See Christine Carpenter, ed., *Kingsford's Stoner Letters and Papers, 1290–1483* (Cambridge: Cambridge University Press, 1996). See also Thomas Stapleton, ed., *The Plumpton Correspondence* (The Camden Society, 1839, series I, no. 4 [rpt. New York: AMS Press, 1968]).

Another English woman of note is Margery Kempe. Although illiterate, she dictated her spiritual testimony to a priest probably in the 1430s. Beyond a spiritual account of her life, however, her "book" includes fascinating details of her daily life: her arguments with her husband, her pilgrimage to the Holy Land, and the difficulties her religiosity caused. See B. A. Windeatt, ed., trans., *The Book of Margery Kempe* (New York: Penguin Books, 1985).

3. To study Renaissance art and skill, perception, and value of art, have students read Michael Baxandall, *Painting and Experience in Fifteenth-Century Italy*, 2d ed. (Oxford: Oxford University Press, 1988).

4. For the origins of humanism, students should read the first two chapters in Jill Kraye, ed., *The Cambridge Companion to Renaissance Humanism*: Nicholas Mann, "The Origins of Humanism"; and Michael D. Reeve, "Classical Scholarship." This entire book would also be useful for more advanced studies of humanism.

5. Elaborate ceremonies surrounded fifteenth-century monarchs and their families. Emphasizing the divine nature of kingship, they were also an immediate and tangible display of secular power and authority. Burgundy was accounted the most sophisticated court in Europe, and France and England vied to compete on the same level. For royal ceremony in Burgundy, see Peter Arnade, *Realms of Ritual: Burgundian Ceremony and Civic Life in Late Medieval Ghent* (Ithaca: Cornell University Press, 1996); Rolf Strom-Olsen, "Dynastic Ritual and Politics in Early Modern Burgundy: The Baptism of Charles V," in *Past and Present*, no. 175 (2002), pp. 34–64; and Edward A. Tabri, "The Funeral of Duke Philip the Good," in *Essays in History*, vol. 33 (1990–1991) (http://www.lib.virginia.edu/journals/EH/EH33/tabri33 .html); and Christine Weightman, *Margaret of York: Duchess of Burgundy, 1446–1503* (Stroud: Alan Sutton,

1989 [rpt. 1993]). For French coronation ceremonies, see Richard A. Jackson, *Vive le Roi! A History of the French Coronation from Charles V to Charles X* (Chapel Hill: University of North Carolina Press, 1984). For English ceremony and ritual generally, see Brian R. Price, "The Manner and Form of the Coronation of the Kings and Queens of England," *Archeologia*, vol. 57, Part 1 (1996) (http://www.chronique.com/Library/Knights/coronation.html). For Henry VII's coronation, see William Jerdan, ed., *The Rutland Papers* (The Camden Society, 1842, series I, vol. 21 [rpt. New York: AMS Press, 1968]). For further information on royal ceremonies, see biographies of individual monarchs and their consorts.

6. Exploration can be approached in several ways. One effective method is to go review everything students already know about exploration and piece those facts together with a few that they may not be aware of to develop a picture of why Europeans began to explore. These additional issues include: the rediscovery of classical geography texts and world maps; the use of the printing press for dissemination of information; the impending and eventual fall of Constantinople to the Ottomans, and the continual threat to the west by the Turks; the growth of capitalism; the rise of the middle class; the merger of Atlantic and Mediterranean ship technology; and the creation of a superpower with the marriage of Ferdinand and Isabella.

7. Why was Portugal the first nation in Europe to begin exploration? The answer is the same as the real-estate answer to why a house sells: location, location, location. Discuss all the relevant aspects of Portugal's location, such as its position far from the Ottoman Empire; close to the African coast; at the point of contact between the Mediterranean and Atlantic (convenient for the merger of the two technologies and navigational knowledge); next to larger, more powerful neighbors; and jutting out into the water like a peninsula.

Making Connections

1. *Where were the centers of Renaissance creativity located? Why did the Renaissance arise there"?* There are a number of reasons why the Renaissance was centered in Italy. Although a small European intellectual elite had studied classical texts since the beginning of the fifteenth century, interest in classical antiquity became widespread when Constantinople fell to the Muslims (1453) and the city's scholars fled to Italy. Linking east with west by virtue of its commercial interests, Italy also proved to be fertile ground for new ideas. Finally, a number of city-states had rulers, like Cosimo de Medici in Florence, who were sympathetic to these new ideas and artistic sensibilities and gave their patronage to intellectuals and artists.

2. *How did Renaissance and medieval culture and society differ? How were they similar?* Both cultures were

war-oriented, and many aspects of ordinary life changed very little. Marriage, for example, remained a political, socioeconomic contract—not just between two people —but between their families as well. The differences between the two periods, however, are striking. The Renaissance was a period of discovery that was reflected not only in monumental voyages of exploration, but also in the world of art and intellectual thought. Artists were no longer considered mere "craftspersons": they reintroduced perspective and mythological subject matter into painting, glorified the human form in sculpture, and built classically inspired architecture. The invention of movable type slowly changed society into a print culture, disseminating ideas, for good or ill, far and wide. Man became the "measure of all things."

Writing Assignments and Class Presentation Topics

1. The progress of the Renaissance is especially apparent in the three sculptures of *David* by three different artists: Donatello (c. 1430), Verrochio (1465), and Michelangelo (c. 1501–1504). Ask students to first briefly explain what the story of David and Goliath is all about. What is most important in the story? Next, have them describe Donatello's *David*. What is emphasized in his work? Then, have students compare Verrochio's version of *David* to Donatello's. How are the statues similar? How do they differ? Finally, have students compare Michelangelo's *David* with the other two. What physical changes have taken place? How do those changes reflect the intellectual changes of the Renaissance? Students should understand that in the story, David overcomes the giant Goliath through inner, spiritual strength. This central idea is captured in Donatello's earlier version of *David*. Over time, however, the physical attributes of David came to equal his spiritual strength, until they are represented equally in Michelangelo's version. The physicality of Michelangelo's *David* is in itself a reflection of inner spirituality.

2. Ask students whom they would want to interview if they could travel back to the Renaissance. Ask them to explain their choice and elaborate on the questions they would like to ask their person. Or, whom would students like to be if they could travel back to the Renaissance? Again, ask them to explain their choice.

3. How did the invention of the printing press affect religion, politics, university study, humanism, and overall knowledge? Which occupations were most affected by the printing press? least affected?

4. Renaissance paintings were often rich in symbolic references that most persons today would not notice or be able to interpret. Without reference either to textbooks or the Internet, ask students to consider Jan van Eyck's *The Arnolfini Marriage*. Ask them to try and explain every single item in the painting, from the bed to the dog at their feet. Also ask students to explain the posture of the couple.

5. Ask students to choose the Renaissance artist they would most like to capture their likeness in a portrait. Which medium would they want their chosen artist to use? Which criteria did they use to select their artist? To get students to think beyond the most commonly known artists, exclude Michelangelo, Leonardo, and Raphael.

6. Why did Europeans begin to explore in the fifteenth century rather than in the fourteenth century? Include technological, economic, and political motivations.

Research Assignments

1. If Europe was such a backwater provincial area of the world in 1300, what changes enabled Europeans to begin to discover and then dominate much of the world by 1500?

2. The Renaissance is sometimes presented as an artistic movement that had little influence on the lives of most people in Europe. By 1500, however, the Renaissance impacted nearly everyone in Europe in some way. Explain why this was the case.

3. What was the role of art and material goods during the Renaissance? The best book on the subject is Lisa Jardine, *Worldly Goods: A New History of the Renaissance* (New York: W. W. Norton, 1996).

4. Ask students to write an essay answering the following question: If an explorer traveled to South America (or to India) in the fifteenth century, what differences would be most noticeable between the new land and Europe? Students should include in their essay the differences in geography, plant and animal life, and human society, as well as all inanimate objects, such as clothing, houses, farming, industry, and political structures.

Literature

Bondanella, Julia Conaway and Peter Bondanella, trans., *Giorgi Vasari: The Lives of the Artists*. 1998.
Caponigri, A. Robert, trans., *Giovanni Pico della Mirandola: Oration on the Dignity of Man*. 1996.
Connell, William J., trans., *The Prince by Niccolò Machiavelli with Related Documents*. 2005.

Films and Videos

The Agony and the Ecstasy (1965; VHS, 2 hrs., 20 min.). The painting of the Sistine Chapel's ceiling serves as the backdrop for the war of wills fought between

Pope Julius II and Michelangelo in this lavish production.

1492–Conquest of Paradise (1992; VHS, 2 hrs., 25 min.). This film is a largely accurate retelling of Christopher Columbus's discovery of the New World.

Mad Love (2001; DVD, 1 hr., 58 min.) This is a lavish dramatization of the life of Juana la Loca, a daughter of Ferdinand of Aragon and Isabella of Castile, who became queen of Castile on her mother's death. She supposedly became unbalanced with the death of her handsome and powerful husband, Philip the Fair of Burgundy, and was placed in confinement by her father, who assumed control of the Castilian crown. The story line has been enhanced, but the main events are depicted accurately enough. Spanish with English and French subtitles

Empires: The Medici: Godfathers of the Renaissance (2004; VHS/DVD, 4 hrs.). This excellent four-part series explores the Medici family's rise to power in Florence. Special emphasis is placed on their artistic patronage, which contributed to the flourishing of the Renaissance.

Historical Skills

Map 14.4, *Early Voyages of World Exploration, p. 537*

The Portuguese explored the coast of Africa and India, whereas the Spanish explored the New World. Why did the Portuguese restrict themselves to trade wherever they went? Why did the Spanish conquer wherever they went?

Mapping the West: *Renaissance Europe, c. 1500,* p. 541

After examining this map of Europe circa 1500, can you explain why power was shifting from the Mediterranean to the Atlantic? Note the size of the countries and their locations in relation to lands and seas surrounding them.

Madonna and Child, *p. 513*

The style of this painting is Renaissance, but the content is medieval. Explain, by noting the description.

Michelangelo's David, *p. 514*

Michelangelo's *David* is such a good example of the Renaissance rebirth of classical ideals that it might be difficult to distinguish it from a Greek statue. How would you know that it must not be Greek but rather Renaissance art?

Expansion of Burgundy, *1384–1476, p. 525,* and The Burgundian Court, *p. 526*

Burgundy's heyday occurred during the period generally considered to be the Renaissance, and yet this illustration seems to suggest an earlier period. Explain why this is so and how this may have happened.

OTHER BEDFORD/ST. MARTIN'S RESOURCES FOR CHAPTER 14

The following resources are available to accompany Chapter 14. Please refer to the Preface of this manual for detailed descriptions of all the ancillaries.

For Instructors

Transparencies

The following maps and images from Chapter 14 are available as full-color acetates.

- Map 14.1: The Spread of Printing in the Fifteenth Century
- Map 14.2: Italy, c. 1450
- Map 14.3: Eastern Europe in the Fifteenth Century
- Map 14.4: Early Voyages of World Exploration
- Map 14.5: European Explorations in the Americas in the Sixteenth Century
- *Sacred & Social Body*
- Botticelli's *Spring*

Instructor's Resources CD-ROM

The following maps and image from Chapter 14, as well as a chapter outline, are available on disc in both PowerPoint and jpeg formats.

- Map 14.1: The Spread of Printing in the Fifteenth Century
- Map 14.2: Italy, c. 1450
- Map 14.3: Eastern Europe in the Fifteenth Century
- Map 14.4: Early Voyages of World Exploration
- Map 14.5: European Explorations in the Americas in the Sixteenth Century
- *Sacred & Social Body*

Using the Bedford Series with The Making of the West

Available in print as well as online at bedfordstmartins.com/usingseries, this guide offers practical suggestions for using **Carol Quillen**, *Petrarch's Secret* in conjunction with chapters 13 and 14 of the textbook; **Geoffrey Symcox and Blair Sullivan's** *Christopher Columbus and the Enterprise of the Indies: A Brief History with Documents* in conjunction with Chapter 14 of the textbook; and **William J. Connell, trans.,** *The Prince by Niccolò Machiavelli with Related Documents* in conjunction with Chapter 14 of the textbook.

For Students

Sources of The Making of the West

The following documents are available in Chapter 14 of the companion sourcebook by Katharine J. Lualdi, University of Southern Maine.

1. Leonardo Bruni and Giovanni Rucellai, *Florence in the Quattrocento* (1427 and 1457)
2. Giovanni Pico della Mirandola, *Oration on the Dignity of Man* (1496)
3. Alessandra, *Letters from a Widow and Matriarch of a Great Family* (1450–1465)
4. Bernardino of Siena, *An Italian Preacher: Sins against Nature* (1380–1444)
5. *Gomes Eanes de Zurara*, Chronicle of the Discovery of Guinea (c. 1453)

Study Guides

The print **Study Guide** and the **Online Study Guide** at bedfordstmartins.com/hunt, both by Victoria Thompson (Arizona State University) and Eric Johnson (University of California, Los Angeles), help students synthesize the material they have learned as well as practice the skills historians use to make sense of the past. The following Map, Visual, and Document activities are available for Chapter 14.

Map Activity

- Map 14.4: Early Voyages of World Exploration

Visual Activity

- *Sacred & Social Body*

Reading Historical Documents

- A Merchant's Advice to His Sons
- Columbus Describes His First Voyage, 1493

The Struggle for Reformation Europe
1500–1560

CHAPTER RESOURCES

Main Chapter Topics

1. The turmoil of the previous century and the threat by the Ottoman Turks led many in early-sixteenth-century Europe to believe that the apocalypse ("Last Judgment") was imminent. This belief, in turn, led individuals to search intensely for religious comfort and meaning.

2. The established church was unable to meet the needs of individuals and society in the sixteenth century because of internal corruption. Focus on money, sale of indulgences, overemphasis on veneration of relics, nepotism, simony, and lack of clerical professionalism and integrity weakened the church at a time when socio-economic and political changes caused a great demand for explanation and consolation.

3. Christian humanists believed that the corruption of the church and the ignorance of the people could be ameliorated through education. Men such as Desiderius Erasmus (c. 1466–1536) and Thomas More (1478–1535) encouraged reform within the Catholic church.

4. When Martin Luther (1483–1546) made public his complaints concerning the church in 1517, the church's hierarchy underestimated Luther as a mere discipline problem, whereas the people saw an opportunity to break free of Rome's monetary demands and other deficiencies.

5. Luther's break from the Catholic church encouraged other reformers to take stands on their beliefs, creating multiple strains of Protestantism, such as Calvinism and Anabaptism.

6. Frustration with the dire socioeconomic conditions common in the sixteenth century merged with the calls for church reform to produce social unrest, rebellion, and severe retaliation by the governments of Europe.

Summary

At the beginning of the sixteenth century, many persons were searching for more meaning in their religion and greater comfort from the trials of everyday life. Internecine warfare and the advancing Turks led people to believe that the apocalypse ("Last Judgment") was imminent. Some searched for more meaning in Christianity via pilgrimages, devotional acts, increased dependence upon the value of relics, vernacular prayer books, and belief in miracles. The church often placed more weight on behavior than spirituality, and this contributed to the uncertainty people felt about salvation. Feeding into this sense of insecurity was the sale of indulgences which, in theory, could reduce the time a person spent in purgatory. Reform efforts from within the church were usually limited and localized, but merchants and artisans were more strategic in their calls for change. Yearning for edifying sermons and a moral clergy, they criticized the church for its simony (especially when it came to appointing children of the nobility to lucrative church offices) and poor pastoral care, and funded young clerics from their own background in university posts who advocated reform at the highest levels. These young clerics were dedicated and thoroughly schooled in Christian humanism.

The leading Christian humanists of this period were the Dutchman Desiderius Erasmus (c. 1466–1536) and the English lawyer Thomas More (1478–1535). Both men combined a love of the classics with Christian piety and desired reforms within society and the church. For Erasmus, education was the key to accomplishing both. His *Adages* (1500) provided wise and pithy sayings on human experience; his *Colloquies* (1523), set out as Latin dialogues, criticized a wide range of subjects, including manners, clerical corruption, and the ambition of Christian princes. Erasmus wanted a united, peaceful Christendom where charity and good works combined with learning and piety were the mark of true religion. These ideas found expression in his *Handbook of the Militant*

Christian (1503). Erasmus continued to criticize the church for its pomposity, power, and wealth in *Praise of Folly* (1509), where he concludes that the wise appear foolish because their values are not of the secular world. He continued his campaign for reform, and published a Latin translation of the Greek New Testament (1516), counseled the future Emperor Charles V (1500–1558) to rule as a Christian prince, and sharply criticized the warrior pope, Julius II. Vacilating between both camps, Erasmus eventually chose Catholic unity over reform and schism, and his writings were condemned by both Protestants and Catholics.

Thomas More shared Erasmus's values. A lawyer, he was well educated and had a long governmental career, serving in Parliament and as a royal ambassador. But More resigned as Lord Chancellor (a prestigious office) in protest over Henry VIII's control of the English clergy, and also because he refused to accept Henry's divorce from Catherine of Aragon as legal. More had earlier set out his vision of reform in *Utopia* (literally, "no place") (1516). A critique of More's own society, Utopia was a just, equitable, and hardworking community. Because there was an equal distribution of goods and services, which included public schools, communal kitchens, hospitals, and nurseries, Utopians had no need of money or private property. They were dedicated to the pursuit of knowledge and natural religion. Utopians loathed war, but were willing to protect their way of life militarily if necessary. Erasmus and More envisioned an enlightened Christendom, but instead got violent and radical change.

Martin Luther (1483–1546) was a young law student when he was caught one day in a storm. He vowed to St. Anne to enter a monastery if he survived. As an Augustinian monk, Luther was greatly troubled by an overwhelming sense of human weakness and his own sinfulness. A superior sent him to study theology, which gave him insight on salvation. He became a professor of theology. Still troubled, though, by church practices, Luther spoke out against indulgences, specifically their sale in 1516 by Johann Tetzel (1465–1519) on behalf of Albrecht of Brandenburg (1490–1545), the new archbishop of Mainz. The money raised was earmarked for the rebuilding of St. Peter's in Rome and to help defray Albrecht's purchase of the archbishopric. Luther drafted ninety-five theses, or points for discussion, criticizing this practice. Intended only for academic debate, the ninety-five theses entered into the mainstream and was seized upon especially by young, educated, urban, middle-class evangelicals. Although seeing himself as the pope's "loyal opposition," Luther wrote three tracts in 1520 that attacked church doctrine and practice: *Freedom of a Christian* expounds that salvation comes not through good works but by faith alone, emphasizes the Gospels, and talks of a "priesthood of all believers"; *To the Nobility of the German Nation* calls on Germans to reject the corruption of the Italians in Rome and reform and defend their church; and *On the*

Babylonian Captivity describes the papacy as the embodiment of the antichrist. Luther defended his position at the Diet of Worms in 1521 in front of the nineteen-year-old emperor, Charles V. Although not immediately excommunicated, it was clear that he shortly would be. Fortunately, Luther enjoyed the protection of the Elector Frederick the Wise of Saxony.

Luther's ideas spread rapidly, especially in German cities that were publishing and trade centers. His ideas were popular among men, women, commoners, and princes, but they resonated especially with urban dwellers who tended to possess higher levels of literacy than their country counterparts and a more highly developed sense of resentment against clerical privilege. Luther's message fit in well with the spiritual needs and social visions of townspeople.

Other reformers, independent of Luther, were also calling for change. Huldrych Zwingli (1484–1531), one-time priest and army chaplain, was greatly influenced by Erasmus and, like him, believed social renewal could be achieved through education. In 1520, Zwingli declared himself a reformer and began attacking, clerical celibacy, ritual fasting, and corruption among the ecclesiastical hierarchy. Zurich soon became the center of the Swiss reform movement. Zwingli worked for a theocracy and fused the concept of the ideal citizen with the perfect Christian. At the Colloquy of Marburg in 1529, an attempt was made to reconcile doctrinal differences between Zwingli and Luther. Although some differences were resolved, no agreement could be reached regarding the Eucharist. Luther believed that Christ was both truly and symbolically present in the sacrament, whereas Zwingli viewed it as a ceremony symbolizing Christ's unity with believers. This would remain a stumbling block between Lutherans and other reform groups.

John Calvin (1509–1564), like Luther, initially studied law, but then experienced a crisis of faith. Influenced by French humanists, Calvin questioned Catholic doctrine. He posted broadsheets denouncing the Mass on Paris churches. The Affair of the Placards provoked royal persecution of religious dissenters, some of whom were executed while many more fled into exile. Calvin sought refuge in Geneva, which had already renounced allegiance to its bishop. Calvin and a local reformer, Guillaume Farel (1489–1565), failed in their first attempt to turn Geneva into a theocracy and, even though driven out of the city in 1538, Calvin was welcomed back in 1541. *The Institutes of a Christian Religion*, written earlier in 1536, became the foundation of Geneva's Christian republic. In it Farel expounds the doctrine of "predestination"—the idea that God knew from the beginning of time who would be among the "elect" or saved. To its supporters, Geneva was a model community. To its critics, who disliked the persecution of dissenters like the Spanish physician Michael Servetus (c. 1509–1553) it was despotic. Geneva, notwithstanding, became the center of reform and Calvinism spread to France, the Netherlands, England, Scotland, Germany, Poland, Hungary, and, eventually, New England.

Some within reform groups desired even more radical change. The German Peasants' War of 1525 was sparked by peasants unhappy at being taxed by both their lord and the church. Some urban workers and artisans also joined in the rebellion, which soon became a mixture of religious and social protest. Luther tried to mediate, warning that even tyrannical rulers had to be obeyed because God appointed them to rule. The German princes wanted reform, but on their terms. And, with Luther's support, they ruthlessly crushed the revolt. In 1529, Charles V declared the Roman Catholic faith the only recognized religion of the empire. Because the Lutheran German princes protested this, they became known as "Protestants."

Out of Zurich came another radical group: the Anabaptists. They rejected the notion of infant baptism because only adults could exercise reason and free will, which were considered integral parts of faith. Anabaptists were baptised again when they reached adulthood. Led by artisans, Anabaptists were drawn from the middle and lower classes. Pacifists, they were persecuted by Zwingli for refusing to bear arms or take oaths of allegiance, and generally for challenging his authority. Zwingli persuaded magistrates to impose death sentences on Anabaptists. Yet, the movement spread and, in 1534, Anabaptists seized the city of Munster in an attempt to return the church to its early roots. They briefly abolished private property and allowed men to take more than one wife. In June 1535, a combined Protestant and Catholic army recaptured Munster, and Anabaptist leaders who survived the skirmish were executed. The Anabaptist movement rekindled in northwest Europe under the Dutch reformer Menno Simons (1496–1561), whose followers were later known as the Mennonites.

The production of vernacular bibles was an important component of the Reformation. The Vulgate Bible contained errors of translation, but the Catholic church resisted more accurate and accessible translations because textual revision threatened church authority. Using Erasmus's 1516 edition, Luther translated the New Testament into German in 1522. Over 200,000 copies were sold in twelve years. In 1534, Luther published his translation of the Old Testament. To counter these, Catholic bibles were also published in German translation. Under the patronage of Guillaume Briconnet, bishop of Meaux, Jacques Lefèvre d'Etaples (c. 1455–1536) translated the Vulgate's New Testament into French. The bishop hoped to spur reform of the French church without breaking with Rome. At first, the English government was slow to accept a vernacular bible, but William Tyndale (1494–1536) published one in Germany and the Low Countries and smuggled copies into England. Although Tyndale was burned as a heretic, after England's break from Rome an official English bible was issued based on his work. Bible reading, however, did not become widespread until the seventeenth century because of low literacy rates and concerns by Protestant clergy that laypersons would challenge their authority.

The Reformation sparked renewed interest in education. State schools replaced medieval church schools. The goal was to train obedient, pious, hardworking Christian citizens, through force if necessary. Parish primary schools taught children age six through twelve, whereas higher schools (*gymnasia*) trained older boys (future pastors, scholars, and officials) in humanist subjects in preparation for university study. Primary education in Catholic countries was uneven. Most Italian boys and girls received some education, but knowledge of Spanish and French was fragmentary. Jesuit colleges, founded in opposition to Protestant *gymnasia*, dominated secondary education and the elite of Catholic Europe attended these schools.

Responsibility for poor relief in both Catholic and Protestant countries was gradually assumed by secular governments. The fourteenth-century's Black Death had been devastating but, between 1500 and 1560, Europe saw rapid population and economic growth and, consequently, also wider gaps between rich and poor. Moralists made distinctions between wandering vagabonds who were often labeled charlatans and criminals, and "God's poor" who should be forced to work if able-bodied. Secular authorities in Nuremburg (1522) and Strasbourg (1523) certified who were genuinely deserving poor and distributed funds to them. Poor relief transcended religious divisions. Similar measures were introduced in the Low Countries, Italy, Spain, and England.

Marriage also underwent changes during the Reformation. Previously, marriages were often conducted privately, which made enforcement difficult if women were later abandoned because no witnesses existed. Common-law marriages among the urban poor were not unusual. Protestant governments regularized marriage and Catholic countries followed suit. Legitimate marriages required registration by both secular and religious authorities. In many Protestant countries, marriages also required parental consent. Although women could seek divorce for reasons of desertion, impotence, and abuse, reconciliation was urged. The monastery was no longer open to Protestant women whose roles were now limited to those of wife, companion, and mother.

The Reformation witnessed changes even in music. The Catholic church often commissioned compositions for religious services, but Protestant congregations provided their own music. The chorale ("harmonized hymn") became the hallmark of Protestant services, and Luther, an accomplished musician, composed numerous hymns, including "A Mighty Fortress." Protestant martyrs sang hymns at their executions, and many urban, German households owned hymnals.

Powerful, princely courts arose alongside and in the wake of the Reformation. The largest was that of Francis I (r. 1515–1547). His court consisted of smaller households for the queen, queen mother, and each of the royal children, all staffed with numerous royal servants. By 1535, the French court numbered 1,622 members. The court was peripatetic, and moved frequently among the many royal palaces. Hunting and mock combat kept the court entertained. Italians Ludovico Ariosto (1474–1533) and Baldesare Castiglione (1478–1529) outlined the cult of "courtesy" ("courtly behavior"). Ariosto's epic poem, *Orlando Furioso* ("The Mad Roland") is a fusion of medieval chivalric romance and classical epic. Concepts of combat, valor, and love are expressed through various characters and stories. Castiglione's *The Courtier* describes, through a series of dialogues, the qualities of the ideal male and female courtier. These were to be a synthesis of military virtues and literary and artistic cultivation.

Catholic Europe also had a vision of a Christian knight. The Emperor Maximilian I (r. 1493–1519) commissioned Albrecht Dürer (1471–1528) to paint a triumphal carriage, in 1518, that incorporated the personified figures of Justice, Temperance, Prudence, Fortitude, Reason, Nobility, and Power. Charles V, Maximilian's grandson, was painted four times by Titian (1477–1576) and, in two of them (1548 and 1550) Charles is depicted as being victorious over Protestants. In Italy, Michelangelo (1475–1564) received numerous religious papal commissions that glorified a papacy very much under siege.

Coinciding with the Reformation was the struggle between France and Spain for dominance over Italy. Most battles were fought in Italy and the Low Countries. In 1525, Francis I was captured at Pavia and held in honorable captivity by Charles V until he agreed to a treaty giving up his claims to Italy. Back in France, though, Francis renounced the treaty and fighting began again. Because of the pope's alliance with France, Charles V seized Rome (1527) and permitted his troops, many of whom were German Protestant mercenaries, to sack the city. Other belligerents in the Italian wars, like England and Italian city-states (who wanted their independence), were drawn into the quarrel for political and religious reasons at various times and on different sides of the conflict. The Italian wars, which began in 1494, ended in 1559 with the Treaty of Cateau-Cambresis, in which the French conceded defeat. The Ottoman Turks viewed this period of warfare as an opportunity to expand their own territory. Under Sultan Suleiman I "the Magnificent" (r. 1520–1566), Muslim forces defeated a Hungarian army at Mohacs (1526) and laid siege, unsuccessfully, to Vienna. Hoping to best Charles V, Francis I briefly allied itself with the sultan (to the scandal of Europe), and Muslim forces besieged imperial troops at Nice. The Franco-Turkish alliance reflected new realities—religion was now but one factor in power politics. With the intro-duction of new military technologies, like heavier artillery pieces, the cost of war rose substantially in the sixteenth century. Money was raised through taxation, the sale of offices, and outright confiscation, but all that was insufficient. On the brink of bankruptcy, England devalued its currency in the 1540s, whereas Charles V and Francis I negotiated huge loans. The German-based Fugger bank established itself under Maximilian I who, in his lifetime, borrowed so much money from them that he had to pawn the crown jewels. The Fugger bank spearheaded a consortium of German and Italian bankers to secure Charles V's election as Holy Roman Emperor in 1519. The new emperor became literally indebted to Fugger. By 1547, Fugger's assets were worth seven million guldens, and over half of that came from Habsburg, especially Spanish loans. War debt had prompted the end of the Italian wars.

Many European realms were divided over religion. France had a growing Calvinist (Huguenot) population by the 1540s, and many of its new members were noble born. Francis I and his son, Henry II (r. 1547–1559), tried to maintain a balance between Protestants and Catholics but, after 1560, the country plunged into religious wars. In England, Henry VIII (r. 1509–1547) had strenuously resisted the Reformation, writing a tract against Luther that earned him the title "Defender of the Faith" from Pope Leo X. But Henry felt the lack of a male heir keenly (he had a daughter, Mary Tudor [Mary I]) and, when he fell in love with Anne Boleyn (1502–1536), he sought a divorce from his first wife, Catherine of Aragon (1485–1536), who was Charles V's aunt. When Rome refused to grant the divorce, Henry VIII appointed Protestants Thomas Cranmer as archbishop of Canterbury and Thomas Cromwell as chancellor. Together these men legislated a separation from Rome. In the Act of Supremacy (1534), Henry was declared head of the English church. The Act of Succession (1534) disinherited Princess Mary and recognized the Boleyn marriage. The dissolution of the monasteries was accomplished with legislation in 1536 and 1539. Thomas More was executed in 1535 for refusing to recognize Henry's leadership of the church and his divorce. A year later Queen Anne, who gave birth to the future Queen Elizabeth I in 1533, was also executed on trumped-up charges of adultery. Henry married four more times and, in 1537, finally fathered a son: Edward VI (r. 1547–1553). Under Henry, the Anglican (English) church was nominally Protestant, but with remnants of Catholic doctrine and ritual. Under Edward VI, the Anglican church became more decisively Protestant. His sister and successor, Mary I (r. 1553–1557), returned England back to the Catholic fold. Over three hundred Protestants were martyred during her reign while many more fled to the continent. Under Elizabeth I, Protestantism was reestablished.

In Scotland, Marie de Guise (1515–1560), the French Catholic widow of James IV, ruled as regent for her daughter, Mary Stuart, who was married to Henry II's heir. The Scottish lords opposed the regent's pro-French policies and formed an alliance with Protestant England. Initially only a small minority group, Protestant numbers grew and, in 1557, the Scottish lords, spurred on by John Knox (1505–1572), imposed a Protestant "covenant" and prayer book on the regent. In 1559, the regent moved against the Protestants, and the Scottish assembly declared her deposed. In the ensuing mayhem (with both French and English troops joining in), Mary Stuart conveniently died, and the Protestant lords assumed control of parliament.

In the German states, the Protestant princes and cities formed the Schmalkaldic League in 1531. In 1541, Charles V convened the Diet of Regensburg, which was aimed at reconciling theological differences between Protestants and Catholics within his empire. When negotiations between the two broke down, Charles militarily defeated the forces of the Schmalkaldic League, and declared freedom of worship for Catholics in Protestant territories. Ironically, some Catholic countries were alarmed at this success, fearing that imperial forces might next be turned on them. In 1552, the Protestant princes regrouped and forced Charles to retreat to Italy. The ensuing Peace of Augsburg (1555) recognized the Lutheran church and the right of the German princes to determine the religion of their respective states. Calvinists, Anabaptists, and other dissenting groups were excluded from this agreement. Although fragile, peace lasted into the early seventeenth century. Charles V abdicated his territories in favor of his son, Philip II in 1555 and, in 1556, retired to a monastery.

After years of seeming inaction, the Catholic church began to renew itself in the 1530s and 1540s. Catholic reformers stressed biblical ethics and moral discipline. Under the auspices of Pope Paul III and Charles V, a general church council was called at Trent. The Council of Trent sat sporadically from 1545–1563, and basically reasserted church authority. It also reaffirmed the doctrine of transubstantiation, which had been a particular dividing point between Catholics and Protestants, and thus dashed any hope at religious reconciliation.

Out of a reinvigorated Catholic church came the Society of Jesus, known as the Jesuits. Its militaristic outlook came from its founder, Ignatius Loyola (1491–1556), who had been a soldier. Formally recognized by the papacy in 1540, the order quickly attracted followers. At the time of Loyola's death, the Jesuits numbered a thousand. Hundreds of Jesuit colleges educated future Catholic leaders and Jesuit missionaries helped spread Catholicism literally around the world, but especially within the Portuguese maritime empire. For some indigenous people, Catholicism seemed an alien, coercive force, whereas to others it was a sweet sign of reason and faith, but there was some attempt by the Spanish crown to protect indigenous peoples. The Portuguese were highly receptive

to the idea of indigenous persons as missionaries, but other Catholic countries discriminated against native populations, especially in Africa and the Americas. This was less of an issue in Asia, where missionaries admired Chinese and Japanese culture and were not supported militarily by their home countries.

Suggestions for Lecture and Discussion Topics

1. How could the Catholic church be forced to reform its ways from within? Could a reformation have taken place internally as had happened many times over the centuries of the church?

2. Discuss the differences in the Protestant beliefs, including views on communion and church governance. There are three different positions on communion: (a) the bread is the spiritual and physical body of Christ (Catholic and Lutheran beliefs); (b) the bread is the spiritual body of Christ (Calvinist belief); and (c) the bread is symbolic of the body of Christ (Anabaptist belief). Governance also has three different forms: (a) the clergy have the authority (Episcopal form); (b) an elected council has the authority (Presbyterian form); and (c) the entire membership holds the authority (Congregational form).

3. Why did the Protestant movement fracture into so many separate sects? Some of the fractures resulted from differing religious beliefs, such as those on communion, but regional and national differences also had an impact. Students might discuss how easy it is to find fault with the existing system, but how difficult it is to agree on a replacement.

4. Have students discuss the deterioration of the role of women in the sixteenth century, especially in Protestant lands. What were the causes? How could this have been avoided?

Making Connections

1. *Contrast the ways in which the Christian humanists and the Protestant reformers tried to change society.* Christian humanists wanted reform of both church and society, and believed that education would be key to doing both. They also believed that the church should reform itself rather than be subjected to lay amendment. To facilitate reform, men like Thomas More and Erasmus published works that gently and indirectly criticized the Catholic church. But when reform was not forthcoming, prominent figures, like Martin Luther, and their followers broke away from the Catholic church and established their own religious sects. These new Protestant sects promoted vernacular bibles, improvements in education, and marriage reform.

2. How were the religious and political conflicts of the early sixteenth century related? Politics and religion were virtually inseparable during this period. The Catholic regimes of France, Scotland, and the Holy Roman Empire all faced Protestant opposition led mainly by a proactive nobility that clamored for official recognition and sometimes a complete shift in state religion. In England under Queen Mary I, the Protestant opposition mainly took the shape of exiles abroad, although like their European counterparts, they, too, were vocal in their condemnation of their ruler and her policies.

Writing Assignments and Class Presentation Topics

1. Assign some students David Herlihy, *Women, Family and Society in Medieval Europe* (New York: Berghahn Books, 1995); and have other students read Roland Bainton, *Women of the Reformation in Germany and Italy* (Boston: Beacon, 1974). Then, ask students to make presentations on the role of women in the periods.

2. William J. Bouwsma, *John Calvin: A Sixteenth-Century Portrait* (Oxford: Oxford University Press, 1988) makes a strong case for Calvin as a person torn between the Middle Ages and the modern era. Students examining this topic can better understand the dramatic changes that were taking place.

3. Assign small groups of students different Christian denominations, such as Catholic, Lutheran, Calvinist, Anabaptist, or Anglican. Ask each group to present the major principles on which their assigned religion is based and to argue why that religion is the correct or best religion.

4. Discuss with the class, or ask students to write about which came first: the Protestant Reformation or the Catholic Reformation. As they examine this question, they should see that the early Protestant reformers were Catholic reformers originally. Additionally, you might ask students to explain why the Catholic church did not reform until after the 1550s, and why it did so at that time.

Research Assignments

1. Have students write an essay on whether or not the Reformation improved the lives of Europeans. Richard Marius, *Martin Luther: The Christian between God and Death* (Cambridge, MA: Belknap, 1999) is a good starting point. Marius believes that Luther's Reformation caused terrible devastation that might have been avoided.

2. Assign an essay on whether the Reformation was more medieval or Renaissance. In some ways, the Reformation was medieval, such as in its total reliance on God and God's power to save one's soul, while in other ways the Reformation was Renaissance, such as in its emphasis on education and the power of education to change people's lives. Start by having the class read William J. Bouwsma, *John Calvin: A Sixteenth-Century Portrait* (Oxford: Oxford University Press, 1988).

3. Have students write an essay on how the Reformation affected women in Europe. The following will help students with this assignment: Olwen Hufton, *The Prospect Before Her: A History of Women in Western Europe* (New York: Alfred A. Knopf, 1998); and Elisja Schulte van Kessel, "Virgins and Mothers between Heaven and Earth," in Natalie Zemon Davis and Arlette Farge, eds., *A History of Women in the West*, vol. 3, *Renaissance and Enlightenment Paradoxes* (Cambridge, MA: Belknap, 1993). Hufton makes a case for the continued opportunities in convents, while van Kessel makes an equally strong case for the deterioration of opportunities for women in Reformation Europe.

4. Assign students an essay in which they support or oppose a move to call the first half of the sixteenth century the "Age of Charles V." Have students begin by reading Roland Bainton, *The Reformation of the Sixteenth Century* (Boston: Beacon Press, 1952 [rpt. 1985]); W. S. Maltby, *Reign of Charles V* (Palgrave Macmillan, 2002); W. P. Blockmans and P. Blockmans, trans., *Emperor Charles V* (Oxford: Oxford University Press, 2002); and I. van den Hoven-Vardon *Renaissance Monarchy: The Reigns of Henry VIII, Francis I, and Charles V* (Oxford: Oxford University Press, 2002).

5. England's Reformation differed from that which occurred on the continent, owing to the fact that it was sparked by Henry VIII's desire for a divorce and his need for a male heir. Ask students to write an essay in which they examine the issue of the degree to which the English Reformation was a government-led movement. Begin by looking at J. J. Scarisbrick's, *The Reformation of the English People* (Oxford: Blackwell, 1984 [rpt. 1985]); C. Haigh, ed., *The English Reformation Revised* (Cambridge: Cambridge University Press, 1987); D. MacCulloch, *Suffolk and the Tudors; Politics and Religion in an English County 1500–1600* (Oxford: Oxford University Press, 1986); and M. C. McClendon, *The Quiet Reformation* (Stanford: Stanford University Press, 1999).

Literature

Bull, George, trans., *Conte Castiglione Baldassare: The Book of the Courtier*. 1976.

Dolan, John P., ed., *The Essential Erasmus*. 1964.

Sacks, David Harris, ed., *Utopia by Sir Thomas More*. 1999.

Waldman, Guido, trans., *Ludovico Ariosto: Orlando Furioso*. 1999.

Films and Videos

A Man for All Seasons (1966; Fred Zinnermann, dir.; with Paul Scofield and Robert Shaw). Although it captures the setting of the English Tudor period well, this film romanticizes Sir Thomas More and the events of the last years of his life.

Anne of a Thousand Days (1969; Charles Jarrott, dir.; with Richard Burton and Genevieve Bujold). This film, rich in atmospheric detail, traces the stormy relationship between King Henry VIII and his second wife, Anne Boleyn.

The Six Wives of Henry VIII (1970; VHS/DVD, approx. 9 hrs.). Each 90-minute episode takes as its subject one of Henry VIII's six wives. Although some of the material is dated in places—especially the sixth episode on Katherine Parr—this series remains the best film drama to date of Henry VIII and his wives. The costumes of the main characters have been carefully researched and accurately reproduced.

Lady Jane (1985; Trevor Nunn, dir.; with Helena Bonham Carter). This film nicely captures the feel of the English Tudor period. Some events are accurately depicted, such as the physical beatings Jane Grey was subjected to, but the love story between Jane and her husband (John Dudley) and their sympathy for the poor are pure fantasy.

Luther (2003; expected release date, spring/summer 2004, 1 hr. 52 min.). This film is about Martin Luther and the Protestant Reformation. Although events are confused chronologically, the film does capture the atmosphere of the period.

Historical Skills

Map 15.1, Spread of Protestantism in the Sixteenth Century, p. 558

Protestantism spread in ways that differed from place to place. After examining the map, explain how Protestantism spread in Germany, France, England, and Scotland. Explain why Protestantism gained little ground in Italy and Spain.

Mapping the West: Reformation Europe, c. 1560, p. 576

Why did the spread of Protestantism dissipate by 1560? How did the existing balance affect politics? How did politics affect the religious balance?

Persecution of the Anabaptists, p. 561

The Anabaptists were persecuted and martyred more than any other group during the Reformation. Does this illustration condone or decry the executions? How can one tell what the artist's viewpoint is?

The Field of the Cloth of Gold, p. 569

The meeting between Henry VIII of England and Francis I of France was painted by an unknown artist. Would you guess that the artist was English or French? Explain why. What was the purpose of these monarchs' display of pomp and ceremony?

Thomas More, Utopia (1516), p. 551

Ask students what More considered to be wrong with his society based on this passage from *Utopia*. More is concerned about the fragmentation of the social fabric, whether through a breakdown in traditional relationships, or a population that lacks necessities. Vanity, where one person believes that he or she is superior to another, negatively affects both situations.

OTHER BEDFORD/ST. MARTIN'S RESOURCES FOR CHAPTER 15

The following resources are available to accompany Chapter 15. Please refer to the Preface of this manual for detailed descriptions of all the ancillaries.

For Instructors

Transparencies

The following maps and images from Chapter 15 are available as full-color acetates.

- Map 15.1: Spread of Protestantism in the Sixteenth Century
- Map 15.2: The Peasants' War of 1525
- Map 15.3: Habsburg-Valois-Ottoman Wars, 1494–1559
- Mapping the West: Reformation Europe, c. 1560
- Dürer's *The Knight, Death & the Devil*
- *Luther as Monk*

Instructor's Resources CD-ROM

The following maps and image from Chapter 15, as well as a chapter outline, are available on disc in both Power-Point and jpeg formats.

- Map 15.1: Spread of Protestantism in the Sixteenth Century
- Map 15.2: The Peasants' War of 1525
- Map 15.3: Habsburg-Valois-Ottoman Wars, 1494–1559
- Mapping the West: Reformation Europe, c. 1560
- Dürer's *The Knight, Death & the Devil*

Using the Bedford Series with The Making of the West

Available in print as well as online at <u>bedfordstmartins.com/usingseries</u>, this guide offers practical suggestions for using *Utopia by Sir Thomas More*, edited with an introduction by David Harris Sacks textbook; *Victors and Vanquished: Spanish and Nahua Views of the Conquest of Mexico*, edited with an introduction by Stuart B. Schwartz, in conjunction with Chapter 15 of the textbook; and *The Trial of Mary Queen of Scots: A Brief History with Documents by Jayne Elizabeth Lewis* in conjunction with chapters 15 and 16 of the textbook.

For Students

Sources of The Making of the West

The following documents are available in Chapter 15 of the companion sourcebook by Katharine J. Lualdi, University of Southern Maine.

1. Martin Luther, *Letter to the Three Nuns at Wittenberg* (1524)
2. Argula von Grumbach and John Hooker, *Women's Actions in the Reformation* (1520s–1530s)
3. *Iconoclasm and Reparations during the Reign of Francis I* (1515–1547)
4. Saint Ignatius of Loyola, *A New Kind of Catholicism* (1546, 1549, 1553)
5. John Calvin, Articles Concerning Predestination (c. 1560) and The Necessity of Reforming the Church (c. 1543)

Study Guides

The print **Study Guide** and the **Online Study Guide** at bedfordstmartins.com/hunt, both by Victoria Thompson (Arizona State University) and Eric Johnson (University of California, Los Angeles), help students synthesize the material they have learned as well as practice the skills historians use to make sense of the past. The following Map, Visual, and Document activities are available for Chapter 15.

Map Activity

- Mapping the West: Reformation Europe, c. 1560

Visual Activity

- Dürer's *The Knight, Death & the Devil*

Reading Historical Documents

- Thomas More, *Utopia*, 1516
- Erasmus Writes to Martin Luther, 1519

A Century of Crisis
1560–1648

CHAPTER RESOURCES

Main Chapter Topics

1. The Peace of Augsburg (1555) officially recognized Lutheranism within the Holy Roman Empire but did not recognize Calvinism. Nonetheless, Calvinism expanded rapidly after 1560, not only altering the religious balance of power in Europe, but also producing political repercussions—including civil war and revolt—in the Netherlands, France, Scotland, and other parts of Europe.

2. Philip II of Spain, the most powerful monarch of his time, did not succeed in his quest to restore Catholic unity in Europe or in his efforts to destroy political enemies in France, the Netherlands, and England. England and the Netherlands emerged from the conflict as great European powers in economic and military terms.

3. The Thirty Years' War, the last and most deadly of the wars of religion, began in 1618. By its end in 1648, much of central Europe lay in ruins and the balance of power had shifted away from the Habsburgs—the monarchs of Spain and Austria — toward France, England, and the Dutch Republic. The war's large armies necessitated bureaucracy and powerful centralized states.

4. The Thirty Years' War exacerbated the economic crisis already under way in Europe. Famine and disease also contributed to the suffering. The war shifted the economic balance of power; as it ended, northwestern Europe began to dominate international trade, but the Spanish and Portuguese retained preeminence in the New World.

5. Even as religious wars raged, thinkers posited nonreligious theories of political authority and scientific explanations for natural phenomena. In this revolution, the Dutch Republic, England, and, to a lesser extent, France led the way. Nevertheless, many still believed in magic and witchcraft and accepted supernatural explanations for natural phenomena.

6. The scientific revolution overturned the theories of Ptolemy and Aristotle, which had passed unquestioned for centuries. More important, however, was the early-seventeenth-century insistence on deductive and inductive scientific investigation that created the basis for rapid expansion of knowledge.

Summary

The peace established within the Holy Roman Empire through the Peace of Augsburg (1555) was maintained until the early seventeenth century, but Protestant inroads into France, the Spanish-ruled Netherlands, and England, along with accompanying political agendas, sparked almost continuous warfare in these countries between 1560 and 1648. Coinciding with the Thirty Years' War was an economic downturn that led to food shortages, famine, and disease—especially in central Europe. Religion was increasingly losing ground to secularized approaches to art, science, and philosophy.

Calvinism spread rapidly in France during the 1550s, and included at least one-third of the nobility, whose women took a particular interest in religion. In 1562, the French Calvinist, or Huguenot, church fielded an army that warred against a rival Catholic army. Both sides looked to great noble families for leadership: the Huguenots to the Bourbon family, who were close relatives of the French king; and the Catholics to the Guise family. The death of Henry II (1559) and the rule of his wife Catherine de Medici as regent for the underage Charles IX (r. 1560–1574) created an atmosphere of political uncertainty that led to civil war in 1562. On St. Bartholomew's Day (August 24, 1572), during festivities to celebrate the marriage of the king's Catholic sister Marguerite de Valois to the Huguenot Bourbon prince, Henry of Navarre, a botched attempt to assassinate the Huguenot leader, Gaspard Coligny, led to three days of mass killings of Protestants. During the St. Bartholomew's Day Massacre, three thousand Huguenots were killed in Paris, and ten thousand more were murdered in the provinces over the following six weeks. Huguenot pamphleteers proclaimed their right to resist a tyrant. This fed into the developing doctrine of constitutionalism, that called for a constitution or contract between ruler and ruled. Both Protestants and Catholics saw the French Wars of Religion as requiring the aid of coreligionists in other countries.

None of Henry II's sons produced an heir to the throne. Caught between the Guises and the Catholic League on the one hand, and the Bourbons and the Huguenots on the other, Catherine de Medici (1519–1589) and her sons attempted to maneuver between the two factions. After Henry III, the youngest of Catherine's sons, was assassinated (1589), Henry of Navarre took the throne as Henry IV (r. 1589–1610) and repelled the Spanish who intervened militarily to block his accession. To control France, Henry IV converted to Catholicism but, in 1598, he granted the Huguenots a large measure of religious toleration in the Edict of Nantes. This measure, which had the support of neutral Catholics and Calvinists who were *politiques*, dealt realistically with a minority too large to ignore and impossible to eradicate. In the years before his assassination in 1610, Henry did much to strengthen the monarchy, including creating a strong bureaucracy to offset the fractious nobility and the use of pageantry and festivals to impress his subjects. Wealthy, middle-class merchants and lawyers were brought into the bureaucratic fold through their purchases of offices, which they could sell or bequeath on to their heirs.

Philip II of Spain (r. 1556–1598) wanted to restore Catholic unity in Europe and lead a Christian Europe against the Muslims. He headed a great naval force against the Ottoman Turks at Lepanto (1571), the success of which enabled him to crush a Muslim revolt in southern Spain led by the Moriscos—Muslim converts to Christianity who had remained secretly faithful to Islam. But Philip could neither prevent Henry IV's accession in France, nor put down the revolt of the largely Calvinist Dutch provinces that began in 1566. After unpaid Spanish troops sacked Antwerp (1576) over a period of eleven days that became known as the "Spanish Fury," the northern and southern provinces cooperated long enough to expel the Spanish. The southern provinces, largely Catholic and French-speaking, were returned to Spain in 1579, but the northern provinces formed the Dutch Republic. Although not formally recognized until 1648, by the end of the century it was a self-governing state sheltering several religious groups. Decentralized government meant that local provincial elites (regents) possessed more power in the Dutch Republic than the ruling prince of Orange. In the seventeenth century, the Dutch Republic's seaborne, trade-based economy thrived. Contact with other cultures made the Dutch Republic tolerant of religious diversity. Catholics could worship privately and Jews openly in most Dutch provinces.

Relations between England and Spain were also strained. Queen Mary's husband, Philip II, had supported England's brief return to the Catholic fold. After Mary's death, Philip proposed marriage to her sister and successor, Elizabeth I. She rejected him, restored Protestantism, and spent much of her reign steering a middle road between Catholicism and extreme Calvinism. But the Puritans steadily gained influence and urged Elizabeth to support the Dutch rebellion against Spain, much to Philip's chagrin. Domestically, Mary, Queen of Scots had fled to England (1568) after being forced by Scottish Calvinists to abdicate her throne on behalf of her infant son, James. In 1587, after nearly twenty years in English captivity, Mary offered Philip her right of succession to the English throne. The plot was discovered and Parliament finally persuaded Elizabeth to execute her cousin in 1587. With Pope Sixtus V's blessing, Philip II sent an Armada of 130 ships against the "English Jezebel" in May 1588. English fire ships scattered the fleet, after which a gale blew the Spanish fleet around Scotland and decimated it. At Philip's death (1598), his empire was still extensive, but he had failed to restore Catholic unity to Europe and his empire had lost much of its luster. In *Don Quixote* (1605), Migel de Cervantes captured the sadness of Spain's loss of grandeur. By the time of Elizabeth's death (1603), on the other hand, Shakespeare was writing some of his most brilliant plays, while James VI of Scotland, England's new king (James I), inherited a country growing in international prominence and power.

In Russia, the Orthodox church faced no direct opposition, although Ivan IV (Ivan the Terrible [r. 1533–1584]) tortured and killed priests (and many others besides) for reasons other than religion. Under Ivan IV, the Russian Empire expanded down the Volga River and eastward into Siberia, but attempts to expand to the west were thwarted by Sweden and especially Poland-Lithuania, which had united into a single commonwealth in 1569. Unlike other European monarchs, the power of Polish-Lithuanian kings was limited and religious toleration promoted. After Ivan's death came the "Time of Troubles," during which the king of Poland-Lithuania tried to enthrone his son as tsar. In 1613, Russian nobles drove out the invaders and installed another nobleman, Michael Romanov (r. 1613–1645), thus beginning the Romanov dynasty.

The Thirty Years' War was the last great war of religion and was sparked by disputes between Boehmia and the Austrian Habsburgs. The Peace of Augsburg had established a balance between Catholics and Lutherans within the Holy Roman Empire but, as Jesuit missionaries won back Catholic cities and as Calvinism made inroads into still Lutheran areas, religious tensions once again resurfaced. That the empire comprised eight major ethnic groups further complicated matters. When Archduke Ferdinand, the Catholic king of Protestant Bohemia, was elected Emperor Ferdinand II (r. 1619–1637), the Bohemians deposed him in favor of the Calvinist Frederick V (r. 1616–1623) of the Palatine. Frederick and Bohemia lost to imperial forces at the battle of White Mountain (1620). From there the war spread largely because much of Protestant Germany was plundered by a mercenary army led by Albrecht von Wallenstein (1583–1634), a Protestant Czech in the pay of the Catholic emperor Ferdinand II. The Lutheran Danish king Christian IV (r. 1596–1648) joined in ostensibly to protect German Protestants, but also to extend his territory. After his defeat by Wallenstein, Gustavus Adolphus of Sweden (r. 1611–1632) stepped in, funded by the Catholic French government under Cardinal Richelieu (1585–1642) who put "reasons of state" well ahead of religious considerations. France worried more about Habsburg power, especially in Spain, than Catholic unity. In 1635, France declared war on Habsburg Spain and aided the Dutch in their struggle for independence.

By 1648, Spain and France were financially and militarily exhausted. Spain had lost Portugal, France had an underage king (Louis XIV), and both countries faced rebellion at home. The lives of ordinary people had been brutally disrupted by war and unpaid soldiers (who rampaged through towns) were on the verge of mutiny. Although some fighting continued beyond 1648, the Peace of Westphalia, negotiated by a diplomatic congress, provided a comprehensive settlement and also a model for resolving conflict among European states. France was a major winner, replacing Spain as the paramount power on the continent; Sweden gained territories in the north. The Habsburgs lost the most: the Spanish Habsburgs recognized Dutch independence after eighty years of war, and the Austrian Habsburgs granted autonomy to the German princes in the Holy Roman Empire. The Peace of Westphalia marked the end of religion as a major factor in war. State interests, national security, commerce, and dynastic pride, among other factors, now dominated policy.

Peace had come to Europe's political powers, but the war had been devastating for ordinary people, especially the peasants. Soldiers were often mercenaries and, because governments were often not able to pay them, they staged mutinies; looted villages; stole from farm families; and raped, tortured, and murdered at will. Armaments and tactics changed and the size of armies increased dramatically. The size of the armies and length of the war produced a need for more revenue and more officials, especially university-educated individuals, to supervise the maintenance of armies, the collection of taxes, and the repression of resistance to the new impositions. The expanding bureaucracy made rulers dependent upon ministers like Cardinal Richelieu, who were capable of managing it all. Rulers also paid a great deal of attention to their royal images and to court protocol and spectacle—which called for still more revenue and even higher taxes.

The last half of the 1500s featured not only religious and political turmoil, but also population growth and rising prices. A flood of precious metals from the Americas inflated food prices, but wages could not keep up. Most governments overspent revenues and ended the century with deep deficits. Recession appeared at different times in various parts of Europe. Foreign trade slumped, prices leveled off, population growth slowed, and production of manufactured goods dropped. The Dutch and the English fared best in the new economic situation, the former through agricultural innovation and seaborne trade, the latter because it had not relied on New World gold and silver and was spared the Thirty Years' War. Causes of the recession have been widely debated, and range from overpopulation and the Thirty Years War to high taxation and climatic change. For many ordinary people, the recession brought food shortages and outbreaks of famine and disease. It also contributed to the deepening of a division between prosperous and poor peasants. Poor harvests resulted in many indigent persons simply abandoning their homes to take to the road in search of food. Malnutrition meant that the poor were especially susceptible to disease. In particular, many peasants became landless laborers. Poor women were also hard hit, with new restrictions placed on their labor. The crisis further resulted in a new pattern of late marriages and smaller families generally, but especially for the poor.

The seventeenth century ended the domination of Mediterranean economies and shifted dominance to the Atlantic economies of northwestern Europe. Spain and northern Italy lost the lead; whereas England, the Dutch Republic, and France competed to become the top mercantile power. There was also an important east-west difference. In the west, economic recovery and labor shortages ultimately worked in favor of the peasants who gained greater independence. In the east, the aristocracy and crown cooperated in completing the subordination of the peasants. In Russia, the law code of 1649 formally reduced peasants to serfs.

England, France, and the Netherlands came late to colonization in the New World. They were largely restricted to the North American continent and the Caribbean. By the 1640s, the British North American colonies contained more than fifty thousand people. French Canada, by contrast, had only about three thousand because France would not allow Protestants to emigrate from France. Both England and France developed their possessions in the Caribbean in the 1620s and 1630s. Some colonists justified the settlement of the New World through missionary work. Native Americans were most receptive to Catholicism, with its emphasis on shared rituals, than to Protestantism, which emphasized individual conversion. But the Spanish were not left behind. Even before the flood of English and French colonists, Spain had explored the Pacific coast as far as northern California, moved inland reaching New Mexico, and competed with Muslim rulers over the heart and soul of the Philippines.

Secularization, the idea that there are nonreligious explanations for political authority and natural phenomena, took root first in those countries that were economically strong: England, the Dutch Republic and, to a certain extent, France. Two major new forms of artistic expression, developed at the end of the sixteenth century, exemplifying the move toward secularization. One was the permanently based professional theater. Hundreds of new plays were written during this period, although the best known were those of William Shakespeare (1564–1616). His plays, often set in the past or foreign lands, nevertheless reflected the concerns of his age: the heartening and sometimes crushing reality of human relationships, the exercise of power in changing times and circumstances, and the rise of the modern state. Opera, the second new art form, was first prominent in the Italian states and combined music, drama, dance, and scenery. It made few intellectual demands because it generally took its plots from familiar stories and mythology. Other artistic shifts were originating in Italy. "Mannerism" was a theatrical style whereby artists distorted perspective to emphasize a message or theme. The work of El Greco, which featured elongated figures, crowded canvases, and bizarre visual effects, epitomized mannerism. Whereas the Renaissance had emphasized balance, unity, and clarity, Baroque art featured curves, exaggerated lighting, intense emotion, and flamboyance. It was closely tied to the Counter-Reformation and particularly embraced by Catholic countries. The Catholic painter Peter Paul Rubens (1577–1640) was the first great Baroque painter. The work of Protestant painters of the period, like Rembrandt van Rijn (1606–1669), was more realistic and focused on everyday life.

Secularization had perhaps its greatest impact on political and natural science. The French Catholic magistrate and politique, Michel de Montaigne (1533–1592), borrowed from the ancient philosophy of skepticism, which helped his argument for religious toleration. He invented the essay (from the French verb *essayer*, "to try") as a brief but memorable means of expressing ideas. Another French Catholic politique, the lawyer Jean Bodin (1530–1596), defended monarchy as the political system most likely to maintain order. Bodin rejected the idea that people had the right to resist tyrannical authority and thus laid the foundation for absolutism. The jurist Hugo Grotius (1583–1645), however, contended that government should be conducted according to natural law, which was valid independent of religious dictates or the decrees of authorities. Natural law protected natural rights, which Grotius defined as life, body, freedom, and honor. Grotius followed his natural laws and rights to attack the use of torture by both church and state. Because he separated religion out of natural law, Grotius's writings were often condemned by both Catholics and Protestants.

Religious authorities also condemned new approaches and discoveries in astronomy and medicine. Nicolaus Copernicus (1473–1543) first challenged the geocentric model of the solar system accepted by Ptolemy and Aristotle. His student Giordano Bruno was burned at the stake for teaching the heliocentric theory. Although rejecting heliocentrism, the Dane Tycho Brahe (1546–1601) added further to the debate through the invention of new instruments that enabled direct observation of the planets and stars. His assistant, Johannes Kepler (1571–1630), embraced heliocentric theories and built on Brahe's work by formulating three laws of planetary movement that promoted the idea that orbits were elliptical, not circular. Galileo Galilei (1564–1642) furthered heliocentric theories by questioning the idea that the heavens were perfect and unchanging in a closed universe. The Catholic Inquisition placed Galileo under house arrest and forced him to recant his theories, but he continued to publish them in the Dutch Republic. Breakthroughs in medicine, anatomy, and pharmacology also took place in the latter part of the sixteenth and first part of the seventeenth centuries. Through his dissection work, the Flemish Andreas Vesalius (1514–1564) refuted the ideas of the Greek physician Galen, whose theories had dominated medicine up to the sixteenth century. Theophrastus Bombastus von Hohenheim, better known as Paracelsus (1493–1541), experimented with new drugs, and laid the foundation of modern pharmacology. The English physician William Harvey (1578–1657) uncovered the workings of the body's circulatory system. The English politician Francis Bacon (1561–1626) and the French mathematician and philosopher René Descartes (1596–1650) contributed to the exposition of the scientific method: Bacon, attacking reliance on ancient writers, practiced inductive reasoning through observation and experimental research; Descartes, through the application of mathematics and logic, developed deductive reasoning through self-evident principles. Descartes, in particular, wished to go beyond the radical skepticism of Montaigne to establish principles for finding certain knowledge. Hounded by Catholic authorities, Descartes fled to the Dutch Republic where he could work more freely. The experiences of Descartes and Galileo highlight the religious division between Catholicism and Protestantism regarding scientific discovery.

Despite scientific discoveries, the division between science and magic was not always clear during this period. Many believed firmly in witchcraft, and witchcraft trials, which significantly were concentrated in the territories of the Holy Roman Empire, and peaked in Europe between 1560 and 1640. Providing an outlet for social stress and anxiety, it was perhaps no coincidence that this peak also coincided with the rapid spread of religious reform. The victims of persecution were mostly women. Historians disagree about whether this represented men's fundamental fear of and hostility toward women, or persecution of the socially marginal, or something else entirely.

The devastating wars of the period produced as a by-product stronger states and a shift in the center of European power from the south to the northwest. An important shift in attitudes also occurred. Many Europeans accepted secular themes and authorities in science, politics, and art without giving up their personal religious views. Religion was still vitally important, but it took a back seat to other causes of war between nations.

Suggestions for Lecture and Discussion Topics

1. The latter half of the sixteenth century includes the Counter-Reformation, the spread of Calvinism, the French Wars of Religion, and the Dutch revolt. What makes this period both dynamic and brutal are the ways in which strong defenses of religious ideas intertwine with more mundane political and economic motives. To expose your students to the importance of this material, examine the impact of Calvinism on politics in this period, particularly the idea of the right to resist tyrants. This idea could be presented in the abstract initially, but then placed in the context of either the French Wars of Religion or the Dutch revolt. While religious motives are important in this era, it is also worth reminding students that political considerations, personal or family ambitions, and the like remain important factors.

On the idea of the right to resist tyrants, see Chapter 6, section 5 (pp. 153–162) of Perez Zagorin, *Rebels and Rulers, 1500–1660*, vol. 1, *Society, States, and Early Modern Revolution: Agrarian and Urban Rebellions* (Cambridge: Cambridge University Press, 1982); and Chapter 12 of H. G. Koenigsberger and George L. Mosse, *Europe in the Sixteenth Century* (London: Longman, 1968). Zagorin and Koenigsberger and Mosse cover many other topics in a clear, dependable way.

For the French Wars of Religion, in addition to titles cited in the bibliography for Chapter 16 of *The Making of the West*, see Chapter 1 of Robin Briggs, *Early Modern France, 1560–1715* (Oxford: Oxford University Press, 1977) for a competent survey. See also Bernard Chevalier, "France from Charles VII to Henry IV," in Thomas A. Brady Jr., ed., *Handbook of European History, 1400–1600: Late Middle Ages, Renaissance, and Reformation*, Heiko A. Oberman and James D. Tracy, vol. 1, *Structures and Assertions* (Grand Rapids, MI: William B. Eerdmans, 1996), a good survey with an extensive bibliography.

For the Dutch revolt, Jonathan Israel's book is excellent (see chapter bibliography). Other good discussions include the essay by J. W. Smit, "The Netherlands Revolution," pages 19–54, in Robert Forster and Jack P. Greene, eds., *Preconditions of Revolution in Early Modern Europe* (Baltimore, MD: Johns Hopkins University Press, 1970); and Chapter 11 in Perez Zagorin, *Rebels and Rulers, 1500–1660*, vol. 2, *Provincial Rebellion, Revolutionary Civil Wars, 1560–1660* (Cambridge: Cambridge University Press, 1982). A far more detailed discussion by an expert on the period is Geoffrey Parker, *The Dutch Revolt*, rev. ed. (New York: Viking Penguin, 1989).

2. Philip II is a central and somewhat tragic figure in the latter part of the sixteenth century. His own story is certainly worth reviewing and, in the process, it is possible to comment on major developments throughout western Europe and in the New World. Henry Kammen's biography, cited in the chapter bibliography, is superb. A survey of Spain in the sixteenth century, also by Henry Kammen, "The Habsburg Lands: Iberia," is in *Handbook of European History, 1400–1600*, cited in suggestion 1. Appended to the essay is an extensive bibliography. Also useful is Chapter 11 of H. G. Koenigsberger and George L. Mosse, *Europe in the Sixteenth Century* (cited in suggestion 1). More detailed coverage may be found in H. G. Koenigsberger, *The Habsburgs and Europe, 1516–1660* (Ithaca: Cornell University Press, 1971).

An exciting focus for a discussion of Philip and events in western Europe during his reign is the Spanish Armada of 1588 (there were additional armadas). In addition to Garrett Mattingly's highly readable account (cited in the chapter bibliography), several studies were published during the four-hundredth anniversary in 1988. One that presents the Armada from the Spanish perspective is Felipe Fernandez-Armesto, *The Spanish Armada: The Experience of War in 1588* (Oxford: Oxford University Press, 1988). Colin Martin and Geoffrey Parker, *The Spanish Armada* (New York: W. W. Norton, 1988) is an evenhanded presentation of the event.

3. Elizabeth I of England continues to fascinate and intrigue students. How was she able not only to succeed in ruling England for decades, but also to succeed brilliantly? How much did she contribute to England's rise to great power status by the end of the sixteenth century? What was she like as an individual? What was it like to live in Elizabethan England?

Two good introductory studies are Susan Watkins, *The Public and Private Worlds of Elizabeth I* (New York: Thames and Hudson, 1998); and Geoffrey Reagan, *Elizabeth I* (New York: Cambridge University Press, 1988). A very readable book that presents Elizabeth and her England is Peter Brimacombe, *All the Queen's Men: Elizabeth I and the English Renaissance* (New York: St. Martin's Press, 2000). An excellent but long biography is that of Wallace T. MacCaffrey, *Elizabeth I: War and Politics, 1588–1603* (Princeton: Princeton University Press, 1992). Finally, students would enjoy viewing *Elizabeth* (New York: PolyGram Video, 1999, 2 hrs., 4 min.), with Cate Blanchett as Elizabeth. Whether you screen some or all of the film, it could furnish the basis for a discussion of what

Elizabeth was like as a person and what England was like as a country. It would also, of course, be necessary to discuss the problems and possibilities of presenting history in feature films. (Students who cannot get enough of Elizabeth I will also enjoy *Elizabeth R,* with Glenda Jackson in the lead role [Beverly Hills, CA: CBS Fox Video, 1995, six videocassettes, 90 min. per segment].)

4. To pair Elizabeth with Ivan IV (the Terrible) may seem perverse. Ivan was, however, not only a contemporary, but actually tried at one point to win Elizabeth's hand. He is a fascinating character in his own right, and his reign offers a good point at which to introduce the Russian Empire into the discussion of western civilization. His reign—that of Boris Godunov, the "Time of Troubles," and the founding of the Romanov dynasty—would make an interesting session and a vivid contrast to the stories of rulers in western Europe.

Two essays — Nancy Shields Kollmann, "Muscovite Russia, 1450–1598," and Hans-Joachim Torke, "From Muscovy towards St. Petersburg, 1598–1689" — furnish essential background and interpretation. They are both part of Gregory L. Freeze, ed., *Russia: A History* (Oxford: Oxford University Press, 1997). See also Part One of W. Bruce Lincoln, *The Romanovs: Autocrats of All the Russias* (New York: Dial Press, 1981) for good coverage of the first Romanovs. The essay by Michael Cherniavsky, "Ivan the Terrible as Renaissance Prince," *Slavic Review,* vol. 27 (1968), pp. 195–211, presents Ivan as a person of considerable learning and sophistication, an important point to make in view of his later bizarre behavior. *The Modern Encyclopedia of Russian and Soviet History* is an excellent source for dependable articles on people, events, and institutions from Russian history (Gulf Breeze, FL: Academic International Press, 1976–). (As of volume 56, the encyclopedia was retitled *The Modern Encyclopedia of Russian, Soviet, and Eurasian History.*) Finally, students should see at least a few scenes from Sergei Eisenstein's masterpiece, *Ivan the Terrible* (New York: Janus Films, 1999, 3 hrs., 4 min.), parts 1 (1944) and 2 (1946). While Eisenstein's film says as much about the times in which it was made (Stalin's Russia) as about Ivan's time, it offers an intriguing interpretation of Ivan as an individual. It is also a landmark film in the history of cinema (the script and a good deal of background information are available in an edition published by Simon & Schuster, New York, 1970).

5. The Thirty Years' War is a short title for a series of complicated, interlocking events of high drama and great significance in European history. Students will probably find a detailed discussion of battles and alliances confusing. You may wish to present an outline using the phases mentioned in the text and stressing the mixture of religious, political, and other motives. There are, of course, dramatic events beginning with the defenestration of Prague (and here you may wish to mention the next defenestration of Prague, which took place 330

years later in 1948, when the foreign minister of Czechoslovakia, Jan Masaryk, either jumped or was thrown out of the window of his office; this event was part of the Communist takeover of Czechoslovakia that year); the period also provides fascinating historical figures, such as Gustavus Adolphus and Richelieu, and many stories of atrocities and great suffering. This would also be a good time to review the Peace of Westphalia and to assess the relative strength of the various European powers.

The Treaty of Westphalia (or Peace of Westphalia) is readily available online. A book that takes a topical approach to war in this period (chapters include "The Changing Art of War," "Recruitment," and "Life and Death in the Armies") is Frank Tallett, *War and Society in Early-Modern Europe, 1495–1715* (London: Routledge, 1992). E. Neville Williams, ed., *Facts on File Dictionary of European History, 1485–1789* (New York: Facts on File, 1980), may be of some use as well.

6. The development of the French state in the first half of the seventeenth century is a process worth following in some detail. During this period, the theory and practice of absolutism began to take shape. Although Louis XIV took developments much further, it is worthwhile tracing what one scholar calls "the birth of absolutism" in this period.

The major figure in the development of the French state is Cardinal Richelieu, one of the all-time great practitioners of politics. For two good biographies, consult Anthony Levi, *Cardinal Richelieu and the Making of France* (New York: Carroll & Graf, 2000); and Joseph Bergin, *The Rise of Richelieu* (New Haven: Yale University Press, 1991). A good biography of Louis XIII is A. Lloyd Moote, *Louis XIII, The Just* (Berkeley: University of California Press, 1989). In addition to Robin Briggs (cited in suggestion 1), see Yves-Marie Berce, *The Birth of Absolutism: A History of France, 1598–1661* (New York: St. Martin's Press, 1996). James B. Collins, *The State in Early Modern France* (New York: Cambridge University Press, 1995) continues the story all the way to 1789.

7. The three major figures of the early scientific revolution are Francis Bacon, René Descartes, and Galileo Galilei. Each man has been the object of a good deal of attention in the past decade and the subject of excellent, very readable books. Their life histories and major ideas make for interesting comparisons, and they each offer important insights into the broader circumstances of their time.

To begin with Galileo: Dava Sobel, a talented writer about science and technology, has recently published *Galileo's Daughter: A Historical Memoir of Science, Faith, and Love* (New York: Walker & Co., 1999), a book based on more than a hundred letters from Galileo's oldest daughter, a nun, to her father. In addition, there is Michael Sharratt, *Galileo: Decisive Innovator* (Cambridge: Cambridge University Press, 1996). Two outstanding reference works are Peter K. MacHamer, ed., *The Cambridge Companion to Galileo* (Cambridge: Cambridge University Press, 1998); and Maurice A. Finocchiaro, ed., *The Galileo Affair: A Documentary History* (Berkeley: University of California Press, 1989).

It is difficult to discuss Francis Bacon without also mentioning René Descartes, but to deal with Bacon, Descartes, and Galileo may make for an overcrowded session. Although reviewing Bacon's and Descartes's contributions to the scientific method may be more practical, doing so omits Bacon's career as a courtier (a point of comparison with Galileo and an opening for a discussion of early-seventeenth-century England). On Bacon, in addition to the book by Perez Zagorin, there is a recent biography by Lisa Jardine and Alan Steward, *Hostage to Fortune: The Troubled Life of Francis Bacon* (New York: Hill & Wang, 1999). See also Markku Peltonen, ed., *The Cambridge Companion to Bacon* (Cambridge: Cambridge University Press, 1996). For Descartes, see John Cottingham, ed., *The Cambridge Companion to Descartes* (Cambridge: Cambridge University Press, 1992). Also by Cottingham, who has turned studying Descartes into a cottage industry, are *A Descartes Dictionary* (Oxford: Blackwell Reference, 1993); and *Descartes* (Oxford: Oxford University Press, 1998), a collection of articles. Finally, two good biographies are Stephen Gaukroger, *Descartes: An Intellectual Biography* (Oxford: Oxford University Press, 1995); and Genevieve Rodis-Lewis, *Descartes: His Life and Thought* (Ithaca: Cornell University Press, 1999).

8. Many of Shakespeare's plays, especially his history plays, reveal much about how the English interpreted and related history to contemporary events and circumstances. Some possible topics for discussion include the relationship between church and state in late-sixteenth-century England, the evolving concept of "commonweal" and "commonwealth," the limits and responsibilities of monarchical authority, traditional versus "modern" views on warfare, and gender relationships. All of Shakespeare's plays are available in Bedford-St. Martin editions, which include critical essays with each text. Also see Russ McDonald, *The Bedford Companion to Shakespeare: An Introduction with Documents* (Boston: Bedford-St. Martins, 2001). There are also some relatively recent and notable film productions of many of Shakespeare's plays, including *Henry V* and *Hamlet* with Kenneth Branagh, *King Lear* with Ian Holm, and *Richard III* with Ian McKellan, which might be the basis of further discussion.

Making Connections

1. *How did the balance of power shift in Europe between 1560 and 1648? What were the main reasons for this shift?* The religious wars of the period altered the balance of power as Catholic countries faced increasingly well-armed, well-organized Protestant forces. During the Thirty Years' War, however, political agendas soon replaced religious differences as the propelling force of international conflict. Habsburg lands in central Europe were devastated by the Thirty Years' War and, at the end of the war, power shifted away from the Habsburgs in Austria and Spain to France, England (which had been spared the destruction of the war), and the Dutch Republic (which gained its independence from Spain).

2. *Relate the new developments in the arts and sciences to the political and economic changes of this period of crisis.* There was an artistic and intellectual divide between Catholic and Protestant Europe during this period. The religious wars created political, economic, and social turmoil in predominantly Catholic countries and, as a result, art increasingly emphasized the emotional and spiritual aspects of Catholicism. Scientific ideas that contradicted Catholic teaching were harshly suppressed. In mainly Protestant countries, secularization informed art and intellectual thinking. Drama and art focused on everyday life, which was realistically portrayed. Protestants believed that God had created a rational and knowable universe, and scientists in Protestant countries were free to seek rational explanations for natural phenomena. The development of a political philosophy rooted in nature was a further extension of this mindset. As the Thirty Years' War progressed, there was a shift away from the traditional Mediterranean-based economies of Catholic countries to the Atlantic-based economies of northwestern Europe, especially in the Protestant nations of England and the Dutch Republic.

Writing Assignments and Class Presentation Topics

1. Assign students an essay on Henry IV of France as a leader. Emphasize that the essay is not to be a capsule biography of Henry, but an assessment of those characteristics that allowed him to lead effectively both before and after he became king. As preparation for the essay, ask the class to list and discuss characteristics they believe contributed to effective leadership. While the focus should be as much as possible on leadership in the late sixteenth century, some reference to the present will be unavoidable and probably useful.

2. Was the defeat of the Spanish Armada in 1588 a turning point in history? Ask students to write a counterfactual essay arguing that the Spanish Armada was successful. Then, what happened? Why? Help students understand that this is more than an exercise in creative writing. They must have, for example, some basis for deciding that Philip would or would not have proceeded to invade England, or for deciding that Henry would or would not eventually become king of France.

3. Set up a discussion of motives in the Thirty Years' War. Each student or small group of students is assigned a country or an individual to investigate before the discussion. In the first part of the discussion, students should represent the country or individual. In the second part of the discussion, students should attempt to survey the Thirty Years' War as a whole in terms of motive and try to reach a conclusion about the decline of organized religion as a reason for war.

4. Ask students to pretend they are living in 1648 and represent one country at the court of another. They are to report on that other country and compare it to the country they are representing. For the essay, students should use maps and the terms of the Peace of Westphalia as well as information from *The Making of the West* and class discussions.

Research Assignments

1. What did it take to be a scientist in the early seventeenth century? Ask students to do a research project on Galileo's career as a scientist. They should pay particular attention to the sources of his funding and to the politics, including church politics, of doing science. The sources listed in the chapter bibliography and in suggestion 6 of "Suggestions for Lecture and Discussion Topics" are good starting points.

2. Divide students into three or four groups and assign each group a country. Each group then investigates trials for witchcraft in that country and produces a fifteen-minute courtroom drama, which they perform before the rest of the class. Use Alan C. Kors and Edward Peters, *Witchcraft in Europe, 1100–1700: A Documentary History* (Philadelphia: University of Pennsylvania Press, 1972); and Brian P. Levack, *The Witch-hunt in Early Modern Europe* (London: Longman, 1987) as starting points.

3. In reference to assignments 1 and 2 above, students may want to investigate notable astrologers of the period, like Dr. John Dee at the English court, and Nostradamus at the French court. How and for whom did these men divine the future? What differentiated their activities from witchcraft? See Gerald Suster, *John Dee* (Berkley, CA: North Atlantic Books, 2003); Benjamin Woolley, *The Queen's Conjurer: The Science and Magic of Dr. John Dee, Advisor to Queen Elizabeth I* (New York: Henry Holt & Co., 2001); and Damon Wilson, *The Mammoth Book of Nostradamus and Other Prophets* (London: Robinson Publishers, 1999).

Literature

Grossman Edith, trans., *Miguel de Cervantes: Don Quixote*. 2003.

Screech, M. A. trans., *Michel de Montaigne: The Complete Essays*. 1993.

Wells, Stanley, et al., eds., *William Shakespeare: The Complete Works*. 1999.

Films and Videos

Elizabeth R (1971; VHS, DVD, 9 hrs.). This series of six episodes of approximately 90 min. each chronicles the major events of Elizabeth I's life including her establishment on the throne of England, the marriage negotiations with the duc d'Alencon, the execution of Mary, Queen of Scots, and the Spanish Armada. Although made in 1971, the series remains the best film drama to date of Elizabeth's life. The queen's gowns are stunningly re-created from surviving portraits.

Mary, Queen of Scotland (1971; Charles Jarrott, dir.; with Vanessa Redgrave). Although inaccurate on some details, the film does accurately reflect the queen's strained relations with the Scottish nobles, the Protestant John Knox, and her reprobate husband, Henry Darnley.

La Reine Margot (1994; DVD, 2 hrs., 24 min.). This is a dramatization of Alexandre Dumas's novel about Marguerite de Valois, her marriage to Henri of Navarre, and the Massacre of St. Bartholomew's Day in 1572. Although the plot has been embellished, it is a largely accurate retelling of those events. Care has been lavished on costumes and settings. The film is in French with English subtitles.

Dangerous Beauty (1998; VHS/DVD, 1 hr., 52 min.). This film is set in sixteenth-century Venice and focuses on the life of a prominent courtesan. The film nicely captures the culture of the period, especially religious sensibilities and the restrictions placed on women. Care has been taken to re-create accurate costumes and settings. The film is in English and French, with subtitles.

Shakespeare in Love (1998; John Madden, dir.; with Gwyneth Paltrow and Joseph Fiennes). Because so little is actually known about Shakespeare's early years as a playwright, this fictional account seems plausible, even if it is also unlikely. Great care has been lavished to get the costuming and setting right.

Elizabeth (1998; Shekhar Kapur, dir.; with Kate Blanchett and Joseph Fiennes). Although the plot is extremely garbled, Blanchett's likeness to known portraits of Elizabeth is striking, and suggests what the queen might have looked like in the flesh.

Galileo's Battle for the Heavens (2002; VHS, 2 hrs.). Dava Sobel's novel, *Galileo's Daughter*, is the basis for this dramatized biography of Galileo. The film uses the letters Galileo wrote to his illegitimate daughter to explore his life and work.

Elizabeth (2003; DVD, 3 hrs., 17 min.). This excellent series, presented by the Tudor historian David Starkey, traces Elizabeth's life up to her accession using archival material and reenactments.

In Search of Shakespeare (2004; VHS/DVD, 4 hrs.). Michael Woods provides a historical context for William Shakespeare's plays by tracking down the playwright in the historical records and in the places he visited. Although a bit breathless in his enthusiasm, Woods does an excellent job of piecing together what is known about the playwright's life in this four-part series.

Historical Skills

Map 16.2, The Empire of Philip II, r. 1556–1598, p. 586

Ask students to review Philip's possessions, both in Europe and in other parts of the world. What does the map suggest about Philip's difficulties in accomplishing his goals? Remind students of the differences in opinions and understandings between the Dutch and Philip, then ask them to consider how serious these kinds of problems might be in other parts of Philip's empire.

Mapping the West: The Religious Divisions of Europe, c. 1648, p. 616

Ask students to compare this map to Map 16.3, The Thirty Years' War and the Peace of Westphalia, 1648 (p. 595). Which religions gained from the fighting in the Thirty Years' War? Which religions were not affected by the fighting? For which religions might the Thirty Years' War present a mixed picture of wins and losses?

Taking Measure: The Rise and Fall of Silver Imports to Spain, 1550–1660, p. 598

You may wish to point out that prices in the seventeenth century continued to rise even as the import of precious metals from America fell (see Fig. 2.09, p. 82, in David Hackett Fischer, *The Great Wave: Price Revolutions and the Rhythm of History* [Oxford: Oxford University Press, 1996]). What would be the implications of continuous inflation and a decrease in the supply of precious metals for the Spanish king from about 1620 onward? Ask students to consider as well what the graph cannot show: Spain continuously at war with a shifting group of opponents.

Massacre Motivated by Religion, p. 585

Ask students to contrast this painting to the engraving depicting *The Horrors of the Thirty Years' War* (p. 594). While both show terrible brutality and cruelty, the first event, the St. Bartholomew's Day Massacre, has a purpose, direction from people in authority, and a kind of logic. Can the same be said about the event shown in Jacques Collot's engraving? Ask students to discuss whether this difference makes the one event justified, at least in comparison to the other.

Rembrandt's Depiction of Dutch Life, p. 588

The Night Watch, the feature attraction of the Rijksmuseum in Amsterdam, is one of the most famous paintings in the world. Originally, it was meant only to commemorate the existence of a militia company. What does the painting indicate about the Netherlands and the prosperous middle-class members of the militia by the 1640s? Ask students to comment on why the painting has become such a famous piece of art.

"Savages" of the New World, p. 605

What do students think is the theme of Paolo Farinati's *America*? Is it perhaps something to do with the advance of Christianity? What is the symbolic meaning of the figure to the left of the Christianized native American?

The Trial of Galileo, p. 612

Why did the Catholic church want Galileo to recant his ideas, based on Copernicus's heliocentric theory, that Earth revolved around the sun? Should Galileo have refused to recant? Would this have been in keeping with the way he had lived his life before the trial? Was Galileo treated differently from the way in which someone on trial for witchcraft would have been treated?

The Horrors of the Thirty Years' War, p. 594

The people who suffered most during the Thirty Years' War were those who were least directly involved in the conflict. Students can examine the effect Hans Grimmelshausen's use of a "simpleton" has on his account. Grimmelshausen uses a literary device that reflects sage wisdom of the time, which held that the simpleminded, or "foolish," were wise and the wise were foolish. This heightens the account because there is no reason or logic to the brutality of marauding soldiers who destroy for the sake of destroying.

Other Bedford/St. Martin's Resources for Chapter 16

The following resources are available to accompany Chapter 16. Please refer to the Preface of this manual for detailed descriptions of all the ancillaries.

For Instructors

Transparencies

The following maps and images from Chapter 16 are available as full-color acetates.

- Map 16.1: Protestant Churches in France, 1562
- Map 16.2: The Empire of Philip II, r. 1556–1598
- Map 16.3: The Thirty Years' War and the Peace of Westphalia, 1648
- Map 16.4: European Colonization of the Americas, c. 1640
- Mapping the West: The Religious Divisions of Europe, c. 1648
- *Elizabeth I*
- *The Life of the Poor*

Instructor's Resources CD-ROM

The following maps and image from Chapter 16, as well as a chapter outline, are available on disc in both Power-Point and jpeg formats.

- Map 16.1: Protestant Churches in France, 1562
- Map 16.2: The Empire of Philip II, r. 1556–1598
- Map 16.3: The Thirty Years' War and the Peace of Westphalia, 1648
- Map 16.4: European Colonization of the Americas, c. 1640
- Mapping the West: The Religious Divisions of Europe, c. 1648
- *Elizabeth I*

Using the Bedford Series with The Making of the West

Available in print as well as online at bedfordstmartins.com/usingseries, this guide offers practical suggestions for using **Jayne Elizabeth Lewis, *The Trial of Mary Queen of Scots***, in conjunction with chapters 15 and 16 of the textbook.

For Students

Sources of The Making of the West

The following documents are available in Chapter 16 of the companion sourcebook by Katharine J. Lualdi, University of Southern Maine.

1. Henry IV, *Edict of Nantes* (1598)
2. Galileo, *Letter to the Grand Duchess Christina* (1615)
3. *The Trial of Suzanne Gandry* (1652)
4. Map of Guaxtepec, Mexico (c. 1580)
5. David Pieterzen DeVries, *Voyages from Holland to America* (1655)

Study Guides

The print **Study Guide** and the **Online Study Guide** at bedfordstmartins.com/hunt, both by Victoria Thompson (Arizona State University) and Eric Johnson (University of California, Los Angeles), help students synthesize the material they have learned as well as practice the skills historians use to make sense of the past. The following Map, Visual, and Document activities are available for Chapter 16.

Map Activity

- Map 16.2: The Empire of Phillip II, r. 1556–1598

Visual Activity

- *Elizabeth I*

Reading Historical Documents

- The Horrors of the Thirty Years' War
- Galileo Writes to Kepler

State Building and the Search for Order

1648–1690

CHAPTER RESOURCES

Main Chapter Topics

1. Louis XIV personified the idea of absolutism. Louis established his personal rule by manipulating courtiers, employing middle-class officials, creating Europe's largest army, and dealing ruthlessly with any opposition.

2. Central and eastern European rulers followed Louis XIV's model of absolutism. The ruler of Brandenburg-Prussia worked to rebuild after the Thirty Years' War and unite far-flung territories, the Austrian Habsburgs fought off the Ottoman Turks and governed many ethnic and religious groups, and the Russian tsars controlled a large but poor empire through enserfment of the peasants.

3. English kings failed to establish absolutism. Rather, revolution between 1642 and 1660, and again in 1688 to 1689, confirmed the institution of an elected parliament with constitutional powers. The revolutions also led to the guarantee of certain rights under the law.

4. The Dutch Republic also founded a strong constitutional system. After William and Mary came to the English throne, the Netherlands joined England to block Louis XIV's efforts to dominate Europe. The Dutch economy, learning, and arts flourished together.

5. Still shaken by the upheavals of the wars of religion, Europeans sought new bases for authority in politics, science, and the arts. Although seeking greater freedom, they labored to balance freedom with order. The new worldview emphasized order and regularity.

6. Isaac Newton's synthesis of astronomy and physics was not merely a breakthrough in science. It also made science and its activities a means for beneficial changes and gains in secular understanding.

Summary

There were two main models of state building in the seventeenth century: absolutism and constitutionalism. France, under Louis XIV, epitomized absolutism, which was a system of government wherein the ruler claimed sole and uncontested power. England exemplified constitutionalism, wherein the ruler shared power with parliaments made up of elected representatives. While still claiming a divine right to rule, absolutist and constitutional monarchs were also turning to secular justifications for their authority. Both forms of government were responses to the threat of disorder that followed the Wars of Religion. Louis XIV came to the throne of France in 1643 at age five. For several years, his mother, Anne of Austria, and her adviser, Cardinal Mazarin (1602–1661), ruled in his name. But, as the financial burdens of the Thirty Years' War increased, Mazarin's policies were challenged (1648) by a charter of demands that would have given the parlements (high courts) the right to approve new taxes. When Mazarin arrested the leaders of the parlements, a series of revolts erupted that involved nearly every social group in France.

The Fronde (1648–1653) was an uprising by nobles who wanted more local control, and the middle and lower classes in the cities who protested constantly rising taxes. Queen Anne was forced to take Louis XIV and flee Paris. Private armies fought the crown and each other. The monarchy survived mainly because no one wanted it overthrown, but it left deep scars on Louis XIV and fed into his absolutist policies—he would not be forced to flee again. After Mazarin's death (1661), Louis XIV decided to rule without the assistance of a first minister. He made himself the center of French power and culture, using court ritual to domesticate the fractious nobility and bind them to him through the exercise of his personal favor or displeasure. Louis also paid a great deal of attention to his image, calling himself the "Sun King," and using the arts adroitly to magnify his grandeur. He especially cultivated the image of a Roman emperor. Under Louis's direction, the arts practically became a branch of government. Writers like the dramatist Molière who, in *Tartuffe* (1664), sharply criticized the church, were in the patronage of the king who extended his protection from critics to them. Other playwrights like Pierre Corneille (1606–1684) and Jean-Baptiste Racine (1639–1699) set tragedies in ancient Greece and Rome and highlighted the classical virtues of order and self-control that Louis fostered at court. The king also commissioned many operas, and even performed major roles in some court ballets. He further sponsored many public works projects, like the construction of veterans' hospitals, but the most important and massive of these was the new palace at Versailles. Versailles and its elaborate, geometrical gardens embodied the idea that order and control defined the exercise of power; it symbolized Louis's success in reining in the nobility and his cultural and military domination over Europe.

Orthodox Catholicism was a pillar of Louis XIV's rule, and he clamped down on religious dissenters. He focused first on the Jansenists, named after Cornelius Jansen (1585–1638). The Jansenists were Catholics whose austere religious beliefs resembled those of the English Puritans. Louis rejected any doctrine that did not stress obedience to authority. Significantly, some noble supporters of the earlier Fronde had embraced Jansenism. Louis closed down Jansenist theological centers and forced the Jansenists underground. In 1685, Louis revoked the Edict of Nantes (1598), which had given Huguenots (French Calvinists) religious freedom and some political independence. He hoped the Huguenots would convert to Catholicism, but thousands instead emigrated to England, Brandenburg-Prussia, and the Dutch Republic.

Louis XIV formed a nationwide bureaucracy under his personal supervision using the intendants (officials who held their positions directly from the king) to reduce local power, improve the collection of taxes, and bring order and control to the kingdom. Additionally, Louis decreed, in 1673, that parlements could no longer vote or even speak against proposed laws. Louis was a suspicious man and employed men from relatively humble origins, whose promotion depended entirely on him, to discover information and run the government. The most important of these men was Jean-Baptiste Colbert (1619–1683) who emphasized mercantilism, which held that governments should do everything possible to increase national wealth. Among other measures, this entailed establishing overseas trading companies, granting manufacturing monopolies, enacting high tariffs, subsidizing shipbuilding and, in 1663, taking over the trading company that had founded New France in Canada and forcibly colonizing present-day Quebec with French peasants. Troops were also garrisoned there. The Iroquois were subdued by force and French exploration of

North America undertaken. In 1684, Sieur de la Salle (1643–1687) claimed territory along the Mississippi River and Gulf of Mexico for Louis XIV, calling it "Louisiana." Virtually every government in Europe embraced mercantilism at this time.

Fearing the Spanish and Austrian Hapsburgs, Louis XIV built up a massive army and instituted military reforms, including special hospitals built for the care for veterans, standardized uniforms, a militia draft, and a centralized system for the distribution of supplies. In 1667–1668, Louis fought the War of Devolution, claiming that because the dowry of his Spanish wife had not been paid, the Spanish Netherlands should "devolve" to him. Louis defeated the Habsburgs in the Spanish Netherlands but had to make peace because England, Sweden, and the Dutch Republic joined the war. But, in the Treaty of Aix-la-Chapelle (1668), Louis gained control of some towns along the Spanish Netherlands border. Seeking to further extend his territories, Louis attacked the Dutch (1672) and Spain (1673), and marched troops into parts of the Holy Roman Empire. Religious differences were set aside, and a Dutch, Spanish, and German coalition formed against him. Under the Treaty of Nijmegen (1678–1679), Louis acquired several Flemish towns and Franche-Comte, which linked Alsace to the rest of France. Still, Louis continued to pursue his expansionist ambitions, and he seized Strasbourg (1681), invaded Lorraine (1684), and attacked some cities of the Holy Roman Empire (1688). Finally, between 1689 and 1697, the League of Augsburg—England, Spain, Sweden, the Dutch Republic, the Austrian emperor, and various German princes—forced Louis to return most of his newly won territories in the Peace of Rijswijk (1697). What thirty years of war illustrated was that absolutism and warfare fed each other. Military success both required and justified ever-expanding state power, but it also eroded state resources, prevented administrative and legal reform, and took a heavy toll on peasant and urban families who were forced to billet soldiers and pay ever-higher taxes.

Elsewhere, others tried to follow Louis XIV's example. Frederick William of Hohenzollern, the Great Elector of Brandenburg-Prussia (r. 1640–1688), shaped territories on the Rhine and along the Baltic coast into an absolutist state during his long reign. He came to an agreement with the Junkers (Prussian nobles): in exchange for allowing him to collect taxes, Frederick gave them complete control over their enserfed peasants and exempted them from taxation. This had the effect of reducing the estates (representative assemblies) to merely a ceremonial institution. He then concentrated on building a large army and an efficient bureaucracy. Although Frederick followed the model of centralizing state power, he did not imitate Louis's ostentatious court. And, as a Calvinist, Frederick William welcomed French Huguenot refugees after Louis revoked the Edict of Nantes.

Sweden, which included modern-day Finland, Estonia, half of the Ukraine, and much of the Baltic coastline of Poland and Germany, flip flopped between absolutism and more representative government. Under Gustavus Adolphus, Sweden was an absolutist state, but after his death (1632), his daughter, Queen Christina (r. 1632–1654), conceded much authority to the estates. When Christina abdicated after converting to Catholicism, her successors returned to absolutism, and Sweden once again became a formidable military power. It spent the next forty years warring with its neighbors and, by the 1690s, had, like France, exhausted itself financially.

For the Habsburg emperor Leopold I (r. 1658–1705), the challenge was consolidating an empire that encompassed different territories, ethnicities, languages, and religions. He promoted a new nobility made up of Czechs, Germans, Italians, Spanish, and even German-speaking Irish; turned Bohemia into a virtual colony; and gained almost all of Hungary in campaigns against the Ottoman Turks. The Hungarian crown was joined to the Austrian, and together they formed the core of the Habsburg Empire until 1918. Finally, Leopold formed a permanent standing army to replace the mercenaries he formerly used.

The Turks also pursued state consolidation, though by means that differed from European monarchs. The Ottomans expanded into the Balkan peninsula through forcible settlement and military control. Local converts to Islam gradually took over local administration, and peasants often served as mercenaries in the Turkish army. Ottoman rulers kept power through a divide-and-conquer process; elites were played off against one another, and various levels of authority battled for power. This shifting political and social system is what made the Ottoman Empire appear weak to European powers.

The Russian Empire also seemed quite different from France, yet its rulers followed an absolutist path similar to the rest of Europe. The response of Tsar Alexei (r. 1645–1670) to a bloody revolt over new administrative structures and taxes was to set the law code of 1649 in place, which established a strict social hierarchy and stripped peasants of most of their rights turning them into serfs. Opposition to enserfment was brutally crushed. The peasants were sacrificed to bring their noble landlords under the control of the tsar. Alexei also increased the size of the Russian army and imposed strict control over the Orthodox church. One religious group, the Old Believers, opposed measures to bring the church into line with Byzantine tradition, and they were ruthlessly suppressed. Still, modern western influences began to penetrate Russia under Alexei and his daughter Sophia, and the government increasingly regulated the minutiae of daily life.

Poland-Lithuania was a notable exception to the absolutism of eastern Europe. Ukrainian Cossacks revolted against the king (1648) and, during a twenty-year period known as the "Deluge," confrontations between the Cossacks and the Polish nobles eventually involved Russia. In 1667, at the end of a Russo-Polish war, the tsar annexed eastern Ukraine and Kiev. Other countries—including Sweden, Brandenburg-Prussia, and Transylvania—tried to take advantage of the chaos. Many Polish towns were destroyed and as many as one-third of the population died. Jewish and Protestant minorities suffered especially; some 56,000 Jews were killed by the Christian combatants, while victorious Catholics hounded Protestants into exile. The commonwealth revived briefly when Jan Sobieski (r. 1674–1696) was elected king, but he could not compete with the power of the great nobles, who controlled parliament. Poland-Lithuania remained weak.

Constitutionalism and absolutism clashed head on in England. Charles I and Parliament fought early in the reign when Parliament resisted new taxes and insisted on being consulted about future taxation. Charles's response was to rule without Parliament from 1629 to 1640, squeezing out as much money as possible from existing taxation laws. In those years, Charles's archbishop of Canterbury, William Laud (1573–1645), pushed the English church toward Catholicism. Puritan critics of Laud and his policies were brutally punished. Scotland actually rebelled over the imposition of Laud's religious policies and, needing funds to fight the war, Charles called a Parliament. While the Parliament of 1640 did not intend revolution, it did work toward reform. To that end, it repealed taxes Charles had enacted without their approval, removed the unpopular William Laud from office, and required Parliament to assemble at least once every three years. Charles's attempt in January 1642 to invade Parliament and arrest the leaders of the opposition produced a state of civil war.

Members of the king's army were known as "Cavaliers"; Parliament's forces were known as "Roundheads" (because of their short hair). Presbyterians wanted Calvinism with some kind of centralized authority, while Independents wanted autonomous congregations free from any hierarchy. Although religiously divided, the Puritans united behind the MP Oliver Cromwell (1599–1658). Cromwell reorganized parliamentary troops and formed the New Model Army, which defeated royalists at the battle of Naseby (1645). Charles surrendered in 1646. When Parliament, dominated by the Presbyterians, tried to disband the army controlled by Independents, disgruntled soldiers began engaging their officers in debates about political authority. Known as "Levellers," they demanded an annual Parliament, pay for MPs (so that the poor could afford to hold office), and enfranchisement for male heads of household.

Fearing the abolition of property rights, Cromwell turned on them. Divisions among the Puritans sparked new religious sects, like the Baptists and Quakers, that emphasized individual religious experience and disdained hierarchical authority. These sects attracted women especially who, by virtue of advocating their religious beliefs, became political activists. Parliament feared the overturn of the social order by these new religious sects. In late 1648, the Rump Parliament (formed when the Independents purged the Presbyterian members) tried the king and executed him in January 1649. The Rump Parliament set up a Puritan republic headed by Oliver Cromwell (1599–1658). Regarding himself as God's agent, Cromwell eliminated political opposition, suppressed the Levellers, allowed some freedom of worship to nonconformist religious sects (though not to Catholics), reconquered Scotland, and crushed Ireland. In actions that are still known today as "the curse of Cromwell," entire Irish Catholic garrisons and their priests were massacred and Catholic-owned property confiscated. Cromwell tried to restrict Dutch trade with England, and even warred against them (1652–1654). These wars resulted in even greater taxes than Charles had required. When Parliament objected (1653), he dismissed it and made himself Lord Protector. Cromwell's death (1658) revived the specter of civil war and, in 1660, the newly elected Parliament invited Charles II (r. 1660–1685) to return from exile and restore the monarchy.

In the 1670s, Charles II and Parliament sparred over the possibility of a Catholic monarch and tolerance for Catholicism and dissenting Protestant sects. In 1673, Parliament forced Charles to rescind his Declaration of Indulgence, and passed the Test Act requiring governmental officials to swear loyalty to the English church. Parliament feared the succession of James, Charles's Catholic brother and heir, and split into two factions: Tory (slang for Irish Catholic bandit), who wanted a strong hereditary monarchy and the restored ceremony of the Anglican church; and Whig (Irish Catholic designation for a Presbyterian Scot), who wanted parliamentary supremacy and tolerance for Protestant dissenters. After Charles died (1685), his Catholic brother James II (r. 1685–1688) favored pro-Catholic and absolutist policies. The birth of a male heir to James led both the Tories and the Whigs in Parliament to invite William of Orange—the husband of James's eldest, Protestant, daughter Mary — to invade England. In what is called the "Glorious Revolution," James fled, and William and Mary accepted both the throne and, in 1689, a bill of rights guaranteeing Parliament's full partnership in a constitutional government. Further, the Toleration Act granted freedom of worship to all Protestants (but not to Catholics).

In the Netherlands, representatives were sent from each of the provinces to the Estates General, which directed foreign policy. The Estates General usually chose the stadholder (executive officer) from among the princes of the House of Orange, although he was more like a president than a king because most power remained in the hands of local authorities. The Dutch Republic dominated overseas commerce and developed into Europe's finance center. The Dutch middle class consisted of merchants, artisans, and shopkeepers who were prosperous and well educated. They idealized middle-class domestic life and were patrons of artists, like Rembrandt van Rijn (1606–1669), who painted scenes ordinary, daily life. Prosperity also brought clear divisions in gender roles, with women confined to the home. Dutch presses printed material censored elsewhere in Europe, like the work of Benedict Spinoza (1633–1677), Galileo, and Descartes. The golden age of the Netherlands could not, however, be maintained indefinitely and, by the end of the century, class divisions started to appear, intolerance of deviations from Calvinism grew, and French styles began to dominate.

In the New World, slavery became crucial to the economic systems of Caribbean colonies. Both the English and French came to deny legal rights to slaves. With wide cooperation from Catholic and Protestant churches and European governments, seventeenth-century slave trade expanded about 400 percent, preparing the way for an Atlantic economy based on slavery. In the English colonies on the North American continent, representative government and a relatively open society developed among the white colonists. At the same time, black slaves were used in most of the colonies, and the native American population faced death through disease and warfare with the settlers. The dichotomy between the principles of representative government and the practice of slavery troubled few.

The wars of the seventeenth century, and the disruptions these caused, prompted a major effort to redefine the relationship between freedom and order. The two most prominent political theorists were Thomas Hobbes (1588–1679) and John Locke (1632–1704). In *Leviathan* (1651), Hobbes emphasizes the need for a central authority, whether a monarch or a parliament, to prevent the miseries of chaos. There was no room for political or religious dissent in his theories. In his *Two Treatises of Government* (1690), which justified the Glorious Revolution in 1688, Locke argued against absolutism. Locke presents the case for constitutionalism and for government as the guarantor of citizens' rights, specifically the right to life, liberty, and property. Both Hobbes and Locke argue, although from different angles, that political authority is the product of a "social contract" among citizens and their chosen rulers. But Locke took his theories even further. In his *Essay Concerning Human Understanding* (1690), Locke asserts human beings are born with a *tabula rasa* ("blank slate"), and that knowledge is not inherent but learned. Locke also promotes the idea that "all men are created equal." These ideas had tremendous implications for educational theories.

Political philosophies were complemented by breakthroughs in natural science. The English natural philosopher, Sir Isaac Newton (1642–1727), developed a new branch of mathematics called "calculus," which enabled him to formulate a single law of gravity. Using this law, which he discusses in *Principia Mathematica* (1687), Newton explains not only Kepler's elliptical planetary orbits but also the motion of ordinary objects on Earth. Newton formulates three fundamental laws of physics: in the absence of force, motion continues in a straight line; the rate of change in the motion of an object is a result of the forces acting upon it; and the action and reaction of between two objects are equal and opposite. Some claimed he had disproved the existence of a divine force, but Newton argued that the regular operation of the universe proved the existence of God. Newton's work helped establish science as an important contributor to social progress. Interest in science grew, both through governmental support, as with the patronage of Frederick William of Brandenburg-Prussia; and the establishment of the Royal Society of London (1662) and the Royal Academy of Science in France (1666), and through the efforts of private individuals to explore common interests.

Artists and intellectuals also sought to make sense of their changing world. During the English civil war, John Milton (1608–1674) embraced individual liberty, advocated divorce, and, in *Areopagitica* (1644), defended the freedom of the press. In retirement after Charles II's restoration, Milton wrote *Paradise Lost* (1677), which continues the discussion of human freedom and tragedies of rebellion. Artistic styles varied considerably, but often had similar aims. The baroque lent itself to public displays of faith and power. It was associated with the Austrian and Spanish Habsburgs and with the papacy. The work of Gian Lorenzo Bernini (1598–1680), which included the square facing St. Peter's Basilica in Rome, reflected the power of Catholicism. Classicism, with its emphasis on geometric shapes, order, and harmony of lines, and its implicit references to the grandeur and power of the classical world, was adapted into a French national style. The work of French painters Nicolas Poussin (1594–1665) and Claude Lorrain (1600–1682) reflected classical ideals. Dutch painters, like Rembrandt and Jan Vermeer (1632–1675), often sold to private individuals or received commissions from civic groups, and favored smaller-scale works featuring ordinary subjects, which they infused with transcendent, even religious beauty and significance. The natural sciences benefited from art through precise drawings of insects and flowers.

The cultivation of manners ordered and defined the social hierarchy. Aristocratic men were expected to act in some ways as women had, in the sense that they learned how to please the monarch or their patron by displaying proper manners, conversing in an elegant and witty way, and demonstrating an interest in the arts. They learned to reject the vulgar and the lowly. The greatest French playwright of the seventeenth century, Molière (1622–1673),

satirizes the cult of manners in many of his plays, particularly in *The Middle-Class Gentleman*. The message was that true gentlemen were born, not made. But while the middle-class rich sometimes aspired to live nobly, the middle class as a whole began to establish a distinctive middle-class style of living, paying considerable attention to what it considered appropriate behavior.

Women contributed to the new emphasis on manners and became involved in intellectual and cultural matters. Socially prominent women presided over salons—informal gatherings in private homes for discussions of love, literature, and philosophy. Women also became artists and writers and developed a new type of literature: the novel. They often wrote under pseudonyms to avoid social scandal. And prominent men did indeed criticize women's learning and growing public influence, and recommended the "salutary yoke" of marriage to curb them. One target of abuse was Aphra Behn (1640–1689), who was one of the first professional, female author and playwright. She was successful in spite of criticism. Her short novel *Oroonoko* (1688), about an African prince wrongly sold into slavery, was adapted by playwrights and produced successfully for the following two centuries.

The lower classes were mainly interested in pursuing three things: the skills and knowledge to farm or work in trade, popular forms of entertainment (like fairs and dances), and religion. The social elites tried to reform the behavior of the lower classes, whom they viewed as a threat to order. Protestant and Catholic religious authorities campaigned against "paganism," ignorance, and superstition. The poor were increasingly regarded as dangerous and lacking in character—a dramatic reversal because poverty and charity to the poor were once respected Christian virtues. Governments separated beggars from the rest of society, confining them in hospitals that were essentially prisons in an attempt to reform their behavior.

Economic growth, social change, and the extension of state power — whether in an absolutist or a constitutional political system — all arose from and intensified a search for order in the seventeenth century. By the end of that century, however, a rough equilibrium had been established in most parts of Europe and its colonies.

Suggestions for Lecture and Discussion Topics

1. How did Louis make himself into the indispensable center of the French political system? What did he hope to accomplish through this and other means? This would be a good point at which to discuss Versailles, which became something like a giant stage for Louis's long-running play. Who else contributed to Louis's system? How important were they, whether prominent

individuals like Colbert, or groups of people like the intendants? How might we assess Louis's efforts?

In addition to the sources listed in the chapter bibliography, William Beik, *Louis XIV and Absolutism: A Brief Study with Documents* (Boston: Bedford/St. Martin's, 1999) presents a detailed look in a book slightly over two hundred pages. Robin Briggs, *Early Modern France, 1560–1715* (Oxford: Oxford University Press, 1977) offers a good overview; and David J. Sturdy, *Louis XIV* (New York: St. Martin's Press, 1998) is also a useful source. Finally, Robert W. Berger, *A Royal Passion: Louis XIV As Patron of Architecture* (Cambridge: Cambridge University Press, 1994) includes a wealth of information on Louis's many construction projects.

2. Although seventeenth-century Russia offers many points of contrast with western Europe, it, too, attempted to create an autocratic political system in which the tsar was all-powerful. Perhaps the most important point is that the consolidation of serfdom not only allowed the aristocracy and the monarch to live in great luxury, it also enabled them to mobilize the relatively scarce resources of Russia and eventually make it into one of the great European powers.

The reign of Alexei as tsar is important for the law code of 1649; for the attempts to reform the Russian Orthodox church, which gave rise to the Old Believers; and for the rebellion led by Stenka Razin. In all these instances, the state became more powerful. Yet, it all fell apart after Alexei died. During the interim between Alexei and Peter, Peter's older half-sister, Sophie, was regent. Sophie was a very interesting figure in her own right and worth spending time on.

In addition to the books listed in the chapter bibliography, Part 1 of W. Bruce Lincoln's *The Romanovs: Autocrats of All the Russias* (New York: Dial Press, 1981) has an excellent discussion of the Romanov tsars in the seventeenth century. Chapter 3, by Hans-Joachim Torke, "From Muscovy towards St. Petersburg, 1598–1689," in ed. Gregory L. Freeze, ed., *Russia: A History* (Oxford: Oxford University Press, 1997) is a good survey. Richard S. Hellie, ed. and trans., *Muscovite Law Code (Ulozhenie) of 1649*, vol. 1 (Irvine: University of California Press, 1988) makes available this seminal document. Paul Avrich, *Russian Rebels, 1600–1800* (New York: Schocken Books, 1972) contains a very good account of Stenka Razin's rebellion. Finally, Lindsay Hughes, *Sophia: Regent of Russia, 1657–1704* (New Haven, CT: Yale University Press, 1990) is the definitive biography.

3. Students should understand the events of both the English civil war and the Glorious Revolution. So much of what occurred during the American Revolution had its roots in seventeenth-century England. At the same time, it is important not to present a view of these events that suggests they are inevitable steps along the way to democratic politics. A distinction should also be made between these events and those of the French Revolution in the following century. The situation in England, which involved both political and religious issues, led to some highly radical doctrines by such groups as the Levellers and the Diggers, but most supporters wanted to defend the rights of Englishmen. Events in eighteenth-century France began with a discussion about revising political arrangements but quickly moved in more radical directions with the radicals gaining power. It may also be worthwhile to compare the revolution of 1688 with the civil war and subsequent events of the 1640s and to ask why England of 1688 did not take the same path as England of the 1640s.

There is no shortage of books about the events of the 1640s and 1650s. A good overview of the entire period is Wilfrid R. Prest, *Albion Ascendant: English History, 1660–1815* (Oxford: Oxford University Press, 1998). Ann Hughes, *The Causes of the English Civil War* (New York: St. Martin's Press, 1999) is a good discussion of the important question of how the civil war began. Conrad Russell, in *The Fall of the British Monarchies, 1637–1642* (Oxford: Clarendon Press, 1991) downplays political conflict and restricts the revolutionary period to the late 1630s and early 1640s. He also stresses the extent to which the English revolution was a British problem. David Underdown, *A Freeborn People: Politics and the Nation in Seventeenth-Century England* (Oxford: Clarendon Press, 1996) offers a modified Marxist overview. Michael Walzer, *The Revolution of the Saints: A Study in the Origins of Radical Politics* (New York: Atheneum, 1975) is an important study of seventeenth-century Puritanism as a factor in revolutionary politics. A scholarly study of the revolution can be found in W. A. Speck, *Reluctant Revolutionaries: Englishmen and the Revolution of 1688* (New York: Oxford University Press, 1988).

On Oliver Cromwell, the central figure of the English civil war, see Peter Gaunt, *Oliver Cromwell* (Oxford: Blackwell, 1995). John Dunn, *The Political Thought of John Locke* (Cambridge: Cambridge University Press, 1969) presents a careful study of *The Two Treatises of Government* and other political writings by Locke.

4. Despite the upheavals caused by civil war and revolution, the seventeenth century proved to be a period of liberation for many Englishwomen. With their men away fighting in the civil war, or in exile during the Commonwealth, women assumed the management of households and businesses both small and large. They petitioned Parliament, sometimes directly, for the restoration of confiscated property, and joined nonconformist religious sects that encouraged political action as an extension of their religious beliefs. Many Englishwomen also took up the pen for public as well as private reflection and testimony. Nor were women silenced after the restoration. As a consequence, a remarkable amount of primary material concerning Englishwomen survives from the seventeenth century. A good deal of this has been published, and it reveals women's experiences in

vivid detail. An in-depth exploration of this subject would help right the balance of a period that is often weighted toward men's experiences. See Antonia Fraser, *The Weaker Vessel* (New York: Alfred A. Knopf, 1984); Mary Prior, ed., *Women in English Society 1500–1800* (London: Methuen, 1985); Patricia Crawford, *Women and Religion in England 1500–1720* (London: Routledge, 1993 [rpt. 1996]); Ann Laurence, *Women in England 1500–1760* (New York: St. Martin's Press, 1994); and Sara Mendelson and Patricia Crawford, *Women in Early Modern England, 1550–1720* (Oxford: Oxford University Press, 1998). Some of the printed primary material from the period could be assigned to students in order to provide a common text for class discussion. See Elspeth Graham, et. al., eds. *Her Own Life: Autobiographical Writings by Seventeenth-Century Englishwomen* (London: Routledge, 1989 [rpt. 1992]); D. J. H. Clifford, ed., *The Diaries of Lady Anne Clifford* (Stroud, Gloucestershire: Alan Sutton, 1990 [rpt. 2003]); James Fitzmaurice, et. al., eds., *Major Women Writers of Seventeenth-Century England* (Ann Arbor: University of Michigan Press, 1997); Sylvia Brown, ed., *Women's Writing in Stuart England: The Mothers' Legacies of Dorothy Leigh, Elizabeth Joscelin and Elizabeth Richardson* (Stroud, Gloucestershire: Sutton Publishing, 1999 [rpt. 2000]); and Patricia Crawford and Laura Gowing, eds., *Women's Worlds in Seventeenth-Century England: A Sourcebook* (London: Routledge, 2000).

5. The Netherlands in the seventeenth century managed not only to establish an unusual constitutional system of government, but also created a vibrant and relatively tolerant urban culture. For a brief moment, it was the European center of art, finance, and commerce. What did Dutch society look like? How far down the social hierarchy did the prosperous, comfortable way of life extend?

Depending on your level of comfort with art history, you might find it relatively easy to discuss Dutch society and economics in terms of paintings. In addition to the books by Schama and Israel listed in the chapter bibliography, see Paul Zumthor, *Daily Life in Rembrandt's Holland* (Stanford: Stanford University Press, 1994); Michael North, *Art and Commerce in the Dutch Golden Age: A Social History of Seventeenth-Century Netherlandish Painting* (New Haven, CT: Yale University Press, 1997); and Mariet Westermann, *A Worldly Art: The Dutch Republic, 1585–1718* (New York: Harry Abrams, 1996). A very useful overview of the history of this period is J. L. Price, *The Dutch Republic in the Seventeenth Century* (New York: St. Martin's Press, 1999). Another, more specialized title is Mike Dash, *Tulipomania: The Story of the World's Most Coveted Flower and the Extraordinary Passions It Aroused* (New York: Crown Publishers, 2000).

6. The cultivation of manners as a way to reestablish order and define the social hierarchy is an interesting topic that could easily be connected to present-day concerns about behavior in social situations. A great deal of information on how life was lived and what constituted proper behavior is given in the books listed in suggestion 4. In addition to the pioneering work of Norbert Elias cited in the chapter bibliography, there is the somewhat spotty book by Roger Chartier, ed., *A History of Private Life*, vol. 3, *Passions of the Renaissance* (Cambridge, MA: Belknap Press, 1989), organized thematically and chronologically wide-ranging. Anna Bryson, *From Courtesy to Civility: Changing Codes of Conduct in Early Modern England* (Oxford: Clarendon Press, 1998) offers a great deal of information and an extensive bibliography. Also very useful are the overview and first two essays in Part 1 of Marilyn J. Boxer and Jean H. Quataert, eds., *Connecting Spheres: Women in the Western World, 1500 to the Present* (New York: Oxford University Press, 1987). Food was also wrapped up in issues relating to social class and manners. There are many good Internet sites on the history of food, but see also C. Anne Wilson, ed., *"Banqueting Stuff"* (Edinburgh: Edinburgh University Press, 1991); Peter Brears, *Food and Cooking in Seventeenth-Century Britain, History and Recipes* English Heritage, 1985); and Gilly Lehmann, *The British Housewife*, author's draft of Part I *Cookery Books and Cookery before 1700*, http://www.kal69.dial.pipex.com/shop/pages/048right.html.

7. Isaac Newton is the central figure of the latter part of the scientific revolution and should receive top billing in any discussion of the breakthroughs associated with that movement. Yet, as Lisa Jardine shows in *Ingenious Pursuits: Building the Scientific Revolution* (New York: Nan A. Talese, 1999), ingenious devices often lie behind the theory, observations, and mathematics associated with scientific discovery. Jardine provides a context for Newton by portraying a world in which there are increasingly accurate clocks, improvements in microscopes and telescopes, navigational advances, attempts to chemically analyze unknown substances, and other developments that advanced theory and made possible practical applications. Newton should probably receive the lion's share of attention in any lecture or discussion, buy it would also be useful to introduce someone like Robert Boyle whose basic contributions to chemistry depended in large part on the equipment created and made by Robert Hooke, an important scientist in his own right. Jardine is also useful in demonstrating that most scientists in the seventeenth century, even Newton, were very much a part of their times. See also Edward G. Ruestow, *The Microscope in the Dutch Republic* (Cambridge: Cambridge University Press, 1996).

For more on Newton, see Richard S. Westfall, *The Life of Isaac Newton* (Cambridge: Cambridge University Press, 1993); Michael White, *Isaac Newton: The Last Sorcerer* (Reading, MA: Addison-Wesley, 1997); and I. Bernard Cohen and Richard S. Westfall, eds., *Newton: Texts, Background, Commentaries* (New York: W. W. Norton, 1996).

Making Connections

1. *What are the most important differences between absolutism and constitutionalism as political systems?* Absolutism in the last half of the seventeenth century was epitomized by the uncontested power of the ruler, a lack of representation of the people in government, and large standing armies. Most absolutist states of this period embraced traditional religion—that is, Catholicism and Orthodoxy—although Prussia was a notable exception. France is the best example of absolutism in this period. The principal elements of constitutionalism included a monarch with limited powers, parliamentary rule (through which the interests of mainly wealthy or landed people were represented), and generally smaller armed forces. England and the Dutch Republic are the best examples of constitutionalism in this period.

2. *In which ways did religious differences still cause political conflict?* Although the Thirty Years' War demonstrated that religion had to be separated out of international politics, religious conflict nevertheless remained a domestic issue, and this was especially true for England. The English civil war (1642–1646) and the Glorious Revolution (1688) were, to a large extent, conflicts over religion.

3. *Why was the search for order a major theme in science, politics, and the arts?* Every aspect of life seemed chaotic after the Thirty Years' War, and artists and intellectuals sought to make sense of the changing world. Hobbes and Locke sought a political philosophy rooted in nature, whereas scientists like Newton attempted to explain the workings of the universe. Artists were employed to emphasize the power, authority, and, significantly, control of the Catholic church and absolutist states like France.

Writing Assignments and Class Presentation Topics

1. Assign students William Beik, *Louis XIV and Absolutism: A Brief Study with Documents* (Boston: Bedford/St. Martin's, 1999) and have them write an essay on Louis's understanding of absolutism as a political system. What did he believe were its uses? How did he set about constructing it? Did he see it as the means to other goals or as an end in itself? It would probably be helpful to discuss absolutism and touch on Louis's version in a preliminary way. You may wish to limit the number of questions students pursue in their essays. For example, the last question will raise several different issues and may well be enough to serve as the basis for a short essay. Consult Beik's book, which contains a fine list of questions following the primary source documents, for additional ideas about assignments.

2. Students should enjoy doing presentations on individuals, groups, and events in the English civil war. This assignment will work better if the class spends a session outlining the major events, people, and some of the more important interpretations of the English civil war before they present their reports. Students should prepare their reports before this session, and use the review as a way of checking their understanding of the material and clarifying points that are not yet clear. Encourage them to bring in documents, illustrations, and other material that will help their audience grasp the information in the reports more quickly.

3. Select four paintings by Jan Vermeer and make reproductions of them readily available (you might use links to established Web sites). Students are to choose one and write informally about what the painting tells them about life during the seventeenth century in the Netherlands. Stress that the essay is not intended to be written from the perspective of art history; comments about Vermeer's blues or yellows are not what you are looking for. Although students may wish to read about the paintings they have chosen, the essays should be based mostly on what each student learns about seventeenth-century life in the Netherlands.

4. Ask students to consider the connections between manners and social hierarchy. Are manners primarily a way of distinguishing one group from another? Students should choose a seventeenth-century example and a twenty-first-century example and explain how they perceive each. Let them know that the examples may be seen in different ways. Using a handkerchief in the seventeenth century, for example, set one apart from most other people. Talking on a cell phone in a restaurant in the twenty-first century may likewise be connected to social hierarchy.

Research Assignments

1. Historical fiction is often much maligned by historians. It is certainly difficult to do well, but when good writing is combined with historical accuracy, such fiction can be a wonderful entrée into the study of history. Four recent novels deal with paintings and other aspects of the Netherlands in the seventeenth century. Provide students with a brief synopsis of each novel and with a short bibliography of readings they may use in ascertaining the skill of a particular novelist in making use of historical fact (draw from the chapter bibliography and from "Suggestions for Lecture and Discussion Topics," number 4). The novels are Tracy Chevalier, *Girl with a Pearl Earring* (New York: Dutton, 1999); Deborah Moggach, *Tulip Fever* (New York: Delacorte Press, 2000); Susan Vreeland, *Girl in Hyacinth Blue* (Denver: MacMurray & Beck, 1999); and Katherine Weber, *The Music Lesson* (New

York: Picador USA, 2000). The novels by Chevalier and Moggach are set in the seventeenth century, Vreeland's book tells the story of a fictitious Vermeer across time, and Weber deals with a real Vermeer in a twentieth-century setting. Vreeland and especially Weber may move further away from the seventeenth century than is useful, so some care should be taken in setting up the assignment.

2. Ask students to investigate England, France, and the Dutch Republic in the 1670s and 1680s in order to decide which country they would most like to have lived in and which country they would least like to have lived in. It might be helpful to have a discussion beforehand about criteria. For example, is political stability the main criterion, or should it be economic development, social opportunity, or cultural and intellectual vitality? This is a research project that might be done by individuals or by groups. Further, it may result in a traditional essay, some type of statistical or visual presentation, or perhaps a combination of all three. Another related assignment is to divide the class into three real-estate companies, which then make presentations on the country they believe provides the best way of life in the late seventeenth century. Each company would organize itself into those who did the basic research, those who wrote the copy or created the presentations, and those who actually made the pitch. Each member of the company would be required to write a short essay commenting on the experience.

Literature

Cobb, Walter J., trans., *Madame De Lafayette: The Princesse de Cleves.* 1992.

Frame, Donald M., trans., *Tartuffe and Other Plays by Molière.* 1967.

Leonard, John, ed., *John Milton: Paradise Lost.* 2003.

MacPherson, C. B., ed., *Hobbes: Leviathan.* 1982.

Montgomery, George R., trans., *Gottfried Wilhelm Leibniz: Discourse on Metaphysics and the Monadology.* 1992.

Shapiro, Ian, ed., *Two Treatises of Government and a Letter Concerning Toleration by John Locke.* 2003.

Films and Videos

Restoration (1994; VHS/DVD, 1 hr., 58 min.). The court of Charles II of England serves as a backdrop to this film. Although the plot is fiction, some historical events are chronicled, such as the Great Plague of 1665. The film is strong on such details as setting and costuming.

The Last King (2004; DVD, 3 hrs., 8 min.). Although the events of Charles II's life and reign are compressed, this is an excellent and largely accurate account of the English king. The contradictions of the king's character have been nicely captured, and care has been lavished on costuming and sets.

Historical Skills

Map 17.1, Louis XIV's Acquisitions, 1668–1697, p. 630

Ask students to examine the map and consider what goals Louis may have had in the various campaigns. Why were the Spanish Netherlands and the lands of the Holy Roman Empire tempting to Louis?

Taking Measure: The Seventeenth-Century Army, p. 631

How would students explain the outliers in this figure —that Sweden has one soldier for every 25 people and England has one soldier for every 410 people? How could the Swedish and the Prussian armies be competitive against the much larger armies of France, Russia, and Austria? Finally, what made England such a formidable military force?

17.2, State Building in Central and Eastern Europe, 1648–1699, p. 633

How would the expansion of Austrian Habsburg territories to the east change the nature of that empire? (Discuss with students the ethnic composition of the empire's population, both in the older segment and in the newer territories.) The Austrian Habsburgs acquired vast new territories outside the boundaries of the Holy Roman Empire. What changes did this foreshadow for the position of the Austrian Habsburgs within the Holy Roman Empire? Finally, ask students to speculate about Brandenburg-Prussia's next moves within the Holy Roman Empire.

Mapping the West: Europe at the End of the Seventeenth Century, p. 660

Ask students to rank the European powers as military powers, as economic powers, and as centers of intellectual and cultural life. Then, ask students to justify their rankings. Would any of the European powers occupy the same position on all three lists? Ask students what other kinds of information they would like to have available for constructing the lists.

Louis XIV in Roman Splendor, p. 624

What kind of image did Louis wish to fashion by having himself portrayed as Mars, the Roman god of war? To what extent did Louis see himself as semidivine? Ask students to examine also the view of the Palace of Versailles (p. 626). If the palace is an extension of Louis, what does this say about his understanding of himself and his goals?

The Siege of Vienna, 1683, p. 634

The siege of Vienna in 1683 is still regarded by many Austrians and other central Europeans as a turning point in European history in that it stopped the advance into Europe of a powerful non-Christian civilization. Ask students whether they believe this interpretation is justified. What reasons do they give to support their positions? What kinds of cultural biases might they be bringing to a discussion of this sort of question?

Artemisia Gentileschi, Painting (an allegorical self-portrait), p. 637

What must it have taken for a woman, even a woman as obviously talented as Gentileschi, to achieve the success she enjoyed as a painter in the seventeenth century? Encourage students to investigate her life. Did it matter, for example, that her father was a well-known painter? Perhaps her best-known painting is *Judith Beheading Holofernes*. Students might want to think about what statement it makes and how it compares to her self-portrait.

Oliver Cromwell, p. 642

What made Cromwell the remarkable leader that he was? His religiosity certainly was one factor. Perhaps another was his ruthlessness in defense of a cause he regarded as just. Were there other reasons?

Why was it important to exhume Cromwell's body and hang it after the restoration of Charles II? What was the symbolism behind the display of his head? Ask students to consider as well the campaign to hunt down and execute everyone who had signed the death warrant of Charles I.

A Typical Dutch Scene from Daily Life, p. 648

Ask students to consider how lifestyles are portrayed in this painting. How would they consider this to be representative of the Dutch Republic? Why?

John Milton, Areopagitica (1644), p. 654

Milton's passionate defense of a free press continues to resonate with western societies today. Students might be asked to consider the importance of likening censorship to murder, and to examine the kind of censorship issues the press face today. For Milton, to kill a man is to kill the image of God, but to censor ideas is to kill the spirit, which like the soul God intended to transcend the physical. Censors commit blasphemy in limiting the press just as surely as they do when they murder a person. Today, the practice of western nations occasionally censoring the press in the name of "security" has drawn a lot of criticism. But another, more insidious kind of censorship is taking place as media conglomerates buy up newspapers and radio and television stations because this limits the dissemination of which facts and ideas are reported, and to a single point of view.

OTHER BEDFORD/ST. MARTIN'S RESOURCES FOR CHAPTER 17

The following resources are available to accompany Chapter 17. Please refer to the Preface of this manual for detailed descriptions of all the ancillaries.

For Instructors

Transparencies

The following maps and images from Chapter 17 are available as full-color acetates.

- Map 17.1: Louis XIV's Acquisitions, 1668–1697
- Map 17.2: State Building in Central and Eastern Europe, 1648–1699
- Map 17.3: Dutch Commerce in the Seventeenth Century
- Mapping the West: Europe at the End of the Seventeenth Century
- *Typical Dutch Scene from Daily Life*
- Gian Lorenzo Bernini, *Ecstasy of St. Teresa of Avila*

Instructor's Resources CD-ROM

The following maps and image from Chapter 17 as well as a chapter outline, are available on disc in both PowerPoint and jpeg formats.

- Map 17.1: Louis XIV's Acquisitions, 1668–1697
- Map 17.2: State Building in Central and Eastern Europe, 1648–1699
- Map 17.3: Dutch Commerce in the Seventeenth Century
- Mapping the West: Europe at the End of the Seventeenth Century
- *Typical Dutch Scene from Daily Life*

Using the Bedford Series with
The Making of the West

Available in print as well as online at <u>bedfordstmartins</u> <u>.com/usingseries</u>, this guide offers practical suggestions for using **William Beik, *Louis XIV and Absolutism*** in conjunction with Chapter 17 of the textbook.

For Students

Sources of The Making of the West

The following documents are available in Chapter 17 of the companion sourcebook by Katharine J. Lualdi, University of Southern Maine.

1. Louis de Rouvroy, Duke of Saint-Simon, *Memoirs* (1694–1723)
2. British Parliament, *The English Bill of Rights* (1689)
3. Ludwig Fabritius, *The Revolt of Stenka Razin* (1670)
4. *A True and Exact Relation of the Raising of the Siege of Vienna and the Victory obtained Over the Ottoman Army* (1683)
5. Madame de Lafayette, *The Princess of Clèves* (1678)

Study Guides

The print **Study Guide** and the **Online Study Guide** at <u>bedfordstmartins.com/hunt</u>, both by Victoria Thompson (Arizona State University) and Eric Johnson (University of California, Los Angeles), help students synthesize the material they have learned as well as practice the skills historians use to make sense of the past. The following Map, Visual, and Document activities are available for Chapter 17.

Map Activity

- Mapping the West: Europe at the End of Seventeenth Century

Visual Activity

- *Typical Dutch Scene from Daily Life*

Reading Historical Documents

- John Milton's *Defense of Freedom of the Press*
- Aphra Behn, *Oroonoko*

The Atlantic System and Its Consequences
1690–1740

CHAPTER RESOURCES

Main Chapter Topics

1. An Atlantic system involving the exchange of manufactured goods, slaves, and plantation commodities such as coffee, sugar, cotton, and tobacco linked western Europe, the western coast of Africa, and the Western Hemisphere together in a commercial network. It created a powerful impetus for economic expansion in the first half of the eighteenth century.

2. The growth in commerce and population helped to create new social and cultural patterns, most readily visible in the cities of western Europe. A more literate public demonstrated interest in concerts, novels, and the often-critical views of writers and artists.

3. The new balance of power that emerged after Louis XIV's death (1715) resulted in greater stability for European states, less frequent and ruinous wars, and increased opportunity to expand control both at home and in the colonies.

4. Within the new balance of power, Russia and Prussia emerged as claimants to the status of great powers, Sweden and the Dutch Republic lost ground and could no longer be considered great powers, and Poland-Lithuania began a gradual weakening process that led to its disappearance by the end of the eighteenth century. Successful mobilization of political and military resources produced great-power status, while failure to mobilize adequate resources led to decline relative to the great powers.

5. The European Enlightenment owed its origins and development—at least in part—to the new balance of power and economic expansion. It emphasized a secular, scientific, critical, but also optimistic attitude as it began to gain momentum in the 1730s and 1740s. It also stimulated debate concerning the condition of women and their place in society.

6. Europe crossed a major threshold in the first half of the eighteenth century, moving from an economy governed by scarcity to one that promised increasing growth and improvement.

Summary

By the end of the seventeenth century, Europe had largely left behind the religious quarrels, political strife, disease, and famine that characterized a large part of that century. In the first part of the eighteenth century, Europe enjoyed important connections with other parts of the world, political stability together with rapid social and economic change, and an overall optimism. The period as a whole could easily be called the "era of coffee," so representative was this new drink with the political debates, economic prosperity, and social attitudes at that time. As coffee became popular, coffeehouses sprang up all over the cities of Europe and became places where individuals could meet to discuss politics. Coffee production was also a major product of the Atlantic system, whereby slaves were taken from West Africa to the Caribbean and North America to work on plantations that produced goods—like coffee—that were exported to Europe. Finally, coffee reflected new social patterns where middle-class persons, prosperous through economic growth, had extra income to spend on luxuries like coffee.

Plantations formed an important component of the expanding and changing economy of the Atlantic system. By using slave labor, plantations produced large quantities of commodities at low prices. The slave trade grew rapidly in the seventeenth and eighteenth centuries. More than eleven million Africans were sold into slavery before the slave trade began declining in the 1850s. Many plantation owners lived opulent lives in Europe, employing agents to run their overseas operations, but life was harsh for slaves. Slaves were forced to accept new identities, beginning with new names; expected to do any work assigned them; and forced to live in squalid conditions. Some slaves became runaways, more resisted as best they could by stealing food, breaking tools, or feigning stupidity. Some observers condemned slavery, but, by the eighteenth century, an increasing number of Europeans accepted the idea that Africans were inferior. The Atlantic system expanded trade and altered consumption patterns in Europe with the introduction of new products like tobacco and sugar. It also encouraged Europeans to emigrate and settle in many different parts of the world. Because of the difficult conditions immigrants faced, many more men than women emigrated from Europe to America. In Spanish and Portuguese territories, interracial marriages and sexual contact between the colonists and the natives were tolerated and fostered greater racial diversity than in British or French colonies. The Spanish were especially successful in converting native populations to Christianity in their territories.

Growing trade in the Atlantic also increased piracy. Buccaneers (from the French *boucan* ["strips of cured beef"]) targeted all shipping, regardless of origin. There were even instances of women dressing up and serving on pirate ships. In Asia and Africa, where trade rather than colonization was paramount, white settlements remained small. Europeans had little contact with East Africa, and almost none with the African interior. But the Portuguese established a few trading places in Angola, and Dutch settlers farmed on the Cape of Good Hope. In China, Catholic missionaries had initially been welcomed at the imperial court, but they lost credibility by squabbling among themselves and associating with European merchants who were looked down upon by the Chinese. The Dutch gained footholds in Java and the East Indies, and competed with Britain, France, Portugal, and Denmark for spices, cotton, and silk from India. Ultimately, the British and French became the leading rivals for control of India, just as they were in North America. Population growth in western Europe was also an important factor during this period. A decline in the death rate was responsible for most of the surge. This decline, in turn, stemmed from changes in weather patterns that created a warmer climate generally more favorable to agriculture. Improvements in agricultural techniques and the disappearance of the plague after 1720 also helped to increase population.

The agricultural revolution of this period made it possible to feed more people with a smaller agricultural workforce. It entailed, first, an increase in cultivated areas by draining wetlands and growing crops on what had previously been common land. Second, it also involved the consolidation of landholdings into larger, more efficient units. Third, farmers used fodder crops like clover to add nutrients to the soil so that fields did not have to remain fallow periodically. Fourth and finally, improved breeding techniques led to larger and better herds. New crops were not a factor until late in the

century. As a consequence of these changes, rural social structure became more hierarchical. Widespread moves to enclose land—especially community land—by large propertyowners became common and some peasants were forced off land their families had worked for generations. Other peasants were forced into tenant status. These new techniques and approaches spread from Britain and the Low Countries to the rest of western Europe, but with only limited acceptance. In eastern Europe, some aristocratic landlords produced for the general market, but little changed in most of the region and serfs lived lives that did not differ significantly from that of slaves on American plantations.

The landed nobility played an important role in rapidly growing cities in the eighteenth century. Their conspicuous consumption kept thousands of artisans, shopkeepers, and servants employed. Population growth, coupled with larger supplies of certain goods, produced a consumer revolution. Tea, coffee, and chocolate came to be considered almost as necessities. Coffeehouses and cafés became familiar institutions in cities and towns. The new consumer society was not without its critics, but many saw it as the basis for a new prosperity. The middle classes of officials, merchants, and professionals formed a vital element as well. Some aspired to live nobly, but most developed a distinctive way of life that was modest compared to the lifestyle of the aristocracy, but more comfortable than the lives of peasants or laborers. The lower classes included artisans and shopkeepers — most of whom were organized in professional guilds — then journeymen and apprentices, and, finally, servants (most of whom were women) and laborers. The very poor, often unemployed, were at the bottom of the social hierarchy.

Social class distinctions were reflected in various ways, including differences in housing, clothing, and literacy. Literacy increased considerably in the eighteenth century, but this trend was limited by social, regional, religious, and gender differences. In general, persons in the upper classes were more literate than those in the lower classes, city people were more literate than peasants, and Protestants were more literate than Catholics. Few children attended school beyond the elementary grades. Growth in literacy rates spurred an increase in the production of books and periodicals; Britain and the Dutch Republic led the way at the end of the seventeenth century. The first London daily newspaper appeared in 1702, and the first literary magazine in 1709. Coffeehouses induced thousands to read newspapers.

The growing middle classes became a new source of support for art, music, and literature, supplementing elite patronage. Public music concerts began in England in the latter part of the seventeenth century and, on the continent, in the first quarter of the eighteenth century. Opera continued to grow in popularity. Although composers still depended largely on court or church patrons, they also composed works for the general public. George Frederick Handel (1685–1759) was one of the first musicians to move successfully in this direction. His oratorios, like the *Messiah* (1741), combined the drama of opera with the majesty of religious and ceremonial music and were hugely successful. There was a shift in painting as well, from the baroque to rococo (from the French word *rocaille* ["shellwork"]). Rococo painting, which often depicted scenes of intimate sensuality rather than the grander themes favored by baroque and classical painters, reflected the tastes of the new public. Working on a smaller, subtler scale, rococo painting could be hung on the walls of their homes.

Early in the eighteenth century, the modern novel took form. Authors concentrated more on individual psychology and social description than on picaresque adventure. Women figured prominently as characters, and were also frequently authors. Eliza Haywood (1693–1756) wrote a number of novels in the first half of the eighteenth century emphasizing the role of women as models of virtue in a changing world. Her counterpart, Daniel Defoe (1660–1731) was best known for *Robinson Crusoe* (1719). The novel's main character very much reflected the times, someone who must deal with the unexpected by improvisation and behave like an ingenious entrepreneur.

Not surprisingly in a time of rapid change, religious revival flourished. Among Protestants, Pietism—a more emotional religion that emphasized Bible study—gained popularity. The Catholic counterparts were Quietism and Jansenism, which emphasized miracles as well as an emotional approach to religion. Jansenism, even though discouraged by Louis XIV and condemned by the papacy, soon outstripped Quietism in popularity and became politicized by mid-century in opposition to the religious policies of the French crown.

In international politics, the death of Charles II of Spain (1700) led to the War of the Spanish Succession (1701–1713). Because Charles left no direct heirs, rival claims were put forward by Louis XIV of France and Leopold I of Austria. Most of Europe allied against France, fearing what would happen should France gain control of Spanish territories. After defeat in several major battles, France agreed to the unfavorable terms of the Peace of Utrecht (1714). Louis XIV's grandson Philip, duke of Anjou, became king of Spain but renounced any claim to the French throne. Spain surrendered its territories in the Netherlands and Italy to Austria, and gave Gibraltar to Britain. France ceded territory in North America to Britain.

No longer in a position to dominate Europe, Louis XIV faced criticism in France for the excesses of his court, the country's constant involvement in war, and the misery of the populace. After his death (1715), his five-year-old great-grandson succeeded him as Louis XV. The duke of Orléans became regent and worked to appease

aristocratic critics. After failing to establish a national bank, France eventually achieved financial stability by avoiding war abroad and social unrest at home. French absolutism was now in decline, and the nation entered into nearly a century of prosperity.

Queen Anne (r. 1702–1714) followed William and Mary as ruler in England. After Anne died leaving no children, the throne passed to the elector of Hanover, a Protestant great-grandson of James I, who became George I (r. 1714–1727). The fear of "Jacobitism," a movement supporting the Catholic son of James II, led Scottish Protestants to agree to the Act of Union in 1707. This act abolished the separate Scottish parliament and recognized the Hanoverian line. A Scottish Jacobite rebellion in 1715 was suppressed, although the Jacobites continued to be active in Scotland into the 1740s. Ireland, having a population of whom 90 percent were Catholics, was by this time little more than a colony. It had supported James II (1689) when the former king of England launched an attempt to regain his crown. Over the following few decades, the Protestant-controlled Irish parliament passed restrictive laws against the native Catholic population.

In the constitutional monarchy of the early eighteenth century, the monarch had considerable power. Both George I and George II, however, relied on Sir Robert Walpole (1676–1745) to help them manage Parliament. Walpole named himself the first or "prime" minister. He also helped to create the parliamentary system of government in which the prime minister is drawn from the leading party in the House of Commons. During the first half of that century, Britain employed its navy and, through the Bank of England with its unique ability to finance war cheaply, became a great world power. At the same time, the Dutch Republic underwent a decline, at least in relative terms. The Dutch dropped out of great-power rivalries to concentrate on international trade and finance.

In Russia, Peter I ("the Great" [r. 1689–1725]) concentrated on building a modern army and establishing a navy. To accomplish these goals, he reorganized government and finance along western lines and greatly increased taxation. Peter also gained control over the Russian Orthodox church and made it a part of the bureaucracy. The Russian nobility were required to participate in state service, either in the military or the administration. Peter also set out to westernize the nobility by insisting that western style clothing be worn at court, that upper-class Russians learn German and French, and that aristocratic women participate in court functions. Although many resisted him, others, eager for social advancement, cooperated. The many foreigners who came to Russia to work with Peter also aided him. St. Petersburg, the new capital, symbolized the changes Peter brought to Russia. But, while Peter had westernized and modernized much of Russia, life for the serfs who made up the vast majority of the population, remained largely unchanged. Peter's methods could also be cruel: men were "pressed" or forced into the army and any suspicion of treason was enough to condemn a person, even the tsar's own son, to torture or death.

Peter's reforms created an army that could hold its own against one of the great military leaders of the age: Charles XII of Sweden (r. 1697–1718). Although Russia defeated Sweden at the battle of Poltava (1709), it was only after Charles XII's death (1718) that negotiations for the Treaty of Nystad (1721) began. After this, Sweden, once dominant in the Baltic region, could no longer be considered one of the great powers.

As Sweden declined, Prussia rose. Under Frederick William I (r. 1713–1740), Prussia doubled the size of its army. Although still a small army, it was the best trained and most up to date in Europe. Such a high percentage of Prussia's male population served in the army that it seemed almost as if the state existed for the sake of the army. Frederick William, however, did not employ his army foolishly, and Prussia stayed out of the War of Polish Succession (1733–1735) taking place just beyond its borders. The war pitted France, Spain, and Sardinia against Austria and Russia. Ultimately, France agreed to accept the Austrian candidate for the Polish throne in exchange for the province of Lorraine. This settlement left Austria unencumbered to fight with the Turks over Hungary and Transylvania.

European powers recognized the necessity of maintaining a balance of power. This had been the compelling force underlying the campaigns against Louis XIV but, even after his death, European nations continued to work against any one nation becoming too powerful. Diplomacy was a masterful tool for this purpose, and diplomatic services developed regular procedures, with France leading the way. Some theorists stressed the idea of harmonizing the interests of the countries concerned but, in practice, the use of secret diplomacy was often involved. At the very least, states recognized that diplomatic means were available to end wars.

Enjoying its better health, the population at large played an important role in military and diplomatic affairs. Governments made efforts to improve the health of their subjects. Public sanitation in urban areas was an increasingly serious challenge. Hospitals during this period slowly changed from charitable to medical institutions; the practice of medicine also improved as diagnoses became more precise and physicians furthered their understanding of the human body through dissection. However, physicians still competed with quacks and patients were as likely to die from diseases contracted in the hospital as to be cured there. Insanity was considered a physical rather than mental illness and there were virtually no treatments for infectious diseases. Personal cleanliness was also relative. The poor rarely washed themselves or changed their clothes and lived in unsanitary conditions. Even among the upper classes bathing was considered dangerous, and most considered themselves clean after they had merely washed their face, changed their clothes, and perfumed themselves.

The Enlightenment, which grew out of the economic prosperity and political stability of the period, first worked to popularize the new science and the scientific method. Lectures and journals on mathematics and science appealed to the fashionable interest. The prestige of science helped to foster a skepticism toward religious conformity. Pierre Bayle's *Historical and Critical Dictionary* (1697) calls for religions to meet the test of reasonableness instead of relying on faith. Others challenged the authority of the Bible by subjecting it to historical, geological, and astrological criticism. Such works tended to challenge traditional secular as well as religious authority. Many critical works were written in French, but were often published in Protestant countries such as the Dutch Republic, Britain, and Switzerland because of French censorship.

The most influential figure in the early Enlightenment was Voltaire (1694–1778), a middle-class opponent of the church and critic of the state. Voltaire admired England and referred to its values and practices when he criticized the state and society in France. He was particularly interested in Newton and his *Elements of the Philosophy of Newton* (1738), which did much to popularize the English scientist, but was condemned by the French government and Catholic theologians. Travel literature also emphasized the idea that customs varied and that Europe and Christianity offered merely one of many perspectives that could be subscribed to on issues of morality and authority. Travel literature was also a forum for political commentary; for example, Montesquieu used his *Persian Letters* (1721) as a means for commenting on political affairs in France. As Enlightenment writers challenged various institutions and customs, some women questioned their situation in their writings. Britain's Mary Astell (1666–1731) published *A Serious Proposal to the Ladies* (1694) advocating the founding of a private women's college. She later questioned the subjugation of women within the institution of marriage. Inspired by Astell, other women also wrote movingly about the situation of women and used the language of oppression and tyranny to make their points. Although most men continued to hold the traditional view that women were limited by their biology, an important debate on the nature of women and their appropriate social roles had begun.

By the 1740s, Europe had witnessed a growing economy, a greater degree of political stability, and new developments in science and social and cultural life. Considerable optimism existed about the possibilities of continued economic expansion and general improvement.

Suggestions for Lecture and Discussion Topics

1. Instructors may approach the large and fascinating topic of the Atlantic system from different vantage points. One such starting point is the Caribbean sugarcane plantation. A look at the Caribbean sugarcane plantation might first involve a discussion of the growing of the sugarcane, then the process of refining sugar, and, finally, the system by which the end product—refined sugar—was exported to England. It could also include an examination of the lives of the planters. A good source to consult for a closer look at the lives of the planters and the production of sugar is Richard S. Dunn, *Sugar and Slaves: The Rise of the Planter Class in the English West Indies, 1624–1713* (Chapel Hill: University of North Carolina Press, 1972); see particularly chapters 6 and 8. Dunn's book also offers a detailed examination of slavery as it was practiced on sugarcane plantations (Chapter 7). Slavery, of course, differed from crop to crop as well as from region to region, so that generalizations must be made with care. Sidney W. Mintz, *Sweetness and Power: The Place of Sugar in Modern History* (New York: Viking Penguin, 1985) is a classic study of sugar, capitalism, and power. Its range is wider than Dunn's book, but Chapter 2, "Production," will be helpful in discussing the production of sugar.

2. The new items of consumption — sugar, coffee, and tea — and the ways in which these staples changed urban social and cultural life can be the subject of an interesting class session. Besides looking at historical patterns, one might refer to present-day habits and institutions connected with these items. Sidney Mintz's *Sweetness and Power* (see suggestion 1) contains a chapter on the widespread consumption of tea, coffee, and chocolate. Mark Pendergrast offers an informative if somewhat breezy book on coffee, *Uncommon Grounds: The History of Coffee and How It Transformed Our World* (New York: Basic Books, 1999). Consult Chapter 1 for an overview of the history of the spread of coffee drinking. Chapter 10 of Wilfrid R. Prest, *Albion Ascendant: English History, 1660–1815* (New York: Oxford University Press, 1998) places consumption of coffee, chocolate, and tea in the first half of the eighteenth century in a British context. Prest's book is part of J. M. Roberts, ed., series *The Short Oxford History of the Modern World.*

3. In his many careers and his novels, Daniel Defoe offers interesting approaches to social and cultural patterns in England of the late seventeenth and early eighteenth centuries. Most students will already know, or be familiar with the plot of *Robinson Crusoe* even if they have not read the book. The novel can be used to introduce a variety of pertinent themes: capitalism, colonialism, and racism, among others. A good place to begin is Peter Earle's interesting and informative *The World of Defoe* (London: Weidenfeld & Nicolson, 1976), particularly parts 3 and 4, which discuss society and the economy in England and the life cycle of the individual. Paula Backscheider offers a comprehensive investigation of Defoe's stranger-than-fiction life in *Daniel Defoe: His Life* (Baltimore: Johns Hopkins University Press, 1989). John J. Richetti, *Daniel Defoe* (Boston: Twayne Publishers, 1987) is a useful, brief biography and analysis of Defoe's major works. Finally, Max Byrd, ed., *Daniel Defoe: A Collection of Critical Essays* (Englewood Cliffs, NJ: Prentice-Hall, 1976); and Frank H. Ellis, ed., *Twentieth-Century Interpretations of Robinson Crusoe: A Collection of Critical Essays* (Englewood Cliffs, NJ: Prentice-Hall, 1969) are both good introductions to literary criticism of Defoe and his most famous novel.

4. The divergent careers of Johann Sebastian Bach and George Frederick Handel offer opportunities for an exploration of the disparate worlds of music in the early eighteenth century. These explorations can open up discussions of religion, commerce, urban developments, and leisure activity. Some knowledge and feeling for the music of the times would be an advantage, but not a necessity. Playing recorded compositions by these composers is highly recommended. For Bach, a good place to start is Denis Arnold, *Bach* (Oxford and New York: Oxford University Press, 1983), a brief biography in the *Past Masters* series. Jan Chiappusso, *Bach's World* (Bloomington: Indiana University Press, 1968) is a very useful book. Other possibilities include the recent, full-length biography by Christoph Wolff, *Johann Sebastian Bach: The Learned Musician* (New York: W. W. Norton, 2000); and Wolff's revised and enlarged edition of Hans T. David and Arthur Mendel, *The Bach Reader: A Life of Johann Sebastian Bach in Letters and Documents* (New York: W. W. Norton, 1966 [rev. ed., 1998]). See also a review of Wolff's biography that serves as a good introduction to major issues connected with Bach's life: Robert L. Marshall, "In Search of Bach," *The New York Review of Books* 47.10 (June 15, 2000), pp. 47–51. For Handel, one might begin with Dean Winton, *The New Grove Handel* (New York: W. W. Norton, 1982), a short biography; or H. C. Robbins Landon, *Handel and His World* (Boston: Little, Brown, 1984). Other possibilities include Paul Henry Lang, *George Frideric Handel* (New York: W. W. Norton, 1966), a comprehensive biography; and Otto Erich Deutsch, *Handel: A Documentary Biography* (New York: DaCapo Press, 1974).

5. Just as Louis XIV was the dominant personality of the latter part of the seventeenth century, Peter the Great was the larger-than-life figure for the first part of the eighteenth century. Almost single-handedly, Peter made the Russian Empire one of the major powers of Europe and created in St. Petersburg a new city destined to play an extraordinary role in Russian history over the following four centuries. An excellent overview of Peter's career can be found in Chapter 4 of W. Bruce Lincoln, *The Romanovs: Autocrats of All the Russias* (New York: Dial Press, 1981). Chapter 5 deals with the planning and

construction of St. Petersburg. M. S. Anderson, *Peter the Great*, 2d ed. (New York: Longman, 1995) is an excellent short biography. The best book on Peter and his Russia is Lindsey Hughes, *Russia in the Age of Peter the Great* (New Haven: Yale University Press, 1998). It is divided by topics, of which probably the most interesting are "Peter's People" (Chapter 6), "St. Petersburg and the Arts" (Chapter 7), and "Peter: Man, Mind, and Methods" (Chapter 11).

6. Voltaire is probably the best-known literary figure of the Enlightenment, and his career encompassed many of the different facets of that movement. A particularly fascinating account of the young Voltaire is found in the first chapter of Peter Gay, *Voltaire's Politics: The Poet As a Realist* (Princeton: Princeton University Press, 1959). Theodore Besterman's biography, listed in the chapter bibliography, should also be consulted. A good overview of the early Enlightenment may be found in Leonard Krieger, *Kings and Philosophers, 1689–1989* (New York: W. W. Norton, 1970). Part 1 of Krieger's book also contains a good discussion of the political and military history of the period from 1690 to 1740.

Making Connections

1. *In which ways did the rise of slavery and the plantation system change European politics and society?* It soon became apparent to European countries that colonization, and the new products that came with it, was more profitable than mining for precious metals. European countries competed with each other, issuing state charters for the founding of colonies. There was a growing European market for plantation goods, such as sugar, tobacco, and coffee, all produced by cheap slave labor. In turn, these new products changed European consumption habits. Smoking became widespread and coffeehouses, where people could meet socially and discuss business and politics, became popular.

2. *Why was the Enlightenment born just at the moment that the Atlantic system took shape?* The optimism generated by rapid economic and territorial expansion, the emergence of a new consumer society, and the stabilization of the European state system all generated optimism about the future. This, in turn, stimulated a renewed interest in ideas, especially in the area of science. Skepticism, which was an integral part of scientific inquiry, was quickly extended to other areas, including religion. At the same time, people became more familiar with foreign cultures and ideas through travel literature.

3. *What were the major differences between the wars of the first half of the eighteenth century and those of the seventeenth century (refer to chapters 16 and 17)?* Religion had been a major factor in the wars of the seventeenth century. By the first half of the eighteenth century, na-tions went to war mainly for political and territorial reasons. These battles tended to be localized; they did not encompass huge areas of conflict and the countryside was not ravaged in the way it had been in the Thirty Years' War. Nations during the eighteenth century also formed alliances to balance the perceived power and ambitions of countries outside the alliances. By then, diplomatic services had also developed regular procedures, which aided the negotiation of international differences.

Writing Assignments and Class Presentation Topics

1. Using the material in Chapter 18, including Figure 18.1 (p. 669) and Figure 18.2 (p. 670) and relevant illustrations, have the class contrast the view of slavery a plantation owner might have with that of one of his slaves.

2. Ask students to compare and contrast the agricultural practices of western Europe with those of eastern Europe and the New World. Have the class discuss the social and economic implications of these practices. Make use of figures 18.1 and 18.2 and other relevant features in the chapter.

3. Ask students what city life was like in the early eighteenth century. In an essay, have students describe it as fully as possible, including the physical layout, the different groups inhabiting the city, new items of consumption, and opportunities for cultural and leisure activities.

4. Ask students to analyze the reasons for the rise of the British and the decline of the Dutch in a brief essay. Which are the most persuasive, and why? Students may need to do additional reading for this assignment. In addition to a selection from Prest's *Albion Ascendant* (see "Suggestions for Lecture and Discussion Topics," number 2), have the class read an excerpt from Jonathan Israel, *The Dutch Republic: Its Rise, Greatness, and Fall: 1477–1806* (Oxford: Clarendon Press, 1995).

5. In a presentation, have students evaluate Peter the Great's efforts to transform Russia into a modern European state. The discussion should particularly include whether or not the price paid by Russian society was worth the result. Ask students to use relevant maps and illustrations as part of their presentations.

Research Assignments

1. Have students write an essay or present a report on the world of one of the following: Johann Sebastian Bach, George Frederick Handel, Antoine Watteau, François Boucher, Daniel Defoe, Pierre Bayle, Voltaire, or Lady Mary Wortley Montagu. For Bach and Handel, see the "Suggestion for Lecture and Discussion Topics,"

number 4. For Watteau and Boucher, begin with H. W. Janson and Anthony F. Janson, *History of Art*, 5th ed. (New York: Harry N. Abrams, 1999 [rev. ed.]). For Voltaire, see the bibliographical suggestions for "Lecture and Discussion Topics," number 6. Also, for Voltaire and Pierre Bayle, see Peter Gay's important book on the Enlightenment, *The Enlightenment: An Interpretation*, vol. 1, *The Rise of Modern Paganism* (New York: Alfred A. Knopf, 1967), with its remarkable bibliography. For Lady Mary Wortley Montagu, see the bibliographical suggestions in the segment in "Historical Skills" on "Did You Know?: Lady Mary Wortley Montagu and Inoculation for Smallpox."

2. Ask students to do a research project on Peter the Great's grand tour of western Europe in 1697–1698. They should chose one of the locations Peter visited and report on what he experienced and learned there. In addition, as a follow-up to Peter's visit, students can write a commentary on what Peter might have wanted to know about that location's politics, economy, and society. See the bibliographical suggestions in "Suggestions for Lecture and Discussion Topics," number 5. Students will require additional help with bibliography. For the Netherlands and for Britain, see the books listed in "Writing Assignments and Class Presentation Topics," number 4; and in "Lecture and Discussion Topics," number 3. For the Austrian Empire, see Robert J. W. Evans, *The Making of the Habsburg Empire, 1550–1700* (Oxford: Clarendon Press, 1979); and Robert A. Kann, *A History of the Habsburg Monarchy, 1526–1918* (Berkeley: University of California Press, 1974).

Literature

Allen, Robert J. (ed.), *Addison and Steele: Selections from the* Tatler *and the* Spectator. 1997.

Allison, Robert J., ed., *The Interesting Narrative of the Life of Olaudah Equiano. Written by Himself.* 1995.

Betts, C. J., trans., *Persian Letters by Charles Louis de Secondat Montesquieu.* 1977.

Defoe, Daniel, *Moll Flanders.* 1722.

Defoe, Daniel, *Robinson Crusoe.* 1719.

Hill, Bridget, ed., *The First English Feminist: Reflections upon Marriage and Other Writings by Mary Astell.* 1986.

Moseley, C. W., ed., *Travels of Sir John Mandeville by John Mandeville.* 1984.

Oakleaf, David, ed., *Eliza Haywood: Love in Excess.* 2000.

Scholar, Angela, trans., *Abbe Prévost: Manon Lescaut.* 2004.

Films and Videos

Longitude (2000; VHS/DVD, 3 hrs., 20 min.). This film retells the true story of eighteenth-century clockmaker John Harrison's search for a way to determine longitude. The film reflects Harrison's frustration, which was as much with the English naval authorities as it was with himself. Care has been taken to recreate the period accurately.

Historical Skills

Map 18.2, Europe, c. 1715, p. 685

Why did France prefer to cede vast territories in Canada rather than its relatively small island possessions in the Caribbean? What was important about the Mediterranean outposts, particularly Gibraltar, that Great Britain gained from Spain?

Mapping the West: Europe in 1740, p. 701

Ask students to discuss what "decline" meant to Spain, the Dutch Republic, Poland-Lithuania, and Sweden. How would they rank the five major powers of Great Britain, France, Austria, Prussia, and Russia? Why would they rank them this way? Ask students to review the map on page 660 and to comment on the differences between Europe in 1740 and Europe at the end of the seventeenth century. Which differences do they regard as the most significant? Why?

Figure 18.1, African Slaves Imported into American Territories, 1701–1810, p. 669

The caption for this figure states that "[t]he vast majority of African slaves transported to the Americas ended up in either the Caribbean or Brazil." How would one explain the graph, and especially the overwhelmingly large number of slaves going to the smallest area, the Caribbean?

The Exotic As Consumer Item, p. 676

The title of the painting is *Africa*, and the continent is represented as an attractive, young, black woman wearing a turban. The painting is part of a series in which attractive, young women represent Europe, Asia, and America. What impression would the viewer get of Africa and other faraway lands? What impression would the viewer get of international commerce? Of slavery?

Sir Robert Walpole at a Cabinet Meeting, p. 687

Ask students to reflect on the implications of government by cabinet. How much power does the king retain at this point? What is Walpole's standing within the cabinet? What does the small size of the bureaucratic apparatus serving the cabinet say about government and its responsibilities at this time?

The Origins of the Enlightenment: Voltaire, Letters Concerning the English Nation (1733), p. 699

Discussion can center on why philosophy and religion were increasingly seen as being separate from each other during the Enlightenment and whether there continues to be a divide between the two in public life. In the face of relatively recent scientific discoveries and, after centuries of trying to reconcile faith with reason, the Enlightenment demonstrated that following the tenets of one did not necessarily mean a rejection of the other. People today can point to Islamic countries where religion and politics are clearly mixed, but there is also a subtle mixing of religion and public life even in Western countries. Orthodoxy is recognized as the state religion in Russia, and chaplains are attached to the legislative chambers of government in Britain the United States. There are references to God in the Pledge of Allegiance and on the paper currency in the United States. Clashes between church and state are constantly in the news and courts and will likely continue to be so.

OTHER BEDFORD/ST. MARTIN'S RESOURCES FOR CHAPTER 18

The following resources are available to accompany Chapter 18. Please refer to the Preface of this manual for detailed descriptions of all the ancillaries.

For Instructors

Transparencies

The following maps and images from Chapter 18 are available as full-color acetates.

- Map 18.1: European Trade Patterns, c. 1740
- Map 18.2: Europe, c. 1715
- Map 18.3: Russia and Sweden after the Great Northern War, 1721
- Mapping the West: Europe in 1740
- *Exotic as Consumer Item*
- *Hogarth*

Instructor's Resources CD-ROM

The following maps and image from Chapter 18, as well as a chapter outline, are available on disc in both PowerPoint and jpeg formats.

- Map 18.1: European Trade Patterns, c. 1740
- Map 18.2: Europe, c. 1715
- Map 18.3: Russia and Sweden after the Great Northern War, 1721
- Mapping the West: Europe in 1740
- *Exotic as Consumer Item*

Using the Bedford Series with The Making of the West

Available in print as well as online at bedfordstmartins .com/usingseries, this guide offers practical suggestions for using **The Jesuit Relations: Natives and Missionaries in Seventeenth-Century North America, edited with an Introduction by Allan Greer**, in conjunction with chapters 17 and 18 of the textbook, and **Margaret C. Jacob, The Enlightenment: A Brief History with Documents**, in conjunction with chapters 18 and 19 of the textbook.

For Students

Sources of The Making of the West

The following documents are available in Chapter 18 of the companion sourcebook by Katharine J. Lualdi, University of Southern Maine.

1. Olaudah Equiano, *The Interesting Narrative of the Life of Olaudah Equiano Written by Himself* (1789)
2. Tsar Peter I, *Letter to His Son, Alexei* (October 11, 1715), and *Alexei's Response* (October 31, 1715)
3. Montesquieu, *Persian Letters: Letter 37* (1721)
4. Mary Astell, *Reflections upon Marriage* (1706)
5. *Hymn from The Spiritual Songbook* (1705)

Study Guides

The print **Study Guide** and the **Online Study Guide** at bedfordstmartins.com/hunt, both by *Victoria Thompson (Arizona State University) and Eric Johnson (University of California, Los Angeles)*, help students synthesize the material they have learned as well as practice the skills historians use to make sense of the past. The following Map, Visual, and Document activities are available for Chapter 18.

Map Activity

- Map 18.1: European Trading Patterns, c. 1740

Visual Activity

- *Exotic as Consumer Item*

Reading Historical Documents

- Lady Mary Wortley Montagu, Smallpox Inoculation in the Ottoman Empire
- Voltaire, Letters Concerning the English Nation, 1733

The Promise of Enlightenment
1740–1789

CHAPTER RESOURCES

Main Chapter Topics

1. The philosophers, the most influential figures in the Enlightenment, were private intellectuals dedicated to solving the real problems of the world.

2. Most of the *philosophes* subscribed to the idea that humans could, through the use of reason, understand and improve society and politics.

3. Many nobles concentrated on reasserting their privileges and resisting the Enlightenment. A large number of the expanding middle classes enthusiastically participated in the movement as a means of both demonstrating their position in society and bringing about change and reform. In general, the lower classes, buffeted by economic change, and particularly the rise in prices, had little to do with the Enlightenment.

4. Taken together, the War of the Austrian Succession and the Seven Years' War confirmed Prussia's status as a great power and reinforced Britain's standing as the leading colonial power at the expense of the French Empire.

5. In addition to traditional forms of popular discontent, governments now had to respond to a broad and informed public opinion, one of the most important results of the Enlightenment.

Summary

In the eighteenth century, even absolutist rulers like Catherine the Great of Russia endorsed Enlightenment ideas for reform. In order for humanity to progress, reason, religious tolerance, education, and justice had to prevail over superstition, religious fanaticism, ignorance, and legal torture. The lives of the lower classes, though, were far removed from Enlightenment ideas. When forced to choose between preserving state authority and reforming daily life for peasants, eighteenth-century rulers who wanted to be perceived as modern and progressive, nevertheless reinforced state power and control.

The Enlightenment, which began before 1740, peaked in the last half of the century. It was a cosmopolitan movement, with adherents in all parts of Europe as well as the British colonies in North America. Philosophes (French for "philosophers") were public intellectuals, united by the ideals of reason, reform, and freedom, trying to solve real problems of the day. In 1784, the German philosopher Immanuel Kant (1724–1804) summed up the movement with *sapare aude* ("dare to know" [or "think for yourself"]). The philosophes objected to religious intolerance, but also believed that religion hindered reform. Only reason could point to needed reforms by bringing critical, informed, and scientific thinking to bear on social issues and problems. The spread of knowledge would be key to comprehensive reform. Central to spreading knowledge was the new multivolume *Encyclopedia* (published 1751–1772), edited by Denis Diderot (1713–1784), which aimed at bringing together information about science, religion, industry, and society. Philsophes desired freedom of the press and freedom of religion, but they wanted intellectual freedom most of all. With a few notable exceptions, like Rousseau, philosophes came from the upper classes. Some were even women, like Emilie de Chatelet (1706–1749), who wrote about the mathematics and physics of Leibniz and Newton. Most philosophes did not hold university appointments. Scottish and German universities were open to Enlightenment ideas, but not French institutions, which were dominated by Catholic clergy. The Enlightenment flourished via personal contacts (including letters); correspondence in published journals; and especially the salons, where intellectuals, aristocracy, and others gathered in the homes of educated women, like M. Marie-Thérèse Geoffrin (1699–1777), to share ideas. Salons, headed by wealthy middle-class and aristocratic women, sprang up all over Europe.

Most influential individuals looked to religion for the foundation of a good society and government, but David Hume (1711–1776), in *Natural Religion of Philosophy* (1755), argued that belief in God was based on superstition and fear rather than reason. Some agreed with him. From Newton's theories, people could conceive of a universe that operated mechanically without the need for God's intervention (even though that conflicted with Newton's position). Out of that notion came atheists who did not believe in God, and deists who did believe in God but did not instill him with an active role in human affairs. Writers at this time disputed the common view that atheism inevitably led to immorality, and deists increasingly criticized both Catholic and Protestant authorities for religious intolerance. Voltaire's motto was *Ecrasez l'enfame* ("crush the infamous thing"), the "thing" being bigotry and intolerance. But attacking the church often meant attacking the state. In France, Voltaire became involved in a case where a Calvinist father had been accused of murdering his own son because it was erroneously believed that the young man was going to convert to Catholicism. The all-Catholic parlement of Toulouse had the father hideously tortured to exact a confession, which he would not give, and then executed him. Voltaire intervened to rehabilitate the father's name and restore his confiscated property to the family. His efforts helped bring about the extension of civil rights to French Protestants and energized the movement to abolish torture.

Critics, like abbe Guillaume Raynal (1713–1796) in his *Philosophical and Political History of European Colonies and Commerce between in the Two Indies* (1770), also took church and state to task for their involvement in the slave trade. But colonization and exploration continued, and James Cook (1728–1779) charted the coast of New Zealand and Australia. Enlightenment ideas fueled the antislavery movement. Freed slaves were encouraged to write of their experiences, and *The Interesting Narrative of the Life of Olaudah Equiano* (1788) was an international bestseller. With these kinds of publications in hand, abolitionists petitioned governments to end the slave trade.

Enlightenment critics were reformers rather than rebels, who looked to educated elites and enlightened rulers rather than to peasants, who were thought to be ignorant and violent, to reform society. This did not prevent their writings from having revolutionary implications concerning democracy, secular states, and individual rights. In his *Spirit of the Laws* (1748), Montesquieu warned against despotism, opposed the divine right of kings, and advocated constitutionalism. The Enlightenment emphasized the secular study of society and the importance of the individual — an emphasis that advanced the secularization of European politics begun in the previous century and laid the foundation for the social sciences of the modern era. Soon,

reason was viewed as the sole foundation for secular authority, which is why the Enlightenment is considered to be the origin of modernity.

Two of the most influential Enlightenment thinkers were Adam Smith (1723–1790) and Jean-Jacques Rousseau (1712–1778). Smith's book, *An Inquiry into the Nature and Causes of the Wealth of Nations* (1776), assumed laws of supply and demand would work as an "invisible hand" to harmonize individual interests with those of society. Perhaps his most consequential insight involved the importance of the division of labor in manufacture, an assembly-line approach to producing goods like pins. To let the system work free of state-imposed obstacles, Smith advocated laissez-faire ("to let alone") economics. The state was to provide national defense, internal order, and public works. Rousseau resisted the urban spirit of the Enlightenment and believed society itself threatened freedoms: "Man is born free, and everywhere he is in chains." He thought science and art were barriers between people and their natural state and extolled the virtues of the simple, rural life. Rousseau explored the tension between the individual and the demands of society first in *The New Heloise* (1761), a best-selling novel; then in *Emile* (1762), another novel, which he used to introduce ground-breaking educational approaches. Rousseau continued the theme in *The Social Contract* (1762), where he delved further into political theory. He argued that citizens enter into a social contract with one another and gain freedom by adhering to "the general will," living under a law to which all consent. Rousseau derived his theories from nature, not history, tradition, or the Bible. He implied people would be most free and moral in a republic with direct democracy, but did not provide for individual rights. Rousseau made no distinctions in social class and roundly condemned slavery. *The Social Contract* was banned in Geneva and Paris for undermining political authority. Still, Rousseau's works inspired French revolutionaries in the 1790s, and Communists like Karl Marx, and continue to generate controversy to this day.

The centers of Enlightenment—London, Amsterdam, and Paris—diffused outward to the rest of Europe and North America. The movement had less of an edge in constitutional countries, where the focus was on economics, philosophy, and history rather than politics and/or social relations. The Enlightenment's major constituents were the educated middle class. In France, educated elites—like Voltaire, Diderot, and Rousseau—faced arrest, exile, and imprisonment for their writings—had much to complain about: the lack of ways in which to make their criticisms known, and a government torn between censoring dissident ideas and wanting to appear progressive. After 1760, the French government ignored books it would once have banned. Additionally, illegal books—pornographic as well as philosophical—were smuggled into France. The Enlightenment movement was less confrontational in the German states. Still, the playwright, literary critic, and philosopher Gotthold Lessing (1729–1781) complained about the lack of freedom to criticize the Prussian government. He advocated religious toleration for Jews, and introduced the Jewish writer Moses Mendelssohn (1729–1786) into Berlin salons. Mendelssohn believed reason would end Jewish persecution and discrimination. Reason was critical to the thinking of Immanuel Kant (1724–1804) who, in his most influential work, *The Critique of Pure Reason* (1781), established the doctrine of idealism—the belief that true understanding comes only by examining the ways in which ideas are formed and then shaped in the mind. For Kant, reason alone could not answer the greatest philosophical questions, like whether or not God exists. But he stressed that moral freedom came from living in society and obeying its laws.

Excessive reliance on reason began to wear thin, and fed into a new movement—romanticism—which emphasized individual genius, deep emotion, and the joys of nature. Rousseau's autobiographical *Confessions* (1782), revealing as it did the writer's inner life, captured the essence of romanticism. Occultism was also an outgrowth of romanticism, but emotion was key. Johann Wolfgang von Goethe (1749–1832) glorified emotion in *The Sorrows of Young Werther* (1774), the story of a young man unhappy in love who commits suicide. It was hugely popular and even the young Napoleon read it several times. Beginning in the 1740s, religious revivals in much of the Protestant world underlined the limits of reason's scope and appeal. Pietists founded new communities in Germany, and revivalists in the North American colonies clashed with established churches, causing each side to establish colleges (like Princeton, Columbia, Brown, and Dartmouth) to further their respective beliefs. In the 1740s and 1750s, the mystic and charismatic Ba'al Shem Tov (1700–1760) rejected the synagogue system and founded the Hasidic (Hebrew for "most pious") sect among Polish Jews. In England, John Wesley (1703–1791) founded Methodism, which took its name from the disciplined and methodical approach to religious study and observance. Methodism, which sought a conversion experience while teaching hard work and temperance, became a major religious movement, especially among the working classes.

Responses to the Enlightenment varied greatly, as the rise of romanticism and religious revival demonstrates. Nobles composed only a very small proportion of the population, but lived disproportionately opulent lives. To pay for this lifestyle, aristocrats on the continent converted their legal rights, called seigneurial dues (from the French *seigneur* ["lord"]), to cash payments. In England, where there were no such dues, aristocrats protected their exclusive right to hunt. Harsh game laws were strictly enforced against poachers, and certain violations of those laws were considered capital crimes. Everywhere, aristocrats insisted on retaining all rights and privileges, whereas peasants were charged and taxed for virtually everything. Many of the nobility retained their special privileges with the help of the state. Frederick II (the Great) of Prussia (r. 1740–1786) packed the officer corps and civil bureaucracy with nobles, while Catherine II of Russia (r. 1762–1796) enshrined aristocratic privileges in the Charter of the Nobility (1785) in exchange for their subservience to the state. In Austria, Spain, the Italian states, Poland-Lithuania, and Russia, most of the nobility either ignored the Enlightenment or feared it might lead to reforms that would challenge their dominant position. A significant noble minority in Britain, France, and the western German states, though, were open to the new ideas.

The bourgeoisie (middle classes) lived primarily in towns or cities, working as doctors, lawyers, or governmental officials; or earning a living through investment in trade, land, or manufacturing. A portion of the middle classes, together with liberal nobles, began to form a mixed elite with new cultural tastes and a common interest in reform. This new, mixed elite often met in the Masonic lodges that had begun in Britain early in the eighteenth century and spread across the continent. The mixed elite also met in local, learned societies or academies, which discussed concrete reforms as well as scientific innovations. In art and architecture, the mixed elite favored neoclassicism—a cultural movement sparked by the recent discovery of Pompeii, Herculaneum, and Paestum. Architecture, furniture, wallpaper, and even pottery soon reflected the ideas of neoclassicism. The neoclassical pottery designs of the Englishman Josiah Wedgewood (1730–1795) became hugely popular and the British queen, Catherine the Great of Russia, and aristocratic and wealthy middle-class families in Europe and North America all owned his wares. While Frederick the Great of Prussia clung to baroque styles, the middle classes became preoccupied with the depiction of ordinary private life in paintings and literature. Court portraits, though, were still in such high demand that the French painter Marie-Louise-Elizabeth Vigee LeBrun (1755–1842) had a waiting list.

Changes were also occurring in the listening publics' tastes. Polyphonic, baroque music gave way to the clear melodic lines of the classical movement. Stringed instruments now dominated the orchestra and public concerts gradually replaced private recitals. There was a shift away from "occasional" music, written for private consumption or specific events, to music that would endure. This meant that composers wrote fewer symphonies as the classical period transitioned to the romantic. Composers like the Austrians Franz Joseph Haydn (1732–1809) and Wolfgang Amadeus Mozart (1756–1791) continued to work for noble patrons but, by the early 1800s, their compositions had entered the canon of concert classics.

Opera also gained in popularity during the last half of the century. Like concert halls, books grew in popularity. Far more people read many more books at the end of the century than at the beginning, and this included women who were now also becoming authors. Catherine Macaulay (1731–1791) wrote best-selling histories of England; whereas, in France, Stephanie de Genlis (1746–1830) focused on children's books.

As economies expanded through booming trade, life worsened for the indigent. Population increased and, although wages also rose, they did not keep up with inflation. At least 10 percent of Europe's urban population depended on charity. Governments were overwhelmed. Beggars and vagabonds were forced into workhouses that were part workshop, part hospital, and part prison. Fear of crime increased with the rise of rural burglary and banditry. The poor who had employment or land to work could participate to some extent in the new tastes and ideas of the period. In reading, the tastes of the lower classes ran to religious rather than secular works. Peasants continued to attend fairs and festivals, while the urban lower classes went to taverns or cabarets. In Britain, bullbaiting, dogfighting, and cockfighting remained popular. In 1744, the first rules for cricket were initiated.

Attitudes toward sexual behavior changed as people poured into the cities and encountered new opportunities and risked new vulnerabilities without the village community to monitor their actions. Out-of-wedlock births jumped from 5 percent to 20 percent. Women who worked as domestic servants were particularly vulnerable to abuse by masters and male servants, and numbers of abandoned babies soared. Desperate to keep their jobs, some women attempted abortion, while others resorted to infanticide. The state tried to regulate sexual behavior—prostitution, adultery, fornication—and infanticide, but made little headway. Male homosexuality, though, was rigorously prosecuted, and the stereotype of the effeminate, male homosexual apparently emerged in the eighteenth century. Attitudes about children changed, and childhood was perceived as being distinctly separate from adulthood. Parents began to concern themselves with repressing childhood sexuality and enhancing education. Children's toys, puzzles, and clothing, appeared, as did books like Tom Telescope's (an obvious pseudonym) *The Newtonian System of the Universe Digested for Young Minds* (1761).

Industrialization began in Britain in the 1770s and 1780s with four interlocking trends: a population increase of over 50 percent in the last half of the century, the introduction of steam-driven machinery, the concentration of laborers in factories, and the shift from woolen to cotton material. In 1733, the Englishman John Kay (1704–1764) invented the flying shuttle, which was faster than hand-drawing the yarn back and forth across the loom. It was in wide use by the 1760s and, as weavers

increased productivity, and because spinners could not keep up, there was a thread shortage. This prompted the invention of the spinning jenny and water frame, a power-driven spinning machine. These machines displaced women who had been doing the work by hand. In 1776, the Scottish engineer James Watt (1736–1819) introduced an improved steam engine and, in the 1780s, the Englishman Edmund Cartwright (1743–1823) designed a mechanized loom so simple that it could be operated by a small boy and was fifteen times more productive than an adult weaver.

No single explanation suffices for England's leadership in the Industrial Revolution; however, improvements in agriculture, capital generated from foreign trade that was expanding, and innovations in technology and organization were important. Although the rest of Europe did not industrialize until the nineteenth century, textile production, notwithstanding, increased significantly through the spread of the "putting-out" or "domestic" system, whereby manufacturers provided the raw materials to families who worked together at home to produce cloth. This system, which is sometimes called "proto-industrialization," was applied to other industries, like glassware, baskets, nails, and guns. Thousands of persons worked full and part time under this system to supplement meager incomes. As cloth became cheaper, the working class could afford more clothes, which were now made in white, red, blue, yellow, green, and even pastel colors, supplementing black, gray, and brown.

Commerce and war, however, remained the ways by which states competed with each other. Many sovereigns of the period were "enlightened depots," like Catherine the Great of Russia, who embraced Enlightenment ideas whenever they did not conflict with their absolutist powers. But rulers were also still militarily aggressive. The unstable balance of power during this period led to two major wars and important changes in status and alignments among the major powers. In the War of the Austrian Succession (1740–1748), Prussia and France fought Austria and Great Britain over Maria Theresa's ascension to the imperial throne. At stake was Silesia (seized from Austria by Prussia). Further, France and Great Britain fought each other in North America and in India and vied for control over the Caribbean. The 1748 Peace of Aix-la-Chapelle established Maria Theresa as empress, recognized her husband, Francis I, as Holy Roman Emperor, and ceded Silesia to Prussia. But this did not resolve colonial conflicts between England and France. The Diplomatic Revolution of 1756 reversed alliances—with former adversaries Prussia and Great Britain allied against long-time enemies Austria and France who joined former foes Russia and Sweden. When Prussia invaded Austria's ally Saxony, long-simmering hostilities between England and France evolved into the Seven Years' War (1756–1763) and soon spread around the globe (in North America, this conflict was called the

French and Indian War). Frederick was saved from certain defeat only by the unexpected death of Empress Elizabeth of Russia (r. 1741–1762). Her successor, Peter III, a great admirer of Frederick and all things Prussian, immediately withdrew Russia from the war. Prussia emerged from the war as a great power. British naval superiority led to a decisive defeat of France in the contest for colonial supremacy. In the Treaty of Paris (1763), France ceded Canada to Britain and agreed to remove its army from India, but kept its valuable West Indian islands. France later took its revenge by supporting the American Revolution against England in 1776.

Prussia emerged from the Seven Years' War as a great power. Through the use of cantonists ("reservists") who trained two or three months annually, Prussia had the third or fourth largest army in Europe, which consumed two-thirds of the state's budget to support it. Noblemen, who paid their own way, were officers in the army and, on retirement, oversaw the cantonist system and served in local offices. This military stranglehold kept peasants enserfed and blocked middle-class access to estates and governmental jobs. In 1772, Frederick the Great proposed the division of Poland-Lithuania among Austria, Russia, and Prussia. Fearing growing Russian influence in Poland and the Balkans, the empress Maria Theresa agreed. Religious divisions in Poland were used as an excuse.

A number of European rulers instituted administrative and legal reforms. Frederick II introduced a uniform civil justice system that administered laws efficiently and consistently. Joseph II of Austria (r. 1780–1790) ordered the compilation of a uniform law code. Catherine II of Russia formed a commission to consider reform proposals contained in the *Instruction*. These legal reforms were based on the ideas of Montesquieu who argued for appropriate punishments and against legal torture, and the Italian writer Cesare Beccaria (1738–1794) who, in *On Crimes and Punishments* (1764), also rejected torture and promoted the concept of being innocent until proved guilty. Ultimately, Catherine was unwilling to undertake substantial legal reforms.

States also sought more control over church affairs, and used Enlightenment criticisms to achieve it. There was much resentment against the power wielded by the Jesuits, and Pope Clement XIV (r. 1769–1774) was pressured into disbanding the order (it was revived in 1814). Joseph II went further and required Austrian bishops to swear fidelity and submission to him as Holy Roman Emperor. Under Joseph II, the Austrian state supervised Catholic seminaries, abolished contemplative monastic orders, and confiscated monastic property to pay for education reform and poor relief. Education was important to Joseph II, to Frederic II of Prussia, and to Catherine II of Russia, and in their countries the state subsidized schools.

Efforts at religious toleration were more mixed. In 1781, Joseph II extended freedom of worship to Protestant, Orthodox Christians, and Jews. In France, Louis XVI signed an edict, in 1787, restoring civil rights to Protestants, but they were still barred from holding political offices. In England, Catholics were still denied the right to worship openly and hold seats in Parliament. Jews continued to be widely discriminated against. They were even looked down on by many philosophes.

Interested parties often resisted reform. In 1781, Joseph II lifted restrictions on serfs, allowing them to travel about freely, enter trades, and marry with permission from the lord. He abolished tithes to the church, shifted more of the tax burden onto the nobles, and converted peasants' labor into cash payments. Joseph's brother and successor, Leopold II, was forced by the nobles to repeal these measures. Frederick II of Prussia encouraged agricultural innovation, but his nobles were only interested in expanding their estates at the expense of the peasants. In France, the physiocrats urged the deregulation of the grain trade, the abolition of urban trade guilds, and a more equitable tax system in order to stimulate agricultural production. In 1763, the government lifted price controls on grain, but had to reverse itself (1770) in the face of grain shortages and famine. The most important effort at reform came when Louis XV, aiming at impartiality, replaced the parlements with courts in which the judges no longer owned their offices. Louis XVI (r. 1774–1792) reversed this reform under aristocratic pressure. Louis's chief minister, Jacques Turgot (1727–1781), attempted reform once more along earlier physiocratic lines. He also planned to introduce a system of elected local assemblies. Aristocratic resistance, coupled with riots against rising grain prices, led to Turgot's dismissal. The French middle class was growing increasingly frustrated at having their hope for reform raised and then dashed.

Governments were increasingly held accountable for their actions by a wider range of individuals who were willing to riot and even rebel under certain circumstances. Grain was a particularly touchy subject. Deregulation and a free market meant that during shortages, grain prices would soar beyond the reach of ordinary persons and farmers accumulated huge profits by selling outside their areas. Riots were the typical response to this type of situation, and farmers were forced to sell their goods locally at fair prices set by the rioters. Women often led these "popular price fixings," as they were called. Food riots occurred frequently in France and Britain in the last half of the century, the most famous being the so-called Flour War in France (1775). In Russia, Emelian Pugachev (1726–1765), a Cossack, led a massive uprising in the 1770s. Claiming to be Peter III, the dead husband of Catherine II, he rallied thousands of Cossacks, mine workers, Muslim minorities, and serfs in a rebellion against the crown. Pugachev encouraged peasants to attack the nobility and seize their estates, and hundreds of aristocrats were killed. But the peasant uprising was not well coordinated with the activities of Pugachev's army, and he was eventually captured and his army defeated. Catherine cracked down, giving nobles even tighter control of the serfs.

Public opinion began to affect politics. Monarchs turned to public opinion to gain support for reforms opposed by the aristocracy. Newspapers supplied political news and supported positions on the issues of the day. In Sweden, Gustavus III (r. 1771–1792) proclaimed a new constitution dividing power between the king and legislature, abolished the use of torture, and assured freedom of the press. In France, the monarch and supporters of parlement used the printed word to square off. One French newspaper, *Le Journal des Dames* (*The Ladies' Journal*) was published by women and combined short stories and reviews with demands for women's rights. The Wilkes affair in the 1760s demonstrated just how powerful public opinion could be. John Wilkes (1725–1798), a member of Parliament, had been arrested for criticizing the government in his paper, *North Britan.* He successfully sued the crown and won damages. When he was reelected, Parliament denied him his seat. His cause was taken up in print, and major reforms were called for, including more frequent elections, more representation for the counties, the abolition of "rotten boroughs" (voting districts in the pocket of local patrons), and restrictions on royal pensions used to garner support. Public opinion was not always used to support reform. In 1780, the Gordon riots protested a bill passed by the House of Commons to grant limited toleration to Catholics. After seven days of rioting, three hundred people were dead and fifty buildings destroyed. Political opposition could also take a literary form. In the play, *The Marriage of Figaro* (1784), by Pierre-Augustin Caron de Beaumarchais (1732–1799), the main character, a servant, gets the better of his employer and mocks government. Marie Antoinette had it read it to her friends, but Louis XVI banned its production.

The failure of the Wilkes's campaign convinced the Americans opposing British rule that the English Parliament was hopelessly corrupt. Americans paid a fraction of the taxes Britons paid and, when Parliament tried to even the balance through such legislation as the Stamp Act (1765), rioting erupted. After the act was repealed, another new tax appeared: the Tea Act (1773). To demonstrate their opposition the Tea Act, colonists (disguised as Indians) boarded British ships and dumped their cargo of imported tea into Boston's harbor. In 1774, when Britain threatened military intervention, the First Continental Congress convened and unsuccessfully petitioned for redress. The following year, the Second Continental Congress organized an army under the leadership of George Washington and, in 1776, it proclaimed the Declaration of Independence. Britain was then pressed on all sides. France and the Dutch Republic aided the Americans, while indirect support for the colonists came when Spain

declared war on Britain. The American colonies achieved independence in 1783. Many viewed the American Revolution as a triumph for Enlightenment ideas.

After the Articles of Confederation failed to provide the new nation with a government sufficiently strong, a constitutional convention drafted a new Constitution in 1787. The new government extended rights only to property-owning, white males—thus excluding women and slaves. This new government was a radical departure from European models. In 1791, a Bill of Rights was appended to the Constitution outlining essential rights, such as freedom of speech. The American Revolution was the most significant, practical result of the Enlightenment. For most Europeans, however, the Enlightenment remained more a promise rather than a reality.

Suggestions for Lecture and Discussion Topics

1. Voltaire is one of the most interesting and broadly representative of the philosophes. Over his long career, he used various methods to reach the public and the powerful. *Candide*, a short and entertaining satire, exemplified one approach. Students might read the entire text or only a selection. Alternatively, selections from Voltaire's *Philosophical Dictionary* might be used as a basis for discussion, or you can use selections from both *Candide* and *Philosophical Dictionary*. Discussions of Voltaire's satire on optimism, his emphasis on the importance of a realistic approach and hard work, and other aspects of his views might best be understood when prefaced by introductory comments on his life and career.

Daniel Gordon's translation of *Candide* features such an introduction and useful documentary material (Boston: Bedford/St. Martin's, 1999). Another useful edition is that by Robert M. Adams (New York: W. W. Norton, 1966). The edition of Voltaire's *Philosophical Dictionary* by Peter Gay is highly recommended (New York: Harcourt Brace & World, 1962). See Chapter 1 in Peter Gay, *The Party of Humanity: Essays in the French Enlightenment* (New York: W. W. Norton, 1971 [originally published in 1959]) for an excellent introduction to Voltaire and his *Philosophical Dictionary*. Other useful books include Peter Gay, *Voltaire's Politics: The Poet As Realist* (New York: Vintage Books, 1965 [originally published in 1959]); William F. Bottiglia, ed., *Voltaire: A Collection of Critical Essays* (Englewood Cliffs, NJ: Prentice-Hall, 1968), which includes several useful short essays; Hadyn Trevor Mason, *Voltaire: A Biography* (Baltimore: Johns Hopkins University Press, 1981), a dependable short biography; and Theodore Besterman, *Voltaire*, 3d ed. (Chicago: University of Chicago Press, 1976), a comprehensive study.

2. Because Thomas Jefferson is someone most students are familiar with. His career is useful as a good introduction to the Enlightenment. Query number eleven,

"Aborigines," from Jefferson's *Notes on the State of Virginia,* which is concerned in large part with his investigation of Indian burial mounds, should provoke a discussion about how the Enlightenment functioned. Students can be asked to consider how Jefferson's investigation reflects the methods of the Enlightenment. Effective visual presentations might be built around Jefferson's plans for the University of Virginia, his main residence of Monticello, or his summer home in Poplar Forest.

A comprehensive biography of Jefferson is Willard Sterne Randall, *Thomas Jefferson: A Life* (New York: Henry Holt, 1993). At three hours, Ken Burns's video portrait *Thomas Jefferson* (Alexandria, VA: PBS Video, 1997) is too long to be shown in one class period, but selections from it would be useful to a consideration of Jefferson as a participant in the Enlightenment. It can be put on reserve for students to watch, or perhaps be shown outside of class if students are interested. *Notes on the State of Virginia* is available in an edition published by Viking Penguin Books (New York, 1998). It is also included in the Library of America edition of *Jefferson's Writings* (New York, 1984). Jefferson in Paris is the subject of Howard Crosby Rice, *Thomas Jefferson's Paris* (Princeton: Princeton University Press, 1976). Pauline Maier provides a good discussion of Jefferson's role in writing the Declaration of Independence in *American Scripture: Making the Declaration of Independence* (New York: Alfred A. Knopf, 1997). See also Garry Wills, *Inventing America: Jefferson's Declaration of Independence* (Garden City, NY: Doubleday, 1978). In a time when Jefferson's attitude toward slavery, his relationship with Sally Hemings, and his treatment of native Americans have been the subjects of searching critiques, Joseph J. Ellis offers a helpful examination of Jefferson's character in *American Sphinx: The Character of Thomas Jefferson* (New York: Alfred A. Knopf, 1997). Also useful in this regard is Jan Lewis and Peter S. Onuf, eds., *Sally Hemings & Thomas Jefferson: History, Memory, and Civil Culture* (Charlottesville: University of Virginia Press, 1999). Finally, S. Allen Chambers, *Poplar Forest and Thomas Jefferson* (Forest, VA: The Corporation for Jefferson's Poplar Forest, 1993) is a fascinating, detailed architectural history of Jefferson's central Virginia summer home.

3. Mozart's career as a child prodigy and a phenomenally gifted composer continues to fascinate students. He exemplifies the artist caught in a changing world where patronage is still important, but opportunities to reach a wider public are also present. Mozart's life also offers the possibility of examining changes in society when new groups arise to challenge the dominance of the aristocracy.

Amadeus, or at least a portion of the film (Burbank, CA: Warner Home Video, 1997), is a good place to start. Can this silly person be the musical genius we all associate with neoclassicism? Was competition between composers really so fierce? What does the relationship between Mozart and Salieri tell us about neoclassicism? Is there a bit of the Romantic in the brooding, passionate Salieri? Is the relationship a metaphor for a struggle between good and evil? Two short biographies are available: Peter Gay, *Mozart* (New York: Lipper/Viking Books, 1999); and John Rosselli, *The Life of Mozart* (Cambridge and New York: Cambridge University Press, 1998). Howard Gardner takes a very different approach in *Extraordinary Minds: Portraits of Four Exceptional Individuals and an Examination of Our Own Extraordinariness* (New York: Basic Books, 1997). Other useful titles include H. C. Robbins London, ed., *The Mozart Compendium* (New York: Schirmer Books, 1990); and the rather lengthy study by Daniel Heartz, *Haydn, Mozart, and the Viennese School, 1740–1780* (New York: W. W. Norton, 1995).

4. How the Enlightenment actually operated is a highly important topic. One way to approach it is by examining a list of the different venues of the Enlightenment:

- Encyclopedias and dictionaries
- Short stories and novels
- Pamphlets
- Newspapers, journals
- Almanacs, books on etiquette, books on how to write letters
- Coffeehouses, reading rooms, lending libraries, book-sellers
- Salons, scientific societies, academies
- Letters and conversation
- Theater and opera
- Engravings and other works of art

Examples of some of these could be provided for the class, or students could be assigned to report on various venues. Students should also be encouraged to discuss how opinion is formed and information exchanged today: How much is new? How much has been discarded? How much from the past is still utilized?

Some resources have already been mentioned in the segments dealing with Voltaire and Jefferson. Other possibilities include Thomas Munck, *The Enlightenment: A Comparative Social History, 1721–1794* (London: Arnold, 2000), which includes an extensive bibliography; Sarah Maza, *Private Lives and Public Affairs: The Causes Célèbres of Prerevolutionary France* (Berkeley: University of California Press, 1993); Robert Darnton, *The Business of the Enlightenment: A Publishing History of the Encyclopedie, 1775–1800* (Cambridge, MA: Belknap Press, 1979) and his *The Forbidden Best-Sellers of Pre-revolutionary France* (New York: W. W. Norton, 1995); and Dena Goodman, *The Republic of Letters: A Cultural History of the French Enlightenment* (Ithaca: Cornell University Press, 1994).

5. Catherine the Great is a fascinating historical figure. A consideration of her life and reign opens up many

possibilities, including an examination of the attempt in Russia to construct an effective central government (which could easily become a comparative examination by bringing in the efforts being made in Prussia, France, or Austria); the problems entailed by rapid social change (which would involve a discussion of the causes of the Pugachev rebellion); the nature of serfdom in Russia; and, of course, the extent of Catherine's commitment to the Enlightenment.

A very useful overview of Catherine's career can be found in Part 2 of Bruce Lincoln, *The Romanovs: Autocrats of All the Russias* (New York: Dial Press, 1981). The best biography of Catherine is by Isabel de Madariaga, *Catherine the Great: A Short History* (New Haven, CT: Yale University Press, 1990). De Madariaga is also the author of a comprehensive study, *Russia in the Age of Catherine the Great* (New Haven, CT: Yale University Press, 1981). Part 1 of Gregory L. Freeze, *From Supplication to Revolution: A Documentary Social History of Imperial Russia* (New York and Oxford: Oxford University Press, 1988) contains a wonderful selection of documents on the nobility, the peasantry, the bureaucracy, and women, among other groups. Other documents, including Catherine's Nakaz or *Instruction*, Pugachev's "Emancipation Decree," and Catherine's Charter to the Nobility, can be found in Basil Dmytryshyn, ed., *Imperial Russia: A Source Book, 1700–1917*, 3d ed. (Ft. Worth, TX: Holt, Rinehart & Winston, 1990). Two outstanding essays are available on the causes and the course of the Pugachev rebellion: Paul Avrich, *Russian Rebels, 1600–1800* (New York: Schocken Books, 1972), Part 4; and Marc Raeff's essay in Robert Forster and Jack P. Greene, eds., *Preconditions of Revolution in Early Modern Europe* (Baltimore: Johns Hopkins University Press, 1970).

6. Frederick II of Prussia is an equally fascinating historical figure and perhaps of more greater overall importance than Catherine. In any case, his life and career might serve as the basis for lectures and discussion on the topics of enlightened despotism, Frederick's relationship with Voltaire, and Prussia and great-power politics at the end of the eighteenth century. Chapter 2 of Holger H. Herwig, *Hammer or Anvil: Modern Germany 1648–Present* (Lexington, MA: D. C. Heath, 1994) is an excellent overview, placing Frederick and Prussia in the context of mid- to late-eighteenth-century Europe. Biographies include Theodore Schieder and Sabina Berkeley, *Frederick the Great* (New York: Longman, 1999), a good introduction; and the recent publication, Giles MacDonogh, *Frederick the Great: A Life in Deed and Letters* (New York: St. Martin's Press, 2000), where the emphasis is on intellectual matters, particularly Frederick's love-hate relationship with Voltaire. Two older studies worth consulting are Sidney B. Fay and Klaus Epstein, *The Rise of Brandenburg-Prussia to 1786* (Malabar, FL: R. E. Krieger, 1981); and Hans Rosenberg's classic study of the Prussian royal bureaucracy, *Bureaucracy, Aristoc-*

racy, and Autocracy: The Prussian Experience, 1660–1815 (Cambridge, MA: Harvard University Press, 1958). Finally, for either Frederick or Catherine, Marc Raeff, *The Well-Ordered Police State: Social and Institutional Change through Law in the Germanies and Russia, 1600–1800* (New Haven, CT: Yale University Press, 1983) is very useful. This book is not about the police state as we have come to know it in the twentieth century, but rather, as the subtitle indicates, about earlier efforts to regulate various aspects of citizens' lives in an attempt to improve them.

7. Protests in western Europe in the last half of the eighteenth century can form the basis for interesting class meetings in which participants discuss the social structure of France and England, popular protest movements, the role of the Enlightenment, and the validity of using a Marxist approach to these questions. Two English historians stand out for their contributions to debates about popular protest in this period. One is E. P. Thompson, whose major book, *The Making of the English Working Class* (New York: Random House, 1963), is a classic. While very long, it is well worth reading. Two articles provide many of Thompson's insights, although without the wealth of detail: "The Moral Economy of the English Crowd of the Eighteenth Century," *Past and Present* 50 (May 1971), pp. 76–136; and "Eighteenth-Century English Society: Class Struggle Without a Class?" *Social History* 3.2 (May 1978), pp. 137–165. The other English historian is George Rude, whose best-known book is *The Crowd in History: A Study of Popular Disturbances in France and England, 1730–1848* (New York: John Wiley & Sons, 1964). Also very useful are his *Paris and London in the Eighteenth Century: Studies in Popular Protest* (New York: Viking Press, 1970); and *Hanoverian London, 1714–1808* (Berkeley and Los Angeles: University of California Press, 1971). Finally, Jack A. Goldstone, *Revolution and Rebellion in the Early Modern World* (Berkeley and Los Angeles: University of California Press, 1991) discusses eighteenth-century France from a demographic and economic point of view and tries to locate the causes of the crisis that becomes the French Revolution. It is not an entirely convincing argument, but the reader learns an enormous amount. Goldstone also provides an extensive bibliography.

Making Connections

1. *Why would rulers experience ambivalence about the Enlightenment, supporting reform on the one hand, while clamping down on political dissidents on the other?* Some of the absolutist rulers of this period, like Catherine the Great of Russia, Frederick II (the Great) of Prussia, and Joseph II of Austria, wanted to be perceived as modern and progressive. But while they were interested in reform to at least some degree, and embraced Enlightenment

ideas they deemed useful in that regard, they rejected anything that had the potential to threaten their personal power and authority. So, while Catherine, Frederick, and Joseph were interested in education, and instituted education reform in their countries, they (or their successor in Joseph's case) backed down on other reforms that were opposed by their powerful nobility, like legal reform in Russia, serf reform in Habsburg territories, and agricultural reform in Prussia.

2. *Which major developments in this period ran counter to the influence of the Enlightenment?* Although absolutist rulers were "enlightened despots," military aggression (in the form of the War of the Austrian Succession [1740–1748] and the Seven Years' War [1756–1763]) rather than reasoned negotiation continued to be the means by which international disputes were settled. The nobility across Europe also continued to insist on their traditional rights and privileges, at the expense of those at the bottom of the socioeconomic hierarchy. Slavery continued to run counter to Enlightenment ideas and there were calls for its abolition. Excessive reliance on reason also began to wear thin, and this discontent fed into a new movement—romanticism—which emphasized individual genius, deep emotion, and the joys of nature. Reaction to the Enlightenment also took the form of religious revival. The Pietists in Germany, revivalists in the United States, and the Methodists in England, were all a response to the growing rejection of reason.

Writing Assignments and Class Presentation Topics

1. Ask students to reflect on the kinds of activities that preoccupied a philosophe. They should be asked to try to make some general statements about what philosophes did, what they believed in, and which changes they wanted to make. These statements should be based on the activities and characteristics of particular individuals. For example, Denis Diderot's work as editor of the *Encyclopedia* can be seen as an attempt to collect useful knowledge about various topics, as an example of the collective work many philosophes engaged in, and as an indication of the value philosophes placed on education. Remind students that the philosophes differed from one another. For example, while most were vitally interested in improving government, their ideas about this topic varied widely. A variation on this assignment is to ask students to write essays or give reports on particular philosophes, emphasizing the extent to which a particular philosophe was a representative figure.

2. Provide students with the list of the different venues of the Enlightenment (see "Suggestion for Lecture and Discussion Topics," number 4) and ask them to reflect on why and how one or more venues was useful in spreading ideas of the Enlightenment. This topic would

work well as an in-class writing assignment if, after the class had discussed the means for acquainting people with Enlightenment ideas, each student was asked to write more expansively on one of the venues. A variation on this topic is to ask students to write an essay on how they currently learn about the world around them (the Internet, TV, conversations with friends, and so on) and what venue is particularly influential as they form opinions about current issues. Which venue or venues are most like Enlightenment models? Least like? Which would a philosopher prefer? Why?

3. Using the visual material available in Chapter 19 (see the suggestions on p. 725 for *Broken Eggs*), students could be asked to write about morality and sexuality in the eighteenth century, including new ideas about marriage and about raising children. Ask students to reflect on the differences caused by factors such as gender and social groups.

4. The War of the Austrian Succession and the Seven Years' War, taken together, produced significant changes in the European balance of power. Ask students to write an essay discussing how these wars affected the relative standing of one of the following major powers: Austria, France, Great Britain, Prussia, or Russia.

5. Rousseau's ideas on education, especially as they are represented in *Émile* and elsewhere in his writings, conflict with his treatment of his own children and his relationships with their mothers. Ask students to explore this issue, keeping in mind such questions as whether his behavior or personality traits can be reconciled with his writings. Is it important that we be able to do so?

Research Assignments

1. For Voltaire and many others, the enlightened despot offered the best opportunity for the Enlightenment to fulfill its various goals. An enlightened despot would have the intelligence to see the benefits the Enlightenment could provide and the power to bring those benefits into being. Students could be asked to choose an enlightened despot from the list below and identify and investigate a specific issue that especially concerned that ruler; for example, religious freedom, freedom of the press, economic reform, education reform, or women's issues. Students should not merely describe the enlightened despot's thoughts on the particular subject, but also to evaluate that person's treatment of the issue. To what extent was the ruler "enlightened" as opposed to "despotic"?

- Catherine II
- Frederick II
- Maria Theresa
- Joseph II
- Louis XVI

Suggested readings for Catherine II and Frederick II have already been listed in "Suggestions for Lecture and Discussion Topics," numbers 5 and 6, respectively. For Joseph II and Maria Theresa, see Charles Ingrao, *The Habsburg Monarchy 1618–1815* (Cambridge: Cambridge University Press, 1994). For Maria Theresa, see C. A. Macartney, *Maria Theresa and the House of Austria* (Mystic, CT: Verry, 1969). For Joseph II, see T. C. W. Blanning, *Joseph II and Enlightened Despotism* (London: Longman, 1970). For Louis XVI, see John Hardman, *Louis XVI* (New Haven, CT: Yale University Press, 1993).

2. The use of images to supplement text has a long tradition in Europe but became far more widespread during the eighteenth century. Students can be assigned research projects on some of the more popular illustrators from the period, such as William Hogarth, James Gillray, or Thomas Rowlandson; or even on a particular series, such as Hogarth's *The Rake's Progress* (1733–1734) or *Marriage à la Mode* (1743). Another possibility is to review the literature on the impact of satirical prints and political caricatures. Students might begin by reading chapters 2 and 3 in Thomas Munck, *The Enlightenment: A Comparative Social History, 1721–1794* (London: Arnold, 2000). These chapters take up traditional popular and elite culture along with what the author calls "broadening the horizon," a variety of cultural changes. From there, students might go to Ronald Paulson, *Hogarth*, 3 vols. (New Brunswick: Rutgers University Press, 1991–1993); Jennifer S. Uglow, *Hogarth: A Life and a World* (New York: Farrar, Straus, & Giroux, 1997); David Bindman, *Hogarth and His Times: Serious Comedy* (Berkeley: University of California Press, 1997); and Sean Shesgreen, ed., *Engravings by Hogarth* (New York: Dover Publications, 1973). Less is available on Gillray and Rowlandson. For Gillray, see Draper Hill, *Mr. Gillray the Caricaturist* (Greenwich, CT: Phaidon, 1965). For Rowlandson, see the ubiquitous Ronald Paulson, *Rowlandson: A New Interpretation* (New York: Oxford University Press, 1972). A broader perspective is offered by Louise Lippincott, *Selling Art in Georgian London: The Rise of Arthur Pond* (New Haven, CT: Yale University Press, 1983); and Diana Donald, *The Age of Caricature: Satirical Prints in the Reign of George III* (New Haven, CT: Yale University Press, 1996). Also useful are E. E. C. Nicholson, "Consumers and Spectators: The Public of the Political Print in Eighteenth-Century England," *History* 81 (1996), pp. 5–21; and R. Porter, "Seeing the Past," *Past and Present* 118 (1988), pp. 186–205.

Literature

Allison, Robert J., ed., *The Interesting Narrative of the Life of Olaudah Equiano. Written by Himself.* 1995.

Atkins, Stuart, trans., *Goethe: Faust.* 2002.

Cranston, Maurice, trans., *Jean-Jacques Rousseau: The Social Contract.* 1968.

Gordon, Daniel, ed., *Voltaire: Candide.* 1999.

Hutter, Catherine, trans., *Johann Wolfgang von Goethe: Sorrows of Young Werther and Selected Writings.* 1987.

Krueger, Alan B., trans., *Adam Smith: The Wealth of Nations.* 2003.

Luvaas, Jay, trans., *Frederick the Great on the Art of War. By himself.* 1999.

Meiklejohn, J. M. D., trans., *Critique of Pure Reason.* 1990.

Roche, Daniel, trans., *Jacques Louis Ménétra: Journal of My Life.* 1986.

Schechter, Ronald, trans., *Gotthold Ephraim Lessing: Nathan the Wise.* 2004.

Films and Videos

Dangerous Liaisons (1988; VHS/DVD, 2 hrs.). This lush adaptation of Choderlos de Laclos's 1782 novel thoroughly captures the maliciousness and sexual depravity of the aristocracy on the eve of the French Revolution.

Ridicule (1996; VHS/DVD, 1 hr., 43 min.). This film is set at the court of Louis XVI, where wit is prized above all other qualities. The film nicely captures the sense of decadence of the period, and is especially strong on such details as costuming and setting (in French with English subtitles).

Historical Skills

Map 19.1, Centers of the Enlightenment, p. 719

Ask students to comment on the geographic extent of the Enlightenment. What might they infer from the map about the participation of men and women in the Enlightenment? Do they have any suggestions for changing the inset map that shows Enlightenment centers in North America?

Mapping the West: Europe and the World, c. 1780, p. 742

Ask students to compare this map with a map in Chapter 18, Europe in 1740 (p. 701). What reasons can they suggest for changing the focus from Europe to the world? Ask students to keep in mind the locations and results of the Seven Years' War and the American War for Independence as they think about this question.

Among the reasons that might be cited: the Seven Years' War was a world war with important ramifications beyond Europe. Among other results, the French were ousted from Canada and India, and the British Empire took the lead in imperial affairs. Also, the American War for Independence led to the creation of the United States of America, with both short-term and long-term implications. The European situation had also changed in various respects, but the major powers remained the same as they were in 1740.

Catherine the Great, p. 707

Catherine had only one child, so she could not be portrayed surrounded by children as Maria Theresa is in the portrait (p. 730). Students might be asked to comment, based on what they know of Catherine, on whether she would have ever allowed a portrait of herself similar to that of Maria Theresa. What is the purpose of the painting of Catherine the Great? What is the background figure to Catherine's left meant to symbolize?

Bookbinding, p. 709

The caption notes that the hundreds of plates in the *Encyclopedia* (which are gathered in separate volumes) tried to depict every stage of the artisan's work — in this case, bookbinding. What does this effort tell us about the purpose of the *Encyclopedia* in particular and the Enlightenment in general?

Broken Eggs, p. 725

Ask students to compare this painting to that of Maria Theresa and her family (p. 730). What similarities and differences do they note? How might they explain these? What is the purpose of each piece of art? Who is the intended audience? What do all of these illustrations suggest about social classes in the eighteenth century?

Thomas Jefferson, Declaration of Independence, July 4, 1776, p. 740

Students can be asked to identify the Enlightenment ideas encapsulated in the *Declaration of Independence*. The idea that a social contract existed between citizens and their government, and that individuals had certain natural rights and duties in relation to it, was rooted in Enlightenment thinking. According to Jefferson, people had a right to life, liberty, and the pursuit of happiness. When the social contract was broken through the tyranny of government, people had a right, even a duty, to rebel against it. The participation of the persons involved in the political process especially distinguishes the document as an Enlightenment work.

OTHER BEDFORD/ST. MARTIN'S RESOURCES FOR CHAPTER 19

The following resources are available to accompany Chapter 19. Please refer to the Preface of this manual for detailed descriptions of all the ancillaries.

For Instructors

Transparencies

The following maps and image from Chapter 19 are available as full-color acetates.

- Map 19.1: Centers of the Enlightenment
- Map 19.2: War of the Austrian Succession, 1740–1748
- Map 19.3: The Seven Years' War, 1756–1763
- Mapping the West: Europe and the World, c. 1780
- Jean-Baptiste Greuze, *Broken Eggs*
- Neoclassical Style

Instructor's Resources CD-ROM

The following maps and image from Chapter 19, as well as a chapter outline, are available on disc in both PowerPoint and jpeg formats.

- Map 19.1: Centers of the Enlightenment
- Map 19.2: War of the Austrian Succession, 1740–1748
- Map 19.3: The Seven Years' War, 1756–1763
- Mapping the West: Europe and the World, c. 1780
- Jean-Baptiste Greuze, *Broken Eggs*

Using the Bedford Series with The Making of the West

Available in print as well as online at bedfordstmartins .com/usingseries, this guide offers practical suggestions for using **Margaret C. Jacob, The Enlightenment: A Brief History with Documents**, in conjunction with chapters 18 and 19 of the textbook; **Candide by Voltaire, translated, edited, and with an Introduction by Daniel Gordon**, and **Nathan the Wise by Gotthold Ephraism Lessing with Related Documents, translated, edited, and with an Introduction by Ronald Schechter**, in conjunction with Chapter 19 of the textbook.

For Students

Sources of The Making of the West

The following documents are available in Chapter 19 of the companion sourcebook by Katharine J. Lualdi, University of Southern Maine.

1. Marie-Thérèse Geoffrin and M. d'Alembert, *The Salon of Madame Geoffrin* (1765)
2. Jacques-Louis Ménétra, *Journal of My Life* (1764–1802)
3. Adam Smith, *An Inquiry into the Nature and Causes of the Wealth of Nations* (1776)
4. Frederick II, *Political Testament* (1752)
5. Thomas Jefferson, *Letter to Colonel Edward Carrington* (1787)

Study Guides

The print **Study Guide** and the **Online Study Guide** at bedfordstmartins.com/hunt, both by Victoria Thompson (Arizona State University) and Eric Johnson (University of California, Los Angeles), help students synthesize the material they have learned as well as practice the skills historians use to make sense of the past. The following Map, Visual, and Document activities are available for Chapter 19.

Map Activity

• Map 19.3: The Seven Years' War

Visual Activity

• Jean-Baptiste Greuze, *Broken Eggs*

Reading Historical Documents

• Jean-Jacques Rousseau, *The Social Contract*, 1762
• Thomas Jefferson, *Declaration of Independence*, July 4, 1776

The Cataclysm of Revolution
1789–1800

CHAPTER RESOURCES

Main Chapter Topics

1. All across Europe and in the United States, people steeped in the Enlightenment discussed constitutions and representative government but, in Europe, only France's government succumbed to a full-fledged revolution.

2. French revolutionaries were the first to establish a constitutional monarchy based on Enlightenment principles. The failure of the National Assembly eventually gave way to the more radical National Convention and the establishment of a republic.

3. Under the pressure of war and resistance to the revolution, the National Convention centralized government to provide food, prosecute the war, and punish counterrevolutionaries, thus beginning the Terror.

4. Maximilien Robespierre, leader of the government during the Terror, tried to create a "Republic of Virtue," through a massive and often violent program of political reeducation and de-Christianization.

5. In the continual wars between 1792 and 1815, France dominated Europe using new means of mobilizing soldiers and through the rise of talented officers, including the brilliant Napoleon Bonaparte. French military campaigns also spread reforms based on Enlightenment principles.

6. After Robespierre's downfall, the Directory could not long manage France. The Directory's weakness afforded Bonaparte the opportunity to establish another, new form of government.

Summary

By the 1780s, Europeans—especially the Dutch, French, and Belgians—were wealthier, healthier, more numerous, and better educated than ever before. While many greeted the American experiment in republican government with enthusiasm, few considered it a model for European states. European monarchies seemed securely established. The Dutch, Belgian, Polish, and French revolts between 1787 and 1789 are called the "Atlantic revolutions" because these occurred on the shores of the North Atlantic. France was the richest and most powerful state in western Europe, and its revolution was more violent and influential than the others.

The Dutch Patriot movement (1787) sought to reduce the power of the *stadholder*. What began as a protest among pro-American middle-class bankers, merchants, and writers grew into a popular movement through a petition campaign and the formation by the Patriots of citizen militias: the Free Corps. The Free Corps forced new local elections in order to oust pro-Orangists from office. In 1787, after the Free Corps defeated the stadholder's troops, Frederick William II of Prussia, brother-in-law of the stadholder, intervened and restored the power of the house of Orange. Many of the wealthy Patriots feared the growing power of the Free Corps who desired more democratic reforms. Lower-class mobs pillaged the homes of wealthy Patriot leaders and many of were forced to flee the country.

Belgian elites in the Austrian Netherlands reacted against the Enlightenment reforms Joseph II introduced, which enhanced his power at the expense of the upper classes. The resistance that began in defense of historic local liberties soon attracted democrats. In late 1789, delegates from the ten provinces declared themselves the United States of Belgium. This movement soon split, however, between the democrats and the aristocracy. The nobles aligned with the church and the peasants who demonstrated against the democrats relentlessly. Faced in 1790 with a choice between the Austrian emperor and "our current tyrants," democrats called for the Austrians to return.

In Poland, Patriots comprising middle-class leaders, some nobles, some clergy, and the king sought to reform the Polish state. In 1788, with Russia preoccupied with Ottoman armies, a reform-minded parliament enacted the constitution of May 3, 1791, which granted the monarchy greater power and freed the two-house legislature from the nobles' individual veto power. Catherine II would not permit even this modest revolution on her borders; she therefore defeated the Patriots and engineered a second and third partition of Poland with Prussia and Austria. After the third partition, Poland was no longer a viable country but remained an unstable element in European politics.

The French Revolution began as a fiscal crisis that stemmed from France's support of the American Revolution. Unlike Britain, which had a national bank, France relied on short-term, high-interest loans and an inadequate taxation system. Interest on the national debt consumed half the national budget. The crown tried to overhaul the taxation system without success, in part because Louis XVI was considered ineffectual, and his wife Marie-Antoinette was, by 1789, a target of widespread hatred for her Austrian birth and extravagant tastes. Louis first tried the Assembly of Notables and then the parlements to back his uniform land tax and other reforms. Repulsed by both bodies, Louis called a meeting of the Estates General, which had not met for 175 years. The main issue quickly became how it would vote. When it had last met in 1614, the three Estates (clergy, nobility, and everyone else) had voted separately, allowing the clergy or the nobility, who together made up only 5 percent of the population but owned about 35 percent of the land, to veto any decision of the Third Estate, which represented 95 percent of the population. Louis doubled the number of Third Estate delegates, making their numbers equal to the First and Second Estates combined, but he still only allowed them one, collective vote. This prompted a pamphlet campaign calling for individual voting, which would then give the deputies of the Third Estate a numerical advantage in parlement. Local meetings were held to elect deputies to the parlement, and peasants gave full reign to their grievances over taxation.

After the elections, expectations were high that the Estates General would resolve all problems. Then, a bad harvest in 1788 caused food shortages and drove up the price of bread. Additionally, a slump in textile production threw hundreds of thousands out of work.

The Estates General began meeting in May 1789, but were soon at a stalemate because the deputies of the Third Estate insisted on individual voting. In June 1789, the deputies of the Third Estate broke away and declared themselves the "National Assembly." Two days later, the clergy narrowly voted to join them. A constitutional revolution was under way. Denied access to their meeting hall, the new National Assembly met on a nearby tennis court and took an oath not to disband until France had a constitution.

The movement of troops into Paris and Louis's dismissal of popular minister Jacques Necker caused people to fear a plot to arrest the deputies. The common people of Paris attacked those places they believed grain or arms were stored. On July 14, an armed crowd attacked and liberated the Bastille prison, a hated symbol of royal authority. All over France, local revolts led to committees of "patriots" replacing local governments. National guard units, composed of civilians, attempted to restore order. In the countryside, however, many peasants, who had long been overburdened with church tithes and secular taxes, feared aristocratic plots and attacked châteaux and burned seigneurial records, an event known as the "Great Fear."

On the night of August 4, 1789, in response to peasant violence, noble deputies announced their willingness to give up tax exemptions and seigneurial dues. The abolition of the feudal burdens satisfied the peasants. The National Assembly also mandated that, henceforth, talent rather than birth would be the path to office.

On August 26, 1789, the National Assembly passed the Declaration of the Rights of Man and Citizen, a stirring statement of Enlightenment principles. The Declaration granted freedom of religion and of the press, equality of taxation, and equality before the law. It established the principle of national sovereignty. In pronouncing all "men" free (Protestant and Jewish men were also granted the vote), the Declaration raised questions about the rights of women and slaves among others. Women were considered citizens, but they could not vote. Still, women took part in revolutionary acts and also authored petitions, published tracts, and organized political clubs. In 1791, Olympe de Gouges (1748–1793) published her *Declaration of the Rights of Women*.

The new constitution divided white men into "active" and "passive" citizens. Only "active" citizens—a designation based on wealth—could vote in the new constitutional monarchy. The old divisions of the provinces were abolished in favor of a national system of eighty-three departments, with identical administrative and legal structures. The practice of purchasing offices was abolished, and officials were now elected. The National Assembly also passed a Civil Constitution of the Clergy in July 1790. Church property was confiscated and pay scales put into place for the clergy. The impounded property was to underpin the new paper money (*assignats*), but inflation set in when the state began selling church land. The taking of monastic vows was outlawed, and monks and nuns were encouraged to leave their cloisters for state pensions. Few nuns took advantage of this offer. In November 1790, the National Assembly required all clergy to swear an oath of loyalty to the constitution. Pope Pius VI condemned the constitution, and half the clergy refused to take the oath; many previous supporters of the Revolution now chose the church over the revolution. Louis XVI, unhappy with the restrictions placed on his power, attempted to flee the country with his family on June 20, 1791. Recognized at Varennes, forty miles from the French border, Louis and his family were captured and returned to Paris.

After the election of a new Legislative Assembly, for which the deputies of the National Assembly had declared themselves ineligible, France moved to war. On April 21, 1792, Louis declared war against Austria. Prussia entered on the side of Austria. In the initial battles, the Austrian armies routed the French. When the war did not go well, the Legislative Assembly came under fire, and a mob invaded the assembly hall and threatened the royal family. Marquise de Lafayette returned from the front to quell the protestors. As the duke of Brunswick and his forces crossed the border, he issued a manifesto (the Brunswick Manifesto) threatening to level Paris if the royal family were harmed.

Political clubs proliferated after the founding of the first one: the Jacobin Club (1789). The *sans-culottes* (men of the artisan class) also participated in political clubs and in the local district governments (sections). On August 10, 1792, the leaders of the sections organized an insurrection and attacked the Tuileries palace, the king's residence. In response, the Legislative Assembly abolished the property qualifications for voting and ordered new elections for a national convention. The new National Convention abolished the monarchy on September 22, 1792, and established the first French republic. As Prussian forces neared Paris, mobs searched out supposed traitors in the prisons. Eleven hundred inmates were killed in the September massacres.

In the first months of the republic, the deputies of the National Convention, most of whom were middle-class lawyers and professionals active in the national network of Jacobin Clubs, split into two factions. The Girondins resisted the power of the Parisian militants. The Mountain took the militants' side. In the trial of the king, the Girondins argued for clemency or exile. The Mountain, however, won a narrow victory, condemning Louis XVI to the guillotine in January 1793. The conflict between the Mountain and the Girondins continued until June 2, 1793, when armed Parisian militants invaded the National Convention and forced the arrest of twenty-nine Girondin deputies. The purged Convention also established paramilitary bands, the "revolutionary armies," and expedited the revolutionary courts.

The Committee of Public Safety was established by the Convention (April 1793) to oversee such things as food distribution, the conduct of the war, and the rooting out of counterrevolutionaries. In July, country lawyer Maximilien Robespierre (1758–1794) joined and became its guiding spirit, the advocate of the Terror, and the effective head of the government. He was also the chief architect of the Republic of Virtue, which aimed to teach citizens, through force if necessary, how to be good republicans. Steeped in the classics of republicanism,

Robespierre defended democratic government, but supported emergency measures that restricted liberties. He favored a free market, but was willing to enact price controls during a crisis. Robespierre spearheaded the move for a General Maximum, which set maximum prices of thirty-nine essential commodities and wages. He also believed that without terror, virtue was impotent, and this became the philosophy of the "Terror." Dishonest officials were purged and political suspects tried and executed. In October 1793, Marie-Antoinette, Olympe de Gouges, and Girondin leaders were sent to the guillotine. Austria, Prussia, England, Spain, Sardinia, and the Dutch Republic, fearing that revolution would spread to their countries, formed a coalition against France. Robespierre was successful in rousing the nation and, by the end of 1793, France had halted the advance of the allied powers; in the summer of 1794, it invaded the Austrian Netherlands and crossed the Rhine, ready to carry the revolution beyond France's borders.

The government spared no effort to extol the revolution and establish it culturally. A new national anthem, "La Marseillaise," was one of a range of means to convey revolutionary slogans and symbols. Foremost among the new symbols was the figure of Liberty. Like Rousseau, Robespierre believed that the republic had to reform its citizens by establishing a new civic religion. Jacques-Louis David (1748–1825) used elaborate revolutionary festivals to destroy the monarchical mystique and make the republic sacred. Some revolutionaries participated in a campaign of de-Christianization, which included closing churches (Protestant and Catholic), selling church buildings, and forcing the clergy out of the religious life. But the Committee of Public Safety, concerned about offending the rural populations, halted that campaign and replaced it with the Cult of the Supreme Being in June 1794. Neither the de-Christianization Cult of Reason movement nor Robespierre's Cult of the Supreme Being attracted many followers.

All aspects of life in France became politicized. The Convention took education out of the hands of the Catholic church and voted for free and compulsory primary education for both boys and girls. But these attempts at secularizing education suffered from the lack of trained teachers to replace those who had been previously provided by Catholic religious orders. The tricolor —the combination of red, white, and blue that eventually became the flag of France — was devised (July 1789) and citizens were required to wear cockades in those colors. Biblical and saints' names gave way to classically inspired ones, like Brutus and Cornelia. Patriots now used the informal *tu* ("you") in place of the formal *vous* and *Citoyen* ("Citizen") for *Monsieur* and *Citoyenne* for *Madame*. A new secular calendar eliminating all Christian references was introduced, but only remained in use for twelve years. The new metric system, however, endured and was eventually used in most parts of the world. Family law was also reformed: births, deaths, and marriages required civil registration; divorce was permitted; and girls as well as boys were permitted to inherit family property equally.

Women especially suffered most in times of war. Women led protests over high prices, food shortages, and moves against the Catholic church. Charlotte Corday took matters into her own hands when she assassinated the outspoken deputy Jean-Paul Marat in his bath in July 1793. Corday was sent to the guillotine.

The arrest of the Girondin deputies (June 1793) sparked insurrection in several departments and in important cities like Lyon. In the Vendée region of western France, civil war broke out in 1793. Peasants, artisans, and weavers joined under noble leadership to form a Catholic and royal army. In addition to the counterrevolutionary army in the Vendée, guerrilla bands supplied by Britain operated in nearby Brittany. In many ways, the civil war was a war of the countryside against the town; townspeople had grown wealthy during the Revolution, whereas peasants—earlier grateful just for the abolition of seigneural dues—now resented increased taxes, the draft, and attacks on the church. Both sides committed atrocities, but the worst were inflicted by Republican troops who viciously put down the peasant insurgents. Controversy still rages today about the numbers of persons killed—estimates range from 20,000 to 250,000 and higher —but it seems clear that this was the worst part of the Terror.

Robespierre weeded out opposition among the deputies. In the fall of 1793, the Convention cracked down on popular clubs and societies, beginning with women's political clubs. The Convention associated women's participation in the public sphere with political disorder and social upheaval, and used biological differences between men and women as an excuse to abolish women's clubs. In the spring of 1794, the Committee of Public Safety moved against critics in Paris and in the Convention. It first arrested and executed the so-called ultrarevolutionaries, local Parisian politicians inclined to demagoguery. Then, it turned against the "indulgents," so-called because they favored a moderation of the Terror. This group included Georges-Jacques Danton (1759–1794), a flamboyant politician whose oratory had swayed opinions at several crucial moments during the Revolution.

Although the emergency was easing, the Terror became even more intense, and executions increased. Even the slightest show of dissent could be interpreted as a capital crime. The official Terror cost the lives of at least 40,000 people, with a further 300,000 suffering imprisonment. The clergy and aristocracy suffered disproportionally. The final crisis came in July 1794. When Robespierre appeared before the Convention on the ninth of Thermidor, Year II (July 27, 1794), with a list of deputies to be arrested, the Convention shouted him down and ordered his arrest. On the following day, Robespierre and his followers were executed.

With Robespierre's death, the Terror collapsed. The Thermidorian Reaction (Thermidor being the revised calendar's name for July) witnessed the reversal of many of Robespierre's policies. Jacobins were purged from office, the Paris Jacobin Club closed, and Robespierre's supporters were harassed and even murdered. Yet another constitution appeared in 1795, calling for a two-house legislature and the Directory, or five-member executive body. For the following four years, the Directory maintained power against both Jacobins and royalists. Pleasure became the order of the day in France.

France might have been defeated in 1793 if Prussia, Austria, and Russia had not been preoccupied with developments in Poland. By the end of that year, France, using the new national draft, had an army of 700,000. It still faced many problems, however, including desertion and inadequate clothing and food. The army's great advantage was that it fought for a revolution it had helped to make, and also because it was staffed by officers who had risen through the ranks by merit rather than by inheriting or purchasing their positions.

The French armies that crossed the Rhine in the summer of 1794 proclaimed a war of liberation, but "liberated" people often viewed the French as an army of occupation. Those near the northern and eastern borders of France—Austrian Netherlands, Mainz, Savoy, and Nice—reacted most positively, petitioning for French annexation. These areas, which remained French until 1815, were within what most deputies in the National Convention considered the "natural frontiers" of France.

The Directory wavered between defending the new frontiers and launching a more aggressive policy of creating "sister" republics. In 1795, the French conquered the Netherlands and created the Batavian Republic. In northern Italy, Napoleon Bonaparte defeated the Austrian army and created the Cisalpine Republic in 1797. In 1798, the Helvetic Republic was created out of Swiss territory, and the Roman Republic out of the conquered Papal States (the Pope fled to Siena). The next year, Bonaparte took an army to Egypt. The social costs of the various campaigns were high: thousands of men were killed (most died in hospital from their wounds rather than on the battlefield) and trade and shipping disrupted.

The Revolution provoked strong reactions elsewhere. In Great Britain, the London Corresponding Society, founded in 1792, corresponded with the Paris Jacobin Club and became the center of reform agitation in England. Pro-French feeling ran even stronger in Ireland, where Catholics and Presbyterians, both excluded from the vote, joined together in 1791 to form the Society of United Irishmen, which called for secession from England. When the French monarchy and nobility were abolished, the nervous British government suppressed the new political societies. In 1798, an Irish rebellion, timed to correspond with an attempted French invasion, was put down brutally. The German Rhineland was generally sympathetic to the Revolution. Many leading German intellectuals initially welcomed the revolutionary cause, but turned against it after 1793. Indeed, sharp, anti-French nationalism sparked a German renaissance. Areas far from France were generally not much affected by the French Revolution, with two notable exceptions. Opinions on the Revolution were sharply divided in the United States, while in Sweden, Gustavus III (r. 1771–1791) was assassinated by a nobleman who claimed the king had violated his oath.

Russia decided to battle Jacobinism in Warsaw. It easily defeated Poland and abolished the constitution of May 1791. Prussia and Russia helped themselves to new slices of Polish territory in the Second Partition of Poland (1793). In the spring of 1794, Tadeusz Kosciuszko (1746–1817) led a national revolt. Needing the assistance of the peasantry but not wanting to alienate the nobility, Kosciuszko summoned the peasants to the national cause on May 7, 1794, promising a reduction of their obligations as serfs, but did not offer freedom. Because most peasants failed to respond, the uprising eventually collapsed. The Third Partition of 1795 by Russia, Prussia, and Austria, completely removed Poland from the map as a viable country.

The Revolution in France spread to the French Caribbean colonies. In August 1791, a large-scale revolt was started by the slaves in St. Domingue. In an effort to end the revolt, the National Convention extended civil and political rights to blacks. This offended white planters who, in 1793, signed an alliance with Britain. Spain, which controlled the other half of the island of Hispaniola, offered freedom to any black slave who would serve in their army, but also support the slavery system. Also in 1793, the French commissioner in St. Dominque freed all slaves in his jurisdiction. In February 1794, the National Convention formally abolished slavery and extended full rights to all black men in the colonies. One of the ablest black generals, the ex-slave François Dominique Toussaint L'Ouverture (1743–1803), changed sides, committed his troops to the French, and eventually became governor. By 1800, however, whites had fled the island and the economy was in ruins. Former slaves were now bound to the land like serfs. In 1802, French troops regained control of the island and arrested Toussaint. Toussaint, who later died in a French prison, became a symbol of black struggles for freedom. The attempt to restore slavery, however, met with defeat, and the Republic of Haiti was proclaimed in 1804.

Napoleon Bonaparte (1769–1821), a penniless artillery officer in 1795, parlayed early military successes and Parisian political connections into command of the French army in Italy in 1796. His success in the Italian campaigns (1796–1797) launched his meteoric career. Bonaparte took an army initially raised for a British inva-

sion to Egypt, where he abolished torture, introduced equality before the law, eliminated religious taxes, and proclaimed religious toleration. Scientists accompanied this expedition to conduct research, and an ordinary soldier uncovered the Rosetta Stone which, for the first time, enabled scholars to decipher Egyptian hieroglyphs. But the military failure of the Egyptian campaign did not harm Bonaparte's prospects; when he returned to France in October 1799, he found an opportunity to advance his fortune. Disillusioned members of the government used Bonaparte to overturn the Constitution of 1795. The coup on the eighteenth of Brumaire, Year VIII (November 9, 1799), nearly failed, but the rump legislature voted to abolish the Directory and set up a three-member consulate. Bonaparte was named First Consul. A new constitution was approved, but millions of voters abstained and the results were falsified to make support appear greater than it had been. It was an unpromising start but, within five years, Bonaparte had crowned himself Napoleon I, emperor of the French, instituting a new order and setting out on a path of conquest and expansion.

Suggestions for Lecture and Discussion Topics

1. The origins of the French Revolution are worth discussing. Contemporary historians have abandoned the Marxist approach, and now view the Revolution's origins in the politics of the 1780s, a politics deeply affected by the currents of the Enlightenment and the socioeconomic issues of that time. A good place to begin is Colin Lucas's article "Nobles, Bourgeois, and the Origins of the French Revolution," *Past and Present* 60 (August 1973), reprinted in Douglas Johnson, *French Society and the Revolution* (Cambridge: Cambridge University Press, 1976). William Doyle, *Origins of the French Revolution*, 2d ed. (Oxford: Oxford University Press, 1988), offers in Part 2 a brief account of the origins from 1786 to the end of the summer of 1789. P. M. Jones's very useful book *Reform and Revolution in France: The Politics of Transition, 1774–1791* (Cambridge: Cambridge University Press, 1995) presents the monarchy as an institution actively engaged in reform. Along these same lines, Simon Schama, *Citizens: A Chronicle of the French Revolution* (New York: Alfred A. Knopf, 1989) offers in Part 1 a more favorable picture of the France of Louis XVI than is usually the case.

Several titles are useful not only for this topic, but also for subsequent topics (and cited in following suggestions). One is William Doyle, *The Oxford History of the French Revolution* (Oxford: Oxford University Press, 1989). A second synthesis is Donald Sutherland, *France, 1789–1815: Revolution and Counterrevolution* (Oxford: Oxford University Press, 1986). A good selection of relevant documents may be found in Laura Mason and Tracey Rizzo, eds., *The French Revolution: A Document*

Collection (Boston: Houghton Mifflin, 1999). The essays in François Furet and Mona Ozouf, eds., *A Critical Dictionary of the French Revolution* (Cambridge, MA: Harvard University Press, 1989) are very helpful. Jacques Sole, *Questions of the French Revolution: A Historical Overview* (New York: Pantheon, 1989) is a handy compendium of questions and answers.

2. Ask students to consider which event in 1789 best marks the beginning of the French Revolution. Did it come as early as the publication of the Abbé Sieyès's incendiary pamphlet, *What Is the Third Estate?* Was it when the Third Estate declared itself the National Assembly or when the Bastille fell? Or, did it only come with the Declaration of the Rights of Man and Citizen in August? Still worth reading, although set in a Marxist framework and a little too schematic, is Georges Lefebvre, *The Coming of the French Revolution* (New York: Random House, 1947). On Sieyès, see William H. Sewell Jr., *A Rhetoric of Bourgeois Revolution: The Abbé Sieyès and What Is the Third Estate?* (Durham, NC: Duke University Press, 1994). On the Declaration of the Rights of Man and Citizen, see Lynn Hunt, *The French Revolution and Human Rights: A Brief Documentary History* (Boston: Bedford Books, 1996). In addition to the two books by Doyle listed in suggestion 1, see also Chapter 4 of Michel Vovelle, *The Fall of the French Monarchy, 1787–1792* (Cambridge: Cambridge University Press, 1984). An important book on the development of the National Assembly in the first two years of the Revolution is Timothy Tackett, *Becoming a Revolutionary: The Deputies of the French National Assembly and the Emergence of a Revolutionary Culture (1789–1790)* (Princeton: Princeton University Press, 1996).

3. Many nineteenth-century observers commented favorably on the moderate period of the Revolution, but decried the period of the Terror as radical, bloody, and excessive. It is important, first, to outline why the attempt at constitutional monarchy failed. Second, it is necessary to distinguish in the Terror those efforts to preserve the Revolution from the threat of war and civil war and also from the more radical efforts to create a Republic of Virtue. In addition to Vovelle, listed in suggestion 2, see Marc Bouloiseau, *The Jacobin Republic, 1792–1794* (Cambridge: Cambridge University Press, 1983). A classic account of 1793–1794 is R. R. Palmer, *Twelve Who Ruled: The Year of the Terror in the French Revolution* (Princeton: Princeton University Press, 1970), first published in 1941. Another classic account, heavily Marxist but still useful, is Albert Soboul, *The Sans-Culottes: The Popular Movement and Revolutionary Government, 1793–1794* (Princeton: Princeton University Press, 1980). Two books helpful for understanding the perspectives of the revolutionaries are Patrice Higonnet, *Goodness beyond Virtue: Jacobins during the French Revolution* (Cambridge, MA: Harvard University Press, 1998); and Lynn Hunt, *The Family Romance of the French Revolution* (Berkeley: University of Califor-

nia Press, 1992). See also the essays in Volume 4, "The Terror," in Keith Michael Baker, ed., *The French Revolution and the Creation of Modern Political Culture* (Oxford: Pergamon Press, 1994).

4. Maximilien Robespierre is a key figure of the French Revolution. Was he simply a ruthless but pragmatic dictator, or was he a fanatical revolutionary, the prototype of the totalitarian ruler who sought to control every aspect of life? Several good biographies and studies are available, including David Jordan, *The Revolutionary Career of Maximilien Robespierre* (New York: Free Press, 1986); George Rude, *Robespierre* (New York: Viking, 1975); and Colin Haydon and William Doyle, eds., *Robespierre: History, Historiography, and Literature* (Cambridge: Cambridge University Press, 1998).

5. A good place to begin study of women in the French Revolution is Joan B. Landes, *Women and the Public Sphere in the Age of the French Revolution* (Ithaca: Cornell University Press, 1988), which demonstrates that the Revolution in some ways provided less room for women in the public sphere than had the Old Regime. See also Chapter 4, "The Bad Mother," in Lynn Hunt, *The Family Romance of the French Revolution*, and her *The French Revolution and Human Rights* (cited in suggestions 3 and 2, respectively). Sara E. Melzer and Leslie W. Rabine, eds., *Rebel Daughters: Women and the French Revolution* (Oxford: Oxford University Press, 1992) contains a number of interesting essays on women and the French Revolution. Additionally, Dominique Godineau, *The Women of Paris and Their French Revolution* (Berkeley: University of California Press, 1988) is a detailed study of that topic.

6. Although the French Revolution dwarfs similar events of this period, it would be worthwhile to examine other revolutions, both those that were contemporaneous and those that were responses to the French Revolution. R. R. Palmer, *The Age of Democratic Revolution: A Political History of Europe and America, 1760–1800*, two volumes (Princeton: Princeton University Press, 1959, 1964), is the major work on the events of this period. Simon Schama has written an excellent study of the Dutch revolutions of this period: *Patriots and Liberators: Revolution in the Netherlands, 1780–1813* (New York: Alfred A. Knopf, 1977). The impact of the French Revolution in the Caribbean is covered in David Gaspar and David P. Geggus, eds., *A Turbulent Time: The French Revolution and the Greater Caribbean* (Bloomington: Indiana University Press, 1997); its impact in the Western Hemisphere is explored in Lester Langley, *The Americas in the Age of Revolution, 1750–1850* (New Haven, CT: Yale University Press, 1996). See also Joan Wallach Scott, *Only Paradoxes to Offer: French Feminists and the Rights of Man* (Cambridge, MA: Harvard University Press, 1996); and François Furet, *Revolutionary France 1770–1880* (Oxford: Blackwell, 1992).

Making Connections

1. *Should the French Revolution be viewed as the origin of democracy, or the origin of totalitarianism (a government in which no dissent is allowed)?* There were elements of both democracy and totalitarianism in the French Revolution. The revolutionaries intended democratic reforms, but they stalled on how to achieve them. The resulting vacuum gave strong men, like Robespierre, the opportunity to seize control and embark on a totalitarian agenda.

2. *Why did other European rulers find the French Revolution so threatening?* The Revolution represented a model of government that was in theory more representative than in many places in Europe. The seeming success of the Revolution generated agitation for reform along similar lines in other countries. For many of these same countries, the Revolution was virtually next door, and it was feared that the conflict could easily spread beyond French borders. Neither had the conflict entirely resolved pre-Revolution problems of a poor economy, social unrest, and a weak and nonresponsive government. Additionally, the killing field in France was on a scale hardly imaginable, and the aristocracy and middle classes in other countries were concerned literally for their own heads.

Writing Assignments and Class Presentation Topics

1. Assign students to write an essay on the summer of 1789 in France based on Chapter 20 and selected documents from Mason and Rizzo (see "Suggestions for Lecture and Discussion Topics," number 1). This essay should be an analysis of the development of revolutionary momentum in this period. Students should comment on whether any individual or group controlled, or had the opportunity to control, the direction of the Revolution at this time.

2. Use Lynn Hunt's *The French Revolution and Human Rights* as the basis for a discussion on the meaning of the Declaration of the Rights of Man and Citizen. The discussion might range over the entire Revolution, or be confined to a particular group that did not seem to be included in the Declaration. Ask students to particularly consider the universal language employed in the Declaration and the sociopolitical implications of that language. Encourage students to also link their thoughts about the Declaration with present-day concerns about identity politics.

3. Have students view *La Nuit de Varennes* (*The Night of Varennes* [1983]), a film that brings together Casanova, Thomas Paine, Nicolas Edme Restif de Bretonne, among other figures of the Enlightenment era.

Restif, a journalist and printer, is following a coach that contains the royal family as they attempt to flee the country. The others do not realize they are involved in an event of historic importance. After viewing the film, students might write an essay on the different points of view presented by the characters in the film. It would be helpful to prepare a brief guide to the characters for the students to review before they view the film.

4. Students might base reports on the essays contained in François Furet and Mona Ozouf, *A Critical Dictionary of the French Revolution*. These essays go well beyond the simple provision of information to discuss the issues and questions involved. They might be supplemented with documents from Mason and Rizzo (see suggestion 1) or with material selected from one or more of the sources cited earlier.

5. Some of the excesses of the French royal family and aristocracy can best be understood visually. Students should analyze Fragonard's *The Swing*, painted in 1765. What is the relationship between the woman in the swing and the man on the ground? Exactly what is the man doing? Is there anything in the picture that might indicate whether this is a licit or illicit meeting? What is the servant's job? Is there anything in the picture that might cause resentment among the lower classes?

Research Assignments

1. The Terror is a dramatic and critical period of the French Revolution. How one understands and evaluates the Terror often determines how one views the Revolution as a whole. Ask students to first become acquainted with the outlines of the Terror by reading William Doyle or Donald Sutherland (see "Suggestions for Lecture and Discussion Topics," number 1). Then have them choose a month from July 1793 to July 1794 to investigate. What were the major events that occurred in that month? Who were the most prominent leaders? What documents, images, accounts, and descriptions can they find that inform them about that month? The finished product might be a standard research paper; a mockup of a newsmagazine reporting on the events and personalities of that month; a diary of a fictional character who has just experienced that month; or some other approach that requires students to assimilate and make sense of the information they have assembled. See "Suggestions for Lecture and Discussion Topics," numbers 3 and 4, for bibliographical citations.

2. The period after the Ninth of Thermidor, the time of the Thermidorian reaction and the Directory (1794–1799), generally receives little attention. Yet, it is a period in which the French Revolution spreads beyond France and also begins, somewhat haltingly, a process of consolidation. It is also the period when Napoleon Bonaparte

first makes his mark. Have students again begin with a broad history of the Revolution, such as Doyle or Sutherland (see "Suggestions for Lecture and Discussion Topics," number 1), to obtain an overview of Thermidor and the Directory. Then, have students select topics and do a research project on an aspect of Thermidor and the Directory. A useful source for more detailed information is Denis Woronoff, *The Thermidorean Regime and the Directory, 1794–1799* (Cambridge: Cambridge University Press, 1984). Other good sources include Martyn Lyons, *France under the Directory* (Cambridge: Cambridge University Press, 1975); and Colin Lewis and Gwynne Lewis, eds., *Beyond the Terror: Essays in French Regional and Social History, 1794–1815* (Cambridge: Cambridge University Press, 1983).

Literature

Brody, Miriam, ed., *A Vindication of the Rights of Women.* 1992.

Lamport, F. J., trans., *Friedrich von Schiller: Robbers* and *Wallenstein.* 1979.

Mainland, William F., trans., *Friedrich von Schiller: Wilhelm Tell.* 1972

Historical Skills

Map 20.2, Redrawing the Map of France, 1789–1791, p. 760

Have students carefully examine and compare the maps showing France in 1789 and in 1791. They should be able to discuss the differences made by the change from organization by provinces to that of organization by departments. Ask students to comment on the substitution of new names for the old. Is the redrawing of the map a project of which the philosophes would have approved? Why or why not?

Map 20.3, French Expansion, 1791–1799, p. 771

Ask students to consider this paradox: the French republic not only completed the project of Louis XIV to establish a France that had expanded to its natural frontiers (such as the Rhine River), but also accomplished the old dream of reestablishing the Roman Empire (in the form of sister republics). Was there a contradiction between extending the Revolution by liberating peoples and doing so by creating an empire (even if it was not called an empire)?

Mapping the West: Europe in 1800, p. 782

Ask students to comment on the differences caused by events in the last two decades of the eighteenth century.

The map of Europe and the World, c. 1780 (p. 742), shows a rough balance of power in Europe and British imperialism dominant outside Europe. What does the map of Europe in 1800 seem to indicate about the balance of power in Europe? Ask students to think about what it does not show; that is, the balance of imperial power in the rest of the world. What was the situation of France as an imperial power at this point?

The Third Estate Awakens, p. 755

How does the message of this image compare to the message of the pamphlet by the Abbé Sieyès, "What Is the Third Estate?" The Third Estate is shown here as powerless and at the mercy of the other two estates. Is this what Sieyès suggests about the Third Estate? Ask students to consider which presentation of the Third Estate might be more effective as propaganda and why.

Women's March to Versailles, October 5, 1789, p. 747

Have students compare this image with "A Women's Club" (p. 759) and "Representing Liberty" (p. 765). Ask them to discuss which image male revolutionaries would be likely to prefer and why they think this would be the case. Why was the participation of women in revolutionary politics frowned upon and eventually forbidden?

The Guillotine, p. 763

As the caption points out, the guillotine became an important symbol of the French Revolution, both for its supporters and its critics. Ask students to comment on the use of the guillotine as a means of execution and on the events after the fall of the Bastille that led to the head of the governor of the fortress being displayed on a pike. Both are examples of revolutionary justice, but one — the use of the pike (and the events preceding its use) — is connected with an irregular form of justice; the other, the use of the guillotine, comes after a trial is held, a verdict is reached, and a sentence pronounced. What might these actions imply about the relationship between society and government?

The Rights of Minorities, p. 758

A discussion can focus on the reasons why Tonnerre argued for the extension of civil rights to Jews, but was careful to distinguish between Jews as individuals and Jews as a nation, and why some western countries are careful to make similar distinctions today. Tonnerre argues that a nation could not exist within another nation; French citizens had to be loyal first and foremost to France since divided loyalties could be dangerous to the state. Recently, the French government banned elementary and high school students from wearing to class symbols (crosses, headscarves, and so forth) that emphasize ethnic and religious separateness. The government is trying to keep issues of church and state separate in order to promote citizenship as a unifying sociopolitical force.

OTHER BEDFORD/ST. MARTIN'S RESOURCES FOR CHAPTER 20

The following resources are available to accompany Chapter 20. Please refer to the Preface of this manual for detailed descriptions of all the ancillaries.

For Instructors

Transparencies

The following maps and images from Chapter 20 are available as full-color acetates.

- Map 20.1: Revolutionary Paris, 1789
- Map 20.2: Redrawing the Map of France, 1789–1791
- Map 20.3: French Expansion, 1791–1799
- Map 20.4: The Second and Third Partitions of Poland, 1793 and 1795
- Mapping the West: Europe in 1800
- *Third Estate Awakens*
- *Fall of the Bastille*

Instructor's Resources CD-ROM

The following maps and image from Chapter 20, as well as a chapter outline, are available on disc in both Power-Point and jpeg formats.

- Map 20.1: Revolutionary Paris, 1789
- Map 20.2: Redrawing the Map of France, 1789–1791
- Map 20.3: French Expansion, 1791–1799
- Map 20.4: The Second and Third Partitions of Poland, 1793 and 1795
- Mapping the West: Europe in 1800
- *Third Estate Awakens*

Using the Bedford Series with The Making of the West

Available in print as well as online at bedfordstmartins .com/udinhdrtird, this guide offers practical suggestions for using **The French Revolution and Human Rights: A Brief Documentary History, edited, translated, and with an Introduction by Lynn Hunt,** in conjunction with Chapter 20 of the textbook.

For Students

Sources of The Making of the West

The following documents are available in 20 of the companion sourcebook by Katharine J. Lualdi, University of Southern Maine.

1. Abbé Sieyès, *What Is the Third Estate* (1789)?
2. *Political Cartoon: "The People Under the Old Regime"* (1815)
3. National Assembly, *The Declaration of the Rights of Man and of the Citizen* (1789)
4. Olympe de Gouges, *Letters on the Trial* (1793)
5. François Dominique Toussaint L'Ouverture, *Revolution in the Colonies* (1794–1795)

Study Guides

The print **Study Guide** and the **Online Study Guide** at bedfordstmartins.com/hunt, both by Victoria Thompson (Arizona State University) and Eric Johnson (University of California, Los Angeles), help students synthesize the material they have learned as well as practice the skills historians use to make sense of the past. The following Map, Visual, and Document activities are available for Chapter 20.

Map Activity

- Map 20.3: French Expansion, 1791–1799

Visual Activity

- *Third Estate Awakens*

Reading Historical Documents

- The Rights of Minorities
- Address to the National Assembly in Favor of the Abolition of the Slave Trade

Napoleon and the Revolutionary Legacy
1800–1830

CHAPTER RESOURCES

Main Chapter Topics

1. Napoleon Bonaparte ended the French Revolution and created an authoritarian state. At the same time, he made many improvements in the administration of France and oversaw the making of a new civil code.

2. Napoleon's astute use of a highly mobile army enabled him to construct an impressive empire that did not, however, endure because he insisted on treating conquered areas as little more than colonies.

3. The Congress of Vienna (1814–1815) set the boundaries of European states and scheduled periodic meetings of major powers to oversee international affairs. Although this congressional system, or "concert of Europe," did not long work as planned, it did, however, help to prevent a major war until the 1850s. The congress promoted domestic stability until the revolutions of 1848.

4. Ideologies—like nationalism, socialism, liberalism, and conservatism—addressed changes produced by the Industrial Revolution and the aftereffects of the Napoleonic Wars including the conservative Vienna settlement.

5. Although romanticism was primarily an artistic movement that glorified nature, emotion, genius, and imagination, it frequently supported nationalist aspirations in the first half of the seventeenth century.

6. Revolts in the 1820s and the revolutions of 1830 sought autonomy, national unity, and constitutional guarantees of individual liberties. Few succeeded except the Serbs, the Belgians the Greeks, and the Latin American colonies.

Summary

Napoleon Bonaparte dominated, stabilized, and extended key elements of the French Revolution; made enduring changes in French government and law; and created an empire that incorporated most of Europe. Even after his fall from power, he left a legend that exerted a powerful influence over the whole of Europe for decades.

One of the more successful generals of the Directory, Napoleon seized power in November 1799 (the eighteenth of Brumaire by the reformed French Revolution calendar). He was chosen as one of three co-consuls, but soon dominated the other two in the drafting of a new constitution (the fourth since 1789), which made him First Consul with the right to select the Council of State. The republic came to an end as Napoleon built a government staffed by men loyal to him. His 1801 concordat with Pope Pius VII validated the earlier sale of church property, appeased Catholics alienated by the Revolution, and recognized Catholicism as the main religion of France. Napoleon centralized government administration, created the Bank of France to facilitate borrowing, and based the currency on gold and silver coinage. Political expression, though, was severely limited. Newspapers were reduced from seventy-three to four progovernment publications, and operas and plays were subject to censorship. Political dissidents were closely watched and sometimes arrested.

In 1804, with the pope's blessing, Napoleon crowned himself emperor. In the tradition of Louis XIV, he embarked on a building campaign that included the Arc de Triomphe, the stock exchange, fountains, and even slaughterhouses. He cultivated a reputation as an efficient, hardworking administrator with intellectual interests in science, law, and art. He appointed men who had served with him in the military to chief governmental positions and placed the bureaucracy on a "client-patron" footing, with himself at its center. Napoleon established a new social hierarchy based on talent and personally chose the country's most illustrious generals, scientists, and wealthy men as well as former nobles to serve as senators. The Legion of Honor was an outgrowth of this emphasis on talent, although military men overwhelmingly dominated the institution. Napoleon introduced a new hierarchy of noble titles. Title could be inherited, but they had to be supported by wealth. Favored generals were often rewarded with estates in conquered territories. Napoleon also advanced his siblings to the kingdoms of Holland, Naples, and Spain. His stepson was made viceroy of Italy. Lacking an heir, Napoleon divorced Josephine de Beauharnais in 1809 and married Marie-Louise of Austria in 1810. A son was born in 1811, and immediately given the title king of Rome.

Napoleon's most impressive and long-lasting accomplishment was the Civil Code (Napoleonic Code) completed in 1804. This code assured property rights, guaranteed religious freedom, and established uniform laws for France that provided equal treatment for adult males, but sharply reduced the rights of women, children, and employees. Fathers were now required to provide for their children, and government-supported foundling hospitals were established as a means of discouraging abortion and infanticide. Women fared worst under the new code, and some rights they had previously held under the monarchy and republic were now curtailed. Women could not sue in court, sell or mortgage personal property, or contract a debt without their husbands' permission. The code also enshrined a double standard for sexual misconduct. Widely imitated throughout Europe, women did not achieve legal status equal to their husbands until 1965. Because women were confined to the home, the educational emphasis was on boys who attended state-run secondary lycees ("schools") that had a strong, military curriculum. Employees were treated with suspicion, forced to carry work cards, forbidden to form organizations, and required to have foremen and shop attendants represent them in labor disputes.

Napoleon supported French scientific inquiry. Under his patronage, laws regarding the expansion of gas were formulated, research on fossils prepared the ground for later theories of evolution, and new amputation and medical techniques were developed. However, Napoleon viewed writers as dangerous, and many who were critical of him and his policies voluntarily went into exile, like, for example, M. Germaine de Staël (1766–1817) who retreated to Germany. M. de Staël's novel, *Corrine* (1807), which featured a brilliant heroine thwarted by an oppressive patriarchal system, was banned in France. Although strong state authority and Catholicism had been restored, many royalists and Catholics considered Napoleon an impious usurper. François-René de Chateaubriand (1768–1848), in his *Genius of Christianity* (1802), criticized Napoleon for not understanding the need to defend Christian values against the Enlightenment's excessive reliance on reason.

Napoleon created a sizable army through conscription: 1.3 million men age of twenty and twenty-four were drafted between 1800 and 1812. Another million were conscripted in 1813–1814. Yet, Napoleon attributed his military success primarily to the high morale of the troops. French troops were not only patriotic, but also fanatically loyal to Napoleon, who fought alongside them, displaying both tactical daring and great physical courage. One opponent said that his presence on the battlefield was worth fifty thousand troops. Tactically, Napoleon preferred one massive, lightening-strike battle against an enemy. He failed, though, to take any of his officers into his confidence regarding strategy, and this later hampered his campaigns. Maintaining so large an army also proved problematic. But Napoleon had an advantage in the disorganization of the allies (England, Austria, Prussia, and Russia) who he could take on diplomatically or militarily one by one.

By 1802, Napoleon had defeated Austria and, with this defeat, the short-lived Treaty of Amiens with Britain was at an end. He sent troops to St. Domingue to quell a rebellion there, but they were driven back by continual resistance of the black population and his troops being exposed to yellow fever. Giving up on his dream of creating an empire in the Western Hemisphere, Napoleon sold the Louisiana Territory to the United States in 1803, using the funds received to resume the war in Europe. The British navy under Horatio Nelson defeated the French at Trafalgar (1805), but Napoleon continued his winning streak on land. He defeated the Austrians at Austerlitz (1805), the Prussians at Jena and Auerstadt (1806), and the Russians at Friedland (1807).

In the Treaties of Tilsit, Alexander I temporarily came to terms with Napoleon at Prussia's expense. The kingdom of Westphalia was carved out of Prussian lands and given over to Napoleon's brother Jerome. Prussia's Polish provinces became the duchy of Warsaw. After defeating Austria, Prussia, and Russia, Napoleon reorganized the areas of Germany and Italy. In 1803, he formed the Confederation of the Rhine, which soon included all of the German states except Prussia and Austria. The Holy Roman Emperor gave up his title for that of emperor of Austria. Napoleon established three unities in Italy: territories directly annexed to France, and the satellite kingdoms of Italy and Naples. He forced reforms on both the annexed territories and the satellite kingdoms. These reforms included ending serfdom, eliminating seigneurial dues, introducing the Napoleonic Code, suppressing monasteries, subordinating the church to the state, and extending civil rights to Jews and other religious minorities.

Roads were improved, public works undertaken, education reformed, and the economy opened up via the removal of internal tariffs. Although Napoleonic reforms often improved the quality of life in these areas, they also went against local customs and were frequently resisted, sometimes even by Napoleon's own family. When his brother Louis was perceived as being too sympathetic with his Dutch subjects, Holland was annexed directly to France. Napoleon's success moved the Prussian king to reform from above in order to compete with the French.

Serfdom was abolished and the army overhauled. Although they gained some personal freedoms, peasants' lives did not improve significantly. In Russia, Alexander I created western-style ministries, lifted restrictions on the import of foreign books, and founded six universities. Other reforms were studied and discussed, but came to nought, and Alexander I's early interest in reform dwindled.

Resistance to the French began almost immediately. The Continental System, inaugurated in 1806, banned all trade with Great Britain by France and its dependent states and allies, and was intended to bankrupt the British economy, but it could not be enforced. There was also resistance to France in dependent states. The *carbonari* ("charcoal-burners") were secret societies in Italy working against the French. In 1807, while the French were fighting British troops in Portugal, Napoleon installed his brother Joseph as king of Spain to replace the senile Charles IV (r. 1788–1808). This action provoked the Spanish clergy and nobility to lead an armed peasant rebellion that raged for six years during which atrocities were committed on both sides. In 1812, already committed to a war in Spain, Napoleon opened a second front and invaded Russia. The Russians drew the French deep into their territory by retreating, and the one major battle—at Borodino—was bloody but inconclusive. Napoleon entered Moscow only to find that the Russians had set it afire. By October, the Grand Army was forced to retreat and lost tens of thousands troops to cold, starvation, and capture. Constantly harassed along the way by Russian troops, the French abandoned artillery and supplies to speed their march homeward. By December, only one hundred thousand French troops remained, just one-sixth the original invasion force. Organized by Britain and Russia, a coalition—that also included Prussian and Swedish forces—defeated Napoleon at Leipzig (1813), a confrontation commonly known as the Battle of the Nations. In 1814, as allied troops approached Paris, the French Senate deposed Napoleon who abdicated when his remaining generals refused to support Napoleon's desire to continue the war. He was exiled to Elba off the coast of Italy. Louis XVIII (r. 1814–1824 [the brother of Louis XVI, uncle of Louis XVII, who never ruled]) became king and tried to establish a British-style monarchy with a two-house legislature and a guarantee of civil rights. But Louis was beset by strife between ultraroyalists, especially returning nobles who wanted their power and property restored, and those who had supported either the republic or Napoleon. In 1815, Napoleon escaped Elba and returned to Paris to popular acclaim, ushering in the "Hundred Days," the period of his return. The allied forces of Prussia, Belgium, Holland, Germany, and Britain—led by Sir Arthur Wellesley, duke of Wellington (1769–1852)—defeated Napoleon at Waterloo whereupon he was sent into a second exile on remote St. Helena, where he died in 1821.

But the issues raised by Napoleon's rule, such as legal reform, social welfare reform, and nascent nationalism, set the agenda for nineteenth-century Europe.

The Congress of Vienna, made up of Austria, Russia, Prussia, Britain, and France, worked to establish a long-lasting negotiated peace. Prince Klemens von Metternich (1773–1859), chief negotiator for Austria, shaped the post-Napoleonic order more than any other delegate. He and British prime minister Robert Castlereagh (1769–1822) sought to check French aggression, yet also to make it part of the new equilibrium to balance the ambitions of Prussia and Russia. The chief representative of France, Prince Charles Maurice Talleyrand (1754–1838), an aristocrat and former bishop who had embraced the French Revolution, represented France even though he had been Napoleon's foreign minister.

Whenever possible, the congress restored traditional rulers, and this period is sometimes referred to as the "restoration." Where restoration was impossible, it rearranged territory in a way such as to balance the interests of the great powers without trampling on the smaller nations. The duchy of Warsaw once more became the kingdom of Poland, but with the Russian tsar as its ruler. The Dutch Republic and Austrian Netherlands united to become the kingdom of the Netherlands under the restored *stadholder*. Austria now headed the German Confederation, which replaced the Holy Roman Empire and included Prussia. The kingdom of Piedmont-Sardinia took Genoa, Nice, and part of Savoy. Sweden received Norway from Denmark, but lost Finland to Russia. The congress followed Britain's lead and condemned the slave trade although, in practice, it continued in many places until the 1840s. The congress inaugurated a new diplomatic order, one in which legitimacy of states depended on the treaty system and not on divine right—Tsar Alexander's proposed Holy Alliance calling upon divine assistance notwithstanding.

The French Revolution and the Napoleonic era called for investigation into the proper sources of authority. Conservatism became the political doctrine that justified the restoration. Conservatives (Tories) favored monarchy over republicanism, tradition over revolution, and established religion over Enlightenment skepticism. Conservatism's most influential theorist was Edmund Burke (1729–1799). In his view, governments had to be rooted in long experience and change must be gradual. Burke and other Conservatives defended hereditary monarchy and the established church, believing that they and the patriarchal family were the best guarantees for an enduring social order capable of admitting change without experiencing chaos. France became the first test case of conservatism, and results were mixed as Louis XVIII faced ultraroyalists who adamantly pushed for a complete repudiation of the revolutionary past.

Religion revived as peace returned to Europe. In France, the Catholic church held open-air "ceremonies of reparation" to express repentance of the outrages of revolution. The Jesuit order was reestablished. Religious societies of laypersons formed in Spain and the Italian states to combat reformers and nationalists. But revivalism also challenged authority, especially in Protestant countries. In Britain, the Methodists, or Wesleyans (named for founder John Wesley (1703–1791) attracted merchants and laborers—men and women—by the thousands. Separated from the established Anglican church (the Church of England), Methodism fostered a sense of democratic community and rudimentary sexual equality. Methodist Sunday schools taught poor children to read and write, thus stimulating demands for greater political participation by the working classes. The United States experienced a second "Great Awakening" beginning in 1790 through huge revival meetings, often led by Methodists. American Protestant sects began systematic missionary work in other parts of the world. Missionary activity by Catholics and Protestants would feed into nineteenth-century imperialism.

What writers began to call the Industrial Revolution in the 1820s spread from Great Britain to the continent but, by the 1830s, it significantly affected only northern France, Belgium, and the Rhineland. Factories with steam-powered machinery appeared first in Britain's textile industries. Families of farmers, soldiers demobilized after the Napoleonic Wars, artisans displaced by machinery, and children of the earliest factory workers, formed the workforce. This new workforce formed a distinct new socioeconomic class: the working class. Working conditions were brutal and grueling. Many hand-loom artisans found their livelihood threatened by the new economic system. Some, the Luddites (after "Ned Ludd" whose signature appeared on their manifestos), destroyed machines and burned mills in protest. Other British workers pressed for the reform of Parliament. Reform clubs led large, open-air meetings and, at one of them, held at St. Peter's Fields in Manchester (August 1819), sixty thousand people attended. In an action that became known as the Peterloo massacre, the authorities sent in troops to break up the illegal meeting; eleven people were killed and hundreds injured. The Six Acts that followed made large political meetings illegal, restricted press criticism, and set the reform movement back a decade.

The railroad first began to use steam engines in the 1820s and was vital to the Industrial Revolution. In 1830, the first railroad line opened between Liverpool and Manchester. The construction and operation of railroads created demand for many goods and services, especially for the railways' components. Railroads also rapidly improved the transportation of goods and passengers, and raw material to factories. The railroads soon became the most striking symbol of the new industrial age.

The French Revolution and Industrial Revolution caused many to reflect deeply about the changes taking place. Answers to questions about the social and political order were called *ideologies*, a word coined during the French Revolution. An *ideology* is a coherent set of beliefs about the way a society's social or political order should be organized. The 1820s and 1830s saw the rise of several ideologies.

Liberalism was one of the important new ideologies of the early nineteenth century. Adherents, especially the leaders of the rapidly expanding middle class, supported constitutional guarantees of personal liberty and free trade. They generally favored the Industrial Revolution but opposed the violence of the French Revolution. The foremost proponent of liberalism, Jeremy Bentham (1748–1832), called his brand of liberalism *utilitarianism* because he believed the best policy was one that produced the "greatest good for the greatest number." He called for parliamentary and penal reform. The slave trade seemed incompatible with liberalism, and many Liberals (Whigs) in Britain and the United States called for its abolition in the West Indies and America. In 1833, Britain abolished the slave trade in its colonies.

Socialism (Marxism), the newest of the ideologies, criticized the division of society into two classes: the new middle class, or capitalists who possessed the most wealth; and the working class, the capitalists' downtrodden, impoverished employees. Many socialists during this period were utopian socialists who believed ideal communities should be based on cooperation rather than competition, and that society would be better off if private property did not exist. In New Lanark, Scotland, Robert Owen (1771–1758), the founder of British socialism, set up a model factory town where employees worked ten hours instead of the usual seventeen, and children between age five and ten attended school instead of working. Owen moved his factory to New Harmony, Indiana, in the 1820s, but it failed after three years due to internal squabbling. Owen's *The Book of the New Moral World* (1820) helped inspire producer cooperatives, consumer cooperatives, and a national trade union.

In France, Claude Henri de Saint-Simon (1760–1825) coined the words *industrialism* and *industrialist* to help describe the new economic order. He believed that work should be controlled not by politicians but by scientists, engineers, artists, and manufacturers. Charles Fourier (1772–1837) urged the emancipation of women and the establishment of utopian communities that would replace state. After Saint-Simon's death, some of his followers set up utopian communities. In 1830, Saint-Simonian women founded the newspaper, *The Free Woman*. Nationalism, because it could be based on liberalism, conservatism, or socialism, was an especially powerful ideology. It held that a people derive its identity from the nation, which is defined by a common language and shared cultural traditions. The fact that nations did not often correspond to the boundaries of states produced much violence and warfare. The French

Revolution and Napoleonic Wars stirred nationalism in the peoples they conquered. Indigenous populations turned against outside rulers: the Turks in the Balkans, the Russians in Poland, and the Austrians in Italy. Nationalism was especially problematic in the Austrian Empire, which encompassed Germans, the Magyars of Hungary, and Slavs (who were further divided into different nationalities, such as Poles, Czechs, Croats, and Serbs). Further, Austria included Italians in Lombardy and Venetia, and Romanians in Transylvania. Metternich's domestic policy attempted to restrain nationalistic movements, an effort largely successful until the 1840s. Nationalistic resistance appealed to Italians eager for freedom from Austria and national unity and, although censorship existed writers stirred nationalistic sentiment and secret societies like the *carbonari* increased in membership. Resistance also appealed to Germans, especially university students who formed nationalistic societies, or *Burschenschaften*. Metternich mistakenly believed that the *Burschenschaften* and *carbonari* were intentionally conspiring against him and pushed for the Karlsbad Decrees that closed down student societies and stepped up censorship. Although Tsar Alexander I had agreed to a Polish constitution that provided for an elected parliament, a national army, and guarantees of free speech and a free press, he had begun retracting his concessions by 1818.

Romanticism—an artistic movement—was, in part, a reaction against the rationalism and formality of the classical style. Romantics glorified nature, emotion, genius, and imagination. The genres perhaps most closely associated with romanticism were poetry, painting, and music, which reached greatness in the poems of George Gordon, Lord Byron (1788–1824), and William Wordsworth (1770–1850), all of whom celebrated overwhelming emotion and creative imagination; the paintings of Joseph M. W. Turner (1775–1851), Eugene Delacroix (1798–1863), and Caspar David Friedrich (1774–1840), all of whom idealized nature; and the music of Ludwig von Beethoven (1770–1827) who scaled emotional heights. Romantics frequently expressed anxiety about the Industrial Revolution's effects on nature and human nature. There were contemporary critics of romanticism, among them Johann Wolfgang von Goethe (1749–1832) in his epic poem *Faust* (1832) and, perhaps, Mary Shelley (1797–1851) in her novel, *Frankenstein* (1818). If there were any common political threads among romantics, it would be the support of national aspirations. Lord Byron, in fact, died of a fever while fighting for Greek independence, and Beethoven's *Ninth Symphony* (1824) included a chorus singing the German poet Friedrich Schiller's (1759–1805) verses in praise of universal human solidarity. Romantic poets and writers residing in the German states, Austrian Empire, Russia and other Slavic lands, and Scandinavia collected old legends and folktales that expressed a shared cultural and linguistic heritage that dated back to the Middle Ages,

thus demonstrating that "nations" long existed even when formal, national boundaries did not. In Britain, Sir Walter Scott (1771–1832) published a collection of Scottish ballads, and wrote popular, influential novels chronicling events in Scottish and English history.

Liberalist, socialist, and nationalist exasperation at the restorations occasionally boiled over in the 1820s. When Ferdinand VII was restored to the Spanish throne (1814), he reestablished the power of the nobility, church, and monarchy, and cracked down on imported books and newspapers. In 1820, disgruntled soldiers demanded that Ferdinand reaffirm the 1812 constitution, which he had abolished. Revolt spread, but Ferdinand patiently waited them out. In 1823, with the consent of the great powers, a French army restored him to absolute power. Rebellious soldiers in Naples joined with the *carbonari* and demanded a constitution. Rebellion spread to Piedmont-Sardinia and, in 1821, after meeting with with Prussia, Russia, and Britain, Austria quelled both revolts. In December 1825, as Russian troops assembled to take the oath of loyalty to the new tsar, Nicholas I (r. 1825–1855), brother of Alexander I, rebel soldiers proclaimed another brother, Constantine, instead, hoping he would favor constitutional reform. Nicholas easily put down the "Decembrists."

Other revolts were more successful. By 1817, Serbs had won virtual independence from Turkish rule. The Turks faced two revolts in Greece: one led by a Russian general that failed; and a second, more substantial peasant uprising in 1821 that succeeded. Atrocities were committed by both sides, but public opinion sided with Greece and sparked British, French, and Russian intervention in 1827; the Turks were defeated at the battle of Navarino Bay. In 1830, Greece was proclaimed independent, and the son of King Ludwig of Bavaria became King Otto I. In Latin American, colonies from Mexico to Argentine revolted and, led by Simon Bolívar (1783–1830), became independent states between 1821 and 1823. In 1823, U.S. president James Monroe (1758–1831) proclaimed the Monroe Doctrine, which prohibited further European intervention in the Americas.

In 1830, a more powerful wave of liberal and national revolt appeared in Europe. The French Revolution of 1830, which ended the reign of Charles X, was the most wide-ranging. In 1825, Charles had passed the Law of Indemnity compensating nobles, who had emigrated during the French Revolution, for property losses. The Law of Sacrilege, passed the same year, imposed death sentences for certain crimes, like stealing from churches. Further, Charles dissolved the legislature, disenfranchised wealthy and powerful voters, and imposed strict censorship. Spontaneous disturbances erupted in 1830, at the end of which, Charles had been deposed in favor of his cousin, Louis-Philippe, duke of Orleans. Although Louis-Philippe extended political and voting rights, still only a fraction of the male population could vote; this so-called July monarchy, a constitutional monarchy, did not offer much relief to the poor and the working classes. Disaffected, these classes rose in rebellion in Lyon (1831), but were quashed.

Belgians also rose in revolt. King William of the Netherlands appealed to the great powers for aid, but Great Britain and France convened a conference that guaranteed Belgian independence in return for its neutrality in international affairs. Belgian neutrality remained a cornerstone of European diplomacy that continued until the beginning of World War I.

Poland was also inspired by the French to revolt against Russian rule. Polish aristocrats formed a provisional government but, without British and French support, Tsar Nicholas I easily put down the rebellion, abolishing the constitution his brother had earlier granted in the process.

In Great Britain, the crown's reputation was seriously tarnished when George IV tried to divorce his unfaithful wife, Caroline, and public opinion took her side in the matter. Politically, however, parliamentary reform was the major agenda. In the 1820s, Sir Robert Peel (1788–1850) revised the penal code and abolished death sentences for minor crimes. In 1824, laws prohibiting labor unions were repealed. Laborers could not strike, but they could bargain collectively with employers. In 1829, Catholics were permitted to hold most public offices and sit in Parliament.

By the 1830s, Metternich's vision of a Conservative Europe still held. Yet, it was also apparent that the revolutionary legacy was not to be extinguished. Additionally, the Industrial Revolution was transforming European life. Although few would have predicted it at the time, the Metternichean order would not continue for much longer. Mass demonstrations in favor of an extension in the voting rights took place in the early 1830s, but the Reform Bill of 1832 passed only after the king threatened to create enough new peers to gain passage for it in the House of Lords. It was hardly revolutionary, but still extended the right to vote by 50 percent, gave industrial cities in the north parliamentary representation for the first time, and set a precedent for further expansion of suffrage. The Reform Bill of 1832 marked the developing power of a mixed elite responsive to the needs of an industrial society.

Suggestions for Lecture and Discussion Topics

1. Napoleon is, of course, the dominant figure of this period. Even after his defeat at Waterloo and exile to St. Helena, he continued to exert considerable influence through the romantic myth associated with him. A session on Napoleon should attempt to answer all or most of the following questions: Why was Napoleon successful in bringing an end to the period of revolutionary turmoil? How much credit should go to the Directory? What were Napoleon's most important contributions to the administration of France? How successful was he in his imperial ventures? What were the main factors leading to the collapse of the empire? What made a romanticized, Napoleonic myth possible? Another way of organizing this session would be to ask how best to characterize Napoleon. Was he a son of the Enlightenment? A revolutionary? A conservative? Simply an opportunist?

In addition to sources cited in the bibliography for Chapter 21, a rather critical biography of Napoleon is Alan Schom, *Napoleon Bonaparte* (New York: HarperCollins, 1997). Other useful studies include Louis Bergeron, *France under Napoleon* (Princeton: Princeton University Press, 1981); and Robert B. Holtman, *The Napoleonic Revolution* (Philadelphia: Lippincott, 1967), a survey of Napoleon's administrative changes. A useful documentary source is Somerset de Chair, ed., *Napoleon on Napoleon: The Autobiography of an Emperor* (London: Cassell, 1991). Among the many reference books available is David Nicholls, *Napoleon: A Biographical Companion* (Santa Barbara: ABC-Clio, 1999), which includes a lengthy essay on Napoleon and his importance in history and entries in alphabetical order; Owen Connelly, Harold T. Parker, Peter W. Becker, and June K. Burton, eds., *Historical Dictionary of Napoleonic France, 1799–1815* (Westport, CT: Greenwood Press, 1985); and also David G. Chandler, *Dictionary of the Napoleonic War* (New York: Simon & Schuster, 1993). Two interesting books written for a wider audience should be mentioned. First is Carolyn Erickson's biography, *Josephine: A Life of the Empress* (New York: St. Martin's Press, 1999), which stresses the more sensational aspects of Josephine's life. Second is the book by Ben Weider and David Hapgood, *The Murder of Napoleon* (iUniverse.com, 1998), guaranteed to provoke discussion.

A close examination of the many portraits of Napoleon painted during his lifetime immediately illustrates the essence of his character and ambitions and would complement any of the suggested topics above. See, in particular, the portraits done by Jacques-Louis David (*An Unfinished Portrait* [c. 1798], *Crossing the St. Bernard* [1804], *The Coronation of Napoleon and Josephine* [1806–1807], and *Emperor in His Study* [1812]); and Jean-Auguste-Dominque Ingres (*First Consul* [1804]; and *Emperor* [1806]). For an interesting contrast, see English political cartoons of Napoleon, especially those done during the Napoleonic Wars.

Napoleon (PBS, 2000), a four-hour video documentary, offers a great deal of striking visual material. The Napoleonic era is also the setting for the immensely popular Aubrey/Maturin series of novels by Patrick O'Brian. See also the widely popular Horatio Hornblower films, based on C. S. Forester's ten novels. The films feature Ioan Gruffud as a British naval officer, with storylines set against revolutionary and Napoleonic France.

Overviews of this period include Charles Breunig, *The Age of Revolution and Reaction, 1789–1859* (New York: W. W. Norton, 1970); older but still useful, Eric J. Hobsbawm, *The Age of Revolution: Europe, 1789–1848* (New York: Praeger, 1969), part of a very fine series; and Robert Gildea, *Barricades and Borders: Europe 1800–1914* (New York: Oxford University Press, 1987), part of *The Short Oxford History of the Modern World* series.

2. Studying the Congress of Vienna provides a good opportunity to survey the European situation between 1815 and 1848. Among other tasks, you might indicate which areas were affected by the French Revolution (and in which ways), and which areas would thereafter soon be affected by the Industrial Revolution. Metternich and the Congress System (the concert of Europe) must first be reviewed. To what extent: was Metternich successful in making the concert of Europe work? Did his success depend on the dominant position of Austria in Germany and Italy? Did Metternich dominate European affairs in order to maintain political stability in the Austrian Empire?

In addition to the sources cited in the chapter bibliography, Alan W. Palmer, *Metternich* (New York: Harper & Row, 1972) continues to be useful. Part 3 of James J. Sheehan, *German History, 1770–1866* (New York: Oxford University Press, 1989); and Part 1 of David Blackbourn, *The Long Nineteenth Century: A History of Germany, 1780–1918* (New York: Oxford University Press, 1998), provide good coverage of Austria and Germany during this period. Part 2 of Gordon Wright's classic *France in Modern Times*, 3d ed. (New York: W. W. Norton, 1981) is an excellent source. Part 3 of W. Bruce Lincoln's *The Romanovs: Autocrats of All the Russias* (New York: Dial Press, 1981) places Nicholas I in context. See also Lincoln's full-scale biography, *Nicholas I: Emperor and Autocrat of All the Russias* (Bloomington: Indiana University Press, 1978).

3. Utopian socialism, especially if viewed as part of the foment of ideologies in the period between 1815 and 1848, can encourage a lively session. It provides an opportunity to discuss some fascinating characters and their often-eccentric ideas and, more important, it provides an opportunity to survey the broad range of responses—optimistic to pessimistic—to the Industrial Revolution. It may also provide useful background for a later discussion of Karl Marx and Friedrich Engels.

Robert L. Heilbronner, *The Worldly Philosophers: The Lives, Times, and Ideas of the Great Economic Thinkers*, 3d ed. (New York: Simon & Schuster, 1967), is an excellent beginning point. Chapter 4 presents Thomas Malthus and David Ricardo, and Chapter 5 the utopian socialists. See also Frank E. Manuel, *The Prophets of Paris* (New York: Harper, 1965) for more detailed discussions of the utopian socialists; and Nicholas V. Riasanovsky, *The Teaching of Charles Fourier* (Berkeley: University of California Press, 1969) for a full-length discussion of Fourier.

4. Romanticism is a protean topic, but it can be made manageable by dealing primarily with its political aspects. As *The Making of the West: Peoples and Cultures* notes, romanticism was associated with conservatism, liberalism, nationalism, and revolution. A session on romanticism might begin by discussing the varying ways in which followers of the movement viewed the world. While most Romantics emphasized nature, emotion, and genius, even this common basis might lead the discussion in different directions. The session might then focus on whether romanticism was largely a conservative or even reactionary movement in the first two decades of the nineteenth century, and a liberal or even radical movement in the following two decades. Finally, the connection between romanticism and nationalism should be given some attention. In which ways did the two movements complement one another? At some point, it might, of course, be helpful to emphasize that romanticism is a far larger topic than just its connections with politics in the first half of the nineteenth century.

A comprehensive introduction to romanticism is Maurice William Cranston, *The Romantic Movement* (Cambridge, MA: Blackwell, 1994). Another broad study, written for the nonspecialist, is Howard Mumford Jones, *Revolution and Romanticism* (Cambridge, MA: Belknap Press, 1974). See also Martin Travers, *An Introduction to Modern European Literature: From Romanticism to Postmodernism* (New York: St. Martin's Press, 1998); Nicholas V. Riasanovsky, *The Emergence of Romanticism* (New York: Oxford University Press, 1992); Roy Porter and Mikulas Teich, eds., *Romanticism in National Context* (New York: Cambridge University Press, 1988); and Charles Rosen, *The Romantic Generation* (Cambridge, MA: Harvard University Press, 1995). Among the many books available on British romanticism are Laura Dabundo, ed., *The Encyclopedia of Romanticism: Culture in Britain, 1780s–1830s* (New York: Garland, 1992); Stuart Curran, ed., *The Cambridge Companion to British Romanticism* (New York: Cambridge University Press, 1993); and two edited by Duncan Wu—*Romanticism: An Anthology*, 2d ed. (Malden, MA: Blackwell, 1998), and *A Companion to Romanticism* (Malden, MA: Blackwell, 1999). See also E. P. Thompson, *The Romantics: England in a Revolutionary Age* (New York: New Press, 1997). For France, see D. G. Charlton, ed., *The French Romantics*, 2 vols. (New York: Cambridge University Press, 1984). For Russia, see *History of Russian Literature of the Romantic Period* (Ann Arbor, MI: Ardis, 1986). More specialized but highly interesting are Ronald Paulson, *Representations of Revolution, 1789–1820* (New Haven, CT: Yale University Press, 1983); Gregory Dart, *Rousseau, Robespierre, and English Romanticism* (New York: Cambridge University Press, 1999); Emily W. Sunstein, *Mary Shelley: Romance and Reality* (Boston: Little, Brown, 1989); and John Hardman, *The Double in Nineteenth-Century Fiction: The Shadow Life* (New York: St. Martin's Press, 1991).

5. One session might be used to compare the French Revolution of 1830 to the British Reform Bill of 1832. Why did France turn to revolution in 1830? How different was the situation in Great Britain, where passage of the Reform Bill of 1832 ended the major urban protest movement? How might we assess the progress achieved by the European revolutionary movement at the time of the 1830s? To what extent had the labor movement developed by this time? A good place to begin is Clive H. Church, *Europe in 1830: Revolution and Political Change* (London: George Allen & Unwin, 1983). For the French Revolution, see David H. Pinkney, *The French Revolution of 1830* (Princeton: Princeton University Press, 1972); John M. Merriman, ed., *1830 in France* (New York: Franklin Watts, 1975); and Robert Bezucha, *The Lyon Uprising of 1834* (Cambridge, MA: Harvard University Press, 1976). William H. Sewell Jr., *Work and Revolution in France: The Language of Labor from the Old Regime to 1848* (Cambridge: Cambridge University Press, 1980) shows the extent to which working-class socialism in the nineteenth century derived from the guild structure of the eighteenth. Craig Calhoun, *The Question of Class Struggle: Social Foundations of Popular Radicalism during the Industrial Revolution* (Chicago: University of Chicago Press, 1982) presents evidence of the importance of artisan communities in early-nineteenth-century protest movements in England. Eric Hobsbawm and George Rude, *Captain Swing* (New York: Pantheon Books, 1968) is a fascinating discussion of the agricultural uprising of 1830. Fortunately for the British government, the agricultural unrest and the urban political protest remained a largely separate phenomena.

Making Connections

1. *What was the long-term significance of Napoleon for Europe?* The Napoleonic Wars had demonstrated that regimes could be overturned virtually overnight. This led to the rise of conservatism, wherein the ideas of both the Enlightenment and French Revolution were rejected: monarchy was favored over republicanism, tradition over revolution, and religion over reason. But after the Napoleonic Wars, a return to authoritarianism in the face of emerging ideologies (including liberalism, socialism, and nationalism) only created further tensions that periodically erupted into civil conflict during the 1820s and 1830s, and finally boiled over completely in the revolutions of 1848.

2. *In which ways did Metternich succeed in holding back the tide of forces for change? In which ways did he fail? Which of these forces for change made the most difference?* Metternich tried to hold back forces for change by restoring traditional rulers, returning countries to their prewar boundaries wherever possible, and when restora-

tion was impossible, rearranging territories in a way such as to balance the interests of the great powers without trampling on the smaller nations. He also sought to check French aggression yet keep it strong enough to balance the ambitions of Prussia and Russia. This arrangement may have prevented the outbreak of widespread European conflict until 1914, but it did not prevent smaller wars—like the Crimean War—between individual countries. Neither was the Congress of Vienna able to anticipate, much less control or prevent, the rise of powerful forces, such as industrialization and the emergence of new, galvanizing ideologies. Industrialization and competing ideologies would most directly determine the configuration of Europe in the latter part of this century.

Writing Assignments and Class Presentation Topics

1. After discussing with students Napoleon's efforts to create a heroic image for himself, ask them to write a short essay comparing the creation of Napoleon's image with American techniques of political image-making. American politicians have immensely greater media resources, but can they do the kinds of things Napoleon did to enhance his image?

2. Metternich was called "the coachman of Europe." Ask students to write an essay that assesses the extent of his power and its limits between 1815 and 1848. Students should reflect not only on the diplomatic and military considerations, but also on the difficulties states experienced in controlling the circulation of ideas and information after 1815. You may wish to assign some additional reading in either Gildea or Hobsbawm for this essay (see "Suggestions for Lecture and Discussion Topics," number 1).

3. Assign a class presentation on conservatism. Those students involved in the presentation should first agree on a definition of conservatism (ask them to think about whether it is a single ideology or perhaps several closely related ideologies) and then select figures to present to the class. They must decide how to present these representative figures, but they should provide a short quotation for each that will help other students get a better sense of what that particular person believed.

4. Have each student find an example of romanticism that he or she can present to the class. Find out beforehand what each student plans to present because there may be some logistical problems to deal with. For example, one student may wish to play a polonaise by Chopin, which, of course, requires an instrument or tape/CD player. Each student should find out as much as possible about his or her example and be prepared to answer questions.

Research Assignments

1. Ask students to investigate Napoleon's impact outside France. You will probably want to restrict the time frame to the period of Napoleon's greatest activity, 1800–1814, but exceptions may be made if students wish to trace Napoleon's influence during the nineteenth century. There are many possibilities in Europe itself, both in countries or areas closely associated with France, and in countries that were considered sovereignties. Outside Europe, students might investigate the failure of France to regain Haiti, the sale of the Louisiana Territory to the United States, the spread of the Napoleonic Code to other parts of the world, and various other topics. Use the bibliographic citations in "Suggestions for Lecture and Discussion Topics," number 1, to get started.

2. The Romantic poets did not live or write in a vacuum, and many of them were highly critical of the society in which they lived. Assign students to look at William Blake's "Holy Thursday," "The Chimney Sweeper," "Nurse's Song" in *Songs of Innocent* and compare them to their counterparts in *Songs of Experience*; or have students read Percy Bysshe Shelley's "Lines Written during the Castlereagh Administration," "Similes for Two Political Characters of 1819," "Song to the Men of England," "Sonnet: England 1819," "The Mask of Anarchy," "Ode to Liberty," "Sonnet: To the Republic of Benevento," "Written on Hearing the News of the Death of Napoleon," all written between 1819 and 1821; or have students study William Wordsworth's "1801 I Grieved for Buonaparte," "London. 1802," "On the Extinction of the Venetian Republic," "The World is Too Much With Us," and "Thought of a Briton on the Subjugation of Switzerland." Have these poets strayed from their Romantic ideals, or do you see evidence of them in these socially and political charged pieces? See David V. Erdman, ed., *The Selected Poetry of Blake* (New York: Meridian, 1976; rpt. 1981); *The Complete Poetical Works of Percy Bysshe Shelley*, vol. II (Blackmask Online, 2002); Jack Stillinger, ed., *Selected Poems and Prefaces by William Wordsworth* (Boston: Houghton Mifflin, Riverside Editions, 1965).

3. Assign a research project on utopian socialism. Ask students to discuss a utopian socialist or an experiment in utopian socialism at length and also to place their subjects in historical context. Were the subjects responding to particular events or developments? What kind of impact did they have in the short term? In the long term? To what extent were they successful? Use the bibliographical citations in "Suggestions for Lecture and Discussion Topics," number 3, to get students started. Remind students that there were a number of communities established in the United States to test the theories of utopian socialists. These communities and figures associated with the theories would also make good topics for research papers.

Literature

Garnett, Constance, trans., *Tolstoy: War and Peace*. 1994.

Gill, Stephen, ed., *Wordsworth: The Major Works*. 2000.

Goldberger, Avriel H., trans., *Madame de Staël: Corinne, or Italy*. 1987.

Hugo, Howard E., ed., *The Romantic Reader*. 1957.

Kaufmann, Walter, trans., *Goethe: Faust*. 1962.

Marchand, Leslie A., ed., *Selected Poetry of Lord Byron*. 2002.

Penman, Bruce, trans., *Manzoni: The Betrothed*. 1984.

Shelley, Mary, *Frankenstein, or the Modern Prometheus*. 1818.

Walter Scott, *Ivanhoe*. 1791.

Waterfield, Robin, trans., *Alexandre Dumas: The Count of Monte Cristo*. 1996.

Films and Videos

War and Peace (1968; VHS/DVD, 6 hrs., 50 min.). This version of Tolstoy's novel (published 1863–1869), set in Russia during the Napoleonic Wars, is considered to be the most faithful of the versions made. Five years in the making, it is a lavish production and an interesting perspective on the wars.

The Count of Monte Cristo (1998; VHS/DVD, approx. 8 hrs.). Gerard Depardieu stars in this dramatization of Alexandre Dumas's 1844–1845 novel set between the years 1813 and 1838. Care has been lavished on the costumes and sets, and the details of everyday life during the period have been reasonably captured.

Napoleon, the Myths, the Battles, the Legend (2001; VHS/DVD, approx. 3 hrs.). This biographical portrait of Napoleon includes letters, diary extracts, and dramatic re-creations of important events in his life.

An Empires Special: Napoleon (2000; VHS/DVD, 4 hrs., 16 min.). This is a thorough PBS documentary on Napoleon.

Napoleon (2003; VHS/DVD, 9 hrs., 20 min.). This lavish series dramatizes the main events of Napoleon's life.

Sharpe's Rifles (1990s; VHS/DVD). Bernard Cornwell's novels about the adventures of Richard Sharpe, an English soldier during the Napoleonic Wars, are chronicled in fourteen made-for-television movies, each lasting approximately 100 minutes each. The films are excellent for their attention to detail in costuming and setting, and for weaving an ordinary soldier's experience of the Napoleonic Wars into the narrative.

Horatio Hornblower (1990s, 2000s; VHS/DVD). C. S. Forester's novels about a young seaman's experiences as he works his way up the ranks during the Napoleonic Wars are dramatized in a series of television movies, each lasting approximately 100 minutes. Excellent on such details as costuming and setting, the plots are infused with historical detail about life in the English navy.

Films from Jane Austen's Novels

All of Jane Austen's (1775–1817) novels have been dramatized, some of them several times over. Like her novels, these films concentrate on the lives led by Englishwomen from gentry families and the contemporary issues of inheritance, marriage, manners, and social conventions that so affected their lives. In the following list (arranged chronologically by date of publication), the date that immediately follows the title refers to the date of its first publication.

Sense and Sensibility (1811). (1995; VHS/DVD, 2 hrs., 16 min.)

Pride and Prejudice (1813). (1995; VHS/DVD, approx. 5 hrs.)

Mansfield Park (1814). (1999; VHS/DVD, 1 hr., 47 min.)

Emma (1816) (1997; VHS/DVD, 1 hr., 45 min.)

Northanger Abbey (1818) (1986; VHS/DVD, 1 hr., 30 min.)

Persuasion (1818). (1995; VHS/DVD, 1 hr., 44 min.)

Historical Skills

Map 21.1, *Napoleon's Empire at Its Height, 1812*, p. 798

Ask students to compare Napoleon's empire with previous empires they have studied. Focusing on the enemies of the French, particularly Portugal, Great Britain, and the Russian Empire, what problems does the map suggest Napoleon faced in 1812?

Map 21.2, *Europe after the Congress of Vienna, 1815*, p. 807

What changes have taken place in the extent of territories controlled by the Austrian Empire and Prussia? What are the possible repercussions of the transformation of the Holy Roman Empire into the Germanic Confederation? Did the new boundaries of the Russian Empire make any appreciable difference in its interactions with western Europe over following decades?

Map 21.4, *Latin American Independence, 1804–1830*, p. 822; and Mapping the West: *Europe in 1830*, p. 824

Ask students to consider why revolutionary movements were almost completely successful in liberating the Latin American colonies, whereas in Europe these movements resulted in only one new state—Belgium, and one new government—in France.

Napoleon as Military Hero, p. 787

What does David do in Napoleon Crossing the Alps at St. Bernard to indicate Napoleon's heroic stature? Ask students to consider Napoleon's gesture and his posture, as well as the horse, the rocks (which are inscribed with the names of Bonaparte, Hannibal, and Charlemagne), and the men and the cannon in the near distance.

Following the Wars, p. 799; and Napoleon's Mamelukes Massacre the Spanish, p. 803

Students should compare the way war is presented in Boilly's painting to its presentation in Goya's painting. What might each artist have hoped to accomplish in his painting? Bring in or put on reserve in the library Goya's *Disasters of War* (1810–1813), a powerful series of etchings that lay bare the realities of war during the Napoleonic era.

Lord Byron, p. 815

Ask students to compare this portrait of Lord Byron with the portrait of M. Germaine de Staël (p. 795). What differences do they note in the portraits? Both Lord Byron and M. de Staël might be classified as public intellectuals, in this case writers who help to shape public opinion. Have students reflect on the possibilities open to Lord Byron that would not be open to M. de Staël.

Caspar David Friedrich, Wanderer above the Sea of Fog (1818), p. 818; and Eugène Delacroix, The Death of Sardanapalus (1826–1827), p. 794

Each painting is a fine example of the Romantic style, yet the two are very different. Students should comment on the differences. What do the paintings suggest about the sources of romanticism and the fundamental characteristics of this approach to art?

An Ordinary Soldier on Campaign with Napoleon, p. 804

A comparison can be made between Jakob Walter's account of the Napoleonic Wars and Hans Grimmelshausen's description of the Thirty Years' War. Grimmelshausen's accounts describe the massive waste and loss of life that comes with war and is quite explicit about how the soldiers behaved. Walter does not recount the blow-by-blow action; rather, he fixates on the immediate aftereffects of war, the innumerable corpses, half-dead cattle, and razed villages and cities. He has left a good deal out of his account, perhaps as much for his own as for his reader's. Nothing much had changed between the Thirty Years' War and the Napoleonic Wars.

OTHER BEDFORD/ST. MARTIN'S RESOURCES FOR CHAPTER 21

The following resources are available to accompany Chapter 21. Please refer to the Preface of this manual for detailed descriptions of all the ancillaries.

For Instructors

Transparencies

The following maps and images from Chapter 21 are available as full-color acetates.

- Map 21.1: Napoleon's Empire at Its Height, 1812
- Map 21.2: Europe after the Congress of Vienna, 1815
- Map 21.3: Revolutionary Movements of the 1820s
- Map 21.4: Latin American Independence, 1804–1830
- Mapping the West: Europe in 1830
- *Third Estate Awakens*
- *Fall of the Bastille*

Instructor's Resources CD-ROM

The following maps and image from Chapter 21, as well as a chapter outline, are available on disc in both Power-Point and jpeg formats.

- Map 21.1: Napoleon's Empire at Its Height, 1812
- Map 21.2: Europe after the Congress of Vienna, 1815
- Map 21.3: Revolutionary Movements of the 1820s
- Map 21.4: Latin American Independence, 1804–1830
- Mapping the West: Europe in 1830
- *Third Estate Awakens*

Using the Bedford Series with The Making of the West

Available in print as well as online at bedfordstmartins.com/usingseries, this guide offers practical suggestions for using **The French Revolution and Human Rights: A Brief Documentary History, translated, edited, and with an Introduction by Lynn Hunt,** in conjunction with chapters 20 and 21 of the textbook.

For Students

Sources of The Making of the West

The following documents are available in Chapter 21 of the companion sourcebook by Katharine J. Lualdi, University of Southern Maine.

1. Abd al-Rahman al-Jabartî, *Napoleon in Egypt* (1798)
2. T. B. Macaulay, *Speech on Parliamentary Reform* (1831)
3. Robert Owen, *Constitution of the Preliminary Society of New Harmony* (1825)
4. Joseph Mazzini, *Life and Writings of Joseph Mazzini* (1805–1872)

Study Guides

The print **Study Guide** and the **Online Study Guide** at bedfordstmartins.com/hunt, both by Victoria Thompson (Arizona State University) and Eric Johnson (University of California, Los Angeles), help students synthesize the material they have learned as well as practice the skills historians use to make sense of the past. The following Map, Visual, and Document activities are available for Chapter 21.

Map Activity

- Map 20.3: French Expansion, 1791–1799

Visual Activity

- *Third Estate Awakens*

Reading Historical Documents

- The Rights of Minorities
- Address to the National Assembly in Favor of the Abolition of the Slave Trade

Industrialization, Urbanization, and Revolution
1830–1850

CHAPTER RESOURCES

Main Chapter Topics

1. In the 1830s and 1840s, after witnessing Great Britain's success with industrialization, European states encouraged the construction of railroads and the mechanization of manufacturing. At the same time, and due in large part to industrialization, urban growth accelerated and soon created a host of problems, some of which were unprecedented.

2. In response to new social problems, including child labor, overcrowding, inadequate sanitation, an inadequate water supply, and the consequent diseases and epidemics, some governments—particularly the British —undertook massive studies, passed ameliorative laws, and began public works. Europeans began to organize reform movements designed to alter the ways in which the lower classes lived and targeted alcoholism, prostitution, and illiteracy. Similar movements attempted to deal with slavery, which was made illegal in the British and French empires. Depictions of social problems in art and literature formed an important impetus to the interest in reform.

3. Nationalism looked past the problems associated with industrialization and urbanization and toward political autonomy and self-determination for groups identified by common languages and cultures.

4. All socialists in the 1830s and 1840s considered liberalism an inadequate response to the problems caused by industrialization and emphasized the importance of organizing the working classes and restructuring society. Communists called for the abolition of private property and communal ownership.

5. During the revolutions of 1848, a series of demonstrations and uprisings toppled governments in France, Italy, Germany, and Austria, affording liberals, socialists, and nationalists opportunities to put their ideas into practice. Their inability to mutually work with one another created openings through which their rulers and armies were able to retake power.

6. The revolutions of 1848 failed and conservative governments returned, but the ideals and goals behind these revolutions were neither discredited nor eradicated. Moreover, Britain saw its slow liberalization justified; many of the German states gained constitutions; France recognized the impossibility of government without popular approval; and revolutionaries had learned the importance of planning beyond the overthrow of the government in power.

Summary

As workers streamed into cities looking for work, epidemics and social problems became endemic. Painters, poets, and novelists graphically depicted the need for social reform. Middle-class women also highly involved themselves in reform-minded activities. Nationalists, liberals, socialists, and communists offered their own visions of change. Food shortages and constitutional crises, combined with these competing ideologies, came to a head in 1848.

In the 1830s and 1840s, industrialization, previously confined largely to Great Britain, spread to the continent. The spread occurred initially in Belgium, northern France, and northern Italy; then moved eastward toward Prussia, Austria, and Russia.

Railroad construction was vital to industrial expansion and, by mid-century, planet Earth had over twenty-five thousand miles of track laid, most of which was in western Europe. New railroads and rolling stock, paid for by state and private funds, demanded increased production of coal and iron and so shifted the emphasis in the Industrial Revolution away from textiles. Britain remained the leader of the world in manufacturing at mid-century, perhaps as much as twenty years ahead of industrial development on the continent. Progress was slowest in eastern Europe; Russia was especially slow to follow because serfs were bound to the land and the aristocracy was disinclined to invest in industrialization.

The new class of factory workers was only a small minority within a working class still largely engaged in agriculture. Factory work could be uncertain at times, many workers therefore divided their time between factory and agricultural labor. Despite the growth in the use of steam-powered machinery on the continent, a large part of the economy also continued to rely on "putting-out," or cottage industries. A major change in these industries was the reorganization of artisan crafts. The former process, in which a skilled craftsperson made a product from start to finish, was broken down into smaller steps that unskilled or semiskilled persons, often women, could perform on a piecework basis for lower wages. Factories began to generate criticism as centers of pollution, noise, and human degradation, which simultaneously created great wealth and extreme poverty. Governmental investigations found very poor conditions, both at work and in the living quarters of the factory workers. The British led the way enacting laws intended to protect women and children from extreme exploitation. The Factory Act of 1833 limited the number of hours children could work, and the Mines Act of 1842 prohibited the employment of women and children underground.

Most cities grew rapidly during this period. In some cases, industrial development spurred the growth of cities, but cities grew even where industrial development was limited. As population in the countryside rose, competition for farmwork intensified, and men and women moved to cities looking for work. Emigration to other countries was also significant: many Irish moved to England, for example, and millions left Europe entirely. Cities could not comfortably or even decently absorb all the new arrivals. Available housing could not keep pace and overcrowding was severe. Aggravating sanitation problems made cities vulnerable to disease; the major killer among diseases was tuberculosis. Cholera epidemics killed tens of thousands—over a million in Russia—and caused panic, but also forced governments to seek solutions to the public-health crisis.

The middle and upper classes often considered the lower classes to be morally degenerate. They viewed the lower classes as lacking in sexual restraint, prone to alcoholism, and likely to be involved in crime. Rates of illegitimacy were high, and those for infanticide were also believed to be elevated. Alehouses proliferated. Reformers who collected data also reinforced stereotypes; reformers also noted and warned of the growing tensions between rich and poor. Although agricultural yields increased by 30 percent to 50 percent during this period, production still could not keep pace with population growth, which increased by 100 percent. Some peasants managed to purchase small landholdings, but large

landowners—often the nobility—enlarged their personal landholdings substantially, sometimes via the purchase of formerly public lands. Rural power remained in the hands of elites who dominated their tenants and controlled local clergy and political assemblies.

Art and literature reflected the concern about the "social question," a term for the problems associated with industrialization and urbanization. Elizabeth Barrett Browning (1806–1861) denounced child labor in her poem "The Cry of the Children" (1843). Sir Charles Barry's (1795–1866) rejection of industrialization was expressed through the rebuilding of the Houses of Parliament, which had burned down in 1834. The structure was a Victorian interpretation of the medieval Gothic style, as were the interior decorations, provided by A. W. N. Pugin (1812–1852). Joseph M. W. Turner (1775–1851) depicted the tension between the untouched, romanticized landscape and industrialization in his paintings. But the novel, which could reach a large reading public by the 1830s, was the form best suited to present social problems. Whereas Honoré de Balzac (1799–1850) presented a panorama of society in his ninety-five novels, Charles Dickens (1812–1870) often focused on the conditions of the working class. Dickens supported charitable organizations and actively pressed for reform. Charlotte Brontë (1816–1855) and George Sand (Amandine-Aurore Dupin [1804–1876]) wrote about the difficult situations women faced. All of these artists and writers were part of a culture explosion that included popular theater, museums, art collecting, and a rapidly expanding print culture. With the introduction, in 1839, of the daguerreotype, named after French painter Jacques Daguerre (1787–1851), photography further heightened the public's awareness of the effects of urbanization and industrialization.

Religion was another powerful motivator for social reform. The Sunday school movement helped thousands of children learn to read, although most of the working class were indifferent to organized religion. Women played a prominent role, whether as nuns in Catholic religious orders or as members of Protestant missionary and reform societies. They targeted prostitution and the consumption of alcohol, and advocated the education of children as a solution to social problems. Above all, the elite sought to impose discipline and order on the lower classes. Popular, lower-class sports, such as bullbaiting, were outlawed. In 1834, the British government passed a new poor law that was commonly known as the "Starvation Act." It established workhouses where the environment was so unpleasant that the poor would actively seek better employment.

Society sought to impose another kind of order in the doctrine of domesticity, according to which men were suited for the public sphere and women only for the home. Under law, women were subjugated to the control of fathers or husbands. Distinctions between men and women were most noticeable in the privileged classes and were reinforced by differences in dress and education. Men's clothes became more practical, while women's clothes became more restrictive and decorative; boys were professionally educated, while girls were tutored in domestic subjects at home or in church schools. Scientific and medical opinion agreed on women's physical and mental inferiority to men. Although feminists protested this ideology of domesticity, few middle-class women had alternatives, barred as they were from higher education, most occupations, and, naturally, political power. Lower-class women, however, generally had to work, whether in the home or outside it.

Overseas, the older patterns of colonialism began to change to *imperialism*, a word coined only in the midnineteenth century. Imperialism usually employed indirect economic exploitation rather than slavery. Slavery was abolished in the British colonies in the 1830s, and in the French colonies in the 1840s, but continued in Brazil, Cuba, and the United States. In this same period, the French invaded Algeria, colonized it, and imposed a protectorate government on Tahiti; while Britain annexed Singapore (1819) and New Zealand (1840), increased its control over India, and fought the Opium War with China, this last ending with the forced Treaty of Nanking, which gave Europeans access to more ports, and Britain Hong Kong but, above all, afforded the British unhindered access to China as a market for opium.

When social reform groups failed to resolve the problems of urbanization and industrialization, people began turning to the political ideologies—liberalism, socialism, but especially nationalism—that grew out of the French Revolution. Several ethnic groups—persons linked by a common language and cultural traditions—pursued nationalist goals in the 1830s and 1840s. After the revolution in Poland failed in 1830, Polish exiles followed poet and ardent nationalist Adam Mickiewicz (1798–1855) in viewing their country as a crucified nation with a Christian mission. A Polish uprising in Galicia foreshadowed the problems of leadership in the revolutions of 1848: the Galician peasants attacked not the Austrians who ruled them, but their Polish masters. Giuseppe Mazzini (1805–1872), an Italian nationalist opposed to Austrian rule, founded Young Italy, a nationalist secret society attracting the interest of thousands of supporters. The Austrian Empire, comprised as it was of a volatile mix of ethnic groups, faced a particularly difficult problem with nationalism. Nationalism in the German states followed the general nationalist program of revived interest in vernacular languages, folklore, and history, but the German states also united over trade matters in the formation of the *Zollverein* ("Customs Union") in 1834. The nagging question of political union was, however, whether or not Prussia or Austria or both could be included. In Russia, nationalism took the

form of opposition to western ideas. Slavophiles ("lover of the Slavs") favored maintaining rural traditions infused by the values of the Orthodox church in the face of western-style industrialization. In Ireland, a group of writers founded the Young Ireland movement aimed at recovering Irish history and preserving the Gaelic language. Daniel O'Connell (1775–1847), a British member of Parliament, called for the abolition of the Act of Union (1801), which would make Ireland independent. O'Connell was arrested and convicted on charges of conspiracy and, although his sentence was later overturned, withdrew from politics for medical reasons. Other nationalist leaders took his place.

Liberalism was strongest in the industrialized countries of western Europe. British liberals wanted to limit the government's economic role to maintaining the currency, enforcing contracts, and financing major enterprises. Liberals stirred animosity among the middle-classes toward the Corn Laws, which benefited large landowners by limiting foreign grain imports. In 1843, *The Economist* was founded to aid liberals in their fight for the repeal of the Corn Laws, which came in 1846 after the election of a new prime minister, Sir Robert Peel (1788–1850). Liberalism in France managed only disappointing results. King Louis-Philippe's government had antagonized middle-class and working-class Frenchmen alike by suppressing opposition groups and increasing censorship in the first instance, and repressing insurrections in the second. The Hungarian count Stephen Széchenyi (1791–1860) campaigned for British-style changes in economics, agriculture, and industrialization. Lajos Kossuth (1802–1894) took this even further and, in 1844, founded the Protective Association, which encouraged a boycott of Austrian goods. Kossuth held up American democracy and British political liberalism as prototypes. In Russia, liberal and even socialist opposition appeared in the 1830s and 1840s, even though Tsar Nicholas I (r. 1825–1855) banned all western, liberal writings.

Socialism perceived liberalism as an inadequate response to industrialization's social and economic problems. While they acknowledged the potential of industrialization, socialists hoped for a future of harmony, cooperation, and prosperity for all. Women were often active in socialist movements, even though socialist men tended to share widespread prejudices against women's political activism. Prominent socialists advocated various forms of organization including trade unions and producers' cooperatives. After 1840, some socialists began calling themselves "Communists" to emphasize their desire to replace private property by communal, collective ownership. Karl Marx (1818–1883) and Friedrich Engels (1820–1895) began a collaboration of great importance in the 1840s. The *Communist Manifesto*, published in 1848, distinguished them from other socialists whom they considered to be unscientific utopians. Marx and Engels supported industrialization because they believed would bring on the proletarian revolution and lead to the abolition of exploitation, private property, and a class-based society.

This period witnessed an upsurge in working-class associations. In Britain, the People's Charter demanded comprehensive electoral reform. Many women set up Chartist societies. When the government refused to act on Chartist petitions for reform, Chartists allied with working-class strike movements and distanced themselves from women workers. Continental workers were less organized although, in France, they formed mutual aid societies aimed at providing insurance, death benefits, and education. In central and eastern Europe, socialism and organized labor had less of an impact.

Nationalism sparked a renewed interest in history. Historical novels, like Alexandre Dumas's (1802–1870) *The Three Musketeers* (1844), became especially popular. Historical paintings linked the present to a glorious past. Nationalism also influenced music; Frédéric Chopin (1810–1849) interwove Polish folk rhythms and melodies in his compositions. Operatic librettos, once based on classical mythology, now emphasized passionate tragedy set against an idealized medieval or Italian Renaissance backdrop. Under the direction of Leopold von Ranke (1795–1886), a professor at the University of Berlin, history as a discipline became more formalized and objective, and emphasized original, primary documents rather than legend and tradition as the basis on which to study history. The study of geology was also transformed, particularly through the work of Charles Lyell (1797–1875), who argued that Earth was far older than the Bible suggested. Under Lyell's influence, Charles Darwin (1809–1882) began sketching out his theory of evolution through natural selection.

Poor harvests in the mid-1840s resulted in famine being experienced by persons both the countryside and the cities. The Irish famines of 1846, 1848, and 1851, were especially harmful and as many as one million may have perished. High food prices reduced demand for manufactured goods, which resulted in widespread unemployment. These developments created conditions ripe for revolution. The actual cause of revolution in France, however, was Louis-Philippe's refusal to consider calls for electoral reform. In February 1848, the people of Paris took to the streets in protest and quickly forced Louis-Philippe to abdicate. The February Revolution made France a republic once again; poet, orator, and historian Alphonse de Lamartine (1790–1869) headed the new, provisional government.

Liberals controlled the new republic and only reluctantly ventured past liberal reforms. They did, however, approve universal, adult male suffrage. They also approved "national workshops" that offered income from public works but, even though the income was not a living wage, the workshops were inundated with ten times the number of applicants expected. The Revolution politicized many segments of the urban population, and many new political clubs and newspapers appeared.

The National Assembly—newly elected in April 1848—was largely composed of middle-class professionals and landowners, and took a conservative line. Attempting to deal with the rapid growth of national workshops, the government would no longer accept new members and directed those already enrolled to move to the provinces or to join the army. In the June Days, the army, the National Guard, and the new mobile guard crushed the working-class uprising. Ten thousand casualties and thousands of arrests and convictions followed. Louis-Napoleon Bonaparte, nephew of Napoleon, won the next presidential election and, in 1852, he declared himself Emperor Napoleon III. Political differences and mutual class suspicion had doomed the Revolution and the Second Republic.

In Italy, the dream of national unification drew together some groups, but regional differences, class conflicts, and varying political goals hamstrung the leadership. Charles Albert, king of Piedmont-Sardinia, was not able to defeat the Austrians in the north. The Roman republic in the south attracted leaders like Mazzini, but also the attention of Louis-Napoleon who sent an expedition to place Pius IX back on the papal throne.

Revolution in France touched off revolutions in Austria, Prussia, and the smaller German states. Middle-class leaders, however, feared lower-class demands for democracy and social reform and were also distracted by nationalistic aspirations. For a time, it was hoped that the federal parliament meeting in Frankfurt would be able to unite Germany. Unfortunately, the delegates lacked political experience and had no army at their disposal. Frederick William IV, initially unnerved by the demonstrations in Berlin, recovered his confidence and crushed the revolution in Prussia, then intervened elsewhere in Germany to reinstate deposed rulers. He contemptuously refused the crown that the Frankfurt assembly offered him. Revolution in Austria, initially successful (Széchenyi and Kossuth became government ministers), could not contend with the ethnic divisions of the empire. By 1849, military force succeeded in destroying that revolution in Hungary, Italy, and elsewhere.

Although the revolutions failed, they did prepare the ground for German and Italian unification and a longer lasting French republic after 1870. Revolution failed to materialize in Britain, the Netherlands, and Belgium, primarily because those governments were already responding to workers' complaints. Neither was there revolution in Russia, although this was mainly due to tight governmental control. But other trends, such as the growth of the bureaucracy in each state, continued. The reassertion of conservative rule reflected the continued dominance of the aristocracy. It also hardened gender discrimination and inhibited the feminist movement.

The international Exhibition of the Works of Industry of All Nations at London's Crystal Palace (1851) indicated that many nations were ready for alternatives to revolutionary politics.

Suggestions for Lecture and Discussion Topics

1. It is important for students to understand both the forces of change and the forces of continuity in the 1830s and 1840s. A good way to do this is by carefully analyzing the spread of the Industrial Revolution to the continent. Although the British industrial economy was still well ahead of the economies of other European nations, by the 1851 exhibition at the Crystal Palace, France, Belgium, several of the German states, and the Austrian Empire had achieved some important advances. The fact that the Russian Empire does not belong on this list is worth noting. Comment on the differences between the continent and Great Britain, especially in connection with the roles of government, finance, and tariffs versus free trade.

There are two particularly good starting points for this topic. One is Chapter 3 of David S. Landes, *The Unbound Prometheus: Technological Change and Industrial Development in Western Europe from 1750 to the Present* (Cambridge, MA: Harvard University Press, 1969). Chapters 8 to 10 of Rondo Cameron, *A Concise Economic History of the World: From Paleolithic Times to the Present* (New York: Oxford University Press, 1989) provides a comprehensive chronological and global context for its discussion as well. Cameron also provides a quite useful bibliography. Peter N. Stearns and John H. Hinshaw, *The ABC-Clio World History Companion to the Industrial Revolution* (Santa Barbara, CA: ABC-Clio, 1996); and a recent overview by Peter N. Stearns, *The Industrial Revolution in World History* (Boulder, CO: Westview Press, 1993) are likewise fine sources to consult. See also Mikulas Teich and Roy Porter, eds., *The Industrial Revolution in National Context* (Cambridge: Cambridge University Press, 1996) and the absorbing and original book by Wolfgang Schivelbush, *The Railway Journey: Trains and Travel in the Nineteenth Century* (New York: Urizen Books, 1979).

2. As the factory system and the mechanization of production spread to countries outside Great Britain, the composition of the working classes changed in important ways. The factory worker, or proletariat, became an increasingly large part of the workforce, but was not yet an important political force. Generally speaking, factory workers in the early industrial period were neither well organized nor politically radical. The more important changes took place among the artisans and craftspersons, many of whom found competition from machine-made goods devastating to their trade. It is important to convey to students the many different paths working-

class lives might have taken during this period. Those who possessed the skills needed by industrial capitalists made up a new labor aristocracy. Others—unskilled or semiskilled—endured cyclical unemployment and the problems of illness or injury. Those who had been skilled artisans often fought a losing battle against changes in the economy.

A good place to begin a presentation of the changing circumstances of the working classes is Peter N. Stearns and Herrick Chapman, *European Society in Upheaval: Social History Since 1750,* 3d ed. (New York: Macmillan, 1992). The bibliography is extensive and helpful. See also John R. Gillis, *The Development of European Society, 1770–1870* (Boston: Houghton Mifflin, 1977), which takes a more topical approach. E. P. Thompson's wonderful book, *The Making of the English Working Class* (New York: Pantheon Books, 1963), offers a wealth of information for those with the time to make their way through it. William H. Sewell Jr., *Work and Revolution in France: The Language of Labor from the Old Regime to 1848* (Cambridge: Cambridge University Press, 1980) describes the extent to which working-class socialism in the nineteenth century derived from the guild structure of the eighteenth. John M. Merriman, ed., *Consciousness and Class Experience in Nineteenth-Century Europe* (New York: Holmes & Meier, 1979) deals with the situation of the artisan. See also Gareth Stedman Jones, *Languages of Class: Studies in English Working-Class History, 1832–1982* (Cambridge: Cambridge University Press, 1983), a series of essays that looks at the development of class consciousness.

There is less material available on social conditions and living standards. One useful book is Katherine Lynch, *Family, Class, and Ideology in Early Industrial France: Social Policy and the Working-Class Family, 1815–1848* (Madison: University of Wisconsin Press, 1988). Another is Colin Heywood, *Childhood in Nineteenth-Century France: Work, Health, and Education among the "Classes Populaires"* (Cambridge: Cambridge University Press, 1988). A very useful overview is Louise Tilly and Joan W. Scott, *Women, Work, and Family* (New York: Holt, Rinehart & Winston, 1978). See also Enid Gauldie, *Cruel Habitations, A History of Working-Class Housing, 1790–1918* (New York: Barnes & Noble, 1974). One very fine source that makes clear the desperate plight of many artisans by mid-century is Eileen Yeo and E. P. Thompson, eds. *The Unknown Mayhew* (New York: Schocken Books, 1972), a selection from the eighty-two letters Henry Mayhew published in the *Morning Chronicle* (1849–1850).

3. Most women did not manage to improve their situation to any great degree during this period. Thomas Mann's novel *Buddenbrooks,* about a German merchant family, features Antonie (Tony) Buddenbrooks whose two disastrous marriages weaken the family fortunes. Yet, Tony is the one who cares most about the family, its

place in society, and its reputation. The only way for most women to maintain or improve their living situations was through marriages that were regarded as "successful," which more often than not meant they brought money into the family. Notwithstanding, there are changes in the period worth discussing. In 1848, for example, Elizabeth Cady Stanton and Susan B. Anthony met with other women at Seneca Falls, New York, and passed the Declaration of Sentiments, which demanded equality with men, the right to vote, and full participation in civic life. Students should find it interesting to discuss the polarity of the growing cult of domesticity at one end of the spectrum of opinion, and the simultaneous efforts of a few women to open new doors on the other.

A useful point of departure is Louise Tilly, *Industrialization and Gender Inequality,* in the American Historical Association's series *Essays on Global and Comparative History* (Washington, DC: American Historical Association, 1993). Tilly discusses the impact of socioeconomic changes on gender inequality through a comparison of Britain, China, France, Germany, Japan, and the United States. See also the books by Tilly and Scott, and by Stearns and Chapman, both cited in suggestion 2 above. Chapters 4 and 5 in Bonnie G. Smith, *Changing Lives: Women in European History Since 1700* (Lexington, MA: D. C. Heath, 1989) provide a good introduction to women and work and the cult of domesticity. Bonnie S. Anderson and Judith P. Zinsser, *A History of Their Own: Women in Europe from Prehistory to the Present,* vol. 2 (New York: Harper & Row, 1988) is organized topically. Parts 7 and 8 have much to offer, including an extensive bibliography. Books on women in the working class or the peasantry include Angela V. John, *Unequal Opportunities: Women's Employment in England 1800–1918* (New York: Blackwell, 1986); and Martine Segalen, *Love and Power in the Peasant Family: Rural France in the Nineteenth Century* (Chicago: University of Chicago Press, 1983). Several books use a national approach to this topic. Among them are Ute Frevert, *Women in German History: From Bourgeois Emancipation to Sexual Liberation* (New York: Berg, 1988); and Catherine M. Prelinger, *Charity, Challenge, and Change: Religious Dimensions of the Mid-Nineteenth Century Women's Movement in Germany* (New York: Greenwood Press, 1987). See also Martha Vicinus, ed., *Suffer and Be Still: Women in the Victorian Age* (Bloomington: Indiana University Press, 1973); Martha Vicinus, ed., *A Widening Sphere: Changing Roles of Victorian Women* (Bloomington: Indiana University Press, 1977); and David Ransel, ed., *The Family in Imperial Russia* (Urbana: University of Illinois Press, 1976). Several other important works are cited in the chapter.

4. The appearance and development of nationalist movements is a major feature of this period. Poles, Greeks, Italians, Germans, Czechs, and other groups actively founded nations or attempted to found nations. Perhaps the most important theme unifying these movements is a blending of the romantic ideas about the past with nationalist ideas about the future. Another important theme is the strain and tension multinational empires experienced during this period.

Chapter 7 of Eric J. Hobsbawm's *The Age of Revolution, 1789–1848* is a good overview of nationalist movements and ideas in this period. See also Eric J. Hobsbawm, *Nations and Nationalism Since 1780: Programme, Myth, Reality* (New York: Cambridge University Press, 1990). Alan Sked, *The Decline and Fall of the Habsburg Empire, 1815–1918* (London: Longman, 1989) provides a dependable survey of the situation in central Europe. More specialized sources include George Barany, *Stephen Széchenyi and the Awakening of Hungarian Nationalism, 1791–1841* (Princeton: Princeton University Press, 1968); and Joseph Zacek, *Palacky: The Historian As Scholar and Nationalist* (The Hague: Mouton, 1970). On the Greek revolt, see Douglas Dakin, *The Greek Struggle for Independence, 1821–1833* (Berkeley: University of California Press, 1973); and Richard Clogg, ed., *The Struggle for Greek Independence* (Hamden, CT: Archon Books, 1973). For Italy, an excellent source is Denis Mack Smith, *Mazzini* (New Haven, CT: Yale University Press, 1994). For Germany, see chapters 7 and 10 of James J. Sheehan, *German History, 1770–1866* (Oxford: Clarendon Press, 1989); and Chapter 2 of David Blackbourn, *The Long Nineteenth Century: A History of Germany, 1780–1918* (New York: Oxford University Press, 1998).

5. Karl Marx came of age during this period, and a review of his life to age thirty (that is, 1848) is an excellent way to give students a sense of the focused discussion in this period. (Charles Darwin or Alexander Herzen could also be discussed for much the same purpose.) Marx was thoroughly familiar with the German idealist philosophers of the period, a student of the French Revolution at a time when the first great histories of that event were being written and published, and deeply interested in the Industrial Revolution and the development of capitalism. Like so many of his contemporaries, Marx was not only busy making sense of the present, he was also at work on his own grand theory of history that was meant to point the way to the future.

A recent, highly readable biography of Marx is Francis Wheen, *Karl Marx: A Life* (New York: W. W. Norton, 2000). Wheen is good on biographical information but not always very dependable in his discussion of Marx's ideas. Isaiah Berlin, *Karl Marx: His Life and Environment,* 3d ed. (New York: Oxford University Press, 1963) is a very good short study. David McLellan, *Karl Marx: His Life and Thought* (New York: Harper & Row, 1973) is probably the best book overall, but it is long. Jerrold Seigel, *Marx's Fate: The Shape of a Life* (University Park: Pennsylvania State University Press, 1993) is a difficult but rewarding biographical study. The best anthology of

[margin annotation: Women's Rights vs Cult of Domesticity]

Marx's writings (and Friedrich Engels's as well) is Robert C. Tucker, *The Marx-Engels Reader*, 2d ed. (New York: W. W. Norton, 1978). Also useful is Eugene Kamenka, *The Portable Karl Marx* (New York: Penguin Books, 1983). Helpful editions of *The Communist Manifesto* are John E. Toews, ed., The Communist Manifesto *by Karl Marx and Frederick Engels with Related Documents* (Boston: Bedford/St. Martin's, 1999); and Frederic L. Bender, *The Communist Manifesto* (New York: W. W. Norton, 1988). For a critical evaluation of Marx, see Paul Johnson, *Intellectuals* (New York: Harper & Row, 1989). For Engels in this period, see Steven Marcus, *Engels, Manchester, and the Working Class* (New York: Vintage Press, 1974).

6. Rather than attempting to cover all the revolutions, it might be better to take a closer look at the revolutions of 1848 by concentrating on one or two that deal with important issues. The revolution of 1848 in France not only refers back to the French Revolution and Napoleon, it also introduces the importance of the social issue in that France is the one location where that issue is not obscured by national aspirations. The German insurrections of 1848 call up the crucial issue of German nationalism. The "German question" — that is, who will control the German states and to what purpose — is placed on the agenda and will remain there for the next century and a half.

In addition to the excellent books cited in the chapter bibliography, see also Peter N. Stearns, *1848: The Revolutionary Tide in Europe* (New York: W. W. Norton, 1974); and the recent collection edited by Robert Evans and Hartmut Pogge von Strandmann, *The Revolutions in Europe, 1848–49* (Oxford: Oxford University Press, 2000). On France, see Maurice Agulhon, *The Republican Experiment, 1848–1852* (Cambridge: Cambridge University Press, 1983); John M. Merriman, *The Agony of the Republic: The Repression of the Left in Revolutionary France, 1848–1851* (New Haven, CT: Yale University Press, 1978); and Mark Traugott, *Armies of the Poor: Determinants of Working-Class Participation in the Parisian Insurrection of June 1848* (Princeton: Princeton University Press, 1985). For Germany, see Wolfram Siemann, *The German Revolution of 1848–1849* (New York: St. Martin's Press, 1998); and Jonathan Sperber, *Rhineland Radicals: The Democratic Movement and the Revolution of 1848–1849* (Princeton: Princeton University Press, 1991).

7. In the summer of 1858, the odor emitting from the Thames River, which flowed with raw sewage, was so overwhelming that sheets soaked in disinfectant were hung over the windows of Parliament. In the following year, the situation even worsened, and Parliament was actually forced to adjourn for the summer. The problems of sanitation in London were long standing, and measures were undertaken to improve it after major cholera epidemics killed thousands in the city in 1832 and 1849. A discussion can begin with the work of Sir Edwin Chadwick, author of the report of a parliamentary commission, *The Sanitary Condition of the Laboring Population of Britain, 1842*, which marks the beginnings of comprehensive waste-management systems in Europe. There are also many published histories of the "water closet" available should a discussion lead in that direction.

Making Connections

1. *Which of the ideologies of this period had the greatest impact on political events? How can this be explained?* Nationalism had by far the greatest impact on political events. Nationalism looked past the problems associated with industrialization and urbanization, issues that preoccupied liberals and socialists, toward political autonomy and self-determination for groups identified by common language and culture. Nationalism was a more inclusive and unifying force than either liberalism or socialism.

2. *In which ways might industrialization be considered a force for peaceful change, rather than for revolution?* Factories became the object of public criticism as centers of pollution, noise, and human degradation. Governmental investigations found that very dire conditions existed both at work and in the living quarters of the factory workers. The British led the way in passing laws intended to protect women and children from extreme exploitation. The British also undertook major public works projects, such as the construction of sewers, to help improve the lives of the poor. Real, substantive changes were formulated by the leadership of the country, not by the citizens.

Writing Assignments and Class Presentation Topics

1. Ask students to imagine that they have the opportunity to travel back in time to the 1830s and 1840s to conduct interviews for oral histories of the working class. Each student should provide an introduction to the person he or she interviews, a list of questions to be asked, and read aloud or hand in a transcript of the "interview." It may be a good idea to draw up a list of several types of workers based on primary and secondary sources readily available to students. Students could then select from the prepared list or you could assign a particular type of worker to each student. See "Suggestions for Lecture and Discussion Topics," numbers 2 and 3, for bibliographical citations.

2. An annotated timeline, which students will be familiar with from the Study Guide, is a useful exercise. Each student selects a country or a theme, such as the development of the railroad or romanticism in literature, and prepares a timeline that briefly identifies and discusses major events, institutions, persons, and so forth.

The timeline would also make a good class presentation (if you do this as a presentation, limit the number of students covering the 1830s and 1840s, and assign the others to do later periods). Students will probably need some bibliographical pointers. Introduce them to such publications as William L. Langer, ed., *An Encyclopedia of World History,* 4th ed. (Boston: Houghton Mifflin, 1968); or Richard B. Morris and Graham W. Irwin, eds., *Harper Encyclopedia of the Modern World* (New York: Harper & Row, 1970).

3. Divide the class into several groups, and ask each group to write, rehearse, and present a fifteen-minute play based on the idea of domesticity in the context of a specific family situation, such as a middle-class family or a working-class family. Each member of the group would have one major role (for example, a writer, director, actor, and/or producer). The each group's play could be based on an actual historical family (see, for example, Phyllis Rose, *Parallel Lives: Five Victorian Marriages* [New York: Vintage, 1983]) or be fictional but factually based; that is, the family might be fictional, but the experiences of the characters should be historically factual. Each student would then write a short essay discussing the experience of putting together their group's play and evaluating what he or she learned about family dynamics from the play. See "Suggestions for Lecture and Discussion Topics," number 3, for bibliographical citations.

4. Discuss in class the types of indices that would prove useful for comparing European nations in the 1840s. These data might include population figures, miles of railroad track, the number of steam engines used in factories, and so forth. Students should then select a country, find as many relevant statistics for it as possible, and present these in graphs or tables. Students should also write a brief essay explaining what they believe the statistics show about their chosen country. In addition to the bibliographical notations in "Suggestions for Lecture and Discussion Topics," number 1, students should become familiar with B. R. Mitchell, *European Historical Statistics, 1750–1970* (New York: Columbia University Press, 1975).

Research Assignments

1. In addition to Marx and Engels, many other seminal figures in European life came of age in the 1830s and 1840s. Students might be assigned to write a research essay on the formative years of one of the following persons: Charles Darwin, Alexander Herzen, John Stuart Mill, George Eliot, Florence Nightingale, or George Sand. For Darwin, see Janet Browne, *Charles Darwin: Voyaging* (Princeton: Princeton University Press, 1995), a very fine biography that concentrates largely on the voyage of *HMS Beagle,* but takes the story into the 1850s. Another useful source is Philip Appleman, *Darwin: A Norton Critical Edition* (New York: W. W. Norton, 1970), which includes writing by Darwin and writing about him. For Florence Nightingale, students might begin with Nancy Boyd, *Three Victorian Women Who Changed Their World: Josephine Butler, Octavia Hill, Florence Nightingale* (New York: Oxford University Press, 1982). Another useful source is Martha Vicinus and Bea Nergaard, eds., *Ever Yours, Florence Nightingale: Selected Letters* (Cambridge, MA: Harvard University Press, 1989). Students should, of course, develop their own list of sources, but it may be useful, as with Darwin and Nightingale here, to supply them with two or three good sources to help them get started.

2. The revolutions of 1848 provide a rich and varied array of possible topics for research and writing. Students might choose to analyze the origins of a particular revolution. This analysis could range from a discussion of the events and developments of the 1840s to a more tightly focused dissection of the particular events in 1848 leading to the temporarily successful revolution in Prussia. In the latter case, of particular interest is William L. Langer, "The Pattern of Urban Revolution in 1848," in Evelyn M. Acomb and Marvin L. Brown Jr., eds., *French Society and Culture Since the Old Regime* (New York: Holt, Rinehart & Winston, 1966). Another direction students might take would involve following an individual through 1848. Who was Louis-Napoleon Bonaparte? What role did he play in 1848? Or, what was Friedrich Engels, coauthor of *The Communist Manifesto,* doing in 1848? Students might also look at countries or areas where there was no revolution: Why was this the case? Use "Suggestions for Lecture and Discussion Topics," number 6, for bibliographical leads. Sperber and Stearns both have extensive bibliographies in their books.

Literature

Dickens, Charles, *Oliver Twist.* 1837–1839.

Forster, Margaret, ed., *Selected Poems of Elizabeth Barrett Browning.* 1988.

Ives, George Burnham, trans., *George Sand: Indiana.* 1978.

Katz, Michael R., trans., *Ivan Turgenev: Fathers and Sons.* 1995.

Keach, William, ed., *Samuel Taylor Coleridge: The Complete Poems.* 1997.

Krailsheimer, A. J., trans., *Honoré de Balzac: Père Goriot.* 1991.

Milligan, Barry, ed., *Thomas de Quincey: Confessions of an English Opium Eater and Other Writings.* 2003.

Films and Videos

Middlemarch (1994; VHS/DVD, approx. 6 hrs.). This excellent dramatization of George Eliot's 1871–1872 novel explores a number of themes, including the political tensions that followed the Great Reform Bill of 1831, the hypocrisy of those who took up religion as a profession, and the restrictions placed on women in England in the 1830s.

Jane Eyre (1997; VHS/DVD, 1 hr., 45 min.). This is an excellent adaptation of Charlotte Brontë's 1847 novel about a young woman trying to make her way in the world as a governess. It graphically depicts the restrictions on and limited opportunities for intelligent but impoverished young women in mid-Victorian England.

Charles Dickens (2003; DVD, 8 hrs., 30 min.). This three-part series examines Dickens's life and the motivations behind his writing by interviewing actors portraying Dickens and those persons who knew him. Dickens's overwhelming concern for the poor, who suffered most from industrialization, is especially emphasized.

Films of Charles Dickens's Novels

Virtually all of Charles Dickens's novels have been dramatized, some of them several times over. Like the novels, the films capture the vagaries of fortune and the hardship of life for the poor and impoverished in the Victorian period. In the following list (arranged chronologically by date of publication), the date that immediately follows the title refers to the date of its first publication.

Oliver Twist (1837–1838). (1997; VHS, 6 hrs.)

Nicholas Nickleby (1838–1839). (2002; VHS/DVD, approx. 3 hrs., 20 min.)

Martin Chuzzlewit (1843–1844). (1994; VHS, 4 hrs., 48 min.)

David Copperfield (1849–1850). (2000; VHS/DVD, approx. 3 hrs.)

Bleak House (1852–1853). (1988 VHS, 6 hrs., 31 min.)

Hard Times (1854). (1994; VHS, 1 hr., 42 min.)

Little Dorrit (1855–1854). (1988; VHS, 6 hrs.)

Great Expectations (1860–1861) (2001; VHS, 3 hrs.)

Our Mutual Friend (1864–1865). (1998; VHS/DVD, approx. 5 hrs., 30 min.)

Historical Skills

Map 22.1, Industrialization in Europe, c. 1850, p. 833

Ask students to think about industrialization and peasant emancipation. How might the two be related? Also ask them to discuss the connections between railroad construction and industrialization. What does this map indicate about the advantages possessed by the British industrial economy around 1850?

Map 22.4, The Revolutions of 1848, p. 858

Using the map, each student should choose five sites of revolution and then rank them, one through five, without revealing the basis for their ranking system. These ranks could then be tabulated for the class as a whole. After the results are in, ask students to comment on why they chose a particular site as first or second or third on the list. Should Paris be first because it was the site of a revolutionary tradition that reaches back to the French Revolution? Should Frankfurt be first because the failure there to create the basis for a united Germany leads to a much different solution under Bismarck?

Mapping the West: Europe in 1850, p. 868

Which areas show the most rapid increase in population in the period between 1800 and 1850? Does there appear to be a correlation between population growth and power?

Bearbaiting, p. 846

What does this engraving suggest about popular culture in the first part of the nineteenth century? Why were reformers often drawn from the middle classes? Why would reformers want to suggest that activities like bearbaiting and bullbaiting were lower-class sports? Compare this engraving to "The Temperance Movement" (p. 845). What might account for the interest in reform movements of all kinds in this period?

The Vésuviennes, 1848, p. 861

Were men more or less anxious about the possibility of liberated women in this period than before? What connections might there be between the various reform movements and the satirical treatment of women's political ambitions?

The Crystal Palace, 1851, p. 867

Ask students to reflect on the messages that the Crystal Palace and the exhibitions it contained were meant to send. What was the purpose of the Exhibition of the Works of Industry of All Nations? To what extent did the exhibition reflect the social and economic reality of Great Britain? Other participating countries? Their colonies?

Marx and Engels, The Communist Manifesto *(1848),* p. 856

Marx and Engels assert that class struggles are a recurring historical phenomenon. Students can be asked to point to some examples to support their claim, and consider whether or not the United States is a classless society. Obvious examples of class struggles include most civil uprisings, like the American Revolution (1776), the French Revolution (1789), the revolutions of 1848, and the Russian Revolution of 1918. More subtle instances of class warfare include the Crusades, the persecution of Jews, and the Protestant Reformation. That there is talk of a "middle class" is proof enough that society in the United States is stratified. In the case of the United States, wealth, education, and celebrity status are key factors in determining class.

OTHER BEDFORD/ST. MARTIN'S RESOURCES FOR CHAPTER 22

The following resources are available to accompany Chapter 22. Please refer to the Preface of this manual for detailed descriptions of all the ancillaries.

For Instructors

Transparencies

The following maps and images from Chapter 22 are available as full-color acetates.

- Map 22.1: Industrialization in Europe, c. 1850
- Map 22.2: The Spread of Cholera, 1826–1855
- Map 22.3: Languages of Nineteenth-Century Europe
- Map 22.4: The Revolutions of 1848
- Mapping the West: Europe in 1850
- Turner's *Fighting Temeraire Tugged to Her Last Berth to Be Broken Up*
- *The Crystal Palace*

Instructor's Resources CD-ROM

The following maps and image from Chapter 22, as well as a chapter outline, are available on disc in both PowerPoint and jpeg formats.

- Map 22.1: Industrialization in Europe, c. 1850
- Map 22.2: The Spread of Cholera, 1826–1855
- Map 22.3: Languages of Nineteenth-Century Europe
- Map 22.4: The Revolutions of 1848
- Mapping the West: Europe in 1850
- Turner's *Fighting Temeraire Tugged to Her Last Berth to Be Broken Up*

Using the Bedford Series with The Making of the West

Available in print as well as online at bedfordstmartins.com/usingseries, this guide offers practical suggestions for using *The Communist Manifesto by Karl Marx and Frederick Engels, with Related Documents,* edited with an Introduction by John E. Toews, in conjunction with Chapter 22 of the textbook.

For Students

Sources of The Making of the West

The following documents are available in Chapter 22 of the companion sourcebook by Katharine J. Lualdi, University of Southern Maine.

1. *Factory Rules in Berlin* (1844)
2. Sarah Stickney Ellis, *The Women of England: Social Duties and Domestic Habits* (1839)
3. Frederick Engels, *Draft of a Communist Confession of Faith* (1847)
4. Sándor Petofi, *National Song of Hungary* (1848)

Study Guides

The print **Study Guide** and the **Online Study Guide** at bedfordstmartins.com/hunt, both by Victoria Thompson (Arizona State University) and Eric Johnson (University of California, Los Angeles), help students synthesize the material they have learned as well as practice the skills historians use to make sense of the past. The following Map, Visual, and Document activities are available for Chapter 22.

Map Activity

- Map 22.1: Industrialization in Europe, c. 1850

Visual Activity

- Turner's *Fighting Temeraire Tugged to Her Last Berth to Be Broken Up*

Reading Historical Documents

- A Romantic Poet Mourns the Fate of the Workers
- Marx and Engels, *The Communist Manifesto*

Politics and Culture of the Nation-State

c. 1850–1870

CHAPTER RESOURCES

Main Chapter Topics

1. The concert of Europe dissolved in the 1850s, in part because Napoleon III worked to weaken its hold over France. Napoleon III helped to engineer the Crimean War (1853–1856), which, by splitting the alliance between Russia and Austria, shifted the distribution of European power.

2. Both the German and the Italian states used the changed circumstances of the 1850s and 1860s, combined with Realpolitik and nationalism, to unify their countries quickly through war. The United States was obliged to wage a civil war to restore national unity.

3. Governments undertook urban improvements— from opera houses to sewers—to avoid revolution and epidemics by attending to the well-being of their citizens. These efforts were generally popular, yet disturbed and dislocated many of the poor, who were, of course, resentful.

4. Governmental attempts to impose order extended as well to colonial enterprises. The British, Russians, and French instituted direct rule over their colonies, expanding the colonial bureaucracies and, in some cases, providing more services.

5. Realism in both art and literature claimed to look at society objectively and to depict it starkly and accurately, claims similar to those of Realpolitik and positivism.

6. Charles Darwin revealed and extended the power of science. His ideas were misunderstood and distorted into Social Darwinism, an application of "survival of the fittest" to modern society that opposed aiding the "unfit." Marxism, with its doctrines of class struggle and the social evolution of history was also a scion of Dar-

winism. Evolution was even used to justify racism and imperialism.

7. Karl Marx attacked socialists and anarchists and encouraged workers to think in terms of a revolution that would destroy bourgeois society and the nation-state.

Summary

In the wake of the failed revolutions of 1848, European statesmen and a politically conscious public rejected the politics and theories of idealism and embraced Realpolitik, a politics of tough-minded realism aimed at strengthening the state and tightening social order. The Realpolitik approach to nation-building, however, meant warfare, dislocation, new inroads into the personal lives of people around the world, shrewd policy, and heated debate. Realism and hard facts fed into the new mind-set of ordinary citizens and elected politicians alike.

In the 1850s, Napoleon III, nephew of Napoleon Bonaparte, reasserted the grandeur of France, revived the cult of his famous uncle, and contributed to the end of the concert of Europe. Napoleon III combined economic liberalism and nationalism with authoritarian rule. His rubber-stamp legislature (Corps législatif) reduced representative government to a façade. While politically old-fashioned, Napoleon III advanced modern economic ideas including innovative investment banks, a free-trade agreement with England, and an ambitious project to rebuild Paris. In the 1860s, after an economic recession, Napoleon III pragmatically tried to find new political allies by liberalizing his politics. In matters of foreign policy, Napoleon III sought to overcome the containment of France imposed by the Congress of Vienna, realign continental politics to benefit France, and acquire international glory.

Napoleon III intervened in the quarrel between the Russian and Ottoman empires, goading the Russians toward war and persuading Austria to remain neutral rather than give aid to Russia. Around the same time, Britain prodded the Ottoman Empire to stand up to Russia. Russia easily defeated the Ottomans at the sea battle of Sinope in the fall of 1853, prompting France and Great Britain to declare war on Russia (1854), ostensibly to protect the Ottoman Empire's sovereignty, but really to thwart Russia's ambition and secure Mediterranean trade routes. British and French troops laid siege to Sevastopol, which took a year to capitulate. Both sides in the conflict were plagued by incompetent generals and insufficient supplies, munitions, and medical care. Approximately three-quarters of a million soldiers died—more than two-thirds from disease and starvation. When Alexander II (r. 1855–1881) became tsar, he had little choice but to sign the Peace of Paris (1856). Russia lost its naval bases in the Straits of Dardanelles and the Black Sea, and Moldavia and Walachia (which soon merged to form Romania) became autonomous, Turkish provinces under the victors' protection.

During the Crimean War, a number of new military technologies were introduced. The telegraph changed the speed at which news from the front lines reached home. The most important figure in the Crimean War was Florence Nightingale (1820–1910) who organized a battlefield nursing service and transformed the appalling sanitary conditions of the troops. The major political change involved the end of the alliance between Russia and Austria and their control of European affairs, and opened the way for reform and national unification movements.

In Russia, during the decade before the Crimean War, hundreds of peasant insurrections erupted. Art and literature fed into serf discontent: Ivan Turgenev's *Hunter's Sketches* (1852) depicted serfs sympathetically, and Harriet Beecher Stowe's *Uncle Tom's Cabin* (1852) was translated into Russian in the 1850s. Defeat added to growing serf defiance and, in 1861, Alexander II felt compelled to emancipate the serfs, ushering in a period of Great Reforms. Communities of former serfs received land to work and distribute as they saw fit. Emancipation was, however, relative in that the peasants and their lands were organized into village communes or *mirs*, and were forced to "redeem" the land by paying off long-term "loans" to the government. Hence, Russia still lacked a fully free, mobile, labor pool. Emancipation was the first of several reforms that included the creation of regional and district self-government *zemstvos*, which were regional councils through which aristocrats could direct neglected local matters such as education, public health, and welfare. Judicial reform gave all Russians—even former serfs—access to modern civil courts, and the principle of equality of all persons before the law finally found its way to Russia. Military reform shorted conscription terms from twenty-five years to six years and saw to it that recruits were educated and treated humanely. Re-

form led to rebellion among aristocratic, Russian youths and also among the national minorities. Some upper-class children embraced manual labor; while some young women entered into phony marriages so they could study in foreign universities. Turgenev labeled these young people "nihilists" because they seemingly lacked a belief in values. Rebels among national minorities within the Russian Empire were addressed with intensive programs of "Russification."

After 1848, the issue of Risorgimento ("rebirth") continued to agitate the Italian peninsula. Piedmont-Sardinia's prime minister Camillo di Cavour (1810–1861) led the movement for Italian unification. The pragmatic Cavour developed a healthy Piedmontese economy, a modern army, and a liberal political climate, then turned to making unification a reality. Assured of the support of France, Piedmont provoked an Austrian invasion of northern Italy in 1859. Although the allies defeated Austria in June 1859, Napoleon III, fearing Piedmont's growing power, signed a treaty that granted Lombardy—but not Venetia—to Piedmont and left the remainder of Italy seemingly disunited. But Parma, Modena, Tuscany, and the Papal States (not Rome, which was occupied by French troops) threw off their rulers and elected to join Piedmont. Giuseppe Garibaldi (1807–1882) further forced the issue by using volunteers to liberate Sicily, then landed his Red Shirts on the mainland. Cavour sent Piedmontese troops south to keep Garibaldi from reaching Rome. Then, Garibaldi endorsed King Victor Emmanuel II (r. 1861–1878) and, in 1861, the kingdom of Italy was proclaimed. Problems soon emerged: 90 percent of the peninsula's population communicated using local languages or dialects, and an economic gulf opened between the wealthy, commercial north and the impoverished, agricultural south.

Otto von Bismarck (1815–1898), a member of the landed nobility and the architect of German unity, only acquired a seriousness of purpose in 1846 after marrying a pious, Lutheran woman. Establishing Prussia as a respected and dominant power became Bismarck's cause. In 1862, William I (king of Prussia, r. 1861–1888; German emperor, r. 1871–1888) appointed Bismarck prime minister to deal with the parliamentary Liberals' opposition to military reforms; Bismarck enlarged the military over their objections. Wars followed with Denmark (1864), Austria (1866), and France in (1870). These wars kept the disunited German states from choosing Austrian leadership and instead united them around a rising Prussia. The war against Austria and most of the small states in the German Confederation was particularly important. The modernized Prussian army decisively defeated the Austrian army. Bismarck drew smaller states into a new North German Confederation, and excluded Austria from German affairs. War with France—nominally over the Prussian candidate for the vacant Spanish throne—brought the new German Empire the southern

German states that had remained outside the North German Confederation. France was quickly defeated, after which Napoleon III was sent into exile and the Second Republic collapsed. King William of Prussia was proclaimed kaiser ("emperor") in the Hall of Mirrors at Versailles in January 1871. In the peace treaty signed in May 1871, France ceded the rich, industrial provinces of Alsace and Lorraine to Germany. Without France to defend the papacy, Italy incorporated Rome. Germany's new, complex constitution ensured continued dominance by the monarchy and aristocracy. Liberals had been silenced by Germany's military successes.

Francis Joseph (r. 1848–1916) ascended the throne in the wake of the revolutions of 1848 and 1849. Although autocratic and resistant to change, under his rule government corruption was minimized and public education promoted. The government respected the rights of minorities to receive education and communicate with officials in their native language. The economy flourished. But liberals criticized the use of police informers, the Catholic church's dominance in education and marital issues, and the lack of representation—especially in matters of taxation and finance. Liberals blocked funding for modernizing the military. After the Prussian victory in 1866, Francis Joseph was forced to grant Magyar home rule to the Hungarian kingdom in 1867, and the Habsburg Empire became a "dual monarchy." Hungary now had its own parliament to decide internal matters. The Czechs and several other national groups desired similar arrangements, but the government was strong enough to deny their wishes. Dissatisfied ethnic groups embraced Pan-Slavism (transnational loyalty of all ethnic Slavs), and looked to Russia as a focal point for potential unity.

Great Britain furnished a sharp contrast to the continent. Its parliamentary system now incorporated new ideas and new ranks of male voters into a system stabilized with economic prosperity and an expanding empire. The marriage of Queen Victoria (r. 1837–1901) and Prince Albert provided a fitting symbol of domestic tranquility that was used as a model by her subjects. The Tory Party evolved into the Conservative Party and, in 1867, led by Benjamin Disraeli (1804–1881), they passed the Second Reform Bill and extended male suffrage. The Whigs also changed names, and became the Liberals. A number of groups, many of whom were from the middle class, pressed for a variety of reforms, several of which were social in origin (including divorce and women's property rights). A sufficient number of demands were met to give the populace a sense of participation in political affairs. Although the monarchy was promoted and the aristocracy kept its privileged position, British politicians embraced Realpolitik, and continued to expand their empire, sometimes by violence.

In the Western Hemisphere, the United States expanded westward, where it faced problems concerning the native American Indians and how to deal with issue of slavery in these new territories. Slavery became the dividing point between the North and the South, and the United States entered the devastating Civil War to preserve the Union. Although the war was not originally intended to liberate the slaves, President Abraham Lincoln took this step in his Emancipation Proclamation (1863). After the Civil War, and as Southern whites regained control over state politics, interest in granting political rights to African Americans waned in the North and racism became entrenched nationwide. To ward off annexation by the United States, Great Britain granted Canada self-government (1867). Also that year, Mexico defeated the attempts by Napoleon III to establish Maximilian, Francis Joseph's brother, on the throne.

European states in search of internal unity and order exerted a major effort to reconstruct the urban environment, particularly in the capital cities. In 1857, Francis Joseph replaced the old city walls in Vienna with concentric boulevards lined with grand, public buildings. Napoleon III sponsored similar efforts in Paris. In peacetime, wider streets afforded the populace room to observe state-organized spectacles of power; whereas in wartime, wider streets better accommodated troop movements. Extravagant buildings and expansive parks further advertised the state's power. In the process of urban reconstruction, however, many old neighborhoods were razed and thousands of less-fortunate people were displaced.

Despite all this grandeur, Europeans continued to be exposed to periodic episodes of epidemics: cholera, typhus, and so on. Louis Pasteur (1822–1895) introduced his germ theory of disease, and pasteurization process of milk and wine. Joseph Lister (1827–1912), an English surgeon, applied Pasteur's theories to medicine and developed antiseptics to kill the germs that caused wounds to become infected. Governmental projects began to replace and improve old sewer systems and drainage and were also employed to provide cities with fresher water. Personal hygiene improved among the middle and lower classes.

The new urban programs required an expanded state bureaucracy. Regular censuses allowed governments to gather data that could be used to determine such things as quotas for military conscription and the need for new prisons. Decision making could now be based on hard facts. Governments took the initiative in dealing with social problems such as the spread of venereal disease, especially syphilis; civil service examinations were initiated so as to select those best qualified for positions, rather than have governmental positions filled via influence.

Increased emphasis on knowledge, science, and objective standards raised the status and changed the nature of certain professionals like doctors, lawyers, managers, professors, and journalists. Governments began to allow professionals to influence state policy and to determine rules for admission to their fields. However, it also had the effect of driving experienced amateurs, like midwives, out of their fields. Nation-building required major improvements in the education of all citizens, whether or not professional. Sunday school could not meet the state's needs. To cohere as citizens of a nation the young (poor as well as rich) had to learn their nation's language, literature, history, and responsibilities of citizenship. Bureaucrats and professionals called for radical changes in the scope, curriculum, and faculty of schools. Instruction in practical knowledge for careers in science and industry became available. Educational opportunities for women expanded thanks to the kindergarten movement and the opening to women students of some liberal arts and professional schools—like Girton and Newnham at Cambridge, and the medical programs at the universities in Zurich and Paris. But education for and by women remained controversial.

Native peoples often resisted the growing power of colonial officials but, frequently, this resistance led to the imposition of an even more powerful colonial government. Perhaps the best example of this phenomenon is the Indian (or Sepoy) Mutiny of 1857. Muslim and Hindu troops were forced to handle gun cartridges greased with animal fat, an affront to both religions. This fed into a rebellion over tightening British control. Smaller rebellions erupted, prompting the British to take over direct rule of India from the East India Company. Close to half a million Indians came to govern the Asian continent under the supervision of only a few thousand British men. Segregation between whites and the native Indians was enforced, and Britain forced India to supply it with cheap raw materials. The British frowned on infanticide, child marriages, and sati, and some upper-class Indians abandoned these practices. Some Indian families sent their children to England to be educated.

France worked to solidify control over Cochin China (modern southern Vietnam). Although French literature, theater, and art became popular among the Indochinese elite, France exploited the area economically, and imposed French models of urban planning on cities like Saigon. Napoleon III promoted the building of the Suez Canal which, when it opened (1869), popularized all things Egyptian. France occupied all of Algeria by 1870. Many native persons cooperated with the colonial powers, hoping for an improvement in their lives, but others resisted and engaged in attacks on soldiers and immigrant settlers.

Christian missionaries made inroads into a weak Qing China. Contact with the west stimulated the mass movement known as the Taiping (Heavenly Kingdom), which advocated an end to the Qing rule, the elimination of foreigners, improved equality for women, and land reform. The Qing regime requested French and British help in putting down the movement in exchange for granting greater influence in their country. The resulting civil war killed some 30 to 60 million Chinese and established western influence in China.

Japan, keen on industrial, military, and commercial innovations, fostered trade agreements with the United States and other countries. Japanese reformers forced the Tokugawa shogun to abdicate and, in 1868, the emperor was restored to full power. The emperor took the name Meiji ("enlightened rule") and worked to establish Japan as a modern, technologically advanced nation free from western control.

Realism dominated the era's fiction and art. Charles Dickens (1812–1870), gained both commercial and literary success with novels such as *Bleak House* (1852) and *Hard Times* (1856) depicting a broad array of social classes and their interlocking problems. George Eliot (pseudonym of Mary Ann Evans) examined contemporary moral values and deeply probed private, "real-life" dilemmas in such works as *Mill on the Floss* (1860) and *Middlemarch* (1871–1872). Many writers on the continent wrote about society as they experienced it then and often roused great controversy. Gustave Flaubert (1821–1880) described the emptiness of middle-class life in *Madame Bovary* (1857), in which a bored, small-town wife (Emma) turns to affairs, fads, and overspending to fulfill her Romantic longing. When Emma cannot pay her debts, she commits suicide. French poet Charles-Pierre Baudelaire shocked society when he wrote about sex explicitly. In Russia, Ivan Turgenev (1818–1883) explored the "generation gap" between nihilistic offspring of Romantic, idealistic parents in *Fathers and Sons* (1862). His contemporary, Fyodor Dostoevsky (1821–1881), whose novels include *Crime and Punishment* (1866), often wrote about the antihero who cannot find a suitable place in society. Visual artists also turned to realism. Gustave Courbet (1819–1877) often depicted laborers at backbreaking work. Édouard Manet (1823–1883) shocked polite society in works such as *Déjeuner sur l'herbe* (1863) and *Olympia* (1865) by painting nude women without mythologizing or romanticizing them. Operas, too, conveyed realism and reached large audiences. Giuseppe Verdi's (1813–1901) *La Traviata* (1853), about a courtesan who falls in love with a married man, stunned audiences. Richard Wagner (1813–1883) fused music and drama to arouse an audience's fear, awe, and engagement with his material. *Der Ring des Nibelungen*, one of four operas that make up the Ring Cycle, reshaped ancient German myths into a modern, nightmarish allegory of a world doomed by its obsessive pursuit of money and power, redeemable only through unselfish love. Wagner's *Tristan and Isolde* is infused with Buddhist ideas and imagery. Wagner and his works promoted a national, German culture and became a force in the realms of philosophy, politics, and art and helped unite a community with shared values.

Church and state clashed in the heated atmosphere of Realpolitik. Bismarck, alarmed at church influence, mounted a Kulturkampf against religion (1872–1887). The Jesuits were expelled from Germany (1872), state power over the clergy was increased in Prussia (1873), and obligatory civil marriages introduced (1875). Resistance to change and reform by the Catholic church was encapsulated by Pope Pius IX in *The Syllabus of Errors* (1864). In 1870, the First Vatican Council approved the doctrine of papal infallibility. But, in 1878, Pope Leo XIII began the process of reconciliation with reform by encouraging up-to-date scholarship in Catholic institutes and universities, and accepting aspects of democracy; this ended the Kulturkampf.

The place of organized religion in everyday life was changing—particularly among the workers and artisans. Spirituality was strong especially among women. In 1858, a young peasant girl, Bernadette Soubirous, began experiencing visions of the Virgin Mary at a grotto in Lourdes (southern France). At Mary's request, Bernadette began to dig and, later, a spring appeared. By 1867, a new railroad had transported millions of pilgrims to the site. Cultural unity of the nation-state could be achieved and enhanced by traditional institutions such as the church.

Charles Darwin (1809–1882), with the publication of *On the Origin of Species* (1859), had an impact that went far beyond the confines of the biological sciences. Darwin's ideas about evolution and natural selection called into question the literalness of the creation story in Genesis. In the 1860s, while working with pea plants, Gregor Mendel (1822–1884) was able to propound his theory of heredity. Subsequent German studies uncovered the principle of spontaneous ovulation from which scientists drew the erroneous conclusion that women were passive and lacked sexual feelings. Similar misconceptions occurred with Darwin's work. Darwin's theory—that all species struggled for survival—was mistakenly believed to also have implications for politics and social structures. Social Darwinism, a set of ideas based on Darwin's theories of evolution and struggle for survival, was used to justify ideas about the superiority of white, middle-class males were superior to all other races and females of any race.

Darwin's work encouraged people to accept Auguste Comte's (1798–1857) claims for "positivism"; that is, a careful study of facts would generate accurate, or "positive," laws of society. It was positivism that could solve the problems caused by economic and social change. This approach was especially attractive to women. Positivism led to the development of the social sciences, anthropology, psychology, economics, and sociology. The two major publications of John Stuart Mill (1806–1873)—*On Liberty* (1859) and *The Subjection of Women* (1869)—contributed in important ways to ideas about social reform, especially as it related to women. Unfortu-

nately, ideas associated with Social Darwinism overwhelmed the tolerant liberalism of writers like Mill. Even before *On the Origin of Species* had been published, Herbert Spencer (1820–1903), in *Social Statistics* (1851), promoted laissez-faire and unadulterated competition to weed out the "unfit" in society. Spencer opposed public education, social reform, and anything that would ease the harshness of the struggle to survive.

One result of government-sponsored education was a better-educated, more politically aware workforce. Secret worker organizations began to reform in the 1850s and embraced a variety of ideas. Pierre-Joseph Proudhon (1809–1865), under the rallying cry "Property is theft," called for society to be organized around natural groupings of men in artisan workshops that would lead to a mutualist society. There would be no formal government, and women would be confined to the home. Anarchism, which advocated the destruction of all state power, was also popular; Mikhail Bakunin (1814–1876) was one of its proponents. Believing that his theories about socialism were scientific, Karl Marx (1818–1883), in the 1860s, condemned doctrines like mutualism and anarchism as being emotional and wrongheaded. His position was especially clearly expressed in *Das Kapital.* Marx emphasized a materialist approach according to which the class relationships arising from work created the basis for everything else, including politics and culture. Where liberals saw the free market producing a harmony of interests, Marx saw the social organization of production (or mode of production) clashing eventually with the means of production. The workers (or the proletariats) would eventually revolt against their oppressors, Marx believed that a proletariat revolution would end private ownership of the means of production; this, in turn, would end class struggle. The possibilities Marx set forth inspired many working-class men to organize, but conditions of working-class life remained harsh.

The Paris Commune of 1871, in large part a reaction to the Haussmannization that had deprived the poor of their homes and workplaces, and to national political trends in the wake of defeat in the Franco-Prussian War, did involve a social revolution. Unfortunately, the Communards (members of the Paris Commune) disagreed on the means by which society could be changed. Despite Marx's recognition of the Commune, socialism was only one among the various routes considered by the Communards. The French provisional government sent troops into Paris at the end of May, and thousands were killed in the government's efforts to end the social experiment. Marx viewed the Commune as a class struggle between workers and upper-class interests, but women (traditional scapegoats in French society) were ultimately blamed for the Commune's rise. These events divided the country and created obstacles to national unity that would take decades to overcome.

Suggestions for Lecture and Discussion Topics

1. The unification of Germany under Bismarck is one of the most important topics covered in Chapter 23. Besides being an excellent example of realism in politics, it also provides an opportunity for students to become acquainted with the "German question." Germany quickly became the most powerful country in Europe in military, economic, and/or cultural terms. The German question refers to the implications for the rest of Europe of a very powerful, somewhat restless Germany. Bismarck was, of course, one of the great figures of the nineteenth century. The influence of his activities in the 1860s extended well into the following century.

There are many biographies of Bismarck available, but two biographies stand out: Lothar Gall, *Bismarck: The White Revolutionary*, 2 vols. (London: Allen & Unwin, 1986); and Otto Pflanze, *Bismarck and the Development of Germany*, 3 vols. (Princeton: Princeton University Press, 1990). Part 4 of James J. Sheehan's *German History, 1770–1866* (Oxford: Clarendon Press, 1989) covers developments in Germany between 1848 and 1866. The initial chapter in Gordon A. Craig, *Germany, 1866–1945* (New York: Oxford University Press, 1980) deals with the unification of Germany between 1866 and 1871. Chapter 5 of David Blackbourn, *The Long Nineteenth Century: A History of Germany, 1780–1918* (New York: Oxford University Press, 1998) is a highly useful discussion of German unification. A very different perspective on German unification may be found in the early chapters of Patricia Kollander, *Frederick III: Germany's Liberal Emperor* (Westport, CT: Greenwood Press, 1995). Frederick, the son of Wilhelm I, did not always agree with the policies of Bismarck and his father. See also the convenient selection of primary sources in Theodore S. Hamerow, ed., *The Age of Bismarck: Documents and Interpretations* (New York: Harper & Row, 1973). A good introduction to German unification and nation-building in general can be found in Chapter 7 of Robert Gildea, *Barricades and Borders, Europe 1800–1914* (Oxford: Oxford University Press, 1987).

2. The reorganization of Russia during this period is also of great importance. Although Alexander II was a reluctant reformer, he did realize the necessity of emancipating the serfs and so also instituted several other reforms which, under different circumstances, would have helped to create a Russian Empire far different from the one that eventually emerged.

On the emancipation of the serfs, see first Gregory L. Freeze, "Reform and Counter-Reform, 1855–1890," in Gregory L. Freeze, ed., *Russia: A History* (Oxford: Oxford University Press, 1997). Daniel Field, *The End of Serfdom* (Cambridge, MA: Harvard University Press, 1976) presents a good study of the give and take between the state and the nobility in working out emancipation. W. Bruce Lincoln, *The Great Reforms: Autocracy, Bureaucracy, and the Politics of Change in Imperial Russia* (DeKalb: Northern Illinois University Press, 1990) is the best overview. Lincoln was a prolific and highly readable writer on Russian history topics. Ben Eklof and John Bushnell, eds., *Russia's Great Reforms, 1855–1881* (Bloomington: University of Indiana Press, 1994) is an important collection of essays on the reforms. S. F. Starr, *Decentralization and Self-Government in Russia, 1830–1870* (Princeton: Princeton University Press, 1972) offers a good discussion of the *zemstvos'* reforms of the 1860s. Part 2 of Gregory L. Freeze, *From Supplication to Revolution: A Documentary Social History of Imperial Russia* (New York: Oxford University Press, 1988) brings together an excellent collection of documents on Russian society in the 1860s. Finally, Ivan Turgenev's great novel *Fathers and Sons* is useful in understanding the temper of the times in Russia. The Norton Critical Edition, Michael R. Katz, ed. (New York: W. W. Norton, 1995) reprints the novel along with many documents and critical essays.

3. Efforts to improve public health, particularly in urban areas, extended the power of the government to intervene in the lives of citizens in important ways. This topic has not yet been fully explored, but sufficient material is available for an interesting lecture and discussion. See first a book that explores the period when Edwin Chadwick, an English pioneer in the field of public health, was active: Christopher Hamlin, *Public Health and Social Justice in the Age of Chadwick, Britain, 1800–1854* (Cambridge: Cambridge University Press, 1998). Chadwick's own book, *The Sanitary Condition of the Laboring Population of Britain* (1842), paints a grim picture of working-class life, but also proposes a solution to the important problem of waste management. In addition, see also the study by Jean-Pierre Goubert, *The Conquest of Water: The Advent of Health in the Industrial Age* (Princeton: Princeton University Press, 1989). Somewhat more specialized, but full of fascinating material, is Donald Reid, *Paris Sewers and Sewermen: Realities and Representations* (Cambridge, MA: Harvard University Press, 1993). Two books deal with theories about disease: Michael Worboys, *Spreading Germs: Diseases, Theories, and Medical Practice in Britain, 1865–1900* (Cambridge: Cambridge University Press, 2000); and Andrew Robert Aisenberg, *Contagion: Disease, Government, and the "Social Question" in Nineteenth-Century France* (Palo Alto, CA: Stanford University Press, 1999). See also Patrice Debre's highly useful biography of the father of the germ theory: *Louis Pasteur* (Baltimore: Johns Hopkins University Press, 1998).

4. Much has been written about the British in India. A good beginning is Stanley Wolpert, *A New History of India*, 6th ed. (New York: Oxford University Press, 1999). Another good survey is that by Judith M. Brown, *Modern India: The Origins of an Asian Democracy*, 2d ed. (Oxford: Oxford University Press, 1994). A more specialized study is David Arnold, *Colonizing the Body: State*

Medicine and Epidemic Disease in Nineteenth-Century India (Berkeley: University of California Press, 1993). Arnold discusses not only the introduction of western medicine to India, but also efforts to adjust western practices to Indian customs and expectations. Thomas R. Metcalf, *Ideologies of the Raj* (Cambridge: Cambridge University Press, 1994) covers the various attempts to justify British rule in India. Rajnarayan Chandavarkar, *Imperial Power and Popular Politics: Class, Resistance, and the State in India, c. 1850–1950* (Cambridge: Cambridge University Press, 1998) examines an aspect of colonialism in India not often discussed: the growth of industrial capitalism and a working class.

5. The theories of Charles Darwin have, in one way or another, virtually taken over many disciplines in the past few years. Even during Darwin's lifetime, Social Darwinism was a powerful force. Students should be introduced to Darwin's life, career, and main ideas. Although his life after the voyage on the *Beagle* was one of few excitements, there were enough interesting developments, particularly after the publication of *On the Origin of Species*, to make a review of his career useful and interesting. A good place to begin is Janet Browne, *Charles Darwin: Voyaging* (Princeton: Princeton University Press, 1995), a very fine biography that concentrates largely on the voyage of *HMS Beagle* but also continues the story into the 1850s. Another useful source is Philip Appleman, *Darwin: A Norton Critical Edition*, 3d ed. (New York: W. W. Norton, 2000), which includes writings by Darwin and writings about him. Another Norton publication along these lines is Mark Ridley, ed., *The Darwin Reader*, 2d ed. (New York: W. W. Norton, 1996). See also *The Autobiography of Charles Darwin*, reissue ed. (New York: W. W. Norton, 1993); and Frederick Burkhardt, ed., *Charles Darwin's Letters: A Selection, 1825–1859* (Cambridge: Cambridge University Press, 1998). Helpful for placing Darwin's ideas in the context of his times is Michael Ruse, *The Darwinian Revolution: Science Red in Tooth and Claw* (Chicago: University of Chicago Press, 1999). Mike Hawkins, *Social Darwinism in European and American Thought, 1860–1945: Nature As Model and Nature As Threat* (Cambridge: Cambridge University Press, 1997) will be invaluable for tracing the influence of Darwin's ideas. Also on the subject of influence, see Peter J. Bowler, *Charles Darwin: The Man and His Influence* (Cambridge: Cambridge University Press, 1996). A biography of Thomas Henry Huxley by Adrian J. Desmond, *Huxley: From Devil's Disciple to Evolution's High Priest* (Reading, MA: Addison-Wesley, 1997) is useful in tracing the spread of Darwin's ideas by one of his chief admirers.

6. Karl Marx and John Stuart Mill are perhaps the two most important political thinkers of the 1850s and 1860s. Marx has, of course, received far more attention than Mill. On Marx, see first David McLellan, *Karl Marx:*

His Life and Thought (New York: Harper & Row, 1973), probably the best book overall, but long. A recent, highly readable biography of Marx is Francis Wheen, *Karl Marx: A Life* (New York: W. W. Norton, 2000). Wheen is good on providing biographical data, but not always dependable in his discussion of Marx's ideas. Isaiah Berlin, *Karl Marx: His Life and Environment*, 3d ed. (New York: Oxford University Press, 1963) is a very good, short study. Jerrold Seigel, *Marx's Fate: The Shape of a Life* (University Park: Pennsylvania State University Press, 1993) is a difficult, but rewarding biographical study. A very informative source is Terrell Carver, ed., *The Cambridge Companion to Marx* (Cambridge: Cambridge University Press, 1992). The best anthology of Marx's writings (and Friedrich Engels's as well) is Robert C. Tucker, *The Marx-Engels Reader*, 2d ed. (New York: W. W. Norton, 1978). Also useful is Eugene Kamenka, *The Portable Karl Marx* (New York: Penguin Books, 1983). Robert C. Tucker, *The Marxian Revolutionary Idea* (New York: W. W. Norton, 1969) is an excellent overview of Marxist theory.

For Mill, a good place to begin is William Stafford, *John Stuart Mill* (New York: St. Martin's Press, 1999). John Skorupski, *The Cambridge Companion to Mill* (Cambridge: Cambridge University Press, 1997) has much to offer. Anthologies include Alan Ryan, ed., *Mill: Texts, Commentaries* (New York: W. W. Norton, 1996); and David Spitz, ed., *On Liberty: Annotated Text, Sources and Background, Criticism* (New York: W. W. Norton, 1975). See also John Stuart Mill, Harriet Hardy Taylor Mill, and Helen Mill, *Sexual Equality: A John Stuart Mill, Harriet Taylor Mill, and Helen Taylor Reader* (Toronto: University of Toronto Press, 1994); and Harriet Taylor Mill, *The Complete Works of Harriet Taylor Mill* (Bloomington: Indiana University Press, 1998).

Making Connections

1. *How did realism in social thought break with Enlightenment values?* Philosophes of the Enlightenment intellectualized the problems of the world, whereas realists took action and dealt with the world as they found it, whether it was the Realpolitik politician, who did what he had to do to achieve his goals (like Bismarck and unification); or the artist, who depicted in excruciating detail the lives of the working poor (like Dickens in his many novels). Stimulated by the thinking of Charles Darwin, positivism grew out of the attempt to understand the world outside religious constraints. It was believed that social scientists could construct knowledge of the political order as they would an understanding of the natural world; that is, according to informed secular investigation. This idea inspired persons to believe that they could resolve the social problems spawned by economic and social change.

2. *Some nation-states tended to follow secularism. Earlier kingdoms were, however, based on religion. Why do you believe this was true?* Religion was the legitimizing force for rulers in early, modern kingdoms; whereas nation-states, like Germany and Italy, were based on the secular concepts of nationalism and Realpolitik. National unity was based mainly on such things as language and culture.

3. *How did the Paris Commune relate to earlier revolutions in France? How did it differ?* As with previous French uprisings, the situation seemed dire prior to the establishment of the Paris Commune. Prussian forces marched on Paris and, lacking bare necessities, the citizens demanded republican reforms. The provisional government, set up after the departure of Napoleon III, reacted in a typical, traditional way: troops were dispatched to quell the unrest. The Paris Commune was declared in the face of this military threat from Prussia but, as in the past, commune leaders argued over how to proceed, which gave the provisional government time to take action. The Paris Commune was suppressed, as were those communes that had been formed in other French cities. As with earlier revolutions, there was a good deal of violence involved on both sides of the conflict. And, as with the French Revolution, the worst of the atrocities committed during the commune were later blamed on women agitators.

Writing Assignments and Class Presentation Topics

1. Ask students to reflect on Bismarck's actions during the process of unifying Germany. To what extent was he merely attempting to resolve the constitutional crisis by demonstrating the value of the Prussian military reforms? Was it important to Bismarck to enhance the prestige of the Hohenzollern dynasty? to increase the power of Prussia? Why or why not? Why did Bismarck decide it was necessary to create the German Empire as such?

You may wish to assign students short selections from one or more of the biographies and studies mentioned in "Suggestions for Lecture and Discussion Topics," number 1. Excerpts from primary sources would also be helpful. See the convenient collection of material in Theodore S. Hamerow, ed., *The Age of Bismarck: Documents and Interpretations* (New York: Harper & Row, 1973).

2. Student presentations on different aspects of the 1860s in Russia offer many possibilities. Students might report on the process by which the government decided to emancipate the serfs, on the other major reforms, on the Polish revolt of 1863, and on the individuals most closely associated with the reforms. The chapter by Gregory L. Freeze mentioned in "Suggestions for Lecture and Discussion Topics," number 2, is a good place to

begin. Students will find Joseph Wieczenski, ed., *The Modern Encyclopedia of Russian and Soviet History*, 60 vols. (Gulf Breeze, FL: Academic International Press, 1976–1996) indispensable.

3. Have students write a short essay describing why there was intense interest in the 1850s and 1860s in realism in fiction. It may be useful to remind students about the overwhelming influence of the idea of Realpolitik in national and international politics and the fascination with scientific and technological advances, especially after the publication of *On the Origin of Species*. To provide focus to the essay, students should refer to the work of realist novelists, such as Charles Dickens and George Eliot.

4. Assign students a three-part essay in which they are to summarize the views of Marx, Mill and, in the third part, point out the ways in which these two men differed. Preface the assignment with an in-class discussion of the views of Marx and Mill. During the discussion, help students understand that Marx presented a complete picture of human history moving inexorably to a predetermined end by means of revolution. Mill, by contrast, subscribed to change, reform, and progress, but presented no overarching picture or predetermined end.

Research Assignments

1. A comparative study of serfdom in Russia with slavery in the United States offers a challenging assignment. Students' studies might compare living and working conditions of serfs with those of slaves; investigate the possibilities for gaining freedom in the period before emancipation in each country; compare the impact of Harriet Beecher Stowe's *Uncle Tom's Cabin* with that of Ivan Turgenev's *A Hunter's Sketches*; or examine the realities of the period after emancipation as experienced by serfs and slaves. Published comparative works are available. Students may wish to begin with Peter Kolchin, *Unfree Labor: American Slavery and Russian Serfdom* (Cambridge, MA: Belknap Press, 1987).

2. During this period, society and government devoted much energy to achieving social order. Students might investigate efforts to eradicate venereal disease. These efforts always involved issues of gender, class, and power. A good starting point would be Bonnie Smith, *Changing Lives: Women in European History Since 1700* (Lexington, MA: D. C. Heath, 1989), Chapter 4, "The Rise of the Woman Worker: The Early Years," and the bibliography for the chapter. See also Peter Gay, *The Tender Passion*, vol. 2 of *The Bourgeois Experience: Victoria to Freud* (New York: Oxford University Press, 1986); Chapter 6, "The Price of Repression," and the relevant section of Gay's bibliographical essay. There are, of course, several other good, country-specific studies available in print.

3. Another sphere in which it was thought that order and control could be brought to bear was on the homefront. Have students research the subject of domestic life in Victorian England, looking first at Mrs. Beeton's *Book of Household Management* (1861). What sort of instructions does Mrs. Beeton give to housewives? How practical would Mrs. Beeton's advice have been at that time? How does "class" figure into Mrs. Beeton's worldview? Compare these instructions to 1950s exhortations to American housewives. Are there any similarities? Would Mrs. Beeton's instructions resonate anywhere in the world today? See Nicola Humble, ed., *Mrs. Beeton's Book of Household Management* (Oxford: Oxford University Press, 2000). In a related subject, have students research the subject of manners—especially food and table etiquette in Victorian England. How had food preparation and storage changed since the beginning of the century? How was food served and eaten at the table in the mid-Victorian period? What role did science and technology play in the changes in food and how people consumed it during this period? Students can begin with Maggie Black, *Food and Cooking in Nineteenth-Century Britain: History and Recipes* (English Heritage, 1985); and Pamela A. Sambrook and Peter Brears, eds., *The Country House Kitchen 1650–1900* (Glourcestershire: Alan Sutton [in association with the National Trust], 1997).

4. Ask students to research and compare the careers of Florence Nightingale and Mrs. Seacole, the daughter of a free, black, Jamaican woman and a Scottish army officer. What were Nightingale's contributions to the medical field? Mrs. Seacole's contributions? Why did Mrs. Seacole, quite well known in her own time through her medical work and her autobiography, *not* become the same kind of iconic figure as Florence Nightingale? Were class and race factors in their achievements and how they are remembered by posterity?

5. Have students research the subject of realism in art in the 1850s and 1860s. What was meant by *realism*? What were John Ruskin's opinions on the subject? What role did scientific and technological advances play in artists' work? How did the pre-Raphaelite movement fit into their desire to depict realism? Compare the work of pre-Raphaelite painters such as Dante Gabriel Rossetti, John Everett Millais, and William Holman Hunt with the work of continental painters, such as Gustave Courbet and Édouard Manet.

Literature

Ashton, Rosemanry, ed., *George Eliot:* Middlemarch. 1994.

Bair, Lowell, trans., *Gustave Flaubert:* Madame Bovary. 1982.

Dubas, Danielle, ed., *Charles Dickens: Four Complete Novels:* Great Expectations, Hard Times, A Christmas Carol, A Tale of Two Cities. 2003.

Katz, Michael R., trans., *Ivan Turgenev:* Fathers and Sons. 1995.

Magarshack, David, trans., *Fyodor M. Dostoevsky:* The Possessed. 1954.

McGowan, James, trans., *Charles Baudelaire: "The Flowers of Evil."* 1998.

Pevear, Richard and Larissa Volokhonsky, trans., *Fyodor Dostoevsky:* The Brothers Karamazov. 2002.

Sklar, Kathryn Kish, ed., *Harriet Beecher Stowe: Three Novels:* Uncle Tom's Cabin Or, Life Among the Lowly; The Minister's Wooing; Oldtown Folks. 1982.

Films and Videos

Edward the King (1975; VHS, approx. 13 hrs.). This thirteen-part series (approximately 1 hour each part) chronicles the life of King Edward VII of England. It is strong on detail and the plot, costumes, and settings are vibrant and realistic.

A Tale of Two Cities (1991; VHS/DVD, 3 hrs., 15 min.). Charles Dickens's 1857 novel diverges from his other works in that it is an epic tale of love and sacrifice during the French Revolution. It is particularly interesting for its Victorian perspective on the Revolution some sixty-five years later. This film is largely faithful to the novel.

Wives and Daughters (1999; PBS, VHS/DVD, approx. 6 hrs.) An adaptation of Elizabeth Gaskell's 1864–1866 novel about a young woman tried by her father's remarriage and initially rebuffed in love.

Victoria and Albert (2001; VHS/DVD, 3 hrs., 20 min.). This is a highly entertaining and largely factual biographical dramatization of Queen Victoria and her husband, Prince Albert during their married years. Care has been lavished on the costumes and sets.

Charles Dickens (2003; DVD, 8 hrs., 30 min.). This three-part series examines Dickens's life and the motivations behind his writings. Dickens's overwhelming concern for the poor, who suffered most from industrialization, is especially emphasized.

Virtually all of Charles Dickens's novels have been dramatized, some of them several times over. Like the novels, the films capture the vagaries of fortune and the hardship of life for the Victorian poor and impoverished. In the following list (arranged chronologically by date of publication), the date that immediately follows the title refers to the date of its first publication.

Oliver Twist (1837–1838). (1997; VHS, 6 hrs.)

Nicholas Nickleby (1838–1839). (2002; VHS/DVD, approx. 3 hrs., 20 min.)

Martin Chuzzlewit (1843–1844). (1994; VHS, 4 hrs., 48 min.)

David Copperfield (1849–1850). (2000; VHS/DVD, approx. 3 hrs.)

Bleak House (1852–1853). (1988; VHS, 6 hrs., 31 min.)

Hard Times (1854). (1994; VHS, 1 hr., 42 min.)

Little Dorrit (1855–1857). (1988; VHS, 6 hrs.)

Great Expectations (1860–1861). (2001; VHS, 3 hrs.)

Our Mutual Friend (1864–1865). (1998; VHS/DVD, approx. 5 hrs., 30 min.)

Historical Skills

Map 23.2, Unification of Italy, 1859–1870, p. 882

Ask students to use this map as a basis for discussing the extent to which Cavour's plans for unification succeeded. Help them understand that it was not only a matter of the territories remaining outside the new kingdom of Italy (Venetia, Rome), it was also the incorporation of southern Italy that would have to figure in any assessment of Cavour's plans and activities.

Map 23.3, Unification of Germany, 1862–1871, p. 885

Ask students to use this map as a basis for discussing Bismarck's actions and intentions during the unification process of Germany. Have students particularly discuss the differences between the outcome of the Austro-Prussian War of 1866 — that is, the North German Confederation, and the Franco-Prussian War of 1870 — the German Empire.

Mapping the West: *Europe and the Mediterranean, 1871, p. 910*

Ask students to consider the consequences of a Europe organized into nation-states. Is there any room left for nations to expand without interfering with the interests of other nations? The only area left in Europe proper was in southeastern Europe: the Balkans. As the Ottoman Empire continued to decline, this area grew in its importance to both major and minor powers.

The Mission of Mercy, p. 878

Why, in an era when most persons and countries were perceived as being realistic and/or tough-minded, are the images of Florence Nightingale generally romantic? Is it part of an effort to find room for a woman taking on unexpected responsibilities? Or is it simply a tendency to see great individual figures as different from ordinary human beings?

Emperor William I of Germany, 1871, p. 884

Contrast this painting with the painting of Napoleon III and his court (*Napoleon III and Eugénie Receive the Siamese Ambassadors*, p. 876). What impression do we gain of the new German Empire from the one painting and of the re-created Napoleonic empire from the other? These paintings might also be compared to the photograph of Queen Victoria and Prince Albert (p. 889).

Vienna Opera House, p. 892; and Paris Sewer, p. 893

How did the opera house and the sewer, each in its own way, contribute to the quality of life in Vienna? Should one be seen as more important than the other? Were they complementary? Explain why.

Édouard Manet, Déjeuner sur l'herbe (Luncheon on the Grass), 1863, p. 902

What is more provocative about this painting: that the men are fully clothed and the women are not? That the scene is one of everyday life and not drawn from history or mythology? What does the painting suggest about women's sexuality?

Woman Incendiary, p. 909

Compare this illustration to the painting of Florence Nightingale (*The Mission of Mercy* [p. 878]). To what extent is this illustration a comment on common ideas about women's place as well as an illustration of "the disorderliness of the commune's resistance to the state"?

Mrs. Seacole: The Other Florence Nightingale, p. 879

The common interests and yet radically different experiences of these two women could be the subject of a discussion. Both women were exceptionally knowledgeable about nursing but, while Nightingale worked under the auspices of the British army during the Crimean War, racial prejudice kept Seacole on the sidelines in an unofficial capacity. When her personal savings ran out, Seacole had to charge soldiers for her services. Well known and well funded, Nightingale established nursing organizations and continued her nursing work after the war; whereas the lesser-known Seacole was virtually destitute. Only a public appeal for funds and the publication of her autobiography saved Seacole from utter poverty.

OTHER BEDFORD/ST. MARTIN'S RESOURCES FOR CHAPTER 23

The following resources are available to accompany Chapter 23. Please refer to the Preface of this manual for detailed descriptions of all the ancillaries.

For Instructors

Transparencies

The following maps and images from Chapter 23 are available as full-color acetates.

- Map 23.1: The Crimean War, 1853–1856
- Map 23.2: Unification of Italy, 1859–1870
- Map 23.3: Unification of Germany, 1862–1871
- Map 23.4: U.S. Expansion, 1850–1870
- Map 23.5: The Paris Commune, 1871
- Mapping the West: Europe and the Mediterranean, 1871
- *Darwin Ridiculed*
- *Napoleon III and Eugenie Receive the Siamese Ambassadors*

Instructor's Resources CD-ROM

The following maps and image from Chapter 23, as well as a chapter outline, are available on disc in both PowerPoint and jpeg formats.

- Map 23.1: The Crimean War, 1853–1856
- Map 23.2: Unification of Italy, 1859–1870
- Map 23.3: Unification of Germany, 1862–1871
- Map 23.4: United States Expansion, 1850–1870
- Map 23.5: The Paris Commune, 1871
- Mapping the West: Europe and the Mediterranean, 1871
- *Darwin Ridiculed*

For Students

Sources of The Making of the West

The following documents are available in Chapter 23 of the companion sourcebook by Katharine J. Lualdi, University of Southern Maine.

1. Rudolf von Ihering, *Two Letters* (1866)
2. Peter Kropotkin, *Memoirs of a Revolutionist* (1899)
3. Krupa Sattianadan, *Saguna: A Story of Native Christian Life* (1887–1888)
4. Charles Darwin, *The Descent of Man* (1871)

Study Guides

The print **Study Guide** and the **Online Study Guide** at bedfordstmartins.com/hunt, both by Victoria Thompson (Arizona State University) and Eric Johnson (University of California, Los Angeles), help students synthesize the material they have learned as well as practice the skills historians use to make sense of the past. The following Map, Visual, and Document activities are available for Chapter 23.

Map Activity

- Map 23.1: The Crimean War, 1853–1956

Visual Activity

- *Darwin Ridiculed*

Reading Historical Documents

- Mrs. Seacole: The Other Florence Nightingale
- Bismarck Tricks the Public to Get His War

Industry, Empire, and Everyday Life
1870–1890

CHAPTER RESOURCES

Main Chapter Topics

1. A series of downturns in business, beginning in 1873, created problems for both entrepreneurs and the working classes. Businesspersons, in search of answers, turned to innovation, new managerial techniques, and significant changes in marketing techniques, such as the department store. Advances in industry and the rise of a consumer economy changed the working lives of millions.

2. The "new imperialism," which brought direct rule by European nations to Africa and Asia, was closely connected with both industrial prosperity and the formation of national identity.

3. The middle classes prospered, enjoyed travel, and invested in their children's education. For millions in the working class, emigration presented possibilities for a new, perhaps better, life overseas or in the city.

4. In the 1870s and 1880s, artists and writers explored the results of imperialism and industrialization using techniques associated with realism. These individuals sometimes interpreted results on the basis of a gloomy Social Darwinism that focused on decline and degeneration perhaps as much as on progress.

5. The expansion of the franchise, still limited to men during this period, marked the beginnings of mass politics. Other characteristics of mass politics included extensive election campaigns, political clubs, and other organizations designed to mobilize voters; and the ready availability of inexpensive newspapers.

6. To differing extents, mass politics and the phenomena associated with it did not develop fully in Germany, Austria-Hungary, and Russia.

Summary

The decades between 1870 to 1890 were an era of industry and empire in the west. Western powers rapidly expanded farther into Africa and Asia. Emigration increased and, in this "new imperialism," European countries tried to imprint other continents with European names of places, architecture, clothing, language, and customs. Urban populations became more self-aware and more informed by reading inexpensive newspapers and took common pride in their nation's expansion.

Innovations in products, technologies, and commerce characterized nineteenth-century Europe. New products included the bicycle, the internal combustion engine, and the telephone. The application and uses of electricity varied widely during this period. Leading industrial nations—out of necessity—mined massive amounts of coal and iron ore and produced large quantities of iron and steel. Outwork, where products like porcelain painting were finished at individuals' homes, persisted in some economic sectors. Industrial innovations—from chemical fertilizers to barbed wire to refrigeration technology—transformed agriculture.

Both Germany and the United States challenged Britain's predominance of industry. Germany, which spent as much money on education as it did on the military, developed productive electrical and chemical engineering industries. The United States benefited from its vast natural resources and from the resourcefulness of citizen-entrepreneurs like Andrew Carnegie (1835–1919) and John D. Rockefeller (1839–1937). French industry grew steadily, but remained less extensive than that of the three leading industrial powers. In other countries, such as Spain, Austria-Hungary, and Italy, industry was primarily a local phenomenon. Although Scandinavia remained largely rural in character, Sweden and Norway did become leaders in hydroelectric power and the development of electrical products. Russia made considerable progress in the latter part of the century, especially in railroads, and the metallurgical and mining industries—yet, all came at the expense of the peasantry.

Despite innovation and expansion, this period was mainly characterized by the crisis of 1873, which, in turn, was followed by almost three decades of economic fluctuations. Economic downturns resulted primarily from industrial and financial setbacks rather than from crop failures, as had been the case earlier; and downturns were felt globally because world economies were interdependent. Part of the problem stemmed from the fact that economists at that time did not understand just how interrelated economies had become. Economic difficulties were further exacerbated by the high start-up costs of new enterprises, which were becoming increasingly capital-intensive rather than labor-intensive. A second problem concerned the extent to which supply outpaced demand. Limited liability corporations and new sources of capital invested in the stock market were two responses to economic problems. Another response was cartels and trusts, which were formed to control prices and impede or reduce competition. When imports began exceeding exports, high deficits wee incurred. Governments therefore ended free trade and imposed tariffs on imported goods. Companies employed managers who specialized in one aspect of their business, such as sales and distribution. Workplaces also depended on increasing numbers of "white-collar" workers — secretaries, file clerks, and typists —to guide the flow of business data. Office workers were increasingly women. This trend was part of a process in which certain categories of jobs were predominantly filled by men and other categories of jobs were filled by women. This also marked widespread pay inequities, where women were paid less than men, sometimes even for performing the same tasks.

The department store introduced consumption on a scale never before possible for an average individual. Department stores set out to create demand by appealing mostly to women who, after all, were enjoined by the cult of domesticity to enhance their homes and the lives of their families. Glossy, mail-order catalogues brought the luxuries of the department store to rural communities. Imperial ventures added many items to the lists of products that had become available for mass consumption.

Fueled in part by a desire for profit and also by the connections made between imperial expansion and national identity, European nations competed for territory in Africa and Asia. In 1879, Britain and France seized Egypt's treasury as security for their investments in the Suez Canal and in other businesses. In 1882, ostensibly to put down Egyptian nationalists who protested the seizing of their government's treasury, Britain took control of Egypt's government. Britain ran Egypt from behind the scenes, reshaping its economy to suit British interests at the expense of the rural population, which barely eked out a living. The French extended their control over Algeria and occupied Tunisia (1881). An influx of cheap consumer goods drove skilled artisans into low-paying employment, such as building railroads or processing tobacco. British, French, and German businessmen sowed anti-colonial seeds by basing local wages—not on gender, as in Europe, but on ethnicity and religion: Muslims were paid less than Christians, and Arabs less than other ethnic minorities.

In the 1880s, European powers jockeyed to dominate the peoples and lands of sub-Saharan Africa. King Leopold II of Belgium (r. 1865–1909) claimed the Congo region of central Africa, provoking competition with the French. Bismarck perceived colonies as political bargaining chips. The British were consolidating their position "from Cairo to Cape Town."

Bismarck attempted to defuse tension among the European powers through a series of meetings in Berlin (1884, 1885). One major decision allowed those nations occupying lands along a coast to claim territory in the interior. Alien nations (imperial powers) paid no attention to indigenous boundaries when establishing colonies. European technology might be used to save lives, as with the use of quinine in the treatment of malaria; or to take lives, as with newly developed machine guns. The result, in any case, was further European expansion. Cecil Rhodes (1853–1902), initially going to South Africa for his health, cornered the diamond market there and claimed for Britain a vast interior territory that was later named Rhodesia in his honor (Zambia and Zimbabwe today). Concepts of European racial superiority (Social Darwinism) were used to justify conquest and political control. Europeans considered native Africans barely civilized, and ruled as if local traditions of political and economic life did not exist. Europeans seized land and forced Africans to work for them.

The expansion of European power also took place on the Asian continent. In India, colonial rule meant not only direct rule, but also considerable intervention in everyday life. Half a million Indians governed India under the supervision of only a few thousand British men. Britain forced an end to any indigenous production of goods that competed with British manufacturing, and required India to supply that country instead with cheap, raw materials. Many Indians came to reject their native customs such as child marriage or *sati*, which required a widow to immolate herself on her husband's funeral pyre. However, British rule also led to segregation and to the relegation of all Indians to an inferior status. In 1885, the Indian elite founded the Indian National Congress—the center of a new Indian nationalism—which successfully challenged the British in the following century.

Britain took control of the Malay peninsula (1874) and of the interior of Burma (1885), thus securing those regions tin, oil, rice, teak, and rubber, as well as interior trade routes to China. British colonization in Asia was intended to counter the activities of other European countries. Russia was absorbing small, Muslim states in central Asia (such as Turkestan) and extending its influence in Persia, India, and China. France consolidated the ancient states of Cambodia, Tonkin, Annam, and Cochin China into the Union of Indochina (1887). Although French literature, theater, and art became popular among the Indochinese elite, France exploited the area economically, and imposed French models of urban planning on cities like Saigon.

Japan escaped the "new" European imperialism by its rapid transformation, after the Meiji Restoration (1868), into a modern, industrial nation with its own imperial agenda. The Japanese state embraced certain aspects of Western culture. Western-style clothing became requisite at the imperial court, and samurai traditions—such as spiritual discipline and the drive to excel—were adapted for a technologically modern military. A constitution drafted in 1889 along German models emphasized state power over individual rights. The state stimulated economic development by building railroads and shipyards, and establishing financial institutions. When the state exhausted its finances, it auctioned off its businesses to private entrepreneurs, like Iwasaki Yataro (founder of Mitsubishi), to develop heavy industries like mining and shipping. As with Europe, patriotism fed into the rise of Japan's industry and the country's increasing intervention in Asia.

The European powers practiced imperialism for various reasons. Its economic benefits were uneven, considerable for port cities and some manufacturing sectors, for example, but a tax burden for many citizens. Imperialism provided a means of displaying national might, but could also lead to disastrous war. Some Europeans viewed imperialism as bringing Christianity and the blessings of "civilization" to inferior colonial peoples. A few romanticized the colonial peoples as somehow unspoiled by civilization. The paradox was, of course, that Europeans who believed in national independence in their home country denied that right to the peoples whose territories they invaded.

In Europe, new middle-class persons joined the upper classes, or "best" circles. The line between aristocrat and bourgeois became blurred; both by the awarding of titles to outstanding members of the middle classes and by usually arranged marriages between aristocrats and the *nouveau riche* ("newly rich"). The wealthiest members of the middle classes lived like the aristocracy and indulged in conspicuous consumption. Big-game hunting became an important way to parade wealth and prove masculinity.

The lives of upper-class women involved marrying within their own social sphere, having and raising children, directing staffs of servants, and maintaining standards of etiquette and conduct. Furnishing the home, overseeing the creation and maintenance of gardens, and keeping up with fashions in clothing occupied much of their time. Some women were also active outside their

homes in religious and philanthropic activities. The middle class was expanding and, for them, domesticity substituted cleanliness and polish for upper-class conspicuous consumption.

Professional sports attracted increasing attention from all sectors of society. Support of a soccer, rugby, or cricket team brought together people who otherwise had little in common and provided a diversion from daily life. Bicycle races and then automobile races proved very popular with much of the population. Individual and team sports were viewed as important for national well-being and strength. Sports activities also promoted a social order based on a distinction between the sexes. Women, for example, played field hockey or rode horses, whereas men played rugby or raced horses. The middle classes often pursued sports that were seen as edifying as well as fun. The lower classes adopted middle-class habits and used trains or river steamships as means to enjoy fresh air, exercise, and rural locales.

Emigration was a major phenomenon during this period. Millions left their homelands to begin over again in more prosperous areas, such as North and South America, Australia, or New Zealand, or to participate in colonial administrations in Asia and Africa. Immigrants arrived in large numbers from Sicily, Ireland, and central Europe, including Russia where many immigrants were Jews who were fleeing brutal pogroms (systematic anti-Semitic attacks). Railroads and steamship lines played a large part in promoting emigration. Once established, immigrants often sent money back to their families in their home countries. Immigrant men and children were more likely than women, who stayed within the home, to adapt to a new foreign language and culture. Internal migration to the rapidly growing cities was even more common than emigration overseas. Migrants to cities often went seasonally, returning home for the harvest.

Changes in technology and management practices required changes in work patterns. Workers complained about the need to work harder and faster, but also about the proliferation of managers who sometimes sexually harassed women workers. These changes and practices sometimes devalued old skills while simultaneously demanding new skills, and frequently created large categories of unskilled workers who received minimal pay. Even worse off were the many outworkers, many of whom were women, who remained at home working for low piece rates. They were among the first to be laid off during slack periods. Middle- and upper-class reformers and reform groups worked to alleviate working-class problems by establishing settlement houses and maternal and child welfare societies. The Fabian Society, founded in London in 1884, was committed to socialism via reform and state planning rather than revolution, and founded the Labor Party (1893) as a way of incorporating social improvement into politics. Some reformers were motivated by a sense of Christian mission, others were impelled by a Social Darwinist argument: a strong, competitive nation required all its citizens to be healthy and hardworking. Reformers paid particular attention to the health and well-being of women, and this included the dissemination of information about contraception. It was believed that small, working-class families had the best chance to survive the rigors of urban life, although the church was against birth control and the reformers themselves were divided on the issue. Reproductive issues also fed into restrictions placed on women's labor. Women were barred from night work and other jobs that they had done previously, like pottery work, were now deemed "dangerous." These and other jobs were now closed to them, the result being that it became even more difficult for women to earn a living.

Industrialization and imperialism often led artists and writers to view their society pessimistically. Émile Zola (1840–1902), for example, produced a series of novels about a French family plagued by alcoholism and madness. The environment — in particular, the urban, industrial environment — was a powerful factor in shaping human lives in Zola's novels. Although it shocked audiences, playwright Henrik Ibsen (1828–1906) allowed his character Nora in *A Doll's House* (1879) to find the courage to leave a loveless and oppressive marriage. Writers envisioned a widespread deterioration that threatened all society. Emilia Pardo Bazan (1859–1921) penned dramas of incest and murder among wealthy, landowning families in rural Spain. The main character in Thomas Hardy's *The Mayor of Casterbridge* (1886) sells his wife at a market. He later rises to a local position of importance, but loses everything when his past catches up to him. The heroine of Olive Schreiner's (1855–1920 [pseudonym, Ralph Iron]) *The Story of an African Farm* (1889) rejects the role of submissive housewife in rural Africa.

The "arts and crafts" movement was a reaction to industrialization. Folk motifs attracted architects and designers who turned to rural artistic styles for models of household goods, decorative objects, and clothing. William Morris (1834–1896) and his daughter May Morris (1862–1938) were leaders in this movement and produced fabrics, wallpaper, and household items based on natural styles and motifs. The emphasis on "craft" harkened back to earlier periods when goods were handmade.

Visual artists consciously sought to make painting differ from photography while continuing to comment on social issues and urban realities. Postimpressionist Georges Seurat (1859–1891) applied pigment to his canvas via tiny dots (pointillism) to depict white-collar workers dressed in their store-bought clothing with their bicycles, books, and newspapers, spending their Sunday leisure time in the park. Edgar Degas (1834–1917) depicted women—from ballet dancers to laundresses—in various states of exertion and fatigue. The fuzzy lines of

Degas's paintings capture the mental haze of physical labor. Édouard Manet (1832–1883) often painted scenes of urban life, and it was from his work that the term "impressionism" derived. It described the artist's attempt to capture a single moment by focusing on the ever-changing light and color found in ordinary scenes. Impressionists moved away from the precise realism of earlier painters. Claude Monet (1840–1926) was fascinated by the way light transformed an object and often painted the same locale at several different times of the day. Vincent Van Gogh (1853–1890) loaded his painting knife with vibrant colors and thickly applied his oils to canvas using emphatic swirls that distorted reality. Industry and science helped create this style through the development of a wider ranger of colors and paints that could be used outdoors. Artists like Monet, Degas, Van Gogh, and the American ex-patriot, Mary Cassatt (1845–1926), were also highly influenced by Asian art and drew on the Japanese concept of *mono no aware* (serenity before and sensitivity to the fleetingness of life).

Although different groups of workers responded to nationalistic messages, the working class as a whole found ways to strive for better working conditions and rates of pay. Unions, often with Marxist platforms, formed at national and transnational levels. From the 1880s onward, the pace of collective action for better pay, lower prices, and improved working conditions accelerated. The new unionism of the 1880s established national organizations that brought together workers in differing sectors of the economy. As workers went on strike for better working conditions, housewives confiscated overpriced merchants' goods and sold them at a reasonable rate, hid children who were working at home from truancy officers, and fought the eviction of themselves, their neighbors, and their friends. Political activism arose out of the home as well as out of the workplace.

New political parties, such as the Labor Party in England, the Socialist Party in France, and the Social Democratic parties of Sweden, Hungary, Austria, and Germany, reached out to the working class who were potentially a collective force in national politics. International workers' organizations also formed to address common interests. Working women, however, were generally excluded from political parties or placed in an auxiliary role because they could not vote or afford union dues. Parties wanted their support, but women's work issues were not perceived as being important. Socialist parties, usually inspired by Marxist theories, attracted the working class, often because of the lack of a moderate alternative to conservative parties. Anarchism was a serious rival, especially in less industrialized countries such as Russia, Italy, and Spain. Socialist parties sponsored many organizations that supported popular community activities, among them gymnastics and choral singing. Informal neighborhood organizations and actions also provided support.

Mass politics involved more than just the working class. Mass journalism appealed to every strata of society. Inexpensive daily newspapers, often emphasizing the sensational, provided Europeans with ready access to information. Journalism helped create a national community of citizens.

Britain pioneered the idea of election campaigns. The introduction of the secret ballot (1872), and the doubling of the electorate through another reform act (1884), meant that politicians had to convince voters they had answers to the problems of the day. William Gladstone (1809–1898), leader of the Liberal Party, conducted the first, modern political campaign (1879). Between campaigns, national political clubs, along with unions and businessmen's associations, brought pressure to bear on political parties. No longer could small cliques easily control politics behind the scenes. That this was now true was evidenced by Ireland. The Irish National League was formed in 1879, and immediately protested absentee English Protestant landlords evicting tenants off the land in order to raise rents. The league voted as a block and elected nationalist representatives to the English Parliament. In a position to block legislation proposed by either the Conservatives or Liberals, MP Charles Stewart Parnell (1846–1891) demanded home rule in return for Irish votes. Independence, however, was not forthcoming and Irish home rule remained a divisive issue.

In France, the Third Republic seemed from its beginnings in 1870 always about to collapse because of intrigue and scandal. The republic survived its first decade mainly because the leading monarchist candidate refused to accept the tricolor. A new constitution, in 1875, created a ceremonial presidency and a primiership dependent upon support from an elected chamber of deputies. Economic downturns and political scandal, often blamed on Jewish businessmen, kept the republic weak throughout the latter part of the nineteenth century. The state worked earnestly to create national unity with civic institutions, most notably free public schools whose doors were open to girls as well as to boys. Mandatory military service also helped fulfill this purpose and turned peasants into Frenchmen.

Liberalism, constitutionalism, and efficient government did not always result in universal male suffrage in Europe. Spain and Belgium granted universal suffrage in 1890 and 1893 respectively, but other monarchies, like Denmark, Sweden, and the Netherlands, continued to limit political participation. In 1887, Italy granted the vote to all men who possessed a primary school education, but this affected only 14 percent of the men in the country.

Bismarck's Germany, although superficially a participant in the new mass politics, emphasized maintenance of the political status quo through the Three Emperors' League: a three-way alliance between Germany, Russia, and Austria-Hungary. While externally Bismarck sought security in Europe, internally he strongly opposed the influence first of the Catholic church (though the Kulturkampf) and then of the Social Democratic Party. Giving up the struggle with the Catholic church, Bismarck turned to the Social Democrats, outlawing the party in 1878. In a more positive vein, Bismarck set Germany on the road toward the welfare state with an accident and disability insurance program in the early 1880s. In the meantime, he moved away from Liberal political support and established a Conservative coalition in the Reichstag. Protective tariffs for both agriculture and industry were the major product of the new alignment.

Liberals were also temporarily successful politically in Austria-Hungary. Under Count Edouard von Taaffe, prime minister from 1879 to 1893, a coalition of clergy, conservatives, and Slavic parties weakened the power of the Liberals. Taaffe's policy of playing nationalities against one another kept the monarchy predominant as the necessary mechanism for holding together groups with competing interests. Pan-Slavism, which Russia did much to support, threatened the stability of the empire, however.

In the Balkans, Russian support for the Slavic nationalities led to war with the Ottoman Empire. Other powers intervened after Russian victory led to the creation of a pro-Russian Bulgaria via the Treaty of San Stefano (1878). Bismarck presided over the Congress of Berlin, which partitioned the enlarged Bulgaria created by the treaty. However, the settlement only temporarily defused the situation. Nothing was done to resolve the conflict between Russian and Austro-Hungarian interests or the problems caused by Slavic nationalism in both the Ottoman and Austro-Hungarian empires.

Following the Congress of Berlin, European powers formed defensive alliances. Austria-Hungary joined with Germany (1879) to form the Dual Alliance against Russia. Italy joined the alliance (1882), which then became known as the Triple Alliance. To protect Germany from Austria-Hungary's aggression, Bismarck signed the Reinsurance Treaty (1887) with Russia to stifle any Habsburg notions about having a free hand to deal with pan-Slavism within their territories.

Russia was relatively untouched by the new political institutions and ideas prevalent in western Europe. By the 1870s, the era of the Great Reform had ended, although some reforms, such as the *zemstvos*, continued as a locus for practical work. Writers such as Leo Tolstoy (1828–1910), author of *War and Peace* (1869) and *Anna Karenina* (1877); and Fyodor Dostoevsky (1821–1881), author of *The Possessed* (1871), opposed violence as a means to reform, but many idealistic, young Russians did turn to the idea of revolution. Some decided terrorism — in particular, the assassination of high officials — would bring down the regime. In 1881, the People's Will succeeded in assassinating Alexander II in a bomb attack. Under his son, Alexander III, Russia entered an era of conservative reaction and a new wave of repression of religious and ethnic minorities, especially Jews.

Suggestions for Lecture and Discussion Topics

1. One approach to examining the changes in industry and commerce that occurred during this period would be to compare the Universal Exposition of 1889 in Paris to the Crystal Palace Exhibition of 1851 in London. To take one example, electricity, particularly in the form of electrical lighting, characterizes the 1889 exposition and sets it apart from the earlier exhibition. Comparing the two offers possibilities for lecturing on or having the class discuss new products, new technologies, new management techniques, and new patterns of consumption.

2. The Belgian Congo, the private property of King Leopold II, exemplifies colonialism practiced at its worst. Joseph Conrad's (1857–1924) *Heart of Darkness*, based on his experiences in the Belgian Congo, offers a way of examining colonial practices in the Congo as well as a range of issues including imperialism, Social Darwinism, racism, sexism, and the nature of European civilization. On the Congo itself, an excellent source is Adam Hochschild, *King Leopold's Ghost: A Story of Greed, Terror, and Heroism in Colonial Africa* (Boston: Houghton Mifflin, 1998). See also Lewis H. Gann and Peter Duigan, *The Rulers of Belgian Africa, 1884–1914* (Princeton: Princeton University Press, 1979). On Conrad, the literature is vast. Start with Adam Gillon, *Joseph Conrad* (Boston: Twayne, 1982); and Gary Adelman, Heart of Darkness: *Search for the Unconscious* (Boston: Twayne, 1987). Other good, introductory sources include Owen Knowles and Gene M. Moore, eds., *The Oxford Reader's Companion to Conrad* (Oxford: Oxford University Press, 2000); J. H. Stape, ed., *The Cambridge Companion to Joseph Conrad* (Cambridge: Cambridge University Press, 1996); and Robert Kimbrough, Heart of Darkness: *An Authoritative Text; Background and Sources; Criticism,* 3d ed. (New York: W. W. Norton, 1988). More specialized titles include Sven Lindqvist, "Exterminate All the Brutes" (New York: New Press, 1996); Susan Jones, *Conrad and Women* (Oxford: Clarendon Press, 1999); Chris Bongie, *Exotic Memories: Literature, Colonialism, and the Fin de Siècle* (Stanford, CA: Stanford University Press, 1991); Peter Finchow, *Envisioning Africa: Racism and Imperialism in Conrad's* Heart of Darkness (Lexington: University of Kentucky Press, 2000); and John W. Griffith, *Joseph Conrad and the Anthropological Dilemma: "Bewildered Traveler"* (Oxford: Clarendon Press, 1995).

3. City life is an important topic that may be presented in interesting ways. Berlin and Paris underwent rapid and extensive changes during this period in terms of architecture and physical layout, transportation, cultural venues, and other aspects of life. Either Berlin or Paris or a comparison between the two would form a good subject for a lecture, especially one with illustrations.

There has been an explosion of books published on Berlin. See, among others, David Clay Large, *Berlin* (New York: Basic Books, 2000); Alexandra Richie, *Faust's Metropolis: A History of Berlin* (New York: Carroll & Graf, 1998); and Giles MacDonogh, *Berlin* (New York: St. Martin's Press, 1998). See also a very useful study by Ronald Taylor, *Berlin and Its Culture: A Historical Portrait* (New Haven: Yale University Press, 1997).

For city life in Paris, there are many sources. A good place to begin would be Donald J. Olson, *The City As a Work of Art: London, Paris, Vienna,* rpt. ed. (New Haven: Yale University Press, 1988). Useful overviews are Johannes Willms, *Paris, Capital of Europe: From the Revolution to the Belle Époque* (New York: Holmes & Meier, 1997); and Norma Evenson, *Paris: A Century of Change, 1878–1978* (New Haven: Yale University Press, 1979). Anthony Sutcliffe, *Paris: An Architectural History* (New Haven: Yale University Press, 1993) offers a detailed discussion. On Paris and art, see T. J. Clark, *The Painting of Modern Life: Paris in the Art of Manet and His Followers* (New York: Knopf, 1984). On the working class in Paris, see Lenard R. Berlanstein, *The Working People of Paris, 1871–1914* (Baltimore: Johns Hopkins University Press, 1984); and W. Scott Haine, *The World of the Paris Café: Sociability among the French Working Class, 1789–1914* (Baltimore: Johns Hopkins University Press, 1996). For the Bohemian world of Paris, see Jerrold Seigel, *Bohemian Paris: Culture, Politics, and the Boundaries of Bourgeois Life, 1830–1930* (New York: Viking Press, 1986).

4. Themes of decline, decay, and degeneration are not limited to art and literature, but appear as well in discussions about society, politics, and economies. Why these themes should be so prevalent in an era of industrial innovation and imperial conquest should furnish the basis for a good discussion.

A good place to begin is Chapter 1 of Eugen Weber, *France: Fin de Siècle* (Cambridge, MA: Belknap Press, 1986). Daniel Pick, *Faces of Degeneration: A European Disorder, c. 1848–c. 1918* (Cambridge: Cambridge University Press, 1993) is the best recent study. An older but still useful study is Koenraad Wolter Swart, *The Sense of Decadence in Nineteenth-Century France* (The Hague: M. Nijhoff, 1964). See also Robert A. Nye, *Crime, Madness, and Politics in Modern France: The Medical Concept of National Decline* (Princeton: Princeton University Press, 1984). Max Simon Nordau, *Degeneration* (Lincoln: University of Nebraska Press, 1993), a reprint of the 1895 edition with an introduction by George L. Mosse, is a classic polemic from the era. See also Carl E. Schorske, *Fin-de-Siècle Vienna: Politics and Culture* (New York: Alfred A. Knopf, 1980). Asti Hustvedt, *The Decadent Reader: Fiction, Fantasy, and Perversion from Fin-de-Siècle France* (Cambridge, MA: MIT Press, 1998) is a convenient introduction to the literature of the times. Mike Jay and Michael Neve, eds., *1900: A Fin-de-Siècle Reader* (New York: Penguin, 2000) is also a useful collection of sources.

5. France may serve as a good example of the problems and potential of mass politics. The Third Republic experienced a difficult birth and continued to struggle for existence in the 1880s and later. Some discussion of the self-conscious effort to forge a nation and loyalty to the republic would be useful.

Part 3 of Gordon Wright, *France in Modern Times*, 3d ed. (New York: W. W. Norton, 1981) offers an excellent overview of the Third Republic. Eugen Weber, *Peasants Into Frenchmen: The Modernization of Rural France, 1870–1914* (Stanford, CA: Stanford University Press, 1976) is a fascinating examination of the ways in which France was re-created as a nation at the end of the century. Two more specialized studies are Michael Burns, *Rural Society and French Politics: Boulangism and the Dreyfus Affair, 1886–1900* (Princeton: Princeton University Press, 1984); and Steven C. Hause and Anne R. Kenney, *Women's Suffrage and Social Politics in the French Third Republic* (Princeton: Princeton University Press, 1984). Perhaps the best survey is Jean-Marie Mayeur and Madeleine Reberioux, *The Third Republic from Its Origins to the Great War, 1871–1914* (Cambridge: Cambridge University Press, 1984). See also Maurice Agulhon, *The French Republic, 1879–1992* (Malden, MA: Blackwell Publishers). Also useful is Patrick J. Hutton, ed., *Historical Dictionary of the Third French Republic, 1870–1940*, 2 vols. (Westport, CT: Greenwood Press, 1986).

6. Bismarck probably deserves a second look. His activities, both within and without the German Empire, help to determine important later developments. Within the empire, did Bismarck's policies encourage political immaturity and stifle the growth of strong political movements and good political leadership? In foreign policy matters, were Bismarck's policies wise contributions to the maintenance of peace, or were they patchwork efforts to reconcile the ultimately unreconcilable?

The two best biographies of Bismarck are Lothar Gall, *Bismarck: The White Revolutionary*, 2 vols. (London: Allen & Unwin, 1986); and Otto Pflanze, *Bismarck and the Development of Germany*, 3 vols. (Princeton: Princeton University Press, 1990). Chapters 2 through 5 in Gordon A. Craig's *Germany, 1866–1945* (New York: Oxford University Press, 1980) deal with Bismarck's role in the German Empire. A very different perspective on Germany under Bismarck may be found in Patricia Kollander, *Frederick III: Germany's Liberal Emperor* (Westport, CT: Greenwood Press, 1995). Frederick, the son of Wilhelm I, ruled only briefly before he died from cancer. In similar fashion, the first several chapters in Lamar Cecil, *Wilhelm II, Prince and Emperor, 1859–1900*, vol. 1 (Chapel Hill: University of North Carolina Press, 1989) offer a different perspective. See also the convenient selection of primary sources in Theodore S. Hamerow, ed., *The Age of Bismarck: Documents and Interpretations* (New York: Harper & Row, 1973). Dependable, brief overviews are provided by Chapter 4 of Holger H. Herwig, *Hammer or Anvil?: Modern Germany 1648–Present* (Lexington, MA: D. C. Heath, 1994); and Chapter 2 of Dietrich Orlow, *A History of Modern Germany, 1871 to Present*, 3d ed. (Englewood Cliffs, NJ: Prentice-Hall, 1995).

Making Connections

1. *Compare the political and social goals of the newly enfranchised male electorate with those of the men and women in the best circles.* The newly enfranchised male electorate joined unions (at both the local and national levels) to bargain for better pay, lower prices, and improved working conditions. Workers established political clubs, while new political parties formed to represent workers' interests at the highest levels of government. Political campaigns often focused on workers' issues. The middle classes, however, in their new prosperity, joined the upper classes, or "best" circles. The line between aristocrat and bourgeois became blurred, both by the awarding of titles to outstanding members of the middle classes and by marriages between aristocrats and the nouveau riche. The wealthiest members of the middle classes lived like the aristocracy, indulging in conspicuous consumption, and they were interested in maintaining the status quo.

2. *Describe the effects of imperialism on European politics and society as a whole. A direct connection was made between imperial expansion and national identity.* National prestige demanded colonial expansion. Because of this, European nations became increasingly distrustful of each other's colonial ambitions. But colonization was not merely a matter of national pride. It was widely believed that colonial natives were inferior and that it was the duty of European Christians to bring Christianity and "civilization" to them. As a result of "civilizing" colonial people, the products of imperialism poured into Europe by way of Oriental carpets, Chinese porcelain, wicker furniture, rich fabrics, and exotic foods and plants. Imperialism became a part of daily life for many Europeans.

Writing Assignments and Class Presentation Topics

1. Role-playing class presentation assignments are plentiful for this period. Students could assume the role of a department store employee, an emigrant, a colonial official, or a particular person, such as King Leopold II of Belgium, Mary Cassatt, or Charles Parnell. You may wish to suggest a list of possible roles for which source material is available in your library or online.

2. Assign students to write a short essay on arguments for and against emigration. Although most of the essay should be a review of the arguments, students should also discuss the factors that would cause them to personally consider emigration (one possibility is, of course, that they would not consider it under any circumstances). You may wish to supplement the documents in the chapter.

3. Give students an opportunity to present reports on French and British politics in this period. The class may be divided into two groups, one for each country. Students in each group decide what to report on and how to do the reporting. For example, they may present a TV newscast based on stories filed by reporters sent back into the past on one of H. G. Wells's time machines. Reports might cover personalities, scandals, party platforms, and other relevant topics.

4. Ask students to reflect on why Bismarck might be considered the greatest or at least the most important individual in nineteenth-century Europe. The emphasis in the essay should consist not on what he accomplished (although a brief review of Bismarck's more important activities is in order), but on the significance of his acts. What was his impact on Germany and, through Germany, on the rest of Europe?

Research Assignments

1. Students might do a research project on one of the many innovations of the period. The typewriter, bicycle, telephone, electric light, and gasoline engine have been mentioned in the text. Other innovations, such as the sewing machine or the vacuum cleaner, might be the basis for a research project as well. The paper or presentation should focus either on the process of inventing and developing the product or on the significance of the new product in industry or the home.

2. Ask each student to select a writer, artist, or composer active during this period. Set a minimum requirement for the amount of reading, viewing, or listening each student should do for the project. It is vitally important that the student gain at least some acquaintance with some of the work of his or her subject. If an art exhibition or a concert is available at a convenient time and location, you may wish to ask all students to attend and to do further research on the artist or composer. You may find it helpful to draw up a list of people for whom research material is available in your library or, if not in the library, to research online.

Literature

Barash, Carol, ed., *An Olive Schreiner Reader: Writings on Women and South Africa.* 1987.

Ingham, Patricia, ed., *Thomas Hardy:* Jude the Obscure. 1996.

Parmee, Douglas, trans., *Émile Zola:* The Earth. 1980.

Sharp, R. Farquharson, trans., *Four Great Plays by Ibsen.* 1981.

Films and Videos

Edward the King (1975; VHS, approx. 13 hrs.). This thirteen–part series (approximately 1 hour each) chronicles the life of king Edward VII of England. It is strong on detail; plot, costumes, and settings.

The Way We Live Now (2001; VHS/DVD, 5 hrs.). Anthony Trollope's 1875 novel is dramatized in this lavish multi-part series. A financier, who mixes with the best in society and is given a seat in parliament, turns out to be a confidence trickster, while his daughter plays a different commercial game, that of the marriage market. The series captures the commercialism of the Victorian age.

Daniel Deronda (2003; VHS/DVD, 3 hrs., 30 min.). This film adaptation of George Elliot's (Mary Ann Evans) 1876 novel includes as one of its theme the social and financial limits placed on women. Most interesting, however, is the window opened to view Jewish life in Victorian England.

The Mayor of Casterbridge (2003; A&E, DVD, approx. 3 hrs., 30 min.). A compelling adaptation of Thomas Hardy's 1886 novel about a man from humble origins who rises to become a prominent citizen, only to be felled by his own ambition, pride, and early unconscionable acts.

Historical Skills

Map 24.1, Africa, c. 1890, p. 926

Use this map first as the basis for a discussion of the "scramble for Africa." What set off the scramble? How did national attitudes toward colonization differ? Ask students if they know or can guess which powers eventually became the major rivals by the end of the century. Next, use this map as a basis for a discussion of how existing African kingdoms might have made conquest relatively easy, but colonial administration somewhat difficult.

Figure 24.1, European Emigration, 1879–1890, p. 938

Why did people from the British Isles make up such a large proportion of those emigrating in this period? Compare the destinations of Russian emigrants with those from Italy or Germany. What major differences do students note? In connection with this image, see also *Mapping the West*: The West and the World, c. 1890 (pp. 955).

Map 24.3, Expansion of Berlin to 1914, p. 951

Ask students to use the information contained on this map and its caption to describe Berlin in the closing decades of the nineteenth century. In addition to the capital of the German Empire, which other labels might fit it? Draw the students' attention to the groups that comprised the growing population of Berlin and also the extensive transportation network of railroad lines and canals.

Map 24.4, The Balkans, c. 1878, p. 952

Based on changes in the Balkans approved at the Congress of Berlin in 1878, what potential problems do students see in this area? Ask them to review of the status of the major powers — Austria-Hungary, Russia, and the Ottoman Empire — and also the situations in Serbia and Bulgaria.

Mapping the West: The West and the World, p. 955

Have students compare Russian emigration to Siberia with the overseas emigration to the Western Hemisphere. Why was the United States the destination of choice for immigrants of so many different nationalities? Students should also examine Figure 24.1, "European Emigration, 1870–1890" (p. 938), in connection with this question.

Universal Exposition of 1889, p. 918

What did the French mean when they talked about celebrating the "progress resulting from one hundred years of freedom"? Had France actually enjoyed freedom in all the years between 1789 and 1889? Why did socialists pick this date to found the Second International? Ask students to compare the Eiffel Tower to the Crystal Palace from the Crystal Palace Exhibition of 1851.

The Great Staircase of the Bon Marché (c. 1880), p. 924

What connections exist between the new consumerism exemplified by the department store and urbanism on the one hand, and imperialism on the other? Ask students to reflect on the reciprocal relationship between institutions such as the department store and the cult of domesticity.

The Violence of Colonization, p. 927

How typical were the policies followed by the agents of King Leopold II in the Belgian Congo? Were the differences between policies in the Belgian Congo and elsewhere only a matter of degree, or were they differences of kind?

An ABC for Baby Patriots (1899), p. 932

What kind of "imperial sensibility" would this image help to inculcate? In particular, what impression might a child gain from the way the African is depicted?

Did You Know?: Polo and Social Class, p. 935

Polo is a good example of a native tradition (Indian) that was adopted and adapted by a colonial power (England). How did the sport become so closely associated with the British aristocracy's way of life? Polo was a team sport that was useful for keeping men and the horses in a cavalry unit in good shape. Transplanted to Britain by those who had learned the sport in India, it was almost ideal for the aristocracy. It was first and foremost a test of manliness and athleticism. Further, considerable wealth was required to purchase and maintain the necessary string of polo ponies.

Contrasting Views: Experiences of Migration, pp. 940–941

In addition to the "Questions for Debate," the following may be useful for class discussion.

1. How might the contrast between the official Hungarian position on emigration and the Swedish charges against emigrants be explained?

The preamble to the Hungarian census of 1890 presents emigration as beneficial both for those leaving and those remaining behind. The two Swedish sources, which defend the emigrant's right to seek better possibilities, present political arguments. No one should be forced to remain in Sweden simply to maintain a source of cheap labor for the benefit of those who were already well-off. None of the documents appears to envision the possibility that an expansion of the domestic economy might permit emigrants to remain at home.

2. To what extent were the expectations of the emigrants and those left behind fulfilled?

The preamble to the 1890 Hungarian census leaves the impression that both those leaving and those staying experienced improved situations. However, the Polish wife left behind experienced considerable hardship. Much depended on when or whether she was able to join her husband. The Swedish journalist asserts the right of poor Swedes to try their luck in America, and the Swedish poem takes an optimistic view: "opportunity has knocked." The Slovak song, by contrast, is a cautionary tale: life is hard in America, and there are dangers for the unwary.

OTHER BEDFORD/ST. MARTIN'S RESOURCES FOR CHAPTER 24

The following resources are available to accompany Chapter 24. Please refer to the Preface of this manual for detailed descriptions of all the ancillaries.

For Instructors

Transparencies

The following maps and images from Chapter 24 are available as full-color acetates.

- Map 24.1: Africa, c. 1890
- Map 24.2: Expansion of Russia in Asia, 1865–1895
- Map 24.3: Expansion of Berlin, to 1914
- Map 24.4: The Balkans, c. 1878
- *Mapping the West*: The West and the World, c. 1890
- *The Letter*
- *Department Store*

Instructor's Resources CD-ROM

The following maps and image from Chapter 24, as well as a chapter outline, are available on disc in both PowerPoint and jpeg formats.

- Map 24.1: Africa, c. 1890
- Map 24.2: Expansion of Russia in Asia, 1865–1895
- Map 24.3: Expansion of Berlin, to 1914
- Map 24.4: The Balkans, c. 1878
- *Mapping the West*: The West and the World, c. 1890
- *The Letter*

For Students

Sources of The Making of the West

The following documents are available in Chapter 24 of the companion sourcebook by Katharine J. Lualdi, University of Southern Maine.

1. Jules Ferry, *Speech Before the French National Assembly* (1883)
2. Joseph Rudyard Kipling, *The White Man's Burden* (1899) and *San Francisco Call*, Editorial (1899)
3. Ernest Edwin Williams, *Made in Germany* (1896)
4. Margaret Bondfield, *A Life's Work* (1948)

Study Guides

The print **Study Guide** and the **Online Study Guide** at bedfordstmartins.com/hunt, both by Victoria Thompson (Arizona State University) and Eric Johnson (University of California, Los Angeles), help students synthesize the material they have learned as well as practice the skills historians use to make sense of the past. The following Map, Visual, and Document activities are available for Chapter 24.

Map Activity

- Map 24.1: Africa, c. 1890

Visual Activity

- *The Letter*

Reading Historical Documents

- Imperialism's Popularity among the People
- Henrik Ibsen, *A Doll's House*

Modernity and the Road to War
c. 1890–1914

CHAPTER RESOURCES

Main Chapter Topics

1. In the decades preceding World War I, industrialization, the accelerated pace of life, the rise of mass politics, the decline in the rural order, and radical innovations in science, philosophy, and the arts resulted in increased conflicts and heightened anxiety for many Europeans. The assassination of the heir to the Austrian throne Francis Ferdinand (June 1914) was the catalyst for the eruption of the political, cultural, and societal discord that had been simmering for decades.

2. Concurrently with modernization, population patterns began to change. Europe became more urbanized and, due to improvements in sanitation and public health, the population soared. Despite this, however, Social Darwinists and eugenicists feared that the rise in population growth among the "lesser" classes was outpacing that of the middle and upper classes whose birthrates were declining. Efforts were made to encourage women to bear children, which included liberalizing laws governing marriage and divorce. As another inducement, politicians played on the middle and upper classes' fears of ethnic minorities and the poor, polarizing European and American societies that had only recently moved toward nationalism.

3. Those scientists who examined the rapidly changing conditions of modern life became alarmed by individuals' complaints of nervousness, fatigue, and irritability. As a result, sciences of the mind—psychology and psychoanalysis—began to consider the mental health of the entire population, not just that of the insane. Sigmund Freud's conclusions, both optimistic with respect to treatment of patients, and pessimistic with respect to mass psychology, were the most influential of the period.

4. Artists, scientists, and intellectuals at the turn of the century responded to and accelerated the pace of changes in ideas, values, beliefs, and artistic forms. Cubism, fauvism, expressionism, relativity, Freudianism, nihilism, feminism, socialism, anarchism, Marxism, anti-Semitism, and mass politics exacerbated the uncertainty, anxiety, and sense of decay that characterized the era.

5. The new mass politics threatened the old order as disenfranchised groups, like the working class and women, demanded rights and shaped political developments. Demagogues employed virulent anti-Semitism and militant nationalism to win support and elections. As a result, mass politics did not bring harmonizing rational debate and compromise, but instead simplistic, divisive, pernicious and rhetoric and attitudes.

6. Heated competition for colonies, growing tensions among colonial powers, the rise of non-western powers such as Japan, and the increasing resistance of colonial peoples made empire-building diplomatically and financially problematic and potentially explosive.

7. Imperial competition, the arms race, militarism, ethnicity-based nationalism, a tangle of alliances, and conflicts in domestic politics set the stage for World War I. Europeans—facing revolutions, terrorism, violent repression, controversy in the arts and sciences, and industrial conflicts—had come to feel that war would set events back on course and save them from the perils of modernity.

Summary

Even though many Europeans had earlier believed in steadily evolving progress, the turn of the century found many individuals increasingly pessimistic about their future and exhibiting signs of depression and anxiety disorders. Growing class conflict, ethnic chauvinism, anti-Semitism, militant nationalism, imperial competition, and the increasingly strident demands of disenfranchised groups—women, the Irish, the Slavs, and colonized peoples—indicated for many that Europe was on the point of collapse. At the same time, innovations in art, music, science, and philosophy were celebrated by some, but considered offensive and frightening by others. Although it was not recognized as such at the time, the assassination of the heir to the Austrian throne, Francis Ferdinand (June 1914), was the catalyst for the eruption of the political, cultural, and societal discord that had been simmering for decades.

A prime concern at the time of modernization was the changing pattern of population growth. Throughout Europe, populations began to soar due to improvements in sanitation and public health that extended longevity and reduced infant mortality. Sections of many older cities were torn down and new buildings erected to accommodate population demands. But population growth did not occur among all classes. Due to the urbanization, improved condoms and the new diaphragm, the spread of information on birth control, and marriages delayed until women were in their twenties—in addition to the ancient practice of abortion—the birthrate among the middle and upper classes declined. This reduction fostered a great deal of anxiety among European leaders. Influenced by Social Darwinist theories and the new "science" of eugenics, governments and the general public were alarmed that the population growth was most rapid among the classes, ethnic groups, and races labeled "inferior." Despite several incentives—including marriage and divorce reforms, which gave women more control over their lives, livelihoods, and property—these trends persisted. More successful was politicians' use of eugenicist and racist rhetoric in campaign speeches, attracting votes by inflaming fears of ethnic minorities or the indigent, which polarized societies only recently encouraged to unite under the banner of nationalism.

Women's lives varied considerably throughout Europe. Women could earn university degrees in Austria, but not at Oxford or Cambridge. In rural eastern Europe, a father's power remained virtually dictatorial; whereas among the middle and upper classes, children were coming to believe that they had a right to choose their marriage partners and marry for love rather than for economic or social reasons. So-called new women dressed more practically, biked and hiked throughout the cities and countryside, and lived independent lives, disrupting traditional notions of gender in the process. Sexual identity further fueled debate. Havelock Ellis (1859–1939), a British doctor, postulated in his *Sexual Inversion* (1884) a new personality type: the homosexual. Homosexuals joined the debate, and called for recognition of the "third sex." Physicians and intellectuals increasing viewed sexuality as an integral part of human identity. The press labeled homosexuality perverse, and hounded English playwright Oscar Wilde (1854–1900) who was convicted of charges of "indecency" and sentenced to two years hard labor. In Germany, the press

condemned some of the men in Kaiser William II's circle for homosexuality and transvestitism. Sexual issues were becoming politicized.

Scientists who examined the rapidly changing conditions of modern life saw that its repercussions included patient fatigue and extreme stress. They therefore began to apply the teachings of psychology and psychoanalysis to patients suffering from depression, neuroses, and anxiety disorders not just to the insane. Sigmund Freud (1856–1939) revolutionized the approach to such cases by avoiding traditional, moral evaluations of human behavior. He believed that the human personality was made up of three competing parts: the ego (which was most in touch with external reality), the id (or libido), and the superego (the part that serves as conscience). Freud became convinced that all human beings had, from birth, sexual impulses that had to be repressed in order for children to attain maturity and for society to remain civilized. In the case of women, Freud believed that adult gender identity was as much about processing life experiences as it was about biology. And, he argued that girls and women were not passionless, as the Victorians had maintained, but rather had powerful, sexual feelings. At the same time, however, Freud discounted charges of unwanted sexual advances and abuse leveled by girls and women, categorizing them as the result of "penis envy." His theories challenged accepted beliefs and scientific theories by claiming that humans were motivated by irrational drives toward death and destruction and that these shaped society's collective mentality. Freud's theories also undermined the old Enlightenment confidence that society would move in a consistently progressive direction.

Intellectuals and artists who rejected accepted values, beliefs, and artistic forms helped launch the disorienting revolution in ideas and creative expression that we now identify collectively as "modernism." Philosophers, social thinkers, scientists, artists, and musicians exacerbated the sense of uncertainty that characterized the era, further eroding European confidence.

A major element of this revolution in thinking was a rejection of the century-old faith of positivism that one could discover in science enduring social laws based on rationally determined principles. Philosophers such as Wilhelm Dilthley (1822–1911) in Germany, John Dewey (1859–1952) in the United States, and the German political theorist Max Weber (1864–1920), increasingly challenged the concept of fundamental or universal laws and postulated their own theories regarding the human condition. These thinkers were labeled "relativists" and "pragmatists" and influenced the way in which society was viewed throughout the twentieth century. Most radical and influential, though, was Friedrich Nietzsche (1844–1900), who presented his ideas as an individual's aphorisms (or representations), not as a universal truth, and considered himself a nihilist rather than a relativist or positivist. Nietzsche believed that people clung to Apollonian, or rational explanations about life because Dionysian ideas about nature, death, and love (such as those found in Greek tragedy) were too disturbing to contemplate. He also believed that dogmatic truth—especially as it concerned religion—was declining and announced, "God is dead, we have killed him." He thought this would usher in new "poetries of life" to replace worn-out religious and middle-class rules. Nietzsche's ideas, which later fed into the school of thought known as "postmodernism," were deliberately misrepresented after his death by his sister (who served as his editorial and literary conservator) and reduced by racists, nationalists, and militarists into simpleminded dogmas that justified violent anti-Semitism and imperialism.

Discoveries made by pioneering researchers also shook the foundations of traditional scientific certainty and challenged accepted knowledge about the nature of the universe. Max Planck (1858–1947), Antoine Becquerel (1852–1908), Marie Curie (1867–1934), Pierre Curie (1859–1906), and Albert Einstein (1879–1955), among others, called into question scientific assumptions held since the time of Isaac Newton. Although initially rejected by traditionalists, theories on radioactivity and the atom and Einstein's General Theory of Relativity eventually forced a paradigm shift that transformed the foundation of science and the popular view of the universe.

Similar conflicts between tradition and innovation raged in the arts, dance, and music. By the late nineteenth century, many artists distanced themselves from classical western norms and from the conventions of polite society. One such group, led by Henri Matisse (1869–1954), was known as the *fauves* ("wild beasts") because they used vibrant colors to capture the essence of industrial society. Modernism in art proliferated competing artistic styles, ideas, approaches, and techniques as well as disagreements about how art related to society. While some artists tried to use their creations to comfort urbanites caught up in the rush of modern life, others sought to shock people out of their complacent acceptance of the state of the world. Some artists experimented in their work with ideas about the subconscious and with non-western art forms. Paul Cézanne (1839–1906) used rectangular dabs of paint to capture a geometric vision of still life and the human form. Pablo Picasso (1881–1973) took Cézanne's work in another direction and developed *cubism*, which emphasized intersecting planes and surfaces. His best-known cubist work of this period is *Les Demoiselles d'Avignon* (1907), which depicts four women with fragmented bodies and heads. In Norway, Edvard Munch's (1863–1944) *Scream* (1895) captured the horror of modern life. German painter Gabriele Münter (1877–1962) and Russian artist Wassily Kandinsky (1866–1944), both of the so-called Blue Rider group, imitated paintings by children and the mentally ill in order to portray psychological reality. Kandinsky

was also the first to produce a truly abstract painting (1909). Few of these artists or their innovative styles succeeded commercially or even critically at the time; indeed, some pointed to modern art as a sign and symptom of what was wrong with European society. Only one new, innovative style proved to be successful, and that was "art nouveau," which incorporated natural and organic designs, like intertwined flowers and vines, and softly curving female nudes. The work of Gustav Klimt (1862–1918) arose from this movement and captured the psychological essence of dreamy, sensuous women.

Industrialization also had an impact on dance and music. Dancers like American Isadora Duncan (1877–1927) and Russian Vaslav Nijinsky (1890–1950) experimented with form, shocking audiences with their seemingly primitive, awkward, and modernistic styles. Musicians like Claude Debussy (1862–1918), Maurice Ravel (1875–1937), Giacomo Puccini (1858–1924), and Richard Strauss (1864–1949) broke with traditional styles and adopted non-western subject matter and tonalities. Music could also have a political edge, and Bela Bartok (1881–1945) used folk melodies to elevate Hungarian ethnicity above the Habsburg Empire's multinationalism. Arnold Schoenberg (1874–1951) even suggested eliminating tonality altogether, and the dissonance of his compositions outraged audiences.

The political optimism of the nineteenth century was, by the turn of the century, tempered by an apprehensive, even pessimistic feeling about the future, especially among the upper classes. Cracks in the political establishment and changing suffrage and activism had undermined upper-class control of politics. There was concern over the growing political power of the working classes who, in turn, feared they would compromise their beliefs by participating in traditional forms of government. This new era of mass politics soon threatened social unity—especially in central and eastern Europe—where governments often responded to reform demands with repression. Some working-class, political parties and their leaders (like V. I. Lenin [1870–1924]) were forced to function in exile. Anarchist parties also flourished, especially in Russia, Italy, and Spain, and some of their numbers bombed government buildings and assassinated public figures, like Empress Elizabeth of Austria-Hungary (1898), King Umberto of Italy (1900), and U.S. President William McKinley (1901). But, while political representation of the working classes was now a fact, their further demands for reform caused unease among the "best people," who still believed they alone should hold political power.

Along with the growth of labor movements came the suffragette movement. Middle-class women led the fight and, although working-class women joined them, they were most concerned about improving their economic situations. It was thought that only by getting the vote and influencing politics could women hope to fight the inequalities and inequities between women and men enshrined in law. Finland was the first to grant women the vote in 1906. When suffrage in other countries was not forthcoming, suffragettes became more militant. Members of the Women's Social and Political Union (WSPU), founded in England by Emmeline Pankhurst (1858–1928), blew up railroad stations, slashed art, and chained themselves to Parliament's gates. They smashed department store windows, organized parades and demonstrations, and went on hunger strikes when they were arrested.

In 1905, the British Labor Party won the parliamentary election and began introducing reforms benefiting the working classes. The National Insurance Act of 1911 instituted unemployment relief and was funded by new taxes on the wealthy. The power to veto legislation in the House of Lords was abolished in the Parliament Bill of 1911. Irish home rule continued to be hotly debated, and promoters of independence, like the poet William Butler Yeats (1865–1939), emphasized Irish culture, Catholicism, and the Gaelic language. Sinn Fein was founded in 1905 to fight for independence. Parliament approved home rule in 1913, but the outbreak of World War I prevented the legislation from taking effect and cut short dreams of independence.

Liberalism was more seriously under threat in Italy. The Italian government was seriously compromised through corruption at the highest levels: Giovanni Gioletti, prime minister for three terms between 1903 and 1914, used various kinds of bribes to influence deputies in parliament. To quell unrest, Gioletti instituted social welfare programs and, in 1912, extended virtually complete suffrage to men.

Because people feared the working class and women's movements, mass politics did not achieve the promised harmonious debate and compromise; mass politics did, however, engender even more conflict. In the two decades before World War I, many politicians inflamed anti-Semitism to maintain support from certain constituencies and win elections. State-sponsored, anti-Jewish pogroms in Russia, the rise of radical nationalistic and anti-Semitic groups in Germany and Austria-Hungary, and the Dreyfus Affair in France are all examples of "the politics of the irrational." Indeed, throughout Europe, statesmen used hate-filled slogans blaming the Jews for social, economic, and political problems.

Jewish response to anti-Liberal politics varied. In some countries, Jews emigrated, intermarried with Christians, converted to Christianity, or adopted the ways and cultures of their oppressors in order to assimilate themselves into society. Another response was to emphasize their own rich culture and heritage. In the 1880s, Ukranian physician Leon Pinsker (1821–1891), believing the lack of a homeland contributed to the Jews' persecution, advocated emigration to Palestine. In 1896,

Theodor Herzl (1860–1904) called not only for Jewish emigration, but the formal establishment of a Jewish nation-state. The following year, the first International Zionist Congress (1897) endorsed settlement in Palestine and, by 1914, some eighty-five thousand Jews had settled there.

After centuries of global expansion, competition among a greater number of nations for colonies in addition to tensions between the two great colonial powers, Great Britain and France, raised serious questions about the future of imperialism. In addition, the rise of Japan as a major, imperial power eroded Europeans' confident approach to imperialism as the natural right of the west. Finally, resistance to European colonial incursions increased and tarnished the image of colonialism. In South Africa, hoping to secure more territory for Britain, Cecil Rhodes deliberately provoked a confrontation with the Boers (descendants of early Dutch settlers) by raiding the neighboring territory of the Transvaal. It was not a popular war in Britain, and newspapers daily chronicled the abuses inflicted on Boer prisoners. Britain eventually won the war, but at great cost in terms of money, lives, and destruction.

The United States had promoted independence movements in Cuba, Puerto Rico, and the Philippines during the Spanish-American War of 1898; however, when the fighting was over the United States annexed Puerto Rico, Guam, and the Philippines and closely monitored Cuba. In the fight against independence in the Philippines, some two hundred thousand locals were slaughtered by U.S. troops.

In Europe, after a disastrous war with Ethiopia (1896), Italy won a costly victory against the Ottomans in Libya. In the east, Japan extended its power and influence over China. Japan invaded the island of Formosa (modern Taiwan) (1874), and the Sino-Japanese war ended China's domination of Korea, which was annexed outright in 1910. Russian troops in Manchuria provoked the Russo-Japanese War, which Japan quickly won to Russia's humiliation. The Russian defeat, the tensions caused by industrialization, and forced Russification programs fed into the Russian Revolution of 1905. In January, a group of workers gathered outside the Winter Palace requesting an audience with see Tsar Nicholas II so they could tell him personally of typical working conditions. Soldiers, firing into the crowd to disperse them, killed hundreds and wounded many more. This incident—Bloody Sunday—sparked almost a year of turmoil, with workers striking over wages, working conditions, and their lack of political representation. Workers rejected the leadership of socialist parties and formed their own councils ("soviets"). Support for the revolution was particularly strong among artisans, industrial workers, peasants, professionals, and reformers in the upper classes. Many women supported the revolution. To end the violence, Nicholas II created a nominally representative body: the Duma. Several dumas met between 1907 and 1917 and, when elected delegates were not to the tsar's liking, he simply dissolved the body. But under Prime Minister Pyotr Stolypin (1863–1911) some real changes were instituted. Land reforms ended the *mir* system of communal farming and taxation and cancelled land redemption payments (imposed after the emancipation of the serfs in 1961). Government loans were made available so peasants could buy their own land. Stolypin also severely restrained on revolutionaries and intensified Russification programs. Unrest, however, continued, and Stolypin himself was a victim in 1911 of the ensuring violence. Another round of strikes erupted in 1914, on the eve of a much larger conflagration.

In China, after its defeat by the Japanese, the Society of the Righteous and Harmonious Fists formed to restore Chinese dignity. More popularly known as the Boxers, they maintained that ritual boxing could protect them from a variety of evils, including bullets. In the face of a worsening economic climate, and with the encouragement of the Dowager Empress Tz'u Hsi (Cixi) (1835–1908), the Boxers rebelled in 1900, massacring missionaries and Chinese Christians who they blamed for China's troubles. Western powers intervened, put down the rebellion, and forced more concessions upon the Chinese. In 1911, the discredited Qing dynasty was overthrown by revolutionaries led by Sun Yat-Sen (1866–1925) and a year later a republic declared. Yat-Sen called for a revival of the Chinese tradition of correct behavior between the governor and the governed, modern economic reforms, and an end to western domination.

In India, the Hindu leader B. G. Tilak (1856–1920) advocated blatant noncooperation with the British. He promoted Hindu customs and inspired violent rebellion in his followers. In response, Britain favored the rival national group, the Muslim League. Ultimately, Britain was forced to concede the right to vote based on property ownership and to representation in ruling councils. The independence movement had not fully reached the masses and these concessions appeased the best-educated and influential dissenters among the middle and upper classes.

Revolution also undermined the Ottoman Empire. Sultan Abdul Hamid II (r. 1876–1909) tried to use Islam as a uniting force among his Serbian, Bulgarian, and Macedonian subjects. This instead ignited ultranationalism among Turks in Constantinople who emphasized Turkish culture, history, and language. In 1908, a group of nationalists calling itself the "Young Turks" seized control of the government in Constantinople. Simultaneously, other parts of the Ottoman Empire, like Egypt, Syria, and the Balkans, also demanded independence. But the Young Turks, backed by western powers who had interests in the rebellious areas, put down the uprisings. There was further resistance in East Africa against the Germans, and in Indochina against the French. Empires, young and old, faced colonial independence movements in the decade before World War I.

As the twentieth century opened, tensions in Europe ran so high that war seemed inevitable to some. The Triple Alliance that Otto von Bismarck had negotiated for Germany, Austria-Hungary, and Italy confronted an opposing alliance between France and Russia. The one wild card was Britain, which would soon join in on the side of France. Even though Britain and France had been bitter rivals for centuries, after war nearly broke out at Fashoda (1898), both nations were frightened into mutual protection and entered into an agreement called the "Entente Cordiale." German provocations in French Morocco during the First and Second Moroccan crises (1906, 1911) pushed Britain and France into a closer agreement by which they eventually made binding provisions for military deployment in the event of war.

While the Germans concentrated on Morocco, Austria-Hungary and Russia sought to extend their opposing influence in the Balkans just as Balkan nationalism had become virulent. Tensions mounted after the Austrian annexation of Bosnia-Herzegovina in 1908 Greece, Serbia, Bulgaria, Romania, and Montenegro, now autonomous states, wanted to extend their control over Ottoman and Habsburg territories that included their respective ethnic groups. In the First Balkan War (1912), Greece, Serbia Bulgaria, and Montenegro joined forces to gain Macedonia and Albania. An alliance between Greece, Serbia, and Montenegro contested Bulgarian gains and prompted the Second Balkan War (1913). In the peace negotiations, Austria-Hungary prevented Serbia from annexing parts of Albania. The grievances between the Habsburgs and the Serbs (allied with the Russians) now seemed irreconcilable. When the Serbs and other Balkan peoples determined to seek independence from Austria-Hungary, they guaranteed a confrontation between the Habsburgs and Russia.

Added to these international tensions were developments from the past century that had transformed the practice of and rationale for war. Increasing numbers of conscripts, a deadly arms race, and modern weapons created a volatile situation in the first years of the twentieth century. The common belief that a military buildup of land and naval forces provided economic and social stability by creating jobs, profits, and national pride made states unwilling to reduce expenditures or to admit that they could not outpace a rival.

On June 29, 1914, Gavrilo Princip (1895–1918), a Serb, went to Sarajevo in Bosnia and assassinated the heir to the Austrian throne Francis Ferdinand and his wife Sophie. Austria-Hungary wanted to destroy the Serb threat once and for all. Although Serbia accepted nearly all of Vienna's demands, the Austrians, unconditionally backed by the Germans (who fully expected a diplomatic solution), declared war on Serbia on July 28. Despite attempts made to stop the war, war fever broke out in the press, and the Austrians abandoned diplomacy and mobilized. Russia, allied to the Serbs, began to mobilize their forces. The Germans, according to their established military strategy, the von Schlieffen Plan, began to mobilize against both France and Russia. Moving to invade France, the German army met an unexpected Belgian refusal to let them pass through Belgium. The Germans moved into Belgium anyway, violating Belgian neutrality that the British had guaranteed through a treaty. This act brought the British in on the side of the French and Russians. World War I had begun.

Suggestions for Lecture and Discussion Topics

1. One of the significant developments of this period was the explosive growth of the modern city. A good way to develop a discussion on the changes in daily life is to look at how cities evolved and transformed, and how architectural styles changed during the latter part of the nineteenth and the early twentieth centuries. Slides of buildings and cityscapes would add greatly to the discussion. Good sources for this topic are Donald J. Olsen, *The City As Work of Art: London, Paris, Vienna* (New Haven: Yale University Press, 1986); Franco Borsi, *Vienna 1900* (New York: Rizzoli, 1986); William Johnston, *Vienna: The Golden Age, 1815–1914* (New York: Clarkson N. Potter, 1981); François Loyer, *Paris, Nineteenth Century: Architecture and Urbanism* (New York: Abbeville Press, 1988); Alastair Service, *London 1900* (New York: Rizzoli, 1979); and Mark Girouard, *Cities and People: A Social and Architectural History* (New Haven: Yale University Press, 1985).

2. In order to deepen students' understanding of how ordinary Europeans lived, develop a discussion on the lives of the urban working class. One way to accomplish this is to have students read autobiographical accounts written by individuals who lived during this period. Two excellent sources from which readings could be assigned are David Kelly, *The German Worker: Working-Class Autobiographies from the Age of Industrialization* (Berkeley: University of California Press, 1987); and Mark Traugott, *The French Worker: Autobiographies from the Early Industrial Era* (Berkeley: University of California Press, 1993).

3. The lives of European women and the suffrage movement are important topics for understanding some of the social transformations that occurred during this period. What was everyday life like for women? What ideas were common about marriage and family? What role did women play in European society? How was that role changing? What motivated women to take part in the suffrage movement? What were the results of the women's movements throughout the countries of Europe? A good introduction on European women's history is Bonnie G. Smith, *Changing Lives: Women in European History Since 1700* (Lexington, MA: D. C. Heath, 1989). Other useful sources include Ute Frevert, *Women in German History: From Bourgeois Emancipation to Sexual Liberation* (Washington, DC: Berg, 1990); Ann Taylor Allen, *Feminism and Motherhood in Germany, 1800–1914* (New Brunswick: Rutgers University Press, 1991); Jean H. Quataert, *Reluctant Feminists in German Social Democracy, 1885–1914* (Princeton: Princeton University Press, 1979); Nancy Reagin, *A German Women's Movement: Class and Gender in Hanover, 1880–1933* (Chapel Hill: University of North Carolina Press, 1995); Richard Stites, *The Women's Liberation Movement in Russia: Feminism, Nihilism, and Bolshevism, 1860–1930* (Princeton: Princeton University Press, 1978); Linda H. Edmondson, *Feminism in Russia, 1900–1917* (Stanford, CA: Stanford University Press, 1984); Rose Glickman, *Russian Factory Women: Workplace and Society, 1880–1914* (Berkeley: University of California Press, 1984); Philippa Levine, *Victorian Feminism, 1850–1900* (London: Hutchinson Education, 1987); Ellen Ross, *Love and Toil: Motherhood in Outcast London, 1870–1918* (New York: Oxford University Press, 1993); and Judith Walkowitz, *City of Dreadful Delight: Narratives of Sexual Danger in Late-Victorian London* (Chicago: University of Chicago Press, 1991).

4. Slides comparing various examples of modern art with more traditional academic art are a good way to demonstrate how radical these art movements were at the time. Briefly explain the origins and philosophy of each movement and then show the images. In class, ask students to describe the content and style of traditional art and then compare these to examples from a variety of modern movements (for example, fauvism, cubism, and expressionism). There are innumerable books published on artists and art movements from this period. A good introductory text on modern art movements is Nikos Stangos, ed., *Concepts of Modern Art: From Fauvism to Postmodernism*, 3d ed. (New York: Thames and Hudson, 1994).

5. In order for students to understand the motivations for the various revolutionary movements in Russia during this period, discuss in some detail the conditions in Russia in the years just prior to World War I. For evidence of everyday life, good sources include Olga Semyonova Tian-Sahnskaia, *Village Life in Late Tsarist Russia* (Bloomington: Indiana University Press, 1993); and Victoria E. Bonnell, ed., *The Russian Worker: Life and Labor under the Tsarist Regime* (Berkeley: University of California Press, 1983). For sources on Russian women, see suggestion 3 above. Sources on the Revolution of 1905 include Abraham Ascher, *The Revolution of 1905*, 2 vols. (Stanford, CA: Stanford University Press, 1988, 1992); Laura Engelstein, *Moscow 1905: Working Class Organization and Political Conflict* (Stanford, CA: Stanford University Press, 1982); Shmuel Galai, *The Liberation Movement in Russia, 1900–1905* (New York: Cambridge

University Press, 1973); and Walter Sablinsky, *The Road to Bloody Sunday: Father Gapon and the St. Petersburg Massacre of 1905* (Princeton: Princeton University Press, 1976). A good documentary film that will help contrast the conditions of everyday life for the common people with that of the royal family is *Last of the Czars*; a classic, silent, Russian film on an episode of the Revolution of 1905 is Sergei Eisenstein's *Battleship Potemkin*.

6. To help students understand how deeply rooted and heinous anti-Semitism was (and still is in some places), it would be useful to explore the most infamous case of the era. Discuss in some detail the Dreyfus Affair in France and how it demonstrated both divisions within France—especially in the military, and the wider problem of anti-Semitism in Europe. Sources on this topic include Jean Denis Bredin, *The Affair: The Case of Alfred Dreyfus* (New York: George Braziller, 1986); Martin Phillip Johnson, *The Dreyfus Affair: Honor and Politics in the Belle Époque* (New York: St. Martin's Press, 1999); and Michael Burns, *France and the Dreyfus Affair: A Documentary History* (Boston: Bedford/St. Martin's, 1999).

7. Along with discussing the process of European colonization, you should examine how colonization affected the subjugated peoples and how treatment differed according to the colonial power and the region colonized. Good sources for this include Muriel Evelyn Chamberlain, *The Scramble for Africa*, 2d ed. (New York: Longman, 1999); Thomas Pakenham, *The Scramble for Africa: White Man's Conquest of the Dark Continent from 1876 to 1912* (New York: Random House, 1991); Adam Hochschild, *King Leopold's Ghost: The Story of Greed, Terror, and Heroism in Colonial Africa* (Boston: Houghton Mifflin, 1998); Winfried Baumgart, *Imperialism: The Idea and Reality of British and French Colonial Explosion, 1880–1914* (New York: Oxford University Press, 1989); and Raymond F. Betts, *The False Dawn: European Imperialism in the Nineteenth Century* (Lexington, MA: D. C. Heath, 1975).

8. The many forces at work within European society made a coming conflict seem, in retrospect, inevitable. Discuss in some detail the foreign and domestic politics of the great powers in order to demonstrate how Europe could have become embroiled in a world war. General sources on the situation in Europe on the eve of the war include John Keegan, *The First World War* (New York: Alfred A. Knopf, 1999); Martin Gilbert, *The First World War: A Complete History* (New York: Henry Holt, 1994); James Joll, *The Origins of the First World War*, 2d ed. (New York: Longman, 1992); Laurence Lafore, *The Long Fuse: An Interpretation of the Origins of World War I*, 2d ed. (New York: J. B. Lippincott, 1971); Robert K. Massie, *Dreadnought: Britain, Germany, and the Coming of the Great War* (New York: Random House, 1991). Studies of individual countries include V. R. Berghahn, *Germany and the Approach of War in 1914*, 2d ed. (New York: St. Martin's Press, 1993); D. C. B. Lieven, *Russia and the Origins of the First World War* (New York: St. Martin's Press, 1983); John Keiger, *France and the Origins of the First World War* (New York: St. Martin's Press, 1983); Samuel R. Williamson, *Austria-Hungary and the Origins of the First World War* (New York: St. Martin's Press, 1990); and Zara S. Steiner, *Britain and the Origins of the First World War* (New York: St. Martin's Press, 1977).

Making Connections

1. *How did changes in society interact with the development of mass politics?* Fear of the working class and women's movements, which sometimes embraced violence as a means to an end, was not assuaged by mass politics. It was hoped that mass politics would bring more harmonious debate and compromise, but even further conflict resulted. In the two decades before WWI, many politicians deliberately inflamed anti-Semitism to gain support from certain constituencies and win elections. State-sponsored anti-Jewish pogroms in Russia; the rise of radical nationalism and anti-Semitic groups in Germany, Italy, and Austria-Hungary; and the Dreyfus Affair in France, are all examples of "the politics of the irrational." Indeed, throughout Europe, statesmen used hate-filled slogans blaming the Jews for social, economic, and political problems.

2. *How was culture connected to the world of politics?* Across Europe, artists mixed political criticism with radical, stylistic changes in their work. Some artists tried to use their creations to comfort urbanites caught up in the rush of modern life; others sought to shock people out of complacent acceptance of the state of the world. Viewers were intended to reflect on the horrors of modern life and its causes. For example, Picasso and Braque made a collage using newspaper clippings that described battles and murders, thus suggesting the shallowness of western pretensions to high civilization. In eastern and central European artists criticized the growing nationalism that determined which sculptures or paintings would be officially purchased. These purchases tended to be traditional in form and subject matter, rather than reflections of contemporary society. Even music could have a political edge. Bela Bartok used folk melodies to promote Hungarian ethnicity over the Habsburg Empire's multi-nationalism.

Writing Assignments and Class Presentation Topics

1. In order to explore how far-reaching anti-Semitism was during this period, have students research the Dreyfus Affair for a written essay and then reenact one of Captain Dreyfus's trials in class.

2. Divide the class into groups and have each group research the various domestic and foreign policy concerns of the individual great powers before World War I. Each student in the group should write on one of the challenges facing their group's assigned great power. Have each group present the cumulative pressures experienced by their assigned country and its motivations for preparing for war. Beyond the books listed in "Suggestions for Lecture and Discussion Topics," number 8, short works that can be assigned on the debates surrounding the outbreak of the war include David Stevenson, *The Outbreak of the First World War: 1914 in Perspective* (New York: St. Martin's Press, 1997); and Holger H. Herwig, *The Outbreak of World War I*, 5th ed. (Lexington, MA: D. C. Heath, 1991).

3. Ask students to write an essay comparing independence movements against European domination. Movements may include those of the Irish, the Boxers in China, the nationalists in India, or the Young Turks in the Ottoman Empire. Ask students to explain how the colonized people were treated by the colonial power, the origins of the independence movements, and the results of the movements by 1914. Good sources are listed in the chapter bibliography.

4. Have students research and write an essay or give an in-class presentation about an artist of the period. They should provide images of the artist's work and discuss his or her style, philosophy, and contribution to the development of European culture.

Research Assignments

1. The women's suffrage movement was a significant element of international politics before the outbreak of World War I. Ask students to do a research project exploring the origins of the suffrage movement, the membership, the obstacles faced, and the level of success prior to World War I. Sources besides those listed in "Suggestions for Lecture and Discussion Topics," number 3, include Leila J. Rupp, *World of Women: The Making of an International Women's Movement* (Princeton: Princeton University Press, 1999); Richard J. Evans, *The Feminists: Women's Emancipation Movements in Europe, America, and Australasia, 1840–1920* (London: Croom Helm, 1977); Sandra Stanley Holton, *Feminism and Democracy: Women's Suffrage and Reform Politics in Britain, 1900–1918* (New York: Cambridge University Press, 1986); Claire Eustance, Joan Ryan, and Laura Ugolini, eds., *A Suffrage Reader: Charting Directions in British Suffrage History* (Leicester: Leicester University Press, 2000); Angela V. John and Claire Eustance, eds., *The Men's Share?: Masculinities, Male Support, and Women's Suffrage in Britain, 1890–1920* (New York: Routledge, 1997); Sophia A. van Wingerden, *The*

Women's Suffrage Movement in Britain, 1866–1938 (New York: St. Martin's Press, 1999); Patricia Greenwood Harrison, *Connecting Links: The British and American Woman Suffrage Movements, 1900–1914* (Westport, CT: Greenwood Press, 2000); Cliona Murphy, *The Women's Suffrage Movement and Irish Society in the Early Twentieth Century* (Philadelphia: Temple University Press, 1989); Steven Hause, *Hubertine Auclert: The French Suffragette* (New Haven: Yale University Press, 1987); and Steven Hause and Anne Kenney, *Women's Suffrage and Social Politics in the French Third Republic* (Princeton: Princeton University Press, 1984).

2. Anti-Semitism emerged as a major issue in turn-of-the-century European culture and politics. In a research project, ask students to explore the impact of anti-Semitism in a particular European country. Topics include pogroms in Russia, the Dreyfus Affair in France, and the emergence of anti-Semitic parties and organizations in Austria-Hungary. Another topic would be the Jewish response to these developments and the emergence of the Zionist movement. Beyond the works on the Dreyfus Affair listed in "Suggestions for Lecture and Discussion Topics," number 6, other sources include Albert S. Lindemann, *The Jew Accused: Three Anti-Semitic Affairs (Dreyfus, Beilis, Frank), 1894–1915* (New York: Cambridge University Press, 1991); George L. Mosse, *Toward the Final Solution: A History of European Racism* (Madison: University of Wisconsin Press, 1978); John Doyle Klier and Shlomo Lambroza, eds., *Pogroms: Anti-Jewish Violence in Modern Russian History* (New York: Cambridge University Press, 1992); Heinz-Dietrich Lowe, *The Tsars and the Jews: Reform, Reaction, and Anti-Semitism in Imperial Russia, 1772–1917* (New York: Harwood, 1992); Brigitte Hamann, *Hitler's Vienna: A Dictator's Apprenticeship* (New York: Oxford University Press, 1999); Carl E. Schorske, *Fin-de-Siècle Vienna: Politics and Culture* (New York: Alfred A. Knopf, 1980); and Walter Laqueur, *A History of Zionism* (New York: Schocken Books), 1972.

3. Many people, including the monarchs themselves, believed that the family relationships existing between the main royal houses of Europe (Britain, Russia, and Germany) would prevent all-out war. Have students research exactly what those relationships were, beginning first by sorting out who was related to whom. Then see Robert K. Massie, *Dreadnought: Britain, Germany, and the Great War* (New York: Random House, 1992). See also biographies of the main ruling figures of the period. For Nicholas II, see Robert K. Massie, *Nicholas and Alexandra* (New York: Atheneum, 1967; rpt. 2000); and D. C. B. Lieven, *Nicholas II: Twilight of the Empire* (New York: St. Martin's Press, 1996). For Kaiser Wilhelm, see Giles MacDonogh, *The Last Kaiser: The Life of Wilhelm II* (New York: St. Martin's Press, 2000). For George V, see Kenneth Rose, *King George V* (London: Phoenix Press, 2000).

Literature

Eugenides, Jeffrey, ed., *Oscar Wilde:* The Picture of Dorian Gray. 1998.

Hingley, Ronald, trans., *Five Plays by Chekhov.* 1998.

Kaufmann, Walter, trans., *The Portable Nietzsche.* 1977.

Nunally, Tiina, trans., *The Unknown Sigrid Undset:* Jenny and Other Works. 2001.

Pruitt, Ida. *A Daughter of Han: The Autobiography of a Chinese Working Woman.* 1945.

Woods, John E., trans., *Thomas Mann:* Buddenbrooks, The Decline of a Family. 1994.

Films and Videos

Edward the King (1975; VHS, approx. 13 hrs.). This thirteen-part (each part approximately 1 hour) series chronicles the life of king Edward VII of England. It is accurate on detail, plot, costumes, and settings.

Howard's End (1992; DVD/VHS, 2 hrs., 16 min.). This film adaptation of E. M. Forster's 1910 novel nicely captures what life was like for upper-middle-class Edwardians, especially women. Stultifying Edwardian moral and social conventions are essential elements of the plot.

1900 House (2002; VHS/DVD, 4 hrs.) and *Manor House* (2003; VHS/DVD, 6 hrs.). In these two series, contemporary English people find out firsthand what life was like in the early twentieth century. For several months, they live as people would have done over one hundred years ago: they wear authentic clothing of the period, live in accommodations true to the period, and perform the jobs appropriate to their class and position in society. In *1900 House,* the focus is on a family of six. In *Manor House,* the divisions between the upstairs family and downstairs staff makes for an interesting and volatile contrast. Although slightly voyeuristic, these series do highlight in an immediate way what life was like in the early twentieth century.

The Forsyte Saga, Series I (2002; VHS/DVD, 4 hrs., 20 min.). John Galsworthy's early novels about the Forsyte family are dramatized in this excellent series. Eight episodes of approximately 50 minutes each graphically depict the reality of marriage and extramarital relationships in late-Victorian society and the plight of women trapped in a patriarchal world of stultifying manners and loveless marriages. Lavish costumes and sets help re-create the late-Victorian period.

Historical Skills

Map 25.1, Jewish Migrations in the Late Nineteenth Century, p. 983

Ask students to locate and identify centers of Jewish population in late-nineteenth-century Europe. Where were Jews emigrating to? What were their reasons?

Map 25.2, Africa in 1914, p. 986

Ask students to locate and identify the few independent African states on the eve of World War I. Compare this map to a current map of Africa and have students note the tremendous political transformation of the African continent over the past century.

Map 25.4, The Balkans, 1908–1914, p. 994

Ask students to locate and identify the major and minor powers on this map. Given the geography, what potential sources of conflict existed in this region?

Mapping the West: Europe at the Outbreak of World War I, August 1914, p. 998

Ask students to identify Germany on this map. Where are Germany's potential enemies located? How were Germany's political developments and worldview in the late nineteenth and early twentieth centuries affected by these geographical relationships?

Figure 25.1, The Growth in Armaments, 1890–1914, p. 995

What caused such a rapid increase in armaments between 1910 and 1914? Which country had the largest increase in armaments? Why?

Large German Family, p. 963

Have students describe the living conditions presented in this photo. What was the quality of life for the urban working class? How do they think people would respond politically to such conditions?

Sydney Grundy, The New Woman, p. 965

How is the "new woman" depicted in this poster? What makes her differ from a "traditional woman"? Compare this image with the photograph of Marie Curie and her daughter (p. 971).

Pablo Picasso, Les Demoiselles d'Avignon, *p. 973*

Have students describe the painting. How does it differ from representational art? What makes it "modern" art?

Kaiser William and Edward VII's Family, p. 969

What role did the connections of the royal families play in diplomacy in the days before the outbreak of World War I? What does this effect suggest about the role of the royal families in the age of mass politics? What does it say about the role of individuals in history?

OTHER BEDFORD/ST. MARTIN'S RESOURCES FOR CHAPTER 25

The following resources are available to accompany Chapter 25. Please refer to the Preface of this manual for detailed descriptions of all the ancillaries.

For Instructors

Transparencies

The following maps and images from Chapter 25 are available as full-color acetates.

- Map 25.1: Jewish Migrations in the Late Nineteenth Century
- Map 25.2: Africa in 1914
- Map 25.3: Imperialism in Asia, 1894–1914
- Map 25.4: The Balkans, 1908–1914
- Mapping the West: Europe at the Outbreak of World War I, August 1914
- *Boxer Rebellion*
- Picasso, *Les Demoiselles d'Avignon*

Instructor's Resources CD-ROM

The following maps and image from Chapter 25, as well as a chapter outline, are available on disc in both Power-Point and jpeg formats.

- Map 25.1: Jewish Migrations in the Late Nineteenth Century
- Map 25.2: Africa in 1914
- Map 25.3: Imperialism in Asia, 1894–1914
- Map 25.4: The Balkans, 1908–1914
- Mapping the West: Europe at the Outbreak of World War I, August 1914
- *Boxer Rebellion*

Using the Bedford Series with The Making of the West

Available in print as well as online at <u>bedfordstmartins</u> <u>.com/usingseries</u>, this guide offers practical suggestions for using *France and the Dreyfus Affair: A Brief Documentary History* by Michael Burns in conjunction with Chapter 25 of the textbook, and *July 1914: Soldiers, Statesmen, and the Coming of the Great War, A Brief Documentary History* by Samuel R. Williamson Jr. and Russel Van Wyk, in conjunction with chapters 25 and 26 of the textbook.

For Students

Sources of The Making of the West

The following documents are available in Chapter 25 of the companion sourcebook by Katharine J. Lualdi, University of Southern Maine.

1. Friedrich Nietzsche, *The Gay Science* (1882)
2. Emile Zola, *J'Accuse!* (January 13, 1898)
3. The I-ho-ch'uan (Boxers), *The Boxers Demand Death for All "Foreign Devils"* (1900)
4. Emmeline Pankhurst, *Speech from the Dock* (1908)
5. Sigmund Freud, *Infantile Sexuality* (1905)

Study Guides

The print **Study Guide** and the **Online Study Guide** at bedfordstmartins.com/hunt, both by Victoria Thompson (Arizona State University) and Eric Johnson (University of California, Los Angeles), help students synthesize the material they have learned as well as practice the skills historians use to make sense of the past. The following Map, Visual, and Document activities are available for Chapter 25.

Map Activity

- Map 25.2: Africa in 1914

Visual Activity

- Boxer Rebellion

Reading Historical Documents

- Document: Leon Pinsker Calls for a Jewish State
- An Historian Promotes Militant Nationalism

War, Revolution, and Reconstruction
1914–1929

CHAPTER RESOURCES

Main Chapter Topics

1. When war erupted in August 1914, long-standing alliances formed into the Central Powers (Germany and Austria-Hungary, and later the Ottoman Empire) on the one side, and the Allied forces (Britain, France, and Russia, and later Japan and the United States) on the other. Both sides of the conflict utilized modern military technologies such as heavy artillery, machine guns, and airplanes, but clung to obsolete strategies and tactics, notably the Schlieffen Plan and the "cult of the offensive." Looking to earlier, rapid victories by Prussia and Japan, a short, decisive conflict was predicted by all. But the four-year war would be a total war, mobilizing entire societies and causing unprecedented mass slaughter and horror.

2. Ordinary soldiers in World War I were not automatons. Some battalions went for long periods with low casualties. These low casualty rates stemmed from fraternization between opposing troops who fought in fairly close proximity to each other. Throughout the war, soldiers across the trenches agreed to avoid fighting. New male camaraderie alleviated misery, aided survival, and weakened traditional class distinctions. Positive memories of this front-line community survived the war and influenced postwar politics.

3. Initially, nearly all set aside their differences, but divisions reemerged when citizens faced shortages, runaway inflation, and staggering casualties. The populace's relentless suffering pushed Russia into revolution. In March 1917, Tsar Nicholas II abdicated. Bolshevik leader Vladimir Lenin returned to Russia and began calling for the spontaneously elected soviets to overturn the democratic Provisional Government, nationalize all privately held lands, and end the war. Lenin took over the soviets, formed a Communist government, and won a civil war against antirevolutionary forces by 1922.

4. In November 1918, revolutionaries in Germany declared a republic and forced Kaiser William II to abdicate. Although Germany's revolutions—from both the left and right—failed, the Weimar Republic set the dangerous precedent of relying on street violence, paramilitary groups, and protests to resolve problems.

5. At the Paris Peace Conference (1919), Woodrow Wilson presented his Fourteen Points for a new international order and a nonvindictive peace settlement. The Fourteen Points did not, however, suit the European victors. The Peace of Paris (1919–1920), a cluster of individual treaties, shocked the defeated countries and some farseeing experts: eastern and central Europe was destabilized through the formation of states consisting of multiple ethnic groups, such as Czechoslovakia, Yugoslavia, and Poland; broke apart the Ottoman Empire; and treated Germany severely with impossible reparations and a "guilt clause" that placed the blame for the war directly on Germany.

6. During World War I, Europe had lost many of its international markets to overseas competitors, including Japan, which grew even stronger during the 1920s. Although Europe overcame economic problems and enjoyed renewed prosperity by the late 1920s, the United States had become the trendsetter of economic modernization. Adopting some methods and ideas from the United States, European economies modernized, as both the managerial class and the union movement continued to grow.

7. Postwar society had to deal with millions of brutalized, incapacitated, shell-shocked, often resentful veterans who returned to a changed world. Fearful of the threat of widespread discontent, governments wanted to reintegrate these men back into society as quickly as possible. Pensions for veterans, benefits for the unemployed, and housing for the returning soldiers and seaman were all designed to alleviate the people's problems and pent-up anger, which had resulted from the war.

8. Cultural leaders in the 1920s were either obsessed by the horrendous experiences of war or, like the prewar

modernists, held high hopes for creating a fresh, utopian future that would have little relation to the past. In both cases, the art produced broke with tradition, thereby continuing the prewar cultural debates about traditional versus modern art.

9. Despite the hopes of many Europeans for a more democratic world, by the end of the 1920s, political strongmen (like Joseph Stalin and Benito Mussolini) had risen to power in several European states. Using mass communications, these despotic, tyrannical leaders promoted mass politics that were antidemocratic, brutal, and totalitarian. These leaders and their systems would be perceived by many as a precursor of the future—particularly after the stock market crash (1929) and the resulting global economic depression.

Summary

Two sides emerged in World War I, formed roughly out of the alliances developed during the fifty years that preceded. The Central Powers (Austria-Hungary and Germany) faced the Allies (Britain, France, and Russia). Japan almost immediately joined the Allies in 1914 in an attempt to expand its interests in China, whereas the Ottoman Empire sided with the Central Powers against Russia. Italy, also hoping for postwar gain, joined the Allies in 1915. Most combatants had expansionist agendas that they believed would be advanced by the war. The colonies provided conscripted troops and even became battlefronts (especially in Africa and the Middle East).

When war erupted in August 1914, the Central Powers and the Allies fought with the same ferocious hunger for power, prestige, and prosperity that had propelled imperialism. Believing that a decisive battlefield victory would end the war quickly, all combatants retained the old-fashioned "cult of the offensive," in which an army would charge its enemy's position brandishing sabers, lances, and bayonets. However, military technology had far outpaced military planning. Machine guns, rifles, airplanes, battleships, submarines, and motorized transports transformed warfare, as did chlorine gas, tanks, and bombs, which were developed between 1914 and 1918. Military offensives, rather than producing the quick victory all expected, resulted instead in mass slaughter on an unprecedented scale. From 1914 through 1916, offensives on all fronts did not lead to any decisive victories. As the war dragged on, the exuberant patriotism of the summer of 1914 gave way to increased alienation, frustration, and anger.

Germany's confidence in a short war was based on a plan devised by General Alfred von Schlieffen (1833–1913) which was to neutralize France within six weeks by passing though Belgium to attack. According to von Schlieffen's plan, when France had been defeated, troops could be shifted to the Russian front which, until

that point, would be maintained by a smaller holding force. But Belgium unexpectedly resisted and allowed instead French and British forces to mobilize in their country. By September, the British and French faced off against the Germans along Marne River, with neither side able to defeat the other. In the first months of the war, 1.5 million men fell on the western front alone and millions more continued to fight under horrifying conditions in trenches that stretched from the North Sea through Belgium and northern France to Switzerland. On the eastern front, the Russians possessed numerical superiority and, with this advantage, initially pushed deep into East Prussia. But the Russian army was poorly armed and trained and quickly defeated by the German army. The Germans faced stalemate on both the western and eastern fronts.

There was stalemate at sea as well. The Allies blockaded ports to prevent supplies reaching the Central Powers. The Germans launched a submarine campaign against Allied and neutral shipping and, in May 1915, the British passenger ship, the *Lusitania*, was sunk killing 1,198 people, 124 of whom were Americans. Still, U.S. President Woodrow Wilson maintained neutrality, and indiscriminant naval attacks ceased. In 1916, the British and German fleets met in the North Sea at the inconclusive battle of Jutland. Germany could not break Britain's naval power.

Despite the destruction, general military staffs on both sides of the conflict continued to plan major offensives. Indecisive campaigns opened with massive military artillery bombardment, followed by large battalions of troops attacking the enemy who easily gunned them down from the safety of their trenches. Casualties of 100,000 and more became common for a single campaign. In 1916, in the battle for Verdun, French and German losses came to almost 1 million; while at the battle of the Somme, British and German losses numbered over 1.25 million men. By the end of that year, France had sustained over 3.5 million casualties. And still there was stalemate. In the east, the Russians menaced the Habsburg Empire, which began recruiting men in their fifties. Saved by German forces, the German general staff stepped in to direct Austrian military operations compromising Habsburg independence.

The experience of war varied among the soldiers. Some troops on both sides avoided suicidal confrontations, and soldiers fraternized on the front lines, sometimes playing ball and exchanging mementos. The battlefield also shattered social barriers between upper-class officers and working-class draftees. Racial divisions also sometimes dissolved as colonial troops fought in the front ranks where danger was greatest. The perspective of colonial troops changed as they saw their "masters" become decidedly "uncivilized."

As losses on the battlefields mounted, political parties on both sides of the conflict initially set aside their differences and assumed nationalist postures. The nations of Europe mobilized persons from the home fronts in order to ensure the steady production and flow of war matériel. Governments, to varying degrees, regulated production, allocated labor, limited workers' rights, rationed raw material and food, provided work incentives for women, and disregarded work regulation laws. They also established propaganda agencies to increase hatred toward the enemy and enacted sedition laws that made it illegal to criticize governmental policy.

All these acts were designed to prepare nations for total war. Rather than binding peoples together, however, the war effort politicized them further by dividing ethnic groups, nations, and empires as never before. Unfair allocation of resources, high profits for businesses, runaway inflation, shortages of basic necessities, social unrest over the effects of women in the workforce, and growing resentment of the restrictions on civilians fed discontent. Colonial civilians suffered especially because they were forcibly conscripted to work for the war effort. The German resumption of unrestricted submarine warfare in the Atlantic, geared toward blockading Britain, brought the United States into the war in April 1917. Dissent over the war affected both sides. Food shortages in Italy, Germany, Russia, and Austria provoked riots and soaring inflation prompted strikes. The new Habsburg emperor requested secret peace negotiations and, in the summer 1917, the German Reichstag were also making peace overtures. That spring, some French troops mutinied over continued, fruitless offensives.

Although suffering was widespread by 1917, the situation was gravest in Russia, which had been overwhelmed by the war and embittered by the staggering losses and terrible privations. The riots that broke out in March 1917 caused Tsar Nicholas II to abdicate, thus ending the three-hundred-year Romanov dynasty. The democratic Provisional Government sought to pursue the war successfully, better manage internal affairs, and establish a constitutional government while competing with the spontaneously elected soviets (workers' and soldiers' councils). Bolshevik leader V. I. Lenin (1870–1924) returned to Russia at this critical moment urging land reform and an end to the war; he began calling for the soviets to seize power on behalf of workers and poor peasants. In November, the Bolsheviks overthrew the Provisional Government and claimed their right to form a new government. The Bolsheviks made peace with Germany and, in the Treaty of Brest-Litovsk (March 1918), vast regions of the old Russian Empire were ceded to Germany. This enabled Lenin to concentrate on winning the civil war at home. Pro-Bolsheviks (or "Reds") were pitted against an antirevolutionary forces (or "Whites"), which included the tsarist military leadership, aristocrats, intellectuals, businessmen, and non-Russian nationality groups. But the disorganized Whites were no match for Lenin and Trotsky who confiscated the military supplies they needed and set up the Cheka ("secret police") to stamp out dissent. The Bolsheviks solidified their power by 1922 when they crushed all opposition via an authoritarian style of rule.

German military leaders attempted one last offensive in the spring of 1918, but they could not defeat the Allies, which now included the United States. As the Allies pushed forward, the German army collapsed. The German military command helped create a civilian government, hoodwinking the politicians into taking responsibility for the defeat and suing for peace. Amid this political deceit and flux, seamen in Kiel revolted, setting off revolts and demonstrations throughout the country. As a result, the German Social Democratic leaders declared a republic. On November 9, 1918, Kaiser William II fled the country, and the armistice was signed on November 11. Conservative figures put the battlefield toll at a minimum of ten million deaths' and thirty million wounded, incapacitated, or eventually died of their wounds. From 1918–1919, an influenza epidemic left at least twenty million more dead. The flood of war memoirs and poetry emphasized that total war had drained society of resources and population, and set the stage for future catastrophes.

As the war ended, revolutionary fervor swept across Europe, but especially in Germany. In the turmoil, radical groups formed, the most prominent being the Sparticists led by cofounders Karl Liebknecht (1871–1919) and Rosa Luxemburg (1870–1919) who argued for direct worker control of institutions. Under Friedrich Ebert's (1871–1925) guidance, the Social Democratic leadership, desiring a parliamentary republic and fearing a Communist revolution, aligned with the German army and paramilitary units (Freikorps) to destroy the active, leftist opposition. The Freikorps hunted down and murdered Liebknecht and Luxemburg. With the proclamation of the democratic constitution in Weimar, right-wing Freikorps also threatened the new government in the Kapp Putsch (1920). Although both right and left revolutions failed, the Weimar Republic's grip on power was far from secure, and it had set the dangerous precedent of relying on street violence, paramilitary groups, and protests to resolve problems.

As political turmoil engulfed peoples throughout Europe, the Paris Peace Conference opened in January 1919. Fearful of communism spreading from Russia, statesmen approached the future status of Germany and the reconstruction of a secure Europe with incompatible visions of the postwar world and pressured by the desperation of millions of war-ravaged citizens who sought revenge as much as basic necessities. The Fourteen Points of Woodrow Wilson (1856–1924) appealed to European moderates who understood that a treaty must not be vindictive. Wilson pressed for a treaty that balanced the interests of the victors and the vanquished because he believed that a humiliated Germany would someday soon become vengeful and chaotic.

The Peace of Paris consisted of individual treaties that redrew European boundaries. Austria was separated from Hungary, Hungary lost almost two-thirds of its inhabitants and three-quarters of its territory, and the Ottoman Empire was broken up. Carved out of the Habsburg Empire were the weak and internally divided states of Czechoslovakia and Yugoslavia (consisting of Serbia, Croatia, and Slovenia). Poland was created out of former Russian, German, and Habsburg territories. But the centerpiece of the Peace of Paris's individual treaties was the Treaty of Versailles with Germany. Germany lost Alsace and Lorraine as well as other territories and colonies, was deprived of its armed forces and forbidden to manufacture war matériel, had part of its territory occupied, and was ordered to pay war reparations to France and Great Britain. The humiliation Germans felt was compounded by Article 231 of the treaty, which described Germany's responsibility for the damage done by the conflict and allowed the Allies to collect payments from economically viable Germany rather than from decimated Austria. The "guilt clause" made Germany an outcast in the community of nations. Wilson's fears of a humiliating treaty were eventually proved to be prescient.

The Peace of Paris also established the League of Nations. Under the principle of collective security, the league was responsible for maintaining global peace, but it was weak from the beginning. Germany and Russia were initially excluded, and the U.S. Senate, reverting to isolationism, failed to ratify the peace settlement and refused to join the league. The League of Nations organized the administration of the colonies and territories of Germany and the Ottoman Empire (such as Cameroon, Syria, and Palestine) through a mandate system. The political control exercised by European powers over mandated territory was based on the premise that these "primitive" territories were too weak to stand on their own in the modern world and needed protection. Yet, colonial peoples had seen firsthand the brutality and savagery of their "masters" and chafed under the mandate system.

The Peace of Paris's repercussions were felt in the 1920s and beyond. In the aftermath of World War I, Western leaders worried about two interdependent issues: economic recovery and ensuring a lasting peace. Germany quickly found it impossible to pay the reparations specified in the Treaty of Versailles, and reneged on monetary and in-kind payments. In retaliation, France and Belgium occupied the Ruhr basin, which was rich in natural resources. To make up for the loss, the German government issued more and more paper currency, which very quickly became worthless. Soon staggering inflation in Germany gravely threatened international economies. The Dawes Plan (1924) and eventually the Young Plan (1929) reduced payments to the victors and restored the value of German currency. Notwithstanding, inflation had wreaked enduring financial and psy-

chological havoc. The Treaty of Locarno provided Germany with a seat in the League of Nations as of 1926, in return for which Germany promised not to violate French or Belgium borders and to keep the Rhineland demilitarized. To guard against future German, Russian, or Hungarian aggression in the east, Czechoslovakia, Yugoslavia, and Romania formed the "Little Entente" in 1920–1921. Between 1924 and 1927, France joined the "Little Entente" and Poland. And, in 1928, the major European powers, Japan, and the United States signed the Kellogg-Briand Pact renouncing international violence. Although international meetings promoted collective security, these meetings also exposed the diplomatic process to the nationalist press and to demagogues who could rekindle political hatreds.

War had a lasting cultural and linguistic affect. *Lousy* had once meant "lice-infested," but English-speaking veterans applied it to anything bad. Raincoats became *trenchcoats*, and terms like *bombarded* and *rank and file* entered into common usage. Maimed veterans were a common sight. The release evident in the Roaring Twenties and the Jazz Age masked serious sociopolitical problems. In England, women were granted the vote in recognition of their contributions to the war effort, but women in France and Italy would not receive the vote until after World War II. Governments attempted to help stabilize society by extending payments to veterans, families with children, and workers who were unemployed or injured.

The Great War did not resolve Europe's problems as many had hoped, but rather a more pervasive postwar cynicism followed the prewar sense of decline. In response, some westerners turned their back on politics, snapped up consumer goods, enjoyed new forms of entertainment, and personal freedoms. Other individuals found hope in Soviet communism and Italian fascism. Utilizing mass communications, Lenin, Stalin, and Mussolini promoted antidemocratic, militaristic, and totalitarian political systems. Throughout the 1920s, the newly independent states of eastern Europe faced particularly difficult obstacles. Unschooled in self-government, lacking a democratic tradition, ethnically divided, economically backward, and intensely competitive with each other, these states (with the exception of Czechoslovakia) had a very difficult time creating stable and prosperous democratic societies. Economic hardship and strong-arm solutions went hand in hand in eastern Europe.

The postwar period also presented challenges for western Europe. Although the German economy improved and Germany became a center of experimentation in the arts, many experienced nostalgia for imperial glory and loathed the Versailles Treaty's restrictions. Right-wing parties favored violence rather than consensus-building and nationalist thugs murdered with abandon democratic leaders and Jews. Charismatic leaders like Adolf Hitler played on the disaffection of the middle and lower middle classes whose standard of living had declined. In 1923, Hitler attempted a coup, but the Beer Hall Putsch failed and he was jailed for a year. While France had to deal with a loss of population and wartime destruction, Britain had to face the fact that although it had become the world's largest empire, its industries were obsolete. Competition from the Ruhr mines bought down England's coal prices and coal workers went on strike (May 1926). Middle-class workers who were unsympathetic to the strike drove trains, worked on docks, and replaced striking workers in order to keep the economy going. Ireland also remained problematic. Violence had erupted when the British government failed to implement home rule in 1916. In 1919, republican leaders announced Ireland's independence, which the British Parliament refused to recognize. Guerilla warfare erupted on both sides. In 1921, the Irish Free State in the south was granted dominion status, whereas Northern Ireland became self-governing with representatives in Parliament. Other European powers also faced increased rebellions in their colonies and/or protectorates, where people expected more rights and even independence because of the sacrifices they had made during the war. In the main, European powers responded brutally to colonial political activism. Despite colonial resistance, Britain and France were at the height of their global power. They took advantage of Germany's former colonies in Africa and of their hold on the Middle East. Cheap oil fueled growing numbers of cars, planes, and like machinery, and heated homes. Hot chocolate and tropical fruit became regular items in the diets.

Japan did particularly well after the war and took shipping, financial, and other businesses away from Britain and France. And, while not yet strong enough to oppose European policies directly, Japan enjoyed growing prosperity and was beginning to edge Britain out of China.

During the war, Europe lost many of its international markets to overseas competitors. Even though Europe did overcome economic problems and enjoyed renewed prosperity by the late 1920s, the United States set the trends in economic modernization. Many Europeans hoped that usage of Henry Ford's (1863–1947) assembly line and Frederick Taylor's (1856–1915) scientific management methods would increase in European productivity and, in turn, build prosperity, create better labor relations, and diminish the threat of communism. In reality, these methods did not lessen the hours or drudgery of work, and the emphasis on efficiency seemed inhuman to many workers. Nevertheless, European economies modernized, and both the managerial class and the union movement grew.

After the war, millions of brutalized, incapacitated, shell-shocked, and often resentful veterans returned to a changed home world. Civilians—especially women—felt estranged from these returning veterans. Women had

bobbed (cut) their hair, shortened their skirts, taken up the smoking habit, and earned money of their own. In the United States, this postwar woman was called a "flapper." Abandoned by wives and sweethearts, some veterans refused to disband and attacked women in public jobs, such as streetcar conductors. Governments wanted to reintegrate these men into society as quickly as possible. Pensions for veterans, benefits for the unemployed, and housing for the returning soldiers and seamen were all designed to improve the quality of life and defuse pent-up anger.

Freer relationships also characterized the 1920s. Young men and women visited jazz clubs and movies together. Revealing bathing suits, short skirts, and form-fitting clothes emphasized women's sexuality. Although the context for sexuality remained marriage, both men and women expected to enjoy the sexual side of the marital relationship and were given explicit advice on how to achieve it. D. H. Lawrence (1885–1930), in *Women in Love* (1920), and Ernest Hemingway (1899–1961) in *The Sun Also Rises* (1926), glorified men's sexual vigor. In this new atmosphere, personal appearance took on new importance. Personal hygiene improved, the cosmetics industry exploded, and physical fitness was promoted.

Social services, economic prosperity, and the gradual postwar increase in real wages provided the economic underpinnings for the culture of this period. As prosperity returned, the middle and upper classes could afford to buy more consumer goods, such as washing machines, vacuum cleaners, irons, and gas stoves. At the same time, new products that enhanced mass communication—such as automobiles, phonographs, radios, and film—brought unforeseen changes in the public world of culture and mass politics. Mass media could promote and further democracy, but it could also become propaganda tools in the hands of dictators like Benito Mussolini, Josef Stalin, and Adolf Hitler.

The film industry took off in the 1920s. Films of literary classics and political events developed a sense of common heritage among people. British documentaries articulated national goals, while Sergei Eisenstein's (1898–1948) silent films *Potemkin* (1925) and *Ten Days that Shook the World* (1927–1928) presented a Bolshevik view of history to Russian and international audiences. Initially, aspects of music hall entertainment—such as comical characters, farcical plots, and slapstick humor—were incorporated into films, but soon other elements surfaced. Detective and cowboy movies showed heroes who could restore justice to a disordered world. Most popular of all were the films of Charlie Chaplin (1889–1977) whose "Little Tramp" character represented the defeated hero, the anonymous man trying to maintain his dignity in a mechanical world. Films featuring international characters were also popular, as were films of sporting events. Radios became a relatively inexpensive consumer item and radio broadcasts broke boundaries.

Cultural leaders in the 1920s were either obsessed by the horrendous experiences of war or hoped for a utopian future free from the past. Some intellectuals turned to Asian philosophies and religions for inspiration, whereas others fixed on the independence and pacifist leader Mohandas Gandhi (1869–1948). Many artists and intellectuals pursued a brutal and cynical style. For example, German Dada artist George Grosz (1893–1959) produced paintings and cartoons of maimed soldiers and brutally murdered women that reflected his desire to "bellow back." Other avant-garde portrayals of seediness and perversion in everyday life flourished during the 1920s. Popular writers like Ernst Junger (1895–1998) glorified life in the trenches and advocated the militarization of society to restore order. His polar opposite, Erich Maria Remarque (1898–1970), called for an end to all war in *All Quiet on the Western Front* (1928). Postwar poetry rejected the comforting rhymes and accessible metaphors of prewar verse. Postwar life was bleakly depicted in "The Waste Land" (1922) by American poet T. S. Eliot (1888–1965), and in "Sailing to Byzantium," by Irish poet William Butler Yeats. The Czech writer Franz Kafka (1883–1924) captured the hopelessness of civilian life in a heavily industrialized world in *The Trial* (1925) and *The Castle* (1926). Taking their cue from Freud, some writers focused on the inner life, like Marcel Proust (1871–1922) who, in his multivolume *Remembrance of Things Past* (1913–1927), explored the workings of memory, the passage of time, and sexual modernity. James Joyce (1882–1941) in *Ulysses* (1922), and Virginia Woolf (1882–1941) in *Mrs. Dalloway* (1925), used the mental thoughts of their main characters to propel their novels, a technique called "stream of consciousness." In *Orlando* (1928), Woolf explored gender identity and created a male character who traveled forward through time, eventually being reincarnated as a woman. Other, more hopeful artists gloried in the promises of the modern world. For example, the Bauhaus in Germany created streamlined buildings and designed functional furniture, utensils, and decorative objects. European artists who were fascinated by technology and machinery were most often drawn—not to Germany or the Soviet Union—but to the United States. Hollywood films, glossy ads, jazz, and New York skyscrapers represented the promise of modernity for careworn Europeans.

In Russia, counterrevolutionaries protested the policy of war communism whereby the army confiscated what it needed from peasant farmers. Suffering from food and housing shortages, workers in Petrograd (formerly St. Petersburg) and seamen at a nearby naval base revolted, pointing to the higher standard of living Bolshevik managers enjoyed. After defeating the counterrevolutionary opposition, Lenin realized that he had to pull back on some of his Communist ideas in order to create a functioning economy. He therefore replaced war communism of the civil war era with the New Economic Policy (NEP). NEP was a compromise with capitalism that allowed for a limited free market. But the NEP was geared toward agrarian reform and, at the 1921 party congress, a group called the Worker Opposition objected to the party's usurpation of economic control from worker's organizations. Lenin suppressed the Worker Opposition and purged dissidents from the party. At the same time, the Communist Party consolidated its control over culture and society by setting up classes in various of political and social subjects, facilitating equality between men and women, promoting birth control education, making abortion legal, setting up day-care centers, encouraging better hygiene, modernizing industry, and generally regulating every aspect of daily life. In 1924, Lenin died and, although he had specifically requested that Joseph Stalin (1879–1953) be removed from power, Stalin instead exiled Trotsky and emerged as the dictator of the Soviet Union by 1928–1929.

Through the use of his army of Black Shirts (made up of veterans and the unemployed), Benito Mussolini (1883–1945) forced his appointment as prime minister and planted fascism in the soil of poverty, social unrest, and wounded national pride. Although his movement was violent and at times brutal, Mussolini's ability to unite the nation (in part through the use of mass media and public displays of power) and seeming ability to develop the Italian economy and military gained him many admirers in the 1920s. He gained papal support by recognizing the Vatican as an independent state with control over family and marital issues, and influence over education. Mussolini introduced a corporate state that denied individual rights in favor of duty to the state. Independent unions were outlawed and in their place corporatist laws in 1926 gathered together employers, workers, and professionals into official groups and organizations that would settle grievances and determine conditions of work. Women, banned from certain professions, saw their wages reduced.

In Germany, Adolf Hitler admired Mussolini and his reforms and, throughout the 1920s, Hitler established and expanded a paramilitary group of storm troopers and a political organization called the Nationalist Socialist German Worker's Party, or Nazis. While serving jail time after the Beer Hall Putsch, Hitler wrote his personal manifesto *Mein Kampf* (*My Struggle* [1925]), which articulated a virulent anti-Semitism and a political psychology for manipulating the masses.

In spite of the hopes of many Europeans for a more democratic world, by the end of the 1920s political strongmen had come to power in several of the eastern European states, the Soviet Union, and Italy, with Hitler waiting in the wings in Germany. When the U.S. stock market crashed (1929) and economic disaster circled the globe, authoritarian solutions and militarism continued to look appealing. What followed was a series of catastrophes even more devastating than World War I.

Suggestions for Lecture and Discussion Topics

1. In order to help explain why World War I traumatized Europe, ask students to discuss the conditions of life on the front lines. What did the men and women at the front witness? How were they forever changed by the experience? A good way to explore these questions is to have students read the writings of those who lived through the war. Two excellent contemporary novels on the war are Erich Maria Remarque's classic *All Quiet on the Western Front* (Boston: Little, Brown, 1929); and Helen Zenna Smith's answer from a woman's perspective, *Not So Quiet . . . Stepdaughters of War* (New York: The Feminist Press, 1930, 1989). As an alternative to assigning both books, the 1930 film version of *All Quiet on the Western Front* can serve in lieu of the novel. Two excellent collections of World War I poetry are Candace Ward, ed., *World War One British Poets: Brooke, Owen, Sassoon, Rosenberg and Others* (Mineola, NY: Dover, 1997); and Jon Silkin, ed., *First World War Poetry* (New York: Viking Press, 1997). Also, the video set *The Great War and the Shaping of the Twentieth Century* (Alexandria, VA: PBS Home Video, 1996); R. C. Sherriff's play *Journey's End*; and Ernest Hemingway's *In Our Time* (1925), will further illuminate the war for students. Works on the battlefield experience include John Elis, *Eye-Deep in Hell: Trench Warfare in World War I* (Baltimore: Johns Hopkins University Press, 1989); Lyn Macdonald, *1915: The Death of Innocence* (Baltimore: Johns Hopkins University Press, 2000); Lyn Macdonald, *Somme* (London: Michael Joseph, 1983); Robert Graves's autobiography, *Good-Bye to All That* (New York: Doubleday, 1929, 1985); Eric J. Leed, *No Man's Land: Combat and Identity in World War I* (New York: Cambridge University Press, 1979); John Keegan, *The Face of Battle: a Study of Agincourt, Waterloo and the Somme* (New York: Random House, 1967); and Alistair Horne, *The Price of Glory: Verdun 1916* (New York: Penguin, 1993). Works on the cultural impact and memory of the war include Modris Eksteins, *Rites of Spring: The Great War and the Birth of the Modern Age* (Boston: Houghton Mifflin, 1989); Paul Fussell, *The Great War and Modern Memory* (New York: Oxford University Press, 1975); George L. Mosse, *Fallen Soldiers: Reshaping the Memory of the World Wars* (New York: Oxford University Press, 1990); Jay Winter, *Sites of Memory, Sites of Mourning: The Great War in European Cultural Memory* (New York: Cambridge University Press, 1995); and Robert Wohl, *The Generation of 1914* (Cambridge, MA: Harvard University Press, 1979).

2. Another way for students to explore the experience of war is to examine the visual arts of the period. Works by artists such as Otto Dix, Max Beckmann, Kaethe Köllwitz, Ernst Ludwig Kirschner, and George Grosz contain many, often brutal and violent, images of the war and its aftermath. In class, show slides of art-works that depict the war and discuss the artists' imagery. By exploring this art, students will gain a deeper understanding of how and why the war continued to haunt the participants and how it shaped the culture of the following decades and beyond. An excellent source for images and information on these artists is Richard Cork, *A Bitter Truth: Avant-Garde Art and the Great War* (New Haven: Yale University Press, 1994). In addition, Cork's book has an extensive bibliography of works on artists and World War I. A video on Otto Dix that examines his images of the war in some detail is *Otto Dix: The Painter Is the Eyes of the World*. Another excellent source on Otto Dix is "The Work of the Devil," Chapter 1, vol. 4, of *The Great War and the Shaping of the Twentieth Century*.

3. Women's roles changed enormously during the war but, after hostilities had ceased, a debate ensued over women's "proper" role in European society. Discuss how women's status changed during the 1920s. What roles did women play in the Great War? What was the impact of suffrage? Which issues surrounded women's entry into the workforce? How were women depicted differently in the mass media? A good introduction on European women's history is Bonnie G. Smith, *Changing Lives: Women in European History Since 1700* (Lexington, MA: D. C. Heath, 1989). Primary sources include Vera Brittain's classic memoir of the British home front, *Testament of Youth: An Autobiographical Study of the Years 1900–1925* (New York: Penguin Books, 1933, 1989). Other useful sources on women's wartime experiences include Ute Daniel, *The War from Within: German Women in the First World War* (New York: Berg, 1997); Susan R. Grayzel, *Women's Identities at War: Gender, Motherhood, and Politics in Britain and France during the First World War* (Chapel Hill: University of North Carolina Press, 1999); Margaret Randolph Higonnet and Jane Jenson, eds., *Behind the Lines: Gender and the Two World Wars* (New Haven: Yale University Press, 1987); and Angela Woollacott, *On Her Their Lives Depend: Munitions Workers in the Great War* (Berkeley: University of California Press, 1994). Works on the changing status and roles of women during the 1920s include Katharina von Ankum, ed., *Women in the Metropolis: Gender and Modernity in Weimar Culture* (Berkeley: University of California Press, 1997); Victoria de Grazia, *How Fascism Ruled Women: Italy, 1922–1945* (Berkeley: University of California Press, 1992); Mary Louise Roberts, *Civilization without Sexes: Reconstructing Gender in Postwar France, 1917–1927* (Chicago: University of Chicago Press, 1994); and Elizabeth A. Wood, *The Baba and the Comrade: Gender and Politics in Revolutionary Russia* (Bloomington: Indiana University Press, 1997).

4. A good way to gain some insight into the popular images of the changing status of women and the debate over modernity is to show film clips that depict the modern "new woman" of the 1920s. How is the new woman depicted? Is she shown in a positive light? A negative

light? A neutral light? How do the depictions compare among the film clips? How does she differ from "traditional" women? What makes her "modern"? Films that portray the new woman include *Sunrise* (1927), *Pandora's Box* (1928), *Metropolis* (1926), and *The Blue Angel* (1930). See also the many films of the German silent screen actress Louise Brooks.

5. One of the most important events of the era was the Russian Revolution. Discuss in some detail the origins of the revolution, its course, and how the Communists solidified their power during this era. In addition, it would be very useful to detail the society—both the reality and the ideal—that emerged in the Soviet Union during the 1920s. An excellent book to assign on the Russian Revolution and its aftermath is Sheila Fitzpatrick, *The Russian Revolution*, 2d ed. (New York: Oxford University Press, 1994). Other books on the revolution and the developments of the 1920s include Katerina Clark, *Petersburg: Crucible of Cultural Revolution* (Cambridge, MA: Harvard University Press, 1995); Orlando Figes, *A People's Tragedy: A History of the Russian Revolution* (New York: Viking, 1996); Peter Kenez, *The Birth of the Propaganda State: Soviet Methods of Mass Mobilization, 1917–1929* (Cambridge: Cambridge University Press, 1985); W. Bruce Lincoln, *Red Victory: A History of the Russian Civil War* (New York: Da Capo Press, 1999); Richard Pipes, *A Concise History of the Russian Revolution* (New York: Alfred A. Knopf, 1995); Alexander Rabinowitch, *The Bolsheviks Come to Power: The Revolution of 1917 in Petrograd* (New York: W. W. Norton, 1976); Richard Stites, *Revolutionary Dreams: Utopian Vision and Experimental Life in the Russian Revolution* (New York: Oxford University Press, 1989); and John M. Thompson, *Revolutionary Russia, 1917* (New York: Charles Scribner's Sons, 1981).

6. After the horrors of World War I, many Europeans rejected traditional culture. As a result, the United States fascinated many Europeans during the 1920s. Discuss the impact of Americanization on Europe and how Europeans adopted and adapted "America" during this decade. Why was the United States so appealing during this time? What impact did Americanization have on European culture? Did this impact last? Good sources on this issue include Frank Costigliola, *Awkward Dominion: American Political, Economic, and Cultural Relations with Europe, 1919–1933* (Ithaca: Cornell University Press, 1984); Mary Nolan, *Visions of Modernity: American Business and the Modernization of Germany* (New York: Oxford University Press, 1994); and Thomas J. Saunders, *Hollywood in Berlin: American Cinema and Weimar Germany* (Berkeley: University of California Press, 1994).

Writing Assignments and Class Presentation Topics

1. Have students research and write an essay on the so-called war guilt debate. By exploring this issue and then debating it in class, students will not only deepen their understanding of the war, but will also get an insight into issues concerning evidence and interpretation. Sources should include works by Fritz Fischer, whose first book presented a very controversial account of war guilt that sparked the debate that still reverberates today. Fischer's books are *Germany's Aims in the First World War* (New York: W. W. Norton, 1967); *World Power or Decline: The Controversy over Germany's Aims in the First World War* (New York: W. W. Norton, 1974); and *War of Illusions: German Politics from 1911 to 1914* (New York: W. W. Norton, 1975). Other sources include Holger H. Herwig, *The Outbreak of World War I*, 5th ed. (Lexington, MA: D. C. Heath, 1991); John Anthony Moses, *The Politics of Illusion: The Fischer Controversy in German Historiography* (New York: Barnes & Noble, 1975); and Gregor Schollen, ed., *Escape into War?: The Foreign Policy of Imperial Germany* (New York: Berg, 1990).

2. One of the significant developments in the wake of World War I was the dissolution of the Austro-Hungarian Empire. Have the students divide into groups and research one of the successor states from independence through the late 1920s. What challenges did these newly independent states encounter? How did they deal with them? Class presentations will help students understand the issues facing these new states and the problems that continued to plague them through World War II.

3. Ask students to write an essay comparing the propaganda of two of the combatant nations of World War I. Have them address the following questions: What kinds of appeals, messages, and imagery are used? How, for example, are the enemy and the home front depicted? How do the depictions compare from country to country? Which propaganda messages and images are more effective and why? Sources for World War I posters include Joseph Darracott, *The First World War in Posters* (New York: Dover, 1974); and Peter Paret, Beth Irwin Lewis, and Paul Paret, *Persuasive Images: Posters of War and Revolution* (Princeton: Princeton University Press, 1992).

4. To further students' understanding of the peace settlement and its flaws, divide the class into groups and have each group research and then represent individual countries at the Paris Peace Conference. Have students reenact the conference, arguing territorial or reparation issues from their country's unique perspective.

5. Comparative studies are a good way to develop understanding of historical events. Have students write essays comparing Fascist Italy to Nazi Germany. Ask students to investigate the origins of the movements, their agendas, their members, their use of propaganda, and the role of their leader. Three good sources that examine these regimes are Richard Bessel, ed., *Fascist Italy and Nazi Germany: Comparisons and Contrasts* (New York: Cambridge University Press, 1996); Alexander J. De Grand, *Fascist Italy and Nazi Germany: The "Fascist" Style of Rule* (New York: Routledge, 1995); and Bruce F. Pauley, *Hitler, Stalin and Mussolini: Totalitarianism in the Twentieth Century* (Wheeling, IL: Harlan Davidson, 1997).

Research Assignments

1. During the 1920s, an unprecedented explosion of artistic creativity emerged from the cafés, cabarets, and studios of Paris and Berlin. By exploring the output of painters, sculptors, writers, architects, and filmmakers, students can better understand why this era witnessed a cultural flowering that directly challenged centuries-old ideas and conceptions. Have students write research papers on an artist or a movement of the period or focus on the developments in either Paris or Berlin. Examples of topics are Dada, surrealism, postwar literature, film, Art Deco, and the Bauhaus. Sources on general cultural developments in Paris during the 1920s include Charles Rearick, *The French in Love and War: Popular Culture in the Era of the World Wars* (New Haven: Yale University Press, 1997); and William Wiser, *The Crazy Years: Paris in the Twenties* (New York: Thames and Hudson, 1983). Sources on general developments in Berlin include Otto Friedrich, *Before the Deluge: A Portrait of Berlin in the 1920s* (New York: Harper & Row, 1972); Peter Gay, *Weimar Culture: The Insider As Outsider* (New York: Harper & Row, 1968); and John Willett, *Art and Poltics in the Weimar Period: The New Sobriety 1917–1933* (New York: Da Capo Press, 1978). Works on Dada and surrealism include Matthew Gale, *Dada and Surrealism* (London: Phaidon Press, 1997); and such primary sources as André Breton, *Manifestoes of Surrealism* (Ann Arbor: University of Michigan Press, 1969); and Robert Motherwell, ed., *The Dada Painters and Poets: An Anthology*, 2d ed. (Boston: G. K. Hall, 1981). Sources on the Bauhaus include Barbara Miller Lane, *Architecture and Politics in Germany, 1918–1945* (Cambridge, MA: Harvard University Press, 1968); and Frank Whitford, *Bauhaus* (New York: Thames and Hudson, 1984).

2. During the 1920s, Paris became the home of a truly unique international community of American expatriate artists and writers who sought the artistic freedom and inspiration that they found lacking in their homelands. Have students write research papers that discuss why a particular artist or group of artists sought refuge in Paris, what they found there, and the art or literature they produced. Examples of subjects are Ernest Hemingway, F. Scott Fitzgerald, Henry Miller, Man Ray, Gertrude Stein, Djuna Barnes, and Janet Flanner. Important literary works from the period include Ernest Hemingway, *In Our Time*, *The Sun Also Rises*, and *A Farewell to Arms*; Henry Miller, *Tropic of Cancer*; and Gertrude Stein, *The Autobiography of Alice B. Toklas*. Sources for this topic include Shari Benstock, *Women of the Left Bank: Paris, 1900–1940* (Austin: University of Texas Press, 1986); Malcolm Cowley, *A Second Flowering: Works and Days of the Lost Generation* (New York: Viking Press, 1973); Tyler Stoval, *Paris Noir: African Americans in the City of Light* (New York; Mariner Books, 1996); Andrea Weiss, *Paris Was a Woman: Portraits from the Left Bank* (San Francisco: Harper San Francisco, 1995); and George Wickes, *Americans in Paris* (Garden City, NY: Doubleday, 1969).

3. As a "total war," World War I had a direct and lasting impact on the home front. Ask students to choose one European country and write research papers that explore the political, economic, social, and cultural changes that took place in their chosen nation during the war. Sources include Jean-Jacques Becker, *The Great War and the French People* (New York: St. Martin's, 1986); Brian Bond, *War and Society in Europe, 1870–1970* (New York: St. Martin's, 1983); Jürgen Kocka, *Facing Total War: German Society, 1914–1918* (New York: Berg, 1984); Arthur Marwick, *The Deluge: British Society and the First World War* (Boston: Little, Brown, 1965); John Williams, *The Other Battleground: The Home Fronts: Britain, France and Germany, 1914–1918* (Chicago: Henry Regency, 1972); and J. M. Winter, *The Great War and the British People* (Cambridge, MA: Harvard University Press, 1986).

Literature

Bloom, Harold, ed., *Ernest Hemingway:* The Sun Also Rises. 1996.

Clark, David, and Rosalind Clark, eds., *The Collected Works of W. B. Yeats.* 1999–2001.

Joyce, James, *Ulysses* (amended and reprinted). 1961.

Kilmartin, ed., Marcel Proust, 1871–1922.

Kollontai, Alexandra, *Love of Worker Bees.* 1923.

Lawrence, D. H. *Women in Love.* 1920.

Moncrieff, C. K. Scott, and Terence Kilmartin, trans., *Marcel Proust:* Remembrance of Things Past. 1981.

Muir, Willa, and Edwin Muir, trans., *Franz Kafka:* The Trial. 1956.

Murdoch, Brian, trans., *Erich Maria Remarque:* All Quiet on the Western Front. 1994.

North, Michael, ed., *"The Waste Land," by T. S. Eliot.* 2000.

Proust, Marcel, *Remembrance of Things Past.*

Woolf, Virginia, *Mrs. Dalloway.* 1925.

Films and Videos

Testament of Youth (1979; VHS, 3 hrs., 20 min.). This series dramatizes Vera Brittain's 1933 novel of the same name, and chronicles her real-life struggle to get an education at Oxford and her work as a battlefield nurse in World War I.

All Quiet on the Western Front (1979; DVD, 2 hrs., 11 min.). This is a dramatization of Erich Maria Remarque's 1929 novel about the disillusionment of a German soldier during World War I as he experiences the horror of warfare.

Brideshead Revisited (1981; VHS/DVD, approx. 11 hrs.). Based on Evelyn Waugh's 1945 novel, this miniseries charts the relationships a middle-class artist has with a fading aristocratic family in the decadent pre-World War II period.

Out of Africa (1985; VHS/DVD, 2 hrs., 41 min.). This film is based on Danish writer Karen Blixen's (Isak Dinesen) 1937 autobiographical book of the same name. Her relationship with the native peoples and her efforts to set up and run a plantation in Africa in 1914 has been romanticized to some extent, but the film does capture the dichotomy between the white owners and the indigenous people.

Orlando (1992; VHS/DVD, 1 hr., 33 min.). This is an excellent dramatization of Virginia Woolfe's 1928 novel about the limits society has placed on women throughout history. Orlando begins life as a man at Elizabeth I's court and is periodically reincarnated. During one of those reincarnations, he becomes a woman, and faces firsthand the discrimination of society.

Remains of the Day (1993; VHS/DVD, 2 hrs., 14 min.). This film, set in an English country manor house on the eve of World War II. focuses on the relationship between the household's butler and housekeeper, and the minutia of everyday life for people "in service" is brilliantly captured. The film portrays quite literally the end of an era, as large households such as those depicted disappeared forever with the coming of war.

The Great War and the Shaping of the Twentieth Century (1996; VHS, 8 hrs.). This is an exhaustive documentary examination of World War I.

Gosford Park (2001; VHS/DVD, 2 hrs., 18 min.). Although this film is a murder mystery in the tradition of Agatha Christie, it captures to perfection the decadence of life for the upper classes between the war years. Life "below stairs" for servants in an English manor house is meticulous re-created and highly illuminating.

Dr. Zhivago (2003; VHS/DVD, 3 hrs., 45 min.). This two-part adaptation of Boris Pasternak's 1957 novel about two lovers in the midst of the Russian Revolution is lavish in every respect.

The Forsyte Saga, Series II (2003; VHS/DVD, 4 hrs., 45 min.). John Galsworthy's novel, *To Let*, is dramatized in three episodes of approximately 90 min. each and continues the Forsyte story in 1920, as the family continues to struggle with issues of social and moral convention in a world much changed after World War I.

Historical Skills

Map 26.4, Europe and the Middle East after the Peace Settlements of 1919–1920, p. 1023

Ask students to compare this map to the map of Europe at the outbreak of World War I (p. 998). Which empires have been dissolved? Which new states have emerged? What potential problems and conflicts could arise from this geopolitical transformation of Europe?

Mapping the West: Europe and the World in 1929, p. 1044

Ask students to locate and identify the major powers that were *not* members of the League of Nations as of 1929. What potential problems could arise from these states not being members of the league?

Figure 26.1, The Rising Cost of Living during World War I, p. 1015

Why was there a steady increase in the cost of living in these three cities during World War I? What caused the rapid increase in the cost of living in Berlin in the months after the war ended? What was the impact of this sudden rise of costs in Germany?

A French Regiment Leaves for the Front, August 1914, p. 1006

What does the photograph convey about the attitudes toward the outbreak of war? Have students consider how and why attitudes about war changed since the outbreak of World War I.

War Propaganda, 1915, p. 1012

Ask students to name the various images used in the poster. Are they effective in stirring emotions? What might be the long-term results of such atrocity propaganda on French attitudes toward Germans?

Eli Lissitsky, Beat the Whites with the Red Wedge (1919), p. 1040

Ask students to discuss the meaning of this painting. Would such messages be clearly understood by the masses of the Russian people? Encourage your students to suggest other examples of art used for political purposes or as propaganda.

OTHER BEDFORD/ST. MARTIN'S RESOURCES FOR CHAPTER 26

The following resources are available to accompany Chapter 26. Please refer to the Preface of this manual for detailed descriptions of all the ancillaries.

For Instructors

Transparencies

The following maps and images from Chapter 26 are available as full-color acetates,

- Map 26.1: The Fronts of World War I, 1914–1918
- Map 26.2: The Western Front
- Map 26.3: The Russian Civil War, 1917–1922
- Map 26.4: Europe and the Middle East after the Peace Settlements of 1919–1920
- Mapping the West: Europe and the World in 1929
- *Inflation* (German Kids)
- Dix, *The Cardgame*

Instructor's Resources CD-ROM

The following maps and image from Chapter 26, as well as a chapter outline, are available on disc in both PowerPoint and jpeg formats.

- Map 26.1: The Fronts of World War I, 1914–1918
- Map 26.2: The Western Front
- Map 26.3: The Russian Civil War, 1917–1922
- Map 26.4: Europe and the Middle East after the Peace Settlements of 1919–1920
- Mapping the West: Europe and the World in 1929
- *Inflation* (German Kids)

Using the Bedford Series with The Making of the West

Available in print as well as online at bedfordstmartins .com/usingseries, this guide offers practical suggestions for using *July 1914: Soldiers, Statesmen, and the Coming of the Great War, A Brief Documentary History, by Samuel R. Williamson Jr. and Russel Van Wyk*, in conjunction with Chapter 26 of the textbook.

For Students

Sources of The Making of the West

The following documents are available in Chapter 26 of the companion sourcebook by Katharine J. Lualdi, University of Southern Maine.

1. Fritz Franke and Siegfried Sassoon, *Two Soldiers' Views of the Horrors of War* (1914–1918)
2. L. Doriat, *Women on the Home Front* (1917)
3. Vladimir Ilich Lenin, *Letter to Nikolai Aleksandrovich Rozhkov* (January 29, 1919)
4. Benito Mussolini, *The Doctrine of Fascism* (1932)
5. Adolf Hitler, *Mien Kampf* (1925)

Study Guides

The print **Study Guide** and the **Online Study Guide** at bedfordstmartins.com/hunt, both by Victoria Thompson (Arizona State University) and Eric Johnson (University of California, Los Angeles), help students synthesize the material they have learned as well as practice the skills historians use to make sense of the past. The following Map, Visual, and Document activities are available for Chapter 26.

Map Activity

- Map 26.4: Europe in the Mideast Peace settlements

Visual Activity

- *Inflation* (German Kids)

Reading Historical Documents

- Outbreak of the Russian Revolution
- Virginia Woolf, *Orlando*

An Age of Catastrophes
1929–1945

CHAPTER RESOURCES

Main Chapter Topics

1. The Great Depression presented a global challenge to existing economic, social, and political institutions.

2. Some nations turned to totalitarian regimes in their attempts to remedy the problems connected with the depression and other difficulties faced by nation-states during this period.

3. Democratic countries made cautious, largely conventional efforts to combat both the depression and the menace of fascism. Countries using less passive techniques employed radio and film propaganda to mobilize society.

4. World War II began largely because of the fascist powers' aggressions—especially Nazi Germany—and also because of the weakness displayed by the democratic powers.

5. Germany and Japan were initially highly successful in World War II, but, by 1943, the superior economic power of the Allies—particularly that of the United States—made the defeat of the Axis powers inevitable.

6. Efforts displayed at the international conferences of Yalta and Potsdam (1945) to put the world back together faced both a growing cold-war antagonism and national liberation movements in the colonies.

Summary

The 1929 stock market crash in the United States precipitated a global depression, creating crises around the world that finally erupted into World War II. Many individuals who had invested in the stock market had done so on margin (borrowed money). When the government tightened stock market regulations, these loans were called in, causing the market to crash. Between early October and mid-November, the overall value of the stock market plummeted from $87 billion to $30 billion. When the United States called in overseas loans, the depression became global.

The Great Depression of the 1930s brought about economic collapse and massive unemployment. Governments cut national budgets and erected high tariff barriers. While some persons remained employed and others even benefited from lower prices, millions of people lost their jobs. Farmers were unable to continue production because they could no longer pay for fertilizers, agricultural equipment, or seed. Millions of farmers lost their land. There were, however, some pockets of prosperity. Municipal and national governments continued public works projects, and new factories produced popular consumer goods, like synthetic fabrics, electrical stoves, and automobiles. Industrial production in Romania actually increased by 55 percent between 1929 and 1939. Although millions were unemployed, the majority of people had jobs, but the high unemployment rate instilled a climate of fear. Gender roles changed when unemployed men lost their status as the breadwinners for their families and many women found employment, albeit low paid, outside the home for the first time. Many men became resentful over the lack of employment and the consequent decline in their patriarchal authority. As it became more costly to raise children, birthrates declined. Concerns about declining birthrates provided support for eugenics and gave rise to racism and anti-Semitism.

The effects of the depression were felt beyond the west. After World War I, Asia, Africa, and Latin America experienced economic growth, rising population levels, and urbanization. The economic downturn, however, stirred anticolonial sentiments. Resentment over colonial status had been seething since the end of the Great War, and it began to boil over. India was the prime example of visibly rising anger over colonialism. Mohandas Gandhi (1869–1948 [called "Mohatma," or "great souled"]) emerged as a leader of the Indian independence movement. Arrested many times, Gandhi advocated civil disobedience as a means of achieving independence. The Middle East also saw great change. In 1929, Mustafa Kemal (1881–1931 [called "Ataturk" or "first among the Turks"]) led the Turks to found a republic in 1923. Kemal rapidly modernized his country by moving the capital from Constantinople (which he renamed Istanbul) to Ankara, mandating western dress for men and women, introducing a Latin alphabet, abolishing polygamy, and granting women the vote. Persia loosened the European grip on its economy, forced negotiated oil contracts on European countries, updated its government, and changed its name to Iran. Britain ended its control over the Egyptian government (though not the Suez Canal). Totalitarianism spread throughout Europe, while Britain and France were preoccupied with their respective colonial interests.

A few countries—principally Italy, the Soviet Union, and Germany—offered radical approaches to reorient their societies. Dictatorships in these nations promised a superior society based on unity and obedience rather than on the freedom and rights of individual citizens. In the Soviet Union, Joseph Stalin (1879–1953) created a powerful, industrialized state within a very short period of time, but the cost was high: perhaps ten million died in labor camps or of starvation. His five-year plans resulted in the collectivization of agriculture and rapid industrialization. Prosperous peasant families who balked at governmental demands for increased agricultural production were removed. Collective farms, comprised of several families living communally, replaced single-family farms. Unskilled workers displaced from the countryside were forced into new, dangerous, urban, industrial jobs. Inexperienced farm workers and industrial laborers could not meet the government's set quotas, and famine resulted. Stalin fixed the blame on "others," and the hunt for "wreckers," counterrevolutionaries, or saboteurs, eventually led to a series of "show trials" that took place between 1936 and 1938. These purges affected all levels of society. Some of the army's highest ranks of the officer corps in the army were eliminated in 1937. Gulags ("prison camps") were established to hold millions of state prisoners, forced under the harshest of conditions to perform hard labor. Some one million died annually in these camps. Historians have debated whether these purges were initiated solely by Stalin to consolidate his power and establish communism in Russia, or if the rank and file of the Communist Party, engaged in power struggles among themselves, were directly involved. The purges may have even reflected genuine concern by the workers over enemies of their proletarian utopia.

In the midst of economic change and social turmoil, Stalin's regime sponsored a move away from experimentation and reform in cultural affairs, education, and gender relations. In light of the declining population levels, the state restricted access to birth control, promoted marriage, made divorces difficult to obtain, and criminalized homosexuality. The flip side to this was that women made gains in literacy, received better health care, were able to join the lower ranks of the Communist Party, and entered the professions. However, women were also still expected to carry out the traditional duties of a housewife. Socialist realism replaced the avant-garde in art and literature. Stalin called artists and writers "engineers of the soul," and controlled their output through the Union of Soviet Writers, which determined the types and acceptable content of books authors were allowed to write. The common worker became a "social hero" in these works. Some artists and writers went underground, whereas others, like the composer Sergei Prokofiev (1891–1953), tried to accommodate their talents to the state's demands.

In Weimar Germany, the government failed to deal effectively with the depression, which left it vulnerable to harsh and vehement criticism by the competing Communist and Nazi parties. The Nazis scored a breakthrough victory in the Reichstag elections of 1930, and more than doubled their representation in 1932. Viewed as young, idealistic, and dynamic, the Nazi Party and its leader, Adolf Hitler (1889–1945), proved to be masters of mass politics and appealed to all segments of society. After becoming chancellor in 1933, Hitler swiftly consolidated power. When the Reichstag building was gutted by fire, the Nazis blamed the Communists, and used the fire as an excuse to suspend civil rights, impose censorship on the press, and prohibit meetings of the opposition. Although the Nazi Party failed to gain a majority in the March elections, they did manage to intimidate the Reichstag into passing the Enabling Act. This act suspended the constitution for four years and gave Hitler the right to decree laws without obtaining the approval of the president or the Reichstag.

Heinrich Himmler (1900–1945) headed the elite SS (*Schutzstaffel*) that protected Hitler's person (body guards) and commanded the Reich's political police force system; Hermann Goering (1893–1946) ran the Gestapo. These organizations possessed vast powers to arrest individuals and either execute them or send them to concentration camps, the first of which opened at Dachau near Munich in March 1933. The Nazis filled these camps with political enemies like socialists, and with Jews, homosexuals, and anyone else who opposed the Nazi's policies.

By the end of 1933, the last remnants of effective resistance to the Nazi Party had disintegrated and the party and government essentially became one and the same. In the Night of the Long Knives (June 30, 1934), Hitler destroyed the power of the paramilitary troops (SA) within the Nazi Party. This strengthened the defense echelon (SS) and reassured the German army that it would remain in control of military forces. To stimulate the economy, the Nazi government pursued a policy of pump priming; that is, spending money on tanks, airplanes, and the Autobahn; unemployment declined. Additionally, the Nazi Party replaced the independent trade-union movement by governmentally classifying jobs, determining work procedures, and setting wages. Women, however, were encouraged to leave the workforce and to concentrate on bearing children. Single women who remained in the workforce received lower pay than men, whatever job they performed.

The four-year plan, begun in 1936, was intended to prepare Germany for war by 1940. In conjunction with this plan, the party also took steps to reshape social and cultural life to reflect their vision. Racially pure Aryan newlyweds could obtain special loans, provided the wife left the workforce. These loans were cancelled on the birth of a couple's fourth child. Books by Jews, socialists, homosexuals, and out-of-favor writers were banned and publicly burned. Membership in the Hitler Youth organizations was mandatory for children over age ten. These children were encouraged to report adults they suspected of being disloyal to the regime; one hundred thousand adult informers were on the Nazi's payroll. Anti-Semitism also grew increasingly visible and was justified by ideas concerning racial superiority. The Germans believed they were directly descended from Aryans, a people of great distinction who, according to legend, existed in ancient times. Some two hundred thousand elderly and disabled persons were euthanized in the late 1930s in the name of racial purity. But Jews were especially targeted, and the Nuremberg Laws of 1935 deprived German Jews of citizenship and prohibited marriage between Jews and all non-Jews in Germany. In 1938, *Kristallnacht* ("the Night of Broken Glass") showed the violent face of anti-Semitism, when Nazis shattered the windows of Jewish stores and homes and sent over twenty thousand Jews to prisons and camps. The wealth derived from the confiscation of Jewish property and collection of immigration fees paid by Jews to leave the country helped finance Germany's economic revival.

Democratic nations, such as the United States, Britain, France, and Sweden, appeared weak when compared with Europe's totalitarian regimes. President Franklin D. Roosevelt (FDR [1882–1945]) established the New Deal in the United States, an interventionist, governmental policy that included relief for businesses, price supports for hard-pressed farmers, and public works programs for the unemployed. The Social Security Act of 1935 set up a fund to which both employers and employees were required by law to contribute. This act provided retirement benefits to workers; unemployment insurance; and payments to dependent mothers, children, and the disabled. The New Deal's programs only partially succeeded in combating the depression; FDR's use of the media—especially his "fireside chats"—helped to keep the masses committed to a democratic future.

Sweden also instituted central planning for its economic and social welfare programs. It devalued its currency, making its exports attractive to international markets, and otherwise pump-primed the economy. To increase population levels, the Swedish government introduced a loan program for married couples, prenatal care, free childbirth in a hospital, a food relief program, and governmental aid to mothers. Because all families received these benefits, there was widespread support for the developing welfare state.

In Britain, the situation worsened before it got better. Payments were reduced to the unemployed, and denied altogether to women, even though they had paid into the fund. High tariffs further discouraged trade. Pump-priming programs were beginning to have an effect by the late 1930s.

After paramilitary groups rioted around the parliament building (February 1934), France rallied republicans, socialists, and communists in a "Popular Front" to fight fascism. Led by the Socialist premier, Leon Blum (1872–1950), the short-lived Popular Front extended family subsidies and welfare benefits, appointed women to governmental positions (even though they could not vote), and guaranteed workers two-weeks' paid vacations, a forty-hour work week, and the right to collective bargaining. While sparking renewed democratic sentiments, the lack of investment from bankers and businessmen, and the government's refusal to support the fight against fascism in Spain, caused the government to collapse.

The balance between democracy and totalitarianism in central and eastern Europe was a delicate one. In Austria, Engelbert Dollfuss (1892–1934) briefly established a dictatorship, but was assassinated by the Nazis when he refused to give in to their demands. In Hungary, the right-wing general, Gyula Gömbös stirred up anti-Semitism and ethnic rivalries, leaving the ground fertile for pro-Nazism after his death in 1936. When Czechoslovakia was divided, the poorer, less-educated Slovaks formed a strong Slovak Fascist Party. In Poland, Romania, Yugoslavia, and Bulgaria, ethnic tensions simmered.

Mass and elite culture responded to the economic and political challenges of the 1930s and simultaneously diverted people's focus away from them. Women in film were depicted variously as both the cause and the cure for the ills of society. Charlie Chaplin's Little Tramp character became a sympathetic, modern, factory worker in the film Modern Times (1936); George Orwell (1903–1950) wrote about the experiences of the poor in Paris and London, the unemployed in the north of England, and the atrocities committed during the Spanish Civil War (1936–1939); Thomas Mann's (1875–1955) novels depicted the struggle between humanist values and barbarianism; and Virginia Woolf (1882–1941) attacked militarism, poverty, and the oppression of women in her novels. The new idea of indeterminacy in virtually all areas of science was unsettling to those who believed science represented certainties. Religious leaders fostered a spirit of resistance to dictatorship among religious people. Tensions mounted in the 1930s with a surge in global imperialism. Jews from Germany, often denied entry into other European countries, flocked to Palestine, causing an upsurge in pan-Arabism; and Japan, Germany, and Italy displayed expansionist ambitions. In the face of global depression, neither Britain nor France had the resources to protect their colonial interests from aggression, and hoped that sanctions imposed by the League of Nations would maintain peace. Japanese aggression in China (1930s) demonstrated the ineffectuality of the League of Nations.

Because Emperor Hirohito was young, he was also weak and rather powerless. Japan's military leaders proclaimed that the military was an institution unto itself, independent of civilian control. In the 1930s, emotional support for the imperial system in Japan increased; Japanese people believed they were a superior race and deserved an empire reflecting that fact. In 1931, Japan invaded Manchuria and set up a puppet government; the League of Nations did nothing in response. In 1937, Japan undertook another major attack on China, ostensibly to free the country from western imperialism. Hundreds of thousands died in the Rape of Najing, so-called because of the brutality directed at women and girls. FDR immediately imposed an embargo on Japan. Because of their self-proclaimed racial superiority and also because of their territorial ambitions, Japan formed alliances with Germany and Italy.

Hitler and Mussolini set about establishing their own empires. Hitler withdrew from the League of Nations in 1933. In 1935, in violation of the Treaty of Versailles, which he had loudly renounced, Hitler introduced military conscription and openly began rearming (although it had been rearming secretly for years). In early 1936, Italy conquered Ethiopia and Hitler sent troops into the demilitarized Rhineland. Europe's response to these actions was, if anything, weak. In 1931, Spanish republicans overthrew the monarchy, but the republicans were divided among themselves and could not check the powerful right wing. The military rebelled in 1936, and General Francisco Franco (1892–1975)—supported by fascist powers in Europe—unified antirepublican sentiment and force. The Spanish Civil War (1936–1939) emerged as the focal point of the confrontation between fascism and democracy. Hitler and Mussolini militarily supported the Spanish right. The Soviet Union supported the republic with troops and, while Britain and France refused to become involved, volunteers from several less-powerful nations went to Spain to fight for the republic. In the end, the Spanish republicans were defeated, and Francisco Franco established his dictatorship.

In March 1938, Germany annexed Austria, a move welcomed by the Austrians who were eager for the Anschluss ("merger"). Then, Hitler pressured Czechoslovakia into granting autonomy to the Sudeten region, an area containing a large German population. Tension increased in the fall, and a German invasion was only averted by an agreement reached at the Munich Conference by Hitler, Mussolini, French premier Edouard Daladier (1884–1970), and British prime minister Neville Chamberlain (1869–1940) who returned home afterward claiming he had secured "peace in our time." The signed agreement stated that Germany would annex only the Sudentenland. Six months later, however, Hitler sent troops into the rest of Czechoslovakia, which caused the British and French to provide Poland and other at-risk countries with a guarantee of assistance should Germany attack. Historians debate whether concerted resistance to Germany early on would have prevented World War II. Some argue yes, others no because Britain and France needed the extra time to build up their military strength. The Nazi-Soviet Pact (August 1939), which guaranteed the neutrality of one country if the other was attacked, formed the final link in the chain of causation; it allowed Hitler to attack Poland without the danger of opening a two-front war. The two powers (Germany and Russia) also secretly agreed to carve up Poland and the Baltic states as soon as it became feasible.

On September 1, 1939, Hitler launched a Blitzkrieg ("lightening war") against Poland, while the Soviet Union invaded from the east. Poland was quickly subdued but, to Hitler's surprise, Britain and France did not agree to peace terms. In the spring of 1940, after the so-called phony war, Nazi Germany conquered Denmark and Norway, then Belgium and the Netherlands. After Germany defeated France in June, it occupied the northern half of the country, but allowed a new French government, named Vichy after the town that became its capital, to control the southern half. Hoping for territorial gains, Italy had also invaded France from the southeast, while the Soviet Union annexed Estonia, Latvia, and Lithuania.

The battle of Britain (the "Blitz") took place that summer. Britain, led by Prime Minister Winston Churchill (1874–1965), fought off the attacks of the German Luftwaffe. Using the wealth of its colonies, Britain poured resources into the aircraft industry, its code-breaking group, and the development of radar. By year's end, Britain was outproducing Germany by 50 percent. Facing continued losses in the air to Britain, Hitler canceled his planned cross-channel invasion and instead decided to invade the Soviet Union. The attack, in June 1941, was at first highly successful but stalled by the end of the year, in part because Hitler insisted on attacking at several points rather than concentrating his forces on Moscow.

With the start of war, Japan had taken over control of parts of the British colonial empire, bullied the Dutch in Indonesia, and invaded French Indochina. In

December 1941, Japan attacked Pearl Harbor and the United States declared war. By spring 1942, Japan had taken Guam, the Philippines, Malaya, Burma, Indonesia, Singapore, and much of the southwestern Pacific. Germany and Italy declared war on the United States and the United States, Britain, the Soviet Union, and Free French came together to form the Grand Alliance (the "Allies"), which other countries joined to fight the Axis powers (Germany, Italy, and Japan).

Far more civilians than soldiers were killed during World War II mainly because of aerial bombardment. Other civilians were killed when the German ground forces encountered enemies or "racial inferiors." Civilian homes were confiscated and intellectuals shot. The Japanese used similar tactics in China. Jews were targeted early on in the war. Initially, Central European Jews were confined to ghettos where they died of disease or slowly starved to death. Others were taken to remote areas and shot. Anti-Semitic civilians sometimes participated in these killings. By fall 1941, Hitler and the leaders of the Nazi Party had devised the "Final Solution": the plan to annihilate all Jews within the far reach of the Nazis. The Final Solution began operations in 1941–1942 with the construction of six death camps in Poland. Those in the death camps and in the many concentration and work camps did what they could to maintain human dignity within a system specifically designed to rob individuals of their humanity before killing them. However, the combination of anti-Semitism and the industrial, scientific, and quasi-legal methods used against those prisoners proved lethal. Six million Jews and six million gypsies, homosexuals, Slavs, and countless others were murdered by the Nazis.

Resistance to the war took many forms and included partisan groups in rural areas— persons gathering military intelligence—and individuals resisting in small ways in everyday activities. Women used their femininity to disguise resistance activities. While the Catholic church initially supported Mussolini and the slaughter of a million Serbs, Catholic and Protestant clergy were among those who set up resistance networks. Collaboration with Hitler's regime also took on many forms, as some sought advantage or were terrorized into collaborating with the Nazis.

In large part, the Allied powers won the war on the home front. The Allies were far more successful in meeting the demands of modern warfare and also highly successful in using patriotic propaganda to inspire citizens to fight for their country. They were especially successful in mobilizing women for the workforce and other crucial areas. There was rationing of food and material goods, but people were willing to give up these things for the war effort. In the Soviet Union, rationing had devastating effects on its population. Propaganda was used on both sides of the conflict to demonize the enemy. This fed into the mindset that resident aliens of hostile nations needed to be incarcerated; for example, the United States interned citizens of Japanese origins, while the Soviet Union rounded up Muslims and other minority groups suspected of Nazi sympathies. At the same time, colonized men were conscripted forcibly. The governments of the Allies necessarily increased in size in order to sustain the efforts to mobilize society and support the war economy.

The Allies' victory at Stalingrad (early 1943), where ninety thousand German soldiers were captured, marked a turning point in the European theater. German general Edwin Rommel was driven out of Africa, and the Allies landed in Italy. On June 6, 1944, the Allied forces landed in Normandy (known as D-Day) and opened the second front. Nazi Germany now faced a two-front war. In August, Paris was liberated, while the Soviet Union retook Poland and the Baltic states and invaded Bulgaria and Romania. Hitler refused to surrender and instead committed suicide. The war in Europe ended May 8, 1945.

The defeat of the Japanese navy at the battles of Midway and Guadalcanal (1942) marked turning points in the Pacific theater. By mid-1945, U.S. forces were poised to invade the Japanese home islands. With no way to resupply their forces, the Japanese undertook *kamikaze* missions. However, because the high command of the U.S. military were concerned that the war would continue into 1946, with the Japanese fighting to the very last man, and also because any invasion of Japan would cost hundreds of thousands of Allied casualties, the decision was made to drop atomic bombs on Hiroshima and Nagasaki in August as part of a campaign to force Japan to surrender. On August 14, 1945, the Japanese surrendered unconditionally.

Although earlier agreements had been reached, the Yalta and Potsdam conferences in 1945 formally sketched out the postwar settlement. The four Allied powers would occupy Germany. Other agreements attempted to settle the future of Europe but, at war's end, that future was highly uncertain and the wartime partnership of the Allies was already beginning to unravel.

World War II left an estimated 100 million dead and perhaps double that number in refugees. Colonial peoples were in full rebellion or close to it. The pessimism for the future was reflected in George Orwell's novel *1984* (1949).

Suggestions for Lecture and Discussion Topics

1. Most students will already be familiar with Anne Frank, and many will have read *The Diary of a Young Girl.* This autobiography can be used in drawing comparisons between Anne Frank and Etty Hillesum, whose story opens the chapter. Their different yet related experiences make it possible to present the Holocaust in a compelling way. Their experiences also raise questions about gender

issues in the 1930s and 1940s, and the two stories will draw students' attention to the use of autobiography. Finally, the class might consider how Anne Frank's experiences can be used to support various perspectives on the Holocaust (in connection with this, see "New Sources, New Perspectives: Museums and Memory," p. 1082).

In addition to Anne Frank, *The Diary of a Young Girl: The Definitive Edition* (New York: Doubleday, 1995), there is a great deal of useful material in *The Diary of Anne Frank: The Critical Edition* (Garden City, NY: Doubleday, 1989). Also helpful are Ruud van der Rol and Rian Verhoeven, *Anne Frank: Beyond the Diary* (New York: Viking, 1993); Willy Lindwer, *The Last Seven Months of Anne Frank* (New York: Anchor Books, 1992); Hyman A. Enzer and Sandra Solotaroff-Enzer, eds., *Anne Frank: Reflections on Her Life and Legacy* (Champaign: University of Illinois Press, 1999); and the film *Anne Frank Remembered* (Columbia Tristar Home Video, 1996).

Etty Hillesum's diary and letters are conveniently bound together in *An Interrupted Life: The Diaries, 1941–1943 and Letters from Westerbork* (New York: Henry Holt, 1996). Rachel F. Brenner, *Writing As Resistance: Four Women Confronting the Holocaust: Edith Stein, Simone Weil, Anne Frank, Etty Hillesum* (University Park: Pennsylvania State University Press, 1997); and Denise de Costa, *Anne Frank and Etty Hillesum: Inscribing Spirituality and Sexuality* (New Brunswick, NJ: Rutgers University Press, 1998) may also be helpful.

2. It is difficult to deal with the Great Depression in class. Either the discussion is too technical or seems hopelessly vague. One way to engage students is to ask them to look closely at the situation in a particular country and then to compare it with the experiences of other countries. As the basis for a discussion, try using Chapter 5, "'Red Ellen' Wilkinson and the Jarrow Crusade: Great Britain in the Great Slump," in David Clay Large, *Between Two Fires: Europe's Path in the 1930s* (New York: W. W. Norton, 1991). This essay uses a dramatic event—a march on London by the unemployed citizens of Jarrow—to give an impression of how ordinary people experienced the depression, before opening up the topic to include all who were affected throughout Great Britain.

France, because it is atypical of the depression experience, also makes an interesting choice for discussion and should illustrate just how widespread the depression was. Chapters 2 and 3 in Eugene Weber, *The Hollow Years: France in the 1930s* (New York: W. W. Norton, 1994) set the depression in the context of the interwar economy. These also provide a fascinating look at how people lived during this period.

3. Approaches to conducting a class on the major dictators of the interwar period are seemingly endless. For Adolf Hitler and Nazi Germany, 1933 and 1934 are crucially important years. A review of Hitler's efforts to consolidate power in these years, which include the

drama of the Night of the Long Knives, and end with the pageantry and propaganda of the Nuremberg Rally of 1934, could be based on the discussion in Chapter 9, "Hitler's Revolution," of Alan Bullock, *Hitler and Stalin: Parallel Lives* (New York: Random House, 1993). See also Large's chapter on the Night of the Long Knives in *Between Two Fires*, cited in suggestion 2 above. At least a few scenes from Leni Riefenstahl's brilliant documentary *Triumph of the Will* (Embassy Home Entertainment, 1986) should be shown to demonstrate the Nazi Party's amalgam of youth, dynamism, power, and nationalism. This film also illustrates the early use of propaganda by the Nazi Party.

For Stalin, in addition to a class on the five-year plan or the purges, an interesting session might be based on Victoria E. Bonnell's *Iconography of Power: Soviet Political Posters under Lenin and Stalin* (Berkeley: University of California Press, 1997), especially Chapter 3, "Peasant Women in Political Posters of the 1930s," and Chapter 4, "The Leader's Two Bodies: Iconography of the Vozhd." For example, plate 4 of *Iconography of Power*, "Every Collective Farm Peasant or Individual Farmer Now Has the Opportunity to Live Like a Human Being," offers a very useful starting point for a discussion. The poster shows an electric lightbulb; a phonograph; a happy, well-dressed peasant family; books by Maxim Gorky, Vladimir Lenin, and Stalin; and a poster with Stalin's silhouette superimposed on Lenin's silhouette. It is meant to portray how people will live in the new Soviet Union, while also subtly glorifying Stalin by association with Lenin and Gorky. Sheila Fitzpatrick, *Everyday Stalinism: Ordinary Life in Extraordinary Times: Soviet Russia in the 1930s* (New York and Oxford: Oxford University Press, 1999) details in chapters 3 and 4 the gap between the realities of Soviet life and the promise. A particularly interesting section of Chapter 3 discusses the Soviet government's attempts to find heroes: Stalin and also polar explorers, aviators, and "shockworkers" were made larger than life in order to inspire—and also divert—the masses.

4. One approach to talking about the dilemmas democracies faced in the 1930s is to focus on Czechoslovakia in that decade. As an industrialized country with a large urban population, Czechoslovakia maintained a functioning democracy when all other successor states in central Europe had resorted to dictatorships. Joseph Rothschild offers a good discussion of Czech affairs in the 1930s in *East Central Europe between the Two World Wars* (Seattle: University of Washington Press, 1993).

5. A class on the Munich Conference presents the possibility of a role-playing exercise. Using the chapter in Large's *Between Two Fires* (see suggestion 2), students could be assigned to role-play Hitler, Mussolini, Daladier, Chamberlain, Benes, and Stalin in a historical simulation. Other students could act as radio reporters and commentators. The idea would be to present the positions of the leaders and their countries and to explore

contemporary reactions to events. Students should be cautioned against the temptation to use the hindsight they have looking back on events from the vantage point of the twenty-first century.

The Nazi-Soviet Pact is also a compelling and important event. First, the pact itself, the secret protocol, and a conversation held after the signing are all available on the Web site of The Avalon Project at the Yale Law School — a repository for a large number of documents connected with treaty-making. Bullock places the Nazi-Soviet Pact in its full diplomatic context and examines the motives of Stalin and Hitler in Chapter 14, "The Nazi-Soviet Pact," in *Hitler and Stalin* (see suggestion 3). Robert C. Tucker places the pact in the context of Soviet history in the last two chapters of *Stalin in Power: The Revolution from Above, 1928–1941* (New York: W. W. Norton, 1990).

6. Stalingrad is the site of the most important battle of the European Theater in World War II. A major book on this battle is Anthony Beevor, *Stalingrad: The Fateful Siege, 1942–1943* (New York: Viking Penguin, 1998). A useful overview may be found in Gerhard L. Weinberg, *A World at Arms: A Global History of World War II* (Cambridge: Cambridge University Press, 1994). The German view of Stalingrad is vividly portrayed in *Stalingrad*, a film by Joseph Vilsmaier (Fox Lorber Home Video, 1986). Timothy W. Ryback, in "Stalingrad: Letters from the Dead," *The New Yorker* (February 1, 1993), provides another German perspective on Stalingrad based on letters by German soldiers describing conditions there. Finally, Donovan Webster, in Chapter 2 of *Aftermath: The Remnants of War* (New York: Pantheon Books, 1996), looks at recent efforts to identify and bury many thousands of nameless dead left without proper burial in the decades after the battle.

D-Day is, of course, more familiar to American students. Stephen E. Ambrose *D-Day, June 6, 1944: The Climactic Battle of World War II* (New York: Simon & Schuster, 1994), based on fourteen hundred oral histories, is a very useful source. See also Ambrose's comments on the television show *Booknotes* on the Web. Again, Weinberg's *A World at Arms*, cited in suggestion 6, provides a dependable overview.

Making Connections

1. *Compare fascist ideas of the individual with the idea of individual rights found in the American and French revolutions.* Fascist nations promised a superior society based on unity and obedience rather than on the freedom and rights of the individual citizen. The duty of the individual was first and foremost to serve the needs of the state as the state directed. These were ideas that were in sharp contrast to the American and French revolutions, where individual rights were considered to be so

precious and inviolable that they were enshrined in key documents: the *Declaration of Independence* and the *Declaration of the Rights of Man and Citizen*. The citizen-government relationship was overseen by a social contract rooted in nature. When a government violates that contract through tyranny, citizens have a right to overthrow it. Such a concept would have been anathema to the fascists.

2. *What differences exist between World War I and World War II?* The combatants of World War I were largely equal in terms of numbers and armaments and battle stalemates were common. Germany had been secretly rearming for years and was in a much stronger military position than Britain or France at the beginning of World War II. And, whereas World War I had begun more or less accidentally with the assassination of archduke Franz Ferdinand, Hitler had planned a European war since the early 1930s, and deliberately provoked Britain and France in 1939. Rabid anti-Semitism was also a unique feature of World War II.

Writing Assignments and Class Presentation Topics

1. Assign students selected passages from the diaries of Anne Frank and Etty Hillesum to read. Ask students to compare and contrast these passages, allowing for the differences in age, background, and experience between the two authors. Students might consider whether the writing of one author or the other is more powerful, more poignant, or bears a better witness to events. It may be helpful to use the selected passages as a basis for an in-class discussion before students write their essays. You will have to be careful, however, to avoid giving the impression that you favor one approach to the material.

2. Divide the class into several groups and assign each group a country to investigate during the period from 1929 to 1939. Each of these investigations should result in a timeline, capsule biographies of major figures, and a summary of major events. Within a particular group, each student should have a definite assignment to fulfill as his or her contribution to the group effort. Each student should also write a brief essay on how the group worked together and his or her role within the group. The group should jointly present a report to the entire class when finished with their individual research and write-ups. Students might wish to use a series of images and comments in the tradition of *Let Us Now Praise Famous Men: Three Tenant Families* by James Agee and Walker Evans (Boston: Houghton Mifflin, 1980), first published in 1941. Or, students could write and present a series of radio news broadcasts, as they would have been broadcast in the 1930s. The chapter bibliography offers a number of books that may also be used as

starting points. Rondo Cameron, *A Concise Economic History of the World: From Paleolithic Times to the Present* (New York: Oxford University Press, 1989) presents an overview of the depression that you may wish to assign as background reading, and it also contains an extensive bibliography.

3. Sometimes counterfactual history can be instructive. Ask students to imagine that the Munich Conference never took place and, instead, war broke out in the fall of 1938. What do they think the outcome would have been in this case? Would, for example, determined resistance by the Czech army have caused the German generals to lose their nerve and stage a coup against Hitler? Would the Soviet Union and France have come to the aid of Czechoslovakia? What would Great Britain or the United States have done? Ask students to describe what they conjecture would have happened from the fall of 1938 to the fall of 1939 and to provide evidence for the plausibility of their scenarios. You may wish to assign "'Peace for Our Time': Appeasement and the Munich Conference," in David Clay Large, *Between Two Fires: Europe's Path in the 1930s* (New York: W. W. Norton, 1991), as background reading.

4. Was Stalingrad the single most important battle in the European theater in World War II? Ask students to respond to this question in an essay; the essay should not be a retelling of the story of Stalingrad. Students may summarize the major aspects of the battle, but their essays should focus on analyses of the battle's outcome that either support or refute the proposition that it was the most important European battle in World War II. Students may wish to compare the battle of Stalingrad to another battle — the D-Day invasion, for example — as a way of supporting their positions. Call students' attention to Gerhard Weinberg's *A World at Arms*, cited in "Suggestions for Lecture and Discussion Topics," number 6, as a good source for information.

Research Assignments

1. Investigating what life was like in the Soviet Union or Nazi Germany in the 1930s is an obvious, although unwieldy, research assignment. Because this is such a big subject, students should be encouraged to focus on a particular group, such as peasants in the Soviet Union, German Jews in Nazi Germany, or women in either country. Require students to read primary sources (you may wish to set a minimum number of pages) as well as the better secondary sources. Alan Bullock, *Hitler and Stalin: Parallel Lives* (New York: Random House, 1993) is a good place to start. For the Soviet Union, a good introduction is Lewis Siegelbaum's essay "Building Stalinism, 1929–1941," in Gregory L. Freeze, ed., *Russia: A History* (Oxford: Oxford University Press, 1997). Sheila Fitzpatrick, *Everyday Stalinism: Ordinary Life in Extraor-*dinary Times, Soviet Russia in the 1930s (Oxford: Oxford University Press, 1999) is filled with information. For Nazi Germany, a good overview is "The Brown Revolution: National Socialism, 1933–1939" in Holger H. Herwig, *Hammer or Anvil?: Modern Germany, 1648–Present* (Lexington, MA: D. C. Heath, 1994). See also Detlev Peukert, *Inside Nazi Germany: Conformity, Opposition and Racism in Everyday Life* (New Haven: Yale University Press, 1987).

2. The wealth of material available on the Holocaust offers many possibilities for research projects. Students may wish to use the essays in Raul Hilberg, *Perpetrators, Victims, Bystanders: The Jewish Catastrophe, 1933–1945* (New York: HarperCollins, 1992) as a beginning point. Another book that would be useful for this purpose is Michael R. Marrus, *The Holocaust in History* (Hanover, NH: University Press of New England, 1987). Marrus's bibliography, now a little dated, is nonetheless very useful. Students should also be encouraged to investigate the Holocaust Museum Web site listed in the chapter bibliography. There is, of course, abundant memoir and documentary material available once students have selected specific topics. Students may also wish to research resistance to the Holocaust. There are many fact-based films that document collective and individual acts of heroism in this regard: *The Scarlet and the Black* (1983), *The Assisi Underground* (1984), *Escape from Sobibor* (1987), *Schindler's List* (1993), and *The Pianist* (2002), to name but a few. Additionally, students can look at the career of Raoul Wallenberg, a Swedish diplomat who lived in Hungary. Hungary who is credited with saving as many as one hundred thousand Hungarian Jews before his disappearance. Or, students can read Edith H. Beer, *The Nazis Officer's Wife: How One Jewish Woman Survived the Holocaust* (New York: HarperCollins, 2000).

Literature

Frank and Pressler, eds., Massotty, trans., *Anne Frank, The Diary of a Young Girl: The Definitive Edition*. 1995.

Hersley, John, ed., *Hiroshima*. 1946.

Keeley, Edmund, and Philip Sherrard, trans., *Seferis: Collected Poems*. 1995.

Lyell, William, trans., *Diary of a Madman and Other Stories by Lu Xun*. 1990.

Orwell, George, *1984*.

Orwell, George, *Down and Out in Paris and London*. 1933.

Pomerans, Arnold J., trans., *Etty Hillesum: An Interrupted Life*. 1983.

Steinbeck, John, *Grapes of Wrath*. 1939.

Thomas, D. M., trans., *Anna Akhmatova: Selected Poems*. 1992.

Ward, Matthew, trans., *Albert Camus: The Stranger*. 1988.

Films and Videos

Olympia (1938; VHS, 2 hrs., 40 min.). German film-maker Leni Riefenstahl was commissioned by the German government to make this film about the 1936 Berlin Olympics. It glorified German athletes and was used by the government for propaganda purposes.

The World at War (1974; VHS/DVD, 26 hrs.). This multipart series is an expansive examination of World War II and includes rare film footage and interviews with soldiers, housewives, and Holocaust survivors.

The Holocaust (1978). This award-winning miniseries, first televised in 1978, follows two German families between 1935 and 1945. The Jewish family struggles simply to survive, while a member of the non-Jewish family rises in the Nazi regime. This series revitalized Holocaust studies, brought discussion about the Holocaust into the mainstream media, and inspired other important films on the subject.

The Jewel in the Crown (1984; VHS/DVD, 12 hrs., 30 min.). An adaptation of Paul Scott's *The Raj Quartet*, this series follows the lives of the Layton family and their connections who are touched in varying ways by India's struggle for independence during and immediately following World War II.

Good Evening, Mr. Wallenberg (1990; VHS/DVD, 1 hr., 55 min.). Excellent dramatic retelling of the true story of Swedish diplomat Raoul Wallenberg who saved thousands of Hungarian Jews during World War II, only to disappear into the hands of the Soviets who invaded Hungary at the end of the war. The film is in Swedish with English subtitles.

The Complete Churchill (1991; VHS, 6 hrs., 40 min.). Martin Gilbert is considered by many to be the definitive biographer of Winston Churchill. In this multipart series, Gilbert examines Churchill's life using archival footage, new documentary material, and interviews with individuals who knew the prime minister.

The Eye of Vichy (1993; VHS/DVD, 1 hr., 50 min.). Claude Chabrol's film consists of official newsreel footage shot during the German occupation of France. This material, shown in France between 1940 and 1944, is a sobering look at Nazi manipulation of propaganda and the power of mass media.

The Wannsee Conference (1984; VHS, 1 hr., 27 min.). A chilling dramatization of the 1942 meeting held by leading Nazi officials at Wannsee to determine a plan to exterminate the Jews. Based on notes of the meeting, the dramatization unsettlingly runs about as long as the original meeting.

The Final Solution (1999; VHS, 3 hrs., 28 min.). This multipart series is an examination of Hitler's systematic extermination of the Jews through the use of period film and firsthand accounts.

Charlotte Gray (2001; VHS/DVD, approx. 1 hr.). Cate Blanchett stars in this film about the French resistance during World War II. The film well captures the danger that resistance fighters faced during the war.

World War II in Color: The British Story (2001; VHS/DVD, 3 hrs.). Archival film story of Britain and World War II in recently restored color footage.

1940s House (2003; VHS/DVD, 3 hrs.). In this series, a contemporary English family finds out firsthand what life was like during World War II. Although slightly voyeuristic, this series highlights in an immediate way what life was like during the war as the family copes with the rationing of food and clothing, mock air raids in the middle of the night, and women entering the workforce.

Bonhoeffer (2003; DVD, 1 hr., 30 min.). Archival material, on-location shooting, and interviews with individuals who knew him help tell the story of Dietrich Bonhoeffer, a Protestant theologian who openly criticized Hitler and the Nazi regime and participated in a plot to assassinate the Führer.

Cambridge Spies (2003; DVD, 4 hrs.). This short but excellent series focuses on Guy Burgess, Anthony Blunt, Kim Philby, and Donald Maclean, all Cambridge students in the 1930s who became double agents, spying for the Soviet Union. In time, they rose to the highest levels of the English establishment.

The Gathering Storm (2002; DVD approx. 3 hrs.). This film focuses on the relationship between Winston Churchill and his wife Clementine during the 1930s when Churchill was out of office and warning all who would listen about a coming war with Germany.

Foyle's War, Series I and II (2003, 2004; VHS/DVD, approx. 3 hrs. each episode). The Foyle's War series are detective stories set during World War II. Although the stories are fiction, the production staff has been careful to correctly show the costuming and setting and to weave details about everyday life during the war years seamlessly into the narrative. The episodes are self-contained.

Films and World War II

Many of the films made during the 1930s and World War II years were, to some extent, propaganda pieces, and their use in the classroom can add an interesting dimension to any study of this period. Students can be asked to research films of this period and perhaps select one for individual review. The following lists some of the better-known films.

The Great Dictator (1940; VHS/DVD, 2 hrs.). A Jewish barber in World War I saves a German officer and, when their paths cross again twenty years later, the officer tries to protect his old friend in the face of a Hitleresque dictator and a repressive government. This is a scathing satire of Hitler and the Nazi regime.

In Which We Serve (1942; DVD, 1 hr., 54 min.). This is a semibiographical account of Lord Louis Mountbatten and his experiences aboard the HMS *Kelly*, which was torpedoed by the Germans. The film emphasizes courage, teamwork, and resilience in the face of wartime hardship.

Mrs. Miniver (1942; DVD, 2 hrs., 13 min.). Mrs. Miniver is an upper-middle-class English housewife who bravely looks after her family during World War II. Her husband and his small boat are used to help evacuate Dunkirk, her son becomes an RAF pilot, her daughter-in-law (a civilian) is killed in an air raid, and the community where she resides comes to terms with their wartime losses. In terms of propaganda, Winston Churchill reputedly said this film was worth a dozen battleships.

Casablanca (1942; VHS/DVD, 1 hr., 42 min.). Humphrey Bogart plays an American expatriot nightclub owner who struggles with a decision to help an old flame, Ingrid Bergman, and her husband as the Germans solidify their control over this Moroccan outpost.

The Fighting Seabees (1944; DVD, 1 hr., 40 min.). This film highlights a civilian construction company that is drafted into the Navy to help form the U.S. Navy's Construction Battalions (CB). The CBs (Seabees) built, among other things, runways in inhospitable territory for U.S. fighter planes.

The Fighting Sullivans (1944; VHS/DVD, 1 hr., 51 min.). This is the true story of five brothers who served on the same ship in the Pacific theater and who died together when their vessel was sunk. Although the film concentrates on the brothers' transition from boys into men, audiences were shocked by the tragedy, and a law was subsequently passed disallowing brothers from serving on the same ship.

The Story of G.I. Joe (1945; VHS/DVD, 1 hr., 45 min.). This film is based on the columns of wartime correspondent Ernie Pyle who reported home on the experiences of everyday soldiers. Infantrymen who fought in the war thought the film was remarkably accurate in its depictions of soldiers' lives.

Many more films about World War II were made after the war. Some were highly critical of certain aspects of the war; some waxed nostalgic, clearly embracing the camaraderie and patriotism of the period; and some merely used the war as a backdrop for comedy pieces. Again, students can be asked to research post–World War II films and perhaps select one for viewing. The following lists a few of the better-known films.

The Best Years of Our Lives (1946; VHS/DVD, 2 hrs., 52 min.). This film focuses on the difficult readjustments to family and civilian life made by three servicemen returning from the war.

Twelve O'Clock High (1949; VHS/DVD, 2 hrs., 12 min.). This film is about the mental and emotional stresses faced by air force fighter pilots during World War II.

Judgment at Nuremberg (1961; VHS/DVD, 1 hr., 58 min.). This fictional drama about Germans on trial for war crimes harkens back to the war crimes trials of 1948.

In Harm's Way (1965; VHS/DVD, 2 hrs., 47 min.). This realistic film is about the war in the Pacific. It captures the tensions that existed between military commanders, the difficulties facing women who served as nurses, and the sheer horror and destruction of World War II naval battles.

Patten (1970; VHS/DVD, 2 hrs., 51 min.). This biographical film concentrates on the career of General George Patton between the years 1943 and 1945.

Das Boot (1981; VHS/DVD, 1 hr., 25 min.). This film is based on Lothar-Guenther BuchHeim's autobiographical novel about his wartime experiences. The film focuses on a German U-boat and its crew as it seeks out, and hides from, the enemy. The film is in German with English subtitles.

Schindler's List (1993; DVD, 3 hrs., 16 min.). Based on the true story of Oscar Schindler, who, during WWII, personally saved more than one thousand Jews from certain death. This film is a chillingly accurate look at how the Jews were maltreated by the Nazis.

Saving Private Ryan (1998; VHS/DVD, 2 hrs., 50 min.). A combat unit is sent from the D-Day beaches to seek out Private Ryan who is behind enemy lines. Ryan's three brothers have already been killed, and the U.S. government wants to ensure his safe return. The film is notable for its realistic depiction of the carnage of war.

Band of Brothers (2001; VHS/DVD, 11 hrs., 45 min. [including additional features]). This ten-part miniseries, based on Stephen Ambrose's novel of the same name, focuses on the real-life soldiers of Easy Company, an elite paratrooper unit of the First Airborne division. The series follows the unit from basic training to the end of the World War II.

Historical Skills

Map 27.3, The Growth of Nazi Germany, 1933–1939, p. 1076

Ask students to review the enlargement of Nazi Germany from 1935 to the start of World War II in September 1939. Which, if any, changes do they believe were justified or brought about by peaceful means? Which changes would the students consider the most important in causing World War II? Have them explain why.

Map 27.4, Concentration Camps and Extermination Sites in Europe, p. 1080

Which concentration camps were specifically established as "death camps"; that is, camps in which the systematic murder of Jews and others took place (Auschwitz-Birkenau, Belzec, Chelmno, Majdanek, Sobibor, and Treblinka)? Ask students to discuss the differences between death camps and other camps. What do they know about some of the other camps, such as Dachau, Buchenwald, or Ravensbrück?

Mapping the West: Europe at War's End, 1945, p. 1092

Why was the human toll in the Soviet Union so great? Ask students to discuss the implications that Soviet losses may have had for the postwar period. What were the circumstances leading to high casualty figures in Poland and Yugoslavia? Why are civilian casualties so much higher than military casualties in Poland?

Nazis on Parade, p. 1049

Which aspects of this scene would cause ordinary German citizens to become supporters of the Nazi Party? What are some of the emotions an observer might have felt? How would these feelings compare to those you experienced when regarding this scene?

A Fireside Chat with FDR, p. 1065

How did Roosevelt's radio broadcasts help to reassure and unify Americans in the 1930s and 1940s? Which other political leaders used radio broadcasts effectively?

Persecution of Warsaw Jews, p. 1081

The Warsaw Ghetto Uprising was a large, dramatic act of resistance. There were, however, relatively few instances of resistance by Jews during the Holocaust. Ask students to suggest reasons why the Jews staged so few rebellions.

Hiroshima Victim, p. 1090

The dropping of the first atomic bomb on Hiroshima has been the subject of controversy for decades. Did the American officials' belief that dropping the bomb would hasten the end of war justify using the new weapon? Does it matter that Americans, and not the French or the British, for instance, dropped the bomb? Why would some of the same scientists who developed the atomic bomb have had reservations about actually deploying it? Should the use of an atomic bomb or the fire bombing of cities like Tokyo and Dresden be viewed as atrocities or as legitimate acts of war?

Memory of the War on Kulaks, p. 1058

Dolgikh's memory of the Communists coming to her family's farm was still sharp after more than sixty years. A discussion can focus on what the Communists considered to be items of "wealth" among the kulaks and whether their assessment that kulaks were wealthy was accurate. Obvious things, like the family horse and the land itself, were considered valuable, but so apparently were cups, spoons, and ladles. Prosperity is a relative term and has to be contextualized. That people were willing to buy such mundane kitchen items suggests that Dolgikh's family were at least better off than many other peasant families, and that the Communists felt they had to be utterly destroyed to level society.

OTHER BEDFORD/ST. MARTIN'S RESOURCES FOR CHAPTER 27

The following resources are available to accompany Chapter 27. Please refer to the Preface of this manual for detailed descriptions of all the ancillaries.

For Instructors

Transparencies

The following maps and images from Chapter 27 are available as full-color acetates.

- Map 27.1: The Expansion of Japan, 1931–1941
- Map 27.2: The Spanish Civil War, 1936–1939
- Map 27.3: The Growth of Nazi Germany, 1933–1939
- Map 27.4: Concentration Camps and Extermination Sites in Europe
- Map 27.5: World War II in Europe and Africa
- Map 27.6: World War II in the Pacific
- Mapping the West: Europe at War's End, 1945
- *Nazis on Parade*
- Altman, *Anna Akhmatova*

Instructor's Resources CD-ROM

The following maps and image from Chapter 27, as well as a chapter outline, are available on disc in both Power-Point and jpeg formats.

- Map 27.1: The Expansion of Japan, 1931–1941
- Map 27.2: The Spanish Civil War, 1936–1939
- Map 27.3: The Growth of Nazi Germany, 1933–1939
- Map 27.4: Concentration Camps and Extermination Sites in Europe
- Map 27.5: World War II in Europe and Africa
- Map 27.6: World War II in the Pacific
- Mapping the West Europe at War's End, 1945
- *Nazis on Parade*

Using the Bedford Series with The Making of the West

Available in print as well as online at bedfordstmartins .com/usingseries, this guide offers practical suggestions for using *Pearl Harbor and the Coming of the Pacific War: A Brief History with Documents and Essays* by **Akira Iriye**, in conjunction with chapters 27 and 28 of the textbook.

For Students

Sources of The Making of the West

The following documents are available in Chapter 27 of the companion sourcebook by Katharine J. Lualdi, University of Southern Maine.

1. Joseph Goebbels, *Nazi Propaganda Pamphlet* (1930)
2. Neville Chamberlain, *Speech on the Munich Crisis* (1938)
3. Isidora Dolores Ibárruri Gómez, *La Pasionaria's Farewell Address* (November 1, 1938)
4. Sam Bankhalter and Hinda Kibort, *Memories of the Holocaust* (1938–1945)
5. Harry S. Truman, *Harry Truman Announces the Dropping of the Atom Bomb on Hiroshima* (1945)

Study Guides

The print **Study Guide** and the **Online Study Guide** at bedfordstmartins.com/hunt, both by Victoria Thompson (Arizona State University) and Eric Johnson (University of California, Los Angeles), help students synthesize the material they have learned as well as practice the skills historians use to make sense of the past. The following Map, Visual, and Document activities are available for Chapter 27.

Map Activity

- Map 27.3: The Growth of Nazi Germany, 1933–1939

Visual Activity

- *Nazis on Parade*

Reading Historical Documents

- The War on Kulaks
- The Greater East Asia Co-Prosperity Sphere

Remaking Europe in the Shadow of the Cold War

c. 1945–1965

CHAPTER RESOURCES

Main Chapter Topics

1. After World War II, Europe, in essence, surrendered global leadership to the United States and the Soviet Union. These two superpowers divided Europe between them, the Soviet Union imposing Communist rule in the East and the United States exercising a powerful if somewhat benign influence in the West.

2. The breakdown of the agreement that was reached at Yalta and Potsdam led to a divided Germany (and Europe) and to the creation of two large military blocs. The Marshall Plan and the Berlin Airlift were peaceful measures but, notwithstanding, communicated resolve on the part of the United States not to allow further Soviet expansion into Western Europe.

3. Western European countries created the European Economic Community (EEC) or Common Market, which was part of a highly productive postwar economy. Eastern European countries endured repressive political systems; they could industrialize their economies, but they could not match the productivity or prosperity occurring in the West.

4. Colonized peoples expected independence because of their service in the war and because they were certain Western values should apply to them. Frequently disappointed by the powers bent on retaining their empires, colonials willingly used violence to obtain their liberation.

5. Growing affluence and Americanization contrasted with the horrors of the Holocaust and the menace of the cold war in shaping European culture.

6. The cold war came closest to becoming a nuclear war in the confrontation between the United States and the Soviet Union over nuclear Soviet missiles based in Cuba in October 1962. Thereafter, the two powers avoided direct confrontation, while still continuing the cold war.

Summary

At the end of World War II, two atomic superpowers emerged: the United States and the Soviet Union. Some believed the end of the world was near, whereas others were wildly optimistic about the future. As the cold war between these two powers progressed, a reorientation took place, with the *West* being defined as the United States and its client countries in Europe, while the *East* was defined as the Soviet Union and its bloc of allies in Eastern Europe. Paralleling these were other terms: the "first world" represented capitalist-based nations, the "second world" encompassed the Soviet socialist bloc, and the "third world" defined countries emerging from imperial domination.

World War II left physical devastation and millions of people exhausted and struggling for survival; millions were left homeless refugees; and Jewish survivors of concentration camps who often found they could not safely return to their former homes, emigrated. Europe could do little on its own to help either refugees or Holocaust survivors.

The United States, now the richest country in the world, dominated world trade. Americans, confident and prosperous, embraced their new position as global leaders. The Soviet Union, devastated by the war, remained a great military power and took pride in its prominent role in the defeat of the Nazis. But peasant hopes for a better life after the war did not come to fruition. Stalin reasserted brutal Communist control over politics and economics.

The origins of the cold war may have been rooted in the animosity that had existed between Russia and the United States, Britain, and France since the Bolshevik Revolution in 1917. Others point to Stalin's aggressive policies, especially the treaty he signed with Hitler early in World War II. Stalin felt the Soviet Union had borne the brunt of the war and was suspicious of Winston Churchill, Franklin Roosevelt, and Harry Truman. Stalin wanted a "buffer zone" along Soviet borders, and Truman interpreted this as ambition for world domination.

The emerging cold war became a series of moves and countermoves made by countries deeply distrusting one another.

Eastern Europe and Germany became bones of contention between the Soviet Union and the United States. Coalition governments evolved into Communist dictatorships by the late 1940s. The United States, concerned about Eastern Europe—but especially about Western Europe—responded with the Truman Doctrine, which sought to counter political crises with economic and military aid, specifically to Greece and Turkey in 1947. The Marshall Plan (1947) was intended to eliminate the terrible poverty in Europe and forestall communism. Stalin believed the plan was directed specifically against the Soviet Union and tightened his grip on Eastern Europe. Yugoslavia was the exception. Marshall Tito (Josip Broz [1892–1980]) and his partisans had liberated their country without outside help and pursued an independent Communist line.

Although postwar Germany was originally planned to be controlled jointly by the four main powers, serious disagreements about this emerged between the United States and the Soviet Union. The United States undertook a reprogramming of German cultural attitudes to permanently stamp out all authoritarian values; Stalin, who perceived fascism as an extreme form of capitalism, confiscated and redistributed the land and wealth of Germans in their occupation zone. Although the Yalta Conference had agreed to treat the German occupation zones as an economic unit, the Soviet Union reneged on the agreement when it expropriated and exported East German industrial plants and their key personnel to the USSR. The United States used the Marshall Plan to assist the economic recovery of West Germany because it was considered central to economic recovery for the rest of Western Europe.

The Soviet Union responded by closing Berlin's borders, which had also been divided into four zones of occupation even though the city was more than a hundred miles deep in the Soviet zone. All road traffic from the west was cut off, and the plan was to starve the allied zones into submission. The Berlin blockade, beginning in July 1948, gave form to the cold war. The Berlin airlift kept Berlin supplied even during the winter of 1948–1949, turning the cold war into a moral crusade. Even after the blockade was lifted, a divided Berlin came to symbolize the cold war. In 1949, the United States, Canada, and their European allies formed the North Atlantic Treaty Organization (NATO) to defend Western Europe. The Soviet Union formed the Warsaw Treaty Organization in 1955 in response to the rearming of West Germany.

The rehabilitation of Germany became a priority for the West. The process of de-Nazification took place in stages. Vigilante justice prevailed immediately after the war; a more systematic process began later. The Nurem-berg trials of highly prominent Nazis were the most visible part of a process that was never completed. Instead, the advent of the cold war caused the United States and other countries to overlook the Nazi pasts of individuals who would be useful in the new circumstances.

In the democratic revival after the war, France formed the Fourth Republic under General Charles de Gaulle (although he soon resigned), and women were granted the right to vote. In Italy, the monarchy was abolished in favor of parliamentary rule, and women there were also allowed to vote. But the Labor and Socialist governments of both countries gave way to Conservative elements that were more centrist. In Britain, Winston Churchill's Conservative government lost the election to Clement Atlee's Labor Party, which had promised an equitable distribution of growing prosperity among the classes through social welfare programs and the nationalization of key industries. Communist parties in France and Italy had taken part in government coalitions as late as 1947, but leftist parties could not gain a foothold in Germany where the Christian Democrats emerged as the major party. Ironically, it was in the United States that democratic institutions and practices were under siege, propelled by the rabid anticommunism of Americans such as Senator Joseph McCarthy.

The European economies recovered quickly after 1948 with the assistance of the Marshall Plan. By the 1950s, most enjoyed low unemployment rates and astonishingly high rates of growth. New consumer goods were more widely available, thus raising the standard of living and making communism less attractive. West Germany and Scandinavian countries especially witnessed unprecedented growth. The Marshall Plan mandated economic cooperation, which also accelerated economic growth. The European Coal and Steel Community, formed by Italy, France, Germany, Belgium, Luxembourg, and the Netherlands, was the first success of cooperation. The idea behind this kind of economic cooperation was that the bonds of common production would keep France and Germany from entering into another cataclysmic war. The EEC, formed in 1957 by the same six countries, was an even bigger success. Beginning with the reduction of tariffs and the creation of common trade policies, it laid the foundation for more than four decades of economic cooperation and growth.

Welfare states developed on both sides of the Iron Curtain with one common aim: the encouragement of reproduction. Family allowances, free health care and medical benefits, and programs for pregnant women and new mothers were either introduced or expanded. The side effect of these programs was that it made it more difficult for women in the West to work outside their homes. In the East, women were encouraged to combine reproduction with production. Child-care programs, maternity leave, and health benefits meant full-time employment in the workforce. Nevertheless, population levels continued to stagnate in the eastern-bloc countries because the scarcity of consumer goods, the shortage of housing, and lack of household conveniences discouraged women from having large families.

Welfare programs in the West were extended beyond women and new mothers, however. State-funded medical insurance, subsidized medical care, or nationalized health-care systems covered the health-care needs in most industrial nations except the United States. Infant mortality rates declined and, as life expectancy rates rose, the U.S. government established programs for the elderly. There were more doctors and dentists than ever before, and vaccines kept once life-threatening diseases at bay. The standard of living also rose in the West. Electricity came to rural areas, governments legislated better working conditions and paid holiday leave, food was abundant and diets grew more varied, and new housing went up. The Soviet bloc followed Stalin in the economic sphere and emphasized industrialization and collectivization of agriculture. Although the approach did not always work in the best interests of the satellite states, some demographic groups did benefit. The Council for Mutual Economic Assistance (COMECON) operated for the benefit of the Soviet Union, but extreme political, religious repression and persecution accompanied economic guidance along with propaganda.

After Stalin's death and a period of uncertainty, Nikita Khrushchev (1894–1971) emerged as the leader of the Soviet Union. In 1956, Khrushchev gave the so-called secret speech, which opened a campaign of de-Stalinization, that included the opening of the gulags. That summer, Polish workers struck for higher wages. This protest, which quickly took on political implications, was resolved within the Polish Communist movement. Similar protests in Hungary in October led to the return of Imre Nagy (1896–1958) as the leader. When Nagy indicated that Hungary would leave the Warsaw Pact, Soviet troops smashed the uprising, killing thousands and sending many more thousands into exile. Nagy was hanged. In the late 1950s, the Soviet Union and its satellites experienced what came to be known as a "thaw." Khrushchev ended the Stalinist purges, reformed the courts, and reduced the powers of the secret police. The thaw, however, was fragile. Khrushchev forced Boris Pasternak to refuse the 1958 Nobel Prize he had won in literature because his novel *Doctor Zhivago* (1957) degenerated the glory of the Communist revolution and upheld the value of the individual. Yet, in 1961, Khrushchev allowed the publication of Aleksandr Solzhenitsyn's *One Day in the Life of Ivan Denisovitch*, a chilling account of life in the gulag. And, despite successes in outer space and other arenas, the Soviet Union remained suspicious of the West and ambitious for its overall position in world affairs.

After World War II, most colonial areas expected to gain independence. Decolonization would, however, be difficult. Religious and ethnic differences created divisions, while in many places indigenous traditions and cultural ties had been destroyed by imperialism. Britain probably lost the most in the process of decolonization. In 1947, the British granted independence to India and to the separate nation of Pakistan. The victory of the Chinese Communists in 1949 provided tremendous encouragement to national liberation movements elsewhere in Asia. The People's Republic of China distanced itself from the Soviet Union by the late 1950s, but anti-Communist countries like the United States continued to see only a monolithic Communist bloc. In 1950, with the support of the Soviet Union, the North Koreans invaded U.S.-backed South Korea. The UN Security Council approved a "police action," and U.S. forces pushed well into North Korea where they met the Chinese army. A settlement was reached in 1953, restoring the prewar border at the thirty-eighth parallel. Victory by the Communists in China, and the outbreak of the Korean War in 1950, brought cold-war superpowers to Asia. In Indochina, the Viet Minh, lead by Ho Chi Minh (1890–1969), forced the French to leave Vietnam. The Geneva Convention carved out an independent Laos and divided Vietnam into North and South, each free from French control. The Viet Minh was ordered to retreat to an area north of the seventeenth parallel. The superpowers, the United States in particular, undermined the new arrangements, and the United States continued to assist the corrupt government of the south as a means to further bar Communist expansion in Asia.

Their vast oil supplies enabled Middle Eastern peoples to play the superpowers one against the other. British imperial attitudes drove Saudi Arabia to negotiate oil contracts with the United States and, eventually, Middle Eastern countries, mandated to Britain after World War I, gained their independence. Another pressing problem in the Middle East was the Jewish people's desire for a homeland in British-ruled Palestine, a desire made imperative by the Holocaust. The British turned Palestine over to the United Nations, which partitioned it into Arab and Jewish regions in 1947. War followed, and the state of Israel was achieved by military victory in 1948. In Egypt, Gamel Abdel Nasser (1918–1970) nationalized the Suez Canal in 1956. Israel, Britain, and France attempted to regain the canal, but Soviet pressure and American refusal to intervene forced these countries to back down.

In Africa, states like Ghana and Nigeria—where the population was predominantly black—gained independence with relatively little violence. In areas with large numbers of white settlers, however, independence came with violence; Kenya, for example, won its independence in 1964 after a bloody conflict between the colonists and the largely Kikuyu rebels. In the French colonies, areas where there were relatively few settlers and little to be gained economically independence was achieved without bloodshed. The French believed they had too much at stake in Algeria, however, and the fighting there was exceptionally bloody and vicious. Colonial events impinged on the French political system and threatened to destroy the government in 1958. The collapse of the Fourth Republic that year returned Charles de Gaulle (1890–1970) to power. De Gaulle formed the Fifth Republic, which featured a stronger chief executive and a negotiated French withdrawal from Algeria. The Dutch and Belgium colonies also quickly collapsed and the independent states of Indonesia and the Congo (now known as the Democratic Republic of the Congo) emerged.

Throughout this period, the United Nations worked to establish an international forum for the resolution of problems, but this forum was often thwarted by developments in the cold war. Beginning in 1955, nonaligned nations attempted to steer between the two great power blocs.

A thriving economy and labor shortages prompted massive migration throughout Europe. These emigrants, many of whom were from former colonies, were seeking a better life. Some emigrants were classified as "guest workers" and granted only temporary resident status; they often took jobs no one else wanted and, while the wages were low by European standards, they were higher than what the guest workers would have received in their home countries. Clandestine workers—workers without visas, passports, or papers—soon began infiltrating Europe.

For many, victory in World War II represented Western civilization's defense against the barbarism of fascism. The West stressed its roots in ancient Greece and Rome but also focused on constitutional or representative government. Holocaust and resistance literature was widely published in the postwar period and memorials were erected commemorating resistance fighters. Existentialism, a fashionable philosophy in the 1950s, detached the meaning of human existence from the past and religion and placed it solely on the individual. Two leading existentialist writers—Albert Camus (1913–1960) and Jean-Paul Sartre (1913–1969)—had written for the resistance during the war. In the novels of Camus, characters act and make choices in the face of evil even where there is no assurance the choices have meaning. Sartre emphasized political action in support of the left. Simone de Beauvoir (1908–1986), Sartre's long-time companion, published one of the twentieth century's most important books: *The Second Sex* (1949). Beauvoir wrote about the failure of women to create an "authentic self," which led them to be seen as the opposite of the self — an object or "Other." Instead of defining themselves, women had allowed themselves to be defined by men.

The war and the national liberation movements that followed it called into question ideas concerning white racial superiority. Frantz Fanon (1925–1961), a black psychiatrist from the French colony of Martinique, wrote influential books such as *The Wretched of the Earth* (1961) that discusses the violence inflicted by colonialism on the colonized peoples and the colonizers alike. In the United States, the older civil rights movement culminated in the U.S. Supreme Court decision in *Brown v. Board of Education* (1954) that segregated education was unconstitutional. The following year, the bus boycott in Montgomery, Alabama, sparked by Rosa Parks's refusal to give up her seat in the white section of a bus, took the civil rights movement in a new direction: civil disobedience modeled on the tactics of Mohandas Gandhi.

In the 1950s and early 1960s, differing ideas about masculinity competed for attention. Common to many were the ideas of rebellion and alienation. Elvis Presley embodied sexual rebelliousness, whereas James Dean in the film *Rebel Without a Cause* projected sulky alienation. Heinrich Böll's protagonist in *The Clown* (1963) protested against the newly prominent who had casually shed their Nazi past for the new fashion of democracy. *Playboy* unashamedly encouraged a hedonistic male lifestyle zeroed in on good food and drink, fast cars, and fast, beautiful women. The message women received did not correspond to either their experiences during the war or the realities of the postwar period. Even in the United States, where the idea of glamorous, feminine women and perfect housewives was heavily promoted, many women worked outside the home all of their adult lives. New appliances, however, like refrigerators and washing machines, did make domestic life easier, which was a good thing because the days of household help disappeared when women sought work in factories rather than working as domestics during World War II.

The 1950s was the heyday of radio, but the new technology of television was beginning to take root. Radio was an important component of propaganda during the cold war, with both sides promoting their respective ideologies and ways of life. It also brought the cold war into the living rooms of millions with reports about nuclear buildup and methods of preparedness. Children practiced what to do in case of a nuclear attack, and some families even erected bomb shelters.

The cold war was also reflected in literature. George Orwell's (1903–1950) novel *1984* (1949) held a bleak prospect for humanity's future. Ray Bradbury's (b. 1920) *Fahrenheit 451* (1953), the title of which indicates the temperature at which books burn, criticized cold-war curtailment of intellectual freedom. Official writers in the Soviet Union wrote and published spy stories. In the West, Ian Fleming's (1909–1964) spy novels featured James Bond, Agent 007, a sophisticated hero who always triumphed over his cold-war adversaries.

Europeans feared the spread of communism, but also debated the negative effects of Americanization. Both the Soviet Union and the United States sponsored high and popular culture as a means of asserting the superiority of their respective systems. It was obvious in the Soviet Union that virtually every aspect of life was connected with the cold-war competition but, in the United States and Western Europe, the cold war also shaped much of modern life. The cold war came close to becoming a nuclear war in 1962. The failure of the Bay of Pigs invasion to topple Soviet-allied Fidel Castro in Cuba and the erection of the Berlin Wall in 1961 had caused high tension and led to calls in the United States for more and better preparation for the possibility of war. When the United States discovered that the Soviet Union had placed nuclear missiles on Cuban soil in October 1962, the tension escalated enormously. President John F. Kennedy (1917–1963) declared a naval quarantine and economic embargo of Cuba and threatened war if the missiles were not disarmed, dismantled, and removed. In the difficult negotiations that followed, the Soviet Union agreed to remove the missiles in exchange for a pledge that the United States would not invade Cuba. After the near catastrophe, the two countries worked to improve nuclear diplomacy and tacitly agreed to avoid direct confrontations in the future. The cold war continued as a powerful shaping force, but other political, socio-economic, and cultural forces were emerging.

Suggestions for Lecture and Discussion Topics

1. How and why the cold war began is a crucial topic. There are many aspects that might be examined, including what was agreed to at the Yalta and Potsdam conferences, American perceptions of Soviet behavior in 1946, and the announcement of the Truman Doctrine in 1947. The Marshall Plan should be closely examined. When General George C. Marshall spoke about his ideas at Harvard in June 1947, and even when Europeans gathered later that summer in Paris to discuss possibilities, there was suspicion on both sides but no cold war as such. By the time Congress passed the European Recovery Act in 1948, which funded the Marshall Plan, the cold war was rapidly taking shape. Questions to use as a basis for a lecture or as a theme for discussion are: What was the true nature of the Marshall Plan? Was it primarily a humanitarian gesture? Was it a rather disingenuous attempt by American businesses to gain control of the global economy? Was it merely another device in the developing cold war competition with the Soviet Union?

In addition to books on the cold war listed in the chapter's bibliography, Melvyn P. Leffler, *The Specter of Communism: The United States and the Origins of the Cold War, 1917–1953* (New York: Hill & Wang, 1994) is an excellent introduction to the topic. George F. Kennan, *Memoirs 1925–1950* (New York: Pantheon, 1967) devotes a chapter to his part in the origins of the Marshall Plan. George C. Marshall, "Against Hunger, Poverty, Desperation, and Chaos," *Foreign Affairs* 76.3 (May/June 1997), is

a convenient source of the speech Marshall gave at Harvard. (This issue contains a very useful special section, "The Marshall Plan and Its Legacy.") See also Michael J. Hogan, *The Marshall Plan: America, Britain, and the Reconstruction of Western Europe* (New York: Cambridge University Press, 1987); and Charles S. Maier and Günter Bischof, eds., *The Marshall Plan and Germany* (New York: Berg, 1991). *The Marshall Plan: Against All Odds* is an interesting and well-informed documentary film on the topic.

On the cold war in general, see Ronald E. Powaski, *The Cold War: The United States and the Soviet Union, 1917–1991* (Oxford: Oxford University Press, 1998); Edward H. Judge and John W. Langdon, eds., *The Cold War: A History through Documents* (Paramus, NJ: Prentice Hall, 1998); Michael Kort, *The Columbia Guide to the Cold War* (New York: Columbia University Press, 1998); and Thomas S. Arms, ed., *Encyclopedia of the Cold War* (New York: Facts on File, 1994).

2. The Berlin blockade and airlift in 1948–1949 is another good vantage point from which to observe the development of the cold war. Neither the United States nor the Soviet Union understood the other's intentions in Germany after the war. One possible interpretation is that the United States had a German policy that it followed consistently, whereas the Soviet Union lacked one. In this view, the American effort to create a Germany that could pay its own expenses and also help to restart the European economy led directly to the Soviet challenge in the Berlin blockade. The success of the Berlin airlift caused the Soviets to give up the blockade and resulted in the division of Germany into East Germany and West Germany in 1949. The cold war also played a role in the formation of NATO that same year. Berlin remained a flash point, at least through the building of the Berlin Wall in 1961, and the two Germanys remained a major focus of the cold war until 1989.

In addition to titles cited in the chapter's bibliography and Leffler's book noted in suggestion 1, see also the special commemorative section, "The Berlin Airlift and the City's Future," *Foreign Affairs* 77.4, pp. 147–194 (July/August 1998). Recent studies include Michael D. Haydock, *City under Siege: The Berlin Blockade and Airlift, 1948–49* (Dulles, VA: Brassey's, 1999); and Thomas Parrish, *Berlin in the Balance, 1945–1949: The Blockade, the Airlift, the First Major Battle of the Cold War* (Reading, MA: Addison Wesley Longman, 1998). Avi Shlaim, *The United States and the Berlin Blockade, 1948–49* (Berkeley: University of California Press, 1983) is probably the leading study of the Berlin blockade. Jean Edward Smith, *Lucius Clay: An American Life* (New York: Henry Holt, 1992) is a major biography of General Clay. In addition, the Public Broadcasting System, *The Berlin Airlift* (dist. Unapix/Miramar, 1998) is a fascinating account of the Berlin airlift featuring contemporary footage and interviews with some of the participants.

3. The new, prosperous Europe that was created in the 1950s and 1960s and the role of the European Economic Community (EEC) in that process are linked topics well worth investigating. One good approach would be through the life of Jean Monnet, the person most responsible first for the European Coal and Steel Community and then for the EEC. A good place to start is Monnet's *Memoirs* (Garden City, NY: Doubleday, 1978), especially Part 2, chapters 13–16. Two good biographies of Monnet are those by Douglas Brinkley and Clifford P. Hackett, *Jean Monnet: The Path to European Unity* (New York: St. Martin's Press, 1991); and François Duchêne, *Jean Monnet: The First Statesman of Interdependence* (New York: W. W. Norton, 1994). Probably the most useful, single source is Sherrill B. Wells, *Jean Monnet: Visionary and Architect of European Union: A Brief Biography and Documents* (Boston: Bedford/St. Martin's, 2000). Derek W. Urwin, *The Community of Europe: A History of European Integration Since 1945*, 2d ed. (London: Longman, 1995) is an excellent introduction. Two authoritative surveys are Rondo Cameron, *A Concise Economic History of the World: From Paleolithic Times to the Present*, 3d ed. (Oxford: Oxford University Press, 1997); and David S. Landes, *The Unbound Prometheus: Technological Change and Industrial Development in Western Europe from 1750 to the Present* (Cambridge: Cambridge University Press, 1969). In Landes, Chapter 7 provides a good summary of the founding of the EEC.

For insights into life in Western Europe in the 1950s and 1960s, see Laurence Wylie's fascinating *Village in the Vaucluse*, 3d ed. (Cambridge, MA: Harvard University Press, 1977). See also the first book by one of the best American journalists reporting on Europe, Jane Kramer, *Unsettling Europe* (New York: Random House, 1980). Kramer presents the stories of four groups of outsiders in Europe in the 1960s and 1970s, Italian Communists in their own country, Yugoslav guest workers in Sweden, Indians from Uganda in England, and colons from Algeria in France.

4. A session dealing with the Korean War might discuss the differences between the concept of "containment" voiced in the late 1940s and the idea of "rollback" that came to be dominant after 1950. A very helpful book in terms of background for the Korean War is Sergei N. Goncharov, John W. Lewis, and Xue Litai, *Uncertain Partners: Stalin, Mao, and the Korean War* (Stanford, CA: Stanford University Press, 1993). *Uncertain Partners* makes a case that Kim Il-sung, the North Korean leader, had the most to do with starting the war. It also points up the complicated and delicate relationships between Stalin and Mao and the Soviet Union and the People's Republic of China. What makes the Korean War such a fateful event is that it broke out just as American officials were considering a major policy statement, NSC 68, a document that helped turn the cold war into a series of military confrontations. On NSC 68, see the very useful book by Ernest R. May, *American Cold War Strategy: Interpreting NSC 68* (Boston: Bedford/St. Martin's, 1993). On the Korean War itself, useful sources are James I. Matray, *Historical Dictionary of the Korean War* (Westport, CT: Greenwood Press, 1991); James I. Matray, *The Uncivil War: Korea, 1945–1953* (Armonk, NY: M. E. Sharpe, 1999); and Stanley Sandler, *The Korean War: No Victors, No Vanquished* (Louisville: University Press of Kentucky, 1999).

Another possibility is a session focused on France and the Algerian revolution. Because the French considered Algeria an integral part of France, the attempt by the Algerian rebels to liberate their country had a definitive impact on domestic affairs in France. In addition to the books cited in the chapter's bibliography, see also Alistair Horne, *A Savage War of Peace: Algeria 1954–1962* (New York: Viking Press, 1978), an excellent if long account. See also Charles S. Maier and Dan S. White, eds., *The Thirteenth of May: The Advent of de Gaulle's Republic* (New York: Oxford University Press, 1968), a useful collection of documents about the end of the Fourth Republic and beginnings of the Fifth Republic in 1958. De Gaulle's account of 1958 and his successful efforts to end the war in Algeria are contained in his *Memoirs of Hope: Renewal and Endeavor* (New York: Simon & Schuster, 1971). A convenient short biography is Andrew Shennan, *De Gaulle* (London: Longman, 1993).

5. Students will probably be curious about what it was like to live during the 1950s and early 1960s when the threat of nuclear war seemed all too real. One possibility is to show the film *Dr. Strangelove, Or: How I Learned to Stop Worrying and Love the Bomb*, Stanley Kubrick's masterpiece from 1964 (Burbank, CA: RCA/Columbia Pictures Home Video, 1987). Ninety-three minutes long, it will not fit conveniently into most class periods, but it would be worth the trouble to arrange an evening showing with an in-class discussion in class the following day. The screenplay was written by Kubrick, Terry Southern, and Peter George. Peter Sellers plays most of the major parts, including Dr. Strangelove.

There are several books that may be helpful in dealing with *Dr. Strangelove* and American culture in the nuclear age. One is Margot A. Henriksen, *Dr. Strangelove's America: Society and Culture in the Atomic Age* (Berkeley: University of California Press, 1997), a readable and interesting discussion of films, novels, and other cultural artifacts from that period. Another direction is taken by Tom Engelhart, *The End of Victory Culture: Cold War America and the Disillusioning of a Generation*, 2d ed. (Amherst: University of Massachusetts Press, 1998). Engelhart believes the idea that America was always on the side of the good became increasingly difficult to sustain in the nuclear age. See also Philip Jenkins, *The Cold War at Home: The Red Scare in Pennsylvania* (Chapel Hill: University of North Carolina Press, 1999), a case study that is set in the national context; Lisle A. Rose, *The Cold*

War Comes to Main Street: America in 1950 (Lawrence: University of Kansas Press, 1999); Stephen J. Whitfield, *The Culture of the Cold War* (Baltimore: Johns Hopkins University Press, 1991); and Richard Alan Schwartz, ed., *Cold War Culture: Media and the Arts, 1945–1990* (New York: Facts on File, 1998). Many of the titles listed in "Suggestion for Lecture and Discussions Topics," number 1, may also be helpful.

A different approach, which depends to some extent on your familiarity with 1950s rock and roll, is a focus on Elvis Presley. Why was Presley so enormously popular? What did this say about America in the 1950s? Peter Guralnick, *Last Train to Memphis: The Rise of Elvis Presley* (Boston: Little, Brown, 1994), a longish but fascinating book, is the best source. Guralnick charts Presley's downfall in *Careless Love: The Unmaking of Elvis Presley* (Boston: Little, Brown, 1999). See also Karal Ann Marling, *Graceland: Going Home with Elvis* (Cambridge, MA: Harvard University Press, 1996). Other useful sources include Lee Cotton, *All Shook Up: Elvis Day-by-Day, 1954–1977* (Ann Arbor, MI: Pierian Press, 1985); Ernst Jorgensen, *Reconsider Baby: The Definitive Elvis Session-ography, 1954–1977* (Ann Arbor, MI: Pierian Press, 1986); and Erika Doss, *Elvis Culture: Fans, Faith, & Image* (Lawrence: University of Kansas Press, 1999).

6. The Cuban missile crisis is, first of all, a moment of high drama in which the entire world was at risk. It also offers the possibility of looking carefully at the conduct of politics in the Soviet Union and the United States. Finally, it provides an opportunity to examine American, European, and Soviet reactions to the crisis at the time. The motives and responses of the main players in the crisis would form a good basis for discussion on leadership and crisis management.

There is a wealth of material available. Chapter 9 of John Lewis Gaddis, *We Now Know: Rethinking Cold War History* (Oxford: Clarendon Press, 1997) offers a thoughtful review of scholarship on several major issues connected with the crisis. Aleksandr Fursenko and Timothy Naftali, *One Hell of a Gamble: Khrushchev, Kennedy, and Castro, 1958–1964* (New York: W. W. Norton, 1998) is, to a large extent, based on Soviet archival sources and provides a good picture of the Soviet side of the crisis. Laurence Chang and Peter Kornbluh, *The Cuban Missile Crisis, 1962: A National Security Archive Documents Reader* (New York: The New Press, 1992) contains an excellent selection of documents combined with an extensive chronology and other helpful material. See also Robert Kennedy, *Thirteen Days: A Memoir of the Cuban Missile Crisis* (New York: W. W. Norton, 1969); Ernest R. May and Philip D. Zelikow, *The Kennedy Tapes: Inside the White House During the Cuban Missile Crisis* (Cambridge, MA: Belknap Press, 1997); and Michael R. Beschloss, *The Crisis Years: Kennedy and Khrushchev, 1960–1963* (New York: Edward Burlingame Books, 1991).

Making Connections

1. *What was the global political climate after World War II? How did it differ from the global political climate after World War I?* After World War I, no single, dominant power in Europe existed until the rise of the fascists in the 1930s. But, after World War II, both the Soviet Union and the United States emerged as strong powers and embraced their new role as world leaders. Indeed, the standoff between these two nations after World War II seemed to suggest that further conflict was imminent. After World War I, Europe had been divided into independent nations under the protection of varying countries. But, after World War II, Europe was divided into two distinct blocs: many Eastern and Central European countries allied with the Soviet Union, and Western European countries allied with the United States. Colonial peoples had been denied their independence after the first world war but, after the second world war, these colonials demanded and sometimes fought to achieve independence.

2. *What were the relative strengths of the two European sides in the cold war?* Western European economies recovered quickly after the introduction of the Marshall Plan in 1947. The EEC, formed in 1957, was an even bigger economic success. Politically, economically, socially, and militarily, Europe had a strong ally in the United States, which helped to counter the power of the Soviet Union and Soviet-bloc countries. However, the Soviet Union was heavily industrialized, had full employment, and had geared every aspect of life toward cold war competition. It also possessed tremendous resources by way of its satellite countries. It prided itself on technological innovation, and had a thriving space program to prove it.

3. *How did events of World War II shape cultural life after the war?* There was a general sense of release after World War II. Young people embraced rock and roll, and some young men adopted a rebellious anti-establishment stance in music and film. The Beat poets critiqued traditional ideals of the upright and rational male achiever, while the American magazine *Playboy* reflected a changed male identity, where men were independent of domestic life just as they had been in the war. The ideal for women was complete domesticity, but the reality was that women had to continue to work to support their families, just as they had done during the war. The thriftiness of the war years was abandoned in favor of spending on new consumer goods. The United States had played a decisive role in the war and continued to do so as Western Europe was being rebuilt. This had the effect of Americanizing Western European culture.

4. *Why did decolonization follow World War II so immediately?* Decolonization happened swiftly in part because colonials remembered what had occurred after World War I. After helping to fight the war through various means, colonial peoples expected they would be

given their independence. When this did not occur, resentment grew until it erupted at the end of World War II. With leaders steeped in Western values and experienced in military and manufacturing technology, people in Asia, Africa, and the Middle East embraced the cause of independence. Exhausted economically and militarily, most European countries were in no position to fight independence movements. Some countries, like Ghana, achieved independence peacefully; others, like Algeria, clashed directly in bloody combat with Western powers.

Writing Assignments and Class Presentation Topics

1. Ask students to write an essay on the cold war as it developed in 1947. In addition to material in the chapter, you may wish to assign some of the documents in Judge and Langdon and perhaps Chapter 3 of Powaski's *The Cold War*, both cited in "Suggestions for Lecture and Discussion Topics," number 1. In the essay, students should not merely recount what happened in 1947 but try to sort out the more important from the less important events. What caused President Truman to proclaim the Truman Doctrine? Was there a connection between the Truman Doctrine and the Marshall Plan? What led to the formation of the COMINFORM (Communist Information Bureau)? Finally, did 1947 mark the beginning of the cold war? Explain why.

2. Assign teams of students the task of presenting one of the following cold war events: the Berlin blockade and airlift, the formation of NATO, the victory of the Chinese Communist Party and the founding of the People's Republic of China, the Korean War, or the Geneva Conference of 1954. Some additional reading will be necessary, but the material cited at the end of "Suggestion for Lectures and Discussion Topics," number 1, should be adequate. Each student should, in addition to his or her team assignment, write a short essay on the presentation and the experience of working with the team.

3. Require students to write an essay comparing and contrasting the experience of two European countries, one from the West and the other from the East, in the 1950s. One rather obvious possibility is West Germany and East Germany. The discussion will most likely center on the politics of the two countries, but students should also try to ascertain the quality of life in the two countries. For this assignment, you may want to assign students a chapter or two in surveys such as Gordon Wright, *France in Modern Times*, 3d ed. (New York: W. W. Norton, 1981); or Dietrich Orlow, *A History of Modern Germany: 1871 to Present* (Englewood Cliffs, NJ: Prentice-Hall, 1995). For statistics and other material, alert students to publications such as the *Statesman's Year Book* (New York: St. Martin's Press, annual).

4. As part of a 1950s day or week, present students with a selection of possible topics on which they may give five-minute reports. Topics might include political figures like Konrad Adenauer, Nikita Khrushchev, or Martin Luther King Jr.; events such as the coronation of Queen Elizabeth II, the launching of *Sputnik*, or the opening of the first Macdonald's; rock and roll songs, stars, or dances; or movies, magazines, and other cultural phenomena. Students should be encouraged to be creative. For example, someone might decide to come to class wearing the attire of the 1950s. His or her report should be a brief description of the clothing, hairdo, accessories, and functionality—if any—of the way the person was dressed. David Halberstam, *The Fifties* (New York: Villard Books, 1993) would be a good resource to put on reserve.

Research Assignments

1. In addition to the topics in "Writing Assignments and Class Presentation Topics," number 2, there are several other cold-war topics from the 1950s and 1960s that would serve as a basis for interesting research assignments. These might include the East German uprising in 1953, the Hungarian Revolution of 1956, the Suez Canal crisis of 1956, the Berlin crisis of 1958 to 1962, the building of the Berlin Wall in 1961, the Bay of Pigs invasion of Cuba in 1961, and the Cuban missile crisis of 1962. Sources listed at the end of "Suggestions for Lecture and Discussion Topics," number 1 should be sufficient to get students started.

2. Assign students a research project on the process of liberation in a country in Africa or Asia. You may wish to limit the possibilities available. Some areas—the Indian subcontinent, for example—form too large and complicated a topic for a research paper unless it is to be the major paper for the term. Also consider whether you will be able to refer students to available sources in many different areas. Ask students to define a problem or present a tentative thesis. The paper should not simply retell the story of the liberation of a particular country.

In addition to the titles by Vadney, Hargreaves, and McIntyre cited in the chapter's bibliography, see Franz Ansprenger, *The Dissolution of the Colonial Empires* (London: Routledge, 1989). Also useful is the encyclopedic book by J. A. S. Grenville, *A History of the World in the Twentieth Century*, enlarged ed. (Cambridge, MA: Belknap Press, 2000).

Literature

Beauvoir, Simone de, *The Mandarins*. 1956.
Beckett, Samuel, *Waiting for Godot*. 1954.
Bradbury, Ray, *Fahrenheit 451*. 1953.

Farrington, Constance, trans., *Frantz Faron: The Wretched of the Earth.* 1986.

Hayward, Max, and Manya Harari, trans., *Boris Pasternak:* Doctor Zhivago. 1958.

Orwell, George, *1984.* 1949.

Parshley, H. M., trans., *Simone de Beauvoir:* The Second Sex. 1993.

Sidhwa, Bapsi, *Cracking India: A Novel.* 1992.

Vannewitz, Leila, trans., *Heinrich Böll:* The Clown. 1994.

Films and Videos

Dr. Strangelove, Or: How I Learned to Stop Worrying and Love the Bomb (1964; Burbank, CA: RCA/Columbia Pictures Home Video. 1987, 1 hr., 33 min.). Stanley Kubrick's classic cold-war satire.

The Cold War (Hollywood, CA: Turner Home Video, 1998). The ambitious, multipart documentary by CNN.

Historical Skills

Map 28.1, The Impact of World War II on Europe, p. 1101

Discuss with students the reasons that various groups of refugees were on the move. In particular, review the situations many Germans found themselves in after the war ended. Ask students to explain why and how the Soviet Union acquired the various areas along its western borders between 1940 and 1956.

Map 28.2, Divided Germany and the Berlin Airlift, 1946–1949, p. 1107

Point out to students that the British also participated in the Berlin airlift. Ask students if they know which airfields in Berlin were used by the Americans and British (the Americans used Tempelhof and the British used Gatow; Tegel, the current Berlin airport, was built during the airlift in the French sector).

Mapping the West: The Cold War World, c. 1960, p. 1135

Ask students to point out which states beyond those in NATO or the WTO might be counted as supporters of the United States or of the Soviet Union in 1960. What was the situation of Cuba? This might be a good opportunity to discuss the Nonaligned Movement that began at the Bandung Conference in 1955. Various nations, among them India, Indonesia, and Yugoslavia, tried to avoid siding with either the United States or the Soviet Union. Ask students to discuss why this effort was unsuccessful.

Taking Measure: World Manufacturing Output, 1950–1970, p. 1113

What impression do students get about this era from looking at the graph? If we examine the graph from 1950 to 1963 and from 1963 to 1970, in which years is the rate of growth of world manufacturing greater? In which years is overall growth greater; that is, in all sectors? Why is this true?

Figure 28.1, "The Arms Race, 1950–1970," p. 1112

Why did the United States steeply increase its expenditures on arms early in the 1950s? Why was the Soviet Union able to come close to closing the gap between their expenditures for arms and the U.S. expenditures? What else would we know if the size of each nation's gross domestic product (GDP) were also indicated? Why are expenditures by the United Kingdom, France, West Germany, and Italy not only rather low but also virtually flat over this time period?

The Atomic Age, p. 1097

Ask students to reflect on the contemporary reactions to the explosion of the atomic bombs at Hiroshima and Nagasaki. What were the conflicting ideas about nuclear power by the 1950s and the cold war? Ask students what they know about present attitudes toward the use of nuclear power for generating electricity.

The Punishment of Collaborators, p. 1109

The topics of collaboration and resistance have continued to be controversial in France and elsewhere after World War II. Ask students to imagine living in an occupied country during World War II. Would they have been collaborators or members of the resistance? Can they imagine situations where the line between the two might be difficult to discern?

Women Clearing Berlin, p. 1111

This would be a good chance to introduce the concept of Stunde Null ("hour zero"), the beginning of the effort to rebuild. Discuss with students the extent of damage in Berlin and other cities, the economic and social problems with which people had to contend, and the psychological dilemmas many faced. The photograph shows the "rubble women." Ask the students where they believe the men were at this point.

Re-Creating Hungarian Youth, p. 1117

How effective would propaganda such as this poster be in Hungary in 1950? We cannot know with any certainty how many Hungarian young persons found the idea of fighting for peace and socialism attractive. However, we may make an informed guess on the basis of cold-war tensions in 1950 and the attractiveness of communism to groups that had been exploited under the previous regime.

Bomb Shelter, p. 1132

How likely is it that bomb shelters such as this would provide adequate protection in the event of the widespread dropping of nuclear bombs? Encourage students to ask about civil defense measures at their college or in their hometown. Do they know of any films or books that touch on the subject of nuclear annihilation?

Consumerism, Youth, and the Birth of the Generation Gap, p. 1129

Consider the similarities between the reactions of young people after both world wars. Skirts got shorter after both wars, and young people took an interest in new forms of music originating from the United States, like jazz and boogie-woogie. Young people also became more concerned about personal appearance with the introduction of makeup after World War I and hair permanents after World War II. Parents had a difficult time adjusting to what seemed like extreme behavior exhibited by their children. With the popularity of retro music, clothes, and dance styles, students might be asked if a "generation gap" exists today between parents and children.

OTHER BEDFORD/ST. MARTIN'S RESOURCES FOR CHAPTER 28

The following resources are available to accompany Chapter 28. Please refer to the Preface of this manual for detailed descriptions of all the ancillaries.

For Instructors

Transparencies

The following maps and images from Chapter 28 are available as full-color acetates.

- Map 28.1: The Impact of World War II on Europe
- Map 28.2: Divided Germany and the Berlin Airlift, 1946–1949
- Map 28.3: European NATO Members and the Warsaw Pact in the 1950s
- Map 28.4: The Partition of Palestine and the Creation of Israel, 1947–1948
- Map 28.5: The Decolonization of Africa, 1951–1990
- Map 28.6: The Cuban Missile Crisis, 1962
- Mapping the West: The Cold War World, c. 1965
- *Women Clearing Berlin*
- *Re-Creating Hungarian Youth*

Instructor's Resources CD-ROM

The following maps and image from Chapter 28, as well as a chapter outline, are available on disc in both Power-Point and jpeg formats.

- Map 28.1: The Impact of World War II on Europe
- Map 28.2: Divided Germany and the Berlin Airlift, 1946–1949
- Map 28.3: European NATO Members and the Warsaw Pact in the 1950s
- Map 28.4: The Partition of Palestine and the Creation of Israel, 1947–1948
- Map 28.5: The Decolonization of Africa, 1951–1990
- Map 28.6: The Cuban Missile Crisis, 1962
- Mapping the West: The Cold War World, c. 1965
- *Women Clearing Berlin*

Using the Bedford Series with The Making of the West

Available in print as well as online at <u>bedfordstmartins .com/usingseries</u>, this guide offers practical suggestions for using *Pearl Harbor and the Coming of the Pacific War: A Brief History with Documents and Essays* by **Akira Iriye**, in conjunction with chapters 27 and 28 of the textbook; *Charles de Gaulle: A Brief Biography with Documents* by **Charles G. Cogaan**, in conjunction with chapters 28 and 29 of the textbook; and *The Nuremberg War Crimes Trial, 1945–46: A Documentary History* by **Michael Marrus**, in conjunction with Chapter 28 of the textbook.

For Students

Sources of The Making of the West

The following documents are available in Chapter 28 of the companion sourcebook by Katharine J. Lualdi, University of Southern Maine.

1. *The Formation of the Communist Information Bureau (Cominform)* (1947)
2. National Security Council, *Paper Number 68* (1950)
3. Ho Chi Minh, *Declaration of Independence of the Republic of Vietnam* (1945)
4. Simone de Beauvoir, *The Second Sex* (1949)
5. Béla Lipták, *A Testament of Revolution* (1956)

Study Guides

The print **Study Guide** and the **Online Study Guide** at <u>bedfordstmartins.com/hunt</u>, both by Victoria Thompson (Arizona State University) and Eric Johnson (University of California, Los Angeles), help students synthesize the material they have learned as well as practice the skills historians use to make sense of the past. The following Map, Visual, and Document activities are available for Chapter 28.

Map Activity

- Map 28.3: European NATO Members and the Warsaw Pact in the 1950s

Visual Activity

- *Women Clearing Berlin*

Reading Historical Documents

- The Schuman Declaration
- The Generation Gap

Postindustrial Society and the End of the Cold War Order

1965–1989

CHAPTER RESOURCES

Main Chapter Topics

1. Humans were, by the 1970s, highly dependent upon machines, even for ordinary daily life because of the technological advances achieved in industrialized countries. Living conditions and workplaces were particularly changed by the introduction of television receivers and personal and main frame computers. The advances in the biological sciences—especially in the area of reproduction—raised especially difficult ethical questions.

2. Postindustrial society moved from an economy based on manufacturing to one that emphasized the service sectors. This new economy depended on large numbers of highly educated professionals and technical experts to gather and analyze data. Changes in the family, the arts, and politics appeared as products of and responses to the economic transformations taking place.

3. Protests against the status quo—domestic and foreign—exploded in the United States, Western Europe, and in other locations globally, prompting a wide range of reactions. The Soviet Union dealt harshly with dissent and failed to respond adequately to the problems that caused it. In 1968, in France and Czechoslovakia, protests escalated toward revolution but were defused.

4. The 1970s brought dramatic changes to international politics. In addition to an era of détente, which included negotiations to limit the nuclear arms race, other players — the oil-producing states organized in OPEC and loosely connected bands of terrorists — challenged the two superpowers and their allies.

5. Beginning in the late 1970s, Margaret Thatcher's neo-liberalism became the standard Western tactic for dealing with "stagflation." Ronald Reagan built upon Thatcher's policies and applied them in the United States; Sweden and France persisted in welfare-state programs with equal success.

6. By the early 1980s, wars in Vietnam and Afghanistan, the power of oil-producing states, and the growing political force of Islam had weakened superpower preeminence. Yet, the largely peaceful collapse of communism in the Soviet satellite countries—Poland, Hungary, Germany, Czechoslovakia, and Romania—was an utter surprise, even though Gorbachev had introduced glasnost and perestroika to respond to the USSR's multiple problems.

Summary

Information technology, like innovations in textile making and the spread of railroads during the Industrial Revolution, catalyzed social change in the postindustrial period. Television constituted one important component of this new technology. European governments initially controlled TV programming and advertising, but gradually encountered competition from private broadcasters using communications satellites. State-sponsored and commercial television avoided extremes, broadcasting only "official" or "moderate" opinions. Eastern-bloc television broadcasting was more tightly controlled and prominently featured educational programming. In both areas, TV became an important element in politics and heads of state could preempt programs for national addresses. As cultivating a media image became important, media consultants became as ubiquitous as policy experts.

In the 1960s and 1970s, computers simultaneously grew smaller, more powerful, and cheaper. With the technological advances made in computer construction, printed circuit boards and miniprocessors produced smaller computers. This, in turn, made possible the return to the eighteenth-century system of cottage industry in which people worked at home.

From the launching of *Sputnik* in 1957 to the first landing on the moon in 1969, the United States and the Soviet Union competed in an unofficial yet hotly contested "space race." American astronauts like John Glenn and Russian cosmonauts like Yuri Gagarin became instant heroes. Public interest in space exploration was reflected in television programs, such as *Star Trek*; and in fiction, like Stanislaw Lem's (b. 1921) novel, *Solaris* (1971). The space race grew out of cold war competition, but international cooperation in the form of global, satellite networks communication resulted. It also highly contributed to pure science, particularly astronomy. Increasingly sophisticated technology reinforced astronomers' belief in the "big bang" theory of the origins of the universe.

From the discovery in 1952 of the double-helix structure of DNA—the material in a cell's chromosomes that carries hereditary information—to the first successful heart transplant in 1967, scientists and doctors transformed the biological sciences and medicine. Advances in the knowledge of viruses and bacteria helped to eradicate and/or treat dangerous and oftentimes lethal diseases. Serious ethical questions were raised by cloning and also with the advances in birth control and reproduction that produced profound sociocultural changes. In vitro fertilization resulted in the first "test-tube baby" in 1978. If a couple was not able to conceive a child, a surrogate mother could be employed to give birth to a child on their behalf. As sexuality became separated from reproduction, public discussions of sexual matters became increasingly explicit, technical, and widespread. Human sexual activity began at increasingly younger ages.

The multinational corporation, while not a new phenomenon, quickly became the most prominent aspect of the new, postindustrial economy. Producing for a global market and conducting business worldwide, multinational corporations established factories and offices in countries away from their original home bases. Multinational corporations originated in the United States, Europe, and Japan but operated wherever labor was cheap, regulations less strict, or other advantages for higher profits existed. Moving manufacturing to former colonies in order to take advantage of their emerging economies appeared to some like a new form of imperialism. In Europe, governments, businesses, and scientists collaborated on special projects such as the *Airbus* and the *Concorde*.

The working class also changed in the new postindustrial economy. The farm population dropped precipitously in industrialized countries as farms were amalgamated into super farms and became part of the agribusiness. The number of blue-collar workers also declined. As workers increasingly set their own production quotas, union membership fell even though strikes still remained important politically and symbolically. White-collar workers no longer necessarily received better pay than blue-collar workers, but they formed the major part of the workforce. For example, by 1969, the percentage of service-sector employees had passed that of manufacturing workers in the United States, the Netherlands, and Sweden. Guest workers played a crucial role in the postwar boom, taking the least desirabl, lowest paying, job with the fewest benefits. In the Eastern-bloc countries, the differences between professional occupations and those involving physical work remained sizable. A high percentage of women—between 80 and 95 percent—worked in the socialist countries worked outside the home and usually held the most menial and worst-paying jobs.

Education and research became vital to the postindustrial economy. Space programs, weapons development, and economic policy all required research, data management, systems analyses, and complex decision making. Soviet-bloc countries found it difficult to compete or even to keep pace with the West owing to excessive, bureaucratic, red tape. Educational institutions benefited from an emphasis on training experts and on conducting research.

Advances in technology, changes in consumption patterns, and the structures of economies strongly affected family structures, which now varied enormously. One striking change was the decline of the birthrate by the 1970s. Modern appliances theoretically reduced the time it took to do housework, which was still performed largely by women, even if they worked outside the home. Most teenagers and many young adults still depended on their parents for psychological and economic support but, as consumers, enjoyed great economic importance. A "generation gap" developed as a by-product of marketing efforts.

"Pop art" expanded the boundaries of art by blurring and satirizing distinctions between the commercial and the artistic and between "low" and "high" art. New artists such as Andy Warhol (1928–1987) and Niki de Sainte-Phalle found appreciation and commercial success. Composers and musicians, however, paid for their highly intellectual experiments with a largely alienated public, but classical music enjoyed a wider audience than ever through improvements in recording techniques.

Social scientists reached the peak of their prestige during this period and appeared able to explain and/or mold the behavior of individuals, groups, and societies. At the same time, some social scientists rejected the existentialist tenet: that individuals possessed true freedom or that Western civilization was more just or sophisticated than any other. Rather, social scientists embraced structuralism, which held that all societies function within controlling structures that operate according to coercive rules similar to those of the unbreakable conventions in linguistics. In 1962, Vatican II, the Second Vatican Council, convened by Pope John XXIII (r. 1958–1963) aimed at empowering the laity, but only largely symbolic changes were achieved. A Protestant revival, particularly among fundamentalists, took place in the United States; however, interest in Christianity remained slight in Western Europe. Increasingly, Western Europe witnessed an influx and dissemination of other religions, including Islam, Buddhism, and Hinduism.

Western Europeans looked less to the United States for guidance. In Germany, Willy Brandt (1913–1992) pursued Ostpolitik—a friendly stance toward East Germany and openness to better relations with the Soviet Union and Eastern European countries. Charles de Gaulle envisioning an independent role for France, entered into trade agreements with the Soviet Union, became close with China, withdrew French forces from NATO, and pursued the development and sale of nuclear weapons.

In the Soviet Union, Nikita Khrushchev lost power to Leonid Brezhnev (1906–1982) and Alexei Kosygin (1904–1980) in a nonviolent coup. Some of the reforms begun under Khrushchev continued initially, although they were later halted. Although the Soviet Union continued to pour money into defense, it also sought to meet popular demands for consumer goods and better housing. Soviet-bloc countries took advantage of looser controls to pursue national, economic interests. Artist and writers found less tolerance; the Soviet Union harassed artists who followed modern trends and forced writers to resort to *samizdat* (undergound publication using typewriters and carbon paper).

In the United States, the civil rights movement emerged as the major issue of the early 1960s. After John F. Kennedy's (1917–1963) assassination, vice president Lyndon B. Johnson (1908–1973) took office. Johnson moved the Civil Rights Act of 1964 through Congress and began an ambitious program of reform he called the "Great Society." Unfortunately for Johnson, he also increased U.S. involvement in Vietnam. By 1966, half a million American troops were fighting there. In 1968, with the war and constant antiwar protests overwhelming the Great Society, Johnson announced he would not seek the presidency in the next election.

The U.S. civil rights movement took many forms. In California, civil rights leader César Chávez (1927–1993) led Mexican workers in a strike against grape producers for better pay and working conditions. The civil rights movement of African Americans evolved into a struggle for "black power" and a celebration of black identity; in 1965, black activists moved toward confrontation and violence. On campuses, white students in the United States and Europe protested against both the university system and the overarching political and economic arrangements

in their countries. A youth-oriented counterculture based on sex, rock and roll, and drugs ran like wildfire through Western and Eastern Europe. Most participants failed to see that the counterculture was—especially popular music—ironically, a by-product of technology and businesses making money by marketing rebellion.

Politically conservative middle-class women were inspired by *The Feminine Mystique* (1963), written by Betty Friedan (b. 1921), who also helped found the National Organization of Women (NOW) in 1966. Globally, women of all ages, classes, and races emerged as a group with substantive demands for reform ignored by most male protesters. Women protested for abortion rights and the decriminalization of gay and lesbian sexuality. Many women renounced brassieres, high-heeled shoes, cosmetics, and other, traditional feminine items. In Italy, women won the right to sue for divorce, and gained access to birth-control information and abortions.

The year 1968 proved to be an explosive year in the annals of protest. Beginning with the Tet offensive in Vietnam, which convinced many Americans that the Vietnam War was unwinnable, 1968 included assassinations of prominent leaders in the United States (Martin Luther King Jr. and Robert F. Kennedy), and near-revolution in France by bureaucratically alienated students and workers. In France, it appeared that the student demonstrations in Paris and millions of workers on strike throughout the country would bring down the government.

Czechoslovakia's strong challenge to the Soviet Union also occurred in 1968. The "Prague Spring" in Czechoslovakia, originating within the Communist Party, quickly gathered momentum among different elements of the Czech and Slovak populations. On August 20–21, 1968, Soviet tanks rolled into Prague and crushed the revolution. Later that year, the USSR announced the Brezhnev Doctrine, which declared socialist countries had the right to intervene in the politics of any country in which a socialist system was endangered. The Kremlin persecuted dissenters: some were exiled, like Aleksandr Solzhenitzyn (b. 1918), after the publication of the first volume of the *Gulag Archipelago* (1973–1976); others were falsely certified as mentally ill and kept in mental hospitals; some were imprisoned in labor camps. Anti-Semitism revived, and Jews were limited in their educational and employment opportunities.

There was a brain drain of Eastern European intellectuals. Composer György Ligeti (b. 1923), of *2001: A Space Odyssey* fame, left Hungary in 1956; the Czech writer Milan Kundera (b. 1929), living in exile in Paris, enthralled with such works as *The Unbearable Lightness of Being* (1984). These and other artists like them enriched Western culture and eroded any lingering support for communism.

In the United States, the reaction against activists differed from that in France or the Soviet-bloc countries, although it too had its tragic qualities. Richard Nixon's (1913–1994) campaign had centered on bringing peace to Southeast Asia but, in 1970, he ordered U.S. troops to invade Cambodia. Campuses erupted in protest and, on May 4, the National Guard killed four students and wounded others at a demonstration at Kent State University in Ohio. Nixon referred to the victims as "bums," and a growing reaction against the counterculture found many Americans who agreed with him. A peace treaty, finally signed in January 1973, allowed the United States to end the Vietnam War, but South Vietnam collapsed two years later. Nixon and his secretary of state, Henry Kissinger, improved diplomatic relations with the People's Republic of China in 1972. This new détente with its rival led the USSR to agree to the first Strategic Arms Limitation Treaty (SALT I) later that year. Sadly, Nixon's unfounded insecurities about reelection precipitated the Watergate scandal, and Nixon, having been reelected in a landslide, had to resign in disgrace in 1974.

Humiliated by the Israeli victory in the Six-Day War (1967), in which Israel had gained Gaza, the Sinai peninsula, the Golan Heights, and the West Bank, Egypt and Syria attacked Israel on Yom Kippur in 1973. Defeated again by Israel (aided by the United States), the Arab-dominated Organization of Petroleum Exporting Countries (OPEC) imposed an embargo on oil exports to the United States—and quadrupled the price of oil. OPEC's revenge set off a decade of worldwide inflation and economic stagnation.

Jimmy Carter narrowly won the 1976 presidential election. Three years later, in 1979, encouraged by the exiled Aytollah Ruholled Khomeini, a popular uprising drove the shah of Iran into exile. U.S. embassy staff were taken hostage and ultimately held until early 1981.

Activists repeatedly and commonly turned to violence and terrorism. Both the West German Red Army Faction, more commonly known as the Baader-Meinhof gang, and the Red Brigades in Italy kidnapped and murdered prominent officials. In Northern Ireland, Catholics experienced discrimination at all levels of society and took to the streets (January 30, 1972) to protest their treatment. British soldiers opened fire and killed thirteen persons in what became known as "Bloody Sunday." This set off a cycle of violence between Protestant paramilitary groups and the Irish Republican Army (IRA) that left five hundred dead in that single year.

Western democracies survived and even scored important successes with the revival of constitutional government in Spain, Portugal, and Greece. Overall, however, by the end of the 1970s, the Western democracies faced a bleak economic future. In particular, the two superpowers seemed to falter as society approached a new global age.

Margaret Thatcher (b. 1925), leader of Britain's Conservative Party from 1979 to 1990, reshaped political and economic ideas and practices in the West. Thatcher believed that a resurgence of private enterprise offered the best possibility of reviving the British economy. "Thatcherism" was based on monetarist or supply-side theories associated with U.S. economist Milton Friedman (b. 1912). Theoretically, a tight rein on the money supply would keep prices from rising rapidly, and tax cuts for the wealthy would encourage investment. Above all, Thatcher sought to diminish governmental involvement in the economy through "privatization," or the sale of government-owned enterprises. Thatcher's brand of economic policies was called neo-liberalism.

The first three years of the Thatcher government were filled with continued economic difficulties and new social problems. The invasion of the Falkland Islands by Argentina (1982) gave Thatcher the opportunity to invoke patriotism and unify the nation. By the mid-1980s, inflation had decreased; debate continues as to whether this resulted from Thatcher's policies. Her approach nonetheless became the standard, with the Labor Party following her lead in the 1990s.

Ronald Reagan (1911–2004), president of the United States between 1981 and 1989, followed Thatcher's economic model. He sponsored massive cuts in income taxes and large reductions in government spending on the theory that tax cuts would lead to investment and a reinvigorated economy. His approach was dubbed "Reaganomics." A long-time cold-war warrior, Reagan spent much of his time preoccupied by the Communist threat (he described the Soviet Union an "evil empire"), which he believed required huge military budgets to contain. The domestic impact of his "imperial overstretch" is still a hotly debated topic.

Elsewhere, retrenchment of the welfare state and imitation of Thatcher's and Reagan's economic policies took place without suffering the same politically divisive rhetoric. Helmut Kohl (b. 1930), who took power in West Germany in 1982, followed much the same pattern with similar results. In France, François Mitterand (1916–1996), a Socialist, attempted a different approach, increasing the size of the state sector and pumping government funds into the economy. However, the need to share power with Conservatives led to a reversal of Mitterand's policies and the adoption of a modified form of Thatcherism. Uncertainty about economic trends and the influx of Algerians and others from North Africa to France led to the growing influence of Jean-Marie Le Pen's National Front Party from 1985 on. Politics, once shaped by class antagonism, was now more and more shaped by racial and ethnic antagonism. Many of the smaller states, without large commitments to defense, like Austria, Spain and Ireland, prospered in the new economic surge that took place at the end of the early 1980s' recession. Prosperity and a rising death toll led to a political rapprochement between Ireland and Northern Ireland in 1999. Sweden remained an exception to prosperity because of its adherence to an expensive array of social programs.

The Soviet Union also faced difficulties with its economy in the 1980s. These included shortages of basic goods, industrial pollution, and low productivity. When Mikhail Gorbachev (b. 1931) took over the leadership of the Communist Party in 1985, he introduced broad plans to revive the Soviet economy through a program of perestroika ("restructuring"). Gorbachev hoped to streamline management and production, improve productivity and investment, and encourage the use of up-to-date technology. He also hoped to introduce marketing strategies, such as supply and demand and profit and loss. Gorbachev intended glasnost ("openness") to provide Soviet citizens with information and to encourage greater participation in public affairs. Just how critical this new openness was to Soviet policy was seen during the Chernobyl disaster. In the past, such disasters would have been blacked out in the global press. Although threatening to many persons in the massive Soviet bureaucracy (he removed more than one-third of the party's leadership in his first months as leader), this policy enjoyed great success as censorship declined and sources of information about the past and current conditions multiplied. Gorbachev perceived foreign affairs as important in their own right as well as connected to economic reform. He formed a working relationship with U.S. president Reagan that led to some progress in scaling down the cold war. Gorbachev also withdrew the Soviet Union's troops from Afghanistan in 1989.

The emergence of Solidarity, a labor movement founded by electrician Lech Walesa (b. 1943) and crane operator Anna Walentynowica (b. 1929) that included much of the adult population in Poland by the end of 1980, turned out to be the first step toward the demise of the Soviet Empire. Solidarity built on the worker protests of the 1970s, the support of the Catholic Church (which by 1980 was headed by a Polish pope, John Paul II), and the assistance of intellectuals to create a major force in Poland with political as well as economic power. In the face of food shortages and demands that Solidarity be officially recognized, the military under General Wojciech Jaruzelski (b. 1923) declared martial law in December 1981 and outlawed Solidarity, which continued its operations clandestinely.

The year 1989 became the *annus mirabilis* ("year of miracles"), beginning with student protests in Tiananman Square in Beijing. Although put down by the Chinese authorities, it inspired others in the Soviet-bloc states. Solidarity regained its legal status and participated in free elections in the summer of 1989; the Communist Party suffered a near-total defeat. The Soviet Union did not intervene, and Gorbachev's clear message to Soviet-bloc states was that the Soviet Union would not intervene in the affairs of other states. The Brezhnev Doctrine had been put aside. Hungary also carried out a peaceful transition to a non-Communist system. In the German Democratic Republic (GDR), massive protest movements put pressure on the Communist government. On November 9, 1989, new travel regulations were enacted that appeared to allow free passage beyond the Berlin Wall. Tens of thousands of East Berliners took advantage of the situation to visit West Berlin. In Czechoslovakia, the government at first used force against demonstrators in Prague in November 1989, but soon capitulated. The playwright Václav Havel (b. 1936), who had been in prison as recently as January for his activism, became president. Romania was the last to collapse. Conditions had been exceptionally harsh under Nicolae Ceausescu, who had been in power since the mid-1960s. He and his family were utterly corrupt and, in early December 1989, an opposition movement arose. It was soon joined by the army, which crushed the few forces loyal to Ceausescu. On Christmas day, TV viewers around the world watched as the dictator and his wife were tried by a military court and then executed. The very worst of communism was over.

Suggestions for Lecture and Discussion Topics

1. Many instructors in Western Civilization courses are not comfortable with discussions of technology. Nevertheless, there are simply too many extraordinary technological developments in the postwar period to ignore them. One such development, ubiquitous by the 1960s, is television. By this time, television was beginning to produce powerful social, economic, and even political changes. Students will know a great deal about television as popular culture and will have opinions about its sociological and economic importance. Many are also fascinated by television as a technology and astounded to learn that there was some television programming already in the 1930s. Television offers a way to discuss technological change in this period and also to chart the many repercussions in various aspects of life and work.

In addition to titles cited in the chapter's bibliography, you may wish to consult some of the following titles. David E. Fisher and Marshall Jon Fisher, *Tube: The Invention of Television* (Washington, DC: Counterpoint, 1996) offers a solid, readable history of the invention of television. While it concentrates mostly on the 1920s and 1930s, it carries the story into the 1960s and 1970s and also features a useful bibliography. It is a part of the Sloan Technology series, a highly recommended series of books on technology and science for laypersons. Anthony Smith, ed., *Television: An International History* (Oxford: Oxford University Press, 1995) provides a wide-ranging and authoritative collection of essays. Also useful is Jeff Kisseloff, ed., *The Box: An Oral History of Television (1920–1961)* (New York: Viking Press, 1995), which deals largely with television broadcasting. Although not directly relevant, "Big Dream, Small Screen," part of *The American Experience* series (PBS, 1997), is a fine biography of Philo Farnsworth, a self-taught inventor who played a highly important role in the development of television in the 1930s.

Computers form another extremely important topic. You may prefer to discuss computers together with related topics such as the Internet when you deal with Chapter 30. There is, however, much to say about the rapid development of computers in the 1960s and 1970s. The following are a few good sources with which to begin. Martin Campbell-Kelly and William Aspray, *Computer: A History of the Information Machine* (New York: Basic Books, 1996) is an excellent introduction and features an extensive bibliography. Scott McCartney, *ENIAC: The Triumphs and Tragedies of the World's First Computer* (New York: Walker & Co., 1999) is useful mostly for background. McCartney offers a careful study of the development of ENIAC in the 1940s and examines the problems the developers faced in marketing their invention. Arthur L. Norberg and Judy E. O'Neill, *Transforming Computing: The Pentagon's Role, 1962–1987* (Baltimore: Johns Hopkins University Press, 1996) discusses the impact of the cold war and defense contracts on computing.

Although intended for college and high school students in survey courses, Michael D. Richards and Philip F. Riley, *Term Paper Resource Guide to Twentieth-Century World History* (Westport, CT: Greenwood Press, 2000) will probably be of use to instructors as well. A large number of the entries concern topics on technology and science. Each entry contains an extensive bibliography of primary and secondary sources.

2. The space race has many possibilities both as a lecture topic and as a basis for discussion. It could be used as an alternative means for dealing with the cold war. It lends itself to any number of comparative topics, such as exploration and discovery, the search for heroes, or new ways of doing science. Enthralling as the story of the space race is, it is important to emphasize the military imperative behind it. Whatever else it might have been, it was first and foremost a component of the arms race.

The best starting place for the space race is Walter A. McDougall, *The Heavens and the Earth: A Political History of the Space Age* (New York: Basic Books, 1985). Other useful sources include David Baker, *Conquest: A History of Space Achievements from Science Fiction to the Shuttle* (Salem, NH: Salem House, 1984); and Phillip Clark, *The Soviet Manned Space Program: An Illustrated History of the Men, the Missions, and the Spacecraft* (New York: Orion Books, 1988). To emphasize that the Soviet Union hoped to land a man on the moon before the United States, you might show the fascinating documentary *Secret Soviet Moon Mission* (PBS Home Video, 1999, 1 hr.]). It covers the career of Sergei Pavlovich Korolev and focuses on his efforts to land a Soviet cosmonaut on the moon. James Harford, *Korolev: How One Man Mas-*

terminded the Soviet Drive to Beat America to the Moon (New York: John Wiley & Sons, 1997) uses Russian sources and is the best biography in English of this important figure.

Basic sources on the many important developments in biology include, first, these books on the discovery of the structure of DNA: Francis Crick, *What Mad Pursuit: A Personal View of Scientific Discovery* (New York: Basic Books, 1988); James Watson, *The Double Helix: A Personal Account of the Discovery of the Structure of DNA* (New York: Athenaeum, 1968), which has also been published as a Norton Critical Edition (1980); and John Gribbin, *In Search of the Double Helix* (New York: McGraw-Hill, 1985).

Among the many books on reproductive technology, Roger Gosden, *Designing Babies: The Brave New World of Reproductive Technology* (New York: W. H. Freeman, 1999) presents the latest information on reproductive technology in nontechnical language. A good discussion from a historical perspective is that of Margaret Marsh and Wanda Ronner, *The Empty Cradle: Infertility in America from Colonial Times to the Present* (Baltimore: Johns Hopkins University Press, 1996). See also R. G. Edwards and Patrick Steptoe, *A Matter of Life, the Story of a Medical Breakthrough* (New York: William Morrow, 1980), an account of the first "test-tube" baby from the perspective of the doctors. The best book on the birth control pill is Elizabeth Siegel Watkins, *On the Pill: A Social History of Oral Contraceptives, 1950–1970* (Baltimore: Johns Hopkins University Press, 1998).

3. Social change is an important topic, but also one that is sometimes elusive. Two chapters in J. Robert Wegs and Robert Ladrech, *Europe Since 1945: A Concise History*, 4th ed. (New York: St. Martin's Press, 1996) provide a very useful introduction to the topic: Chapter 9, "Postwar European Society: The Managed"; and Chapter 10, "Postwar European Society: The Managers." Each chapter features a good deal of statistical information and an extensive bibliography. Another useful source is Chapter 10, "The Social Revolution, 1945–1990," in Eric Hobsbawm, *The Age of Extremes: A History of the World, 1914–1991* (New York: Pantheon Books, 1994). Arthur Marwick, in *Class in the Twentieth Century* (New York: St. Martin's Press, 1986), offers a general survey.

A quite different approach involves using the Beatles as a focus for an examination of popular culture, much as the suggestion in Chapter 28 for using Elvis as a focus. In this case, the question would be why the Beatles were so popular, and what their popularity says about Europe and the United States (and, to a considerable extent, much of the rest of the world) in the 1960s. Using the Beatles for this purpose is more complicated than using Elvis, in that the Beatles — and especially their manager, Brian Epstein — were quite astute in playing off existing trends and determining what would set the Beatles apart and set new trends.

There is an embarrassment of riches on the Beatles. Here are a few of the most basic sources. The best place to start may be James Miller, *Flowers in the Dustbin: The Rise of Rock and Roll, 1947–1977* (New York: Simon & Schuster, 1999). Miller, a well-known rock critic, devotes five chapters to the Beatles, placing them in the context of the development of rock and roll. Also useful for this purpose is Ian MacDonald, *Revolution in the Head: The Beatles' Records and the Sixties*, 2d ed. (London: Fourth Estate, 1997). In the way of primary sources, there is, first, the massive 1995 ABC network television production available on videocassettes as *The Beatles Anthology* (Turner Home Entertainment, 1996; 8 videocassettes, 10 hrs., 28 min.). The Beatles's first film is available as a CD-ROM: *A Hard Day's Night* (Voyager Co., 1993). John Lennon, *Lennon Remembers:* The Rolling Stone *Interviews* (New York: Popular Library, 1971) presents Lennon, on the Beatles just as they were breaking up. Brian Epstein and Martin Lewis, *A Cellarful of Noise: The Autobiography of the Man Who Made the Beatles, with a New Companion Narrative* (Los Angeles, CA: Byron Press Multimedia Books, 1998) provide some insights into Epstein's highly successful efforts to create and market the Beatles. Also useful is Charles Neises, ed., *The Beatles Reader: A Selection of Contemporary Views, News, & Reviews of the Beatles in Their Heyday* (Ann Arbor, MI: Popular Culture, Ink., 1991).

There are a number of good biographies. Perhaps the best is Philip Norman, *Shout!: The Beatles in Their Generation*, 2d ed. (New York: Simon & Schuster, 1996); also highly regarded is Mark Hertsgaard, *A Day in the Life: The Music and Artistry of the Beatles* (New York: Delacorte Press, 1995). Two books that view the Beatles as serious musicians are Walter Everett, *The Beatles As Musicians:* Revolver *through the* Anthology (New York: Oxford University Press, 1999); and Allan Kozinn, *The Beatles* (New York: Chronicle Books, 1995).

For more general background, see Arthur Marwick, *The Sixties: Cultural Revolution in Britain, France, Italy, and the United States, c. 1958–c. 1974* (Oxford: Oxford University Press, 1998). See also CNN's *Cold War*, Episode 13, "Make Love, Not War: 1960s"; and Neil A. Hamilton, ed., *The ABC-CLIO Companion to the 1960s Counterculture in America* (Santa Barbara, CA: ABC-CLIO, 1997).

4. Domestic politics in the 1960s is a fascinating but also very large topic. Because it would be difficult to ignore the United States in this period (in itself a huge topic), you might consider a discussion of the 1960s in America based on the lives of Martin Luther King Jr. and Lyndon B. Johnson, fellow southerners who were similar in their heroic struggles to recall America to its fundamental values. Fortunately, there are several very fine books with which to work. A basic text is James T. Patterson, *Grand Expectations: The United States, 1945–1974* (New York: Oxford University Press, 1996). Chapter 15,

"The Polarized Sixties: An Overview," is indispensable. Chapters 16 to 21 carry the story to 1968. A good short account is John A. Salmond, *My Mind Set on Freedom: A History of the Civil Rights Movement, 1954–1968* (Chicago: Ivan R. Dee, 1997). On King, see Taylor Branch, *Parting the Waters: America in the King Years, 1954–1963* (New York: Simon & Schuster, 1988); and Taylor Branch, *Pillar of Fire: America in the King Years, 1963–1965* (New York: Simon & Schuster, 1998). Clayborne Carson, ed., *The Papers of Martin Luther King, Jr.* (Berkeley: University of California Press, 1992–) has thus far reached the end of 1958 in four volumes. The *Eyes on the Prize* series consists of two parts, the first with six episodes (Alexandria, VA: PBS Video, 1986), and the second with eight (Alexandria, VA: PBS Video, 1989–1992). See also David Bradley and Shelley Fisher Fishkin, eds., *The Encyclopedia of Civil Rights in America*, 3 vols. (Armonk, NY: Sharpe Reference, 1998). On Johnson, see Robert Dallek, *Flawed Giant: Lyndon Johnson and His Times, 1961–1973* (New York: Oxford University Press, 1998). The literature on Johnson and Vietnam is vast and controversial. David Kaiser, *American Tragedy: Kennedy, Johnson, and the Origins of the Vietnam War* (Cambridge, MA: The Belknap Press, 2000) offers a thorough and careful examination of an important aspect of the topic. An excellent guide to the history of the war is Marilyn B. Young, *The Vietnam Wars, 1945–1990* (New York: HarperCollins, 1991). The best reference source is Spencer Tucker, ed., *Encyclopedia of the Vietnam War: A Political, Social, and Military History*, 3 vols. (Santa Barbara, CA: ABC-CLIO, 1998). *Vietnam: A Television History*, 13 episodes, 780 min. (New York: Sony Corporation of America, 1987) is an extraordinarily useful resource.

5. It may be best to approach 1968 as a series of reports followed by a class discussion. For this possibility, see the "Writing Assignments and Class Presentation Topics," number 3. If you wish to concentrate on a single, crucial development, the Prague Spring is suggested, a turning point that was not allowed to turn. Or, as some wit put it twenty-one years later, "'89 is just '68 turned upside down."

Joseph Rothschild, *Return to Diversity: A Political History of East Central Europe Since World War II*, 2d ed. (New York: Oxford University Press, 1993) is the best book with which to begin. Kieran Williams, *The Prague Spring and Its Aftermath: Czechoslovak Politics, 1968–1970* (Cambridge: Cambridge University Press, 1997) is a comprehensive analysis of the reform movement and its suppression by the Soviet Union that makes use of the archival sources available since the events of 1989. Jaromir Navratil, ed., *The Prague Spring '68* (Budapest: Central European University Press, 1998) is a very good collection of documents. Two excellent studies are William Shawcross, *Dubcek: Dubcek and Czechoslovakia, 1918–1990* (London: Weidenfeld and Nicolson, 1991); and Jiri Valenta, *Soviet Intervention in Czechoslovakia,*

1968: Anatomy of a Decision (Baltimore: Johns Hopkins University Press, 1979 [rev. ed., 1991]), is a useful effort to explain the Soviet decision to invade. Also useful is Alexander Dubcek with Jiri Hochman, *Hope Dies Last: The Autobiography of Alexander Dubcek* (London: HarperCollins, 1993), which covers 1968 from Dubcek's point of view; and Milan Kundera, *The Unbearable Lightness of Being* (New York: Harper & Row, 1984), a brilliant novel that, among many other things, explores aspects of 1968.

France in 1968 is another possibility. It would be worth considering why May 1968 in France came as close as it did to toppling de Gaulle's government. A close analysis of events would show a nation undergoing the stresses of incomplete social and economic change, as well as revealing the unusual degree to which cultural, intellectual, and political affairs were concentrated in Paris. It also might contrast the attractive, even charismatic, anarchy of the student movement with the fumbling and uncertain but brutal response of the government. All of this created a crisis that seemed to be far more momentous than it was.

A good place to start is Chapter 12 of J. Robert Wegs and Robert Ladrech, *Europe Since 1945: A Concise History*, 4th ed. (New York: St. Martin's Press, 1996). See Keith A. Reader and Khursheed Wadia, *The May 1968 Events in France: Reproductions and Interpretations* (New York: St. Martin's Press, 1993). Two useful books on de Gaulle are Charles Cogan, *Charles de Gaulle: A Brief Biography with Documents* (Boston: Bedford/St. Martin's, 1996); and Jean Lacouture, *De Gaulle: The Ruler, 1945–1970* (New York: W. W. Norton, 1992). In addition to David Caute's book cited in the chapter's bibliography, see an oral history put together by Ronald Fraser, ed., *1968: A Student Generation in Revolt* (New York: Pantheon, 1988); and Carole Fink, Philipp Gassert, and Detlef Junker, *1968: The World Transformed* (Washington, DC: German Historical Institute and Cambridge University Press, 1998).

6. The 1970s feature many developments in international politics, of which probably the most important are steps taken to reinforce détente and the impact of OPEC. The two are related in that the increasingly interconnected world economy made it difficult for the two superpowers to conduct the cold war without regard to the rest of the world. In addition, the Soviet Union, which in the 1970s was becoming a "gerontocracy" (government by old men), showed serious signs of social strain. Its aging leaders seemed to respond to domestic difficulties by a kind of international adventurism, including intervention in Afghanistan.

On SALT I, see, first, the memoirs by Henry Kissinger, *White House Years* (Boston: Little, Brown, 1979); Richard M. Nixon, *RN: The Memoirs of Richard Nixon* (New York: Grosset & Dunlap, 1978); and Gerald Smith, *Doubletalk: The Untold Story of SALT* (Garden City, NY: Doubleday, 1981). Smith was the chief American delegate and views Nixon's SALT diplomacy rather critically. See also Anatoly Dobrynin, *In Confidence: Moscow's Ambassador to America's Six Cold War Presidents* (New York: Times Books, 1995). John Morton Blum, *Years of Discord: American Politics and Society, 1961–1974* (New York: W. W. Norton, 1991) is good on the domestic considerations of SALT. William Bundy, *A Tangled Web: The Making of Foreign Policy in the Nixon Presidency* (New York: Hill & Wang, 1998) is a highly critical examination of American foreign policy as practiced by Kissinger and Nixon. Adam Ulam, *Dangerous Relations: The Soviet Union in World Politics, 1970–1982* (New York: Oxford University Press, 1983) provides an overview of Soviet activities in the international arena. John W. Young, ed., *The Longman Companion to Cold War and Détente, 1941–1991* (London: Longman, 1993) is a useful reference work. See also CNN's *Cold War*, Episode 16, "Détente, 1969–1975."

The Helsinki Accords of 1975, which were a notable and promising step at the time, would also be worth discussion. On Helsinki, see Michael B. Froman, *The Development of the Idea of Détente: Coming to Terms* (New York: St. Martin's Press, 1991); and Vojtech Mastny, ed., *Helsinki, Human Rights, and European Security* (Durham, NC: Duke University Press, 1986). See also the books by Bundy, Dobrynin, and Ulam listed in the preceding paragraph.

For OPEC, see Daniel Yergin, *The Prize: The Epic Quest for Oil, Money, and Power* (New York: Touchstone, 1993), a long but fascinating and informative book. See also Terry Lynn Karl, *The Paradox of Plenty: Oil Booms and Petro-States* (Berkeley: University of California Press, 1997); and Ian Skeet, *OPEC: Twenty-five Years of Prices and Politics* (Cambridge: Cambridge University Press, 1988).

The Soviet Union in the 1970s appeared headed toward serious crises on the domestic front. Begin with Gregory L. Freeze, "From Stalinism to Stagnation, 1953–1985," in his *Russia: A History* (Oxford: Oxford University Press, 1997). A highly critical discussion is found in Chapter 10 of Martin Malia, *The Soviet Tragedy: A History of Socialism in Russia, 1917–1991* (New York: The Free Press, 1994). See also Seweryn Bialer, *The Soviet Paradox: External Expansion, Internal Decline* (New York: Alfred A. Knopf, 1986). More specialized titles include Marshall I. Goldman, *U.S.S.R. in Crisis: The Failure of an Economic System* (New York: W. W. Norton, 1983); and Murray Feshbach, *The Soviet Union: Population, Trends, and Dilemmas* (Washington, DC: Population Reference Bureau, 1982). See also Ulam, listed earlier.

Making Connections

1. *What were the differences between industrial society of the late nineteenth century and postindustrial*

society of the late twentieth century? Heavy industrialization was a feature of the late nineteenth century but, in the postindustrial period, society moved from an economy based on manufacturing to one that emphasized services. This new economy depended on large numbers of highly educated professional and technical experts to gather and analyze data. And yet, white-collar workers did not necessarily enjoy better pay than blue-collar workers, even though they made up the majority of the workforce. While many jobs in the late nineteenth century demanded some degree of education, the need was less pronounced for factory work. There was also a significant social and economic divide between white-collar and blue-collar jobs. In the postindustrial society, computers simultaneously were smaller built, more powerful, and cheaper throughout the period, both increasing the pace of work and making it less labor intensive. In some cases, computers transformed the way work was performed. New technological improvements reduced the size of computers, which enabled individuals who owned a PC to perform their jobs at home for the first time since the eighteenth century.

2. *Why were there so many protests, acts of terrorism, and uprisings across the West during these decades?* Prosperity and the rising benefits of a postindustrial, service-oriented economy made people ever more eager for peace. Students, after years of study, did not want to end their lives on some far away battlefield fighting a war that probably could not be won. Still other activists—including women and minorities—simply wanted a fair (or equal) chance at education, jobs, and political influence. Students, blacks, and other racial minorities, Soviet-bloc citizens, women, environmentalists, and homosexuals sometimes brought their societies to the brink of revolution during what became increasingly angry protests. Most were against the cold-war order and wanted to share equally in postindustrial prosperity. When they felt their voices had not been heard, many resorted to violence to get their message across.

3. *What have been the long-term consequences of Communist rule between 1917 and 1989?* For most of its existence, the Soviet Union relied on heavy industrialization, which was tied to its military programs. With so much of its resources committed to the military, spending on welfare programs fell and standards of living slowly declined. Communism stifled creativity and motivation, while a corrupt economic and political system caused many to experience despair. Technologically, the Soviet Union lagged behind other European countries, making its transition from a Communist- to a capitalist-based, postmodern, service economy all the more difficult.

Writing Assignments and Class Presentation Topics

1. Require students to interview at least two individuals about their most vivid memories of such things as the cold war in the 1950s and 1960s, television in the 1960s and 1970s, and, if possible, someone living in Europe during 1989 when communism fell. The subjects should have been at least ten years old during the period being investigated. This would be an opportunity to talk with students about oral history. You may wish to provide them with an article describing how an oral history is collected or make up a brief guide for them. Before they start the project, talk with students about questions they might ask, background knowledge they might need, and so on. It would certainly be useful to talk with them afterward concerning their experiences of interviewing individuals. School children crouching in the hallways, practicing for a nuclear event, is often a prominent memory of those who were young in the 1950s and 1960s. You may want to mention your own vivid memories, if you were at least age ten in 1960. For the record, I remember quite well John F. Kennedy's inauguration in 1961, both his speech and Robert Frost's trying to read a poem he had written for the occasion in the bright sunlight and finally reciting one from memory. I also remember the Beatles' first appearance on the *Ed Sullivan Show* in 1964 and the excitement in 1969 surrounding the report of the first men on the moon. The fall of communism in 1989 was a far more electrifying experience for Europeans than it was for those living in the United States, and interviewing persons who were there would bring an interesting perspective to the subject.

2. The space race in the 1960s should work well as a source for class presentations. These might be relatively brief and focus on the pioneering astronauts and cosmonauts, the various missions, spacecraft, and the technology involved. Reports could make use of material from video documentaries and from Web sites. At the end of the reports, the class might reflect on the meaning of the space race and on its accomplishments. Was it merely an extension of the cold war, or did it speak to larger purposes? Was it money well spent and time and energy used wisely? Does humanity somehow need this kind of enterprise periodically? Explain why or why not.

3. The year 1968 was such a protean year that it might be best to approach it through a series of class presentations. You may wish to limit the possible topics by drawing up a list of those you are already familiar with. Remind students of the vast amount of material available through recordings, video documentaries, and Web sites (see "Suggestions for Lecture and Discussion Topics," number 5). In this case, combining the class presentation with an essay in which the student reflects on his or her topic and discusses how it might be placed in the context of the 1960s. For example, someone giving a report on

the assassination of Martin Luther King Jr. could use television news footage of King at the Memphis sanitation workers' strike and a recording of the speech he gave the night before he was killed. The report could also refer to newspaper or newsmagazine accounts of the riots that followed King's assassination and the eventual capture of the man accused of killing King, James Earl Ray. The paper, however, would reflect on King's role in the 1960s and perhaps at least note the turn toward black power that the civil rights movement took.

4. Assign students a paper on détente between 1969 and 1975. You may wish to have them view Episode 16, "Détente, 1969–1975," of CNN's *Cold War*. (They should at least view the Web site for that episode.) Another possibility is to assign students a relatively brief reading, such as Chapter 24, "Nixon, Vietnam, and the World," in James T. Patterson, *Grand Expectations* (see "Suggestions for Lecture and Discussion Topics," number 4).

Research Assignments

1. Ask students to imagine that they have been given a contract to compile an encyclopedia on the 1970s: *The Seventies in Europe and North America*. Students may wish to see how an actual encyclopedia covering similar ground is laid out. See Carl Singleton, ed., *The Sixties in America*, 3 vols. (Pasadena, CA: Salem Press, 1999). Divide the students into groups and have each group deal with a different European country or with a single category like painting or sports. Each group then draws up a list of topics to be covered and the number of words to be devoted to each topic. It then assigns each individual in the group one or more topics so that each person is writing about two thousand words. For West Germany, for example, topics might include Willy Brandt, Hans Schmidt, the Baader-Meinhof gang, Heinrich Böll, Rainer Werner Fassbinder, and so forth. Students should copyedit each other's work and revise as required. Each entry should have a short bibliography of important sources and be cross-referenced as appropriate. Two books on the 1970s may be useful: Peter Carroll, *It Seemed Like Nothing Happened: The Tragedy and Promise of America in the 1970s* (New York: Holt, Rinehart & Winston, 1982); and David Frum, *How We Got Here: The 70's, the Decade that Brought You Modern Life (for Better or Worse)* (New York: Basic Books, 2000).

2. Have students investigate the lives of prominent figures from the 1960s and 1970s and either write a biographical essay or do a class presentation. While some background information might be necessary, the essay or presentation should focus on what that person was doing during the period and what its significance was. For example, an essay on Betty Friedan would certainly include a discussion of *The Feminine Mystique* (1963) and her work in the National Organization for Women (NOW). It should not mention, except perhaps in passing, her book on aging, *The Fountain of Age* (1993). It probably should mention *Life So Far: A Memoir* (2000) but note that this book is a reflection long after the fact on events of the 1960s and 1970s and therefore a source to be used with care.

Literature

Emecheta, Buchi, *The Joys of Motherhood*. 1980.
Grossman, Edith, trans., *Gabriel García Márquez:* Love in the Time of Cholera. 1999.
Kundera, Milan, *The Unbearable Lightness of Being*. 1984.
Middleton, Christopher, trans., *Christa Wolf:* The Quest for Christa T. 1979.
Rushdie, Salman, *The Satanic Verses*. 1989.
Todd, Albert C., and James Ragan, eds., *Yevgeny Yevtushenko: The Collected Poems, 1952–1990*. 1992.
Whitney, Thomas P., and Harry Willetts, trans., *Aleksandr Solzhenitsyn:* Gulag Archipelago. 1973–1974.

Films and Videos

A Hard Day's Night (1964; VHS, Oak Park, IL: MPI Home Video, 1995, 1 hr., 48 min.). A satire on the Beatles starring themselves.

Historical Skills

Map 29.1, The Airbus Production System, p. 1148

Ask students to discuss the advantages and disadvantages of having components of the Airbus manufactured in four different countries. What difference does it make that all four countries are members of the European Union (EU)? Ask students to compare and contrast this production system with what they may know of the production system used by many multinational corporations.

Map 29.2, The Vietnam War, 1954–1975, p. 1158

Use the map to discuss the Tet offensive with students. Ask them to locate and describe what happened at Hue, Da Nang, Saigon, and My Lai in 1968, and relate why these events were important. Through which countries does the Ho Chi Minh Trail run? What did the United States do to try to stop the North Vietnamese from using the trail?

Mapping the West: Europe and the Mediterranean, 1980, p. 1180

Compare the origins of the guest workers who went to France with the origins of those who went to West Germany. What might be the results of some of the differences? Why were there no guest workers going to the COMECON countries?

Figure 29.1, Fluctuating Oil Prices, 1955–1985, p. 1168

Why was the sudden increase in the price of oil in 1973 so difficult to deal with? To what extent were countries able to cope with later price increases at the end of the 1970s and beginning of the 1980s?

Shrine to Jan Palach, p. 1139

Ask students where Jan Palach might have gotten the idea for self-immolation. Why was his action so shocking? Remind students of Czechoslovakia's long tradition of martyrs.

Valentina Tereshkova, Russian Cosmonaut, p. 1144

Tereshkova traveled into space long before the existence of any female American astronauts. Why was this true? What does this difference suggest about Soviet society and American society? How well known was Tereshkova in the Soviet bloc?

Thalidomide Children, p. 1145

Ask students if they think something like the birth defects caused by thalidomide could happen again in Europe or the United States. What other controversies involving pharmaceutical products or chemical products were current then?

Gay Activists in London, p. 1162

What is the connection between gay liberation and the civil rights movement? Why did gay liberation and other similar movements appear at the end of the 1960s and the beginning of the 1970s? Ask students to comment on the ways in which individuals constructed identities during this era. How would the students compare these ways with the construction of identity in earlier times? In later times?

Margaret Thatcher's Economic Vision, p. 1172

Margaret Thatcher makes a strong argument for the reform of Britain's welfare state. Ask students to argue against the prime minister's position with a view to Enlightenment ideas, and some consideration of the situation in post–World War I Europe. Thatcher's concentration on the private rather than public sector seems contradictory to Enlightenment ideas that government should serve the common good. By reducing or severely limiting benefits for the impoverished and unemployed, Thatcher catered to the resentment of those who were prosperous and created an atmosphere of fear for people living on the edge of society. As after the first world war, the most vulnerable in society, in this case those who were poor and jobless, could be blamed for Britain's post–World War II economic situation.

OTHER BEDFORD/ST. MARTIN'S RESOURCES FOR CHAPTER 29

The following resources are available to accompany Chapter 29. Please refer to the Preface of this manual for detailed descriptions of all the ancillaries.

For Instructors

Transparencies

The following maps and images from Chapter 29 are available as full-color acetates.

- Map 29.1: The Airbus Production System
- Map 29.2: The Vietnam War, 1954–1975
- Map 29.3: The Collapse of Communism in Europe, 1989–1991
- Mapping the West: Europe and the Mediterranean, 1989
- *Thalidomide Children*
- *Berlin Wall*

Instructor's Resources CD-ROM

The following maps and image from Chapter 29, as well as a chapter outline, are available on disc in both Power-Point and jpeg formats.

- Map 29.1: The Airbus Production System
- Map 29.2: The Vietnam War, 1954–1975
- Map 29.3: The Collapse of Communism in Europe, 1989–1991
- Mapping the West: Europe and the Mediterranean, 1989
- *Thalidomide Children*

Using the Bedford Series with The Making of the West

Available in print as well as online at bedfordstmartins .com/usingseries, this guide offers practical suggestions for using *Charles de Gaulle: A Brief Biography with Documents* by Charles G. Cogan, in conjunction with chapters 28 and 29 of the textbook.

For Students

Sources of The Making of the West

The following documents are available in Chapter 29 of the companion sourcebook by Katharine J. Lualdi, University of Southern Maine.

1. Josef Smrkovsk´y, *What Lies Ahead* (February 9, 1968)
2. *Student Voices of Protest* (1968)
3. Nick Ut, Photograph of Children Fleeing Napalm Attack (June 8, 1972)
4. American Embassy in Saudi Arabia, Cable *4663: Saudi Ban on Oil Shipments to U.S.* (October 23, 1973)
5. *Glasnost* and the Soviet Press (1988)

Study Guides

The print **Study Guide** and the **Online Study Guide** at bedfordstmartins.com/hunt, both by Victoria Thompson (Arizona State University) and Eric Johnson (University of California, Los Angeles), help students synthesize the material they have learned as well as practice the skills historians use to make sense of the past. The following Map, Visual, and Document activities are available for Chapter 29.

Map Activity

• Europe and the Mediterranean, 1980

Visual Activity

• *Thalidomide Children*

Reading Historical Documents

• Margaret Thatcher's Economic Vision
• Mikhail Gorbachev and Reform in the USSR

The New Globalism: Opportunities and Dilemmas
1989 to the Present

CHAPTER RESOURCES

Main Chapter Topics

1. The introduction of the Euro in 2002 and the admittance of former Soviet-bloc countries to the European Union (EU) were reflections of the globalization that had occurred in the twenty years that preceded. Globalization raised hopes and opportunities, but it also presented new challenges.

2. The fall of communism in Europe led to a revival of ethnic tensions in former Communist countries. Serbia attempted to dominate the Yugoslav federation by force, resulting in a wave of "ethnic cleansing," or genocide, not seen since World War II.

3. The transition from a command economy to a free market economy was difficult and painful for most former Communist countries, especially Russia, owing to widespread corruption and shortages of essential necessities. The war in Chechnya bogged down and caused further problems for Russia, but Western countries prospered and forged closer ties through the introduction of a common currency (the Euro) and the opening of the EU to new members, some of which were former Communist countries.

4. Global organizations like the World Bank, the International Monetary Fund (IMF), and the World Trade Organization (WTO), along with nongovernmental organizations (NGOs), exercised considerable power and influence over developing nations. The intervention of the global organizations in world affairs was considered highly controversial.

5. Globalization contributed to an increase in pollution levels, and environmentalists urged a list of remedies: conservation, alternative means of transportation, reductions in greenhouse gases, and recycling. Many countries embraced these "green" programs, but the United States and Russia lagged behind other countries in promoting environmentalism. The spread of disease became a world issue. Health care improved in the West for those who were financially better off, but the poor and unemployed were often deprived of such services. Health care became especially dire in African countries where AIDS created a demographic crisis.

6. Western countries clashed with Islam and international terrorism increased. The United States broke off diplomatic relations with Iran after the hostage crisis (1979), and the Soviet Union went to war with Afghanistan. Saddam Hussein's invasion of Kuwait sparked the first Gulf War (1990). After the destruction of the World Trade Center and damage to the Pentagon (2001) was caused by hijacked planes piloted by militant Muslims, the United States invaded Afghanistan and routed the Taliban government, which had been responsible for obtaining the training of the hijackers. In 2003, in a hugely unpopular move, the United States and Britain went to war against Iraq because these countries feared it possessed weapons of mass destruction (WMDs).

7. Globalization blurred cultural and national identities. Although Western culture predominated—especially in film, television, and music—foreign films and literature became widely popular. Music from former Communist-bloc countries was listened to for the first time and the works of dissident writers were reappraised. Postmodernism, where no one, particular style predominated, was reflected in architecture. But postmodernism also referred to a movement away from cherished eighteenth-century ideas regarding individual freedoms and the nation-state. The global age has not resulted in the triumph of Western civilization; rather, such factors as international migration; the information revolution; and the sharing of a global, popular culture have all created a climate in which nationalism paradoxically has been both weakened and strengthened.

Summary

The introduction of a common currency—the Euro—throughout much of Western Europe (January 2002), and the admittance of many new countries from the former Soviet-bloc countries to the European Union (EU) (2004) represented post-cold war unity, opportunity, and hope for the future. Globalization contributed to the climate that made closer relations between European nations possible. With globalization, the West faced new political, economic, and social challenges and opportunities. National and international migration increased significantly, global competition (especially from Asia) exerted pressure on Western economies, and cultural exchanges accelerated. The international impact of environmental degradation, genocide, terrorism, and diseases such as AIDS were also parts of the globalization process. With the decline and fall of the Soviet Union, the United States emerged as the dominant power in the world and, as Asia and the Islamic world rose to resist it, there were predictions of a fundamental clash between Western civilizations and cultures beyond the West. Others predicted a Europe, already in a position of opposition, resisting U.S. influence. The difficulty in assessing the recent past is that events are still being interpreted. The unification of Europe will probably prove to have been momentous. Conflicts between a newly unified Europe and the United States may result in future clashes, and terrorism is likely to remain a global issue.

When the Soviet Union fragmented and Communist countries declared their independence in the late 1980s and early 1990s, it quickly became apparent that ethnic divisions in those countries had been held at bay by sheer force. Opportunistic politicians, who used long-repressed ethnic tensions to further their political careers and nationalistic agendas, replaced communism. In 1990, Slobodan Milosevic (b. 1941) was elected president of Serbia and immediately asserted Serb ascendancy over the Yugoslav confederation, which included Slovenia, Croatia, and Bosnia. In 1991, Slovenia and Croatia seceded from the federation and, in response, the Serb army invaded Croatia. Civil war erupted in Bosnia-Herzegovina as the Muslim majority attempted to create a multi-ethnic state in the face of Bosnian Serb resistance backed by the Serbian government. A UN embargo on military supplies left the Bosnian Muslims defenseless. Tens of thousands died as Serbs under Milosevic's leadership carried out an ethnic cleansing campaign against other nationalities. Women were raped and men of all ages were murdered and buried in mass graves. Having withdrawn from Croatia in the late 1990s, Serbian forces attacked Muslims of Albanian ethnicity in Kosovo. From 1997 to 1999, hundreds of thousands of Albanian Kosovars fled their homes as Serb militias and the Yugoslav Serbian army slaughtered the civilian population. The UN finally took decisive action and forced the withdrawal of Serbian troops. People throughout the world thought this action came far too late. A regime change in Serbia resulted in Milosevic being delivered to the war crimes tribunal that had been set up in the Netherlands. Soon after, the new Serbian president was assassinated by Milosevic's supporters.

As Yugoslavia fell into civil war, the economy of the Soviet Union collapsed. The Russian parliament elected Boris Yeltsin (b. 1931) president of the Russian Republic over the Communist Party's candidate. In the summer of 1991, a group of hard-liners—including members of the Soviet Secret Police (KGB)—placed Mikhail Gorbachev (b. 1931) under house arrest and attempted to overthrow the government. Yeltsin stood atop a tank and called for mass resistance. Hundreds of thousands of people filled the streets to protest, and army units defected to Yeltsin. With the failure of the coup, the Soviet Union quickly disintegrated. Statues of Communist figures were pulled down, the KGB's files were unsealed, and the Communist Party and its newspaper (*Pravda*) were outlawed. The Baltic states of Estonia, Latvia, and Lithuania declared their independence in September, and other former Soviet states followed. Ethnic tensions soon erupted: Armenians in Tajikistan and Azerbaijan were under attack. In the Baltic states, anti-Semitism became a political tool. In Russia, widespread corruption deepened the economic crisis under Yeltsin's presidency in the 1990s. Attacking Muslim dissenters in the province of Chechnya brought new problems, as did the emergence of organized crime. Yeltsin resigned (December 1999) and appointed Vladimir Putin (b. 1952) interim president. Putin won the spring 2000 elections and proceeded to drive from power the regional government's figures who had become powerful and wealthy at the expense of the people. However, Putin continued the devastating war with Chechnya and faced serious economic problems. In Russia and much of Eastern Europe, inflation was rampant, salaries often went unpaid, and food was in short supply. There was a brain drain as young people emigrated, and hundreds of thousands of Russians became refugees as they fled former Soviet countries. People took desperate measures to stay alive.

For former Soviet countries, the transition from a command economy to a market economy was difficult and painful. The shift was easiest for Hungary and Poland, which had taken early measures to effect a smooth transition but, elsewhere, widespread corruption made the transition extremely difficult. Many countries were behind the West technologically and could not compete. The brain drain from these countries made catching up all the more difficult. People emigrated for various reasons, including the lack of jobs, ethnic hatreds, and anti-Semitism. For many, the West seemed to offer a better life in every respect: better jobs, housing, and social services.

The war in Chechnya was a serious political and economic problem for Russia. In 1991, the National Congress of the Chechen people peacefully took power away from the Soviet Union in a course toward their independence. When the Soviet Union collapsed the following year, Chechen rebels absconded with a large stockpile of Russian weaponry. In an effort to maintain control over the oil-rich territory, Russian troops sealed the Chechen borders and invaded in December 1994. In 1996, the KGB assassinated a major Chechen leader. Chechen terrorist activities within Russian cities, and the mounting loss of Russian soldiers, made the war extremely unpopular. In 2002, Chechen loyalists took over a Moscow theater and held the audience as hostage. Nerve gas was pumped into the theater, killing not only the rebels but almost two hundred of the hostages as well. As the Chechen war continued, the newly independent states in Central Asia—Kazakhstan and Uzbekistan in particular—faced the politically volatile mix of oil-rich, anti-Western, radical Islam.

Western Europe prospered as its central and eastern counterparts floundered. In 1992, the traditional boundaries between most Common Market members were eliminated, which allowed travelers to move freely and without the hindrance of passports. In 1994, in accordance with the Maastricht Treaty (1992), the European Community became the European Union (EU) and, in 1999, a common currency—the Eurodollar—was introduced and, in 2002, this currency came into common usage. The EU's parliament negotiated common policies on such diverse things as the price of automobiles to warnings on cigarette packs for most of its member nations. The EU also accepted the role of mediator in European conflicts, such as that between Greece and Turkey, the latter having only recently become a member nation. The EU did have problems, however. The EU did not enforce regulatory practices, and individual governments sometimes placed obstacles in the way of businesses wanting to expand to other countries. Still, the EU's assistance in bolstering the economies of poorer member nations made many Eastern European countries eager to join. Conversely, the low cost of doing business in these Eastern countries attracted Western investment, which made them a good risk. In 2002, the EU admitted ten new members: Estonia, Latvia, Lithuania, Poland, the Czech Republic, Slovakia, Hungary, Slovenia, Malta, and Cyprus. That same year, Russia became affiliated with NATO, the organization originally set up to counter the military power of the Soviet Union. Slowly, the economies of Central and Eastern European countries began to pick up. Central and Eastern Europeans soon became savvy at shopping for the lowest prices, and young people (who often lived with their parents) had disposable income to spend on newly available products. Globalization had reached the rest of Europe.

Cities in the West became globalized and business of all kinds was transacted across international borders. Decent housing became expensive, driving the white-collar workforce into the more affordable suburbs. Workers performing menial tasks remained in the city but lived in squalid housing. Because of their prosperity and diversity, global cities like London, Paris, and New York attracted emigrants from around the world. Emigrants were not always welcomed by the native population who feared the loss of their national identity and culture through dilution. Some emigrants accepted jobs that native persons would not do, whereas others emigrated to new lands because they were transferred by their employers.

The West also saw the emergence of new nations, such as Slovakia and the Czech Republic (1993). Additionally, there were movements aimed at regional autonomy; some Bretons and Corsicans clamored for independence from France; in Spain the Basque separatist group ETA adopted violence in a thus far unsuccessful campaign for independence.

Globalization witnessed the rise of supranational organizations, many of which regulated international finance and trade, whereas others aimed at social issues. The World Bank and International Monetary Fund (IMF) grew in power and stature. The IMF extended loans to developing countries on condition that they restructure their economies along neo-liberal principles. The World Trade Organization (WTO) came into being (1995) and coordinated trade among member nations, often sparking protests in the process. Large, charitable organizations (known as "nongovernmental organizations" [NGOs]) often possessed great international power and helped shape economic, political, and social policies in developing countries. Sometimes NGOs intervened in more immediate ways, like Doctors Without Borders, who regularly minister to the medical needs of refugees like those in what was formerly Yugoslavia.

Responses to globalization varied. The European Union and the United States enacted high tariffs (sometimes against each other) to prevent the influx of cheap consumer goods into their respective countries, but otherwise supported the World Bank, the IMF, and NTOs. Grass-roots organizations, like the Association for Taxation of Financial Transactions (ATTAC), protested against these world organizations on the grounds that they benefited developed nations at the expense of poorer, underdeveloped countries.

It was becoming clear that globalization was a threat on several fronts. The effects of the 1986 nuclear meltdown at Chernobyl were being realized in the 1990s with high rates of cancer in children from that region. A hole in the ozone layer was discovered. Deforestation, ever-deeper incursions into the rain forest, and the use of dangerous chemicals like chlorofluorocarbons, all shared responsibility for acid rain and the ozone layer hole. The world began to experience global warming and the resulting greenhouse effect negatively affected weather patterns, causing both droughts and floods. Dire consequences were predicted and environmentalists like E. F. "Fritz" Schumacher (1911–1977) in Germany and Rachel Carson (1907–1964) in the United States wrote powerful critiques about what technology had perpetrated on the environment and advocated conservation. The formation of the Green Party in Germany (1979) was an outgrowth of this environmentalism, and Green Party candidates are presently featured in elections throughout Europe and the United States. Some European cities, like Paris and Frankfurt, introduced regulations aimed at reducing pollution. Fuel-efficient cars were designed and manufactured, bike lanes introduced, windmills put into place, and recycling encouraged. The Kyoto Protocol (1997) introduced further actions necessary to reduce international pollution levels, but the United States and Russia—among the world's top polluters—refused to sign the treaty.

Rapid, global, expanding growth of the Earth's population was an additional source of pressure. To a large extent, the population boom was caused by a decline in the death rate due to the introduction of Western medical practices and pharmaceuticals. Population levels actually declined in Europe, but increased significantly in less industrialized countries. By the end of the twentieth century, Earth's population was greater than six billion. That number is expected to double by the year 2045. Ironically, longevity levels decreased in the United States and especially in Russia and former Soviet countries. Fertility rates were also dropping, most likely due to the availability and low cost of birth control. While the West enjoyed improved vaccines and pharmaceuticals employed against diseases, poor countries were cut off from such health care benefits. African countries suffered most because they were additionally susceptible to cycles of drought, poverty, and famine. In the West, the focus was on high-tech solutions for health problems, like transplants and chemotherapy, but preventive health care for the masses received less attention. The poor and unemployed were more likely to suffer illnesses than those who were more fortunate, but these indigents were most likely the ones to have restricted access to health care services. By the 1990s, AIDS had become a pandemic disease and it along with the Ebola virus threatened a demographic crisis in Africa. The emergence of Severe Acute Respiratory Syndrome (SARS) in the Orient (2003) created world panic.

During the 1980s and 1990s, it became clear that there was a growing economic schism between the northern and southern hemispheres of the world. With some exceptions, people in the Southern Hemisphere experienced lower standards of living and restricted access to health care. There were notable improvements, however. Apartheid was abolished in South Africa in the early 1990s and, in 1994, Nelson Mandela, imprisoned for almost thirty years for his activism, formed a multiracial government.

The West faced a new crisis involving Islam in the 1990s. The hostage crisis in Iran at the end of the 1970s demonstrated the power of the volatile mix of religion, nationalism, and oil. Islamic fundamentalism, first directly under Iran's Ayatollah Khomeini, then more latterly under Iraq's Saddam Hussein and Saudi Arabia's Osama bin Laden, offered an attractive alternative to Westernization, but power in the Middle East remained fragmented. The area was plagued by war, first between Iran and Iraq (the latter supplied by the United States); then between the Soviet Union and Afghanistan. Islam alone could not bring about unity. With the collapse of the Soviet Union, Hussein attempted to take advantage of the new post-cold war international order by appealing to pan-Arabism. When Hussein annexed oil-rich Kuwait in an attempt to recoup heavy losses from the Iran-Iraq war, he only succeeded in arousing international resistance that included the Soviet Union as well as Western powers. The first Gulf War drove Iraq's troops out of Kuwait.

Tensions also arose between Palestinians and Israelis in the 1980s and 1990s as terrorists bombed European targets in retribution for their support of Israel. In 2001, Muslim militants hijacked airplanes and flew them into the World Trade Center in New York and the Pentagon in Washington, DC, killing over three thousand persons. These terrorist actions prompted the United States to declare a "war" on terrorism. A coalition of international powers, led by the United States, drove out the Taliban regime in Afghanistan, where the hijackers had trained in Osama bin Laden's (b. c. 1957) camps; bin Laden, however, remained at large. The cooperation between the United States and Europe soon collapsed, however, when the United States and Britain claimed Saddam Hussein possessed and was stockpiling WMDs and went to war with Iraq in 2003. France, Germany, and Russia pointedly refused to support the war, which was also hugely unpopular in Britain and the United States.

The global diffusion of industry and technology was another indication of Western fragmentation. Explosive productivity from Japan to Singapore during the 1980s resulted in a shift in economic power from the Atlantic region to the Pacific. Japan led the way with investments in high-tech consumer industries and flourishing financial institutions. By the end of the 1980s, Japan was home to the world's eight largest banks. Even before its economic difficulties of the late 1990s, some questioned the price Japanese and other Asian workers paid for this economic success. Many Asian workers—especially women—labored in sweatshop conditions to produce consumer goods for the West. A severe economic crisis developed in the region, caused in part by irresponsible and corrupt financial practices. By 2001, the economic downturn had spread to Europe and the United States.

The movement of people from one country to another helped to further blur national and cultural identities. Many—more than fifty million in 1995—became refugees from warfare and political persecution. While millions emigrated to Western Europe or to the United

States, other areas—among them nations in the Middle East, Nigeria, and Singapore—brought in millions of foreigners to shore up labor-force shortages. The money migrants sent home supported not only their families, but sometimes their countries as well. The situation of immigrants could be exploitative, especially where it concerned women. As immigrants, they often performed the worst jobs, received the worst pay, and faced rape and other violent crimes against their persons on a regular basis. Women were also more likely than men to be denied political asylum. Children of immigrants faced difficulties over national and personal identity. The influx of new populations also caused political parties with racist agendas to achieve some electoral success in Western Europe.

The rapid expansion of the Internet in the 1990s was yet another component of globalization. The importance of computer skills helped to create a new elite and, of course, a new underclass, although newly Internet-linked countries achieved significant economic gains in a very brief period of time by marketing goods online and providing "help desk" services. The Internet provided not only a new range of buyers, it also provided a new array of consumer goods, thus further globalizing economy and culture. The downside of this picture is that individuals' jobs were threatened. Multinational corporations, now more prolific than before, operated in any country where a competitive edge was to be found. And, with the Internet, companies could "outsource" much of their work literally around the globe.

Popular culture increasingly became a global phenomenon in the latter part of the twentieth century. The political and economic power of the United States made English the dominant international language. Indeed, it is the official language of the EU. Western control of much of the world's media ensured that Western culture spread widely. American films, television, music, and magazines became popular around the world. The West, in turn, absorbed cultural influences from other parts of the world. Foreign films made a profitable headway, and India's "Bollywood" industry thrived. Colombian-born Nobel Prize-winning novelist Gabriel García Márquez (b. 1928) attracted a large audience in the West with his novels, including *One Hundred Years of Solitude* (1967) and *Love in the Time of Cholera* (1988). In some cases, the cultural transfers were quite complicated. When, for example, Naguib Mahfouz (b. 1911), another Nobel Prize-winner, introduced the West to middle-class Egyptian life in his *Cairo Trilogy*, he used the European novel as his vehicle and colonialism as his backdrop. The experiences of immigrants were often the subject of novels. The Nigerian-born writer Buchi Emecheta (b. 1944) explored what it was like for newcomers to Britain in *In the Ditch* (1972) and *Head Above Water* (1986). Salman Rushdie (b. 1947), an immigrant from India (though clearly integrated into British culture), demonstrated in-

advertently the problems one might encounter writing a novel that offended religious sensibilities. His novel *The Satanic Verses* (1988) resulted in the Ayatollah Khomeini's offering a reward for Rushdie's assassination. Nobel Prize-winner Toni Morrison (b. 1931), who wrote about the men and women who were brought as slaves to North America, sparked controversy as "multiculturalism" became a part of school curricula in the United States. Some viewed multiculturalism as a sign of deterioration similar to what would be brought about through mixed-race marriages.

Globalization ushered in an era of culture conflicts. Former Communist countries faced different challenges. Literary dissidents lost their subject matter as communism fell across Europe. When the shadow of communism fell across the face of Europe, authors who could no longer write about the subjects they choose, lost official patronage and either became dissidents, went underground, or into self-exile. But music and other arts, however, flourished. Works long hidden from the state by composers such as Giya Kancheli (b. 1935) and Alfred Schnittke (1934–1998) were now widely performed. The works of composers who had refused to cooperate with the authorities, like Galina Ustvolskaya (b. 1919) and Mikhail Bulgakov (1891–1940), were now listened to for the first time. Works by dissidents, like that of Milan Kundera (b. 1929), written at the height of communism, were reappraised.

Postmodernism in some respects reflected the new global arts, in which various forms coexisted without a central unifying theme or a privileged canon. This is particularly apparent in the AT&T building in New York designed by Philip Johnson (b. 1906); and in the Guggenheim Museum in Bilbao, Spain, designed by Frank Gehry (b. 1929). The term "postmodernism" could also be applied as "reflecting a movement away from various eighteenth-century ideas," such as individualism or belief in the nation-state. Another definition stressed the "unfreedom" or irrationality that shaped human life. Michel Foucault (1926–1984), a prominent French writer, characterized, in his unfinished *History of Sexuality*, the sexual revolution as simply another means by which society controlled individuals. For some, the message was that the rational, independent, and superior West was an illusion. Postmodernism caused people to reexamine and even to reject the Western tradition. After all, the daunting problems of postmodern life—population explosion, resource depletion, North-South inequities, global pollution, ethnic hatreds, and global terrorism—are still with us. However, even though a relatively small number of persons had enjoyed what Western civilization offered in the past, this fact should not blind people to its potential. The West brought democracy, human rights, and economic equality to previously oppressed peoples and countries. The exchange of ideas, made possible by modern technology, increased our understanding of other peoples and cultures, and hopefully made us more tolerant. The future shape of the West cannot be predicted. That it will continue to change and evolve is unquestionable; it is a process that will not cease so long as human history continues.

Suggestions for Lecture and Discussion Topics

1. The challenges of the global age offer opportunities as well as potentials for disasters. A workable approach might involve a review of several of the general trends covered by Paul Kennedy in Part 1 of *Preparing for the Twenty-first Century* (New York: Random House, 1992). Kennedy discusses demographics, the rise of multinational corporations, agriculture and the biotechnology revolutions, and a new industrial revolution, among other topics. Students could also read Kennedy's final chapter, "Preparing for the Twenty-first Century," which asserts that the key elements of the new century are "the role of education, the place of women, and the need for political leadership" (p. 339). This source should produce a good discussion of what is to come and how best to prepare for it. Something similar might be done with Chapter 17, "Goods and Values," and the Epilogue of David Reynolds, *One World Divisible: A Global History Since 1945* (New York: W. W. Norton, 2000). Also useful is T. E. Vadney, *The World Since 1945: The Complete History of Global Change from 1945 to the End of the Twentieth Century* (New York: Penguin, 1999).

A different approach emphasizes the history of the environment over the past few decades. J. R. McNeill, *Something New Under the Sun: An Environmental History of the Twentieth-Century World* (New York: W. W. Norton, 2000) argues that the past century was unusual both for the intensity of environmental change and the role of humans in causing it. He points out the extent to which Western civilization depends on circumstances in the natural world that may be in danger of changing drastically. In this case, you might survey some of the ways in which humanity has altered or is in the process of altering the environment and the resultant repercussions of these alterations. McNeill discusses the different parts of the environment, for example, the atmosphere and the hydrosphere, in Part 1, "The Music of the Spheres." Examining one or two chapters of Part 1 will give students an entirely different perspective on the history of the past few decades and present them with a different context into which to fit European or world history. Lester R. Brown, Christopher Flavin, and Hilary French, eds., *State of the World 2000* (New York: W. W. Norton, 2000) may be used for a somewhat similar purpose. Students could be asked to read and discuss one or more of the chapters. A good overview is "Challenges of the New Century" by Lester R. Brown, whereas "Creating Jobs, Preserving the Environment" by Michael Renner introduces the crucial issue of whether environmental concerns may harm the

economy. Several other chapters might furnish the basis for a lecture or a lively discussion.

2. A major shift in thinking over the past two decades has resulted in a different approach to the welfare state. Essentially, most countries have ceased expanding the welfare state and, instead, have turned large parts of the public sector over to private investors or managers. Opinions vary as to what this produced: a generally prosperous economy that provides opportunity for nearly everyone, or an economy that favors the wealthy and influential at the expense of the poor. It is also unclear whether governmental policies have caused the economic developments in question; prosperity might have come into being regardless of what governments of various countries did or tried to do.

Margaret Thatcher and her policies are at the heart of attempts to revise the welfare state and jump-start the economy. In addition to books listed in the chapter's bibliography, Thatcher's own views on her term in office are worth reading. See Margaret Thatcher, *The Downing Street Years* (London: HarperCollins, 1993). David Cannadine, *History in Our Time* (New Haven: Yale University Press, 1998) has an excellent chapter on Margaret Thatcher and her politics. Eric J. Evans, *Thatcher and Thatcherism* (New York: Routledge, 1997) provides a solid introduction to the former British prime minister's conservative revolution. Paul Pierson, *Dismantling the Welfare State?: Reagan, Thatcher, and the Politics of Retrenchment* (New York: Cambridge University Press, 1996) is useful in showing the ideological connections between the two leaders. Several other titles may also be useful for background. These include Thomas Janoski and Alexander Hicks, *The Comparative Political Economy of the Welfare State* (New York: Cambridge University Press, 1993); A. de Swaan, *In Care of the State: Health Care, Education, and Welfare in Europe and the USA in the Modern Era* (New York: Oxford University Press, 1988); and Theda Skocpol, *Social Policy in the United States: Future Possibilities in Historical Perspective* (Princeton: Princeton University Press, 1995).

3. At the center of events in Europe during the last decade of the twentieth century were the German revolution of 1989 and the subsequent unification of the two Germanys. Students should have some sense of how the German Democratic Republic (GDR) could go from being a success story in the 1970s and then, seemingly overnight, turn into a regime doomed to fall apart in the late 1980s. The drama of the fall of 1989 is certainly worth discussing as are the intricate maneuvers leading to the unification of Germany. Some consideration of the career of Helmut Kohl, whose great moment was the unification process, would be helpful in dealing with the crucial role of Germany in European affairs.

In addition to books cited in the chapter's bibliography, see Mary Fulbrook, *Anatomy of a Dictatorship: Inside the GDR, 1949–1989* (Oxford: Oxford University

Press, 1995) for excellent coverage of the history of the GDR. Charles S. Maier, *Dissolution: The Crisis of Communism and the End of East Germany* (Princeton: Princeton University Press, 1997) is the best book on the events of 1989. Philip Zelikow and Condoleezza Rice, *Germany Unified and Europe Transformed: A Study in Statecraft* (Cambridge, MA: Harvard University Press, 1995) is an authoritative study of the diplomacy involved in the unification of Germany. Unfortunately, there is no good biography of Helmut Kohl. Peter E. Quint, *The Imperfect Union* (Princeton: Princeton University Press, 1997) discusses the impact of the unification process on East Germany. Andreas M. Glaeser, *Divided in Unity: Identity, Germany, and the Berlin Police* (Chicago: University of Chicago Press, 1999) offers a unique perspective on unification by looking at East and West Berliners working together in the Berlin police force. Jonathan P. G. Bach, *Between Sovereignty and Integration: German Foreign Policy and National Identity After 1989* (New York: St. Martin's Press, 1999) surveys the effort by Kohl and others to connect German unification to integration in transnational bodies. Two collections of documents will be useful: Richard T. Gray and Sabine Wilke, eds., *German Unification and Its Discontents: Documents from the Peaceful Revolution* (Seattle: University of Washington Press, 1996); and Konrad H. Jarausch and Volker Gransow, *Uniting Germany: Documents and Debates, 1944–1993* (Providence, RI: Berghann Books, 1994).

If time permits, some discussion of the remarkable career of Václav Havel and of Czechoslovakian politics would be worthwhile. While Havel has his limitations as a political figure and Czechoslovakia had some difficulties in the transition period after 1989 (including the "Velvet Divorce"), both stories are worth retelling. On Havel, see first John Keane, *Václav Havel: A Political Tragedy in Six Acts* (New York: Basic Books, 2000). Havel's views can be easily seen in his *The Art of the Impossible: Politics As Morality in Practice: Speeches and Writings, 1990–1996* (New York: Alfred A. Knopf, 1997). On the revolution of 1989, see first Timothy Garton Ash, *The Magic Lantern: The Revolution of '89 Witnessed in Warsaw, Budapest, Berlin and Prague* (New York: Random House, 1990); see also Bernard Wheaton and Zdenek Kavan, *The Velvet Revolution: Czechoslovakia, 1980–1991* (Boulder, CO: Westview Press, 1992). Useful sources on Czechoslovakia in the 1990s are Robin H. E. Shepherd, *Czechoslovakia: The Velvet Revolution and Beyond* (New York: St. Martin's Press, 2000); and Michael Kraus and Allison Stanger, *Irreconcilable Differences: Explaining Czechoslovakia's Dissolution* (Lanham, MD: Rowman & Littlefield, 2000). Gale Stokes, ed., *From Stalinism to Pluralism: A Documentary History of Eastern Europe Since 1945,* 2d ed. (New York: Oxford University Press, 1996) provides a useful selection of documents for Czechoslovakia and other countries. Tina Rosenberg, *The Haunted Land: Facing Europe's Ghosts After Commu-*

nism (New York: Random House, 1995) presents fascinating reports on the aftermath of 1989 in Czechoslovakia and also in Poland and Germany.

4. The collapse of the Soviet Union (1991) and the struggles of the Russian Republic under Boris Yeltsin are topics that deserve to be covered even if the post-cold-war world no longer pays the same kind of attention to Russia as it paid to the Soviet Union. Some assessment of Gorbachev's role in the collapse would also be useful. Still intensely disliked in Russia, Gorbachev was nonetheless one of the major figures of the latter part of the twentieth century due to his contribution to the end of the cold war and his attempt to reform communism.

In addition to books cited in the chapter's bibliography, there is a wealth of memoirs, reportage, and scholarly studies available. First, Boris Yeltsin has written several autobiographical works: *Against the Grain: An Autobiography* (New York: Summit Books, 1990); *The Struggle for Russia* (New York: Random House, 1994); and *Midnight Diaries* (New York: Public Affairs, 2000). See also the somewhat uncritical biography by Leon Aron, *Yeltsin: A Revolutionary Life* (New York: St. Martin's Press, 2000). Talented and perceptive reporters have provided us with brilliant reports on the Soviet Union and its successors. Among the best is David Remnick, whose books include *Lenin's Tomb: The Last Days of the Soviet Empire* (New York: Random House, 1993); and *Resurrection: The Struggle for a New Russia* (New York: Vintage Books, 1998). J. F. Matlock Jr., *Autopsy on an Empire: The American Ambassador's Account of the Collapse of the Soviet Union* (New York: Random House, 1995) provides a massive, well-informed account. Two books that cover the Yeltsin era are Stephen M. Fish, *Democracy from Scratch: Opposition and Regime in the New Russian Revolution* (Princeton: Princeton University Press, 1995); and Michael Urban with Vyacheslav Igrunov and Sergei Mitrokhin, *The Rebirth of Politics in Russia* (Cambridge and New York: Cambridge University Press, 1997). See also Graeme J. Gill and Roger D. Markwich, *Russia's Stillborn Democracy?: From Gorbachev to Yeltsin* (Oxford: Oxford University Press, 2000); and Thane Gustafson, *Capitalism Russian-Style* (Cambridge: Cambridge University Press, 2000).

5. The disintegration of Yugoslavia may seem a specialized topic, but it involves issues central to the meaning of the twentieth century and even to history in general. For example, what is the price of political ambition? The power wielded by Slobodan Milosevic and Franjo Tudjman in the 1990s resulted from events that recalled the Holocaust in their cruelty and brutality. What role should the great powers play in the affairs of a sovereign nation? How did the reluctance to intervene in Yugoslavia compare with the decision to intervene against Saddam Hussein? Even deeper issues might include questions about human nature and about the impact of historical experience on different groups of people.

A good place to begin would be Carole Rogel, *The Breakup of Yugoslavia and War in Bosnia* (Westport, CT: Greenwood Press, 1998), a solid introduction with some documents and other features. Probably the best overall discussion is that of Sabrina P. Ramet, *Balkan Babel: The Disintegration of Yugoslavia from the Death of Tito to the War for Kosovo*, 3d ed. (Boulder, CO: Westview Press, 1999). Another good book, although not quite as comprehensive, is Laura Silber and Allan Little, *Yugoslavia: Death of a Nation*, revised and updated (New York: Penguin, 1997). Timothy Judah, *The Serbs: History, Myth, and the Destruction of Yugoslavia* (New Haven: Yale University Press, 1998) provides a close look at the Serbian part of the Yugoslavian tangle. Also useful in this regard is Dusko Doder and Louise Branson, *Milosevic: Portrait of a Tyrant* (New York: Simon & Schuster, 1999), a critical biography by two seasoned journalists. See also the recent scholarly study, Robert Thomas, *The Politics of Serbia in the 1990s* (New York: Columbia University Press, 1999). Franjo Tudjman, the president of Croatia until his recent death, was also responsible for much of the horror of the 1990s. Marcus Tanner, *Croatia: A Nation Forged in War* (New Haven: Yale University Press, 1997) offers a useful discussion of Tudjman's role in the making of Croatia and unmaking of Yugoslavia. For Bosnia, see first Noel Malcolm, *Bosnia: A Short History*, updated edition (New York: New York University Press, 1996). Useful for a discussion of the war is Steven L. Burg and Paul S. Shoup, *The War in Bosnia-Herzegovina: Ethnic Conflict and International Intervention* (Armonk, NY: M. E. Sharpe, 1999). Michael A. Sells, *The Bridge Betrayed: Religion and Genocide in Bosnia* (Berkeley: University of California Press, 1998) argues against the idea of ethnic hostility over the centuries. On Kosovo, see first Tim Judah, *Kosovo: War and Revenge* (New Haven: Yale University Press, 2000). A valuable study of the Kosovar experience and human rights is Julie A. Mertus, *Kosovo: How Myths and Truths Started a War* (Berkeley: University of California Press, 1999).

6. It is a bit daunting to suggest a closer look at the last chapter in the book — in effect, the last session of what will have been for some a year-long process. Look at two topics: the Internet, a mostly positive subject, albeit not without its downside; and AIDS, a dark subject to be sure, but one with some potential for good. On the Internet, simply listen to what your students have to say. Some suggestions follow for resources. For AIDS, lay out a few lines of inquiry and then lead the class a discussion.

It seems only fitting to begin with an Internet source. "A Brief History of the Internet," <http://www.isoc.org/internet-history/#Origins>, is at times a little technical, but it is nevertheless a useful overview of the Internet's history, written in many cases by persons who played prominent roles in that history. Probably a better place to start, though, is the last part of Martin Campbell-Kelly and William Aspray, *Computer: A History of the Information Machine* (New York: Basic Books, 1996). Books on the origins of the Internet include Janet Abbate, *Inventing the Internet* (Cambridge, MA: MIT Press, 1999); and Katie Hafner and Matthew Lyon, *Where Wizards Stay Up Late: The Origins of the Internet* (New York: Simon & Schuster, 1998). *Nerds 2.0.1: A Brief History of the Internet* (PBS Home Video, 1999; 3 hrs.) is a good documentary. It does require some prior familiarity with the topic, however.

There is no shortage of information on AIDS. "AEGIS" at <http://www.aegis.com> is a huge Web site filled with information on AIDS. It includes links to documents and reports of all kinds. Three print sources of information are Raymond A. Smith, ed., *Encyclopedia of AIDS: A Social, Political, Cultural, and Scientific Record of the HIV Epidemic* (Chicago: Fitzroy Dearborn, 1998); Darrell E. Ward, *The AmFAR AIDS Handbook* (New York: W. W. Norton, 1998); and Sarah Barbara Watstein with Karen Chandler, *AIDS Dictionary* (New York: Facts on File, 1998). See also Douglas A. Feldman and Julia Wang Miller, eds., *AIDS Crisis: A Documentary History* (Westport, CT: Greenwood Press, 1998). Edward Hooper and Bill Hamilton, *The River: A Journey to the Source of HIV and AIDS* (Boston: Little, Brown, 1999) is a long, compelling, but also controversial book. Its premise is that HIV jumped from simians to humans through the administration of oral polio vaccine in Africa in the 1950s. Douglas Starr, *Blood: An Epic History of Medicine and Commerce* (New York: Alfred A. Knopf, 1998), while not focused on AIDS, includes the scandals connected with HIV-tainted blood. After the international AIDS conference in Durban, South Africa, in the summer of 2000, it is clear that AIDS in Europe and North America is a different problem with different possible solutions than AIDS in developing countries in Africa and Asia. In the developing countries, the challenges are many: the need for better health care and better preventive measures for what will surely be a demographic disaster of mammoth proportions, even in the best of circumstances.

Making Connections

1. *In which ways did the global connections at the beginning of the twenty-first century differ from the global connections at the beginning of the twentieth century?* At the beginning of the twentieth century, many, perhaps most, people traveled short distances by horse and buggy. Railroads were faster, but these were land-locked. For continental travel, slow-moving boats were the only transportation available. There were, however, cultural exchanges between countries, although not instantaneous as they virtually are today. New forms of transportation and communication truly have made the world "smaller." Up-to-date, foreign-based television programs, newspapers, and magazines are widely available in many

parts of the world. People listen to the popular music of different countries by way of radio programs and CDs. Dissident voices from repressive regimes can be heard around the world. In this global economic environment, consumer goods are often made in faraway countries, while economic downturns tend to affect all countries.

2. *How did the Western nation-state of the early twenty-first century differ from the Western nation-state at the opening of the twentieth century?* The Western nation-state of the early twentieth century thought mainly in terms of its own country's interests. Today, nations band together on issues that concern everyone, such as global pollution. The early-twentieth-century nation-state probably actively pursued imperialism, although today Western nations publicly eschew imperial ambitions. The economies of nation-states are today bound much more closely together than they have been in the past. Western countries today embrace the principle of representation for its citizens, regardless of gender or race. As Western countries face immigrant populations, economic downturns, and neofascist groups, care must be taken not to fall prey to the kind of racist nationalism that prompted the World War II.

Writing Assignments and Class Presentation Topics

1. Ask students to reflect on one event they believe is likely to happen in the next decade, based on historical trends. It may be something fairly specific, such as the overthrow of Slobodan Milosevich and the revival of democracy in Serbia, or something far more general, such as the end of the Gutenberg era in the face of electronic books. Ask students to support their predictions on the basis of historical evidence, such as the persistence of opposition groups in Serbia despite persecution, or the increasing number of experiments with publishing on the Internet after the fashion of Stephen King. In effect, they have to show how they extrapolated from known facts to what is not yet known.

2. Organize students into several groups and assign each group the task of presenting to the rest of the class the events of 1989 in a particular country. You will need to set some parameters. Should they deal only with what happened in 1989? Should they be allowed or encouraged to choose an earlier starting date and perhaps also to take the presentation past the end of 1989? What kinds of sources do you want them to examine? Encourage students to use, whenever possible, visual material, primary sources, and material objects (a piece of the asbestos-laced Berlin Wall, for example). Each group should organize itself so that every student has a definite assignment. Every student should write a brief essay critiquing his or her experience.

3. Require students to keep a journal on events in a particular country over a period of at least three or four weeks. Decide whether you wish to receive the journal in paper format or as an attachment to an e-mail. Ideally, each student would put her or his journal on a personal Web site or a course Web site. (This would, however, necessitate that everyone have these skills already or acquire these skills as part of the work for the course.) Set minimum numbers for this journal; for example, students might be required to read or view at least two items each week and write a minimum of two pages of commentary; or students may have four items one week and only one item the following week. Encourage students to cast as wide a net as possible, using not only print sources or Web sites but also art, music, documentaries, and items from the material culture of the country.

4. Present students with a case study of the expansion of NATO or the widening and deepening of the EU (other topics are, of course, possible; these are suggested because they involve transnational questions). Include in the case study a few pages of narrative, mostly to set the scene; and some primary sources. Give students a question to consider; for example, ask them to work through a case study on the Eurodollar and then comment on whether it was a good thing to introduce the Eurodollar at this juncture. Good places to begin putting together a case study are the following Web sites: for NATO, North Atlantic Treaty Organization at <http://www.nato.int>; for the EU, Europa at <http://europa.eu.int>.

Research Assignments

1. The journal mentioned in "Writing Assignments and Class Presentation Topics," number 3, will serve as preparation for a larger research project on a country in the 1990s. Of course, students might simply be assigned a research paper on a specific aspect of the politics and economics of a particular country in the 1990s. It may be useful, if you have not already done so, to invite a reference librarian from your college to demonstrate methods for finding information on recent historical events. There are many useful Web resources, particularly if students know a few techniques for more sophisticated searching, as well as annual publications, compilations, and indexes, that make it possible to find information and analysis.

2. Divide the students into two groups and assign each group the task of designing a magazine (or e-zine if they have the requisite skills) on the twenty-first century. The magazine/e-zine is meant to deal not only with current events but also with past events that have a bearing on the present and, to a more limited extent, with what people might expect in the future given existing lines of development. Each group should collectively choose a title, determine departments that will continue from issue to issue, such as "Technology and the Twenty-first Century," and draw up a list of articles and essays for the

first issue. The groups should then work together to write one or more of the articles and essays, with some students serving as researchers, some as authors, others as editors, picture editors, and so forth.

Present students with a partial model of such a magazine/e-zine. For example, introductory text might include the following:

Clemenceau noted in World War I that "war is too important to be left to the generals." We would change that slightly to note that recent history is too important to be left to the social scientists. *20/20 Vision* covers in each issue significant topics in world history in a manner designed to provide the reader with an introduction, together with suggestions on the best Web sites, videos, books, articles, and other sources of information and analysis. The following topics will be covered in the initial issue.

> Russia: A Funny Thing Happened on the Way to Democracy and Free Enterprise
>
> Nelson Mandela, the End of Apartheid, and the Rainbow Nation
>
> Water
>
> Energy
>
> AIDS
>
> Another WTO to Worry About: The World Trade Organization

Literature

Carson, Rachel, *Silent Spring*. 1962.

Emecheta, Buchi, *The Joys of Motherhood*. 1979.

Grossman, Edith, trans., *Gabriel García Márquez*: Love in the Time of Cholera. 1999.

Kundera, Milan, *The Unbearable Lightness of Being*. 1984.

Morrison, Toni, *Paradise*. 1998.

Rushdie, Salman, *The Satanic Verses*. 1989.

Todd, Albert C., and James Ragan, eds., *Yevgeny Yevtushenko*: The Collected Poems, 1952-1990. 1992.

Historical Skills

Map 30.2, The Collapse of Communism in Europe, 1989–1991, p. 1189

Have students use this map as a basis for comparative discussion of the events of 1989–1990. For example, a comparison of East Germany and Czechoslovakia might emphasize the concentration of demonstrations in Prague (and in Wenceslaus Square in Prague); in East Germany, demonstrations in Leipzig, Dresden, and other cities were as important as those in Berlin. The special role of opening Hungaria's border with Austria is another aspect of 1989 that this map could be used to show. Ask students to reflect on why events in Romania were so much bloodier than those occurring elsewhere.

Map 30.3, The Former Yugoslavia, c. 2000, p. 1192

As with the previous one, this map may be used in discussing the disintegration of Yugoslavia. Ask students to comment on the effect Slovenia's geographic location had on its experiences in the 1990s. Call students' attention to the fact that Serbia, Montenegro, and the province of Kosovo technically constitute the Federal Republic of Yugoslavia. What role did Croatia's geographic location play in its experiences in the 1990s? How does Bosnia-Herzegovina differ from Slovenia? Croatia? Serbia? Macedonia? Note the location of Kosovo and Macedonia, and ask students to comment on Macedonia's role during the expulsion of the Albanian Kosovars and the NATO bombing campaign in 1999.

Map 30.5, The European Union in 2000, p. 1208

Have students use the map as a basis for a discussion of the concepts of "widening" and "deepening" the EU. Ask students to discuss the reasons why various countries joined when they did. Which countries among those applying for membership were more likely to fit in immediately? Why might some observers have reservations about admitting Turkey into the EU?

Mapping the West: The World at the Start of the New Millennium, p. 1221

To what extent is the North-South division a useful concept? Does it oversimplify the complexity of the division of wealth among nations? Is there any correlation between wealth and Internet diffusion? Ask students to comment on any connections they note.

Yugoslavia in 1990, Before Destruction of the Mostar Bridge and After, p. 1190

The Mostar Bridge, a sixteenth-century structure (1566), was a feat of Ottoman engineering. Ask students to reflect on what the bridge and its destruction symbolized. They might wish to think about the importance of history and culture in the lives of the citizens of Mostar and what the destruction of the bridge might have done to a common heritage.

Vaclav Havel Addresses the Citizens of Post-Communist Czechoslovakia, February 21, 1990, p. 1199

As a poor, post-Communist country, there were serious economic reasons to reject Czechoslovakia's membership in the EU. Students can be asked to argue why Czechoslovakia should be included. Havel makes a salient point, that the country's Communist past has strengthened the will of the people to succeed and that they have a greater interest than many other member nations in making the union work. There is also the hint that humanity and common decency demands that Czechoslovakia be included.

OTHER BEDFORD/ST. MARTIN'S RESOURCES FOR CHAPTER 30

The following resources are available to accompany Chapter 30. Please refer to the Preface of this manual for detailed descriptions of all the ancillaries.

For Instructors

Transparencies

The following maps and images from Chapter 30 are available as full-color acetates.

- Map 30.1: The Middle East, c. 2003
- Map 30.2: Eastern Europe, 1990s
- Map 30.3: The Former Yugoslavia, c. 2000
- Map 30.4: Countries of the Former Soviet Union, c. 2000
- Map 30.5: The European Union in 2004
- Mapping the West: The World at the Start of the New Millennium
- *9/11 Newspaper in front of the Colesseum*
- *Gehry Architecture*

Instructor's Resources CD-ROM

The following maps and image from Chapter 30, as well as a chapter outline, are available on disc in both PowerPoint and jpeg formats.

- Map 30.1: The Middle East, ca. 2003
- Map 30.2: Eastern Europe, 1990s
- Map 30.3: The Former Yugoslavia, c. 2000
- Map 30.4: Countries of the Former Soviet Union, c. 2000
- Map 30.5: The European Union in 2004
- Mapping the West: The World at the Start of the New Millennium
- *9/11 Newspaper in front of the Colesseum*

For Students

Sources of The Making of the West

The following documents are available in Chapter 30 of the companion sourcebook by Katharine J. Lualdi, University of Southern Maine.

1. Zlata Filipovié, *A Child's Life in Sarajevo* (October 6, 1991–June 29, 1992)
2. African National Congress, *Statement to the Truth and Reconciliation Commission* (August 19, 1996)
3. Leif Zetterling, Cartoon of *Klasskamrater* ("Classmates") (c. 2001)
4. Amartya Sen, *A World Not Neatly Divided* (November 23, 2001)

Study Guides

The print **Study Guide** and the **Online Study Guide** at bedfordstmartins.com/hunt, both by Victoria Thompson (Arizona State University) and Eric Johnson (University of California, Los Angeles), help students synthesize the material they have learned as well as practice the skills historians use to make sense of the past. The following Map, Visual, and Document activities are available for Chapter 30.

Map Activity

- Map 30.4: Countries of the Former Soviet Union, c. 2000

Visual Activity

- *9/11 Newspaper in front of the Colesseum*

Reading Historical Documents

- Václav Havel Addresses the Citizens of Post-Communist Czechoslovakia
- Petra Kelly, Activist for the Green Party

Appendix: Essays

What Is "The West"?

Michael D. Richards

Sweet Briar College

Edward Said, in his classic study *Orientalism* (1978), asserts that "as much as the West itself, the Orient is an idea that has a history and a tradition of thought, imagery, and vocabulary that have given it reality and presence. . . ." Can it be that "the West" or even "Western civilization" is only an idea that has taken different forms at various times and places? Rather than try to answer the question immediately and directly, it might be helpful to look at several possibilities that allow us to approach it in more indirect ways.

First, perhaps we can establish a geographical basis for the notion of "the West." Immediately, we land in difficulties. A large part of Western civilization, the Judeo-Christian heritage, Greek civilization, and Roman civilization, is "southern," that is, Mediterranean. Even if we ignore this conundrum, we still find little agreement on the question of what, in terms of geography, the West is. Martin W. Lewis and Kären E. Wigen suggest in *The Myth of Continents* (1997) seven different geographical interpretations of the West. The most extreme limits the West to Britain, as in "The Wogs begin at Calais." The second interpretation is a slightly more expansive but still minimal West, confined to the northwest of Europe and including only Britain, France, the Low Countries, and Switzerland. A third possibility is the historical West of medieval Christendom, expanding slowly over time. By the twentieth century, a fourth version is derived from the West of the cold war or, alternatively, Europe and its white settler colonies (both versions often include Japan). The fifth version is a cultural West, a West defined by language, religion, and high culture. This version takes in those parts of Latin America that otherwise would not be included. The penultimate version is the maximum West and includes all areas with a Christian or Islamic heritage. Finally, there is the West as defined by the idea of modernization — those areas with a high concentration of urbanism and industrial capitalism.

Geographical interpretations, as it turns out, do not provide a clear-cut answer. We can see that, at different times and places, the spatial extent of the West has been variously understood. Perhaps we might get closer to a definition if we examine certain processes and institutions that are the common property of different groups. Supposedly, the West is characterized by reason and its chief product, science; by democracy and representative government; and by capitalism. David Gress gives the West (Britain and the Netherlands in particular) credit for "inventing" what he calls "the three pillars of modernity." It may be more accurate to say here that the West developed particularly dynamic and effective versions of these processes, aided in no small way by borrowings from the Islamic and Chinese cultures. In any case, Gress believes these processes are not necessarily connected to European culture, but are universal and can be adopted without having to adopt European culture at the same time. Here, at least, he avoids the triumphalism of recent years in which history is reduced to the story of Western civilization becoming the model the rest of the world will follow in the future. J. M. Roberts's video series, *The Triumph of the West*, the last episode of which is entitled "Capitulation," is a sophisticated version of this latter view.

Perhaps it is not the large processes of science, capitalism, and democracy that set the West apart but smaller items, certain cultural artifacts. We could point to, for example, the Greek and Roman classical sources, which served as a basis for the Renaissance and, later, as one of the inspirations for the Enlightenment. There is additionally the literary canon, today much modified and enlarged, but nonetheless still viable. Similarly, there are the great and beloved bodies of European art and music. Finally, there exist the long philosophical and epistemological traditions that stand behind the large processes discussed above. All of these are familiar elements of something we might call Western civilization. William McNeill puts it this way: "A shared literary canon, and expectations about human behavior framed by that canon, are probably central to what we mean by a civilization" (8).

In the twentieth century, of course, the concept of ideas and values from the past serving as guidelines for behavior has been attacked, first by the Futurists, then by many other movements. Yet, for all those attacks, it is striking that we continue to examine and think about the great body of art and ideas we call Western culture. And while there will always be argument about what to include in that body, there is a rough if continually evolving consensus.

This brings us back to Said's formulation: the West, like the Orient, is an idea that changes from place to place and from one time to another. It built on the Greco-Roman and Judeo-Christian traditions, but only slowly and with great difficulty. The first version of the West was medieval Christendom. It depended heavily on the existence of something different from itself in order to define itself. One important "other" was Islam. When Charles Martel supposedly stopped the advance of Islam in Europe at Tours in about 732, the idea that the West was not Islam began to take hold. The Crusades played a vital role in defining what the West was by the process of clarifying what it was not. Other events, the centuries-long process of the reconquista, in which Spaniards took Spain back from the Moors, and the defense of Vienna against the Ottoman Empire in the late seventeenth century, helped as well to consolidate the idea of Europe as Christendom.

By the seventeenth century, however, Europeans began to use the word Europe in a positive sense, and Europeans viewed the world in terms of Europe by the start of the eighteenth century. Denys Hay illustrates the shift by pointing to the terminology used in two similar documents. When the king of England issued Cabot a patent in 1496, he commissioned him to explore lands hitherto "unknown to all Christians." Two and a half centuries later, Commodore John Byron was ordered to search for "lands and islands of great extent hitherto unvisited by an European power" (Hay 117).

In the process, Europeans had come to see themselves as superior to the people they encountered. This view may have originated in Christianity, in that Christians believed they possessed the keys to salvation, while pagans did not. The Drang nach Osten by the Teutonic Order, which by definition created a West, is one example. In the seventeenth and eighteenth centuries, advanced technology associated with military matters and commerce reinforced this attitude. The Enlightenment, while critical of aspects of Western civilization, set up a process involving the use of human reason that was supposed to lead to greater and greater progress in the future. It was, in a very real way, a secular version of the promise of Christianity.

It is probably in the nineteenth century that the idea of the West and Western civilization became fully developed. One major factor was the Industrial Revolution(s), the several quantum jumps in productivity, beginning in Britain with the production of textiles, continuing with the development of the iron and steel industries, railroads, and steamships, and reaching a temporary plateau at the end of the century with the advent of the electrical and chemical industries and the great expansion of the production of consumer goods. Another factor was the overall success enjoyed by Europeans in dealing with the ancient Chinese empire. Yet another is probably the visibility of the British Empire, with India as its jewel in the crown. Additionally, the "scramble for Africa" contributed to the sense that the West had triumphed. The West now included Europe and its many colonies, several white settler colonies that formed the British Commonwealth, and one former colony, the United States, now an independent and increasingly powerful country. Social Darwinism and eugenics attributed the very real power and seeming superiority to what was believed to be a scientifically justified racial basis.

In the twentieth century, the support of German National Socialism for a racial interpretation of history, and the horrendous policies that came out of that approach, called into question any racial basis for alleged superiority. Marxism, in the form of Soviet communism, actually challenged the idea of the West much more effectively than National Socialism. It also helped to redefine the idea of the West, in that the West and Western civilization became everything that communism was not.

We are left now in a post-Communist, postcolonial world in which many countries seem to be more or less western. David Gress may be correct: these countries may be simply modern and only superficially western. It complicates matters even further when writers from the former colonies win major literary prizes and are well received by the guardians of the Western literary tradition. It is probably simply too early to locate an adequate replacement for the older anti-Communist idea of the West. However, the consensus that exists among historians and other interpreters of Western civilization is striking: certain items are seen as essential to any understanding of the West and Western civilization. These include the Golden Age of Athens; Hellenism; the Jewish faith; the Roman Republic and Empire; medieval Christianity and the beginnings of artistic, musical, and literary traditions; the Renaissance; the Reformation; the scientific revolution; the Enlightenment; the French Revolution, the Industrial Revolution; nationalism; imperialism; war; revolution; and the cold war, among others. We may approach these topics differently, emphasizing the role of women, for example, or looking at mass culture as well as high culture, but we nonetheless believe we see in them the outlines of something we call the West or Western civilization.

That there would be at any given time several distinct ideas about what is the "West" should not be a problem. Americans will have a different sense of what the West is than Poles or Czechs, who may see themselves on the frontiers of the West instead of at its powerful, confident center. Certainly across time there have been different ideas about the West and Western civilization — and this is an important idea to convey to students. We not only have to construct an understanding for ourselves of what the West and Western civilization are, we also have to be aware of the many times in the past when people put together their ideas of the West and Western civilization. This awareness is, of course, fundamental to historical understanding. Every era writes its own history. However, to paraphrase Marx in *The Eighteenth Brumaire of Louis Bonaparte*, each era is not free to write history just as it pleases. The past comes with various aspects already in place that cannot simply be ignored. The West and Western civilization are works in progress. There is no guarantee they will continue to dominate the world as they have for the past two centuries. In fact, it is very likely that the locus of power and development will shift from the Atlantic to the Pacific Rim in the next few decades. Even if this were to happen, however, examining the idea of the West and the reality of Western civilization would still be useful, as it is the only way for large numbers of people to gain true orientation as to their present circumstances and a useful perspective on the future. The West is, as Edward Said states, only an idea with a history, but it has been and continues to be a powerful and significant idea.

Bibliography

Gress, David. *From Plato to NATO: The Idea of the West and Its Critics.* New York: Free Press, 1998.

Hay, Denys. *Europe: The Emergence of an Idea.* 1957.

Lewis, Martin W., and Kären E. Wigen. *The Myth of Continents.* Berkeley: University of California Press, 1997.

McNeill, William. "The Rise of the West after Twenty-five Years." *Journal of World History* 1.1 (1990):8.

Roberts, J. M. *History of the World.* 1993.

———. *The Triumph of the West.* Chicago, IL: Public Media, 1987.

Said, Edward. *Orientalism.* New York: Pantheon Books, 1978.

Active Learning Strategies for the Western Classroom

Dakota Hamilton

Humboldt State University

Two challenges often face instructors of the Western Civilization survey: compulsion and high enrollment. Because many college and university students *must* take Western Civilization courses for their program of study or to fulfill general education requirements, enrollment caps are often set at ridiculously high levels. As a result, instructors often face large classes filled with students who *have to*, rather than *want to*, be there.

From the instructor's point of view, traditional lectures can be the easiest method of instruction for these kinds of classes. These can work well, especially when the instructor has real enthusiasm for the subject matter. During our course of study, we probably all have been the students of brilliant lecturers who enthralled, inspired, thrilled, amused, and moved us deeply. But structuring classes solely around lectures can be problematic from the students' perspective. Studies have shown that attention spans average between ten and twenty minutes for most students, which means that student restlessness, or even sleep, may set in before a class is half over. As opposed to passive learning, which is typically epitomized by the traditional lecture format, active learning has to be part of the classroom, whatever its size. Probably few instructors are scintillating lecturers all of the time, or even want to spend every class lecturing. Fortunately, there are many active learning strategies that can complement traditional lectures.

Active learning strategies are activities designed to elicit direct student participation. Rather than being passive receptors of information, students are encouraged to become active participants in the learning process through carefully designed assignments. Such assignments can be either straightforward—intended to recapture students' wandering attention; or more complex—intended to stimulate critical thinking about a particular issue or subject. Group work is often emphasized because active learning assignments are meant to generate thought-provoking discussions. Instructors wishing to explore the theoretical basis and practical applications of active learning strategies might read John C. Bean, *Engaging Ideas: The Professor's Guide to Integrating Writing, Critical Thinking, and Active Learning in the Classroom* (San Francisco: Jossey-Bass Publishers, 2001).

This is not to say that lectures should be abandoned outright because the traditional lecture format can be transformed into an active learning situation. After lecturing for ten or twenty minutes, instructors could do a number of things to reengage student attention. For example, an instructor could give a quiz on the material presented up to that point, with students referring back to their notes. Or, an instructor could ask students to write a short summary of what has just been presented or to devise true/false or multiple-choice questions for an upcoming exam based on that same material. It is also possible to introduce analysis or critical thinking with a carefully designed question, based on the lecture material that asks students to argue a particular position, either in writing or in a small discussion group or as part of a wider class discussion.

In-class interviews can also be an effective approach to keeping students active and involved. Students can select or be assigned the roles of specific historical figures and be interviewed by the rest of the class at appropriate times during the course. A pair or group of historical figures could take opposing sides of a historical issue. To ensure full participation by the entire class, every student might be asked to contribute by preparing questions a week in advance, which the instructor could then review; or by submitting a short, written report on their historical figure(s). This way, the instructor can review the questions in advance to be sure they are relevant and will give voice to students who might otherwise simply sit quietly in class. Using the Spanish Armada as an example, students might ask "King Philip II of Spain" a mix of factual and speculative questions, such as how many Spaniards made it home after the defeat of the Armada or whether he still believes God is on his side in the conflict between Catholics and Protestants. "Queen Elizabeth I" then might join the discussion, and students could ask whether England was militarily prepared to meet the Armada because it was clearly over a year before the attack that Spain was mobilizing, or whether "Elizabeth" would have executed her cousin if she had known the Armada would have been the result. Other appropriate historical figures for this kind of activity include Pericles, Augustus, Mohammed, Charlemagne, a survivor of the fourteenth-century plague, a medieval monk or nun, Dante, and Joan of Arc. Pairings or groupings of historical figures and issues might include a manorial lord and a peasant discussing medieval justice, Charles I and Oliver Cromwell discussing the tensions between monarchy and parliamentary rule, and Louis XVI and Robespiere discussing the French Revolution. What is particularly engaging about this kind of assignment is that individual interests can be accommodated to some degree because students could work within their own areas of interest. For example, a student studying the natural sciences might choose Newton or Darwin; a student majoring in literature might select Dante or Dickens; an art student might prefer Leonardo or Hogarth; an education major might want Locke or Rousseau; and a musician might select Bach or Mozart. Having students present material and answer questions in front of their peers keeps the classroom lively—the presenters have to know the material well, as do the students asking the question.

Film assignments are another good way to stimulate interesting active learning situations. Students could all view the same film, or each student could select a historically based film from the list of film suggestions provided with each chapter of this Instructor's Resource Manual. Students often feel comfortable critiquing films in a way that they do not feel about other kinds of material. In their reviews, students might consider issues of historical accuracy: Are the characters, whether fictional or based on real figures, appropriately drawn? How close is the plot to real events? If the plot is fictionalized, does the storyline still seem plausible? Does the setting have the right look and feel? Did the researchers working on the film get the details correct? Once the particulars of a film or films have been considered, students could move on to the overarching question of whether films should be as historically accurate as possible. After the instructor has collected the essays, students might then post their reviews on the course Web site, so that they can discuss each other's essays online before bringing the discussion into the classroom. The instructor has the choice of reviewing the online postings for grades, monitoring the discussion but staying out of it, or prompting a new line of analysis at appropriate points. Under the guidance of an instructor, such online postings can really enhance the discussion that takes place in the classroom.

Appropriate visual material could also be introduced after lecturing for ten or fifteen minutes, perhaps with a short, in-class writing assignment based on that material prior to a larger, class discussion. Such assignments have the additional advantages of offering students the opportunity to work with visual material as primary sources and to practice the responses that might be expected of them on an examination. Visual activities could last for ten minutes, followed by a concluding lecture segment, or even for the remainder of the class period.

Visual images or literary texts can also be introduced into the classroom by having students select or perhaps draw by lottery for significant works of art or literature. Rather than writing and presenting a "review" style essay, students might be asked to take a position on a particular work or several related works. For example, the Renaissance artist Albrecht Dürer produced no less than seven portraits of himself between the ages of 13 and 37, including *The Martyrdom of the 10,000* (1508), in which Dürer places himself in the center of the work. Students might be asked to trace Dürer's changing sense of self through these paintings, to compare it with shifting notions of the artist during the Renaissance, and to indicate how Dürer visually signaled his changed view of himself. Alternatively, students might be asked to support or refute the idea that Charles Dickens exaggerated the situation of the working classes in his novels. Because Dickens's novels were initially serialized, many sections actually stand on their own and might serve as appropriate examples, or students might refer to *A Christmas Carol*, which is relatively short. Again, after instructors have collected their essays, students might then post them on the course Web site before an in-class discussion.

Other writing assignments lend themselves to both individual and group work. An instructor might give students contradictory quotations on various historical issues and ask them to wrestle with them, either in an individual essay or as part of a group assignment.

Similarly, an instructor might frame a thesis and ask students, either individually or in groups, to take opposing sides and to debate the issue in front of the class, with the remaining students not directly involved serving as judges.

In addition to eliciting student participation, critical thinking and writing are other important elements of active learning. These elements are intimately connected because it is during the writing process that ideas are thought through and organized into coherent analyses and arguments. If students start writing early in their academic careers, instructors can start them on the journey to becoming sophisticated, critical thinkers. Assignments that are intended merely to elicit data or information do little to help students either remember the information or think critically about it. Students have become all too good at searching the Internet and piecing together papers that are chock full of information but containing little or no analysis. Although these papers may be informative and well organized, this does not make up for the lack of critical thinking. Instead, instructors should construct writing assignments that force students to think critically about an issue and to understand and weigh opposing viewpoints in order to arrive at some personal conclusion. It is important for instructors to structure questions in a way such that there are no "right" or "wrong" answers, and for students to understand that the assignment will be evaluated on the quality of its argument rather than on getting the "right" result.

Instructors of large Western Civilization survey courses should not balk at making such writing assignments because they can be managed even in large classrooms as long as the assignments are carefully thought out. Some fruitful assignments can be made using the primary sources in *The Making of the West: Peoples and Cultures* or its accompanying reader, *Sources of* The Making of the West by Katharine J. Lualdi. Such an assignment might ask students to consider whether they could successfully make the "negative confession" contained in the Egyptian Book of the Dead, or to propose an alternative confession that reflects contemporary culture and values; to write a letter to a friend about why they should or should not enter into public service in today's world after reading Giovanni Rucellai's advice to his sons; to "update" John Milton's *Areopagitica* (1644) by finding more contemporary arguments for a free press, including Thomas Jefferson's *Declaration of Independence* (1776); to rewrite a print document, such as *The Funeral Oration of Pericles* (429 B.C.E.) by Thucydides, or *The Accomplishments of Augustus* (14 C.E.), in the barest of modern-day English; to take the opposite view of that expressed in a primary source, such as writing a letter home from the perspective of the factory worker in contrast to *Factory Rules in Berlin* (1844); or to write "diary" entries for historical figures during a controversial time in their figures' lives, or playing the role of a courtier-chronicler in the mode of Saint-Simon in his *Memoirs* (1694–1723), or Montesquieu in his *Persian Letters: Letter 37* (1721). All of these sample assignments could later be read aloud in small groups or even to the whole class, thus stimulating discussions of related issues. Such assignments require students to have a thorough understanding of the original sources, as well as of their historical context. However, they would also be short (probably no longer than one page), so they would be appropriate for a large class. These kinds of assignments would therefore encourage students to think critically beyond the original source, and yet still be manageable for an instructor of a large class.

Asking students to work with other original documents in their original script can also make for a stimulating exercise. Students may be used to reading primary documents that have been translated or transcribed and then neatly typed into English in their textbooks and readers. However, it is an entirely different experience for them to look at sixteenth-century English documents in their original form. An instructor might begin with a brief overview of the kinds of documents that have survived from this period before moving on to related subjects, such as the production of paper and ink. With a bit of coaching, students might then look at and try to transcribe a few lines from several different kinds of documents, some written in italic form, some in the more difficult "secretary hand." Students might then be asked, by themselves, to transcribe a carefully selected letter, such as the letter by Henry VIII to Cardinal Wolsey in about 1521 concerning the king's fears over the loyalty of several noblemen, including the duke of Buckingham, who was shortly to be executed on charges of treason. The instructor could conclude the lecture by discussing how one might interpret the documents based first on internal evidence and then through context. In addition to engaging students in examining primary source material, this type of exercise helps students to understand that history involves looking at original material, making informed judgments about it, and only then writing a historical narrative.

Studies have shown that groups consisting of no more than five students work best, but group work can still be successfully incorporated into large classrooms. Instructors might assign questions or problems such that each group defends a position or renders an opinion. To combat the difficulties associated with determining the individual contribution of each student, each group member might be required to keep a journal of their research on the topic, including a possible thesis statement, which would then be shared with their group members. Based on the independent research notes, thesis statements, and rough drafts, the group would then collectively formulate and write a paper for presentation. Ultimately, instructors could review the individual journals to determine if a student had participated fully in their group and could be assigned credit for his or her individual contribution, as well as for their final paper. A peer review, where groups read each other's papers for content, argument, and flow, might also be incorporated into this process, but this might depend on how much class time is available to devote to such a project.

Although most students ultimately find it to be a rewarding experience, instructors should be prepared for some degree of resistance when turning a classroom into an active learning environment. Asking students to *think* about what they are doing in a critical way is inherently more challenging than listening to a long lecture. In addition, students are often reluctant to voice an opinion for fear of being "wrong." One further complication is that students tend to be very trusting of what they see in print and asking them to challenge or test what they have read can be unsettling. However, after engaging in some of these active learning activities, most classes appreciate the stimulation, the challenge, and the break from the traditional lecture format.

Working Primary Sources into the Western Civilization Syllabus

Katharine J. Lualdi

University of Southern Maine

Teaching the history of Western civilization at the survey level poses an array of exciting but difficult challenges for instructors. While it is important to construct a narrative that is coherent and engaging, instructors must also fit their coverage of vast expanses of time, place, and culture within the typical one-semester survey format. A textbook can provide a chronological and thematic framework for surmounting this challenge, yet neither it nor any other work alone can adequately elucidate the many dimensions of the past. Primary sources fill this gap with the voices of people who shaped and were shaped by history as it unfolded around them. Documents thus provide an invaluable means of enlivening and deepening the major issues, ideas, and events addressed in the survey narrative while allowing students to see that history is not a static compilation of facts and dates, but rather an ongoing process of discovery and interpretation.

The value of including primary source materials in the Western civilization survey extends beyond their ability to illuminate specific topics and points of view through first-person accounts. They also reveal historians' broad appreciation of the multitude of peoples and societies both within and outside Europe that shaped Western values, institutions, and traditions. Using a collection of documents to place the development of the West on both the European and world stage can thereby enhance students' understanding of the past and its relationship to the present in today's global age.

Compiled specifically to accompany The Making of the West: Peoples and Cultures, the documents included in Sources of THE MAKING OF THE WEST: PEOPLES AND CULTURES were selected with these goals in mind. The collection is organized into individual chapters, comprised of four documents each, which speak to key events and opinions of a specific historical era in important, and often surprising, ways. Traditional political documents are included alongside less conventional sources that elucidate Europe's social and cultural life as well as its increasing interconnectedness with the world at large. The voices of women and minorities were also granted a special place in the selection process because of their crucial yet often undervalued impact on the course of Western history.

Each chapter of Sources of THE MAKING OF THE WEST: PEOPLES AND CULTURES includes several editorial features to facilitate the use of the documents in a classroom setting. A summary situating the documents within the broader historical context and addressing their relationship to each other prefaces every chapter. An explanatory headnote accompanies each document to provide fundamental background information on the author and the source while highlighting its significance. Discussion questions are also included to help students examine the fundamental points and issues in greater depth. Finally, all chapters close with comparative questions to encourage students to see both the harmony and discordance among the document sets.

Together, these editorial features strengthen the coherency of each chapter as a pedagogical unit while still allowing instructors the freedom to choose documents and questions that best suit their own teaching goals and methods. The editorial apparatus is also geared towards strengthening students' analytical skills by encouraging them to consider the connections between the content of each document to a specific author, time, place, and audience. In this way, students learn that all primary sources are unique products of human enterprise and are often colored by personal concerns, biases, and objectives. It is the job of the historian, whether a professional or novice, to sift through such nuances to uncover what they reveal about the past.

Thus, both the content and format of Sources of THE MAKING OF THE WEST: PEOPLES AND CULTURES make it a valuable resource for teaching students not only about the formation of Western civilization but also about the process of historical inquiry. As such, the collection is also intended to be a springboard for more advanced work with primary sources.

The Western and world history titles in the Bedford Series in History and Culture are ideally suited for this purpose. The French Revolution and the Dreyfus Affair, for example, are both treated in the textbook and document reader, but the series volumes on these subjects delve into greater detail and from many more angles. By incorporating these and other relevant titles from the series into a Western civilization survey course, instructors can further engage students in unraveling the historical record in all of its diversity and complexity.

Visual Literacy: The Image in the Western Civilization Classroom

Paul R. Deslandes

Texas Tech University

W e often hear that, for good or bad, the current generation of traditional college-aged students is a group used to digesting (or at least ingesting) a diversity of visual stimuli ranging from fast-paced and remarkably intricate computer games to the music videos offered up to them on MTV and VH1. While some within the academy decry this development as the "dumbing of America," others view it as fertile ground for both research and teaching. Historians who teach general Western civilization surveys can use this reality to their advantage by thinking about their courses as opportunities to promote an understanding of the past through visual as well as written means. By employing a range of visual materials (including films, traditional slides and overheads, and high-tech computer simulations) in new and innovative ways, instructors can move beyond the tendency to use images as "illustrations" alone. The Western civilization classroom needs to be viewed as an ideal environment within which historians can actively promote visual literacy among college students by encouraging them to "read" and analyze images with a critical eye that will broaden their interpretive skills while possibly turning them on to the study of history in a way that document-based exercises alone cannot.

Naturally, resistant instructors might consider such a pedagogical approach as the active encouragement of a dangerous and worrying trend — the tendency on the part of students to avoid serious reading at all costs. What I am proposing in this brief examination of visual media in the Western civilization classroom is not an abandonment of the traditional document study but, rather, a broadened conception of what constitutes a valuable, or even an essential, source. The skills that we hope our students will acquire by reading Jean-Jacques Rousseau's *The New Heloise*, Mary Wollstonecraft's *Vindication of the Rights of Woman*, or Friedrich Engels's *The Condition of the Working Class in England* are nicely complemented by those that are honed by having them examine Sergei Eisenstein's *Battleship Potemkin*, images of the industrial landscape, or photographs of the Victorian family. Indeed, as university and college history departments rethink the utility of teaching Western civilization (by examining, for example, the various ways in which we might incorporate non-Western perspectives and histories into more standard history surveys), we need to consider very seriously a broadening of the parameters of what we define as valid sources.

By encouraging students to read images, films, photographs, and other types of evidence critically, we can go some way toward establishing what is often labeled, by art historians and others, as "visual literacy."[1] While this concept has multiple meanings, it is used here to convey several key points. First, visual literacy in the western civilization classroom is not exclusively about allowing students to further acquire the so-called cultural capital often associated with higher education by teaching them about the great artists in Western history. Rather, it is about encouraging an active and integrative approach to learning that allows students to conceptualize, in the broadest possible sense, what constitutes the material of history. In this way, the use of images, be they static or moving, forces students to think actively about the process of "doing history." Questions about authenticity, motive, intention, and selectivity naturally emerge from a consideration of these sources and thus improve dramatically the Western civilization student's critical capacities. It is the active promotion of the student's ability to ask these sorts of questions that constitutes the first cornerstone of an education in visual literacy.

The second major advantage of this particular form of literacy is that it allows students to actually visualize the past. Images that help to set a context, allow students to attach a human face to social movements, or illustrate clearly the discrepancies in wealth in the European past enrich students' overall understanding of history and, quite possibly, ensure that some of the big themes of our classes actually stay with them beyond the final examination.

Finally, developing visual literacy in the Western civilization classroom renders what we do in these general surveys — which are often populated by history majors and nonmajors in nearly equal numbers — relevant to other departments. By actively encouraging students to "read" images critically in our classroom, we are able to make broader claims about the validity of the Western civilization survey in universities and colleges increasingly under pressure to illustrate the utility of certain courses. Visually literate students are better able to pursue not only the further study of history but degree courses in business, mass communications, fine arts, and the sciences. In this way, the encouragement of this type of learning in our classrooms serves a broader and very important educative function.

Methods of the Presentation of Visuals

Two central questions emerge for any instructor who chooses to pursue a visually oriented approach to the teaching of Western civilization. First, what are the best methods for presenting images to students in classes that may range in size from twenty to five hundred? Second, how does one present images in a fashion that goes beyond the merely illustrative function toward the goal of encouraging visual literacy? While many of the answers to these questions will only be worked out during the course of teaching a Western civilization survey, there are several key issues to consider beforehand.

The way in which instructors might present images is largely dependent upon the types of technologies available to them at their respective institutions. Ranging from the simple and usually ubiquitous overhead projector to the most sophisticated of wired classrooms, the options are indeed numerous. Each method has its own advantages and disadvantages. In the case of the low-tech overhead projector, its chief virtue is its versatility and flexibility. This device, which projects transparencies that can be made professionally or manually by the instructor, allows for any image from a textbook or monograph to be reproduced quickly and easily on a photocopier for classroom presentation. This method facilitates the ability of the instructor to decide on a visual presentation at the very last minute and enables quick additions and shifts in focus. It also has the added benefit of allowing for the integration of visual evidence from recently published books and articles, thus encouraging Western civilization professors to include up-to-date scholarship in their lectures.

Another highly utilized method is the slide projector, the favored device of most art historians even in this age of increasingly sophisticated computer-generated images. Slides, which must be produced in a photographic laboratory, require a little more advanced planning than do overheads. They do, however, provide the Western civilization instructor with some flexibility by allowing for nearly any image from a wide variety of sources to be reproduced cheaply. Slides also allow the instructor to take photographs of historic sites, buildings, and museum exhibits that might then be useful for classroom instruction. Also, while there are some mass-produced overhead sets (usually of maps), there are far more invaluable and highly varied slide collections (generally sold through textbook publishing companies) that focus exclusively on Western civilization images ranging from paintings by the Great Masters to political cartoons to contemporary photography.[2] The equipment required for this sort of image is fairly inexpensive and low-tech. While a little more prone to mechanical problems (such as burnt-out lamps or defective remotes) than the overhead, the slide projector also has the advantage of being highly portable and generally hassle-free.

Of course, at a point in time when discussions of technology and the teaching of history are increasingly frequent, Western civilization instructors must also consider a range of high-tech options when making the decision to "go visual." There are now available a number of computer presentation programs that enable instructors to generate images freely and easily in their classrooms. Most who choose to pursue this route use the PowerPoint option available through the ubiquitous Microsoft Office program found on most university and college computers. This software, most frequently utilized by businesses and corporations to create multimedia presentations, has been adapted by many instructors to construct user-friendly and visually stimulating lectures. Rather than engaging in a full-scale discussion of the merits and disadvantages of this particular type of transmission of knowledge, I would like to focus here briefly on how one might use this sort of software to produce clear and crisp images for classroom discussion. Software of this sort allows instructors to store images that have been either scanned from books and other sources or downloaded from one of several Western civilization image Web sites or CD-ROMs on a computer's hard drive. These images are thus saved permanently and easily used time and again in multimedia lectures. While somewhat problematic in terms of the amount of disk space required, programs of this sort also allow for short video clips to be stored in a computer for classroom use.

Once mastered, these high-tech options can be quite simple to work with, cost-effective, and enjoyable. These newer forms of technology also have the very clear advantage of efficiency. Instead of searching in overcrowded offices for storage space for multiple boxes of slides and files of transparencies, Western civilization instructors can simply have these images scanned (there are, in fact, slide scanners available on the market and in many university computer labs) and stored, centrally and in a far more organized fashion, on the hard drive of a laptop computer.

While undoubtedly useful, this technique is not without its problems. First, there is the expense of the equipment. At the very minimum, the instructor who chooses this option will need to have a laptop computer and portable LCD projector. Increasingly, universities and colleges are creating wired classrooms in which this equipment is permanently installed.

Depending on the financial health of an institution, equipment of this sort may or may not be made readily available. Second, there are the problems of time associated with scanning images and familiarizing the instructor with the software and the methods of presentation. Unless one can hire a graduate or undergraduate assistant to help with the scanning and organization of images, work of this type will divert the attention of the instructor away from other valuable activities, such as research or administration. Finally, there is always the possibility of complete equipment failure in which key files are erased or hard drives crashed, effectively negating all of this time-consuming work. Although the possibility of total failure is remote, it is worthwhile thinking about the relative security of the tangible transparency and slide. Even though projectors might also break down, it is far easier to run down the hall to the audio-visual closet than it is to embark once again on a time-consuming scanning project.

One other method of presentation and storage, also of the high-tech variety, merits some consideration here. Instructors used to working with computers might wish to construct a Western civilization Web site to which images, short video clips, and a whole array of primary sources can be posted. The site can be used to store all of the images drawn upon for lectures and classroom exercises, thus providing a permanent record of visual material that students can consult easily and conveniently for research and study purposes. An individual Web site also enables the instructor to establish direct links to other relevant image Web sites as well as various repositories of primary source materials.

Interpretation of Visuals

While decisions about the method of presentation are indeed crucial, more serious pedagogical questions must also be considered as the instructor decides how to proceed in promoting visual literacy among Western civilization students. There are several approaches to the teaching of images that are worthwhile thinking about.

Image presentation and interpretation in the classroom might be divided into two distinct categories, loosely characterized as either freestanding or complementary exercises. Freestanding exercises are best conceived as entire (or partial) class sessions devoted to the interpretation and discussion of selected images. This sort of format works best in considering topics such as "Fascist Propaganda" or "Everyday Life in the Eighteenth Century." In pursuing such an exercise, the instructor would have students read appropriate textbook chapters and various supplementary background materials. With a solid base, students would then be expected to interpret, in the case of the exercise on fascist propaganda, images of posters and photographs reflecting Fascist and Nazi efforts to organize daily life in Italy and Germany during the 1920s and 1930s. These might include posters produced for the Mussolini-inspired Mothers' and Infants' Day in Italy and pictures of various Nazi youth organizations that encouraged and actively enforced uniformity, physical fitness, and loyalty to the state.[3] Another immensely powerful source that might be used in this particular exercise is Leni Riefenstahl's documentary of the 1934 Nazi Party rally at Nuremberg. As an example of how Hitler attempted to forge a sense of unity in the aftermath of the purges of the SA in June of 1934, Triumph of the Will serves as a powerful example of how the moving image could be used to very explicit political ends. Perhaps most striking for students is the extent to which the film conveys ostensible mass support for enormous party spectacles as well as the orchestrated and choreographed nature of the rally.

Complementary exercises often take on the same form as freestanding exercises, but with a slightly different intent. Rather than asking students to simply acquire background information by reading a textbook, the complementary exercise uses images to broaden and enliven discussions of printed primary source materials. The focus then is on encouraging students to consider the full range of sources at the disposal of the historian in learning about, for example, the social and cultural impact of the Industrial Revolution. An exploration of this particular theme can be effectively accomplished by pairing several different types of sources. An instructor might, for example, provide students with excerpts from several different reports on working conditions in England from the early to mid-nineteenth century, which they would be asked to read in preparation for a class meeting. During the meeting, students could discuss the content of these sources and their historiographical significance by considering them alongside a range of images depicting the industrial landscape, factory conditions, and working-class housing. On its most basic level, this technique tends to serve as a catalyst for discussion by prompting responses to the images that are informed by the student's careful reading of the printed material. On a more sophisticated level, this type of exercise provides students and instructors alike with an opportunity to discuss issues related to veracity, authorial or artistic intent, and the complementary nature of different types of historical sources. It also serves another vital function by ensuring that the images of working-class life and the industrial landscape formulated in students' minds have a tangible relationship to "reality" that transcends what are often excessively romanticized or overdramatized film portrayals.

Substantial planning and advanced thinking is required to execute these sorts of exercises effectively. Any instructor intending to work extensively with visual evidence in the Western civilization classroom should construct a checklist of questions and issues — which should be distributed to students in printed form — to consider when interpreting visual evidence. Robert Levine, a prominent historian of Latin America, has offered some general guidelines for interpreting photographs as historical evidence that can, with some manipulation, be applied to the analysis of a whole range of visual evidence including paintings, films, and political cartoons. Levine states in his book, *Images of History: Nineteenth and Early Twentieth Century Latin American Photographs as Documents,* that there are ten themes to consider when "reading" photographs as historical evidence. These include, among others, the need for students of history to ask the same sorts of questions of visual images as they might of printed material. Levine argues that issues related to attribution as well as questions of time, place, bias, intentions, and audience should emerge as foremost in any consideration of this sort of evidence.[4]

Other questions that should appear on any checklist to be used by students when considering historic images might include:

What does the image tell us about a given society's values, mores, and social norms?

How have these norms changed over time?

How do images demarcate social divisions in a given society or time period?

How are rural and urban scenes portrayed?

What do visual portrayals of a point in the past tell us about material culture in that era?

And, what is revealed about customs, dress, religious beliefs, family organization, and gender roles in historic images?

While the list of questions that can be posed is potentially enormous, instructors should tailor their own checklists to both the demands and abilities of their students and the specific goals of the course. Those intent on integrating visual material into written assignments (such as exams or formal essays) will need to think more seriously about what sorts of "objective" information about each image or set of images they want students to master for the purposes of assessment. This will necessitate a uniform "viewing sheet" which students should be required to complete, for each interpretive exercise, as a component of the class participation grade. While this degree of integration may be preferred, instructors interested in making the transition to a visual classroom more slowly may require a less substantial or formal checklist.

For those students not used to approaching history through visual sources, instructors will also need to impress upon them, from the very beginning, the seriousness of this pursuit. It must be stressed that adequate preparation is as essential for visual exercises as it is for more traditional discussions of course readings. To remind students of this, instructors may find it necessary to build into their syllabi periodic quizzes, graded viewing exercises, and other assignments that will encourage students to take seriously this style of learning about the past. Furthermore, instructors need to be absolutely comfortable with visual analysis in order for this type of learning experience to be effective. Thus, extensive reading will be required in the fields of art history, cultural studies, film studies, and visual theory, all of which have dealt more precisely and explicitly with the promotion of visual literacy in the university and college classroom.

Suggested Exercises for the Visually Oriented Western Civilization Classroom

While there are, quite literally, dozens of possible exercises, the approach taken by any instructor of Western civilization will largely depend on her or his methodological and intellectual interests and predispositions. What follows are three basic exercises that might be adapted to any classroom setting. Each of these exercises could be presented to a class as either complementary or freestanding, depending on the needs of the instructor.

1. The Iconography of the French Revolution

This exercise draws on the numerous political cartoons, prints, and various material artifacts generated during the years of the French Revolution to encourage students to think about the ways in which political ideas could be expressed visually through artistic metaphors and caricatures. Following Lynn Hunt's lead in her book *The Family Romance of the French Revolution*, this exercise might present students with an opportunity to examine how the French Revolution was conceived of, at least by some, as a form of family rebellion and patricide, in which the king, as the symbolic head of the French "family," was ritually executed. The iconography of the French Revolution opens up all sorts of other possibilities. An instructor might ask students, in the classroom, to examine images of "Liberty" in discussing not only revolutionary ideology but also gender roles and ideals in the late eighteenth century.

Possible sources for images, primary documents, and interpretive approaches include: Lynn Hunt, *The Family Romance of the French Revolution* (Berkeley: University of California Press, 1992), and Emmet Kennedy, *A Cultural History of the French Revolution* (New Haven, CT: Yale University Press, 1989). An impressive collection of images and sources has been gathered for a new CD-ROM to be produced by Pennsylvania State University Press. See Jack Censer and Lynn Hunt, *Liberty, Equality, Fraternity: Exploring the French Revolution* (forthcoming). For further information on this CD-ROM, consult the Web site of the Center for History and New Media at George Mason University at <http:/chnm.gmu.edu>.

2. Colonialism and Popular Culture

This particular exercise asks students to analyze a series of images (c. 1880–1920) that help to illuminate ideas about race, cultural superiority, and the civilizing mission in the age of new imperialism. Drawing primarily on examples from European popular culture, these images might consist of the highly evocative advertisements created in Great Britain for Pears' Soap, which drew on ideas about the civilizing nature of European products as well as stereotyped images of the unenlightened (particularly with respect to the emerging consumer ethos) "dark savage." Complementary documentary sources might include the poetry of Rudyard Kipling and other writings by various advocates of empire.

Possible sources for images and interpretive approaches include: Anne McClintock, *Imperial Leather: Race, Gender and Sexuality in the Colonial Context* (London and New York: Routledge, 1995) and Thomas Richards, *The Commodity Culture of Victorian England: Advertising and Spectacle, 1851–1914* (Stanford, CA: Stanford University Press, 1990).

3. Ideology and Film in the Early Soviet Union

This exercise focuses on an interpretation of Sergei Eisenstein's 1925 film, *Battleship Potemkin*, about a revolutionary mutiny that occurred aboard a Russian navy vessel in 1905. By analyzing the film, students are able to examine the impact of the Russian Revolution and communist ideology upon the visual arts. Themes to be covered in analyzing this film might include the filmmaker's portrayal of class antagonism in the relationship between ordinary soldiers and naval officers, the infusion of revolutionary ideology into the plotline, and the power of images in conveying political messages. An exercise of this sort also provides a wonderful opportunity to initiate discussions on the techniques of filmmaking (especially Eisenstein's use of separate and titled acts and alternating close-ups and long shots), encouraging students in the process to think about the method as well as the message of presentation.

Possible sources for film suggestions, primary documents, and interpretive approaches include: Sergei Eisenstein, *Selected Works, Vol. I: Writings, 1922–34*, edited and translated by Richard Taylor (London: British Film Institute, 1988) and Peter Kenez, *Cinema and Soviet Society, 1917–1953* (Cambridge: Cambridge University Press, 1992).

Conclusion

The degree to which it is possible to integrate visual learning into the Western civilization classroom will depend largely on the predilections and predispositions of the individual instructor. For those interested in departing from the "stand and deliver" lecture format, this style of teaching provides invaluable opportunities for integrative and participatory learning. Adding a visual dimension to the standard Western civilization survey enhances the learning experience by encouraging students to broaden their understanding of how historians learn about the past while giving them a sense of what that past (an often abstract concept reflected only in awkward sounding and occasionally confusing documents) "actually" looked like. By expanding the routes through which Western civilization students learn about the past, instructors can actively improve upon the skills of analytical thought, interpretation, and creative and accurate expression that every university and college professor tries to facilitate.

The benefits to the instructor of this sort of approach are equally important. By integrating visual material, new instructors might discover a style of teaching that they will be able to adapt to different situations throughout their academic careers. Similarly, experienced teachers might find that this new approach breathes fresh life into stale lectures, encourages new avenues of inquiry and fields of exploration, and reinvigorates a waning or possibly lost enthusiasm for teaching. While instructors will certainly differ in their opinions on the utility of such an approach, it is certainly one worthy of at least a period of trial and experimentation. The possibilities are endless and the rewards considerable.

Suggested Sources

Readings

Allen, Robert C. "Historiography and the Teaching of Film History." *Film and History* 10–2 (1980).
Carnes, Mark C. "Beyond Words: Reviewing Moving Pictures." *Perspectives* 34.5 (May/June 1996).
Herman, Gerald "History through Film: Making Multi-Media Lectures for Classroom Use." *Film and History* 2.4 (1972).
Hiley, Michael. *Seeing through Photographs.* London: Gordon Fraser, 1983.
Levine, Robert M. *Images of History: Nineteenth and Early Twentieth Century Latin American Photographs as Documents.* Durham and London: Duke University Press, 1989.
Margolis, Eric. "Mining Photographs: Unearthing the Meaning of Historical Photos." *Radical History Review* 40 (1985).
O'Connor, John. "Special Report: The Moving-Image Media in the History Classroom." *Film and History* 16.3 (1986).
———. *Teaching History with Film and Television.* Washington, DC: American Historical Association, 1987.
Rosenstone, Robert. *Visions of the Past: The Challenge of Film to Our Idea of History.* Cambridge, MA: Harvard University Press, 1995.
Schulkin, Carl. "The Challenge of Integration." *Perspectives* 37.2 (February 1999).
Susman, Warren I. "History and Film: Artifact and Experience." *Film and History* 15.2 (1985).
Trinkle, Dennis A. "Computers and the Practice of History: Where Are We? Where Are We Headed?" *Perspectives* 37.2 (February 1999).
Zukas, Alex. "Different Drummers: Using Music to Teach History." *Perspectives* 34.6 (September 1996).

Web Sites

Center for History and New Media. <http://chnm.gmu.edu/>.
Modern History Sourcebook. <http://www.fordham.edu/halsall/mod/modsbook.html>.
Western Culture: Links and Online Book. <http://www.westernculture.com/>.

CD-ROMs

CD-ROM with Presentation Manager Pro. Bedford/St. Martin's.
The Western Civilization CD-ROM. Instructional Resources Corporation <http://www.irclink.com/>

NOTES

[1]The term implies that literacy is acquired through a reading of images and other forms of communication as well as written texts. Visual literacy is, in fact, a specific field of academic study that ranges in focus from reception theory to pedagogic examinations of visual media in the classroom. The diversity of issues that are dealt with by scholars working in this area is reflected in the contents of the *Journal of Visual Literacy,* published by the International Visual Literacy Association. For additional information, see their Web site at <http://www.ivla.org/>.

[2]For one example of these collections see "The Western Civilization Slide Collection" produced by the Instructional Resources Corporation of Annapolis, Maryland.

[3]I have drawn material for this particular type of exercise from Victoria de Grazia, *How Fascism Ruled Women: Italy, 1922–1945* (Berkeley: University of California Press, 1992), and Claudia Koonz, *Mothers in the Fatherland: Women, Family Life and Nazi Politics* (New York: St. Martin's Press, 1987).

[4]For a discussion of these issues, see Robert M. Levine, *Images of History: Nineteenth and Early Twentieth Century Latin American Photographs as Documents* (Durham and London: Duke University Press, 1989).

Literature and
the Western Civilization Classroom

Michael D. Richards

Sweet Briar College

Every time I teach the Western civilization survey, I make it a point to introduce students to at least one classic of Western literature. Even if the students do not remember much about the course, perhaps they will remember reading and enjoying *Candide* or *Madame Bovary* or *One Day in the Life of Ivan Denisovich.* There are times, too, when a novel or play can help students understand a historical issue or situation in ways that the textbook or a historical monograph cannot. And there is probably nothing better than fiction or poetry for drawing students into a consideration of the big historiographical questions: what is right or wrong in a given circumstance, what has or does not have significance, and whether there is purpose or meaning to the history of humanity.

In the next few pages, I will take up some of the problems and also some of the joys of using literature in Western civilization courses. Overall, I mean to encourage anyone who has not tried using literature to utilize this important resource. I also want to reassure those who have used literature in the past that this is a direction they should continue to take. Much of teaching is a process of trial and error, and you must discover what you are comfortable doing and make your own creative mistakes. Nonetheless, I will include a few practical applications for you to consider.

The Colossal Responsibility of Teaching Great Literature

Historians are sometimes daunted by what they see as the huge responsibility associated with the teaching of a novel or a play. My approach to this is roughly that of Georges Clemenceau during World War I when he remarked that "war is too important to be left to the generals." Literature is a vital part of Western civilization, and it also helps us understand better many other aspects of Western civilization. We have an obligation to take a novel or a poem seriously as a source of history and to communicate this significance to our students. We must do the best we can in this regard, but we are not charged with explicating a particular work from a literary point of view. The most crucial piece of advice I can give is simply to read the novel or play or poem carefully. Ideally, you should read it at least twice, once to get a sense of the piece and a second time to take notes.

A couple of examples may be helpful at this point.

Heart of Darkness *by Joseph Conrad*

A few years back, I tried to summarize Conrad's novel in an introduction I was writing for a text on twentieth-century Europe. I contended the book was not so much about the Belgian Congo as it was about the fragility and precariousness of Western civilization. The heart of darkness was not upriver but in every man and woman. When I showed this summary to a good friend, who is a gifted teacher of English literature, she warned me that critical opinion of Conrad was rather unfavorable and that many considered him a racist and a misogynist. Did this mean, I wondered, that I ought not to teach Conrad any longer? If I chose to continue, how much of the new criticism did I need to read and how much did I need to pass on to my students? The answer to the first question is I still teach Conrad. The answers to the second question are "some" and "very little."

The second question is important, and I want to outline here what "some" and "very little" actually meant in this case. I was fortunate in that one of the main feminist critics of Conrad, Marianna Torgovnick, was then teaching at the university where I did my graduate work. About the time I became aware of the new interpretations of Conrad, the alumni magazine featured an excellent article about her. Not too long after that, David Denby wrote about Conrad and the new interpretations in *The New Yorker* ("Jungle Fever," 6 November 1995, pp. 118–129). All this was perhaps serendipitous, but serendipity happens most often to those whose minds are prepared for it. Beyond serendipity, there were many other sources available. For example, there was the Norton Critical Edition of *Heart of Darkness* (New York: W. W. Norton, 1988), third edition, edited by Robert Kimbrough. For most authors or titles, a number of resources are available in libraries or on Web sites (see the "Suggestions for Research and Discussion," on page 180). Time and interest will limit what you realistically should do. There is no need to pursue the study of a novel to the point of publishing a critical analysis of the book, although this did happen to me once.

In the case of Conrad, students will have to know there are controversies, quite important ones. I discuss the controversies briefly, making a case for Conrad and against him. I also indicate that my reading of the book may be incorrect. Since the students have read the book themselves, it is up to them to arrive at their own conclusions. The most important reason for reading *Heart of Darkness* or any piece of fiction in a history course is that students attempt to form and defend some opinions about the work itself and attempt to use it to understand history more fully — in this case, the history of late nineteenth-century imperialism. It gives them practice in what should be a lifelong effort to arrive at and articulate informed opinions. (See manual p. 181 for a more extended discussion of teaching *Heart of Darkness*).

Madame Bovary *by Gustave Flaubert*

That Flaubert is famous for his great effort to find "le mot juste" makes *Madame Bovary* a little daunting. The book is, however, also an extraordinary resource for social history. It has much to say about the practice of medicine in France in the first part of the nineteenth century, the pretensions of small-town intellectuals, the impact of romanticism, and life in provincial France generally. But shouldn't you discuss the wonderful writing? Yes, but only to the extent you can. If you can't, don't try to fake it. In my case, a friend who taught French literature casually mentioned one day the wonderful passage in which Rodolphe begins his seduction of Emma during the agricultural show. Flaubert sets off their romantic blather against speeches about the importance of agriculture and announcements of awards for the best sheep or pig. While I had noted Rodolphe's smooth insincerity, I had overlooked this example of Flaubert's art. Now that this ironic juxtaposition has been pointed out to me, I can mention to students both the literary aspects and the pathetic story of the old servant. While it is certainly advantageous to be alert to the literary aspects, and even to seek out colleagues who may be able to help expand on them, comprehension of these should not be the major goal of the presentation or discussion of the novel.

Teachable Sources versus Unwieldy Novels

After many valiant efforts, I have stopped trying to teach *The Magic Mountain* in a history course. I still spend a portion of a class talking about Thomas Mann and *The Magic Mountain* when we examine Weimar Germany and the rise of Hitler. But the novel itself is much too long and complicated and includes many pages written in French. Rather than the novel, I might have students read "Mario and the Magician," a short story by Mann that lends itself to a discussion of fascism in the interwar period.

It is philistine not to use a novel because it is longer than three hundred pages. Still, a little pragmatism is in order when teaching the Western civilization survey. A novella, a short story, a play, perhaps a few poems, or excerpts from a long novel will generally work better than a lengthy novel, no matter how wonderful the novel. So, try Aleksandr Solzhenitsyn's *One Day in the Life of Ivan Denisovich* instead of *First Circle* or Charles Dickens's *Hard Times* rather than *Our Mutual Friend.*

One Day in the Life of Ivan Denisovich *by Aleksandr Solzhenitsyn*

Solzhenitsyn's novella works almost perfectly in a Western civilization survey. One drawback is that it is now often read in high school; therefore, it may not be new to many students. An additional problem is that there is no longer quite the same interest in the Soviet Union as there once was when the cold war had just ended. In its favor, this book is not only a quick read but is also an absorbing tale. It is also a part of Nikita Khrushchev's efforts to contend with the Stalinist legacy (he personally intervened to allow it to be published in the Soviet literary periodical *Novy Mir*), and therefore it stands as a part of the larger political history. Lastly, it effectively introduces students to the Gulag Archipelago, the vast system of prisons and labor camps created by the secret police in the 1920s and 1930s, and to the disturbing questions this system raises about humanity in the twentieth century.

Anthologies

Anthologies are a staple of Western civilization courses, but the kind of anthology we might use to bring fiction or poetry into our course is not available. Most anthologies for history courses contain documents having to do with politics, economics, and society. Only one that I am aware of departs very far from the familiar mix, and that is *Movements, Currents, Trends: Aspects of European Thought in the Nineteenth and Twentieth Centuries* by Eugen Weber. Some may be familiar with the original version of the book: *Paths to the Present*. This very interesting anthology is a collection of documents about major cultural movements beginning with romanticism. It leans toward prefaces, manifestos, and critical essays. Other anthologies designed for humanities courses cover art and music as well as literature, but they are generally less useful for Western civilization courses.

One series of anthologies, while still not quite what we might wish for, should be mentioned here. I first became acquainted with the series published by Viking Press through *The Portable Twentieth-Century Russian Reader*, edited by Clarence Brown, and, later, *The Portable*

Nineteenth-Century Russian Reader, edited by George Gibian. Most volumes are devoted to particular authors, but there is *The Portable Greek Reader*, edited by W. H. Auden; *The Portable Roman Reader*, edited by Basil Davenport; *The Portable Medieval Reader*, edited by James Bruce Ross and Mary Martin McLaughlin; *The Portable Renaissance Reader*, also edited by Ross and McLaughlin; *The Portable Romantic Poets*, edited by Auden and Norman Holmes Pearson; and *The Portable Victorian Reader*, edited by Gordon S. Haight.

There are often anthologies available for a particular national literary tradition. For example, anthologies of Russian literature include *Twentieth Century Russian Plays: An Anthology*, edited by F. D. Reeve (New York: W. W. Norton, 1963), and *The Penguin Book of Russian Short Stories*, edited by David Richards (New York: Penguin, 1981). There are also anthologies devoted to a particular period or event. Two examples are *The Penguin Book of First World War Poetry*, second edition, edited by Jon Silkin (New York: Penguin, 1981), and *Against Forgetting: Twentieth Century Poetry of Witness*, edited by Carolyn Forché (New York: W. W. Norton, 1993).

To the best of my knowledge, there is nothing comparable to the Viking series of portable readers for all of Western civilization. There are anthologies of western literature such as *The Norton Anthology of World Masterpieces*, seventh edition, edited by Sarah Lawall, but they are designed for a course on comparative literature. *The Norton Anthology of World Masterpieces*, for example, consists of two volumes, each 2,350 pages in length. Given the extraordinary amount of material covered in a Western civilization course, it is more practical for you to choose one novel or perhaps to put together a short reader of your own (in this day of desktop publishing, that is relatively easy to do).

Other Possibilities

You should also keep in mind essays, autobiographies, memoirs, and diaries. I have frequently used Eugenia Semyanovna Ginzburg's *Journey into the Whirlwind*, her account of her experiences in the purges in the Soviet Union in the 1930s, with considerable success. This is more familiar ground for historians in that these genres frequently form the documentary basis for our work.

Resources

You may wish to use one or more of a number of very useful resources to help in dealing with a particular novel or author. One such outstanding resource is the Cambridge Companion series. This series includes, for example, *The Cambridge Companion to Renaissance Humanism*, edited by Jill Kraye, and *The Cambridge Companion to the Eighteenth-Century Novel*, edited by John Richetti. Most of the titles in the series center on individual authors, but a few cover national literary traditions. Other series that generally focus on one book or a single theme or personality include the Oxford Reader's Companion series, the Norton Critical Editions, and the Bedford Series in History and Culture. Twayne Publishers offers both short biographies and critical studies of individual titles. Collections of critical essays on particular authors or titles are also published by Garland Press, Greenwood Publishers, G. K. Hall, and Prentice-Hall.

 Web sites are very important. One excellent site is the GaleNet Literature Resource Center at <http://www.galenet.com/servlet/LitRC?&u=LRC&u=CA&u=ClC&u>. This Web site combines the resources of various Gale Group publications: Contemporary Authors, Contemporary Literary Criticism Select, and Dictionary of Literary Biography. (Note: GaleNet access is only available through libraries; you must see your librarian to obtain a username and password.) The Lycos search engine is also a good way to find information on the Web for a particular author or title. Here, however, you will quickly come upon material that is not relevant, not useful, or simply incorrect. Your students will likely use this resource as well. A discussion of Web sites, and their advantages and disadvantages, early in the course is highly recommended.

Practical Ways to Use Literature in the Western Civilization Classroom

Heart of Darkness *by Joseph Conrad*

There is a plethora of resources for work on *Heart of Darkness*. In addition to the Norton Critical Edition, there are *The Cambridge Companion to Joseph Conrad*, ed. J. H. Stape (Cambridge: Cambridge University Press, 1996), and *The Oxford Reader's Companion to Conrad*, ed. by Owen Knowles and Gene Moore (Oxford: Oxford University Press, 2000). Gary Adelman has published *Heart of Darkness: Search for the Unconscious* (Boston: Twayne, 1987). Marianna Torgovnick's *Gone Primitive: Savage Intellects, Modern Lives* (Chicago: University of Chicago Press, 1990) includes an informative section on the novel. There is also a great deal of useful information on the GaleNet Literature Resource Center. A search on Lycos turned up some interesting and helpful sites as well. If anything, there is almost too much in the way of resources.

One approach is to set the novel in the context of a larger issue or problem. In this case, we can set Conrad's novel in the context of imperialism at the end of the nineteenth century. This gives us more questions to ask and helps to de-emphasize the literary aspects. Before talking about the novel, take a few minutes to tell the class who Conrad was and to make a few comments on the novel itself. In this case, we would need to mention the controversies surrounding the novel, the accusations that Conrad was a racist and a misogynist. You may want to provide students with a few ideas to ponder before they begin reading. For example, you might ask them to consider why the opening of the novel is set on the Thames, or what implicit comparison Conrad makes between the Thames and the Congo. A one-page guide asking students to consider a few basic questions and providing some background will be helpful.

There are two basic ways to deal with the book. One is a discussion of some of the main themes set beforehand. These might include the following questions: What is imperialism? How did Europeans view themselves at the end of the century? How did European men view European women? What was their attitude toward the people that they colonized? How did people deal with power in this period? What was Western civilization to Marlow? What was the "heart of darkness"? If possible, tie the discussion to the text by quoting from the novel.

The other basic approach is an explication of the text, a specialized lecture that takes the students through the book in pursuit of one or more themes. I might wish, for instance, to assert that Conrad believed that civilization was fragile. Unfortunately, in his observation, the lure of power was immensely strong. Heart of Darkness is full of stories of Europeans succumbing to the lure of power. By way of contrast, Conrad introduces the plight of the native crew on the steamboat Marlow is taking up the river. They have all but used up their food supply, which is separate from that of the Europeans, and it may be some time before they find a village on the river where they can trade for food. They are also cannibals, and Marlow wonders why they don't simply take over the boat and have the Europeans for dinner. Something restrains them. He can't name it, but it impresses him that these so-called savages had not given in to hunger (Conrad 114–117). In contrast to the natives' restraint, Marlow descries how the helmsman, whom he liked, lacked restraint and got himself killed as a result. When people on the shore attack the boat, the helmsman throws open the shutter that protected him from the arrows and shoots a rifle at the attackers. The boat is close to the shore, and the helmsman is speared through the open window and dies (Conrad 120–122). Then Marlow identifies the helmsman with Kurtz, the person everyone in the company thought would go far: "'Poor fool! If he had only left that shutter alone. He had no restraint, no restraint — just like Kurtz — a tree swayed by the wind'" (Conrad 129). Speaking of Kurtz directly, Marlow says, "'the wilderness had found him out early . . . I think it had whispered to him things about himself which he did not know, things of which he had no conception till he took counsel with this great solitude — and the whisper had proved irresistibly fascinating'" (Conrad 138).

The third way to approach the novel is simply to let the discussion go where it will, but be prepared to step in occasionally with relevant passages for the students to consider. In the case of such free-form discussion, you would resist the temptation to lay things out to students and only guide them toward the kinds of insights you hope they will take away from the material. You may be surprised at what your student readers will find and point out. This method gives you the opportunity to make what points you might wish to make but allows for the possibility that others will have different insights to contribute. Such an approach actually takes more preparation than the first two methods (and requires you to be quick on your feet), but may well bring greater rewards.

Reference

Conrad, Joseph. *Heart of Darkness.* 1950. Signet Classics Edition. (New York: Penguin, 1997).